ivan allen, jr. department of science
industry and government

PRIMER ON THE LAW OF MERGERS

Earl W. Kintner

PRIMER ON THE LAW OF MERGERS

A GUIDE FOR BUSINESSMEN

THE MACMILLAN COMPANY, New York
COLLIER-MACMILLAN Publishers, London

Printed in the United States of America

The Macmillan Company
866 Third Avenue, New York, New York 10022
Collier-Macmillan Canada, Ltd., Toronto, Ontario

Library of Congress catalog card number: 72-86504

Printing: 1 2 3 4 5 6 7 8 Year: 3 4 5 6 7 8 9

Prologue

Why Read This Book?

In our free enterprise system the allocation of goods and services is not achieved through the dictates of big government, nor do we allow such vital decision making to reside in the hands of private monopoly. Centralized decision making in either form must necessarily result in the three classical evils described by Adam Smith: high prices, a limitation on production, and a deterioration in the quality of the goods produced. For this reason we have sought another means of regulating our economic order. Economic decision making is decentralized. The allocation of goods and services is a function of consumer choice. Businessmen, spurred by the profit motive, compete for the consumer's custom, which thus dictates which goods will be produced and purchased and, in consequence, business success or failure.

With the potential rewards so great, but the consequences of failure so disastrous, it was inevitable that competitive abuses would occur. These abuses took many forms. Price fixing and price discrimination, territorial arrangements, exclusive dealing, and boycotts are but a few examples. Competitors disappeared, monopolization was imminent, and the evils described by Adam Smith were becoming a reality. With free enterprise in jeopardy, American ingenuity provided a unique answer—not government control, not private monopolization, but antitrust, that is, government-imposed ground rules to allow competition to govern the marketplace.

Of course, competition depends upon a choice, and if competitors merge or acquire suppliers or distributors, thus foreclosing sources of supply or outlet to their competitors, or if their aggregate size makes competitors less aggressive, the function of competition is thwarted. It is no wonder, then, that a prime concern of the antitrust laws has been with mergers. Not all mergers are, of course, prohibited by these laws. Some may be pro-competitive or, at least, not anticompetitive. Where, then, is the line to be drawn? Numerous cases and rules and guidelines of the enforcing agencies—the Justice Department and the Federal Trade Commission—deal with this problem. It is the objective of this book to attempt to pull together this mass of information and to present in a clear and easy-to-understand manner this important body of law.

Yet it is not only the aware businessman who is, or should be, concerned with the law of mergers. The so-called merger wave can have consequences to the whole structure of our economy, with a significant effect on all of us. An understandable presentation of the laws relating to mergers thus seems imperative. This was a second reason for undertaking this book.

Though this book is primarily concerned with the antitrust aspects of mergers, other legal aspects of the subject have been examined in Part II. Antitrust is, of course, not the only concern in the decision as to whether to merge or in what form the merger is to take place. Various state and federal laws must be consulted on such topics as choosing the method of purchase, dealing in securities, tender offers and take-overs, accounting procedures, tax considerations, labor considerations, and closing of the deal. Separate chapters examine each of these topics.

In Part III we turn to substantive antitrust law. Beginning with a consideration of antitrust theory—both historical and economic—because this is the backdrop against which the statutory language is interpreted by the courts, we then turn to the substantive standards of each of the laws dealing with mergers: the Clayton Act, the Sherman Act, and the Federal Trade Commission Act. Separate chapters deal with the Celler–Kefauver Amendment, classification of mergers, relevant market, tests of unlawfulness, defenses, miscellaneous corporate amalgamations, mergers involving foreign commerce, and recent developments. Part IV is concerned with enforcement and remedies available to the Department of Justice, the Federal Trade Commission, and private parties injured by the antitrust violations of others. Finally, we examine special industry mergers, that is, mergers involving the so-called regulated industries.

Although every major premise of merger law has been stated, and every leading case examined, my intention is not to teach businessmen how to be their own merger lawyers. The very idea is folly, because these laws are infinitely subtle and appear in an infinite variety of forms. But if the businessman's awareness of these laws can be heightened, and if he is sufficiently aware to consult a specialist *before* the consequences of a contemplated course of action descend upon him, a precious gain has been won.

Acknowledgment

Any book of this character is the product of many minds. I must gratefully acknowledge the assistance of my colleagues Michael C. Addison, Steven V. Berson, Joseph P. Griffin, Hugh C. Hansen, Rich A. Harrington, Jethro K. Lieberman, Joseph R. Sahid, Stephen J. Weiss, Arnold R. Westerman, and Merle F. Wilberding, who contributed valuable research. My colleagues Mark R. Joelson and Eugene J. Meigher assisted in the final review of the text. My wife reviewed several key chapters for layman's understanding and made helpful editorial suggestions. Bernie R. Burrus, Professor of Law at the Georgetown Law Center and my colleague in private practice, rendered invaluable research and editorial assistance as we shaped the substance of this book during the past two years.

E.W.K.

Contents

PART I The Historical Background 1

1 Introduction 3
2 Why Firms Merge 16

PART II The Legal Background of a Merger 25

3 Choosing the Method of Purchase 27
4 Dealing in Securities 43
5 Tender Offers and Take-Overs 64
6 Accounting Aspects of Mergers 98
7 Tax Considerations 109
8 Labor Aspects of Mergers 119
9 Closing the Deal 132

PART III Antitrust 137

10 Antitrust Theory 139
11 Mergers Under the Original Clayton Act 154
12 Mergers Under the Sherman Act 162
13 Mergers Under Section 5 of the FTC Act 171
14 The Celler–Kefauver Amendment 191
15 Classification of Mergers 211
16 Relevant Market 221
17 Tests of Unlawfulness 232
18 Defenses 256

19 Miscellaneous Corporate Amalgamations 273
20 Mergers Involving Foreign Commerce 285
21 Recent Developments in the Antimerger Laws 305

PART IV **Enforcement and Remedies 317**

22 Justice Department Procedure and Enforcement 319
23 Federal Trade Commission Practice and Procedure 348
24 Private Enforcement 360

PART V **Special Industry Mergers 377**

25 Mergers in the Regulated Industries 379
26 Bank Mergers 411
27 Conclusion—A Final Word on the Conglomerate 449

PART VI **Appendixes 455**

Appendix **I** Selected Bibliography 457
Appendix **II** The Sherman Act 482
Appendix **III** The Clayton Act 484
Appendix **IV** The Federal Trade Commission Act 495
Appendix **V** Justice Department Merger Guidelines 506
Appendix **VI** Federal Trade Commission Special Reports Relating to Large Corporate Mergers 516

Index 519

PART I

The Historical Background

In these first two introductory chapters we shall trace the history of the merger movement in the United States and consider the various motivations of businessmen in merging.

1 Introduction

No discussion of corporate mergers and acquisitions should rightfully begin without first turning back the clock to the American Revolution and the early days of the new Republic. Our imagination is drawn to the retreat of the Colonial Army across the farmlands of New Jersey following the Battle of Long Island. As General Washington and his aide, Alexander Hamilton, approached the Great Passaic Falls, located in what is now the city of Paterson, they could not help but be attracted to the potential for power the waterfalls possessed. Hamilton vowed to the future president that, if the war could be won, he would turn the valley into a great manufacturing center which would be a model to the world.

Hamilton did not forget his promise. As the nation's first secretary of the treasury, at the age of thirty-four, he prodded the New Jersey legislature until it passed an act on November 22, 1791, incorporating "The Socicty for establishing useful Manufacturers."

SUM, as it came to be called, was not to be just another corporation. Hamilton, his vision unbounded, sought to create the first truly diversified manufacturing company in the world. The prospectus revealed that he was "optimistically certain that success would be morally certain in the making of paper and pasteboard, paper hangings, sail cloth and other coarse linen cloths, stockings, ribbons and tapes, thread and fringes, blankets, carpets, 'Chip Hats,' women's shoes, pottery and earthenware, brass and iron wire; the printing of cotton and linen goods and some incidental manufacture of such goods for printing"; and, as an afterthought, "a brewery for the supply of the manufacturers" was considered worthy of mention.

Initially, the proposal was met with great enthusiasm. Residents of New Jersey eagerly anticipated "that this hitherto oppressed state may yet rise to importance, and shine with splendor in the new constellation." Pierre L'Enfant, having recently completed the design for the nation's capital, was hired to construct the industrial complex.

Yet before long, doubts and criticism emerged. Friends of small entrepreneurs began to fear the consequences of economic concentration likely to result from such an undertaking. One such critic warned "all manufacturers to view it as a birth of a political monster which if suffered to grow up will destroy their dearest interests." Another urged, "It would be well for our manufacturers of leather, paper, hats, shoes, carriages, in short every article that can be named, so large is the capital, and so extensive are the objects of this institution, to take the alarm. . . ." Businessmen themselves became skeptical of the plan. In a letter to Hamilton, attributable to one Thomas Marshall, the concerns which would be repeated by a later generation of businessmen were revealed:

> I had at first with you the idea that an establishment comprehending a dozen different objects well chosen, conducted by an able direction, enlightened and honest managers and skillful workmen might have the greatest Success, and I still so think; but would not the union of so many qualities, on which the success entirely depends, be an absolute miracle? . . . But if one of them is Wanting, you will find bad goods come out of the hands of unskillful workmen; dishonest managers make a fraudulent advantage at the expense of their employers, which in such a multitude of details will escape the eye of the directors; and directors who for want of particular knowledge of each of the different branches [will] conduct well that with which they are best acquainted, and be continually exposed to be deceived in all the others. The more I think on this affair, the more I am persuaded that there is a great risk in pursuing it in the manner in which it is proposed, and its advantageous execution must depend on fortune, more than on reason.

Unfortunately for the new nation and with the help of this country's first financial panic, Marshall's fears were substantiated. Within five years the experiment ended in failure as SUM suspended all manufacturing activities.

It is doubtful that any subsequent generation of businessmen has had the courage to undertake the construction of another SUM. Yet Hamilton's dream has not been forgotten. We are presently witnessing the creation of diversified corporations by another route, as today's businessmen put together corporate nations by merger.

The present merger movement, which has continued throughout the post-World War II period, was preceded by two earlier waves of accelerated merger activity. These took place at the end of the nineteenth century and during the 1920's. A common thread links each of these three periods of corporate consolidation. Merger activity has tended to coincide with a general heightening of business activity, broad expansion of the economy, increased interest by the public in securities, and a bullish stock market. In short, mergers are the child of prosperity. There are several reasons for this relationship. The incentive to grow is stronger during periods of economic buoyancy, because expectations are heightened, growth is made possible because rising profits add pools of capital to corporate treasuries, and investors are willing to finance adventurous managements.

Moreover, growth by merger often becomes more attractive than internal growth, for at least three reasons. First, because the cost of building new facilities will have skyrocketed, it may be less expensive to acquire the securities of an existing business which, for some reason, may be selling at less than the replacement cost of the company's assets. Secondly, if the acquiring company's stock has been inflated by the stock market, it can use its stock to achieve financial leverage in making acquisitions. Finally, the urge to take advantage of the prosperity prompts businesses to act as quickly as possible. Mergers avoid the time lag inherent in internal growth.

Despite this common theme, each of the three merger movements has had unique characteristics; each resulted from different historical causes, was financed differently, affected industries nonuniformly, and had differing impacts on market structure and competition.

THE FIRST PERIOD: MERGERS AND MONOPOLISTS

The first merger period can be best understood if we briefly review the historical situation. By the late nineteenth century the geographical frontiers of the continental United States had been sealed and the entire country had been laced together by the steel thread of the great railroads. Waves of immigrants since the Civil War settled throughout the country. These new Americans could contact their European relatives through Cyrus W. Field's trans-Atlantic cable and each other by using that familiar new convenience, the telephone.

The internal consolidation and rebuilding of the United States could not have taken place without complete freedom from foreign entanglements. The isolationism of the three decades following the Civil War was due primarily to the thrust of American energy and ingenuity toward internal consolidation and domestic expansion. However, after the frontiers were sealed and the country united from sea to sea, Americans began to look outward for the first time. As this first merger movement began, the cry "Remember the *Maine*" propelled this nation out of its isolation and into Cuba, Puerto Rico, and the Philippines.

After 1850 the form of the business organization changed rapidly. Individual proprietorship and partnership gave way to the corporation chartered under state laws. The early corporate statutes, however, were restrictive—for example, limiting the assets of the corporation in dollar amount, and, in some instances, geographically, to the state of incorporation. But business growth would not be impeded. Lawyers turned to the trust, a common-law device involving the transfer of legal title of assets to trustees who would then operate the business on behalf of the beneficiaries. The similarity to the corporate form—directors operating the business for the shareholders—is evident. Also, there was limited liability to the beneficiaries, as there is to the shareholders in the corporate form. The trust, however, being a common-law mechanism, had the great advantage of not being subject to restrictive state laws, such as governed corporations. The trusts rapidly grew in number and size. With growth came abuse; with abuse, a demand for reform; and ultimately the "antitrust laws."

With the liberalization of corporate laws at the turn of this century, particularly the New Jersey statute, and the public resentment of "trusts" came a return to the use of the corporation, this time on a national and international basis. Clever businessmen, encouraged by the *laissez-faire* policy of the government, had developed complex corporate structures from the basic corporate form. Mass production in manufacturing and vast geographical extensions in marketing had opened new vistas for these emerging giants. Financing was developing on a grand scale and many individuals were achieving sufficient financial security to buy several or more shares of these great corporations.

The first merger wave followed the "trust" movement of the 1880's and the period of railroad consolidation. The public's eagerness to invest in securities prompted promoters, speculators, and underwriters to fashion horizontal, and, to a lesser extent, vertical combinations seeking the control of markets. A *horizontal* merger involves the acquisition by one company of all or part of the stock or assets of a competitor which offers similar goods or services in the same market area—for example, two companies manufacturing and selling tires in Arizona. A *vertical* merger is one in which the acquiring company merges with a supplier or a customer—for example, a company manufacturing tires with a company selling tires. Industries which were formerly atomized were consolidated under the dominance of a few major companies to avoid "destructive" competition. Standard Oil of New Jersey, United States Steel, American Tobacco, and other behemoths backed by investment bankers of titanic size, systematically foreclosed competition in numerous basic industries, including tin cans, copper, chemicals, farm machinery, and, of course, steel and tobacco. Between 1898 and 1902, more than 2,650 mergers were reported in leading financial journals. The year 1899 alone saw more than 1,200 mergers.

Although the Sherman Antitrust Act had been adopted amid great fanfare in 1890, it played almost no role in stemming the first merger tide. The Department of Justice, the agency entrusted with its enforcement, was grossly understaffed and interested in other pursuits. During the first twelve years of its existence, for example, the Sherman Act was used mainly as a weapon against labor unions. Even during Theodore Roosevelt's administration, the government's entire antitrust staff consisted of five lawyers and four stenographers. Nevertheless, public opinion eventually forced the government into action. Predatory practices of the acquiring moguls, in combination with declining economic conditions, which raised prices 50 per cent between 1897 and 1913, generated the first period of "trust-busting." The adverse public attitude toward trusts and monopolies continued to be a major political issue in the first two decades of the twentieth century. Roosevelt's understaffed Justice Department waged a vigorous, highly public campaign against the trusts.

Although some of the most egregious offenders, such as Standard Oil and American Tobacco, were dissolved, the Sherman Act in its infancy had no real impact on the nation's corporate structure. The decline in merger interest was attributable rather to the collapse of the shipbuilding trust in the first years of the new century, which revealed the dangers of fraudulent trust financing. A general decline in stock market prices, culminating in the financial panic of 1907–1908, put an end to this first wave of corporate marriages.

The pattern of consolidation, however, had been established. It was estimated that the 100 largest industrial corporations controlled nearly 18 per cent of the assets of all industrial corporations by 1909. This was in sharp contrast to the situation which had prevailed twenty years earlier. The Rockefellers, the Goulds, and the Morgans had an irreversible impact on our nation's economy.

As indicated, politicians capitalized on the public indignation with the concentration of industry and especially the rise in prices. President Roosevelt had initiated judicial efforts to stem the tide of concentration. William H. Taft campaigned in 1908 on a pledge to continue his predecessor's policy, but his reluctance to exploit the Justice Department's antitrust accomplishments was turned against him in the election of 1912.

Recognizing that the American people had not heard any recent vocal government opposition to the trusts, Woodrow Wilson's campaign included the proposition that "private monopoly is indefensible and intolerable." To carry out his campaign promises, President Wilson urged Congress to clarify and elaborate the Sherman Antitrust Act. Congress responded with the Federal Trade Commission Act and the Clayton Antitrust Act.

Whereas the Federal Trade Commission Act was a preventive measure, the Clayton Act was primarily punitive. The former established an independent commission to eliminate incipient and existing unfair methods of competition. The latter proscribed specific methods of unfair competition and anticompetitive practices. The passage of these two antitrust measures did not completely solve the problems of private monopoly, but these acts, combined with renewed publicity of enforcement efforts, satisfied the public until attention was diverted by World War I.

Other domestic reforms highlighted the first two decades of the twentieth century. The Interstate Commerce Commission, created in 1887 to regulate railroads, was fortified by a series of sophisticated statutes designed to meet some of the ICC's problems. Aided by the Muckrakers, the federal government's Meat Inspection Act and the Pure Food and Drug Act heralded a new sense of concern for the consumer.

The Wilson administration, thoroughly imbued with the president's theory of executive leadership, urged the Congress to effect major reforms. The Federal Reserve Act of 1913 was the direct result of the Aldrich Commission Report, the most prestigious of several studies and discussions pointing toward a "money trust" dominated by a few great banking houses in New York City. The Federal Reserve Act, like the FTC Act and the Clayton Act, definitely bore the mark of the new president. President Wilson also sponsored extensive agricultural and labor reforms.

In the early twentieth century, for the first time in American history, foreign policy developed almost entirely apart from domestic policy. The only common issue was the tariff, which was revised downward by the Payne–Aldrich Tariff of 1909 and more drastically by the Underwood–Simmons Tariff of 1913. These revisions reflected the increasing international role played by the United States. As American economic and political influence extended beyond the Caribbean, involvement in European and Asian affairs seemed inevitable.

The result, of course, was American participation in World War I. Foreign policy and domestic policy were once again merged, but for the first time since the War of 1812, American domestic policy completely depended on its foreign policy.

THE SECOND PERIOD: MERGERS AND STOCK SPECULATION

The second phase of the merger movement was generated during World War I, as wartime controls reminded industries of the benefits of cooperation. The government forgot the clamor which produced its regulation of business and discouraged competition which might damage the war effort. Industries were encouraged to work together to maximize productivity. The overriding importance of foreign policy during the war provided the opportunity for a new wave of mergers. Moreover, the flotation of government bonds to finance the war reacquainted many small investors with the stock market. Once the postwar boom got underway the individual lessons of the past were forgotten as waitresses and barbers looked for opportunities to turn their life savings into a quick profit on Wall Street. Investment bankers were only too happy to assist them, and merger activity proceeded apace during the period of "uninterrupted prosperity," which came to an abrupt halt with the advent of the Great Depression.

Mergers during this "hysteria stage" could not be effected rapidly enough to satisfy the hunger of investors. Wall Streeters chuckled at the thought of uniting Worthington Pump and International Nickel so that they could underwrite the stock of "Pumpernickel." When the smoke from the stock market crash cleared, unfortunately, Wall Street had become a name synonymous with the Biblical cities of Sodom and Gomorrah.

While the boom was on, vertical mergers and the creation of public utility holding companies took place at an accelerated pace. Relatively broad ranges of related product lines were united under one board of directors. Thus, Radio Corporation of America, General Foods, American Cyanamid, and Borg-Warner came into being. Nevertheless, horizontal combinations continued to dominate the merger scene. Nearly 70 per cent of the mergers which took place between 1926 and 1930 involved direct competitors. Unlike the earlier wave of horizontal mergers, however, few monopolies were created by this consolidation. Instead, oligopolies as we know them came into being, rendering the market structure rigid without destroying competition entirely.

More than 4,600 mergers were consummated between 1926 and 1930. The peak year, 1929, rivaled 1899 in the number of mergers which took place. Between 1919 and 1930 nearly 12,000 manufacturing, mining, public utility, and banking concerns disappeared through merger. The number of chain distributors in twenty-six businesses increased from 8,500 to 20,000. Less than 1,600 chains made more than 10,000 acquisitions. By 1930 retail chain stores sold nearly one quarter of all drugs, tobacco, food, clothing, and general merchandise.

During 1921–1933, assets of $13 billion were acquired by merger, representing approximately 17.5 per cent of the nation's total manufacturing assets. There can be no doubt that once again the structure of American industry had been permanently altered. Berle and Means, in their classic work on corporations, estimated that by 1930 the 200 largest nonfinancial institutions controlled nearly half of the nation's nonbanking corporate wealth and nearly one quarter of the total wealth of the country, receiving more than 40 per cent of the income of all nonbanking corporations. Ten groups of holding companies controlled almost three fourths of the country's electric power. Much of the concentration had been attributable to mergers.

Although the motives of some of the architects of these earlier corporate marriages may have been questionable and although the social benefit flowing from some of their creations may have been mixed, there can be no doubt that expansion of the economy during the early days of industrialization would not have proceeded at its somewhat remarkable pace without the consolidation which took place in many basic and production industries. To take advantage of a growing technology large amounts of capital were essential, and capital was controlled by a few major investment bankers. To channel scarce American dollars and foreign investor interest, corporations had to present an appealing image to Wall Street, and consolidation, with a resultant decrease in competition, had always been appealing. Our rapid growth as an advanced industrial nation could not have been possible without some sort of a merger movement.

Moreover, it is generally assumed that true economies of scale were available to many of those firms which expanded their operations. Although this position can be overstated (the rate of merger activity has always coincided closely with stock prices, indicating that the condition of the capital market has a more important influence on mergers than underlying industrial conditions), it seems clear that many mergers did result in better products at lower prices. The wave of mergers during the

1920's, for example, coincided with a rising level of employment, a significant increase in national income, and a steady decline in price levels.

Of course, not all mergers were that romantic. It is questionable whether the formation of such companies as the Lone Pine–Surprise Consolidated Mining Company, the American Saddlery & Harness Company, and the American Hominy Company was essential to our national welfare. Nor can it be suggested that the highest moral values prevailed in the merger marketplace. "Watered" stock, three- and four-tiered pyramiding by holding companies, predatory business practices, and quick exits to Brazil were not uncommon. Yet, through it all, we emerged a strong and advanced industrial nation.

This second merger movement ended like the first, but just as the economic rise far outstripped the economic rise of the first merger period, so did the fall.

The 1930's was a decade for introspection, consolidation, re-evaluation, and reform. Once again all American resources were directed inward, toward rebuilding the nation struck with its worst domestic crisis since the Civil War. Foreign policy existed only to the extent that the United States found it necessary to deny involvement.

One significant difference in the reform legislation of the early 1930's from prior reforms stands out. Big business was not treated as the perpetrator of the problem but rather as a victim. Government reform was directed at the securities system and at banking, but there was no significant legislation designed to limit corporate activity. The National Industrial Recovery Act (the "Blue Eagle") was, in fact, designed to promote cooperation, not competition. The antitrust laws were held in abeyance. Price deviation, or competition, from the Codes promulgated under the Act were illegal. Then two things happened to change the attitude of the president toward business. First, the Supreme Court struck down the NIRA in the *Schecter* case. Secondly, the unemployment rate, which had declined in the early days of the New Deal, began to rise significantly. These events coincided with the 1936 election, and it was at this point that the president began to attack businessmen as "economic royalists" and the real cause of the Depression. Thurmond Arnold was appointed to head the Antitrust Division and a new era of "trust-busting" ensued.

Between 1935 and the outbreak of World War II, Franklin D. Roosevelt consolidated the gains of his New Deal and inaugurated many programs to enhance individual dignity. The Social Security Act (1935) and the Fair Labor Standards Act (1938) are two of the most important accomplishments of this "Second New Deal." Unemployment, however, continued to be a problem until the collapse of neutrality in 1941.

World War II again created the climate in which the merger movement could germinate. Unemployment was eliminated. The labor force was effectively apportioned by the War Manpower Commission, but despite the efforts of the National War Labor Board to stabilize wages, significant salary increases were recorded during the war. Competition was all but eliminated in order to meet the demands of producing the mightiest wartime arsenal the world has ever seen.

In the conversion to a "peacetime" industrial establishment the lessons of cooperation were not forgotten. With only a few momentary lapses the economy of the United States has grown constantly since World War II.

THE PRESENT PERIOD: MERGERS AND THE CONGLOMERATE

The present merger movement began soon after World War II ended. It has grown and persisted, taking only momentary pauses during the economic slowdowns of 1948–1949, 1957–1958, 1966, and 1969–1970. Lasting longer than the earlier movements, it has already surpassed them in absolute and relative size, reaching a peak in 1967–1968.

Unlike the earlier movements, investment bankers have not served as the architects or primary source of funds for present-day corporate acquisitions. The decline of the investment banker's role has been attributable to developments in the financial and industrial communities. During the past forty years capital has tended to concentrate into the hands of institutional investors, including insurance companies and pension funds. Financing, therefore, can be more direct, less complex, and more professional. Corporate managers no longer need to rely on investment bankers, because they have learned to negotiate financing for themselves. Moreover, many basic industries and older companies have become pools of unused capital. Rather than needing more financing, they now face the problem of putting excess capital to work. Thus, between 1957 and 1964 more equity was retired than was issued by American corporations.

The present movement is actually composed of two periods. Activity following World War II resembled the trend of the 1920's, as horizontal and vertical mergers united related product lines. With the passage of the Celler–Kefauver amendment to the Clayton Act, however, the pace of horizontal and vertical mergers declined. The focus shifted to a new type of consolidation pattern which harkened back to the days of Alexander Hamilton. Product relationship between acquiring and acquired firms became harder to find as firms branched out into seemingly unrelated areas of commerce.

Accompanying this development, the trend toward concentration also shifted focus. Following 1947, market concentration actually declined across a broad front in the producer goods sector of manufacturing. Instead, the consumer goods manufacturing industries led the consolidation movement. Whatever economies of scale resulted were thus concentrated in the marketing and distribution functions rather than in production. This, of course, paralleled the advancement of our economy from an orientation toward production to an orientation toward the market.

The First Phase

The first phase of the present movement took place between 1943 and 1947. Concentration was significantly increased in the cement, textile, paper, and distilled liquor industries. More than 2,400 sizable mergers, leading to the acquisition of approximately $5 billion in assets, took place between 1940 and the 1948 recession. The acquired assets totalled more than 5 per cent of all manufacturing assets in the country.

A contemporary study revealed that most sellers were motivated by tax, management, and investment considerations, whereas buyers were most concerned with acquiring new product lines or achieving a greater degree of vertical integration. Nevertheless, a 1948 report of the Federal Trade Commission indicated that the desire to diversify had prompted numerous conglomerate acquisitions, particularly in the food, drug, petroleum, and machinery industries. Thus, for example, a coal mining concern had acquired a manufacturer of male underwear and a manufacturer of household appliances purchased a producer of paper goods. Still, these acquisitions were treated by the business community as bizarre. Critics soon emerged who repeated the 150-year-old warnings of Thomas Marshall.

The Present Phase

Concern with what was regarded as an unhealthy trend toward concentration prompted Congress to enact the Celler-Kefauver Amendment to the Clayton Act in 1950, forbidding certain mergers which might reduce the level of competition in an industry. No sooner had the legislation been adopted than a merger movement which dwarfed all earlier such movements engulfed the nation. This merger movement coincided generally with a period of dramatic growth in the United States economy. From 1948 through 1968 more than 15,000 acquisitions were recorded, representing total acquired assets of nearly $68 billion. In 1968 alone more than 2,400 companies with combined assets exceeding $15 billion were acquired. Twenty-one per cent of all manufacturing and mining assets in the country were acquired by merger between 1953 and 1968.

Although thousands of mergers have taken place, the economic significance of the present merger movement centers on the merger conduct of "large" firms (those having more than $10 million in assets). As the merger movement has accelerated, it has increasingly involved acquisitions of extremely large corporations.

In 1948 only six large firms were acquired by merger. In 1968, 201 such mergers took place, representing the acquisition of more than $12 billion in assets. The assets acquired in these 201 large mergers equaled four fifths of all the assets acquired by merger that year. The number of firms having from $10 to $25 million in assets acquired between 1948 and 1968 equaled 63 per cent of the total number of firms of this size operating in 1968. The merged firms controlled assets equal to 59 per cent of the assets held by firms of this size in 1968. If no large mergers had taken place during this period, there would have been about 50 per cent more firms of this size in 1968 than there actually were.

Approximately 22 per cent of the 500 largest industrial concerns listed by *Fortune* in 1962 had disappeared by merger by the end of 1968. As many corporations with assets of more than $250 million were acquired in 1968 as during the previous twenty years. A small number of very large companies did much of the acquiring. Between 1948 and 1968, 37 per cent of all the acquired companies, controlling 56 per cent of all the assets acquired, were merged with companies having more than $250 million in assets. During this period the nation's 200 largest corporations acquired more than 60 per cent of all the assets involved in large acquisitions. Concurrently, the percentage of assets obtained by new capital investment in relation to assets acquired by merger steadily dropped. In 1953, for example, acquired assets were only 7.4 per cent as much as new capital investment. For the next twelve years the figure averaged between 15 and 20 per cent. It jumped to 38.5 per cent in 1967 and 54.6 per cent in 1968. Thus, it is apparent that corporate managers were focusing an increasing amount of attention on growth by merger rather than growth by internal capital.

Given these figures, it is not surprising that the present merger movement has led to an increase in the level of aggregate concentration. Approximately 2,600 manufacturing companies with assets exceeding $10 million presently own about 86 per cent of all manufacturing assets in the United States and receive 88 per cent of the net profits earned by all manufacturing corporations. The 200 largest industrial corporations own 60 per cent of all manufacturing assets, equal to the share held by the 1,000 largest in 1941. The percentage of total assets owned by the 100 largest manufacturing corporations exceeds the share held by the 200 largest in 1950. Indeed, eighty-seven United States corporations presently own approximately 46 per cent of the assets held by all manufacturing corporations, earning net profits equal to the net profits received by the other 194,000 manufacturing corporations in the country.

Between 1947 and 1960 the 200 largest manufacturing corporations increased their share of total corporate manufacturing assets from 42.4 to 54.1 per cent. Approximately half of this increase was attributable to merger, the rest to industry growth. By 1968 the percentage had risen to 60.9. The share increase from 1960–1968 was due almost entirely to mergers. No termination of this trend toward aggregate concentration is foreseeable. Despite the slump in merger activity during 1969–1970 as a result of a declining stock market, it seems plain that merger activity will continue to be brisk, although blunted by current enforcement activities of the Antitrust Division of the United States Department of Justice and the Federal Trade Commission. If the overall trend resumes, it has been predicted that by 1975 the 100 largest corporations will own more than 55 per cent, and the 200 largest more than 70 per cent, of all manufacturing assets in the United States.

Levels of aggregate concentration, however, do not completely reflect the impact mergers have had on the structure of particular industries. From 1948 to 1964, for example, nearly half of all the assets acquired by merger involved five industries—transportation equipment, chemicals, petroleum, paper, and nonelectrical machinery. In the peak year, 1968, 900 of the total 2,400 mergers took place in the chemicals, fabricated metals, and electrical and nonelectrical machinery industries.

Significantly, the pace of mergers classified as horizontal and vertical has perceptibly slackened. From 1948 to 1951, 62.5 per cent of all large mergers were either horizontal or vertical, compared to 37.5 per cent which were conglomerate. Thereafter, this ratio steadily declined, until by 1968 only 11.5 per cent of all larger mergers were horizontal or vertical, whereas 88.5 per cent were conglomerate. In 1968, 43 per cent of all mergers, small as well as large, were conglomerate in nature.

The new factor on the merger scene was the conglomerate corporation, which became a significant economic force during the 1960's. Between 1961 and 1968, eleven new conglomerate concerns acquired nearly $11 billion in assets as a result of 500 acquisitions. Dominating the financial news for several years, these modern-day descendants of SUM rose to meteoric heights before plunging into disfavor. Only time will tell whether they will ultimately meet the expectations of their creators.

Because so much of the recent merger activity has been conglomerate in nature, the economic impact on markets has not been as readily apparent as during earlier merger periods. Market concentration has taken place on a more selective basis. Despite the merger trend, for example, the number of companies manufacturing producer goods actually increased 23 per cent between 1947 and 1963. Many producer goods industries became less oligopolistic during this period. On the other hand, the number of companies making consumer goods dropped by 8 per cent. Concentration was especially pronounced in industries manufacturing highly differentiated products (those in which one company's product cannot serve as a perfect substitute for another company's product because of consumer preferences). Because the degree of product differentiation depends on the level of advertising expenditures, it can be concluded that marketing factors prompted this consolidation. Thus, a manufacturer of soaps or breakfast cereals might feel a strong incentive to merge, knowing that by pooling advertising campaigns with the campaigns of its partner it could expect to increase its sales.

The implications of the most recent merger movement are the subject of controversy. A head count of mergers or even the number of firms in an industry does not necessarily determine the competitive strength of the economy. Consolidation within a given industry may intensify the rivalry of the survivors. Do these figures, then, indicate a trend toward ultimate concentration or are they indicative of present-day corporate needs which will benefit the consumer? Is power being centralized in the hands of a few industrialized giants or is competition vigorous enough to accommodate the most recent wave of mergers? Are the corporate structures being created structurally sound or are they likely to decrease efficiency and creativeness? We will return to these questions later, after we have gained some understanding of the motives and mechanics of mergers.

2 Why Firms Merge?

The reasons for merging are as varied as the reasons a company may have to expand or diminish its operations. Moreover, in today's economic world, tax and financial considerations unrelated to corporate size, per se, have also spurred what a now famous *Fortune* article described as "The Urge to Merge." So far as mergers affect the public, these reasons may be good, bad, or indifferent.

To place the merger movement in perspective, two premises must be established. Aside from unusual situations, such as an immediate need for cash or for estate planning considerations, an owner usually will only sell his business when he believes that, for whatever the reasons, the business will be worth less to him in the future. Conversely, a prospective purchaser will only be interested in acquiring a business if he believes the acquired firm will be worth more to him in the future. Given these broad premises, we will examine the motives of sellers and buyers in some detail, indicating why merger, rather than internal expansion, may be a preferred method of achieving growth from the buyer's point of view.

SELLER MOTIVATION

When we think of the American economy we generally picture the corporate giant wielding its vast bureaucracy to supply our needs. It is easy to forget that much of our nation's business is conducted by relatively small firms, organized perhaps by a single man, financed and owned by his family and friends, and geared to produce a single product. Indeed, some 1.6 million businesses are today operated in the corporate form.

Although these closely held concerns may grow and prosper, they lack some of the valuable characteristics of larger corporations. First, because no organized market for the securities of the corporation exists, liquidity may be difficult to achieve. If the corporation's stockholders want to terminate their ownership interest, either to use the proceeds for other investments, to pay estate taxes, or to terminate their relationship because they disagree with the policies of the controlling shareholders, they may be forced to sell at distress levels. Executors of controlling shareholders may even be forced to liquidate the business to meet estate taxes. Moreover, because in many instances the controlling shareholder's stock represents the bulk of his estate, his executor may find it advisable to liquidate so that he can reinvest the estate's assets in more diversified holdings for the protection of the estate's beneficiaries.

Second, the business may lack the one characteristic which makes a corporation unique—continuity. Because the business in many cases *is* the founder, chances of its survival after his death are often questionable. His relatives may have begun mentioning something about "diversification."

Selling the business, however, although it would solve these problems, might not be totally satisfactory. The founder might not yet be ready to give up control of the business which has consumed so much of this energy. Even if he is ready to retire, he would have to consider the tax consequences of a sale. His after-tax profit might be considerably less than he would like it to be. A carefully planned merger would avoid all of these problems. Tax could be deferred; liquidity could be achieved if the acquiring firm is a publicly held company. If the acquiring firm is diversified, the security that "spreading the risk" entails could be realized.

Many acquiring corporations would be eager to have the head of the business remain at his post. In fact, some would only be interested in the purchase if the existing management agreed to remain in command. The acquiring firm might supply the capital needed to modernize the business or help it to expand into related product lines to serve its customers better, thus enabling the firm to retain or expand its position in the industry. The expertise that the acquiring firm could make available might help solve technological and managerial problems that the acquired corporation had been unable to master.

Because merger makes available an easy or potentially profitable exit, many entrepreneurs have been encouraged to start a business when they might not otherwise have done so. Undoubtedly, the possibility of merger has sustained the viability of beginning small business operations amid the ever-increasing "bigness" of business.

On the other hand, the owner's reasons for selling might not be so pure. His number-one salesman may have just left his employment and taken a list of the firm's most important customers. His competitor, who had always been rather sleepy, may have patented a new design which threatens to make obsolete existing business relationships. Less dramatic changes may be taking place which he realizes will diminish the profitability of the business in the coming years. The rule of *caveat emptor* certainly applies in the merger field.

Whatever the reason, the decision to sell will not be made lightly. A man who has devoted his life to the business cannot be expected to turn over control of his source of pride to strangers without some trauma. He will be plagued with doubts, wondering if he can really retain control of his business in the days ahead, if he will be subjected to arbitrary supervision by managers in some distant city, whether the sale will demoralize his employees and customers, whether he will have to struggle to get much-needed capital from the acquiring firm, whether the acquiring corporation will milk his business then liquidate it, whether his brother-in-law, who has been on the payroll for ten years without contributing anything, will be fired, whether efficiency experts will wipe out the organizational scheme he so carefully established, and a host of others. Stories of sellers withdrawing from the deal at the last minute or crying at closings are legion. There is a very human element involved.

Even though the business may be larger and publically held, similar reasons may be present which lead to a sale. The need for capital and expert management, the desire to diversify, the urge to participate in markets that are growing faster than the market shared by the selling firm may motivate stockholders and directors to transfer their allegiance to a more powerful corporate entity. Moreover, hoped-for economies of scale and many of the other reasons which prompt a larger firm to acquire a smaller one, to which we now turn, may also be present.

BUYER MOTIVATION

By joining two separate business entities into one, the architects of a merger hope that the resulting firm will be greater than the sum of its parts. That something extra, if it is realized, is called synergy. Synergisms may stem from operating or financial reasons. Operationally, for example, the acquisition of a going concern may bring with it an exceptional management team, a talented research and development group, patents, sources of raw materials, a stock exchange listing, an existing reputation, or desirable physical facilities. Acquiring the selling firm's product might strengthen the acquiring firm's present line either by satisfying customer demands, broadening the customer base, or adding new geographic markets. Adding a new business might increase utilization of existing resources, including unused capital, frustrated management, or physical facilities not operating at capacity levels.

Moreover, enlarging the scale of operations may reduce production and marketing costs and increase sales volume through better use of distribution facilities. Technological, managerial, and service functions can be distributed over a broader base. Thus, the cost of providing legal, accounting, and consulting services; obtaining license agreements; securing capital; approaching new problems such as foreign marketing; and using computers and laboratories can be minimized. Such savings may enable the combined firms to meet competitive pressures better.

Further, there is a growing school of thought which contends that the major problem facing modern-day corporations is the shortage of capable managers. The conglomerate movement, it is suggested, can alleviate these problems by providing expert high-level management to a variety of businesses. Thus, planning, financing, and other major decisions can be made by outstanding people using the most advanced technological tools. One president of a merger-minded company went so far as to state that the conglomerate concept is so desirable that within ten years, 200 conglomerate companies would transact all the nation's industrial business. Justice Douglas in a concurring opinion to the Supreme Court's decision in the *Pabst-Blatz* merger case quoted an article by humorist Art Buchwald describing—at some time in the future—the application to the Justice Department by the two remaining American corporations for permission to merge.

The conglomerate firm, then, seeks mergers so that it may function as a mutual fund and management consulting service. It is questionable, however, how much merger activity is actually generated by these operational considerations. Although we will return to this issue later, it bears noting at this point that a degree of skepticism has greeted those who argue that, given the present state of the American economy, hoped-for operational synergisms explain the present-day merger movement. There is substantial agreement, however, that financial considerations have played an increasingly important role in the decision to merge.

At the most traditional level, a firm may merge to obtain an improved credit standing in the financial community. This will result, for instance, if the equity–debt ratio of the acquired firm is more favorable than that of the acquiring firm. Moreover, it may seek to acquire a firm with a large supply of capital, such as an insurance company. The capital may be used to finance more ventures, or it may be distributed to shareholders as a dividend. In one such raid, dividends of $170 million were extracted from the coffers of an acquired insurance company and paid to the delighted shareholders.

If, on the other hand, the acquiring firm has excess capital, it can put that capital to work by investing in a business which it believes has been underpriced by the market. If the acquired firm's value has been discounted because of internal deficiencies, such as unimaginative management, the acquiring firm may seek to remedy the deficiency and reap the profit.

The desire to diversify has prompted mergers in numerous industries. The essence of business is change, and progressive managements have recognized that the merger vehicle provides a means of maintaining or expanding profits despite fluctuations in the industry in which a company may be currently operating.

Diversification may be a defensive necessity. By gaining a franchise in desirable markets, a firm can decrease its dependence on a single item or offset seasonal or cyclical fluctuations. A mature firm may enter new fields to avoid obsolescence. Diversification may be precipitated by threatened government regulation, as happened in the tobacco and drug industries, or because the firm has relied on the government too much. As James E. Ling, Chairman of the Board and Chief Executive Officer of Ling-Temco-Vought, Inc., described his own company's problem, "As late as 1964, 90% of LTV's business was committed to the military and space agencies. The management of LTV had suffered a number of traumatic experiences as the result of cutbacks in aircraft and missile programs. Thus, we were determined that never again would we be dependent upon any one product, market or technology to sustain our growth and progress." Even without these factors diversification in recent days has become a virtual psychological necessity. Real growth may be realized if the acquired firm is growing at a rate faster than that of the acquiring firm, and companies have attempted to accelerate their rate of growth by seeking out desirable merger candidates.

The competitive structure of the industry in which the firm operates may supply the motive for merger. Firms may wish to combine simply to foreclose competition. If the merger pattern in an industry gains momentum, nonmerging firms may feel compelled to join the merger bandwagon to avoid being left behind in the restructuring the industry can anticipate. This pressure will be especially apparent if a take-over bid is threatened. Managers who stand to lose their jobs if the take-over is successful may seek out a partner more friendly to their interests.

Antitrust considerations have occasionally encouraged merger activity. A merger can short-circuit rigid strictures which have been placed on the conduct of separate legal entities doing business together, such as firms in parent–subsidiary or franchisor–franchisee relationships. In Europe state-sanctioned cartels enable firms to reduce competition to their mutual advantage. Because cartels are not allowed in the United States, merger sometimes provides the only viable alternative.

Yet two other factors—taxes and the stock market—must be considered. If the acquiring firm chooses its partner carefully, its balance sheet and income statement can be made to show real or apparent profits even though the combined firms enjoy no increase in sales or decrease in costs. And few corporate managers have lost their jobs by showing increased profit figures.

To understand how this newest form of alchemy produces instant profits, the current fascination of Wall Streeters with "performance" and the operation of the tax laws must be understood.

Stock-Market Considerations

As one merger-minded executive candidly admitted, "The fashion in acquisitions and mergers these days is to evaluate them primarily on a financial basis. The upper-most questions seem to be: What will the proposed acquisition or merger do for my per-share earnings? What will it do for my image in the financial community in terms of sales-growth curves and earnings-growth curves?" If a company increases its earnings per share of outstanding stock rapidly, the investment community will reward the company by placing a premium on its stock. If it is anticipated that the growth will continue indefinitely, investors may be willing to pay thirty, forty, or even fifty times the current year's earnings per share for a chance to participate in this growth.

Companies which command this spotlight of glamor are in an excellent position to expand by merger. Let us assume that a "glamor" company earns $100 and has 100 shares of stock outstanding. A share of its stock sells for $50, or fifty times earnings. The firm then issues twenty shares of its stock to acquire by merger the stock of a less glamorous concern, which also earns $100 and has 100 shares of stock outstanding, but whose stock sells for only $10 a share. Following the merger, the acquiring firm's accounts reflect $200 earnings with 120 shares of stock outstanding. Strange as it may seem, the investment community, in a leap of faith, has tended to believe that the merged firm has the same growth potential the acquiring firm had. The price of the acquiring firm's stock will therefore rise to resume the same (or similar) price–earnings ratio it had before the merger, which might leave the stock selling for $80 per share. Having reached this plateau, the acquiring firm can make its next acquisition by issuing even fewer shares of its stock. And so the cycle continues, at least until someone realizes that the merged firm cannot achieve the anticipated rate of growth. Members of the investment public and those who received stock for their ownership interest in the acquired companies reap the consequences.

A similar increase in per share earnings can be achieved if the acquiring company "buys" the acquired firm's earnings by issuing debentures, preferred stock, or warrants instead of its common stock. Using the preceding example, if the acquiring firm issued debentures to effect the merger, it could double its earnings without increasing the number of shares outstanding, conceivably doubling the price of its common stock.

Accounting techniques can also be utilized to show an increase in per share earnings. "Adjustments" can be made to the acquired firm's method of accounting, changing a conservative accounting system to one which is less restrained in its computation of earnings. Possibilities along these lines are almost endless, given the variety of accounting principles dealing with depreciation, tax, and other variables which are "generally accepted."

The practice of pooling, which will be discussed in a later chapter, also inflates earnings by deleting from the balance sheet the premium over book value the acquiring firm must pay to effect the purchase. By pooling, moreover, the acquiring firm may hope to submerge details of one of its business lines by publishing consolidated financial statements. This obscures the data from competitors (or from unwary investors).

Tax Considerations

The tax laws encourage the merger game by lowering the ante of corporate growth. They encourage the seller to accept a lower price than he would for a simple sale of his business, and help the buyer pay the purchase price. As a general rule, a sale of business assets is a taxable event. Gain or loss must be recognized in the year of sale. A merger, on the other hand, may qualify as a "tax-free" sale. The gain or loss will not be recognized, but will be deferred until such time as a taxable event does occur.

The benefits of deferred taxation are real. For example, the owner of a closely held corporation, by deferring the tax on the sale of his business, will have a larger estate to pass on to his heirs. At his death, an estate tax is paid that is less than the tax on the sale would have been. His heirs take the ownership interest at a stepped-up basis, thus avoiding tax which would otherwise have been assessed.

Other incentives to merge are created by the tax laws. If a company has suffered losses, it would be presumed that the company's worth has been discounted in the marketplace. Certain tax provisions nevertheless inflate the company's worth in the merger marketplace. To the extent that gains have not been realized against which the losses can be offset, the company will have accumulated a tax loss. That tax loss can be carried forward and applied to income which may be earned in future years.

The presence of a "tax loss carryforward" creates profitable possibilities for merger. The company burdened by the tax loss can acquire a profitable enterprise yet pay taxes on the income of that company which are less than would have been paid by the acquired company until the tax loss carryforward is depleted. Penn-Central Railroad is a classic example. It at one time launched a major acquisition effort based almost entirely on its estimated $500–$600 million tax loss carryforward.

On the other hand, a profitable company may be willing to pay a premium for the opportunity of acquiring the tax loss carryforward, because it can decrease its future tax burden to the extent of the carryforward. In addition, it may be able to liquidate the acquired company, taking advantage of the loss which could not be realized if the acquired firm liquidated, because it would have had no offsetting income.

"Debt–equity switching" offers another avenue for profitable merger activity. In return for the stock of the acquired firm, the acquiring firm issues debentures. We have already indicated that the earnings per share ratio of the acquiring firm's stock benefits from this transaction. In addition, two tax savings are involved. First, by qualifying as a tax-free exchange, tax payments can be deferred until the debentures become due. Secondly, the acquiring firm pays for the purchase with before-tax income. (If it had to pay dividends on stock, the dividends would come from after-tax income, which is only half as much.) The acquiring firm can therefore afford to pay a premium price for the company.

The widely reprinted speech of Richard Cheney, then senior vice president of Hill and Knowlton, Inc., before the Ohio State Bar Association on November 7, 1968, dramatizes this concept:

> A [firm] using subordinated debentures, convertible securities and/or warrants can afford to pay a big premium for an old-line company with no debt. To get the wherewithal for his offer, all he needs is his own printing press to print the securities he is using to make his tender. And he can afford to offer a big increase in investment income to the stockholders of the target because he has the federal tax laws going for him.
>
> He will leap at the chance to offer a $50 debenture paying $3 interest for a stock selling at $40 and paying a $2 dividend. Why not? He actually makes money in the deal. For every share of stock he gets through his tender, he makes $2 in dividends. On this he pays only about 15 cents per share in taxes because the dividend is an intracompany dividend and the Treasury excludes 85 percent of such dividends from taxation. At the same time, the $3 in interest he pays out is a cost of doing business for tax purposes. Each $3 he pays out costs him only $1.50. So he's taking in $1.85 in dividends after taxes and paying out $1.50 after taxes. Thus for every share he gets in his tender he makes 35 cents. He can afford to run his printing presses overtime creating funny money by the truckload.

In 1968, thirty-one major transactions, involving $4.5 billion, were financed using this technique. This represented ten times the number and 100 times the worth of transactions of this nature which had taken place just two years earlier. Undoubtedly, businessmen learn quickly.

Finally, the tax laws assist in the purchase of businesses which have accumulated pools of surplus cash. An obliging acquiring company can use this cash to help pay for the purchase. This bit of wizardry can be described in a grossly simplified way. If the acquired firm distributed its cash surplus to its stockholders, the distribution would be taxed at ordinary income rates. A properly supervised merger can result in having the same distribution made, but this time the distribution will be called a return of capital and thus taxable at the lower capital gains rates. Thus, the acquired firm may literally be willing to sell $1 for 80 cents. Anyone for merger?

Merger v. Internal Growth

Presumably, when a corporation decides to expand by merger rather than through internal growth, it has concluded that this is a cheaper method of achieving its goals. As we shall learn later, the source of this cheapness may be suspect from society's viewpoint.

In addition to the stock-market and tax considerations which prompt mergers, expansion by merger may save time and money and reduce the uncertainty of entering a new field of business. It is much easier to purchase a going concern with its existing facilities, personnel, and technology than to organize a new business. The purchased concern will already have established a market position and demonstrated its revenue-yielding capacity. The danger inherent in combating difficult competition during the early stages of development can be avoided.

The initial cost of a merger is fixed and not subject to unforeseen contingencies. That cost might be lower than the cost of reproducing the necessary facilities. Moreover, future earnings may be used to finance the purchase, allowing the acquiring firm to enter the desired market for a modest initial capital expenditure. By setting up the merger as an installment purchase with payments geared to the acquired firm's future earnings, the acquiring firm's risk will have been minimized.

The Role of Management

Lastly, the human factor has undoubtedly motivated an untold number of mergers. Dreams of building a personal empire or creating the impression of growth to satisfy aggressive stockholders and add "glamour" to the corporation have caused managements to join the merger bandwagon even though real synergisms could not be expected to result. As the president of one merger-minded company candidly admitted, "When I became President I just wanted to make an acquisition— you know, like going out on your very first date; all you want is a girl."

Far from being an incidental motive, it has been suggested that large merging firms have exhibited a tendency to achieve growth by merger even at the cost of the interests of shareholders. The best interests of management are identified with growth and not necessarily with profit making.

This merger syndrome has taken its toll. One management consulting firm concluded that between 1960 and 1965, 11 per cent of those firms which had been acquired were later sold or liquidated and another 25 per cent turned out to be of "doubtful" worth. Other observers estimate that as many as half of the companies that have instituted acquisition programs have not been successful in their endeavors. As in any other business activity, there can be no substitute for thorough planning and careful follow-through.

The remainder of this book, we hope, will help the reader to avoid some of the legal pitfalls which might mar corporate marriages.

PART II

The Legal Background of a Merger

Much has been written to familiarize corporate managers with the difficult business questions involved in all mergers. The materials listed in the Bibliography can help the executive define his company's goals, seek out and screen prospective partners, evaluate personnel and facilities, set a fair price, and determine the method of financing.

Once these questions have been addressed, however, the executive often finds that he has entered unfamiliar territory. Tax and accounting treatment, questions regarding the form the transaction will take, reluctant shareholders, recalcitrant directors, and a host of other problems figuring so prominently in the negotiations, must be dealt with sooner or later. An executive who waits too long before consulting legal specialists might find that he has made unwise commitments. If he calls them in too soon, on the other hand, time and money will be wasted. Because companies experienced in making acquisitions realize that negotiations with numerous candidates may take place before a single merger is completed, the cost of consulting specialists prematurely may be high indeed.

The next few chapters seek to widen the reader's horizon. By presenting in simplified form an introduction to the legal setting in which a merger takes place, it is hoped that the nonlegal executive or the general practitioner will be better able to identify issues that arise during the course of merger negotiations to help him determine when the specialists should be consulted. If unnecessary expense and costly mistakes can thereby be avoided, these chapters will have served their purpose.

3 Choosing the Method of Purchase

Corporations exist because they have been created by the laws of one of the states. Because they are creatures of that state's sovereignty, it has long been conceded that they may be bought or sold only by complying with the laws of that state.

Although the rules governing mergers vary from state to state, they are linked by many common denominators. All states, for example, provide three basic methods by which corporations may be joined:

1. *"Statutory" merger or consolidation.* By complying with the requirements explicitly set out in a state's statutory scheme, a merger results by operation of law. In a *merger,* one of the joining corporations survives, while the others cease to exist as legal entities. In a *consolidation,* all the corporations existing prior to the act of joining cease to exist as legal entities and a new corporation is created. (Because mergers and consolidations are almost identical, both will be referred to hereafter as mergers unless otherwise indicated.)
2. *Purchase of assets.* The acquiring corporation can buy the other corporation's assets, leaving the selling corporation's shell intact.
3. *Purchase of stock.* The acquiring corporation can obtain ownership of the target corporation by buying its shares directly from the shareholders. Unlike the other two merger forms, a stock purchase does not require the approval of the acquired corporation's directors.

It should be noted at the outset that any desired postmerger corporate structure can be achieved regardless of the method of joinder used. Assume, for example, that A and B corporations wish to merge in such a way that they become one corporation for all purposes. They may do this through a statutory merger proceeding in which the shareholders of A receive stock in B in exchange for their stock in A. As an alternative to a statutory merger proceeding, B could purchase A's assets from A in return for B stock. A could then liquidate, distributing the B stock to the A shareholders. As another alternative, B, using its own stock, could purchase the A stock from shareholders of A. B could then liquidate A by distributing A's assets to B. As still another alternative, B could create a subsidiary to perform any of the preceding transactions. The subsidiary could then be reunited with B. And so on.

Although the desired postmerger corporate structure can be achieved by using alternative forms, the methods are not interchangeable. Despite the theoretical similarity in end result, different legal consequences can and do flow from the choice of merger form. Different consequences also flow from the choice of consideration used to pay the purchase price. Whether to use cash, debentures, stock, or some hybrid form of security will thus depend not only on business factors, but also on legal ones. Each method of purchase has advantages and disadvantages. Choosing the most appropriate method or combination of methods is an intensely practical undertaking dictated by the positions and needs of the merging corporations and their stockholders. A review of those considerations can only highlight the factors to be evaluated.

In the following discussion, vagaries of the laws of individual states will not be emphasized. To simplify the presentation, reference will be made to the Model Business Corporation Act, first proposed by the American Bar Association and the American Law Institute and presently adopted with minor variations in numerous states. Of course, no merger should be attempted without first reviewing carefully the statutory and decisional law of the states having an interest in the merger.

PREPARING FOR THE DEAL

A review of every corporation will reveal hurdles to merging which can be alleviated by advance planning. The state of incorporation can be changed to one more amenable to merger; unnecessary restrictions in corporate charters and by-laws can be removed; unwanted assets can be sold or spun off; the capital structure of the company can be simplified and rationalized; the authorization to issue necessary venture stock can be obtained; and other housecleaning can be completed. In short, the corporation should be streamlined for action, removing the layers of crust accumulated during years of business activity.

STATUTORY AUTHORITY

Most states have adopted liberal merger statutes imposing few restrictions on the types of mergers allowed. So long as the procedural rules are followed in these states, little effort is made to interfere with a corporate decision to merge. Nevertheless, substantive restrictions exist in certain situations. Although all states permit domestic corporations to merge with out-of-state corporations, some require that the domestic corporation be the survivor in such a merger. Some states strictly enforce statutory provisions requiring that merging corporations be engaged in "similar" business activities. Moreover, to protect what is loosely called the public interest, special restrictions apply to most mergers involving enterprises in regulated industries, such as public utilities and insurance companies.

A corporation confronted with restrictive state laws regarding mergers can always reincorporate in a state more hospitable to its merger plans. Depending on the disposition of the state, however, less drastic alternatives may be available. For example, the acquiring corporation might be able to create a subsidiary to consummate the merger without running afoul of the state's proscriptions. Similarly, an assets or stock transaction may pass muster even though a statutory merger would not be allowed. Thus, we begin to catch a glimpse of the differences in result flowing from the choice of merger form.

Once it becomes clear that the contemplated merger will not be forbidden by state law, the rights and responsibilities of those more particularly affected by the merger must be considered. We direct our attention at this point to the shareholders of the merging corporations.

OBTAINING STOCKHOLDER APPROVAL

The directors and managers of corporations generally exert a far more powerful influence over corporate activities than do the "owners," who are, of course, the stockholders. Except in closely held corporations or in corporations having a few stockholders owning a significant percentage of the outstanding shares, the managers and directors rarely consult these "owners" when questions regarding the fate of the corporation are at issue. The stockholders usually learn of the decisions only after they have been made. This situation is drastically altered when a merger is in the offing. Reasoning that the very essence of the stockholders' investment will be affected by a merger, legislatures and courts have acted to insure stockholders a voice in merger proceedings.

Depending on the number of stockholders and their willingness to accept the merger, the burden of obtaining their approval may indeed be formidable. It may be necessary to schedule special stockholder meetings, clear proxy materials with the Securities and Exchange Commission, conduct publicity campaigns to secure the necessary stockholder vote, ward off legal attacks by opponents of the merger, and face the creation of an obstreperous minority stockholder interest which might object to dividend policies or the allocation of business or other benefits among the members of the corporate family.

Further, dissenting shareholders might insist on receiving "appraisal" rights—the right to sell their shares back to the corporation (or the surviving corporation) and to be paid a cash sum equal to the "fair market value" of the shares. Establishing the fair market value may be time-consuming and expensive and always raises the possibility of litigation. Moreover, if there are a number of dissenters, the cash drain on the corporate funds may be significant. Most corporations, therefore, provide for withdrawal from the merger if the percentage of dissenters exceeds a permissible level.

It should be noted that the rights granted by statute are interlocking. If a particular merger transaction requires a shareholder vote, dissenters usually have the corresponding right to an appraisal. If appraisal is available, minority interests can be eliminated at the outset. Like buying off an unhappy in-law before a marriage, the resulting harmony may sometimes be worth the price. In addition to these statutory protections, stockholder rights may be amplified by the corporate charter or by-laws, by the terms of a contract or loan agreement, or by stock exchange requirements. Statutory provisions generally establish a floor for stockholders' rights rather than a ceiling. The burden of obtaining shareholder approval will be influenced by the merger form.

Statutory Merger

To complete a statutory merger, in most states approval must be obtained from a specified percentage of the stockholders of *all* the corporate parties to the merger. Until recently, the Model Corporation Act and most states set the required percentage at two thirds. This percentage has now been reduced in many jurisdictions. Stockholders opposing the merger are entitled to appraisal rights.

A different proceeding available in some states is known as the "short-form" merger. By statute, a wholly owned or nearly wholly owned subsidiary (the ownership interest by the parent is usually set at 90 or 95 per cent) can be merged with its parent by a simple vote of the board of directors of the parent, who need not consult their shareholders. Appraisal rights are not extended to the shareholders of the subsidiary.

Purchase of Stock

A stock purchase, because it involves the shareholders directly, does not require the formality of a vote in most states. A tender offer is made to the shareholders of the target corporation, generally offering a premium to encourage them to sell, whether or not the directors and managers of the target corporation favor the merger. The shareholders decide individually whether or not they will participate.

The shareholders of the acquiring corporation are not entitled to vote on the purchase. Nevertheless, the rules of the New York Stock Exchange and the American Stock Exchange require a vote if the acquisition will increase the outstanding shares of the acquiring corporation by 20 per cent or more, or if the directors, officers, or major shareholders of the acquiring corporation have an interest in the acquired corporation.

Appraisal rights are not required by most state statutes in stock acquisition mergers. Because in this type of merger, the distinct possibility exists of minority shareholder interests, various "squeeze-out" methods have been devised to attempt to eliminate this interest. The success of these methods depends on the judicial philosophy in the state in which they will be tested regarding the importance to be given to the protection of minority interests. In *Abelow* v. *Midstates Oil Corp.*, for example, a subsidiary of the acquiring corporation purchased the stock of another corporation. The subsidiary then "sold" the assets of the acquired corporation to its parent for cash, liquidating soon after the sale. As a result of the liquidation the cash was distributed to its shareholders—namely, the parent and the minority interest. The Delaware Supreme Court allowed the corporation to exclude the minority interest by this subterfuge. These legal games have not been as successful in other states, however. In *Kellogg* v. *Georgia-Pacific Paper Corp.*, for example, a federal district judge in Arkansas considered a case in which the subsidiary, following its purchase of another corporation, adopted a plan of liquidation providing for distribution of its assets to the parent and distribution of its cash to the minority interest. The court commented:

> To say that majority stockholders may dissolve a corporation and proceed to take over the business and principal assets for themselves while at the same time forcing the minority to take mere cash for their interests, would be to confer upon the majority the power to confiscate the minority interest, thus depriving the minority shareholders of their interest in an existing business with its attendant possibilities of growth and appreciation in value, an interest which may be worth much more than the present cash value of the minority shares. Such should not be permitted.

A less controversial squeeze-out method may be available in those states providing for short-form mergers. The stock of the acquired corporation can be purchased by a subsidiary, after which the subsidiary is reunited with its parent. The minority interest may be forced to accept appraisal rights in return for its shares.

Purchase of Assets

By statute in most states, shareholders of the selling corporation must ratify an assets sale made other than in the regular course of business by a majority of two thirds. Many states grant appraisal rights to dissenting shareholders. However, appraisal rights are not available in all states. Thus, in these few refuges, it is possible to merge without having to pay dissenting shareholders and without creating minority interests. Stockholders of the acquiring corporation generally have no voting or appraisal rights in an assets transaction. Here again, however, the rules of the stock exchanges may require a vote under the circumstances described previously for stock purchases.

ARE THESE DISTINCTIONS JUSTIFIED?

It is apparent that the form of merger chosen by the directors will have a considerable influence on the rights of the shareholders. Voting and appraisal rights may be avoided, either deliberately or incidentally, because of the flexibility inherent in the law. Given the derivative of Murphy's Law applicable to lawyers—that any flexibility in the law which can be stretched to its breaking point will be stretched to its breaking point—the following transaction can be imagined. Assume that a billion-dollar corporation with 10,000 shares outstanding wishes to merge with a million-dollar corporation with 1,000 shares outstanding. It is anticipated that many of the shareholders of the larger corporation would not oppose the merger. The directors of the smaller corporation "purchase" the stock held by the larger corporation's shareholders, giving ten shares of the smaller corporation's stock for every share of the larger corporation's stock. The "acquired" corporation is thereafter liquidated. The original stockholders of the larger corporation, of course, will be in control of the combined corporation. Theoretically, at least, the entire transaction could be completed without the vote of the smaller corporation's shareholders.

Fortunately, such legal theatrics which would so cavalierly deprive shareholders of their rights simply will not pass muster in most states. Judges have refused to give credence to the rather transparent "upside-down" nature of the transaction and have insisted that the shareholders of the smaller corporation be treated as if they were shareholders of an acquired corporation.

However, other problems are not so easily resolved. As has been pointed out, various transactions produce a corporate structure identical to that which would result from a statutory merger yet which does not guarantee to shareholders the same rights they would have in a statutory merger. This would be true, for example, in an assets or stock purchase followed by liquidation of the acquired corporation, or a short-form merger of a subsidiary following merger of the subsidiary with another corporation. Disgruntled shareholders have occasionally attacked these transactions as unfairly denying them their rights.

In *Farris* v. *Glen Alden,* for instance, the Pennsylvania Supreme Court examined a merger agreement calling for a purchase of B's assets by A, to be immediately followed by a liquidation of B. Although the resulting corporate structure would have matched that which would have resulted from a statutory merger, the acquiring corporation asserted that its shareholders had no right to an appraisal. In its opinion, the court identified some of the conceptual and practical problems involved:

> When use of the corporate form of business organization first became widespread, it was relatively easy for courts to define a "merger" or a "sale of assets" and to label a particular transaction as one or the other. . . . But prompted by the desire to avoid the impact of adverse, and to obtain the benefits of favorable, government regulations, particularly federal tax laws, new accounting and legal techniques were developed by lawyers and accountants which interwove the elements characteristic of each, thereby creating hybrid forms of corporate amalgamation. Thus, it is no longer helpful to consider an individual transaction in the abstract and solely by reference to

> the various elements therein determine whether it is a "merger" or a "sale." Instead, to determine properly the nature of a corporate transaction, we must refer not only to all the provisions of the agreement, but also to the consequences of the transaction and to the purposes of the provisions of the corporation law said to be applicable.

Applying this rationale to the facts of the case before it, the court concluded that, although styled as an assets sale, a "*de facto* merger" had, in fact, been consummated.

The *de facto* merger doctrine is a judicial tool to reach a desired end and has been employed in assets and even stock transactions to protect voting and appraisal rights of dissenting shareholders of both acquiring and acquired corporations. Some judges have gone so far as to imply that a moral question was at issue. As the New Jersey Chancery Court stated in *Applestein* v. *United Board and Carton Corp.*:

> If, in truth and in substance the proposed plan in this case is a "merger," why should the interested parties not frankly and honestly recognize it as such and pursue the statutory procedure . . . for validating the proposal? It is a fundamental maxim of equity that "Equity looks to the substance rather than the form." . . . This court of conscience never pays homage to the mere form of an instrument or transaction, if to do so would frustrate the law or place justice in chains. The courts of equity in New Jersey, and elsewhere, have never hesitated to look behind the form of a particular corporate transaction and find that it constituted a corporate merger, if in fact and in substance it was a merger, regardless of its deceptive outward appearance.

Yet the courts in other states, the most notable being Delaware, have not been as willing to ignore the form of the transaction chosen by the directors, chains or no chains. In *Hariton* v. *Arco Electronics, Inc.*, the Delaware Chancery Court ruled that the shareholders of the acquiring corporation in a situation, which, for our purposes, can be considered similar to the situations in *Farris* and *Applestein,* need not be granted voting and appraisal rights. The court reasoned, "the sale-of-assets statute and the merger statute are independent of each other. They are, so to speak, of equal dignity, and the framers of a reorganization plan may resort to either type of corporate mechanics to achieve the desired end."

This ambivalence in judicial response merits deeper inquiry. If voting and appraisal rights serve important functions in statutory mergers, it seems inconsistent to deny them in assets or stock transactions, especially those followed by liquidation of the selling corporation. There seems to be no reason why shareholders' "rights" should depend for their realization on decisions over which the shareholders themselves have no control. It is, therefore, necessary to identify the function voting and appraisal rights, in fact, serve.

Interestingly, some commentators have argued that these rights incident to a merger serve no useful function. They reason as follows: (1) other corporate decisions, such as a decision to develop a new product line by internal growth rather than by merger, have as much impact on the nature of the shareholders' investment as does a merger; (2) voting and appraisal rights are not granted to stockholders who disagree with these decisions; (3) therefore, voting and appraisal rights incident to a merger are not important enough to merit special efforts by courts to preserve them. Accordingly, these commentators concluded that courts should not interfere with the form of the transaction chosen by the directors.

This argument leaves much to be desired. A more consistent policy may indeed be necessary. But it might be more desirable to achieve that consistency by granting voting and appraisal rights in additional situations, rather than by withdrawing them in mergers.

Beyond that line of argument, however, it seems clear that some mergers present unique problems justifying extraordinary protection. Voting rights, for example, serve an important function when a true merger, rather than an "elephant–flea" acquisition, is contemplated. The corporation resulting from the merger will undoubtedly be quite different from any of the corporations existing prior to the merger; the change will occur too rapidly to enable the shareholders to express their disapproval by way of a vote against the incumbent management at the annual meeting; and the action may be irrevocable for all practical purposes. Similarly, appraisal rights serve an important function when the securities of the merging corporations are not readily marketable. Again, because of the speed involved in a merger, dissenting shareholders in these situations may have nowhere to turn to make their escape except to the corporation.

So long as the merger will significantly affect the shareholders' investment and so long as the securities of the corporations are not readily marketable, therefore, it does not seem unreasonable to grant extraordinary protection to shareholders and to enforce that protection regardless of the form of the transaction chosen by the directors. Unfortunately, few mergers today fit this theoretical mold. Voting and appraisal rights tend to become burdensome when, as is usual, the corporations are of unequal size and the securities of one or both corporations are traded regularly on a national exchange. The situation becomes downright ludicrous when we apply the statutory formula to certain mergers. No justification has ever been advanced, for example, to explain why the stockholders of General Motors must ratify the decision of that company's board of directors to acquire a tiny manufacturer of auto parts or to be paid by General Motors if they disagree with the decision. General Motors before the merger will still be General Motors after the merger. The directors' decision to merge may well have a less significant impact on the corporation's state of affairs than a dozen other decisions routinely made every day not requiring shareholder approval. And if some shareholders are unhappy they can complain to their brokers at the same time they give him a sell order. Thus, in those situations falling outside the theoretical mold for which the merger statutes were presumably intended, attempts to circumvent the statute can be viewed as good-faith efforts by resourceful lawyers to avoid arbitrary limitations on the powers of directors to acquire other businesses. It may be difficult to justify frustrating their efforts by the invocation of a Latin phrase.

The battle taking place in courtrooms is gradually being transferred to legislative halls. Some state legislatures have begun what may prove to be a new trend by restricting appraisal rights to shareholders of corporations whose shares are not listed on a national exchange. The Model Corporation Act was recently amended to reach a similar result.

Voting rights have also been scrutinized in some states. Ohio recently adopted far-reaching revisions to its merger laws providing for a vote by the shareholders in most kinds of corporate fusions but only when the shareholders' investment will actually be influenced to a significant degree (as determined by the amount of equity dilution). Delaware, Connecticut, and Rhode Island are moving in a similar direction.

Although these statutory solutions are not ideal (for example, they do not protect shareholders of companies making a rapid series of small mergers), they are a necessary beginning. Given the present state of the law the choice of merger form frequently depends on legitimate considerations having little relation to the voting and appraisal rights of stockholders. For instance, significant tax and securities registration benefits flow to a corporation and its stockholders if the selling corporation is immediately liquidated following an assets sale. Although corporations desiring to take advantage of these provisions could avoid attacks under the *de facto* merger doctrine by granting voting and appraisal rights to the stockholders of the acquiring corporation whether or not this would later be deemed necessary by a court, it would seem preferable to eliminate the anxiety and wasted motion inherent in these procedural requirements through a clear and reasonable legislative pronouncement.

Until these questions are considered by more legislative groups, it seems clear that the *de facto* merger battle is due to continue. Because the doctrine has only vague parameters in most states, caution and prudence are required.

ASSUMPTION OF LIABILITIES

So long as the books of the corporation to be acquired have been examined by a certified public accountant, or by the acquiring corporation itself, a fairly accurate estimate of outstanding liabilities can be made. The purchase price will be adjusted to reflect these liabilities. Such an examination, however, is not always possible. The management of the selling corporation may be reluctant to open its books, especially during early stages of negotiation, for fear that information will be leaked to its competitors. Some ultracautious entrepreneurs have refused to permit any examination at all, demanding that such an examination be postponed until after the merger has been completed. Although normal prudence would suggest that the acquiring corporation terminate its negotiations if such a position is taken, some adventurous souls have been willing to risk a purchase under these circumstances, gambling on their ability to identify a sound business deal. (A similar problem is regularly encountered in take-over bids, although the risk will be minimized if the target corporation has published financial data certified by an independent accountant.)

Even if an examination can be made, however, all liabilities may not be uncovered. Transactions may have occurred during the acquired company's life leading to claims being made against it at a later time. Tax deficiencies, antitrust violations, patent infringement, or breach-of-contract claims may arise like midnight ghosts to haunt the new owners.

In a statutory merger, the acquiring corporation assumes all liabilities, known and unknown, of its partner. A corporation purchasing the stock of another corporation, although not assuming the acquired corporation's liabilities, accepts the corporation burdened by whatever liabilities it has incurred, because the acquired corporation continues to exist as a legal entity.

The only way to attempt to avoid unknown or contingent creditors of the acquired corporation is by purchasing its assets, leaving the corporate shell of the acquired corporation intact. Theoretically, at least, creditors would be forced to exert their claims only against the selling corporation, because the selling corporation has merely "exchanged" one form of assets for another. This conceptual model is, of course, fictitious. A corporation which has sold all its assets is not the same entity it was when its creditors extended their trust. Moreover, liquidation of the selling corporation generally follows the sale. The proceeds of the liquidation will be distributed to the corporation's stockholders, who may be geographically dispersed, making it difficult for creditors to satisfy their claims.

The possibility for abuse inherent in this form of merger has led to legislative and judicial action seeking to protect the legitimate claims of creditors from defeat by unscrupulous or callous managements. Transfers made to defraud a corporation's creditors will not be upheld. Even if the selling corporation is acting with a legitimate business reason, however, creditors may still be protected; for example, state "bulk-sales" laws, modeled on Article 6 of the Uniform Commercial Code, provide that a significant transfer of assets will not prevent creditors from pursuing the assets in the hands of the purchasers unless attempts have been made to notify them that the sale of assets is about to take place. It is not always easy or desirable, for business reasons, to comply with the bulk-sales laws and many acquiring corporations make no attempt to do so, seeking to protect themselves by other means.

So long as the purchase is for cash and the bulk-sales laws have been complied with, however, the acquiring corporation will usually be protected. Two exceptions to this general proposition should be noted. The acquiring corporation will not escape liability if it makes its payment directly to the stockholders rather than to the corporation. This follows because the acquired corporation's creditors are left, hat in hand, facing a corporate shell with nothing in it. Also, the *de facto* merger doctrine may be available in some states to assist creditors even if payment is made to the corporation. The application of the doctrine in this situation seems unwarranted. The bulk-sales laws should be capable of performing their function without having to be supplemented by the more unwieldy *de facto* merger doctrine.

If the assets are purchased for the acquiring corporation's stock rather than cash, insulation from the selling corporation's creditors, even if the bulk-sales laws have been complied with, cannot be guaranteed. Cash is real, but stocks frequently represent nothing more than someone's wishful thinking. The stock market crash of 1929 taught the dangers of relying on stock as collateral, and some judges have never recovered from the shock. Thus, in some states, courts have invoked the *de facto* merger doctrine to allow creditors of the selling corporation to pursue its assets into the hands of the acquiring corporation when stock has been used to purchase the assets. Use of the *de facto* merger doctrine seems a clumsy way to reach this result. Although it satisfies creditors, it raises problems serving to confuse the situation. If the doctrine is invoked, for example, does it necessarily follow that the required shareholder vote to effect the merger must follow the statutory-merger procedure rather than the sale-of-assets procedure? Should appraisal rights, which might not be granted under the sale-of-assets statute, be granted as under the statutory-merger statute?

To avoid these problems, some states, even those not recognizing the *de facto* merger doctrine, have attempted to protect creditors in other ways. "Trust fund," "implied assumption of liability," and other theories have been invoked to impose liability on acquiring corporations using significant amounts of stock to purchase the assets of another corporation.

One further danger exists in a purchase-of-assets or statutory-merger transaction. Most states have adopted the Uniform Commercial Code's provision allowing for the creation of a lien attaching to "after-acquired" property, that is, any property ever acquired by the debtor until the lien is satisfied. If the acquiring corporation is subject to such a lien, the acquired assets will also be burdened. The reach of the lien can be avoided by merging the acquired corporation into a subsidiary or by purchasing the stock of the acquired corporation.

It should be clear from this short discussion that the danger of a forced assumption of unknown or contingent liabilities exists in all acquisitions. Caution dictates that provision be made at the time of the merger to protect the acquiring corporation. Protection can come in one of several ways. Warranties can be obtained from the acquired corporation or its principal shareholders guaranteeing the nature and amount of liability. Warranties from the corporation, however, will not survive the closing in a statutory merger and will have little value in a stock transaction. In an assets transaction, the protection of the warranty may be defeated for practical purposes if the selling corporation is liquidated. Although the warranties of principal shareholders would offer greater protection to the acquiring corporation, those shareholders may be extremely reluctant to face unlimited liability and possible participation in protracted litigation.

To avoid these problems, it has become common practice for acquiring corporations to withhold or deposit in escrow part of the purchase price for a specified period of time to be used to satisfy unknown or contingent liabilities. This procedure can be simplified further if the purchase price is to be paid in installments. Thus, the uncertainty inherent in any purchase of a going concern can be reduced.

RETENTION OF CONTRACTUAL AND OTHER RIGHTS

One virtue of a stock transaction is that it preserves existing relationships between the acquired corporation and third parties. Thus, rights under a contract, franchise, or lease; agreements with labor unions and employees; use of the corporate name and charter; a stock exchange listing; and experience ratings earned under workmen's compensation and unemployment compensation insurance policies will be retained automatically despite the merger. These contractual and other rights may be assigned by the selling corporation in an assets transaction if assignment is not prohibited by the terms of the original agreement or by law. Some will pass to the acquiring corporation automatically in a statutory merger. But the possibility exists that in transactions other than stock purchases some rights can be preserved only by obtaining the consent of third parties, whereas other rights may be lost entirely.

DILUTION OF SHAREHOLDERS' EQUITY

Acquiring corporations frequently refrain from using voting stock in acquisition transactions to avoid diluting the equity of their shareholders. As we shall learn in Chapter 7, however, *only* voting stock can be used in an assets or stock transaction if the merger is to qualify for tax-free treatment. On the other hand, consideration other than voting stock can be used in a statutory merger without jeopardizing its tax-free nature. Thus, corporations seeking a tax-free merger with a minimum of dilution to equity can achieve these dual goals only through a statutory-merger proceeding.

SPEED, EASE, AND EXPENSE

A purchase of assets can create problems associated with the transaction so complex as to exhaust even the most courageous acquisition team. Each parcel of land must be examined to ensure that title defects do not exist; research in every state in which the corporation does business must be conducted to uncover liens; hundreds of documents may have to be prepared to account for all the assets. Even the most careful planning may inadvertently overlook specific assets and result in clouds being cast over ownership. Moreover, an assets transaction is likely to be the most disconcerting to creditors and employees and the most expensive way to merge, entailing the payment of business, franchise, personal and real property, sales, use, transfer, and license taxes.

A statutory merger likewise involves complying with formal requirements consuming time and effort. Moreover, stockholders of both corporations must be consulted for the necessary voting. This involves notification, proxy solicitation, and potential legal challenges from dissident shareholders. Thus, a stock purchase is often the most convenient, inexpensive, and speedy method, especially if the number of shareholders is small. Accounting for individual assets will not be necessary, and the formal requirements of a statutory merger can be avoided.

USE OF THE "POOLING" METHOD

As will be pointed out in Chapter 6, the "pooling" method of accounting for mergers can be used only in stock-for-stock transactions.

ANTITRUST CONSIDERATIONS

Since the 1950 amendments to Section 7 of the Clayton Act, the legality of a merger under the antitrust laws no longer depends on the form of the merger transaction. For Section 7 purposes, mergers are measured against a single antitrust yardstick whether they result from statutory proceedings or from stock or assets purchases. Nevertheless, different antitrust consequences may flow from the postmerger corporate structure adopted by the participants. For example, a corporate family operating through unincorporated divisions appears to have greater freedom under the antitrust laws than if the components operated as separately incorporated subsidiaries.

The distinction between the alternative methods of doing business was highlighted by the Supreme Court's 1951 decision in *Kiefer-Stewart Co. v. Joseph E. Seagram & Sons, Inc.* Seagram, the well-known manufacturer of alcoholic beverages, had established several wholly owned subsidiaries, Seagram Corporation and Calvert Corporation, to distribute the Seagram products. A competitor charged Seagram with "conspiring" to restrain trade in violation of Section 1 of the Sherman Act by selling liquor only to those wholesalers willing to resell at prices fixed by the two subsidiaries. Seagram denied that its subsidiaries could be guilty of "conspiring," because they were parts of a single entity. It cited in support of its position an established series of cases holding that agents and employees of a single corporation could not be guilty of "conspiring" among themselves. The Supreme Court rejected Seagram's defense. Applying what has come to be called the "bathtub conspiracy" doctrine, the Court ruled in broad language that "common ownership and control does not liberate corporations from the impact of the antitrust laws."

This language, echoed by the Supreme Court in other cases decided both before and since the *Seagram* case, has created concern in many quarters. If accepted at face value it would spell virtually an end to the practice of operating through subsidiaries. No corporation could afford exposure to an antitrust attack alleging that it had "conspired" with its subsidiary to "fix prices" at which the subsidiary would sell its goods to the public or to "divide" the market among various subsidiaries. These internal decisions are, of course, essential to the sound administration of any corporation.

The government enforcement agencies have recognized that such a literal interpretation of the "bathtub conspiracy" doctrine would be unrealistic. In 1965 Assistant Attorney General Donald Turner, then head of the Antitrust Division of the Department of Justice, attempted to reassure antitrust lawyers that a "freewheeling interpretation" of the doctrine would not be forthcoming. Events since that time indicate that the enforcement agencies have accepted Turner's restraint.

What, then, does the *Seagram* decision mean for the businessman? The factual circumstances presented to the Supreme Court in that case may provide some guidance. It is clear that a special relationship existed among the Seagram family of companies. Each of the subsidiaries operated as semiautonomous profit centers, making their own decisions without guidance or direction from above, concerning how and at what price they would sell to wholesalers. The Court found that the subsidiaries, in fact, held themselves out as competitors in the distribution of alcoholic beverages.

Many commentators have concluded, therefore, that the Supreme Court applied an "economic entity" test to determine whether the "bathtub conspiracy" doctrine applied, treating units which operated independently as separate economic entities for purposes of the antitrust laws. Under this analysis it would make no difference whether the entities were subsidiaries or divisions; the only relevant consideration would be whether the economic realities indicated that the subsidiaries acted as independent competitors in relation to the acts charged as unlawful.

This view of the *Seagram* decision draws support from *Sunkist Growers, Inc.* v. *Winckler,* a case decided by the Supreme Court in 1962. There, for various reasons, an agriculture cooperative organized itself into three separate corporations to carry on business. The corporations were charged with conspiracy under the Sherman Act. Using what has been called a reverse analogy to *Seagram,* the Court refused to uphold a finding of conspiracy, recognizing that the economic realities in that case made clear that only one entity existed for business purposes, despite the existence of three legal entities. "To hold otherwise," the Court said, "would be to impose grave legal consequences upon organizational distinctions that are of *de minimis* meaning and effect."

The validity of the "economic entity" rationale was tested in a sequel to the *Seagram* case. Following the Supreme Court's decision, Seagram undertook a corporate reorganization apparently as an attempt to avoid the strictures imposed by the Supreme Court. It dissolved its subsidiaries, transferring their functions to unincorporated divisions. Nevertheless, the divisions continued operating as competitors in the distribution of alcoholic beverages, much the same as the predecessor subsidiaries had acted.

Troubled by the "paper-shuffling" aspects of the reorganization, a federal district judge, in *Hawaiian Oke & Liquors, Ltd.* v. *Joseph E. Seagram and Sons, Inc.,* concluded that the "economic entity" test required him to rule that the unincorporated divisions could in fact be guilty of conspiracy. In so doing, the court quoted the language of Mr. Justice Stewart in *United States* v. *Arnold, Schwinn & Co.,* a conceptually related antitrust case:

> [The Supreme Court] has emphasized in the past that . . . differences in form do not represent "differences in substance." . . . Draftsmen may cast business arrangements in different legal modes for purposes of commercial law, but these arrangements may operate identically in terms of economic function and competitive effect. It is the latter factors which are the concern of the antitrust laws.

On appeal, the Ninth Circuit Court of Appeals rejected this rationale, ruling simply that unincorporated divisions could not conspire among themselves.

The district court's decision at least had the virtue of consistency. Whether or not divisions are separately incorporated seems a slim reed on which to base antitrust liability. Yet one cannot help but get the impression that something more fundamental is wrong with the "bathtub conspiracy" doctrine.

If the "economic entity" test is the correct one to be applied in these situations, corporations could readily avoid antitrust problems by assigning one executive of the parent corporation to "supervise" the operations of the subsidiaries, especially in matters having potential antitrust significance. Certainly this would avoid any claim that the subsidiaries acted as competitors. Yet it is hard to see how the purpose of the antitrust laws would be served by such restrictions on the freedom of corporations to organize internally as they see fit.

If separate incorporation is the key, then a massive restructuring of the American way of doing business might be predicted. It is doubtful that such a restructuring actually will take place. The benefits of operating through subsidiaries are significant, and the antitrust enforcement agencies do not seem terribly eager to force such a restructuring. Most probably, therefore, only an unlucky few would inadvertently be charged under the "bathtub conspiracy" doctrine. This type of sporadic law enforcement would only serve to bring the law into disrepute.

Neither view, however, may describe the meaning of the "bathtub conspiracy" doctrine accurately. Many commentators have gone to great lengths to show that in every case in which the doctrine has been invoked, the conduct declared unlawful could have been found unlawful under some more traditional antitrust theory. These commentators have suggested that the Supreme Court settled on the "bathtub conspiracy" doctrine, deliberately or inadvertently, to strike down particularly reprehensible single-firm conduct. Accepting this view, it is possible that the "bathtub conspiracy" doctrine is not really a doctrine at all and that, when the final vote is in, corporate action otherwise permissible under the antitrust laws will not be held unlawful because the corporation acts through subsidiaries or divisions.

Yet our conjecture should not distract attention from what the Supreme Court has said. As recently as 1968, the Supreme Court, in *Perma Life Mufflers, Inc.* v. *International Parts Corporation,* stated very clearly, "But since [the parent and its subsidiary] . . . availed themselves of the privilege of doing business through separate corporations, the fact of common ownership could not save them from any of the obligations that the law imposes on separate entities." Only time will tell whether this language in fact represents the thinking of the Court.

4 Dealing in Securities

The stock market crash of 1929 and the massive economic depression that followed, brought on at least in part by fraudulent excesses in the unregulated securities market, caused a far-reaching review of the way securities were issued and traded. Although various alternatives were available to the government to attempt to curb these excesses, the regulatory philosophy that emerged stressed reliance on a policy of full and fair disclosure by those issuing and dealing in securities to enable investors to make more informed judgments. Although various substantive standards were imposed, the government by and large assumed a "watchdog" role to assure that the information disclosed was accurate and complete.

The federal government adopted two basic legislative packages during the early years of the New Deal—the Securities Act of 1933 (the "1933 Act"), concerned primarily with initial distributions of securities, and the Securities Exchange Act of 1934 (the "1934 Act") dealing, as its name suggests, with postdistribution trading in securities. Most states enacted related legislation, commonly known as Blue Sky laws, because they were directed at stock having nothing but the blue sky above to give them value.

THE SECURITIES ACT OF 1933

The basic thrust of the 1933 Act is contained in Sections 3, 4, and 5. Section 5 generally makes it unlawful for securities to be *offered for sale* or to be *sold* through any means of interstate commerce, including the mails, unless a registration statement has become effective with the Securities and Exchange Commission and a prospectus meeting the requirements of the 1933 Act has been delivered to purchasers of the securities. Information that must be disclosed when the securities are to be issued in connection with a merger includes material facts relating to the business, management, properties, and financial statements of *both* parties to the merger. Section 3 of the Act exempts certain *securities* (such as those of banks and railroads) from the registration requirements of

Section 5. Section 4 excludes certain *transactions* from the coverage of Section 5. Transactions other than by *issuers, underwriters,* and *dealers* and transactions *not involving a public offering* are all exempt. (The italicized words are words of art and are defined by the 1933 Act, commission rules, and judicial decisions.)

THE SECURITIES EXCHANGE ACT OF 1934

Section 12 of the 1934 Act, as amended, requires the registration of securities listed on a national securities exchange and equity securities traded over the counter if the issuer has more than $1 million in assets and more than 500 shareholders. Section 13 requires the filing by companies having securities registered under Section 12 of current information annually, quarterly, and within ten days after the occurrence of certain reportable events. These reporting requirements are also generally applied to companies which have sold securities pursuant to a registration statement under the 1933 Act and which have not registered securities under Section 12. Section 14 regulates the solicitation of proxies. Section 16 prevents "short-swing" profiteering by insiders of companies which have securities under Section 12 by providing for the recapture of *any* profits made by officers, directors, and shareholders owning more than 10 per cent of *any* class of equity securities, from *any* purchase and sale or sale and purchase of the company's equity securities in a six-month period. Section 10, and SEC Rule 10b-5 implementing Section 10, make unlawful misrepresentation, deceit, and other fraudulent devices and practices by *anyone* in connection with the purchase or sale of *any* security. Violation of these provisions subjects the individual involved to civil liability, injunctive action by the SEC and, possibly, fines and imprisonment.

Having set out the basic statutory scheme, we will examine some of the securities problems associated with mergers and acquisitions.

SECURITIES REGISTRATION

Registration with the SEC is not required if a company acquires another company for cash. By contrast, if securities form the consideration for the acquisition, registration of such securities will be required unless either the security or the transaction is exempted. Principally because registration is time-consuming and expensive, companies frequently seek to avail themselves of these exemptions.

Four exemptions may be available to avoid registration of securities used in acquisitions—the *no-sale* exemption, the *private-offering* exemption, the *intrastate* exemption, and the *small-issue* exemption. The intrastate exemption will be available only in those rare situations where the issuer is incorporated and doing most of its business in the same state where all the stockholders of the acquired company reside and where resales of the securities issued in the transaction to persons outside that state are not anticipated. The small-issue exemption under Regulation A of the 1933 Act, applies only to transactions valued at less than $500,000 (increased from $300,000 in late 1970). Even then, what amounts to a somewhat simplified form of registration will be required as a condition of the exemption. The private-offering and no-sale exemptions, on the other hand, are often used in mergers and acquisitions and will, therefore, be discussed in some detail.

The Private-Offering Exemption

Those who drafted the 1933 Act hoped to protect the masses of unwary and unsophisticated investors. They had no desire to restrict security issuances to small groups of investors who had the financial power and business acumen to fend for themselves. As James Landis observed, "The sale of an issue of securities to insurance companies or to a limited group of experienced investors was certainly not a matter of concern to the federal government. That bureaucracy, untrained in these matters as it was, could hardly equal these investors for sophistication, provided only it was their own money that they were spending." To avoid unnecessary regulatory burdens, therefore, Section 4(2) of the 1933 Act exempts from registration "transactions by an issuer not involving any public offering." Although the Act does not define the term *public offering,* a regulatory and judicial gloss over the years has imparted a relatively understandable meaning, although each case must be decided on its own facts.

What Constitutes a Public Offering?

The SEC in 1935 issued an opinion of its general counsel stating that "under ordinary circumstances an offering to not more than approximately twenty-five persons is not an offer to a substantial number and presumably does not involve a public offering." The number of investors is not determinative, however. Other factors that must be considered include the relationship of the investors to the issuer and to each other, the number of shares offered, and the size and manner of the offering.

In *SEC* v. *Ralston Purina Co.,* the Supreme Court made clear that one of the most important factors to be considered was the investors' *need* for the information contained in a registration statement. Obviously concerned that some issuers might attempt to take advantage of small groups of unsophisticated investors on a "private" basis, the Court announced that it would look to the ability of the investors to obtain "access to the same kind of information that the Act would make available in the form of a registration statement" to determine whether an offering was private. Assume, for example, that a large national concern wishes to acquire the stock of a closely held corporation having assets of $3 million. All of the stock is held by twenty-two people. The founder, his wife, and son together own 51 per cent of the stock. Nine corporate officers each own 1 per cent of the stock. Ten individuals each own 4 per cent. Five of these ten are prosperous businessmen who have held the stock since the corporation was founded. Two of the ten are attorneys for the corporation. The remaining three stockholders are widows who inherited their stock from their husbands, who were among the original investors. All of these women have taken an active part in the affairs of the corporation and are astute businesswomen. The private-offering exemption would be available under these circumstances.

"Taking for Investment"

Assuming that these indicia of a private offering—the size, relationship, and sophistication of the offeree group—are present, the real battle to secure the exemption has just begun. The central purpose of the 1933 Act is to prevent unregistered distributions of securities to the public. A private offering without registration is permitted because it does not involve a distribution to the "public." But if those who receive securities pursuant to a private offering resell the same securities to the public immediately thereafter, the private-offering exemption would soon become a guise to effect wide unregistered distributions of securities. Accordingly, restrictions on resale have been imposed to insure that the securities "come to rest" in the hands of those who receive them in a private offering.

These restrictions are imposed via a *circuitous* route. First, the Act requires underwriters to register securities before they may sell them to the public. An underwriter is defined as someone who purchases securities from an issuer "with a view to distribution." If an underwriter purchases securities from an issuer, the transaction will be considered part of a plan to distribute securities to the public. Accordingly, the private-offering exemption will be unavailable. It is important therefore, to define the key phrase *with a view to distribution.* If *any* of the shareholders of the acquired corporation have such a prohibited "view" in mind when they receive the securities of the acquiring corporation, the private offering exemption will not be available.

It seemed eminently logical to those charged with the early administration of the 1933 Act, therefore, to ascertain what shareholders were thinking at the time they received the securities in question to determine whether they had a "view" to "distribution" of the securities, or whether they intended to hold the securities for "investment." This approach has presented two significant difficulties. First, it is almost impossible to determine what people intend at the time they acquire securities, particularly in light of the self-serving nature of their statements. Second, what they intend to do at that time bears no relationship to the needs of the investing public for disclosure concerning the securities in question or the issuer of such securities. It was partly in answer to this criticism that the SEC promulgated Rule 144.

Briefly, Rule 144, adopted April 15, 1972, provides that a person will not be deemed an underwriter if the restricted securities are sold in accordance with the requirements of the rule. However, in that Rule 144 is both prospective and nonexclusive, it is necessary to examine not only the rule but the traditional methods of transfer of restricted securities.

Means of Determining Investment Intent

The traditional method of determining investment intent has been the documentation of it. Persons acquiring securities under this exemption have been asked to sign "investment letters" in which they represent that they have acquired the securities for investment and not with the view to distributing them. To be sure, a resale of investment securities shortly after they had been acquired would be, in most cases, compelling evidence that these persons did not have the requisite investment intent at the time they acquired their securities. If such is the case, the exemption from registration would be lost retroactively. To avoid the loss of the private offering exemption in this manner, issuers have protected themselves in other ways. Restrictive legends on the face of the share certificates and "stop-transfer" orders to their transfer agents, preventing resale absent the issuer's approval, completed the protective package.

Rule 144 deals solely with the resale of securities, not with the determination as to whether there has been a private placement. In the commission's release adopting Rule 144, however, it states "these devices serve a useful policing function, and the use of such devices is strongly suggested by the Commission."

When Are Resales Permitted?

The requisite "investment intent" does not mean that the shareholders can never sell their shares. Before the adoption of Rule 144, the SEC took the position that resales would be permitted only if a "change of circumstances" had occurred. The rise and fall of the stock market, the rise and fall of the company's earnings, and other foreseeable contingencies were not such a "change of circumstances" as to justify resale. As the SEC stated in *Crowell-Collier Publishing Co.:*

> Holding for the six months' capital gains period of the tax statutes, holding in an "investment account" rather than a "trading account," holding for a deferred sale, holding for a market rise, holding for sale if the market does not rise, or holding for a year, does not afford a statutory basis for an exemption and therefore does not provide an adequate basis on which counsel may give opinions or businessmen rely in selling securities without registration.
>
> Purchasing for the purpose of future sale is nonetheless purchasing for sale and, if the transactions involve any public offering even at some future date, the registration provisions apply unless at the time of the public offering an exemption is available.

In this regard, the SEC generally issued "no-action" letters (formally announcing the staff's intent not to pursue the matter further) if a shareholder encountered a serious and unforeseeable personal financial setback which required him to sell his investment stock *or* if he had held the securities acquired under the private offering exemption for at least three years, although the SEC generally did not pursue resales in the absence of a change of circumstance if the stock had been held for two years.

The resale of restricted securities acquired after the effective date of the rule but not sold pursuant to it should be done only with extreme caution. The commission has stated that "in deciding whether a person is an underwriter, the length of time the securities have been held will be considered, but the fact that securities have been held for a particular period of time does not by itself establish the availability of an exemption from registration." Presumably, the commission could adopt this posture in regard to restrictive securities acquired before the effective date but not sold pursuant to the rule as well.

Resale in accordance with Rule 144 essentially means meeting four requirements. First, the restrictive securities must have been owned by the seller for a period of at least two years. Second, the amount sold must not be more than 1 per cent of the outstanding number of shares of the class, or if the class is traded on an exchange, the lesser of 1 per cent or the average weekly volume of all the exchanges upon which this class is sold during the four weeks preceding the sale. Third, the securities must be sold in ordinary brokers' transactions. Fourth, Form 144 must be filed with the commission concurrently with the sale, in order that adequate information be available to the public in regard to the issuer of the securities. It should be noted that unless Form 144 is filed, the seller must bear the burden of proof that an exemption is available under the commission's statements regarding sales not in accordance with Rule 144.

Although these requirements seem at first to be litmus-paper tests, a brief examination of each shows that this is not so. In regard to the holding period, the person for whose account the securities are sold (remembering that the seller must deal with a broker) must have been "subject to the full economic risks of investment" during the two years. Thus, if the shares were purchased by a note or other obligation to pay the purchase price, the obligation must provide for full recourse against the purchaser, secured by collateral other than the securities purchased, and must have been discharged by payment in full prior to the sale of the securities. Further, the doctrine of "fungibility" will not apply. Thus, if restrictive securities are purchased on January 1 and June 1, the stock purchased on January 1 can be sold two years after that date. The purchase on June 1 does not start the holding period anew. Excluded from the holding period, however, is any period during which the seller had a short position in, or any option to dispose of, any securities of the class, or convertible into it. This is also true of nonconvertible debt securities.

Finally, stock dividends, stock splits, or other securities acquired in connection with or as a result of ownership of the securities are deemed to have been acquired when the original securities were acquired.

The limitation on amount of securities sold is based upon the policy of preventing the private placement from becoming a public distribution. As stated, the amount of security which may be sold in any six-month period, if traded on a registered national securities exchange, is the lesser of 1 per cent of the class outstanding *or* the average weekly reported volume of trading on all exchanges in which the security is traded over the four-week period prior to the date of the filing of Form 144. If the securities are not traded on a registered national securities exchange, then the 1 per cent of the amount of the class outstanding is the sole limitation upon the amount which may be sold in any six-month period.

It should also be pointed out that the resale purchaser in the private placement acquires a new two-year holding period on the date of purchase. Also, in regard to the six-month period, the rule permits sales in successive periods, although there can be no accumulation. As to the manner of sale, a broker's transaction is required in which the broker does no more than execute a sale order as agent and receives no more than the usual commission.

The purpose underlying the requirement of filing notice with the commission simultaneously with the sale of restricted securities is to insure that adequate current information is available to the public. This should present no problem for the holders of restricted securities of companies subject to the reporting requirements of the Securities Exchange Act of 1934. The holder can rely upon the issuers' statements in the latest report in which the information required of the company has been filed. The company must have been subject to these reporting requirements for a ninety-day period prior to the date of the report, and in addition, must have filed the most recent annual report which is required of it. If the securities mentioned in the notice are not sold within ninety days after the filing of it, then another notice amended to reflect current information must be filed.

Holders of restricted securities of small companies may find it more difficult to comply with the public information required by the rule. Although the commission encourages all issuers to register their securities voluntarily, under certain specified conditions the information requirement is deemed to be met when specified information is supplied. In practice, however, this would be most difficult for the small holder of restricted securities. In recognition of this the commission has promulgated Rule 237 for those instances in which Rule 144 is not available.

A sale pursuant to Rule 237 is allowed during any twelve-month period of the lesser of 1 per cent of the securities outstanding, or $50,000, if the following conditions are met:

1. The person has owned and has fully paid for the securities for a period of five or more years.
2. The issuer is a domestic organization which has been actively engaged in business as a going concern for at least the last five years.
3. The securities are sold in negotiated transactions other than through a broker or dealer.
4. The person files the required notice with the appropriate regional office of the commission at least ten days before the sale, with a copy to the issuer.

The noncontrolling investor in small businesses will also find that Regulation A has been broadened to make it more available to him. The small investor should also be aware that a notice under Rule 144 is not required to be filed with respect to transactions during any six-month period which involves the lesser of $10,000 or no more than 500 shares.

For those still interested in the resale of privately placed securities, it should be noted that in the future the SEC will not issue "no-action" letters, nor will they consider the change-of-circumstances doctrine as before. Because of the heavy burden of proof which must be borne by those not selling in accordance with the provisions of Rule 144 (or within the limited application of Rule 237), resale under the rule would certainly be advised.

These restrictions on resale are significant. Any person agreeing to acquire investment stock, whether in connection with a corporate merger or acquisition, or otherwise, should fully understand this in order intelligently to evaluate the proposed transaction. If shareholders do not wish to be bound, or if the private offering exemption is not available, other methods may be pursued in order to style the transaction to exempt it from the registration requirements of the 1933 Act.

The "No-Sale" Exemption

At one time the SEC concluded that securities issued to effect corporate mergers and acquisitions should not necessarily be treated as other securities distributions were treated. In promulgating Rule 133, the commission felt that shareholders voting on an acquisition proposal were less like investors making investment decisions than they were corporate functionaries carrying out a corporate plan under state law. They viewed the individual decision making as overruled by that of the will of the majority. Recently, however, this reasoning has come under increasing criticism. The SEC now feels that the corporate action is derived from the individual consent given by each shareholder in voting on a proposal to merge, consolidate, or reclassify a security. The shareholder who consents to the proposal is thus expressing his acceptance of the new security, whereas the shareholder who votes against the proposal is deferring his decision either to accept the new security or to receive a cash payment. Thus, the corporate action is the aggregate effect of the voluntary decisions made by the individual shareholders. It is in accord with this change of reasoning that the commission has adopted Rule 145, effective on and after January 1, 1973. Rule 133 is rescinded on and after that date, but the rule will continue to be available for completion or consummation of any transaction that was either submitted for vote or consent of security holders or formally submitted for approval to any governmental regulatory agency before January 1, 1973. Rule 133 is also available for resales of securities received by persons in any transaction for which Rule 133 was available, so the operation of Rule 133 as well as Rule 145 will be examined here.

Rule 133 applies to mergers, sale of assets, and certain other transactions requiring, by state law or corporate charter, a favorable vote of a majority of the acquired or transferring corporation's shareholders if such approval is binding on all shareholders (except to the extent that dissenter's rights are available). Thus, *securities issued in statutory mergers and in such sale-of-assets transactions* (where the selling corporation subsequently liquidates, distributing the acquired shares to its shareholders) *need not be registered.* Rule 133 does not by its terms exempt the issuance of securities in acquisitions effected by means of stock for stock exchanges. On the other hand, the resale of securities under Rule 133, subject to certain exceptions, a discussion of which follows, does not *require* registration.

Under the "negotiated transaction" exception to Rule 133 registration is required when a few shareholders of the acquired corporation control the corporation so completely that a vote of the minority shareholders amounts to no more than a mere formality. In *Great Sweet Grass Oils, Ltd.,* the commission said, "in such a case the transaction is not corporate action in the real sense, but rather is action reflecting the consent of the persons in control, and consequently results in a 'sale' to them."

The other major exception to Rule 133 is designed so that an "affiliate" may not resell the securities of the acquiring corporation except in transactions not deemed to involve a "distribution" within the meaning of the rule. An affiliate is defined as a person or group of persons who "control" the seller. (The definition of *control* depends upon the particular factual situation presented.) Thus, affiliates may immediately sell part of their holdings under the "leakage" provisions of Rule 133 (that is, the provisions which describe a transaction which would not constitute a distribution). The leakage rules provide that if the security involved is not traded on an exchange, approximately 1 per cent of the outstanding shares or units may be sold by an affiliate within a six-month period. If the security is traded on an exchange, an affiliate may sell within a six-month period the *lesser* of approximately (1) 1 per cent of the outstanding shares or units or (2) the largest volume of trading on securities exchanges in the security during any one week within the four calendar weeks preceding the order to the broker to sell. As was seen previously in Rule 144, all sales must be made in normal brokers' transactions, and no special compensation to the brokers may be paid. Continued use of the leakage provisions in successive six-month periods, however, may be taken as evidence that a distribution requiring registration is involved. It should also be noted that in certain circumstances two or more affiliates (such as husband and wife) may be grouped so that they will be limited to a single computation of the maximum amount which may be sold under the leakage provisions.

To summarize, no restrictions are placed on resale of stock received in a Rule 133 transaction by noncontrolling shareholders of the acquired corporation. Controlling shareholders of the acquired corporation are limited by the formula contained in the leakage provisions of the rule. The change-in-circumstances doctrine, however, has been used to allow controlling shareholders to effect resale without regard to this limitation. Because of the express renunciation of this doctrine in regard to Rule 144 however, reliance upon it at this time would be risky at best.

The effect of Rule 145 is to require registration and delivery of a prospectus containing accurate and current information concerning the proposed business combination to security holders for securities to be issued in connection with reclassification of securities, mergers, consolidations, or transfers of assets, unless an exemption from these provisions is available. The rule would not operate to make the notice of a meeting of stockholders for voting on proposed transactions a statutory prospectus, as long as the written communication contains no more than certain specified information.

In order to make compliance with the registration requirements less burdensome, the commission has amended Form S-14 to provide that the prospectus to be used shall consist of a proxy or information statement meeting the requirements of the proxy rules. For those companies subject to the commission's proxy or information rule, registration will involve filing a proxy statement and form of proxy or information statement, and the transmittal of such material to security holders. Thus, the commission feels that registration will involve little additional work on the part of companies subject to those rules. For those companies not subject to the proxy rules, or subject thereto but not required to solicit votes from their security holders, the prospectus required would contain the same information which would be required by the proxy rules. This in itself makes registration less burdensome to smaller companies, as the information requirements under the proxy rules are less demanding than are those under the 1933 Act.

For purposes of determining who is an underwriter, and thus subject to the registration requirements of Rule 145(a), Rule 145(c) provides that any party to any transaction specified in Rule 145(a) who offers or sells securities acquired in such transaction shall be deemed to be engaged in a distribution and therefore an underwriter, except for the issuer or any person who is an affiliate of such party at the time any such transaction is submitted for vote or consent. The term *party* is defined to mean corporations, business entities, or other persons whose assets or capital structure are affected by the transaction specified in 145(a), other than the issuer. This is merely a carryover of the Rule 133 thinking for determination of underwriter status for the affiliate of the acquired corporation who "controlled" the seller. Although the definition of *control* depends upon the particular factual situation, officers and directors are held to be within the rule.

In summary, Rule 145 would operate to inhibit the creation of public markets in securities of issuers concerning which adequate current information is not available to the public. The SEC believes that this approach is consistent with the philosophy underlying the 1933 Act, and as a disclosure law this will provide the best protection for investors.

ASSISTING THE LOCKED-IN SHAREHOLDER

The restrictions on resales of securities acquired by controlling shareholders in a Rule 133 transaction and by all security holders in a private-offering transaction can be extremely burdensome. Fortunately, alternative procedures may be available to alleviate these restrictions. The acquiring corporation, for example, might agree to allow these security holders to include their securities in its next registration statement. Further, if the issuer has solicited proxies in connection with a Rule 133 transaction under the SEC's proxy rules, an easily prepared registration statement is available. Using the simplified Form S-14 together with the proxy statement satisfies the normal registration requirements. Because the proxy solicitation material must contain much the same information required by a registration statement (including a description of the business and properties of each party to the acquisition; an explanation of the acquisition plan and of the shareholders' rights, including dissenters' rights, the exchange ratio, market values over a two-year period, financial statements and other financial data; and information about the directors if directors are to be elected as part of the plan), relatively little effort must be expended to convert the merger proxy statement into a Form S-14 registration statement.

Security holders who have their securities registered may not be interested in selling any or all such securities immediately following registration. Delayed sales create problems, however, because the information contained in a registration statement becomes stale with the passage of time. Specifically, if the prospectus covering the registered securities is used more than nine months after the effective date of the registration statement of which it is a part, the information in such a prospectus cannot be more than sixteen months old. The SEC interprets this language to prohibit the use of a prospectus more than nine months old if the *certified* financial information in it is as of a date more than sixteen months prior to such use. Undoubtedly, a registration statement can be amended to update both its financial and nonfinancial contents but this will require substantial effort and expense. For this reason a company filing a registration statement for selling security holders typically requires (or requests, if it has no right to require) these persons to dispose of their securities within a relatively short period of time after the propectus covering their securities becomes available for use.

In December 1970 the SEC adopted an extremely short registration form (Form S-16) which may be used by certain large companies to register securities to be sold by security holders of the company provided that securities of the same class are listed on a national securities exchange and that the security holders dispose of their registered securities "in the regular way" on an exchange. Typically, the prospectus portion of a Form S-16 Registration Statement will consist of but two or three pages.

The conditional exemption from registration contained in Regulation A under the 1933 Act may be available if a number of conditions are met, including, generally, the filing of a Notification on Form 1-A, containing an offering circular which resembles a prospectus. Some, but not much, effort and expense may be saved by utilizing Regulation A as compared with registering the securities involved. It should be kept in mind, however, that the maximum amount of securities which may be offered under Regulation A on behalf of any one person (other than the issuer) is $100,000.

SHELF REGISTRATION BY ACQUIRING CORPORATION

A company engaged in a continuous acquisition program might prefer to register a large amount of securities to be held on the shelf until the individual acquisitions are consummated. Such a procedure is acceptable to the SEC so long as the prospectus is kept current. In view of existing limitations regarding the types of acquisitions in which shelf registration is feasible and the circumstances in which shelf registration may be used, however, the present registration of securities for future issuance in acquisitions may be of little value.

First, an issuer cannot prepare a shelf registration statement for use in stock-for-stock transactions. This is so because a stock swap must be made pursuant to a prospectus which describes in detail both the acquiring and the acquired company. As a practical matter such a prospectus cannot be prepared in advance of the specific acquisition it covers.

Second, securities issued in many acquisitions are exempted from the registration requirements of the 1933 Act by virtue of either Rule 133 or the private offering exemption. Shelf registration of securities issued in these transactions is therefore unnecessary so far as the issuing corporation is concerned. Nor are security holders of the acquired corporation benefited by shelf registration—the SEC has taken the position that a shelf registration statement may not cover resales of stock received in acquisitions. Thus, shelf registration of securities issued in exempted transactions serves no useful purpose.

POSTACQUISITION REPORTING

A company subject to the reporting requirements of the 1934 Act must file a current report on Form 8-K with the SEC (and any exchange on which its securities are listed) within ten days after the close of the month in which it is acquired by another company or in which it makes any "material" acquisition. An acquisition is considered material for the acquiring company if the assets or gross revenues of the acquired company exceed either 15 per cent of the assets or gross revenues of the acquiring company.

STATE SECURITIES LAWS

Although registration of securities issued in mergers and acquisitions may not be required under the 1933 Act, it may be required under state securities laws. The Blue Sky laws of many states contain the equivalent of private-offering and no-sale exemptions just discussed, but this is not uniformly the case. Consequently, the laws of the various states into which shares will be issued must be checked.

IS ALL THIS NECESSARY?

Those who have managed to survive through this chapter to this point probably will be asking themselves if all this complexity is really needed. Why, for example, should distinctions be drawn between stock-for-stock and stock-for-assets transactions for purposes of the registration requirements of the 1933 Act? What function does registration serve when the securities involved are listed on a securities exchange so that the issuer of these securities files registration-statement-quality information every year with the SEC? A reworking of the exemptions from registration as they relate to mergers and acquisitions is clearly needed.

SELLING CONTROL

Those who control a corporation by reason of their stock ownership in all probability will enjoy an enviable position when acquisition negotiations begin. In most cases, the controlling shareholders will be the focal point of the suiter's attention and can often demand a premium for their shares. Although consistent with our general economic philosophy of allowing a person to sell his property at whatever price he can demand for it, the receipt of a premium by controlling shareholders can raise problems under both state and the antifraud provisions of the Exchange Act.

Because controlling shareholders exercise such great power vis-à-vis minority shareholders, various courts have imposed legal liability on the sale of control when it appeared to the court that the controlling shareholders had abused their power. The findings of abuse have rested upon a determination of a breach of a fiduciary duty. The question of the fiduciary duty of the controlling shareholder (or the controlling group of shareholders) has been raised in regard to whether control itself is a corporate assest or one which belongs to the control group. Therefore, sale at a premium by controlling shareholders is not *necessarily* a breach by itself, but particular caution must be exercised if the controlling shareholder is also an officer or director of the corporation. The fiduciary duty of officers and directors, and the breach of that duty, has been much easier for the disappointed minority shareholders to establish, particularly in the light of diversion of "corporate opportunity."

Perlman v. *Feldmann* is a leading case regarding sale of corporate control. It involved the acquisition of Newport Steel Corporation, a steel-producing company, by Wilport Company, a syndicate of end users of steel. The acquisition took place during the Korean War, when steel was in short supply. Minority stockholders of Newport charged that the controlling shareholder, who was also chairman of the board and president, abused his trust by selling his stock to the acquiring corporation at a substantial premium. They pointed out that Newport at the time of the sale had an excellent opportunity to take advantage of the shortage of steel to generate good will by allocating steel to customers in the geographic area in which the company could operate most profitably, and to expand its operations by obtaining interest-free loans from its customers in return for an assured supply of steel. They argued that these opportunities would be eliminated by the acquisition because Wilport's owners would use all of Newport steel in their businesses. The court agreed that, should these corporate opportunities be lost as a result of the sale, the controlling shareholders should be held accountable, phrasing the issue as follows:

> In Indiana, then, as elsewhere, the responsibility of the fiduciary is not limited to a proper regard for the tangible balance sheet assets of the corporation, but includes the dedication of his uncorrupted business judgment for the sole benefit of the corporation, in any dealings which may adversely affect it. . . . Although the Indiana case is particularly relevant to Feldmann as a director, the same rule should apply to his fiduciary duties as majority stockholder, for in that capacity he chooses and controls the directors, and thus is held to have assumed their liability. . . . This, therefore, is the stand-

> ard to which Feldmann was by law required to conform in his activities here under scrutiny. It is true, as defendants have been at pains to point out, that this is not the ordinary case of breach of fiduciary duty. We have here no fraud, no misuse of confidential information, no outright looting of a helpless corporation. But on the other hand, we do not find compliance with that high standard which we have just stated and which we and other courts have come to expect and demand of corporate fiduciaries. In the often-quoted words of Judge Cardozo: "Many forms of conduct permissible in a workaday world for those acting at arms length, are forbidden to those bound by fiduciary ties. A trustee is held to something stricter than the morals of the market place. Not honesty alone, but the punctilio of an honor the most sensitive, is then the standard of behavior. As to this there has developed a tradition that is unbending and inveterate. Uncompromising rigidity has been the attitude of courts of equity when petitioned to undermine the rule of undivided loyalty by the 'disintegrating erosion' of particular exceptions. . . ." The actions of defendants in siphoning off for personal gain corporate advantages to be derived from a favorable market situation do not betoken the necessary undivided loyalty owed by the fiduciary to his principal.

It would seem the safest approach for the controlling shareholders would be to insist that the acquiring corporation propose the same terms to the minority shareholders as they themselves are to receive. In practice, however, this may not be a realistic approach: in most cases, the acquiring corporation only wants to purchase enough shares to have control and thus is not interested in purchasing, or making an offer to purchase, all the shares outstanding. In any case, the controlling shareholder must try to insure that the purchaser will not later "loot" the corporation, and he certainly must not try to conceal the premium he is receiving or otherwise misrepresent the transaction to the minority shareholders.

THE MISUSE OF INSIDE INFORMATION

Those who follow the stock market have long since grown accustomed to watching the price of a stock rise for a few days without apparent reason, only to learn later that unanticipated good news concerning the corporation, such as a favorable merger, has been announced. The cynical treat this with shrugged shoulders, explaining that the market has always been rigged in favor of those with "inside" information. Those who take advantage of such information, however, may someday find themselves in trouble with the SEC.

Prior to the adoption of the federal securities laws, corporate insiders having confidential information were under varying obligations to the public to refrain from trading in securities about which they knew more than the public. Many states allowed them to fleece the public at will. Others put tight restrictions on their stock dealings, forcing them to refrain from trading if they had *any* information not available to the public. Still others required insiders to refrain from trading if they were aware of "special facts" affecting the corporation. Common to all states, however, was the lack of an effective enforcement mechanism to control insider profiteering. Section 10(b) of the 1934 Act has changed this situation profoundly. To implement that section, the SEC adopted its now famous Rule 10b-5, providing that:

> It shall be unlawful for any person, directly or indirectly, by the use of any means or instrumentality of interstate commerce, or of the mails, or of any facility of any national securities exchange,
> (1) to employ any device, scheme, or artifice to defraud,
> (2) to make any untrue statement of a material fact or to omit to state a material fact necessary in order to make the statements made, in the light of the circumstances under which they were made, not misleading, or
> (3) to engage in any act, practice, or course of business which operates or would operate as a fraud or deceit upon any person, in connection with the purchase or sale of any security.

In addition to subjecting insiders to criminal prosecution for "willful" violations of the rule, private parties who have been wronged by an insider's misconduct can maintain civil actions to remedy their losses.

Rule 10b-5 applies to securities transactions made on an exchange, over the counter, or privately. Even making an intrastate telephone call in connection with the sale or purchase generally will provide a sufficient jurisdictional basis to make the rule applicable to the transaction.

Moreover, *all* "persons," whether or not they are directors or officers of the corporation, may come within the purview of the rule. In *Cady, Roberts & Co.*, for example, a stockbroker, who also served as a director of a corporation, learned at a meeting of the board of directors that the corporation was about to release unfavorable news. He shared this knowledge with a partner at his brokerage firm. The partner quickly sold stock in the corporation before the adverse news was released to the public. The SEC found unlawful this sale of stock by the "tippee." It described the application of Rule 10b-5 as follows:

> Analytically, the obligation [to refrain from dealing in stock of a corporation] rests on two principal elements; first, the existence of a relationship giving access, directly or indirectly, to information intended to be available only for a corporate purpose and not for the personal benefit of anyone, and second, the inherent unfairness involved where a party takes advantage of such information knowing it is unavailable to those with whom he is dealing.

One of the most challenging problems raised by Rule 10b-5 involves the identification of that information considered "material" so as to bar trading by those having confidential knowledge of it. Where an acquisition is concerned, those with advance knowledge of its terms, those whose special access to facts places them in a better position than the public to appreciate the significance of those terms, and those who are aware even only of the existence of such proposals may be prohibited by Rule 10b-5 from taking advantage of their knowledge.

Speed v. *Transamerica Corp.* demonstrates the danger involved when an insider fails to reveal information affecting the value of a merger offer. Transamerica, a holding company with a 47 per cent interest in Axton-Fisher Tobacco Co., devised a plan to profit from a corporate situation at the expense of the minority shareholders. Axton-Fisher's tobacco inventory had been carried on its books at substantially below its market value. Realizing this, Transamerica attempted to obtain complete control of the company by purchasing shares from the other shareholders. Having obtained such control, it planned to liquidate Axton-Fisher and pocket the difference between the book value and the market value of the inventory. The Court found that Transamerica's failure to reveal its liquidation plan to the minority shareholders before purchasing their shares violated Rule 10b-5.

Nevertheless, the use of generally known information by insiders is not forbidden. In *Cady, Roberts & Co.,* the SEC stated that no liability attached to an insider whose "perceptive analysis of generally known facts," rather than his use of undisclosed information, motivated his market activity. The Second Circuit Court of Appeals in *SEC* v. *Texas Gulf Sulphur Co.* framed the rule as follows:

> Nor is an insider obligated to confer upon outside investors the benefit of his superior financial or other expert analysis by disclosing his educated guesses or predictions. . . . The only regulatory objective is that access to material information be enjoyed equally, but this objective requires nothing more than the disclosure of basic facts so that outsiders may draw upon their own evaluative expertise in reaching their own investment decisions with knowledge equal to that of the insiders.

The distinction between "basic facts" and "perceptive analysis" of facts can sometimes be illusive.

What duty is imposed on insiders before the terms of an acquisition have been settled? It would be most disruptive if a corporation had to announce publicly every merger proposal that came its way even though the proposal was of the most tentative nature. In fact, were it to do so and then not complete a merger or not complete it on those terms, shareholders who may have acted in reliance on the announcement would be legitimately concerned. But should insiders be allowed to trade in the stock of the companies involved in the acquisition negotiations, even if the negotiations are of the most tentative nature, while the public is unaware that negotiations are taking place?

Questions similar to these were considered at length during the celebrated *Texas Gulf Sulphur* litigation. In late 1963 TGS engineers, after preliminary aerial surveillance, drilled a single test hole for ore in a remote section of Canada. The engineers at the site visually examined the core extracted from the test hole and concluded that it contained an unusually high copper and zinc content. Following normal mining procedures, the hole was camouflaged and further drilling was terminated until the company could acquire additional land in the area.

In the mining industry it is common knowledge that the results of a single test hole are almost meaningless and may well be misleading.

Further drilling is necessary to determine whether a commercially valuable ore body has been discovered. Nevertheless, several officers of TGS with knowledge of the test hole results began heavy buying of the company's stock and passed the news to various friends, who also purchased stock. A chemical assay confirmed the visual examination soon thereafter, and further insider purchases were made.

Drilling was resumed on March 31, 1964, after TGS had acquired additional land surrounding the test hole. Within the next few days it had become clear that a significant ore discovery, one of the richest finds in modern times, had been made. Not until April 16 did the company issue a press release describing the discovery. Thereafter, the price of TGS stock soared.

The Second Circuit Court of Appeals had no trouble finding unlawful those purchases made by insiders just prior to the public disclosure of the discovery, after extent of the ore body had been ascertained. The more significant question, however, concerned the legality of the purchases made between the time the first hole had been drilled and the time drilling was resumed. Because the first hole could at best be considered inconclusive evidence of a commercial ore body, the trial court ruled that information about that hole was not "material" so that the initial insider purchases were not unlawful.

The court of appeals, in a decision that has caused much controversy, disagreed. The test of materiality it applied, "whether a *reasonable* man would attach importance . . . in determining his choice of action in the transaction in question," was more or less standard dogma. What was unusual was that the court held that the term *reasonable man* is not limited to normally prudent investors, but also includes *speculators.* In the language of the court:

> The speculators and chartists of Wall and Bay Streets are . . . entitled to the same legal protection afforded conservative traders. Thus, material facts include not only information disclosing the earnings and distributions of a company but also those facts which affect the probable future of the company and those which may affect the desire of investors to buy, sell or hold the company's securities.
>
> In each case, then, whether facts are material within Rule 10b-5 when the facts relate to a particular event and are undisclosed by those persons who are knowledgeable thereof will depend at any given time upon a balancing of both the indicated probability that the event will occur and the anticipated magnitude of the event in light of the totality of the company activity.

Further, the SEC has stated that in accordance with the general disclosure policy of the securities acts, disclosure of corporate information, both favorable and unfavorable, must be released. Failure to do so, coupled with the trading of the company's stock by either the company itself or by its insiders, would be a serious risk of violation of the 1934 Act and rule thereunder.

The preceding rationale of *Texas Gulf Sulphur* and the SEC statements regarding disclosure are certainly significant in regard to acquisition negotiations. Since potential acquisitions may affect the market price of a company's stock, insider trading should cease as soon as it becomes apparent that speculators will be interested in *knowing* about acquisition negotiations.

Tippee v. Tipper

Those who pass along information to others expose themselves to another risk. If the information proves to be incorrect, tippees who act on the incorrect information and lose money as a result may recover their losses from the tipper, even though the tippees themselves have violated the law by trading on the basis of the inside information. This, at least, was the holding of the District Court for the Southern District of New York in *Nathanson* v. *Weis, Voisin, Canon, Inc.* There are contrary holdings, based on the fact that the tippee is *in pari delicto* with the tipper, but since the Supreme Court has not yet spoken on the issue, the danger remains.

Disclosure Rule of the Exchange

Rule 10b-5 only requires that inside trading cease once information about such negotiations becomes "material." This rule and the previously mentioned SEC statement regarding release of material information come very close to requiring timely disclosure. The New York Stock Exchange, on the other hand, *does require* timely disclosure of "any news or information which might reasonably be expected to materially affect the market for security." The Exchange Company Manual goes on to state:

> Negotiations leading to acquisitions and mergers, . . . the making of arrangements preparatory to an exchange or tender offer, . . . are the type of developments where the risk of untimely and inadvertent disclosure of corporate plans is most likely to occur. . . . Accordingly, extreme care must be used in order to keep the information on a confidential basis.
>
> WHERE IT IS POSSIBLE TO CONFINE FORMAL OR INFORMAL DISCUSSIONS TO A SMALL GROUP OF THE TOP MANAGEMENT OF THE COMPANY OR COMPANIES INVOLVED, AND THEIR INDIVIDUAL CONFIDENTIAL ADVISORS WHERE ADEQUATE SECURITY CAN BE MAINTAINED, PREMATURE PUBLIC ANNOUNCEMENT MAY PROPERLY BE AVOIDED. In this regard, the market action of a company's securities should be closely watched at a time when consideration is being given to important corporate matters. If unusual market activity should arise, the Company should be prepared to make an immediate public announcement of the matter.
>
> At some point it usually becomes necessary to involve other persons to conduct preliminary studies or assist in other preparations for contemplated transactions, e.g., business appraisals, tentative financing arrangements, attitude of large outside holders, availability of major blocks of stock, engineering studies, market analyses and surveys, etc. Experience has shown that maintaining security at this point is virtually impossible. Accordingly, fairness requires that the Company make an immediate public announcement as soon as confidential disclosures relating to such important matters are made to "outsiders."

The American Stock Exchange has guidelines comparable to those of the New York Stock Exchange. The guidelines look toward the immediate public disclosure of material information and insider trading, as well as requirements for public dissemination and "response to unusual market action."

SHORT-SWING PROFITS

The essence of a Rule 10b-5 violation is the misuse of information available to some but not available to others. Section 16(b) of the 1934 Exchange Act also places restrictions on insiders, but in a far less flexible manner. Under this section, additional trading restrictions are imposed on all officers and directors, and of those shareholders owning more than 10 per cent of the shares of a corporation having securities registered with the SEC under Section 12 of the 1934 Act. To prevent this class of insiders from profiting from short-term swings in the market price of the securities of their corporations, Section 16(b) permits the corporation to recapture *any* profits realized by these insiders from *any* purchase and sale or *any* sale and purchase of the corporation's securities within a six-month period. If a prohibited trade has been made, Section 16(b) applies automatically to strip the insiders of their profit; no amount of "good faith" on the part of those subject to the section can excuse them from its operation.

The automatic six-month test, however, has recently been brought under scrutiny. In *Abrams* v. *Occidental Petroleum Corporation,* the Second Circuit Court of Appeals said that it would look to whether the stock conversion would "have lent itself to speculative abuse." In regard to the merger situation, the court stated that it could "see no reason why this same principle should not apply when the question is whether the receipt of securities of another company . . . constitutes a 'sale.' " In this case, the target company accepted a better offer by one corporation after a first corporation had made a tender offer and had purchased more than 10 per cent of the common stock of the target company. Thus, when the tender offerer sold its recently acquired stock, the newly formed corporation moved to assert 16(b) liability. In essence, the court found that an exchange of this type is not subject to "speculative abuse." Because *Abrams* has only shortened the six-month period in a somewhat limited circumstance, it would still seem to be a wise practice to hold for the minimum period to avoid a possible 16(b) violation.

As an example of a situation to which this section probably would apply, assume that the president of company A purchases 1,000 shares of his company's securities on February 1. On April 1, company A is merged into company B. Any profit realized by the president of A on securities purchased in February and "sold" pursuant to the merger in all probability would be subject to recapture in a shareholders' derivative suit.

As another example, assume that company A's president receives 1,000 shares of company B's securities pursuant to the April 1 merger. Needing cash, he sells 100 shares of the company B stock on September 1. Any profit realized as a result of this sale would be subject to recapture, as *Abrams* would not apply.

5 Tender Offers and Take-Overs

The growing separation of corporate ownership from corporate control first described by Berle and Means in the 1930's has been responsible for a variety of developments in the business world. Among these developments has been the growth of public contests between opposing control groups to win the support of public shareholders. The tender offer, or take-over bid, as it is sometimes called, is one such method of contest.

Tender offers were little known and little used until recently. When thought of at all, they were generally regarded as a convenient way for a corporation to repurchase its own shares. By contrast, they are presently considered an integral part of this country's larger merger movement. As a technique to seize control of a corporation without obtaining the consent of the incumbent management, tender offers now receive widespread attention from corporate managers fearful of losing their jobs, from investors hoping to realize handsome profits, and from acquisition-minded companies seeking to acquire leverage in the corporation marketplace. Tender offers have achieved their popularity because they are so frequently successful.

There are two kinds of tender offers, those involving an offer to pay cash for the securities of the target company (described as cash offers) and those involving an offer to exchange securities of the bidder for securities of the target (described as exchange offers). Cash offers captured the attention of the investment community in the early 1960's and retained their popularity until economic conditions made exchange offers more attractive.

In the seven-year period from 1956 to 1963, for example, only 105 cash tender offers were recorded. By contrast, 186 such offers were recorded during the three years from 1963 to 1966. The value of these offers rose from $186 million in 1960 to $951 million in 1965, a 500 per cent increase.

The number of exchange offers also increased, albeit at a slower pace. Between 1960 and 1965, the value of stock tenders increased from $435 million to $558 million. Thereafter the pace quickened. The twenty-four exchange offers registered in 1965 increased to fifty-four issues aggregating $880 million in 1966 and to 182 such registrations in 1968 having an aggregate value of $11.2 billion. Cash offers, having trailed exchange offers until 1963, again trailed as liquidity worsened and the price of money increased.

The growing respectability and importance of the tender offer soon became apparent. Thus, in 1966, 100 tender offers involved companies having securities listed on national exchanges. Only eight such companies were so involved in 1960. Reflecting the broader merger movement, the number and size of tender offers peaked in 1968. At least 250 firms experienced some form of tender offer that year. The passage of the Williams Act regulating take-over bids in July of 1968, and the decline of the merger fervor generally caused a decline in the number of tenders. Between the date the Williams Act became effective and February 1969, fifty-four cash offers valued at less than $1.5 billion and 104 exchange offers valued at $9 billion were registered with the SEC. In the months from March 1969 to January 1970, only thirty-seven cash tenders were registered, with a parallel decline in the number of exchange offers. Changing economic conditions, however, will undoubtedly restore the popularity of tender offers as a means of obtaining control of publicly held corporations.

ANATOMY OF A TENDER OFFER

A tender offer is simply a public invitation to the shareholders of a corporation to sell their shares. The offer is usually communicated by advertisements published in financial newspapers. The advertisement contains the terms of the offer, directions explaining the mechanics of tendering, and forms, including a "Letter of Transmittal," enabling the shareholders to tender their shares to the purchaser.

Tender offers frequently spring from the ashes of unsuccessful merger negotiations between the two companies. Thus, a company whose merger offer has been rebuffed by the target company's management may believe it desirable to approach the target company's shareholders directly.

Although a tender offer may be made without the blessings of the target company's management, management blessing, or at least management silence, is usually sought. Nothing is more likely to insure the success of the offer than an absence of management opposition.

Prior to the enactment of the Williams amendments to the Securities Exchange Act of 1934, tender offers were rarely made until the purchasing company had acquired a substantial position in the target company stock through open market purchases. These purchases were often made surreptitiously to avoid alerting the target management. However, the introduction of Section 13(d) reporting requirements has foreclosed the ability of the purchasing company to acquire target company stock secretly prior to the public announcement of its tender offer.

The number of shares sought through the offer depends on what the offerer hopes to accomplish. Although many offerers seek only to gain an investment position in the target, most are interested in obtaining some degree of control. If control is obtained, the purchaser will generally propose a merger to buy out the remaining shareholders.

The terms of tender offers are fairly routine. The offerer usually reserves the right to accept any, all, or, in the event too few shares are tendered, none of the offered shares. Escape clauses insure that the offerer will not be handicapped in the event the state of the market or the condition of the target changes for the worse.

Based on a long-standing custom, the offerer will agree to pay brokers who tender shares on behalf of their customers a large (generally double) commission. This generosity on the part of the offerer is motivated by a desire to obtain the assistance of a broker who will actively solicit tenders. Even though tendering shareholders pay no commission, brokers will often become involved in conflict-of-interest problems resulting from their attempts to service both parties to the transaction.

Many shareholders otherwise impressed by the bid price may nevertheless be reluctant to tender. If the offer calls for *pro rata* acceptance, for example, tendering shareholders may be left holding odd lots of the target stock. Others may wish to avoid completing the required forms and awaiting the results of the offer to learn whether or not their tender has been accepted. Moreover, institutional investors may not want to get involved in a contested offer, fearing they will later be blamed for the success or failure of the offer.

Seeking to capitalize on this reluctance, an arbitrage market of major significance to the success of tender offers has developed. Once an offer has been announced, large dealers and brokers stand ready to purchase shares on the open market at a price near the bid price discounted only by their expectations regarding the offer's chance for rapid success. Although the point spread between the bid price and the inflated market price may be small, these arbitrageurs will make substantial profits if the offer is successful.

By accumulating large blocks of shares ultimately to be tendered to the bidder, arbitrageurs not only provide an escape route for uncomfortable shareholders, they also increase the probability that the offer will be successful. It has been estimated that between 60 and 90 per cent of tendered shares are tendered by arbitrageurs, who have facetiously been labeled the "midwives" of tender offers. Obviously, they are an important third force to be reckoned with.

THE ADVANTAGES OF A TENDER OFFER

Tender offers enable corporations to gain control of companies resisting their advances with a minimum of cost and procedural effort in a short period of time and, perhaps most importantly, with a high probability of success. Although both cash and exchange offers share these characteristics, they are accentuated in cash bids. Because of these advantages, tender offers have replaced proxy fights as the principal instrument of corporate combat.

Although attracting considerable attention in the media, proxy fights were never terribly popular. Not only are they more prolonged and more complicated than tender offers, they are also believed by many to be more expensive and are definitely riskier. The insurgent in a proxy fight, for example, must spend large sums of money to hope to succeed. If the incumbent management survives the battle, as the statistics show is likely, the loser has nothing to show for his efforts but his scars. Even if the insurgent wins, his potential gain is limited by the extent of his stock ownership, the salaries he and his friends can secure for themselves as officers of the company under attack, and whatever other pickings can be gleaned from the prize.

By contrast, a tender offerer can publish his bid in a newspaper or two, then sit and wait for a few weeks until the results are finalized. His costs will be limited to the cost of the money committed to the offer and whatever litigation expenses ensue. His initial investment can be limited, because he is interested only in obtaining control, not in obtaining all the outstanding shares. If his offer is successful, and the statistics this time are on his side, he will stand to profit handsomely if his investment judgment was correct.

Most importantly, tender offers can be profitable to the offerer even if the offer is *not* successful. Historically, the stock market has responded favorably to tender offer announcements. Reflecting a "me too" attitude on the part of investors, shares of the target company frequently have risen above the bid price following an offer whether or not the offer is successful. The attacker who has acquired a sizable position in the target company prior to the public offer may find himself holding the shares at an appreciated value after the offer has failed. If he chooses not to remain as a minority shareholder, he can sell the shares on the open market, to a third party also interested in acquiring the target, or back to the target corporation itself, whose management may be more than eager to buy out the potential threat to their job security. Any such sale, however, would be subject to the provisions of Section 16(b) of the Securities Exchange Act which requires that any profit realized on the sale of securities by a person owning more than 10 per cent of any class of security is recoverable by the issuing corporation if the seller has not held them for a minimum of six months.

In April, 1968, for example, Loew's Theatres, with assets of $250 million, announced a tender offer for Commercial Credit, a company whose assets exceeded $3 billion. Commercial Credit was paying dividends of $1.80 per share, and its stock was selling at about $30. Loew's offered $45 convertible debentures paying $2.475, and convertible to

Loew's common at $90. Annual interest after taxes on the debentures cost Loew's approximately $1.25. Commercial Credit dividends after taxes yielded Loew's $1.65 per share. Thus, Loew's stood to realize a 40¢ annual profit on each share tendered.

The market responded favorably to the offer, pushing Loew's shares from about $70 to more than $100. Commercial Credit's shares rose from $30 to $55. At that point, however, Commercial Credit frustrated the offer by merging with Control Data at $65 per share. Yet Loew's could hardly be called a loser. Prior to announcing its tender offer, Loew's had accumulated more than a million Commercial Credit shares, somewhat less than 10 per cent of the shares outstanding, paying approximately $30 per share. Thus, by the end of 1968, Loew's had realized more than $28 million profit on its $30 million investment, had avoided the application of Section 16(b), and still had 5,300 shares of Control Data worth almost $700,000.

Yet the most important reason for preferring tender offers is that they are so often successful. It is clear that proxy contests hold out little hope for success to insurgents. One study, for example, found that of fifty-six contests for control, only fourteen had been successful. Although most observers agree that tender offers are more likely to succeed, quantification has been more difficult.

There is substantial agreement that uncontested tender offers are almost invariably successful. Of those that are contested, most empirical studies to date reveal that at least one in three will fail completely. Beyond that, the studies are not in harmony. The germinal study of contested tender offers, that of Hayes and Taussig, concluded that only one of every three such offers succeeded. Later studies, the most notable being that of Austin and Fishman, refined the concept of success substantially. Noting that the acquisition of a significant investment position as a result of a partially successful tender offer often resulted in the complete absorption of the target within a few years, they rated a tender offer's chance of success as 2 to 1, or 65 per cent.

Part of the reason for this success rate, at least for cash offers, is the position of secrecy from which the offer is launched. Secrecy prior to the announcement of the bid prevents a premature market runup of the target company's stock and hampers the target company's ability to resist. By contrast, exchange offers are considered a "sale" of securities within the meaning of section 2(3) of the Securities Act of 1933, thus requiring advance filing of a registration statement and prospectus with the SEC. Because delays are frequently encountered before a registration statement becomes effective, the element of surprise will be lost. Equally restrictive provisions govern proxy contests.

Neither cash nor exchange offers, of course, are all milk and honey. For one thing, they are more expensive than other acquisition techniques. The offer must include a premium over the market value of the shares to induce shareholders to sell, financing may be expensive, and the costs of waging a contested battle can be significant. Because most tenders will be taxable events to the shareholders, the premium must be large enough to attract shareholders in high income brackets, who are also likely to be the largest shareholders. Smaller and less wealthy shareholders also benefit from this premium, thus contributing to the cost of the bid. Further, because take-overs are launched from secrecy, detailed examination of the target company is precluded. The acquiring company may find unpleasant surprises awaiting.

Finally, because the price of the target company's shares will rise after the offer has been announced, any subsequent attempt to sweeten the offer to attract additional shareholders is likely to be expensive. This results from the fact the offerer must pay the same price to all shareholders who accept the offer. Consequently, the initial price should be established with care.

RAID OR CRUSADE?

Heated debate has surrounded the tender offer's rise to prominence. Opponents describe such offers as a form of legalized rape in which shrewd and cunning upstarts attempt to raid proud old companies for personal plunder. Proponents defend tender offers as the only realistic way to replace entrenched, colorless managements with imaginative, aggressive professionals. As usual when large sums of money are involved, more heat than light has accompanied the debate.

To gauge the impact of tender offers, two measuring sticks must be used. First, are tender offers in general beneficial or disadvantageous to the companies involved? Second, are the techniques employed during tender offers fair to the tendering shareholders? There can be no question at this late date that target companies during the first phase of the take-over boom had little to distinguish them from fossils. It has been observed that most take-overs during this period could have been foreseen by examining the target company's published financial data. Writing in 1967, for example, Taussig and Hayes concluded: "Our detailed analysis . . . suggests that . . . the typical subject company has exhibited disappointing operating performance, paid decreasing dividends and is excessively liquid. In short, vulnerability to a take-over bid may be traceable to inept, or at least overly-conservative management." During this period, therefore, take-over bids could be expected to have a beneficial impact on the business community, because it could realistically be expected that successful tender offers would revitalize these otherwise moribund companies. The optimistic attitude of the investment community toward take-overs undoubtedly reflected these expectations.

As the merger movement gained in popularity, however, a not-so-subtle shift in the thrust of the take-over boom surfaced. Increasingly, profitable and well-managed companies became the targets of tender offers, whereas take-over interest in corporate wallflowers subsided. During this second phase of the tender offer movement, only two characteristics distinguished many target companies from other companies—high liquidity and a low price–earnings ratio.

Seeking out companies with these two characteristics, of course, reflected the more general acquisition strategy pervading the entire merger movement. "Glamour" companies capitalized on this acquisition strategy, because the price of their own stock responded favorably to the acquisition of a company with a low price–earnings ratio. Moreover, high liquidity not only helped the acquiring company finance additional acquisitions, it also helped pay for the purchase of the target company itself.

Debt–equity switching became commonplace. Of the $11.2 billion worth of securities registered for the purpose of exchange offers in 1968, more than half represented convertible bonds or convertible preferred. Eighty per cent of the cash offers filed with the SEC between August 1968 and June 1969 were financed by bank loans. Not infrequently the acquiring company anticipated repaying the loans with the target company's own funds.

"Funny money" also made its appearance on the take-over scene. Complex securities packages, undecipherable to all but the select few, were not uncommon. One wonders what the proverbial widow from Des Moines thought about an offer involving:

- $45 principal amount of subordinated debentures.
- 3/5 of a share of preferred stock having no public market.
- 3/10 of a five-year warrant to purchase one share of common.

All this was in exchange for two shares of common stock of the target company.

It thus became increasingly clear that companies engaged in the take-over game were not necessarily seeking to redeem the investments of oppressed shareholders. More likely, their interest centered on the effect the take-over would have on the price–earnings ratio of their own stock and their ability to engage in future acquisitions. In short, attention shifted from "sleepers"—those companies with an underdeveloped potential because of poor management or other operational deficiencies—to "plums"—companies which, because of high liquidity, sound debt position, or low price–earnings ratio could yield an immediate financial benefit to the acquiring company.

Critics of the take-over phenomenon, although correctly sensing that all was not well, never really appreciated what was in fact taking place. The paradigm of the "raider," that mythological creature who would milk the target and liquidate the remains, was simply not accurate. The critics missed the mark because they failed to realize the relationship of the take-over boom to the larger merger movement.

Moreover, shareholders were no more interested in operational considerations than were acquiring companies. Empirical studies have demonstrated that, at least in recent years, no correlation exists between the target company's operating performance and the chance that the offer will be successful. Although various commentators have tried to find such a relationship undoubtedly to support preconceived notions as to what led to success, the statistics they compiled demonstrate the absence of any such correlation.

Because neither acquiring corporations nor shareholders were much interested in operational considerations, it should not be surprising that tender offers have not proved to be an effective vehicle for corporate reform. Because the motive for the acquisition was not to *improve* the target but only to *acquire* it, it was to be expected that the operating characteristics of targets, even for something as visible as dividend payments, would not change much following take-overs. In short, few take-overs today excite the expectations with which they were once greeted.

Despite this cynical portrait, there are those who contend that the *fear* of being taken over has spurred otherwise anemic managements to new and greater heights of efficiency and creativity, thus benefiting those who have invested in these companies. Although this may have been true in some cases, it is equally clear that much of the creative effort to emerge from the fear of being taken over has been directed toward the development of a highly sophisticated array of defensive measures calculated to insulate managements even more effectively from the fear of losing their jobs.

Whether or not tender offers contribute to the economic well-being of our country is a question that may never be answered fully. But it did become clear to many during the golden years when cash tender offers were virtually unregulated that abuses existed in the manner take-over battles were fought. Insider profiteering, market manipulation, and an inability to control managements more interested in protecting their jobs than the interests of their shareholders brought about the need for remedial action. Federal regulation soon followed.

But whatever else tender offers are, they are above all exciting, if only to those who happen to be involved in them. During January 1969, for example, 100 companies, almost all listed on the New York Stock Exchange, were involved in tender offers. More than 40 million shares of these companies were traded that month, representing 15 per cent of that month's trading activity. To brokers, investors, and acquiring and target companies tender offers are indeed exciting.

THE LEGAL BACKGROUND OF TENDER OFFERS

Evolution of the Williams Act

Despite repeated cries during the late 1960's for federal legislation to control the burgeoning merger movement, Congress seemed to respond very slowly to the challenge. Hearings preceded debate, debate generated further hearings, but the amount of legislation enacted into law remained miniscule. It was, therefore, surprising that Congressional action to regulate tender offers came so swiftly and decisively, especially because tender offers represented only a small portion of the total number of corporate acquisitions. Many observers offered a cynical explanation for this dichotomy of treatment. They pointed out that those companies most likely to be taken over were among the oldest and most established in American society. When incumbent managements of these companies realized that brash young business school graduates threatened to take away their jobs, the theory goes, the hot lines to Washington were opened.

Although the extent to which Congress was influenced by such mundane considerations will never be known, it cannot be denied that the opening Congressional barrage directed against take-overs carried the unmistakable sounds of a shaken corporate aristocracy. Senator Williams of New Jersey led the attack by offering S.2731 in 1965. He introduced the bill, appropriately entitled, "Fuller Disclosure by and Protection Against So-called Corporate Raiders," with the following call to arms: "In recent years we have seen proud old companies reduced to corporate shells after white collar pirates have seized control with funds from sources which are unknown in many cases, then sold or traded the best assets, later to split up most of the loot among themselves."

Although that bill died in the 89th Congress, it managed to capture the attention of the SEC. The commission, although criticizing parts of the bill, announced its strong agreement with the bill's fundamental objectives. Chairman Cohen later vocalized the SEC's position as follows:

> The basic principle of investor protection . . . is simple: Investors should be informed of the identity, background, future plans and other material information about anyone seeking to acquire control of their company before they sell securities to that person. This is necessary if public investors are to stand on an equal footing with the acquiring person in assessing the future of the company and the value of its shares. Further, the bills recognize that the need of investors for full and complete information in arriving at a decision to *sell* securities is just as great as when they are arriving at a decision to *buy* securities—a concept which is inherent in the Exchange Act.
>
> The proposed legislation would, of course, subject a new class of persons to the reporting requirements of the Exchange Act; that is, persons not yet in control. But it would not represent a change in the fundamental policy underlying the federal securities laws that investors should be fully informed of all material facts before reaching an investment decision.

Senator Williams caught the hint and, along with Senator Kuchel, submitted S.510, a bill incorporating many of the SEC's suggestions, to the 90th Congress. Recognizing that his earlier arguments had been too bold to attract much support and, one hopes, responding to a spate of articles criticizing the factual basis for his earlier rhetoric, Senator Williams modified his approach considerably:

> The measure is not aimed at obstructing legitimate takeover bids. In some instances, a change in management will prove a welcome boon for shareholder[s] . . . and . . . it may be necessary if the company is to survive.
>
> I have taken extreme care with this legislation to balance the scales equally to protect . . . corporation, management, and shareholders. . . . Every effort has been made to avoid tipping the balance of regulatory burden in favor of management or in favor of the offeror. The purpose of this bill is to require full and fair disclosure for the benefit of stockholders while at the same time providing the offeror and management equal opportunity to fairly present their case.

When asked if his remarks were not inconsistent with his earlier comments, Williams confessed, "You are absolutely right. But that was during the 89th Congress and I have changed my language." Senator Kuchel, however, did not seem to realize that the party line had been changed. He continued describing the bill as an attempt to prevent corporations from being "financially raped" by the "take-over pirate."

But the overriding Congressional sentiment more closely resembled the "new" philosophy of Senator Williams. As stated in the brief submitted by the SEC to the District Court in *Pan American Sulphur Co.* v. *Susquehanna Corp.,* the Williams Act was "intended to provide full disclosure [for the benefit of investors] without tipping the balance of regulation either in favor of management or in favor of the person making the takeover bid. . . ."

The Williams bill as enacted amends Sections 13 and 14 of the Securities Exchange Act of 1934, by adding subsections 13(d) and (e) and 14(d), (e), and (f). Together with the implementing rules promulgated by the SEC, it regulates tender offers in four ways. First, those making tender offers are required to disclose certain information through statements filed with the SEC and distributed to investors. Second, similar information must be filed by those making recommendations to shareholders, including incumbent managements of the target, regarding the advisability of tendering. Third, broad antifraud provisions circumscribe those involved in tender offers. Finally, moving beyond traditional regulatory devices, the bill imposes substantive requirements regarding the form and content of tender offers in an avowed attempt to achieve a degree of "fairness" for shareholders.

The following sections provide a much-simplified overview of the Williams Act and subsequent amendments.

Scope of the Williams Act

Basically, the Williams Act applies to tender offers for equity securities registered, either under the Exchange Act of 1934 or the Investment Company Act of 1940, with the SEC. Except for the antifraud provisions, the original Williams Act applied only to cash offers. As part of a series of amendments adopted in 1970, the Act's coverage was extended to exchange offers and to offers for securities of insurance companies. The Act does not apply to offers made by a company for its own stock. In addition, the commission has exercised its power under the Act to exclude certain limited categories of offers not affecting corporate control from the Act's coverage.

Any "person" defined by the Act who proposes a tender offer which, if successful, would give him a greater than 5 per cent ownership interest (reduced from 10 per cent in 1970) of the class of security acquired, is governed by the terms of the Act. (Small purchases, defined as those involving less than 2 per cent of the class during a twelve-month period, are excluded from the Act's coverage.)

Person is defined in the Act in unusually broad terms to include any corporation, association, group, syndicate, or partnership, whether formal or informal, whose purpose is to acquire, hold, or dispose of securities. The significance of this all-inclusive definition cannot be underestimated. Frequently in the past a corporation about to make a tender offer would quietly make its intentions known to a select group of friends, including institutional investors and other large dealers in securities. Having received the good news, the recipients of the information were expected to purchase shares of the target company's stock in the market at the pre-offer price for tendering to the offerer after the offer was announced. This practice, known as "warehousing," always raised *Texas Gulf Sulphur* problems and "gun-jumping" problems under Section 5 of the Securities Act of 1933 when an exchange offer was involved, because the purchasing company would not have complied with the filing requirements of the SEC at the time it alerted its friends. The Williams Act restricts the practice even further for both cash and exchange offers, because it would be reasonable to infer the existence of a "syndicate" or "partnership" from such an arrangement. If before meeting the filing requirements of the Williams Act, the "syndicate" purchased more than 5 per cent of the target company's stock, even though the acquiring corporation alone owned less than 5 per cent, a violation of the Act might be found. Moreover, the mere formation of a syndicate, whether express or implied, would constitute an "acquisition" requiring a filing under the Act in the event that its members owned in the aggregate, or as a result of its formation would own in the aggregate, more than 5 per cent of the outstanding equity securities notwithstanding the fact that none of the members had acquired any new shares.

Similarly, a question may arise as to whether the acquiring corporation is the "owner" of 5 per cent of the target's stock. As part of its effort to acquire a substantial position in the target prior to the public offer, the bidder may enter contractual arrangements of many types. In addition to outright purchases, it may acquire transferable or nontransferable options, "calls," or conditional rights to purchase stock after the offer has been made. A transferable option is as good as ownership itself and will be so treated. Conditional contracts and other contractual arrangements might be taken as evidence that the acquirer and the other party to the transaction had formed a partnership. Caution is obviously required.

Curiously, the Williams Act does not define the crucial term *tender offer*. The public tenders to which the financial community has become accustomed are, of course, included. But private offers to purchase the stock of another corporation, whether made by direct approaches to controlling shareholders or large open-market purchases, may be considered within the Act's coverage by the SEC. Although the commission was expected to exercise its rule-making authority to exclude private offers from the Act's coverage, it has not yet done so.

Information Required to Be Disclosed by the Offerer

The offerer must file copies of Schedule 13D with the SEC at the time an offer is made. All soliciting materials must be attached as exhibits, and the following information must be disclosed:

- Routine data describing the securities to be solicited.
- The identity and background, including any criminal record during the preceding ten years of the persons making the offer.
- The source and amount of funds to be used to finance the offer.
- If the purpose of the offer is to acquire control, any plans the offerer has to liquidate the target, to sell its assets, to merge it with another entity, or to make any major changes in its business or corporate structure.
- The number of shares "beneficially" owned, directly or indirectly, by the offerer and its associates, and all transactions in the stock of the target made within the preceding sixty days.
- Information regarding arrangements or contracts for securities of the target, including loans or option agreements, calls, and so on.
- The names of all persons being paid by the offerer to make solicitations or recommendations regarding the offer.

The tender offer itself must include a fair and adequate summary of this information. If the offer is to be financed by a loan made by a bank in the regular course of business, however, the name of the bank need not be revealed to the public.

Restrictions on the Terms of the Offer

The offerer can no longer set the terms of the offer unilaterally. Under the Williams Act shareholders are guaranteed three basic benefits:

- A tendering shareholder has the right to withdraw his shares at any time within seven days, and after sixty days, from the date the offer is made.
- If less than all the outstanding shares are sought, and if more shares than are sought are tendered during the first ten days of the offer, the tendering shareholders are entitled to have their shares accepted on a pro rata basis. (This provision codifies rules of the stock exchanges in effect at the time the Williams Act was adopted.)
- All shareholders, even those who have already tendered, must be given the benefit of any subsequent increase in the bid price. If the bid price is raised, the ten-day proration period is reactivated.

Recommendations by the Target Company Management

Target companies themselves have been restricted by the Williams Act. As a condition to commenting on an offer, the target company must file copies of Schedule 14D with the SEC. All soliciting materials must be attached, and a fair summary of the information contained in the schedule must accompany recommendations to shareholders. The items that must be disclosed include the reasons for the recommendation, a description of any arrangements made with the offerer, and information concerning trading activity in the target company's stock during the preceding sixty days by the target company, its subsidiaries, officers, and directors.

Because some of this information may require time to accumulate, and because the first few days of an offer are often crucial to a target company caught by surprise, the commission permits the target to send a short announcement to its shareholders before Schedule 14D is filed. The announcement may state only that management is studying the offer and that shareholders are requested to defer tendering until a recommendation has been made. If the target company makes such an announcement, it is thereafter obligated to make a recommendation at least ten days prior to the expiration of the offer or within a shorter time if the commission approves. Amendments to Schedules 13D and 14D must be filed if any material change occurs in the facts set forth.

SHORT-TENDERING AND OPEN MARKET PURCHASES

Two significant SEC rules have been promulgated under the Williams Act. Although they have no explicit statutory basis, they nevertheless represent legitimate exercises of the commission's rule-making authority.

The first prohibits the practice known as "short-tendering." The rule is directed at brokers and arbitrageurs who tendered more shares than they owned during offers expected to be oversubscribed. If the offerer accepted only a pro rata portion of the tendered shares, those who short-tendered would have more than their pro rata share accepted. This, of course, put the other tendering shareholders at a disadvantage. The second rule prohibits the offerer from purchasing securities of the target company in the open market and through privately negotiated transactions so long as the offer is outstanding. This obviously increases the cost of an offer since the market price is normally lower than the bid price. At the same time, the rule provides for consistency in the treatment of both the tenderor and the seller in the marketplace. Both skilled and the unsophisticated investors are protected by the broad prohibition. The rule also operates to the benefit of arbitrageurs.

A PARTIAL CRITIQUE OF THE WILLIAMS ACT

The policy of disclosure central to the Williams Act is, of course, the hallmark of the federal securities laws. Since the 1930's, disclosure has been almost an article of faith to those seeking to protect investors. Yet forced disclosure is not *always* justified or desirable. Because disclosure usually imposes a burden on those required to make the disclosure, that burden should be weighed against the need investors have for the information to be disclosed before disclosure is made mandatory.

In the context of tender offers, the cost of disclosure can be measured in terms of the number and types of tender offers that will be discouraged or defeated. Given this cost, what benefits do investors receive from getting the information required to be disclosed by the Williams Act? SEC Chairman Cohen attempted to answer that question as follows:

> It is argued by some that the basic factor which influences shareholders to accept a tender offer is the adequacy of the price. But, I might ask, how can an investor evaluate the adequacy of the price if he cannot assess the possible impact of a change in control? Certainly without such information he cannot judge its adequacy by the current market price. That price presumably reflects the assumption that the company's present business, control and management will continue. If that assumption is changed, is it not likely that the market price might change? An example will show why. Assume that a company's stock sells for $5 per share—its going concern value as assessed by investors. Its earnings are poor; its prospects dim; its management uninspired. Is a cash tender offer of $6 per share adequate? Or do we need more information? Suppose a person believes that with control he can liquidate the company and realize $15 per share, or maybe more. Certainly the company's shareholders would want to know about liquidation plans. Indeed, it is the plan to liquidate which makes the bidder willing to pay more than $5 per share. Whether or not the company's liquidation value is generally known is not important, for without someone to carry out the liquidation, this value is unobtainable. If the company's shareholders, at the time of the tender

> offer, know of the plan to liquidate, would they consider $6 per share adequate? I think a reasonable question arises.
>
> I do not need to make the example so dramatic. Assume simply that the offeror has a proven record of accomplishment in the company's field, as opposed to a present management which has not done well. This factor alone would undoubtedly affect investors' assessments of the future worth of the company's securities.

Such reasoning, although persuasive when applied to exchange offers or proxy contests, does not help explain the function of disclosure during cash offers. An investor who gives up his securities in a company for the securities of another company, or who offers his proxy to another company, is vitally interested in that company's future potential. Maximum disclosure is therefore useful and desirable. An investor who sells his securities for money, on the other hand, cashes in his chips and is no longer interested in the future fate of that company. The kind of disclosure urged by Chairman Cohen for cash offers ignores this reality and therefore raises problems of the highest magnitude. If the offerer reveals plans indicating that it has developed techniques to increase the value of the target substantially, stockholders of the target would be foolish to sell their shares for cash. Acting rationally, they would prefer to retain their interest in the target so as to be able to reap the benefits of the revitalizing effort promised by the offerer. If enough shareholders refuse to part with their shares, the offer will fail and no one will benefit. Conversely, if enough shareholders believe the offerer is a "white-collar pirate" whose only interest is to plunder the target, they will rush to sell out as quickly as possible, making the tender offer a resounding success. Thus, if the Williams Act were to function as intended by its authors, it would have an effect exactly contrary to the wishes of those authors. Only if shareholders had perfect communication and organization among themselves, which they most assuredly do not, could such a perverse result be avoided. Professor Mundheim graphically portrayed these dangers during the Congressional hearings on S.510:

> Suppose A, an outsider, on the basis of his research and analysis, discovers that Company X's chief asset, land presently used to grow fruit trees, could bring twice its present value if sold now to Y, a developer of planned community, who is looking for the site having the characteristics of the land held by X. Y is not aware of the existence of this land. In order to capitalize on his research and analysis by selling the land to Y, A can try to buy the land at its present market price or he can try to buy enough shares in X to give him control of the corporation and then have the corporation sell the land. Under S.510 he will, if he takes the latter route, have to disclose his intentions with respect to the sale of the land. If the contemplated disclosure is sufficiently detailed, no one should tender his shares. The practical result, of course, is that A will never make the tender offer in the first place. He may choose the alternate route of offering to buy the land (in that case no disclosure of future plans has to be made), but management which is happy with the status quo (it gives them comfortable salaries and assured jobs) may not be willing to sell the land—even at a premium above market. The net effect is that the land in this case does not achieve its most economic use and

> the shareholders do not even receive the premium above market which a cash tender offer usually carries.

Yet Congress seemed unimpressed with this and similar warnings.

That the Williams Act has not led to chaos can be attributable to two factors. First, those companies with definite and innovative programs to offer have increasingly engaged in exchange rather than cash offers. By sharing the potential profit with the existing shareholders of the target, they have managed to overcome the problems of disclosure raised by the Act. Although this has reduced their profit, it has, one hopes, increased the credibility of the securities marketplace.

Other companies have learned the art of vagueness. If definite plans do not exist at the time an offer is made, they obviously cannot be revealed. Exquisitely careful draftsmanship by exquisitely careful corporate lawyers has made clear that many offerers now follow the Biblical adage, "Sufficient for the day is the evil thereof." Thus, Chris-Craft Industries stated its intentions regarding its proposed takeover of Piper Aircraft Corporation as follows:

> Chris-Craft is purchasing the Piper shares for investment with a view to control of Piper, but it does not presently have any specific plan or proposal to liquidate Piper, to acquire control of Piper, to sell its assets or to merge with any other companies or to make any other major change in its business or corporate structure. If this Offer is successfully completed, Chris-Craft will give consideration to some form of combination between it and Piper.

Zapata Norness took a slightly different approach when it offered to buy shares of Southdown, Inc.:

> Zapata intends through this Offer to acquire control of Southdown and thereby to implement operational and financial policies for Southdown similar to those applied in recent years by Zapata to its operations, which could include the reinvestment of Southdown earnings in lieu of the payment of dividends. Zapata intends to cause Southdown to operate as a substantially autonomous entity under a management which Zapata feels can best implement the above policies, which management may include present officers of Southdown. Zapata does not intend to increase its ownership of Southdown, to liquidate or sell the assets of Southdown, or merge it into Zapata or any other person, or to make any other major change in its business or corporate structure except changes resulting from implementation of the above policies, including changes brought about by acquisitions by Southdown of other companies or their business.

If Senator Williams labored to bring forth a mountain, one wonders if he really produced a molehill. The substantive provisions of the Williams Act cannot be ignored so easily. The privilege of withdrawal, the right to benefit from any subsequent increase in the bid price, and the right to pro-rata acceptance during the first ten days of the offer undoubtedly give a certain peace of mind to shareholders by eliminating some of the anxiety-producing decisions they would otherwise have to make. Rather than being steamrollered into tendering during the first few days for fear they will lose the benefits of the bid price, they can assess the offer from a more relaxed perspective. The investment decision, however, that must be made during tender offers—whether to sell now or later—is the same decision that must be made every time *any* corporate event of significance occurs. It has never been explained satisfactorily why shareholders should be given special privileges in this regard just because a tender offer has been made.

The only conclusion that can be drawn from the operation of the substantive and disclosure provisions of the Williams Act is that, although the cost of tender offers has been increased to some unknown extent, the only positive benefit has been to eliminate some of the anxieties normally present in the securities marketplace. This, unfortunately, hardly seems reason enough to justify federal intervention into the field of tender offers. On the other hand, the antifraud provisions of the Williams Act contained in Section 14(e), to which we now turn, seem destined to have a major beneficial impact on the way tender offers are conducted.

ANTIFRAUD PROVISIONS

Section 14(e) of the Williams Act reads as follows:

> It shall be unlawful for any person to make any untrue statement of a material fact or omit to state any material fact necessary in order to make the statements made, in the light of the circumstances under which they are made, not misleading, or to engage in any fraudulent, deceptive, or manipulative acts or practices, in connection with any tender offer or request or invitation for tenders, or any solicitation of security holders in opposition to or in favor of any such offer, request, or invitation.

One of the 1970 amendments to the Act corrected an apparent oversight by specifically granting rule-making authority to the SEC to "define, and prescribe means reasonably designed to prevent, such acts and practices as are fraudulent, deceptive, or manipulative." Designed to extend the SEC's Rule 10b-5 to tender offers, Section 14(e) is certain to have a far-reaching impact. It applies to all tender offers, whether stock or exchange, and whether or not the tender offer itself is within the scope of the other provisions of the Williams Act. In fact, no limiting language even requires that the offer affect interstate commerce. Thus, the regulatory scope of Section 14(e) is as broad as the Constitution allows and, some argue, possibly even broader.

Before the Williams Act was adopted, target companies occasionally sought to invoke Rule 10b-5 to attack allegedly fraudulent conduct by offerers during the course of various take-overs. Two major obstacles stood in their way. First was the *Birnbaum* doctrine requiring that the plaintiff be a "purchaser" or a "seller" of securities to claim the protection of Rule 10b-5. Because target corporations had no direct stock dealings with offerers, they were not classified as sellers or purchasers and were thus denied standing to bring suit.

Even if the plaintiff could overcome this hurdle, it still had to prove that the offerer's conduct violated some legally imposed duty. Under the *Cady, Roberts* doctrine, it was held consistently that the offerer, being an "outsider," had *no* duty to disclose any information concerning its bid. Unless the offerer had engaged in affirmative action of some sort to deceive investors, therefore, plaintiffs in these actions could not expect any relief. Thus, in *Mills* v. *Sarjem Corp.*, a federal district court found no violation of Rule 10b-5 even though the offerer had not revealed to tendering stockholders its pre-existing plan to resell the target company's stock at a handsome profit. This decision should be compared with that reached in *Speed* v. *Transamerica,* a case discussed in the chapter on securities, to appreciate its significance.

Both of these obstacles have been removed by the Williams Act. The "in connection with" language of Section 14(e) obviates any requirement that the plaintiff be a purchaser or seller of securities and thus grants target corporations standing to redress alleged antifraud violations. Moreover, offerers have been placed under a specific duty to disclose at least that information required to be disclosed by the Act.

Certain questions still remain. Even before the Williams Act became effective, courts were growing increasingly impatient with offerers who failed to disclose obviously relevant information. Whether the requirements for disclosure under the Act will be extended to data not specifically mentioned by the Act itself remains to be seen. In the absence of the exercise of the SEC's rule-making power or possession by the offerer of confidential data acquired from the target, however, courts will probably be reluctant to extend the disclosure requirements in this way.

Several basic issues arise under Section 14(e). First, when must the existence of a plan to make a tender offer be announced? Second, once an offer has been made, what facts must be disclosed to avoid committing an error of omission? Third, if an affirmative misrepresentation has been made, is the misrepresentation material? Finally, what conduct will be held to be "fraudulent, deceptive, or manipulative"? Because Section 14(e) applies to target companies as well as to offerers, both companies involved in an offer must resolve these questions satisfactorily to avoid running afoul of the Act's mandate.

ANNOUNCEMENT OF EXISTENCE OF TENDER OFFER

As a preliminary problem, because the existence of a plan to make a tender offer is a corporate fact of significance to investors, it has been suggested that once a company has formulated definite plans to launch a tender offer it must disclose its plans under the *Texas Gulf Sulphur* rationale before buying shares of the target on the open market. Perhaps fearing to tread too heavily into an aspect of the market's operation better left to Congress, no court has yet accepted this theory. (Individuals aware of the plan, of course, would be restricted by the *Texas Gulf Sulphur* prohibitions.) Nevertheless, the danger exists that knowledge of such a plan may leak and cause a flurry of excitement in the stock market. The rules of the SEC and the stock exchanges require immediate disclosure in the event such a leak occurs. In all likelihood, disclosure at this point may seriously affect the outcome of the offer and leaks should therefore be guarded against.

Premature disclosure of the existence of an offer may be necessary to accomplish some other purpose. Bangor Punta's planned exchange offer for the shares of Piper Aircraft demonstrates the difficulties confronting the companies involved in these situations. When Piper became the subject of a take-over attempt by Chris-Craft, it scurried to find a friendlier merger partner. The Piper family reached a suitable agreement with Bangor Punta, and a joint press release was prepared whose main purpose, presumably, was to halt the flow of tenders to Chris-Craft. The release included the following statements:

> Bangor Punta has agreed to file a registration statement with the SEC covering a proposed exchange offer for any and all of the remaining outstanding shares of Piper Aircraft for a package of Bangor Punta securities to be valued in the judgment of the First Boston Corporation at not less than $80 per Piper share.
>
> Sales of the combined companies would reach $450,000,000 in fiscal 1969, with approximately $180,000,000, or 40%, in the aircraft, recreational and leisure time fields.

Although the release could have been characterized as a factual and useful description of the agreement that had been reached, the Second Circuit Court of Appeals held that specifying the $80 figure before a registration statement had been filed constituted unlawful "gun jumping." Critics were not pleased with the decision. It was pointed out that under *Texas Gulf Sulphur* disclosure of the $80 figure may have been considered mandatory to avoid charges of insider profiteering. That the parties to the agreement found themselves on the horns of a dilemma at the time the press release was prepared could not be denied. On October 7, 1969, the SEC issued its Release No. 5009 as an effort at accommodation. It provides:

> Disclosure of a material event would ordinarily not be subject to restrictions under Section 5 . . . if it is purely factual and does not include predictions or opinions. . . . [When close questions arise we encourage] issuers and their counsel to seek informal consultation with the Commission's staff which is accustomed to dealing with such questions and is usually able to give rapid and definite responses.

WHEN IS A MISREPRESENTATION OR OMISSION MATERIAL?

Two kinds of subject matter are present in most tender offers—that specifically required to be disclosed by the Williams Act, and that which, although not required, may accompany publicity campaigns designed to influence stockholders.

INFORMATION REQUIRED BY SCHEDULE 13D

Of the items required to be disclosed by the offerer, the one most likely to lead to litigation involves the offerer's statement of its plans regarding the target. The judicial construction so far given this requirement has been moderate and relaxed.

Besides being unwilling to show all its cards at this point in the game, the offerer will be legitimately concerned that investors will seize on every statement concerning the future as an immutable and prophetic fact and thus come to expect more than can be delivered in light of future and unforeseen circumstances. As a result, statements of purpose have been prepared with a view toward litigation. Present knowledge and intent is emphasized, and it is often pointed out that present intentions may change in light of future developments. The offerer might state that it "will give consideration to" various alternatives and that it "reserves the right to" deviate from its stated plans. (This, of course, assumes that information likely to be subpoenaed by an inquisitive opposition, including internal memoranda and communications with lenders who will provide the financing, does not belie these hedges.)

The history of the *Electronics Specialty* litigation demonstrates the problems likely to be encountered. Making one of the first tender offers following the adoption of the Williams Act, the offerer (International Controls) stated its plans in the following language:

> The Company intends through this offer to acquire control of Specialty. It does not presently have any plans or proposals to liquidate Specialty, to sell its assets or merge it with any persons (other than the Company or its subsidiaries), or to make any other major change in its business or corporate structure, except that it intends to continue Specialty's stated plans to sell its Space Conditioning Division and will consider the possible liquidation or sale of any other unprofitable divisions. Upon completion of this offer, the Company will give consideration to a merger between itself or a subsidiary and Specialty.

SEC staff members believed the statement to be too vague. After some discussion, the statement was changed by adding that if a merger was proposed it would be on terms reflecting the "relative market prices . . . during a representative period." The target challenged the sufficiency of the revised statement, alleging that the offerer had already decided that the merger, if consummated, would be at a 1 to 1 exchange ratio.

Although the district court found a violation of the Williams Act, that finding was reversed by the Second Circuit Court of Appeals. Ruling that "it would be as serious an infringement . . . to overstate the definiteness of the plans as to understate them," the court concluded that the language prepared *before* the changes were inserted at the SEC's insistence "seems entirely accurate and the subsequent elaboration unnecessary." Although the matter is still not without doubt, it appears likely that other courts will adopt a similar approach.

INFORMATION REQUIRED BY SCHEDULE 14D

Prior to the adoption of the Williams Act, target managements all too frequently conducted spurious advertising campaigns, or at least engaged in "puffing," to induce shareholders not to tender their shares. Inflated projections of future earnings seemed to be the most frequent form of wishful thinking, if not outright deception. Those shareholders who were persuaded not to tender on the basis of these projections, because they were not buyers or sellers of securities, had nowhere to turn when the difference between the projections and reality became apparent.

The Williams Act, fortunately, has changed this situation. Before recommending for or against an offer, the target in Schedule 14D must reveal the reasons for its recommendations. Presumably, this involves something more than merely stating as in the past, "if the offerer is prepared to offer *x* dollars for your shares, it must believe that your shares are worth more than *x* dollars." It is arguable that this statement is misleading in itself, because a more logical conclusion to be drawn is that the offerer believes the target shares are worth the bid price *only* if the bidder can assume control of the target and perhaps change its policies and management. Any more specific economic predictions must now be based on supportable facts. To avoid charges of deception, therefore, the target would be well advised to have on hand studies prepared by outside consultants evaluating the terms of the offer in light of the target's financial situation.

The target will also have in its possession innumerable operational and financial details not available to outsiders. Naturally it will want to publicize all the favorable information and suppress all that is unfavorable. Two questions must therefore be answered—what *can* the target disclose, and what *must* it disclose? Assume, for example, that an established and successful company offers to buy the shares of the target. The bidder informs the target management that it has no plans to replace them, and, in fact, will grant the incumbent management a large bonus and a substantial salary increase if they agree to stay on in the event the offer is successful. That same day, the target management learns that sales and income for the year, for some unexpected reason, will be 50 per cent below what had been publicly projected by the company two months earlier. Later that afternoon, however, management receives word that what appears to be a marvelous scientific device has just been developed by its research staff; that initial, tentative reports indicate that the device is not protected by existing patents; and that the marketing staff believes that if all the claims made by the scientists are true, and if their preliminary market research is accurate, the target can be expected to quadruple its profits the following year. However, they suggest that this information be kept confidential for a few months to allow further marketing and scientific coordination. As the target management evaluates these developments, another company, attracted by the first offer, initiates its own offer at a substantial premium above the first offer. The chairman of the board of the second offerer, which is a little-known company with a profitable financial history, boasts in a phone conversation with the chairman of the board of the target that his company will fire the incumbent management, whom he describes as "stodgy old men," within an hour after its offer is successful.

How much can the target management disclose if they choose to oppose one or both of the offers? How much must they disclose if they choose to remain neutral? How much must they disclose if they choose to recommend acceptance of one of the offers? Can the management of the target, either on behalf of themselves or the target, buy or sell shares in the target at this point or at some later point, and if they do or do not, must they reveal what they are doing? Can they drop back 5 yards and punt? Clearly, management of the target cannot trade in the target company shares while this information remains confidential without violating the *Texas Gulf Sulphur* prohibitions. Assuming management refrains from trading, the answers to the questions posed must be deduced from a broad philosophical perspective only recently taking shape in the courts.

The court in *Texas Gulf Sulphur* defined *material information* to be that "which may affect the desire of investors to buy, sell, or hold the company's securities." This is obviously a broad definition and would almost assuredly include every item mentioned in the hypothetical situation described. This definition, however, was not devised to apply to contests for corporate control. Other values and considerations at stake in such contests mitigate against so broad a definition.

Projections and optimistic statements, for example, are generally discouraged under the 1933 Securities Act to prevent corporations from manipulating investors. This policy becomes especially important during contests for corporate control where "puffing" can be expected almost as a matter of course. So long as the target management operates in the reasonable belief that the information it disseminates is correct, however, it should not be restricted unduly. Because the target is fighting for its life against an opponent who can be expected to take public issue with any questionable statements, it should not have its hands tied by forcing it to restrict its comments to present data, especially because the present performance of targets is so often dreary.

These considerations do not necessarily apply to that information adverse to the target's interests, such as the unexpected lower earnings in the example. The adversary process will never begin if the target keeps its bad news under wraps. Although it can legitimately be questioned why an offerer should be able to force a target to reveal information it might not otherwise be eager to reveal, this argument is not persuasive if the target decides to make a recommendation. In that situation should it not be required to disclose information which *it* undoubtedly considered, or should have considered, before making the recommendation?

All of these factors seem to have been taken into account by rules promulgated under the Williams Act. By requiring a target making a recommendation to reveal the "reasons" for its recommendation and any arrangements it has with the offerer, it appears that a proper balance may have been reached. For if information, whether favorable or adverse to the target, is of such sufficient importance that a reasonable management would have taken it into account in its calculations, it would seem that it *can* and *must* be revealed without some overriding reason relating to the target's successful conduct of its business. Although doubts may arise as to whether it would be "reasonable" to take a particular item into account, any error should be on the side of caution, and the staff of the SEC will always be available to provide guidance in truly difficult situations.

ITEMS NOT NECESSARILY REQUIRED BY THE SEC

During the course of any hard-fought tender offer, charges and countercharges will be bandied about almost indiscriminately. In the heat of battle, misstatements of fact may be made that may or may not affect the outcome of the offer. In *Electronic Specialty,* the court took a relaxed approach to this problem, indicating that the test to be applied would resemble that which it applied to proxy contests:

> The likeness of tender offers to proxy contests is not limited to the issue of standing. They are alike in the fundamental feature that they generally are contests. This means that the participants on both sides act, "not in the peace of a quiet chamber," . . . but under the stresses of the market place. They act quickly, sometimes impulsively, often in angry response to what they consider, whether rightly or wrongly, to be low blows by the other side. Probably there will no more be a perfect tender offer than a perfect trial. Congress intended to assure basic honesty and fair dealing, not to impose an unrealistic requirement of laboratory conditions that might make the new statute a potent tool for incumbent management to protect its own interests against the desires and welfare of the stockholders. These considerations bear on the kind of judgment to be applied in testing conduct—of both sides—and also on the issue of materiality. As to this we reaffirm the test announced in *Symington Wayne,* . . . whether "any of the stockholders who tendered their shares would probably not have tendered their shares" if the alleged violations had not occurred.

The court in that case found that its test had not been violated, although the offerer had not corrected a clear misstatement about its plans that appeared in the *Wall Street Journal,* and despite a borderline misrepresentation made by the offerer's president to a *Wall Street Journal* columnist concerning whether a tender offer would be announced. Regarding the latter incident, the court believed that "the episode reflects the difficulties commonly experienced in answering skilled and energetic reporters who seek more definiteness than there is, and the frailties inevitable in human communication. . . ."

If a material misrepresentation has been made, certain defenses may nevertheless be available to the violator—such as that it made a good-faith mistake, that investors did not rely on the misrepresentation, and that an injunction would not be appropriate—but these are matters for lawyers and litigation and need not concern us here.

WHAT CONDUCT IS "FRAUDULENT, DECEPTIVE, OR MANIPULATIVE"?

The vagueness of these words is apparent. Some of the problems of definition likely to be encountered will be explored in the sections on tactics.

OTHER LEGAL IMPLICATIONS

State and federal laws other than the Williams Act may also govern certain aspects of tender offers. At least two states, Ohio and Virginia, have adopted legislation more restrictive of tender offers than the Williams Act. Spurred on by local businessmen fearful of take-overs by powerful national concerns, the legislatures in these states have placed serious obstacles in the paths of tender offerers. Whether this legislation represents a trend, or whether the antitake-over movement has run its course, remains to be seen.

Because tender offers so often involve outside financing, attention must be given to the margin requirements of the Federal Reserve Board, including Regulations G, T, and U. Various banking laws must also be considered. And in this day of international financing (thirteen of the ninety-one cash tender offers filed with the SEC between July 1968 and January 1970 involved foreign financing), even such things as Eurodollars must be considered.

Finally, the short-swing profit recapture provision of Section 16(b) of the 1934 Exchange Act must be taken into account. Assume, for example, that corporation A announced an offer for all the shares of corporation B. Many shareholders respond to the offer, and on February 1, A purchases 20 per cent of B's outstanding shares pursuant to the offer. Thereafter, the price of B shares, buoyed by the offer, rises above the bid price. Fearful of A's future plans, the B management proposes a "friendly" merger with corporation C. The terms of the merger call for an exchange of C shares for B shares at a premium above the then market price of the B shares. The shareholders approve the deal, and the merger becomes effective on April 1.

Because the exchange pursuant to the merger normally constitutes a "sale" under section 16(b), A, through no fault of its own, loses the entire profit it would otherwise have realized. Because of the harshness of this result, much behind-the-scenes jockeying, begging, bargaining, and cajoling frequently accompanies take-overs involving the surprise entrance of a third party. Recent decisions, however, indicate that 16(b) does not automatically require the finding of an abuse in such a situation. The absence of advanced knowledge of an impending merger coupled with an inability to control its outcome may result in a finding of lack of the speculative abuse with which 16(b) is meant to deal.

Similar concerns are present if C, rather than merging with B, makes a higher offer for B shares than A has made. If A has accumulated more than 10 per cent of the B shares at the time C's offer is announced, it cannot safely tender its holdings in B until six months after it acquired the B shares.

OFFENSIVE TACTICS

It was mentioned earlier that offerers generally seek to acquire as large a position as possible in the target before announcing their offer, and that they try to surprise the target to hamper defensive moves. Both tactics have lost much of their importance. The 1970 amendments to the Williams Act require a company owning 5 per cent of the stock of another company to make public its ownership interest. And defensive preplanning by potential targets has eliminated much of the value of "surprise" offers. Because these peripheral tactics have faded in significance, acquiring companies have been forced to devote more attention to the terms of their offers. If the offer is not attractive enough to convince shareholders to sell or tender and to convince arbitrageurs that the offer will be successful, the offer most likely will fail.

The premium is, perhaps, the most important term of the offer. Hayes and Taussig found that premiums ranged from 0 to 44 per cent, and that the median for cash offers between 1956 and 1966 was 16 per cent above the market price two days before the offer was announced. Interestingly, however, they also found no correlation between the mechanical percentage of the premium and the ultimate outcome of the offer. Instead, the correlation that emerged matched the outcome with the subjective expectations of shareholders, a far more subtle figure. Some factors influencing those expectations include:

- Whether the target is a declining or a glamour company.
- The state of the stock market.

- The historic price movement of the stock.
- Whether the stock is low priced (below $20) or high priced.
- The season of the year.
- For exchange offers, the condition and reputation of the offerer.
- Whether the stock is widely scattered or narrowly held.
- The thinness of the market for the shares.
- The recommendation of the target company management.

Many of these factors are self-explanatory. The others reflect irrational factors always at work in the marketplace. Thus, if the target stock reached artificial highs several months prior to the offer but is selling at a more normal price at the time the offer is made, perhaps because of a general decline in the stock market, many shareholders will be reluctant to tender, hoping to watch the stock return to its highs. The offerer will be in a better position if it can announce that its bid price represents an all-time high.

Similarly, a larger premium may be required to buy low-priced stock, because the same premium sounds less impressive for low-priced stock than for high-priced stock. For example, American Electric Power offered to purchase all the shares of Michigan Gas & Electric at $100 per share. Michigan's highest bid price two days prior to the offer had been $74.50. The offer, therefore, reflected a 33 per cent premium, or more than $25 per share. Michigan retaliated by declaring a 7-for-1 stock split. The adjusted bid price amounted to $14.30 per share compared to the adjusted market price of $10.65 per share. The new premium, $3.65 per share, while still 33 per cent, definitely proved less interesting to the shareholders. (In addition, the market price of Michigan's stock advanced to reflect the split, further dimming the offerer's prospects.)

Terms of the offer other than the bid price also influence the outcome. For example, if the offer is for all shares of the target, thus obviating the possibility that tendered shares will be accepted pro-rata, arbitrageurs will purchase as many shares as they can to maximize potential profits.

The timing of the offer may also be significant. Hoping to capitalize on the temporary disenchantment of shareholders, for example, the offer may be made to coincide with the target company's announcement of a disappointing earnings report. Similarly, offers made in June and December are believed to be more successful than offers made at other times of the year. The need for cash during these months for summer vacations and Christmas expenses is thought to influence shareholders to tender.

Additionally, offerers try to complete the offer in as short a period of time as possible. This minimizes the time the target has to mobilize its defensive plans, avoids uncontrollable fluctuations in general market conditions, and reduces the possibility that arbitrageurs will develop doubts about the ultimate success of the offer. Reflecting this strategy, offers are generally announced on Monday mornings so that five full trading days will pass before the week end grants a breathing space. But there are limits to this natural tendency to steamroll. If less than all of the shares of the target are solicited, the proration provision of the Williams Act seems to require that the offer remain open for a minimum of ten days. The exchanges have long suggested a minimum time limit of thirty days.

Once the offer has been finalized, the offerer will want to insure that it is communicated to as many shareholders of the target as possible. Full-page advertisements in the major financial newspapers will be seen by many shareholders. More importantly, they will be seen by stock-brokers. Because brokers receive a large financial benefit from their customers' decisions to tender, they can normally be expected to spread the good news.

In the past, much attention was directed at whether offerers could obtain shareholder lists from targets to communicate with the target shareholders directly. Although the laws in most states imposed a duty on targets to supply these lists to at least those offerers who owned a specified percentage of shares in the target, the law was flouted with relative impunity by targets, who depended on the cumbersomeness of court proceedings to frustrate offerers. Nor did the federal securities laws offer any help. The proxy rules require incumbent management either to supply a shareholder list to the insurgents or to send the insurgents' material to the shareholders directly. Despite the grandiose phrases accompanying passage of the Williams Act emphasizing the importance of informing investors fully, no parallel rule has yet been promulgated for tender offers.

This issue has now dwindled in importance. The current fashion among investors of holding stock in "street name" minimizes the value of obtaining shareholder lists. Many offerers no longer even attempt to obtain these lists, concentrating their efforts instead on brokers. Despite the obvious conflict of interest under which they operate in a take-over battle, it is clear that brokers play a valuable role by reaching shareholders who otherwise might not be aware of the offer.

In summary, the offerer's task is really one of planning. If it can catch the target management off balance, if it can formulate an attractive offer, and if it engages in a minimum of publicity, little more will be required. The rest of its battle consists of responding to the many fronts soon to be opened by a resourceful target management.

DEFENSIVE TACTICS

All defensive tactics flow from two basic strategies. Before an offer has been made, potential targets try to make themselves look less attractive to potential offerers. If they do not succeed and an offer is made, they must act to impede the offerer's acquisition of their stock.

Preplanning

Because a target's options are restricted by the time factor once a take-over attempt has been launched, those companies who have recognized their vulnerability to a take-over have mobilized their resources both to discourage take-over attempts and to be prepared to strike back if one is launched. Many ways to discourage take-overs exist. One course of action involves improving profit performance, reducing excess liquidity, and improving the company's stock performance through legitimate efforts—in other words, doing what should have been done all along. Either concurrently with such a plan for improvement, or as a substitute for it, many companies have taken a somewhat easier route. One strategy involves "flogging the multiple" through the manipulation of accounting and financial techniques. Fighting to improve their price–earnings ratios, these companies have run the gamut from transparent bookkeeping changes to debt–equity switching.

Other more fundamental changes might be made. For example, the target's capital structure could be modified to maximize the percentage of shares held by interests friendly to the management. This might be accomplished by increasing the number of target shares held by employee pension funds, increasing the number of stock options issued to management, or even donating shares to agreeable charities. More sophisticated devices have also been used, such as Goodrich employed when it bought the other half interest in a joint venture it was engaged in with Gulf Chemicals, a corporation friendly to the Goodrich management, with Goodrich stock.

The corporate charter and by-laws can also be amended to make it more difficult for another company to acquire control or to merge with the target. In effect, these provisions make it more difficult for a successful offerer to enjoy the fruits of his success. For example, cumulative voting can be abolished, the board of directors can be classified so that elections are staggered, and clauses protecting directors from removal without cause can be adopted.

The most controversial changes to corporate charters involve those establishing extraordinary voting provisions to approve certain types of mergers, such as the following:

- The so-called 80–10 provision, requiring 80 per cent shareholder approval before a merger with another corporation owning 10 per cent of the shares of the target can be effected.
- Provisions requiring as much as a two-thirds favorable vote of shareholders not party to a merger before a merger with a shareholder can be approved. (In effect, nonparty shareholders are given a veto power.)
- The creation of a special class of privately placed preferred stock with voting power to veto a merger.

- Variations of all of the preceding, conditioning the activation of these special voting provisions on a failure of the offerer to reach a prior understanding with the target company management.
- If these provisions are adopted, removal of the provisions can be conditioned on a higher than majority vote.

To date, these "supermajority" provisions have not appeared to raise any concerns under state law. In late 1968, however, the New York Stock Exchange, in a letter sent to the presidents and secretaries of listed corporations, suggested that these provisions discriminated "between shareholders based on the size of their investments," and warned that "these arrangements would appear to raise substantial questions as to whether or not they constitute an infringement upon the voting philosophy of the Exchange." Because the exchange reserves the right to "refuse to list any class of stock which has unusual voting provisions which tend to nullify or restrict its voting," listed companies were understandably concerned. They were even more concerned because in late 1968 many companies listed on the exchange, being among the oldest and most conservative in the country and thus vulnerable to take-overs, were fighting for their corporate lives.

The Corporate Secretaries Association objected to the exchange's letter strenuously and let it be known in no uncertain terms that the board of governors of the New York Stock Exchange should mind its own business. After some thought and discussion the exchange governors announced they had decided "not to adopt a formal policy" at that time but would keep the matter under study. In fact, the governors decided to turn their attention to the kinds of financing used by those companies *making* tender offers. Needless to say, the matter of charter provisions is still under study. As one commentator noted, "The trouble is that the exchange is a political institution, it is not a Galahad."

Even though the states and the exchanges have not interfered with these restrictive charter provisions, however, hurdles must still be overcome. In most cases proxies must be solicited before these provisions can be adopted. Full and fair disclosure will therefore be essential to avoid running afoul of the federal proxy rules.

These charter provisions have only one purpose—to make take-overs more difficult to achieve. If a corporation is not willing to admit this to its shareholders candidly, disaster may result. The harshness of its disclosures can be cushioned, of course, by pointing out that the changes

- Provide greater continuity for those having an intimate knowledge of the business.
- Protect the corporation from being taken over by strangers, perhaps citing excerpts from the legislative history of the Williams Act to show why this is desirable, or evidence showing that take-overs have

not always worked to the advantage of the target company shareholders.

- Make the position of incumbent management more secure.

Perhaps the most persuasive justification for these provisions, however, was given by Babcock & Wilcox:

> These provisions requiring an 80% stockholders vote in the limited circumstances described seek to preserve for public stockholders some of the protections which traditionally have resulted from arm's length negotiations of such major transactions as a merger, consolidation or sale of assets. In the recent past certain corporations have sought to acquire control of other corporations through acquisition of a substantial number of shares of stock and then to force through a merger, consolidation or sale of assets without arm's length negotiation of terms. In such a case the interested party can vote the shares it owns in favor of the transaction it wants to force through. Consequently a requirement for an 80% vote restores a more meaningful franchise to the disinterested shares and thus serves to preserve the voting power of the public shareholders and makes it more difficult for a large stockholder to impose its will on the public stockholders. . . .

The final element of preplanning involves the preparation of a battle plan to meet a take-over attempt if one is made. Watchdog committees provide an early-warning system and minimize the adverse impact of a surprise offer by:

- Monitoring unusual activity in the target company stock.
- Maintaining contact with exchange specialists who handle the target company's stock, with investment bankers who may hear rumors of an impending take-over, and even with "spies" at the more important financial publications.
- Developing personal contacts with large shareholders of the target.
- Lining up possible "friendly" merger partners.
- Preparing an emergency kit that includes
  - Information needed for Schedule 14D.
  - Telephone numbers of larger stockholders.
  - Drafts of advertisements and literature that do not depend on who the offeror is or the offer's details.

Loose-leaf books containing these battle plans have appeared with some regularity at corporations throughout the country. If not prefaced properly, they might make interesting reading during litigation brought by irate shareholders charging management with trying to perpetuate itself in office regardless of the best interests of the corporation.

After an Offer Has Been Announced

It is absolutely essential that the target company management have some reason for opposing a tender offer other than simply a desire to keep their jobs. More legitimate reasons are not difficult to find, but serious problems will be created if they are not identified. Thus, a formal resolution of the target directors, geared to the particular offer then in progress, should precede any action to oppose the offer. The most common reason given is that, in the judgment of the directors, the offering price is "inadequate." With this magic incantation, and protected by the "business judgment" rule, management will be free to roll out a most incredible arsenal of weapons to fight the offer.

Phase One

As its first line of defense, the target management will attempt to discourage shareholders from tendering or from selling their shares on the open market. An advertising campaign directed at the shareholders will point out that

- The offer reflects favorably on the prospects of the target company, because the offerer obviously expects to profit from acquiring shares at the bid price.
- Increased profits under present management are anticipated.
- The bid price is less than a recent market price.
- The exchange will be taxable to the shareholders.
- The offerer has hedged his offer with many conditions while tendering shareholders will be locked into the offer for some time before learning whether or not their shares have been accepted.
- If the offer is pro rata, shares should not be tendered until the last day of the offer.
- Brokers are being paid a handsome commission for each share tendered.
- None of the officers or directors of the target plan will tender any of their shares.
- The company is taking detailed and comprehensive action to defeat the offer.

If an exchange offer has been proposed, management may raise doubts about the condition of the offering company and may even cast aspersions on the parental lineage of the offerer's management. Armour, for example, had this to say: "Historically, a frantic use of the printing press cheapens the value of the currency issued. General Host already has a top-heavy debt structure and would add up to $126,000,000 more. . . . There is substantial doubt as to General Host's ability to meet its interest requirements, including interest on the proposed debentures. . . ."

Yet charges along this line will normally be minimized, and will be omitted entirely in a cash offer. Thus, United States Lines, sounding somewhat like a participant in a United Nations debate, said:

> The value of the tender offer obviously reflects a favorable opinion by Walter Kidde & Co. on the near-term and long-range prospects of United States Lines. In one sense this can be considered a compliment to the company's programs recently developed and announced by your management. You should bear in mind that the acceptance of the tender offer has tax consequences. . . .
>
> Careful projections have been made by "expert analysis," both inside and outside the company which indicate a very dramatic increase in earnings within the five-year period projected. . . . This past year's earnings were unsatisfactory. . . . Your directors and management have great confidence in the future of United States Lines Company. We believe that all shareholders will benefit from the new program of expansion, and before taking action on the tender offer, you should consider whether your interest might be better served by retaining your stock in the company. . . .

But actions still speak louder than words. To highlight the "inadequacy" of the offer, nothing could be more persuasive than to have the market price of the target stock rise above the bid price. Stock splits and special dividends help raise the market price, as do open-market purchases by the target and its friends. If the market price in fact rises above the bid price, arbitrageurs intent on tendering at the bid price will not be interested in purchasing shares on the market and the offer will most assuredly fail.

These techniques have not raised problems under state law. It has become increasingly apparent, however, that defensive devices calculated to raise the market price of the target shares invite problems under the federal securities laws. Declaring special dividends after a tender offer has been announced, for example, could clearly be regarded as a "manipulative" device in violation of Section 14(e) of the Williams Act unless an important corporate justification for such a dividend exists, such as increased earnings or a change of plans regarding the need for surplus funds.

Open-market purchases by the target also raise problems. Initially, *Texas Gulf Sulphur* questions must be explored to insure that the target is not concealing material information. Second, Rule 10b-6 prohibits corporations from purchasing their own stock if the corporation is simultaneously engaged in a "distribution" of its stock. Some SEC staff members, despite severe criticism by members of the securities bar and Congressional observers, believe a distribution is in progress if the corporation has

- Outstanding securities presently convertible into common stock.
- Outstanding warrants presently exercisable for common stock.
- An agreement to issue its common in connection with a merger or an exchange offer.

Finally, the Williams Act requires a target company to file certain information with the SEC before it can repurchase its own shares during a tender offer. The amount of securities to be purchased, whether the shares are to be held in the corporate treasury or otherwise disposed of, and the source of the financing, including a description of any loan transactions, must all be disclosed. Most importantly, the target must also state the *purpose* of the purchase. The real purpose, of course, is to run up the price of the stock and to absorb shares dumped on the market before arbitrageurs can purchase them. Few managements are willing to admit these reasons. If they try to camouflage their motivation, however, Section 14(e) may have been violated.

Phase Two

Despite a corporation's best efforts, many shareholders will not be convinced and will gladly dump their shares on the open market into the waiting hands of arbitrageurs. The target and its friends can absorb some of these shares by entering the market. But the most crucial task facing the target will be to discourage the arbitrageurs from buying. If the market price cannot be run up to exceed the bid price, other tactics must be explored.

Arbitrageurs profit only if the tender is successful and then only if it is successful in a short period of time. If they can be convinced that the offer will fail, or that, even if it ultimately succeeds, success will be at some future indeterminate date, they will turn their attention elsewhere. To discourage arbitrageurs, therefore, targets frequently engage in myriad forms of litigation seeking both to delay the offer and to cast doubts on its ultimate success. Judicial (or governmental) intervention may be sought by charging the offerer with alleged violations of the filing or antifraud provisions of the Williams Act or provisions of state laws, or by urging that the merger will violate the antitrust laws. To increase the possibility of governmental intervention it can acquire a company in competition with the offerer.

The courts have not been blind to the motivation behind such litigation, however. Reflecting an attitude already prevalent, the court in *Electronic Specialty* warned, "district judges must be vigilant against resort to the courts on trumped-up or trivial grounds as a means for delaying and thereby defeating legitimate tender offers. . . ." Because courts regard the motive for bringing suit during tender offers with suspicion, preliminary injunctions are rarely issued except in clear cases.

Phase Three

Moving offensively, the target can direct pressure against the offerer through suppliers, customers, unions, creditors, and others. If it wants to be daring, it might propose a countertender offer for the shares of the bidder. Although such a bid will probably not be successful, it might confuse the situation so thoroughly and raise enough concerns among the management of the bidder that a mutual withdrawal may be proposed.

Phase Four—The Ultimate Defensive Weapon

Experience has taught, however, that all the defensive tactics employed after an offer has been made are mere buckshot against the cannonlike onslaught of a tender offer. Although they may succeed in defeating some offers, they cannot be depended upon to overcome truly sound and well-planned take-over attempts. Only one weapon can be trusted to frustrate an offer completely—a defensive merger with a partner more to management's liking. Although stockholder approval is necessary to effect such a merger, that approval will not be difficult to secure, because friendly mergers can usually be arranged on a tax-free basis. Even arbitrageurs will be agreeable to these arrangements, especially if the friendly merger offers a slight premium above the tender offer. Wise managers of corporations vulnerable to a take-over recognize this reality, and many have negotiated "mutual-aid" arrangements with companies of their choice to avoid last-minute scrambles to find a suitable merger partner.

A FINAL LOOK AT THE WILLIAMS ACT

The Williams Act generated considerable comment as it wound its way through Congress. Many of its supporters, and most of its critics, believed it would give target companies significant new tools to combat tender offers. Understandably, much of the debate surrounding the Act concerned the economic and social desirability of hampering tender offers. As experience under the Act has accumulated, no such result appears to have taken place. In fact, many observers suggest that, if anything, target companies rather than offerers have been more affected by the Act's operation. Until the Williams Act became operative, bidders could not always be sure what conduct of theirs might later be held unlawful under the rather amorphous standards imposed by the then-existing federal securities laws. The Williams Act went far toward crystallizing definite disclosure and substantive standards that can be followed with relative ease. Target companies, on the other hand, operated with relative impunity before the Williams Act. Little in the law restrained their conduct. All this has changed. Increasingly restrictive standards are evolving to hold targets to the same standards as exist for any company that attempts to manipulate the price of stock for personal gain.

Despite its shortcomings, therefore, the Williams Act, by framing livable parameters around the conduct of both offerers and targets, may well have fulfilled the hopes of its most enlightened supporters—to assist shareholders without interfering unduly in the normal market environment of tender offers.

6 Accounting Aspects of Mergers

As the earnings-per-share ratio came to have such overriding importance to the investment community in the 1960's, corporate managers quickly realized that their self-interest depended on their ability to present favorable earnings-per-share growth patterns at the close of each fiscal year. When it became apparent that mergers could trigger certain accounting techniques glamorizing corporate earnings profiles, even without an increase in sales or a decrease in costs, the rush to join the merger bandwagon erupted.

Between overzealous managers and the public stood the accountant, that guardian of corporate morals. Or so the public thought. Unfortunately, the accounting profession proved unable to control the use of techniques capable of misleading or deceiving investors during the years of heightened merger activity. Abuses were widespread and ultimately led to a rude awakening in the investment community, causing the values of the stocks of the worst abusers to plummet. The subsequent mobilization of public opinion against the accounting profession finally forced changes, but only after the proverbial horse had escaped from the barn.

This sad epic in the history of the accounting profession was largely the outgrowth of the peculiar role certifying accountants play in corporate record keeping. Because of a felt need to retain flexibility, a given financial transaction frequently can be described by alternative accounting methods. The choice of method may have a major impact on the earnings results portrayed in the financial statements. Significantly, the decision to choose a particular accounting method is made in the first instance by the corporation. Although certifying accountants review the choice, they will not substitute their judgment for the corporation's judgment so long as the method chosen by the corporation is "generally accepted" and is not prohibited by established accounting rules.

Because almost no standards or rules governing many aspects of merger transactions existed during the heyday of the merger boom, corporations increasingly adopted those accounting techniques that best supported the picture they wished to convey to the public. As they became bolder in choosing methods inflating paper earnings, accountants could do no more than certify that a particular corporation was not alone in its boldness. A kind of Gresham's law emerged; those "generally accepted accounting principles" producing higher paper earnings drove out accounting methods producing lower paper earnings. To the public, an accountant's certification implied that corporate records were more or less fair and accurate; to the accountant, "generally accepted accounting principles" for mergers meant increasingly that a particular scoundrel was doing nothing worse than what some other scoundrels were doing.

Merger masters had at least four accounting techniques at their disposal capable of inflating paper earnings. First, the acquiring corporation could suppress the premium over book value it paid in a merger transaction by the so-called pooling technique (described subsequently). Although inflation and prosperity pushed corporate values far above the book values of the corporate assets, the acquiring corporation could ignore the real cost of an acquisition, thus overstating future profits.

Second, rather than issuing common stock to pay for the acquisition, corporations turned increasingly to convertibles, warrants, rights, and hybrid securities having many of the attributes of common stock. Those examining the company's earnings-per-share ratio received a distorted picture of the investment value of the company's stock, because the potential diluting effect of these securities was ignored.

Third, by preparing consolidated financial reports, the economic data describing the company's various lines of business could be submerged. Receiving a single report showing profitability, investors were lulled into a false sense of security. A mystique soon surrounded merger-minded corporations because they appeared to outsiders to have a Midas touch, sweeping marginal firms into a hopper which produced only profits. Few realized the significant problems swirling behind the scenes which would later spell disaster.

Finally, the acquiring corporation could juggle its accounts after an acquisition to show "instant earnings"—earnings it had not earned—by a variety of methods. For example, earnings of the acquired corporation were added to the acquiring corporation's earnings for the entire year even though the merger may have taken place at the end of the year. By changing the acquired corporation's accounting techniques (for instance, by slowing down depreciation charges or switching from LIFO to FIFO to account for inventories) the subsequent earnings picture could be "improved." Moreover, if the pooling technique had been used, some of the acquired assets valued far above book value could be sold immediately after the merger at a handsome "profit."

Much has been done, however belatedly, to eliminate the potential for abuse in each of these accounting areas. Both the Securities and Exchange Commission and the Accounting Principles Board of the American Institute of Certified Public Accountants have mandated more realistic accounting approaches to the problems raised by mergers.

THE POOLING CONCEPT

A corporation purchasing a new item of equipment records the equipment on its books at the purchase price. It makes no difference, of course, how the item was carried on the books of the selling corporation. The sale, constituting a transaction of independent economic significance, establishes the purchaser's book value.

The "purchase" method of accounting produces similar treatment when a corporation buys another corporation. Under this accounting system, the physical and identifiable intangible assets acquired in the purchase are recorded on the books of the acquiring company at their current worth as reflected by the purchase price. The purchase price of a going concern, however, especially if it is profitable, includes something more than the value of these identifiable assets. A premium based on anticipated future earnings, a differential reflecting the respective bargaining power of the parties, and the state of the stock market influence the transaction so that rarely, if ever, will the purchase price equal the current worth of the selling corporation's assets. The aggregate of all the intangible factors causing the difference between the total value of a business and the value of its identifiable assets is called good will, for accounting purposes. How this good will should be treated by the acquiring corporation has been the subject of intensive debate.

Briefly, many have argued that good will, representing part of the expense of "buying" the earning power of the acquired corporation, should necessarily be amortized (written off) against future earnings, either periodically or in a lump sum when it appears as if the good will no longer has a monetary value. Others would remove good will from the earnings cycle completely, charging it instead on the balance sheet to a surplus account. They contend that good will is a long-term investment of indefinite life and may never be used up at all, because it is not necessarily utilized or consumed in the production of income.

The Securities and Exchange Commission partially resolved the debate by issuing its Accounting Series Release No. 50 in 1945, prohibiting the write-off of good will to capital surplus. Nevertheless, if it could be determined that the good will was not diminishing, the corporation was under no obligation to amortize it. Some companies took advantage of this leeway by treating good will acquired in mergers as a permanent asset, refusing to amortize it at all. Others turned to the pooling method of accounting to exclude good will from their accounts entirely.

The pooling concept evolved in response to mergers between affiliated companies under common ownership. Recognizing that such mergers did not alter existing patterns of business, the merged companies were permitted, and sometimes even required by rate-making bodies, to combine their accounts as if they had been joined all along. Thus, assets and liabilities, as well as the surplus accounts of the combining corporations, were simply added together to form the accounts of the surviving corporation. Under this method, therefore, good will did not arise at all. Moreover, instead of revaluing the assets at current worth, taking into account the unrecorded effects of inflation and the deficiencies of past accounting practices, the surviving corporation retained existing book values.

Many soon urged extension of this accounting treatment to other types of mergers. Thus, when the stockholders of two companies of approximately equal size joined together, or "pooled" their resources, exchanging stock in their separate companies for a proportionate ownership interest in the new entity, it did not seem appropriate to treat the transaction as if one corporation had "purchased" the other, because the purchase accounting method actually distorted the financial picture of the resulting corporation. To illustrate, if all other things remained equal following such a merger, it would be expected that postmerger profits would be portrayed as equaling the total profits of the combining corporations before the merger. Yet if the merger were treated as a "purchase," revaluing the assets at current (higher) worth, the increased depreciation charges would cause the combined business to show a decrease in paper profits.

To avoid this distortion, the AICPA sanctioned extension of the pooling concept to mergers involving two different sets of owners in Accounting Research Bulletin No. 40, published in 1950. Accounting Research Bulletin No. 48, published in 1957, established guidelines to help accountants determine the appropriateness of applying the pooling concept to particular mergers. The criteria suggested continuity of ownership, continuity of management, continuity of business purpose, relative size equivalence of the merging firms, and a stock-for-stock exchange.

These guidelines soon faced attack from many quarters. Because good will could not be deducted for federal tax purposes, its amortization yielded no corresponding tax benefit. As inflation bid up the amount of good will created in mergers, therefore, intense pressure existed to fit as many mergers as possible into the pooling category. Because the guidelines were vague at best and because they were criticized by many as "false gods" having no functional relationship to whether corporations had in fact pooled their resources, they presented a weak front from which to resist these pressures. The criteria established by the AICPA slowly eroded with each passing year until they were no longer recognizable. Thus, in 1968, the owners of Electronic Instrumentation, Inc., received 769 shares of Teledyne, Inc., for their interest in Electronic. This represented 0.0086 per cent ownership interest in the resulting enterprise. Despite this miniscule interest, the merger was accounted for as a pooling.

Of the original criteria established by the AICPA, only the stock-for-stock requirement remained viable, and even that was diluted. It soon became possible for corporations to treat virtually every acquisition as either a pooling or a purchase, at their option. Not surprisingly, the choice was dictated by a consideration of the result which would be most favorable to the acquiring corporation.

The stakes involved were high. As early as 1963, Leonard Spacek, chairman of Arthur Andersen & Co., in a speech before the Second Annual Accounting Forum, demonstrated graphically the consequences of using the pooling instead of the purchase method of accounting:

> A striking example of the diversity in results which could be obtained can be shown by looking at the market price and book value of International Business Machines Corporation. If some other entity were to acquire IBM as other companies are purchased, for its market value of $13½ billion, the assets would be recorded at about $1½ billion under the pooling-of-interests method and at $13½ billion under the acquisition accounting method; under the latter method the additional $12 billion of goodwill might or might not be amortized against earnings. Since amortization or nonamortization are also alternatives, the company that made this purchase could amortize intangibles at the full amount of present income, and, on this basis, it would take about 50 years to remove it from the balance sheet; thus, the alternative practices would permit the purchasing company to have no income at all or to have any amount it wished up to $250 million per year. This wide range of choice under generally accepted accounting principles is what many of my contemporaries in the accounting profession like to call "flexibility."

The opportunity for manipulation was also present when "negative" good will was acquired in mergers. In those cases the purchase method yielded the most favorable results because depreciation charges were minimized. Rapid amortization of the negative good will also produced higher paper profits.

The AICPA commissioned studies in 1963 and again in 1968 to evaluate the accounting treatment given business combinations. A draft opinion suggesting substantial tightening of the rules governing use of the pooling method was circulated in February 1970.

The most controversial provision of the proposed rules would have applied a strict size equivalence test to the merging firms. Adopting the view of many critics that a "significant sharing of risk cannot occur if one combining interest is minor," the draft opinion sanctioned use of the pooling method only if stockholders of the smaller company to the merger received more than a 25 per cent share of the combined common stock interest. Opponents attacked the provision as conceptually unjustified. They contended that the relative interests of the two sets of stockholders in the combined enterprise were irrelevant so long as their proportionate interest was retained, pointing to the stock-for-stock tax-free "reorganization" provisions of the federal tax laws to support their position.

The AICPA succumbed to this criticism. In a later draft it substituted a more relaxed size requirement which would have allowed the pooling method if the smaller company was at least one ninth as large as its acquirer. The final opinion abandoned the size test entirely. In its place, requirements were imposed to insure that the ownership interests of the two sets of stockholders would be preserved.

Opinions No. 16 and 17 of the board, establishing the new guidelines, prohibit the alternative use of the purchase and pooling methods. If a merger meets certain requirements it must be treated as a pooling. If the guidelines are not met, it must be treated as a purchase. Good will acquired in mergers must be amortized systematically but in no event can the amortization period exceed forty years.

The AICPA summarized the conditions attached to use of the pooling method as follows:

> Each of the combining companies is autonomous and independent and has not been a subsidiary or division of another corporation within two years before the plan of combination is initiated.
>
> The combination is effected in a single transaction or is completed according to a specific plan within one year.
>
> A corporation issues only common stock with rights identical to those of the majority of its outstanding voting common stock in exchange for substantially all of the voting common stock interest of another company.
>
> Each of the combining companies maintains substantially the same voting common stock interest; with no exchanges, retirements, or distributions to stockholders in contemplation of effecting the combination.
>
> Each of the combining companies reacquires shares of voting common stock only for purposes other than business combinations, and no company reacquires more than a normal number of shares after the date the plan of combination is initiated.
>
> The ratio of the interest of an individual common stockholder to those of other common stockholders in a combining company remains the same as a result of the exchange of stock to effect the combination.
>
> The voting rights to which the common stock ownership interests in the resulting combined corporation are entitled are exercisable by the stockholders; the stockholders are neither deprived of nor restricted in exercising those rights.
>
> The combination is resolved at the date the plan is consummated and no provisions of the plan relating to the issue of securities or other consideration are pending.
>
> The combined corporation does not agree directly or indirectly to retire or reacquire all or part of the common stock issued to effect the combination.
>
> The combined corporation does not enter into other financial arrangements for the benefit of the former stockholders of a combining company, such as a guaranty of loans secured by stock issued in the combination, which in effect negates the exchange of equity securities.
>
> The combined corporation does not intend or plan to dispose of a significant part of the assets of the combining companies within two years after the combination except to eliminate duplicate facilities or excess capacity and those assets that would have been disposed of in the ordinary course of business of the separate company.

EQUITY DILUTION

The earnings-per-share ratio consists of the numerator, reflecting earnings, and the denominator, reflecting the number of shares of common stock outstanding. Those corporate managers who were not content to await an increase in earnings to demonstrate a pattern of growth learned to accomplish the same result on paper by minimizing the denominator. Because common stock issued in mergers diluted equity, many corporations went to great lengths to find substitute methods of payment.

Cash or debentures, although avoiding the dilution problem, were not necessarily adequate substitutes. Cash was not always available, and debentures could not always compel investor enthusiasm, especially during the boom years of the late 1960's. To attract those wishing to participate in the earnings potential of acquiring corporations without diluting equity, therefore, the use of convertibles, warrants, rights, and financial packages employing various mind-boggling combinations and permutations of these securities became exceedingly popular.

Often the only difference between these securities and common stock was the name given them by the issuing corporation. For example, "preferred" stock might be issued entitling the owner to nominal dividends and liquidation preferences, voting rights equivalent to the holders of the company's common, and convertibility at a price virtually insuring conversion in a short period of time. Because these securities were not labeled *common,* they did not dilute the corporation's earnings-per-share figure.

The Accounting Principles Board of the AICPA expressed concern with this trend in 1966. The board tried to persuade investors, who seemed oblivious to the potential dilution to equity made possible by these securities, to give less attention to the earnings-per-share ratio, urging them to use the ratio only in conjunction with other financial data. This appeal failed. The attraction of investors to EPS figures continued unabaited.

The board finally abandoned this approach in May 1969, promulgating rules governing the calculation of EPS data in Opinion No. 15. Earnings-per-share data must now be shown on the face of the income statement, where it is subject to the scrutiny of the certifying accountant. Corporations with potentially dilutive securities are required to present two earnings-per-share figures representing "primary earnings per share" and "fully diluted earnings per share." The primary figure consists of "outstanding common shares and those securities that are in substance equivalent to common shares and have a dilutive effect." The "fully diluted" figure represents potential dilution from all contingent or convertible securities capable of ripening into common.

Guidelines were established to describe those securities to be treated as "common stock equivalents." Thus, convertible securities whose market price at the time of issuance produces a cash yield less than 66⅔ per cent of the then current bank prime interest rate are to be treated as if they were common. Other guidelines from Opinion No. 15 are as follows:

> Stock options and warrants (and their equivalents) and stock purchase contracts—should always be considered common stock equivalents.
>
> Participating securities and two-class common stocks—if their participation features enable their holders to share in the earnings potential of the issuing

> corporation on substantially the same basis as common stock even though the securities may not give the holder the right to exchange his shares for common stock.
>
> Contingent shares—if shares are to be issued in the future upon the mere passage of time (or are held in escrow pending the satisfaction of conditions unrelated to earnings or market value) they should be considered as outstanding for the computation of earnings per share. If additional shares of stock are issuable for little or no consideration upon the satisfaction of certain conditions they should be considered as outstanding when the conditions are met.

In this way the accounting profession hopes to insure more realistic EPS data.

RESURRECTING SUBMERGED DATA

For some years prior to 1969 corporations filing various forms with the SEC were required to indicate the relative importance of business activities contributing 15 per cent or more to revenues. Disclosure of information regarding the *profitability* of identifiable business segments, however, was not required. Most corporations, therefore, published only consolidated financial reports, combining economic data for many potentially diverse business activities into a single statement.

To the extent that corporations submerged data describing their individual lines of business activity, investors (and government enforcement officials, especially those who enforce the antitrust laws) were prevented from analyzing actual corporate operations. Critics found it difficult to reconcile consolidated financial reporting with the national policy of full and fair disclosure mandated by the Securities and Exchange Acts of 1933 and 1934.

Understandably, corporations resisted more detailed financial disclosure. Prudent managers had no desire to increase the amount of information available to unions, customers, and actual or potential competitors regarding profits in particular segments of their businesses. Many argued that experimentation with new products and innovative techniques, sometimes requiring years of unprofitable operations, would be discouraged if they had to explain the reasons for the losses to stockholders. Further, they pointed to the difficulty in calculating accurate segmented data, explaining that many expenses of a combined enterprise, such as central office overhead, research and development, charitable contributions, and taxes, could not be allocated easily to individual segments of the business. These reasons were not convincing. In one sense, they resembled warmed-over versions of the arguments advanced against the first securities-regulation laws. Many doubted the sincerity of those who argued that reasonably accurate data could not be compiled, because most corporations regularly prepared segmented data for their internal use to identify earnings patterns in corporate units. Nevertheless, certain problems presented formidable obstacles to regulatory efforts. Assuming the data should be segmented, criteria for dividing corporations into meaningful segments had to be established. No uniform criteria seemed available, because American industries are not organized according to a single pattern. For example, the reporting might be by division, product line, functional activity, geographic area, or some other system. Does General Motors have a single passenger automobile line or five passenger automobile lines? Should Safeway report data for its supermarkets in a single city or state or region?

Finally, in 1969, the SEC promulgated Securities Act Release No. 4988. Forms S-1, S-7, and 10, relate to the sale and distribution of securities. Companies engaging in more than one "line of business" were required to disclose the revenues and profitability of each. The commission did not define what a "line of business" was. Instead, it established broad criteria based on rates of profitability, opportunities for growth, and degrees of risk, delegating the problem of definition to management:

> [I]n view of the numerous ways in which companies are organized to do business, the variety of products and services, the history of predecessor and acquired companies, and the diversity of operating characteristics, such as markets, raw materials, manufacturing processes and competitive conditions, it is not deemed feasible or desirable to be more specific in defining a line of business. Management, because of its familiarity with company structure, is in the most informed position to separate the company into components on a reasonable basis for reporting purposes. Accordingly, discretion is left to the management to devise a reporting pattern appropriate to the particular company's operations and responsive to its organizational concepts.

Data for every line of business need not be reported. Borrowing from the commission's summary of the requirements:

> Where a registrant and its subsidiaries are engaged in more than one line of business, the amendments require the disclosure for each of a maximum of the last five fiscal years subsequent to December 31, 1966, of the approximate amount or percentage of total sales and operating revenues and of contribution to income before income taxes and extraordinary items attributable to each line of business which contributed, during either of the last two fiscal years, a certain proportion to (1) the total of sales and revenues, or (2) income before taxes and extraordinary items. For companies with total sales and revenues over $50 million, the proportion will be 10 percent; for smaller companies, 15 percent. Similar disclosure is also required with respect to any line of business which resulted in a loss of 10 percent or more (or 15 percent or more for smaller companies) of such income before deduction of losses. Where the percentage test as applied to both sales and earnings contributions results in more than ten lines of business, the disclosure may be limited to the ten most important lines. Where it is not practicable to state the contribution to income before income taxes and extraordinary items for any line of business, the contribution to the results of operations most closely approaching such income is to be disclosed.

On September 15, 1969, responding to the recommendations of the so-called Wheat Report, the SEC proposed extension of the "line-of-business" reporting requirements to Form 10-K, filed with the commission annually. Many have questioned the usefulness of the information supplied under the "line-of-business" guidelines. Because groupings may be on a large scale (for example, the "lines of business" chosen by the company might be "defense," "industrial," and "consumer"), it is possible that meaningful information may continue to be suppressed. Moreover, it has been suggested that the flexibility of the regulations simply gives corporations another opportunity to mislead investors. Despite these criticisms, the regulations are a step in the right direction. If abuses occur, more stringent action may be forthcoming.

"INSTANT" EARNINGS

Perhaps a classic example demonstrating the exaggeration of paper earnings made possible by the judicious use of "generally accepted accounting principles" can be found in AMK's take-over of John Morrell & Co. AMK's profit for 1967 was $1.8 million on sales of $41 million. It acquired Morrell at the end of the business day on December 31, 1967. By combining Morrell's earnings with its own for the entire year, AMK reported 1967 profits of $7 million on sales of $841 million, a 250 per cent earnings increase over what it would have reported had the merger not taken place.

The following year AMK altered several Morrell accounting practices. Inventory was changed from LIFO to FIFO; depreciation was changed from an accelerated to the straight-line method; and the provision for pension costs was reduced. As a result of these accounting changes, AMK raised its 1968 reported earnings by nearly $5 million, increasing earnings per share by 99 cents, from $1.26, the figure it would have been had these changes not been made, to $2.25. It was no coincidence that AMK stock sold at an all-time high soon after the 1968 fiscal year reports were released, at a price twenty-six times the reported "earnings," despite the fact that, had these accounting changes not been made, AMK would have reported a 15 per cent drop in 1968 earnings.

Several steps have been taken to control the "instant-earnings" problem. SEC Release No. 4910, issued July 18, 1968, restricted the use of comparisons between pooled earnings information and unpooled data for years prior to the merger: "In the opinion of the Commission, it is misleading to . . . invite or draw conclusions as to improvement in a company's operations by comparing pooled figures for a particular year with unpooled figures for a prior year. Comparisons in such case should be made with financial data for the prior period restated on a combined (pooled) basis."

The AICPA has established a certain amount of uniformity in the treatment given pension plans, income tax, and other accounting areas, reducing the possibilities for abuse. Yet there is a limit to this kind of imposed uniformity, because accounting inflexibility breeds atrophy.

Although the "instant-earnings" problem has been the least amenable to regulatory solution, the opportunity for manipulation has been reduced in recent years. Corporations can only profit from these accounting games once. Sooner or later, the day of reckoning must come. Investment analysts, having awakened to the danger, no longer accept this kind of accounting legerdemain unquestioningly. There is reason to hope, therefore, that the most blatant tactics used in the past will be abandoned voluntarily by corporate managers as unprofitable.

7 Tax Considerations

In Chapter 2 the important tax concepts influencing *why* firms merge were discussed. This chapter will focus on the tax considerations and results of mergers and acquisitions. It is important to note, however, that this chapter's discussion will be in general terms only; no in-depth analysis and examination will be set forth. The reason, of course, is that the tax effects of mergers, acquisitions, and reorganizations are a highly technical part of a very intricate tax structure. Because of its complex character and its numerous detailed facets which might affect a particular situation, a complete exposition of the area is beyond the scope of this book. However, this chapter will endeavor to set out the basic tax concepts as applied to mergers, acquisitions, and reorganizations. The businessman should be fully aware that a tax-free reorganization should be planned and implemented only by a lawyer thoroughly skilled in the art of constructing and executing reorganization plans.

From the tax point of view, acquisitions, mergers or reorganizations are either taxable transactions or nontaxable transactions. Those transactions that are taxable do not require an elaborate treatment. The basis of the property transferred and the fair market value of the property received will determine whether the holder has a gain or loss. The length of time the stock or other property has been held will determine whether it is a long-term or short-term capital gain or loss. A very major drawback for a seller to a taxable transaction is that, very often, a significant portion of the proceeds is immediately siphoned off for the payment of taxes on the recognition of gain. In addition, the corporation reasonably may be concerned with the possibility of double taxation, that is, one tax on the corporation and another tax on the shareholder when the money is distributed.

In the merger and acquisition area the stress, of course, is on the nontaxable transactions, that is, the tax-free reorganizations (mergers, acquisitions, and consolidations) as defined in Section 368 of the Internal Revenue Code. Under the rules thereunder, neither the participating corporations nor the shareholders thereof recognize any taxable gain—except to the extent that the shareholders of the acquired corporation might receive property other than the stock or securities of the acquiring corporation or its parent, that is, to the extent that they might receive "boot." The basis of the property transferred is carried over to the property received; in other words, as the result of the typical tax-free reorganization, the individual or corporation will have no tax imposed upon him and will have no change in basis.

The Internal Revenue Code contemplates five different reorganizations that are applicable to corporate acquisitions of unrelated corporations. In addition, there are three more reorganizations which apply to a divisive reorganization, to a recapitalization of a corporation, or to a change in corporate identity or place of incorporation. After discussing those reorganizations relevant to acquisitions and mergers of unrelated corporations, a short discussion of the other types of reorganizations will be set out for informational purposes.

The first type of tax-free reorganization which can be used as a tool in acquiring or merging with an unrelated corporation is the "statutory merger or consolidation," or, as it is more commonly known, an "A" reorganization. The derivation of "statutory merger or consolidation" is the section's requirement that the transaction must be effected pursuant to the corporate law provisions of the United States, or a state or territory or the District of Columbia. This reorganization encompasses two types of transactions: a statutory merger and a consolidation. In a statutory merger one corporation is merged into another corporation. For example, suppose Alpha Corporation is merged into Beta Corporation pursuant to the provisions of a particular state. After the merger Alpha Corporation would be dissolved. The shareholders of Alpha Corporation would exchange their Alpha shares for shares of Beta Corporation. Under this simple example, neither Beta Corporation nor the Alpha shareholders would incur any tax liability or basis adjustment because of the transaction. A valid A statutory merger has been effected.

A *consolidation* denotes the conjoining of two existing corporations into a newly created corporation. For example, following the preceding example, if Alpha Corporation and Beta Corporation were consolidated into Delta Corporation and, after the consolidation, only Delta Corporation remained, the others having been dissolved, a valid A consolidation would have been effected. The shareholders of Alpha and Beta would merely exchange their stock for the stock of Delta.

In spite of the relatively simple requirements set out in the Internal Revenue Code for an A reorganization, there are, by judicial interpretation, three additional prerequisites. First, there must be a "business purpose" for the merger or consolidation. A sham or other thinly veneered device designed solely to achieve a tax-free result will defeat that goal and disqualify the merger or consolidation. Instead, a valid business reason must exist for effecting the transaction. Second, there must be a "continuity of interest," as originally established by the old Supreme Court case of *Pinellas Ice & Cold Storage Co.* Since then it has been implemented in the regulations and requires that the shareholders of the merged corporation maintain at least to some extent their equity interest in the surviving corporation. This test attempts to preclude a merger in which the shareholders of the dissolved corporation receive only cash, notes, and other nonequity remuneration. Under the continuity-of-interest doctrine, the stockholders are required to continue a proprietal interest in the surviving corporation. Generally this is satisfied if, at the effective date of the reorganization, the shareholders of the acquired corporation continue to have an equity interest equal in value to at least 50 per cent of the value of all of the formerly outstanding stock of the acquired corporation. For example, if prior to its merger into Beta Corporation, the value of Alpha's outstanding shares was $1 million, Alpha's shareholders, to satisfy the continuity-of-interest test, would be required to have on the date of the reorganization an amount of Beta's shares equal in value to at least $500,000. The remaining compensation paid to Alpha's shareholders may be in the form of cash or term notes without jeopardizing the reorganization's A status. Third, in order to qualify as an A reorganization, the merger or consolidation must not be characterized as a "step transaction," that is, the use of several transactions which are, in substance, only steps in a single integrated transaction.

In an A reorganization, the tax treatment accorded the corporation is generally nonrecognition of gain or loss; in addition, the surviving corporation takes the same tax basis that the dissolved corporation had for the properties. For the shareholders the general rule is that the tax basis for the stock received is the same as that for the stock surrendered; however, if any "boot" (money or property other than stock) was recognized by the shareholder, his basis is reduced by the amount of the gain recognized.

A reorganizations have several advantages over B and C reorganizations. First, the shareholders of the acquired corporation can receive boot without disqualifying the tax-free status of the merger. (Although a C reorganization permits boot up to 20 per cent of the value of the properties acquired, that exception is often of minimal value because any liabilities assumed by the acquiring corporation are considered boot.) Second, shareholders of the acquired corporation can receive stock other than voting stock; both the B and C reorganization dictate that the stock must be solely voting stock; however, in an A reorganization, the stock can be preferred, or common nonvoting, or any number of other combinations without disqualifying the merger as a tax-free reorganization.

In 1968 Congress added to the Internal Revenue Code Section 368(a)(2)(D) which provided for new type of A reorganization. Referred to in the corporate-tax field by such names as the *two-tier A*, the *baby A*, or the *triangular A*, this new form permits the acquiring corporation to establish a wholly-owned subsidiary into which the acquired corporation is merged:

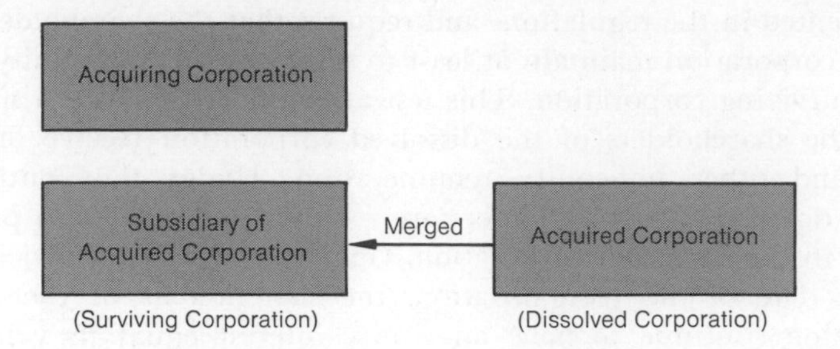

The shareholders of the acquired corporation receive stock of the acquiring corporation—the parent, *not* the subsidiary. After the merger is effected, the subsidiary is the surviving corporation (as well as the parent), and the acquired corporation is dissolved.

The three basic requirements for the triangular A are (1) that the merger would have qualified as an A reorganization if it had been merged into the parent corporation, (2) that no stock of the acquiring corporation's subsidiary can be used—it must be the stock of the parent, and (3) that the acquiring corporation's subsidiary must receive substantially all the properties of the merged corporation.

There are several distinct advantages to the triangular A reorganization. Because the acquiring corporation uses its subsidiary to effect the merger, it does not require a vote of its shareholders, a fact which eliminates any problems of dissenters' rights. Of course, this does not obviate the requirement that the shareholders of the acquired corporation must affirmatively vote for the merger. Another very important advantage of the triangular A is that the acquiring corporation, because it uses a subsidiary, does not expose its own assets to the known, and sometimes unknown, liabilities of the acquired corporation. Further, the use of a wholly-owned subsidiary as the active tool in the merger eliminates the need for costly securities registration procedures because the merger qualifies under Rule 133 of the Securities Act of 1933. In addition, the triangular A avoids the limitations on net operating-loss carryovers that are otherwise often unavoidable in an A reorganization. Of course, the advantages discussed earlier of an A reorganization—that is, receipt of boot without disqualifying merger and receipt of stock other than voting stock—are also present in the triangular A merger. The main drawback to a triangular A merger is the requirement that the subsidiary corporation must assume all the liabilities of the merged corporation. Although shareholder guarantees can be negotiated for unknown or contingent liabilities, those protections are sometimes less than fully effective.

On January 12, 1971, another type of tax-free reorganization was added by Section 368(a)(2)(E). Commonly called the reverse merger, it is, in fact, the converse of the triangular A just discussed. For example, suppose the acquiring corporation, instead of merging the acquired corporation into its wholly-owned subsidiary, wanted to merge its subsidiary into the acquired corporation. Prior to Section 368(a)(2)(E), there was no statutory authority for effecting the transaction tax-free. Although there was a Revenue Ruling which permitted the preceding hypothetical to be treated as a valid reverse B reorganization (assuming the other attributes of a B reorganization were met), that procedure had the drawback of being less than codal authority and, more importantly, it required that the stock be acquired "solely for voting stock" because it was a B reorganization. No cash or stock other than voting stock could be utilized in the acquisition. When the reverse merger was codified, however, it had the effect of excising the requirement that it qualify as a B reorganization: more particularly, it authorizes the reverse of the two-tier A. The newly authorized reorganization structure is as follows:

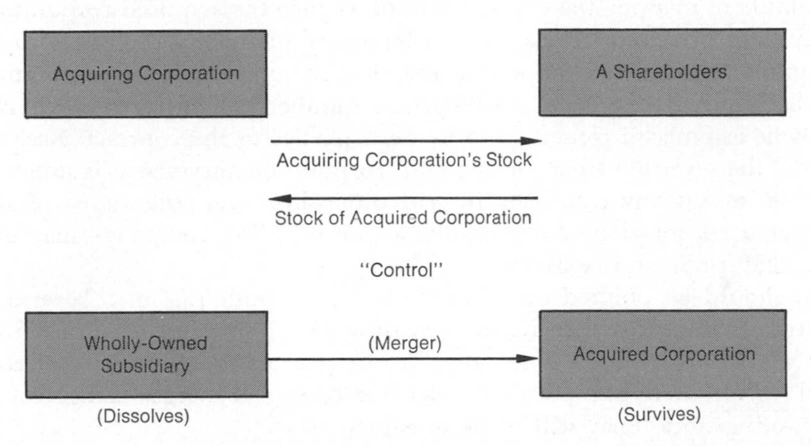

Note that after the merger the subsidiary is dissolved and the acquired corporation survives. It is important to remember that in order to make the transaction tax-free, the shareholders of the acquired corporation are required to surrender "control" stock, within its reorganization meaning, that is, ownership of at least 80 per cent of the total combined voting power of all classes of stock entitled to vote and at least 80 per cent of the total number of shares of all other classes of stock in the corporation. In turn, the acquiring corporation can issue stock of the parent corporation (either voting stock or stock other than voting stock), cash, or "other property." However, as to the latter two alternatives, the shareholders would be required to recognize boot.

The basic requirements for this reverse merger are (1) that the parent must control the subsidiary before the merger, (2) that the parent corporation's stock must be used, (3) that after the merger the surviving acquired corporation must hold "substantially all" of its properties and "substantially all" the properties of the dissolved subsidiary, and (4) that the shareholders of the acquired corporation must exchange an amount of stock constituting "control" of that corporation.

One of the unsolved problems is the meaning of *substantially all* in determining whether sufficient properties are held by the surviving corporation. The judicial interpretation of *substantially all* has generally been directed at the nature, not the quantity of assets; for example, in one instance a court might hold that transfer of the operating assets is sufficient. On the other hand, the Internal Revenue Service, for advance rulings purposes, requires percentage tests. In the case of a reverse merger, it is expected that these percentage tests will require that the acquired corporation hold, at a minimum, 90 per cent of the net assets' fair market value and 70 per cent of the gross assets' fair market value. These percentages are applicable to the assets of both the acquired corporation and the dissolved subsidiary.

The attractiveness of the new reverse merger is the additional flexibility it gives a corporation in effecting a tax-free acquisition. The desirability of merging the existing subsidiary into the acquired corporation may stem from limitations on transferability placed on the assets to be acquired; another very important practical reason is that the corporation to be acquired may have a substantial number of contracts which can only be assigned if consented to by both parties to the contract. Because under the reverse merger the acquired corporation survives, it is unnecessary to assign any contracts. In still other instances, the status of the acquired corporation—for example, a public utility company—may dictate that it remain in existence.

It should be pointed out that the use of subsidiaries in a reverse B merger, first approved in Revenue Ruling 67-448, has not been outlawed by Section 368(a)(2)(E). Therefore, in instances in which transfer of control stock may not be possible, a tax-free reverse B merger using "solely for voting stock" may still be permissible.

The reverse-merger method as well as the forward triangular A reorganization has added new dimensions in corporate planning and flexibility by validating the use of subsidiaries. At the same time, it must be recognized that these additional tools have added to the corporate and taxation complexities of the transaction. Therefore, the businessman should be very careful that great care be taken in the planning and execution of these transactions.

As alluded to previously, another major tax-free method of acquiring an unrelated corporation is a B reorganization. Sometimes called simply a stock-for-stock exchange, the B reorganization can be effected tax-free if the shareholders of the acquired corporation give up their control voting stock in exchange for the voting stock of the acquiring corporation. The following diagram will illustrate the principle of a B reorganization:

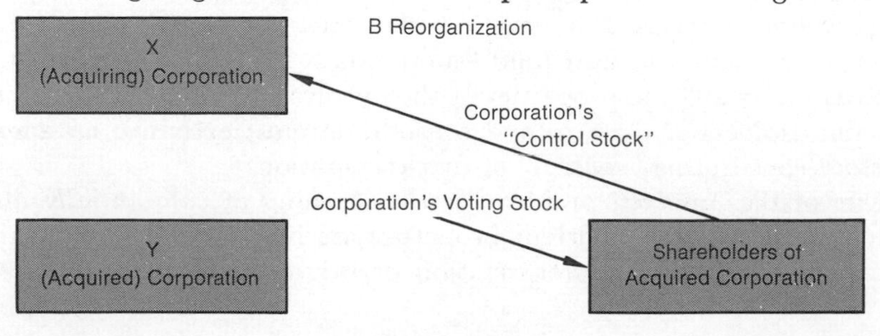

The shareholders of the acquired corporation have exchanged their control stock of Y Corporation for "solely voting stock" of X Corporation, the acquiring corporation. After the transaction, Y Corporation, the acquired corporation, becomes a subsidiary of X Corporation, the acquiring corporation.

In general, there are the same additional judicial tests present in the B reorganization as were present in the A reorganization, that is, there must be a business purpose for the transaction, the continuity of interest test must be satisfied, and the B reorganization must not be merely a "step transaction" in an integrated plan which would not qualify for tax-free treatment. The step transaction doctrine is very important in a B reorganization because it precludes a corporation from first acquiring a portion of a corporation's shares for cash and later attempting to acquire the remaining shares as part of a tax-free exchange. The step transaction would hold that the stock acquisitions were merely two steps in one integrated plan to acquire control of the corporation. Therefore, because cash, in addition to stock, was used to effect the acquisition, it is disqualified from being a tax-free B reorganization.

Because a B reorganization is a solely-for-voting-stock transaction, boot is forbidden. Accordingly, the shareholders will incur no tax liability because they cannot receive boot, only voting stock. The tax basis of the shares the shareholders received is the same as the basis of the stock they surrendered. The corporation does not recognize any gain or loss. Its tax basis for the stock of the acquired corporation which it received from the shareholders is the same as the basis the stock had when it was in the hands of the shareholders. This will, of course, require informational statements from the shareholders stating their tax basis for the surrendered shares.

Because of the requirement of "solely for voting stock," the B reorganization is not as often derailed by the continuity-of-interest test. However, the step-transaction test often is a very serious problem because the form of a B reorganization prescribes the acquisition of the entire corporation, that is, the assets and the corporate shell. Often, however, after the acquisition, the acquiring corporation transfers the acquired assets to itself and liquidates the acquired corporation. Depending on the overall design of the transactions, and the time sequences involved, the acquiring corporation may run the risk that the Internal Revenue Service will hold that these were step transactions and that what in fact transpired was one transaction that is indistinguishable in form from a C reorganization. But if the separate tests of the C reorganization are not met, the entire transaction will be taxable to the shareholders and the corporation. Therefore, the impact of the step-transaction doctrine on a B reorganization can be very important and, at times, devastating.

Another major tax-free form is the C reorganization, essentially a stock-for-assets acquisition. The most common type of C reorganization is the acquiring company's issuance of voting stock in exchange for substantially all the assets of the acquired corporation. In form it proceeds as follows: The acquiring corporation exchanges its voting stock for substantially all the assets of the corporation to be acquired. The acquired corporation, in turn, liquidates and distributes to its shareholders the stock of the acquiring corporation. The net result, of course, is that the shareholders of the acquired corporation have exchanged their stock, tax-free, for the stock of the acquiring corporation.

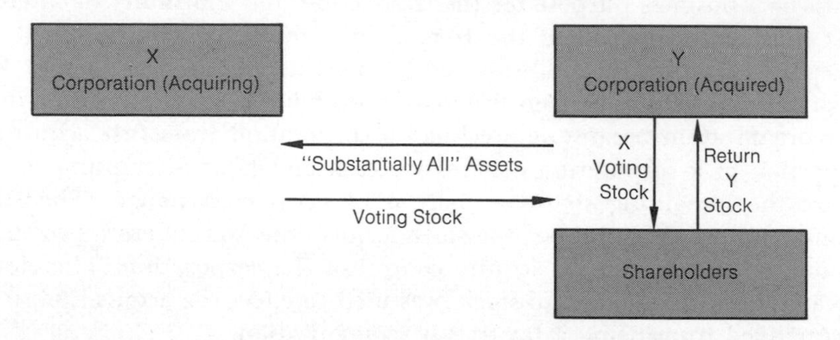

Although the C reorganization is generally believed to have a limitation of using only the voting stock of the acquiring corporation, there is one exception to that rule. Under the exception it is permissible for the acquiring corporation to use boot (cash, or other property) and still qualify as a C reorganization if solely-for-voting stock is used exclusively to acquire at least 80 per cent of the fair market value of the assets. However, for purposes of determining whether this exception is valid, any assumed liabilities are treated as boot. This last factor, of course, has significantly minimized, if not abrogated, the practical availability of this exception.

The two important statutory considerations in the C reorganization are the requirements for voting stock and the requirement that "substantially all" the assets of the unrelated corporation must be acquired. As alluded to in a different context previously, for purposes of procuring an advance ruling on a C reorganization from the Internal Revenue Service, the IRS had held the position that this test is met if there is a transfer from the acquired corporation of 90 per cent of the assets at fair market value *and* 70 per cent of the gross assets at fair market value.

In addition to the statutory tests, there are the three judicial requirements discussed previously, that is, business purpose, continuity of interest, and step transaction. Although these tests have been discussed previously, it is worth noting that the step transaction can play a very important role in the validity of a C reorganization. For example, a corporation may sell a portion of its assets to its shareholders, and then two months later attempt to transfer its remaining assets to another corporation in the guise of a C reorganization. The Internal Revenue Service may well take the position that these two transfers were merely steps in a single integrated transaction which does not fulfill the requirements of a tax-free C reorganization. Of course, the consequences of having a taxable transaction may well be disastrous both to the corporations and to the shareholders, especially if it were executed with the understanding that no tax liability would be incurred thereby.

The importance in using tax-free reorganizations in effecting a merger or acquisition cannot be overemphasized. The tax results, both to the corporation and to the shareholder, can be either benevolent or catastrophic, depending on the structure of the transaction. Each of the previously discussed reorganizations can produce tax-free results. The decision to pursue one particular type should not be made until experienced tax counsel has analyzed the facts and evaluated all the law's nuances.

Mergers and acquisitions are generally accomplished by the reorganizations already discussed. However, Section 368 of the Internal Revenue Code does set out three more tax-free reorganizations which, although not designed for acquisitions or mergers, often play an important role in overall corporate planning. A D reorganization is a divisive transaction designed to siphon off an existing business under the provisions of Sections 354 to 356 of the Internal Revenue Code. These divisions are termed either a *spin-off*, a *split-off*, or a *split-up*. A spin-off is the transfer of the assets to a newly created corporation in exchange for that corporation's stock, which is then distributed to the transferer corporation's shareholders in the form of a dividend. A split-off differs very slightly from a spin-off in that the shares of the newly created corporation are distributed to the shareholders of the transferer corporation in exchange for stock of the transferer corporation which is being redeemed by the sharcholders. A split-up occurs if a corporation transfers all of its assets to more than one corporation in exchange for those corporations' stock; the transferer corporation then liquidates and distributes the shares of the several corporations to its shareholders in exchange for its own stock. The very basic requirements of these divisive reorganizations are that the assets transferred must be part of the "active conduct of a trade or business" which must have been actively conducted throughout the five-year period preceding the distribution of the stock, and that the transaction must not be a device used principally for the distribution of earnings and profits from the corporation.

An E reorganization is merely a recapitalization. Generally this plan is used to rearrange and reconstruct the corporate financial structure and usually involves an exchange of stocks for bonds, or vice versa, or it might significantly enlarge either the debt or equity structure of the corporation.

The final tax-free transaction under Section 368 is the F reorganization, which is defined as a "mere change in identity, form or place or organization, however affected." For example, Alpha Corporation, incorporated in Arizona, might create Delta Corporation under the laws of Delaware. Thereafter, all the assets of Alpha are transferred to Delta, and Alpha shareholders exchange their stock for Delta Corporation stock. This example would be a valid tax-free F reorganization.

Although this chapter has described the tax aspects of acquisitions and mergers in very general terms, we have attempted to set out the basic structures and effects of the different types of tax-free reorganizations. Further consultation with tax counsel is highly recommended to explain and examine all the tax ramifications of a particular proposed merger or acquisition.

8 Labor Aspects of Mergers

The Supreme Court's unanimous 1964 decision in *John Wiley & Sons, Inc.* v. *Livingston* opened a new chapter in the law regulating corporate acquisitions. The Court said:

> Employees, and the union which represents them, ordinarily do not take part in negotiations leading to a change in corporate ownership. The negotiations will ordinarily not concern the well-being of the employees, whose advantage or disadvantage, potentially great, will inevitably be incidental to the main considerations. The objectives of national labor policy, reflected in established principles of federal law, require that the rightful prerogative of owners independently to rearrange their businesses and even eliminate themselves as employers be balanced by some protection to the employees from a sudden change in the employment relationship.

By committing itself to strengthen the position of employees of corporations undergoing fundamental changes in structure, the Court introduced a new dimension to merger negotiations. Despite the thousands of acquisitions consummated since the *Wiley* decision, and despite the importance of labor considerations to virtually every acquisition, however, the ramifications of that commitment are still not entirely clear.

Assume, for example, that two corporations whose employees are unionized propose to merge. Among the questions that must be answered are the following:

- Must the selling corporation consult with the union representing its employees either before or after its decision to sell?
- Following the sale, must the buyer hire the seller's employees?
- If the buyer hires the seller's employees, must he grant them the same benefits previously granted by the seller?
- Must the buyer recognize the union representing the seller's employees?
- Must the buyer abide by the terms of a collective bargaining agreement signed by the seller?
- Must the buyer remedy unfair labor practices committed by the seller?

The answers to these questions will affect the value of the corporation to be sold, sometimes significantly. Few would be willing to acquire a failing company burdened by onerous labor commitments unless those commitments could be avoided. On the other hand, a premium will be offered to acquire a company whose labor force is committed to work at bargain wages for a period of years.

Although the *Wiley* line of cases has still not provided clear rules to define the rights and responsibilities of employers and employees in acquisition transactions, certain guidelines have emerged. Thus, it appears that the answers to many of the preceding questions will be determined by what the purchaser *does* with the company it acquires. If it maintains the company as a separate, going concern, making few operational changes, it may well inherit the rights and obligations of the seller vis-à-vis the seller's employees. If significant operational changes are made, however, the rights and obligations of the seller's employees normally will be terminated.

Before discussing the buyer's labor obligations in greater detail, we will first consider the seller's obligations.

THE SELLER'S DUTIES

No single yardstick exists to judge the merits of a decision affecting a corporate enterprise. Thus, how capital should be invested, how financing should be secured, how production schedules should be established, whether the corporation should be sold to another or should acquire another, are questions that might be answered differently yet logically by different groups affected by the decisions. For example, because employees of the corporation have different interests at stake than shareholders regarding merger proposals, they would be expected, if granted the power, to shape a merger agreement to meet their needs and not necessarily the needs of the shareholders. There is no reason to suspect that the decisions of employees would be any less "right" than the decisions of shareholders.

This is not the economic system the American people have adopted, however. Our system operates on the premise that productivity will be maximized, thereby benefiting the greatest number of people, if owners of private sources of capital enjoy maximum freedom to decide questions involving the fate of a corporate enterprise.

Segments of the corporate world were therefore concerned by the Supreme Court's 1964 decision in *Fibreboard Paper Products Corp.* v. *NLRB*. Fibreboard had a well-established collective bargaining relationship with a union representing its maintenance employees. Because of rising costs, however, the company sought alternatives to its operating procedures. It finally decided to subcontract maintenance responsibilities at its plant to an independent firm. The subcontractor hoped to reduce costs by using its own employees, who were to be more closely supervised and who were to receive fewer fringe benefits than the Fibreboard employees.

The union charged that the subcontracting decision altered a "term or condition of employment" and therefore should not have been reached unilaterally. It insisted that Fibreboard violated Section 8(a)(5) of the National Labor Relations Act by not granting the union an opportunity to bargain over whether the subcontract should have been let.

The Supreme Court, in an opinion prepared by Chief Justice Warren, concluded that collective bargaining in this situation could have served a useful purpose. Had the employees been alerted to the seriousness of Fibreboard's concerns, he reasoned, they might have reduced their demands to preserve their jobs. The company's unilateral action denied the union this opportunity. Nor did he believe that collective bargaining under these circumstances would burden the company significantly. According to the Court:

> The Company's desire to contract out the maintenance work did not alter the Company's basic operation. The maintenance work still had to be performed in the plant. No capital investment was contemplated; the Company merely replaced existing employees with those of an independent contractor to do the same work under similar conditions of employment. Therefore, to require the employer to bargain about the matter would not significantly abridge his freedom to manage the business.

Balancing the small cost to the company to pursue collective bargaining against the potentially great value of bargaining to the employees, the Court upheld the union's contentions.

Limited to its facts, the *Fibreboard* decision should not have raised the furor it did. *Fibreboard* gave no veto power to unions. It merely assured employees a last opportunity to offer concessions that might prevent a loss of jobs to employees who were willing to work at lower wages. But the implications of the Supreme Court's decision were far-reaching. Did the Supreme Court mean to imply that any corporate decision likely to affect the job security of employees, such as decisions regarding corporate sales or acquisitions, must first be submitted to the union for advice and, perhaps, consent?

So close to the surface were these implications that Mr. Justice Stewart felt compelled to prepare a separate, concurring opinion. Joined by Justices Harlan and Douglas, he erected a barrier beyond which he would not go:

> [T]here are . . . areas where decisions by management may quite clearly imperil job security, or indeed terminate employment entirely. An enterprise may decide to invest in labor-saving machinery. Another may resolve to liquidate its assets and go out of business. Nothing the Court holds today should be understood as imposing a duty to bargain collectively regarding such managerial decisions, which lie at the core of entrepreneurial control. Decisions concerning the commitment of investment capital and the basic scope of the enterprise are not in themselves primarily about conditions of employ-

ment, though the effect of the decision may be necessarily to terminate employment.

Capturing the underlying sociological and economic problem confronting the Court, Mr. Justice Stewart wrote:

> I am fully aware that in this era of automation and onrushing technological change, no problems in the domestic economy are of greater concern than those involving job security and employment stability. Because of the potentially cruel impact upon the lives and fortunes of the working men and women of the nation, these problems have understandably engaged the solicitous attention of government, of responsible private business, and particularly of organized labor. It is possible that in meeting these problems Congress may eventually decide to give organized labor or government a far heavier hand in controlling what until now have been considered the prerogatives of private business management. That path would mark a sharp departure from the traditional principles of a free enterprise economy. Whether we should follow it is, within constitutional limitations, for Congress to choose. But it is a path which Congress certainly did not choose when it enacted the Taft-Hartley Act.

For a period of time following *Fibreboard,* the National Labor Relations Board did not seem willing to adhere to the parameters suggested by Mr. Justice Stewart. The *Fibreboard* rationale was extended to plant closings, plant sales, and even the termination of all business operations by a corporation. When the *New York Mirror* concluded it could not endure its losses any longer and sold its assets, for example, the board suggested it had violated its statutory duty by not granting the employees an opportunity to bargain about the contemplated decision to sell. Even though extenuating circumstances convinced the Board to issue no remedial order, management concern grew.

The scare created by the board seems to have passed. To have its orders enforced, the Board must seek assistance from federal courts of appeals. One by one these courts refused to enforce bargaining orders in these circumstances, citing instead Mr. Justice Stewart's concurring opinion in *Fibreboard.* Thereafter, the board seemed to retreat.

Companies and unions had not been idle during this interim, however. The management-prerogatives clauses of many collective bargaining agreements were revised to define more clearly the respective rights of the parties regarding proposed changes in fundamental corporate structure. Accordingly, litigation since *Fibreboard* has dwindled. Future developments have not been foreclosed, however. The pendulum continues to move, and it is not inconceivable that some future court may consider reasonable that which Mr. Justice Stewart decried.

Although at present no duty exists to bargain with a union concerning a *decision* to merge, the management of a corporation that has agreed to be acquired by another should meet with the union to discuss the *effects* of its decision. Questions associated with the end of the bargaining relationship, such as entitlement to severance pay or other rights accruing under the collective bargaining contract, must be resolved. Answers to these questions, however, may be of only secondary importance to the employees. The question of most immediate interest—what comes next—can only be answered by the buyer. Because the scene of action has shifted, the employees will often explore avenues to influence the buyer's decisions.

OBLIGATION OF BUYER

A company that purchases a truck from another company has no legal obligation to the driver who operated the truck for the seller. By contrast, a company that purchases an entire fleet of trucks from a trucking company may have legal obligations to all the seller's employees. This distinction is not some form of legal hocus pocus. During the past half century legislative packages have been fashioned seeking to minimize strife between employees and employers. The sale of an entire enterprise can jeopardize the stability of labor relations in a way not possible when only a few assets of a company are sold. Federal courts have, therefore, imposed safeguards to minimize the potential disruptiveness of an acquisition transaction.

To illustrate the rationale behind such safeguards, assume that employees organize and select a union to represent them. A collective bargaining agreement is thereafter reached with the company management. The collective bargaining agreement establishes pay scales and fringe benefits, provides a grievance resolution procedure, and establishes a measure of job security through seniority provisions. The parties operate under this agreement (as modified) for fifteen years. During that time the employees acquire seniority, accumulate contingent benefits under the pension plan, and generally develop a stable working relationship with the company management. One day, however, the owner of the company announces that tax considerations have prompted him to sell the assets of the company to a large concern. Soon thereafter papers are signed, the letterhead the company uses is revised, and a representative of the buyer begins visiting the plant at regular intervals. The front-line supervisors of the company remain the same (although the former president is now called the plant manager); the name of the company remains the same (although it is now called a division); the working methods and products manufactured by the company remain the same. In fact, so far as the employees are concerned, nothing of substance changes.

Even the least initiated can foresee the dissatisfaction that might result should the employees be told that as a result of this shuffle the collective bargaining agreement has been terminated, they have lost their pension and seniority benefits, their union will no longer be recognized, and they must take salary cuts if they wish to keep their jobs.

Now let us change the facts. Assume instead that our hypothetical company, because of inept management, has allowed labor costs to climb unreasonably and therefore cannot operate profitably. Accordingly, it attempts to sell its assets so that it can withdraw from the marketplace. A potential purchaser, after much hesitation, devises a plan to rejuvenate the company. Immediately following the purchase it plans to hire one third the existing labor force, replacing the others either with skilled craftsmen from one of its own plants or with machines. A drastic overhaul in manufacturing technology is contemplated; plans to terminate unprofitable product lines and add new product lines are devised; the plant itself is to be moved to a more convenient location.

Even given these changes, the potential buyer calculates that it can rescue the company from its doldrums only by drastically reducing wages to bring them more in line with wages paid by other firms in the industry. It, therefore, proposes to pay the employees the same wages it pays its present employees and expects that they will be assimilated into the union representing its employees. If it cannot implement these wage changes the company will not be interested in the acquisition.

In many cases, the conflicts between the employees and the corporate parties to a merger illustrated by these examples will have been resolved by contract. Many collective bargaining agreements treat in detail the mutual obligations of the parties should an acquisition interrupt established relationships. In other cases, negotiations among the parties prior to or immediately after the merger will produce an amicable settlement. Yet contracts are not always explicit, and settlements are not always possible. Resort to litigation may be the only alternative.

As illustrated in the excerpt from *John Wiley & Sons* quoted at the introduction to this chapter, the courts have fashioned a "balancing" test to resolve these kinds of conflicts. The interests of employees are weighed against the interests of employers to determine who shall prevail. The judicial function, therefore, has been to identify the interests at stake and then to construct a system of priorities to evaluate those interests.

Applying the balancing concept to the two examples described previously may illustrate its significance. In the first example, the fear of labor strife seems real. Other than for abstract concepts of contract law, the employer can advance no good reason why the sudden shift in the ownership of the business should override the employees' interests in retaining the gains they have realized during the years. In the second example, the possibility of labor strife seems less likely, because the consequences of the change in ownership are more visible and the bargaining unit no longer exists as an entity. Moreover, other considerations—namely, the importance of encouraging entrepreneurial experimentation—suggest that the interests of the employees be submerged.

Whatever the merits of the balancing concept, it seems to be here to stay. The remainder of this chapter will explore its application to various conflicts likely to arise from the sale of a going concern.

The "Successor" Doctrine and the Duty to Bargain with the Predecessor Union

The NLRB adopted an unspoken balancing test in early cases dealing with the rights of employees to maintain their union representative following an acquisition. Applying the label *successor* to corporations acquiring other corporations in a situation similar to that given in the first example above, the board ruled that such "successor" corporations were required to recognize and bargain with the union that had represented the seller's employees. As the trial examiner stated in *Simmons Engineering Co.:*

> The [original certification of the union by the seller's employees] was the announcement of the designation of employees of their bargaining representative. It cannot be said that a change of management resulted in a change in their preference. If every change in management would nullify a designation of representatives, this would constitute an encouragement of litigation and industrial strife which the act seeks to prevent.

Among the factors the board considers to determine whether the acquiring corporation is a successor are the following:

1. Whether the same plant is used.
2. Whether the same products are manufactured.
3. Whether the same machinery and production methods are used.
4. Whether substantially the same work force and supervisers are used.
5. Whether the same jobs exist.
6. Whether working conditions remain the same.

John Wiley and the Survival of Contract Obligations

In *John Wiley and Sons, Inc.* v. *Livingston,* the Supreme Court adopted something akin to the successor concept to extend additional protection to employees.

In 1962 John Wiley & Sons, Inc., a publishing firm, acquired Interscience Publishers, Inc., pursuant to a statutory merger. Interscience functioned as a going concern for some months following the merger. Few operational changes were made during this time. Thereafter, Interscience's plant was discontinued and the Interscience employees were transferred to Wiley's plant. Under traditional common-law concepts described in Chapter 3, the surviving corporation in a statutory merger or purchase of stock acquisition normally becomes burdened by all contractual liabilities of the selling corporation. When assets are purchased, however, only those liabilities expressly assumed become the purchaser's responsibility. Wiley's statutory merger with Interscience should, therefore, have bound Wiley to honor the existing collective bargaining agreement between Interscience and its employees. Wiley, however, refused to be so bound, and the union representing Interscience's employees brought suit in a federal district court charging Wiley with breach of contract.

Although the case might have been resolved under state law, none of the litigants before the Supreme Court so limited their arguments. The AFL–CIO, acting as a friend of the Court, urged that Wiley be bound by the entire agreement. This was necessary, it alleged, to guarantee the interests of the employees under federal labor law. Wiley insisted that no provision of federal law required it to adhere to Interscience's agreement, because it was not a party to the agreement. The union representing Interscience's employees advanced a compromise position. Citing the well-established federal labor policy favoring arbitration of labor disputes, the union asked that Wiley be required to arbitrate, under the contract's arbitration clause, whether and to what extent it was bound by the contract. Describing the "balancing" test quoted at the introduction to this chapter, the Court upheld the union's bootstrap contentions:

> We hold that the disappearance by merger of a corporate employer which has entered into a collective bargaining agreement with a union does not automatically terminate all rights of the employees covered by the agreement, and that, in appropriate circumstances, present here, the successor employer may be required to arbitrate with the union under the agreement. . . .
>
> Central to the peculiar status and function of a collective bargaining agreement is the fact, dictated both by circumstances . . . and by the requirements of the National Labor Relations Act, that it is not in any real sense the simple product of a consensual relationship. Therefore, although the duty to arbitrate . . . must be founded on a contract, the impressive policy considerations favoring arbitration are not wholly overborne by the fact that Wiley did not sign the contract being construed. . . . There was a contract, and Interscience, Wiley's predecessor, was party to it. We thus find Wiley's obligation to arbitrate this dispute in the Interscience contract construed in the context of a national labor policy. . . .
>
> The transition from one corporate organization to another will in most cases be eased and industrial strife avoided if employees' claims continue to be resolved by arbitration rather than by "the relative strength . . . of the contending forces". . . .
>
> It would derogate from "the federal policy of settling labor disputes by arbitration" . . . if a change in the corporate structure or ownership of a business enterprise had the automatic consequence of removing a duty to arbitrate previously established; this is so as much in cases like the present, where the contracting employer disappears into another by merger, as in those in which one owner replaces another but the business entity remains the same.

Several aspects of the decision should be noted at this point:

1. The Court did not accept the AFL–CIO's argument that Wiley be bound by the entire contract. How much of the contract should bind Wiley was to be determined by the arbitrator "within the flexible procedures of arbitration."
2. Despite delegating this difficult task to arbitrators, the Court did not establish standards to guide their decisions.

3. The "appropriate circumstances" referred to in the opinion (defined by the Court as "substantial continuity of identity in the business enterprise before and after a change") seem to be the same circumstances considered by the board to determine whether a company is a "successor."
4. The last sentence quoted above and the entire rationale of the Court indicate that whether the acquisition takes the form of a merger or of a purchase of assets or stock has no relevance. Subsequent judicial decisions reveal that this interpretation has been adopted by the lower federal courts; it is now clear that *Wiley* applies to asset acquisitions regardless of contrary state law concerning the assumption of liabilities.
5. Wiley's employees were not represented by a union at the time of the merger. Citing the potential problems caused by the presence of a competing union, courts since *Wiley* have refused to impose arbitration in those cases in which the buyer's employees were unionized. This result seems unfortunate. The flexibility of arbitration praised by the Supreme Court seems no less flexible and no less praiseworthy simply because another union is present. If the arbitrator can resolve conflicting claims of management and a union he should also be able to resolve conflicting claims of management and two unions, perhaps in a tripartite arbitration proceeding.

THE UNANSWERED QUESTIONS

By leaving unspecified the standards to be used to determine whether and how much of the contract should bind the successor, the Supreme Court invited experimentation by arbitrators, the courts, and the board.

The first significant case construing *Wiley, Wackenhut Corp.* v. *United Plant Guard Workers,* was decided by the United States Court of Appeals for the Ninth Circuit. The court seemed to interpret *Wiley* as imposing on the successor employer a duty to abide by *all* terms of the collective bargaining agreement:

> The specific rule which we derive from *Wiley* is that where there is substantial similarity of operation and continuity of identity of the business enterprise before and after a change in ownership, a collective bargaining agreement containing an arbitration provision, entered into by the predecessor employer is binding upon the successor employer. . . . It follows that under the rule of *Wiley,* Wackenhut is bound by the collective bargaining agreement entered into by General Plant, and is bound thereunder to arbitrate the union grievances.

This opinion was immediately criticized as removing all discretion from the arbitrator, a result directly contravening the Supreme Court's holding in *Wiley.* Soon thereafter, in *United Steelworkers* v. *Reliance*

Universal, Inc., the United States Third Circuit Court of Appeals took another approach:

> [W]e find implicit in the guarded language of the *Wiley* opinion, recognition and concern that new circumstances created by the acquisition of a business by a new owner may make it unreasonable or inequitable to require labor or management to adhere to particular terms of a collective bargaining agreement previously negotiated by a different party in different circumstances. . . . [A]n arbitrator . . . may properly consider any relevant new circumstances arising out of the change of ownership, as well as the provisions of and practices under the old contract, in achieving a just and equitable settlement of the grievance at hand. The requirements of the contract remain basic guides to the law of the shop, but the arbitrator may find that equities inherent in changed circumstances require an award in a particular controversy at variance with some term of terms of that contract.

This decision, too, was criticized for granting *too much* discretion to arbitrators. The critics wondered what special expertise qualified an arbitrator "to dispense his own brand of industrial justice" simply because an acquisition had been consummated. Would he be free to raise the salaries of employees if he found they were underpaid in relation to the successor employer's wealth?

The NLRB skirted the issue raised by *Wackenhut* and *Reliance* for several years. Nevertheless, it did not remain idle. Spurred on by *Wiley*, it delimited management discretion significantly in a series of rulings. In *Chemrock Corp.*, the employees of the selling corporation insisted that the purchasing employer negotiate with their union as to whether and on what terms they would be hired. The purchasing corporation refused and did not hire *any* of these employees. Because the employees were not hired traditional dogma would suggest that the employer was not a "successor." Nevertheless, the board ruled that the purchasing employer had a duty to bargain with the union representing these employees even though they were not working for him. His refusal to bargain was held to be an unfair labor practice. This ruling places employers on the horns of a dilemma. If they rehire the seller's employees, they will probably be deemed successors. If they fail to bargain about rehiring, the union might charge a violation of the *Chemrock* doctrine. If they bargain and refuse to hire the employees, the union might blame the refusal on an unlawful antiunion animus.

The board did not stop there. In *Overnite Transportation Co.* the new employer hired the seller's employees but on terms less desirable than those the employees had received from the seller. The board ruled these "changes" in wages and working conditions to have been illegal. Instead of unilaterally changing conditions, the board said, the employer should first have bargained with the union. Thus, although the board still did not require the employer to adhere to its predecessor's collective bargaining agreement, the *Overnite* rationale compelled employers to adhere to the *terms* of that agreement until bargaining took place.

In *Perma Vinyl*, the board ruled that a successor employer must remedy unfair labor practices committed by its predecessor. The rationale the board used to justify its decision had far-reaching implications:

> In the exercise of [its] authority the Board is not, of course, restricted to requiring remedial action by the offending employer alone. . . . There can be no doubt, for example, that the successor or assignee who operates as a disguised continuance of the old employer or to whom the business has been transferred as a means of evading liability under the Act may thus be reached. . . .
>
> In imposing this responsibility upon a bona fide purchaser, we are not unmindful of the fact that he was not a party to the unfair labor practices and continues to operate the business without any connection with his predecessor. However, in balancing the equities involved there are other significant factors which must be taken into account. . . . When a new employer is substituted in the employing industry there has been no real change in the employing industry insofar as the victims of past unfair labor practices are concerned, or the need for remedying those unfair labor practices. Appropriate steps must still be taken if the effects of the unfair labor practices are to be erased and all employees reassured of their statutory rights. And it is the successor who has taken over control of the business who is generally in the best position to remedy such unfair labor practices most effectively. The imposition of this responsibility upon even the bona fide purchaser does not work an unfair hardship upon him. When he substituted himself in place of the perpetrator of the unfair labor practices, he became the beneficiary of the unremedied unfair labor practices. Also, his potential liability for remedying the unfair labor practices is a matter which can be reflected in the price he pays for the business, or he may secure an indemnity clause in the sales contract which will indemnify him for liability arising from the seller's unfair labor practices.

The scope of this opinion can best be approached by substituting the clause "adhering to the terms of the existing collective bargaining agreement" for the clause "remedying the unfair labor practices" in the last sentence just quoted.

The board finally ruled in 1970, in *William J. Burns International Detective Agency,* that all terms of an existing collective bargaining agreement bind a successor employer unless there are "unusual circumstances." Wary of the criticism that had greeted *Reliance,* the general counsel of the board argued that exemption from full contract compliance would only be applied to provisions "within the area of impossibility of performance." Believing the board to have stripped arbitrators of the powers given them in *Wiley,* the United States Court of Appeals for the Second Circuit refused to enforce this aspect of the board's order.

While the courts and the board wrestled with the consequences of the *Wiley* decision, the Wiley company and the union representing Interscience's employees finally arbitrated their disputes. Citing *Reliance, Wackenhut,* and *Burns,* the arbitrator ruled that Wiley was bound to the entire Interscience collective bargaining agreement during the time the Interscience plant was operated as a going concern by Wiley. When the plant was disassembled, he added, the contract terminated:

> [W]here the industrial community has remained substantially intact after a change in ownership, the collective bargaining agreement is just as applicable to the enterprise as it was before that event. This was the "substantial continuity of identity in the business enterprise before and after a change" in the ownership that the Court [in *Wiley*] made requisite to obligating the unconsenting successor to arbitrate. The same reasoning would compel the persistence of the contract upon which the employees' rights are dependent, either to its contract termination date or until there is a change of conditions that altered the separate identity within the new business enterprise, whichever occurred sooner.
>
> In the present case, this conversion took place on January 12, 1962, when the former Interscience employees were moved to the Wiley quarters and comingled with the larger Wiley contingent. . . . [T]he former Interscience clerical and shipping employees became a minority accretion to an identical unit of Wiley employees for which the Union was not the chosen bargaining representative. With the loss of the elements necessary for its viability, the collective agreement between the Company and the Union ceased to be enforceable. To have continued the contract and the Union's representational posture into the Wiley plant would have been contrary to the national labor policy referred to by the Court and as manifested in the majority representation principle inherent in the National Labor Relations Act. It also would have created a disparity in treatment among employees having a community of job interest and imposed an administrative problem that could be resolved only by imposing the minority terms upon the others.

WHO SHOULD DECIDE?

From the point of view of the observer, whether these decisions are made by the courts, the board, or by arbitrators seems to have little relevance. It would appear that the outcome will be the same in any event since the criteria developed by these decision makers bear a striking similarity, despite a difference in language. Moreover, one would be hard put to explain why "better" decisions might be reached by judges than by board members or arbitrators. From the point of view of litigants, however, decision by an arbitrator seems clearly preferable. Speedy resolution of the issues is of paramount concern in this area, because the life of a collective bargaining agreement is short. It might take several years for the courts or the board to decide the issues presented. An arbitrator can usually have his opinion prepared in a much shorter time period.

The promise of a speedy resolution of the issues may also have other consequences. So long as the questions remain open, so long as whoever is to decide has a degree of discretion, and so long as there is little to be gained by delay, both parties would profit by negotiating a settlement to the matter on their own.

In the final analysis, this may be the ultimate teaching of the Supreme Court in *Wiley*—that it is far better for the parties to meet *prior* to the merger and reach an amicable settlement among themselves. As in other areas of labor relations, this route will most often lead to an arrangement that can stand the test of time. No mature employer will look forward with pleasure to acquiring a labor force whose animosity toward the employer has already been generated by demoralizing uncertainty. By opening the door slightly, *Wiley* has constructed a foundation upon which sensible negotiations can be conducted.

9 Closing the Deal

The previous chapters have explored specific problems likely to be encountered by a corporation contemplating an acquisition transaction. Once these problems have been resolved, the parties will be ready to finalize their agreement. This chapter outlines some of the legal steps necessary to complete the acquisition.

CHECKLIST

Every acquisition generates considerable paperwork. Almost all the actors involved—including officers, directors, shareholders, accountants, outside accountants, house counsel, local counsel, and other counsel of both the buying and selling corporation—will have some role to play. To avoid confusion and monitor progress, it is desirable to list in advance each task that must be performed, together with the name of the person assigned to perform it. Attention to the following categories of items to be performed may help in the creation of such a checklist.

1. *Officers and directors.* Distribute questionnaire to generate information required for the preparation of proxy and registration statements; arrange for formal resolution authorizing acquisition; establish employment contracts with those executives whose services are to be retained.
2. *Shareholders.* Arrange for proxy solicitation; establish machinery to satisfy rights of dissenters.
3. *Accounting aspects.* Review in detail the financial statements of the seller (and possibly the buyer if stock is to be issued); check methods and accuracy, paying particular attention to special problems (such as inventory) that may affect the value of the seller; obtain certified data for proxy and registration statements; establish whether pooling or purchase treatment will be accorded.
4. *Restrictions.* Review for unusual problems the articles of incorporation, by-laws, minute books, financing arrangements, special provi-

sions regarding rights of security holders, patents, and trademarks and copyrights.

5. *Property.* Review status of titles; prepare papers necessary to effect transfer of seller's assets, including contractual commitments of others to seller (whether by novation, assignment, or otherwise); ascertain the seller's commitments to others; decide which, if any, must or should be assumed by buyer. Determine condition of physical assets and collectibility of accounts receivable.
6. *Labor factors.* Ascertain extent of seller's labor commitments, including collective bargaining agreements, long-term employment contracts, pension plans, option and profit-sharing arrangements; determine the value of severance pay and other commitments which will have accrued at the time of closing; negotiate, if necessary, the postacquisition status of the seller's employees; notify employees of the consequences of the acquisition in a manner calculated to avoid uncertainty.
7. *Securities factors.* Determine and comply with SEC proxy and registration requirements, obtaining investment representations and no-action letters as needed; instruct transfer agents; comply with stock exchange voting, publicity, and listing requirements; notify exchanges and SEC as required; avoid Section 16(b) problems; comply with all disclosure requirements; attend to Blue Sky matters.
8. *Tax factors.* Secure whatever IRS rulings are considered necessary, allowing sufficient time for this purpose before the closing; comply with state tax laws.
9. *Other regulatory matters.* Comply with state laws dealing with acquisitions, filing whatever forms are required; qualify the surviving corporation in those states in which it will do business; adhere to state and federal regulatory laws.

THE ACQUISITION AGREEMENT

The parties to the agreement will execute a contract in writing weeks and even months before the closing is scheduled to take place. The contract will have been prepared by lawyers and its meaning will be clear to other lawyers. Businessmen, on the other hand, may find it hopelessly complex and undecipherable. Although they might prefer to consummate the transaction with a handshake, the complexity of the acquisition transaction itself necessitates a detailed written agreement that can be referred to in the future in the event the expectations of either party to the merger are not met. Rather than bemoan the consequences of our sophisticated business system, this section provides a map to guide the weary executive through the typical purchase agreement.

Every purchase agreement has a single, simple function, to establish what each party will *give* to the other and, therefore, what each party will *get* from the other. To accomplish this function, lawyers frame the language of the agreement in terms of "representations and warranties," "affirmative and negative covenants," "consideration," and "conditions precedent." The terms should not be frightening; the same terms may well appear in the deed or lease nearly everyone signs when purchasing a house or renting an apartment. The concepts involved are equally manageable.

The buyer, for example, needs to know what he is buying. He will therefore ask the seller to "represent and warrant" that it:

- Is properly organized as a corporation and is authorized to carry on its present business.
- Is in good standing in the states in which it does business.
- Is authorized to participate in the acquisition.
- Is in the condition described in its most recent financial statement (i.e., has not issued additional securities, declared a dividend or other distribution, sold material assets, suffered a loss of some kind, increased salaries or other compensation, encumbered property with mortgages, and so on.
- Rightfully owns the assets it purports to own (or, if the acquisition takes the form of a stock purchase, that the shareholders rightfully own their shares).
- Certifies the condition of its physical assets and the collectibility of its accounts receivable.
- Is not aware of adverse information or developments that have not been revealed to the buyer.
- Has paid its taxes and other debts not specifically listed.
- Etc.

The seller may be expected to back up its warranties by establishing an escrow fund or otherwise agreeing to indemnify the buyer in the event that all that glitters turns out to be something other than gold.

Much can happen to the value of the seller between the date the contract is signed and the date of the closing. Accordingly, the seller, by undertaking "negative covenants," promises that it will do nothing to detract from its representations and warranties at least until ownership actually changes hands. For example, it will promise not to increase salaries, change its capital structure, enter new, material contracts, and so on. It will also undertake "positive covenants" to cooperate with the buyer in making records available, to intercede on the buyer's behalf with third parties, such as creditors.

The buyer will not want to go forward with the deal if all is not as it should be when the time set for closing has arrived. The contract will therefore list "conditions precedent" to the closing. If these conditions (such as favorable tax and SEC rulings, absence of threatened governmental action, compliance by the seller with its covenants, and so on) are not met, the buyer will be excused from its obligations under the contract.

The buyer's central obligation to the seller is to pay the purchase price. If the sum is certain and payment is to be made in cash, the contractual clause for providing payment need not be complex. If the purchase price is to be set at some later date based on market value of the buyer's stock or earning performance of the seller following the acquisition, or if the buyer plans to assume only a portion of the seller's liabilities, the seller will insist that the contract contain numerous clauses covering foreseeable contingencies.

Additional problems will be encountered if payment is to be made in the seller's securities. The actual value of the buyer becomes as important as the value of the seller in such a case. Nevertheless, the seller rarely has the bargaining power to demand the same warranties as are routinely given by the seller. It must usually settle for representations concerning the buyer's capital structure and the buyer's covenant that it will not dilute the value of the securities to be issued in the acquisition before the closing. Because the seller normally is concerned with the tax treatment to be accorded the acquisition, it will condition the closing on a favorable tax ruling. Both parties will condition the transaction on favorable opinions of the attorneys regarding a host of matters, especially those treated in the warranties. Finally, certain remedies will be described to deal with a breach of the contract.

Although every acquisition contract contains similar provisions, each contract is unique. Because it is prepared to deal with a particular acquisition, the contract must be geared to the problems peculiar to that acquisition. Thus, if labor considerations, antitrust problems, or matters in litigation are of special concern, the contract will be structured to avoid later disappointments. It should be obvious that the attorneys writing the contract can prepare for these contingencies only if they are made aware of the problems. Rather than regarding the contract as a burdensome exercise in semantics, the wise businessman will work with his attorneys in its preparation, sharing his special concerns with them so that they can better serve his interests.

THE CLOSING

Sooner or later the magic moment arrives when ownership of the business is about to change hands. To be prepared for this moment, everyone and everything must be at the right place at the right time. The documents necessary to a major closing may number in the hundreds. Leases, deeds, other title certificates, opinions and rulings, major contracts, investment letters, stock certificates, financial statements, subsidiary agreements relating to assumption of liabilities, indemnification, nondisclosure, noncompetition, and so on, must all be ready. To expedite the closing a checklist of the required documents should be prepared. In addition, it is often wise for the attorneys to review these documents prior to the closing, placing them, perhaps, in escrow, to avoid last-minute delays. By making the closing as painless as possible, time and tempers can be preserved.

PART III

Antitrust

Having summarized the various aspects of the legal background of mergers, we shall now examine in some detail the substantive antitrust laws in their relation to corporate amalgamations. As we shall see, all three of the basic antitrust laws—the Sherman Act, the Clayton Act, and the Federal Trade Commission Act—have been employed to attack mergers, the effects of which are anticompetitive.

10 Antitrust Theory

Controls and restrictions on economic behavior are no sudden invention of modern man. In the Middle Ages, craft guilds in many countries imposed rigid restraints on the producer, limiting the territory in which he could sell, setting his prices, and imposing quality control on his manufacture. Although they were administered by people within the craft, the guild regulations derived their legal force from royal grants of power. Nor was secular authority the only impediment to free markets; for centuries, widely accepted doctrines of the Church forbade the charging of more than a "just price" and of interest in capital loans. Even as concepts of nationalism and national wealth developed during the sixteenth and seventeenth centuries, developments which portended a material shift in the way people thought about society, the growing national economies of the European states were shaped by a mercantilist philosophy which dictated the necessity of governmental control over trade and commercial practices in order to assure a favorable trade balance (that is, an excess of exports over imports) and a steady influx of precious metals.

To seek a financial and political base independent of Parliament, the crown under King James I and Charles I from the 1620's to 1640's began to grant royal monopolies in England that in a short time infested nearly every area of economic life. In the words of Louis Hacker: "There were monopolies imposed upon the soap, salt, glass, starch, vinegar, wine, alum, cloth-finishing, gold and silver-thread manufacture, and the pin industries; upon the selling of playing cards and dice; upon the importation of tobacco; upon the issuance of licenses for the keeping of taverns, the engrossing of wills, and the printing of linens." Monopolies that had existed prior to this time were expanded beyond all proportions. For example, the theory of "mines royal" summarized the fact that the mining of silver and gold was done only with the permission of the Crown. However, during this time period the term *mines royal* also came to include the mining of iron, lead, copper, and tin. Those who had engaged in such activities before were forbidden to continue without a grant from the king. The monopolies were not limited to the "heavy" industries either. Some examples of the smaller professions granted royal protection are (1) the gauging of red herrings, (2) the gauging of butter casks, (3) the marking of iron, (4) the weighing of straw and hay, and (5) the gathering of rags. Even the powerful bankers and gold merchants found their exchange businesses curtailed by the creation of the old office of the royal exchequer.

The turmoil in England that began with the Civil War of Oliver Cromwell and ended in the Glorious Revolution of 1688 was prompted in no small measure by the crushing burdens imposed by the system of royal monopoly. The invitation by Parliament to William and Mary Orange to accede to the British throne signalled also the ascension of the propertied middle class to political power. State control over manufacture, mining, land, and labor was drastically altered and reduced.

If freedom for the capitalist was to become the rule in England during the next century, the opposite was ordained for the new colonies; subservience to the mother country was deemed vital to her economic well-being. Within the mother country, concern for the domestic economy was secondary to that for foreign trade, which was the paramount economic factor. The mercantilist theory logically required the mother country to exploit her colonies, by prohibiting or limiting colonial manufacturing in order to permit maximum acceptance of exports from the homeland. As early as the 1660's the Navigation Acts forbade any but English vessels from carrying goods to or from the colonies. Export duties and other charges increased the price which colonists were compelled to pay for European products. During the next 100 years, British policy dictated —and British agencies enforced—the rule that the economy of the colonies was to be subservient to that of the home country. The Privy Council, the Board of Trade, and Parliament persisted in concert to deny to the colonies (and to Englishmen as well) the right to invest their capital in American manufacturing enterprises. In 1699 Parliament passed the Woolen Act, which denied colonial woolen manufacturers the ability to sell colonial wool and woolen yarn in intercolonial and foreign commerce. Other important matters that merited the attention of Parliament later on resulted in the passage of the Hat Act of 1732 and the Iron Act of 1750. The thoroughness of such laws was demonstrated by the Hat Act, which forbade the exportation of hats from the colonies, restricted the hat makers to two apprentices, each for a seven-year term, and excluded Negroes from hat making.

Colonial expansion could be frustrated in other ways too, one of which included the vetoing of laws passed by the separate colonies. A Pennsylvania law encouraging growth in the shoemaking industry was disallowed in 1705 on the theory that England should not be subject to competition from the colonies when such competition could be avoided. One year later a New York law concerning the sail-making industry met the same fate, justified by the Board of Trade on the ground that it would be "more advantageous to England that all hemp and flax of the growth of the plantations should be imported hither," in order to manufacture it here. This practice continued on into the middle of the eighteenth century with the disallowance in 1756 of a Massachusetts law designed to increase the production of linen. The scrutiny of colonial enactments was not only practiced across the Atlantic, but even the royal governors were instructed to review all the legislation and to exercise their veto power against those laws that might allow colonial manufacturers to compete one day with England.

Closely aligned to its policy of controlling and curbing colonial manufacturing, the Crown also imposed strict controls over American currency. Because expanding currency gave rise to the possibility of capital investment in manufacturing, British policy during the 1700's was to limit the size of the currency. The Massachusetts land bank was outlawed in the 1740's, and by 1751 Parliament forbade the issuance of bank notes and legal-tender bills of credit in New England, extending the prohibition to all colonies in 1764 (and forbidding the issuance of bills and notes to raise money for the military, which until that time had been permitted). The currency contracted dramatically. In 1765 John Dickinson wrote:

> Trade is decaying and all credit is expiring. Money is becoming so extremely scarce that reputable freeholders find it impossible to pay debts which are trifling in comparison to their estates. If creditors sue, and take out executions, the lands and personal estates, as the sale must be for ready money, are sold for a small part of what they were worth when the debts were contracted. The debtors are ruined. The creditors get back but part of their debt and that ruins them. Thus the consumers break the shopkeepers; they break the merchants; and the shock must be felt as far as London.

As England increased its economic hold over the colonies during the 1760's and 1770's by enforcing the trade acts more closely and by capturing for the Crown western lands that might otherwise have permitted colonists to expand their land dealings and fur trade, the shock wave of Revolution was indeed felt as far as London. The ever-increasing number of duties and other devices that discouraged domestic manufacture and direct colonial trading with non-British ports culminated in the notorious Tea Act of 1763, which permitted the East India Company, on the verge of bankruptcy, to transport in its vessels 17 million pounds of tea for sale in the American market, thus seriously undercutting colonial importers and retailers of British tea, who were obliged to ship on British rather than American vessels.

Local economic interests, wants, and ambitions at long last would not remain subordinated to considerations of foreign trade. Neither could the far-off colonies remain immune from the stirrings of sentiment for independence. In both the economic and political realms, the desire for freedom from unwanted governmental interference in the lives of the people proved to be too powerful in the American colonies to resist successfully.

The rebellion against political and economic restraints may be measured from the tumultuous year 1776, in which the colonists proclaimed their political independence and Adam Smith, in an influential book called *The Wealth of Nations,* proclaimed what is said to be the death knell of mercantilism and the first full-blown account of an economic way of life we have come to call capitalism.

Reacting to the restrictions imposed upon them by the former monarch, the new citizens of the United States saw to it that the energies of manufacturers, businessmen, and tradesmen would not be stifled. After a nearly disastrous experiment with a loose confederation, the states called into existence, through the Constitution, a national economy whose chief virtue seemed to be the probability that, unlike the mercantilist societies now already themselves undergoing change, growth would be by internal development. Reliance would be placed on the encouragement of a self-sufficient local trade and manufacture rather than on a foreign one.

Though we often describe those early days of the Republic as fitting most closely the political theories of the man after whom we name the age—Thomas Jefferson—in the long run the views of Alexander Hamilton, Jefferson's political antagonist, have proved to be more prescient. It was Hamilton who laid in a series of reports the basis for the development of a capitalist economy in the United States. In 1791, at a time when economic theory (and Thomas Jefferson) held that agricultural endeavors were more productive than manufacturing or industrial enterprise, Hamilton published his *Report on Manufactures,* a trenchant analysis of the meaning of productivity. In this *Report* the first secretary of the treasury laid bare the claims of agricultural superiority over manufacturing and found the "distinction . . . rather verbal than substantial." Affirming the economic and social value of industry, Hamilton set out an economic program of tariffs, duties, and bounties that was in no small measure adopted and from which not even Jefferson later significantly turned.

The Hamiltonian vision was not, for all its intellectual vitality, realized immediately on a vast scale, though its impact was felt from the start. Left more or less to themselves, with ample room for geographic expansion, with abundant natural resources, including inland waterways which the Supreme Court rather early on decided were national commercial routes outside the bounds of state regulation, and with an increasing application of technological innovation to economic enterprise, the American people built a nation and an economy, but not a national economy. Power was still in the hands of the landed classes. It took a civil war to prepare the nation for a reorientation of power to the moneyed class, the capitalists. Hamilton's vision was then more than realized, for it was soon recognized that the exercise of new governmental power was required.

The trouble with which we are concerned appeared on the horizon after the Civil War and partly as a result of that war. Production and distribution on a national scale, to meet national exigencies, required massive accumulations of capital to operate large business enterprises. To finance the war more than $2.5 billion in bonds were sold during the war years, and nearly $500 million worth of greenbacks was issued. Much of this $3 billion was invested in manufacturing industry and transportation. Protectionism became rampant during the war as rigid tariffs were enacted by Congress, and they were not repealed, but instead were added to during Reconstruction. The National Banking Act of 1863 was the first step in the creation of a federal banking system (many of whose defects were cured in 1913 by the Federal Reserve Act). But of all federal legislation that would be responsible for the dramatic postwar growth of large corporations, two related clusters of enactments stand out: homestead and railroad laws. The Homestead Act of 1862 promised land to a potentially enormous number of citizens through the relatively simple means of simply settling and building on it. But

> [t]he whole system of land disposal soon became honeycombed with fraud. There was fraud in the filing of homestead entries and in the purchase of land under the Pre-emption Act. There was open theft of the public domain through illegal enclosing, particularly cattlemen. Timber and mineral lands were illegally pre-empted. The land-grant railroads were notoriously culpable: they sought to maintain possession of their sections without troubling to comply with the terms of the awards, and, even after they had laid down their tracks, many continued to hold out the choicest sections for their speculative values.

The railroads profited immensely from the war. To begin with, Southern opposition in Congress to a continental railroad system had successfully prevented federal assistance. The sudden disappearance of that opposition with the outbreak of war permitted the transcontinental roads to be built: "The Republicans were more generous than simply authorizing the laying down of the lines. The rights of way were guaranteed; the Indians' titles were extinguished; military protection was promised against marauding bands; and the builders were given free use of timber, earth, and stone from the public lands." The Union Pacific, authorized to build from Omaha to the California border, was granted 12,800 acres of land adjoining the track for every mile laid. Four railroad corporations were chartered between 1862 and 1871, receiving loans through federal bond offerings; though the roads eventually (1897) agreed to pay back the principal, they defaulted on all but a small part of the $50 million in interest that accrued to 1890. Congress succeeded in giving away more than 150 million acres of land between 1850 and 1873 to land-grant railroads. As Louis Hacker has written:

> The end of the Civil War left American capitalism ready for new advance. With the capital plant and the profits originating in that period, the enterprisers resumed railway building and building construction; and the heavy-goods industries were strengthened and expanded. The manufactures of iron, lumber, brick, petroleum products, and glass were stimulated; so were those of machinery generally, mechanical transportation equipment, and agricultural implements; markets and ready capital gave spur to invention, new processes, and new plants.

Giant economic entities—what we have come to call big business—possess characteristics that are not consonant with the benevolent theories of economic growth and development that were widely shared prior to the Civil War. Big industrial and other corporations—for instance, and notably, the railroads—had a tremendous power to govern large sectors of the economy: they could set prices which customers had to pay, for if they did not they would not be able to utilize the necessary services of the utilities or purchase the necessary commodities of the giant producers. In short, the giants became monopolies, deciding through their pricing, rebating, and other business arrangements who should live and die in the economy.

Among these monopolies were the trusts: the Standard Oil of Ohio Trust was the first in 1882, but before the decade was out Oil was joined by the Whiskey Trust, the Sugar Trust, the Lead Trust, and the Cotton-Oil Trust. The trust is a common-law device that permits a board of trustees to vote the many different companies' shares of stock, whose certificates are deposited with the board. In the nineteenth century, state corporation laws were miserly creatures that usually did not permit companies to operate out of state; the trust arrangement was an extremely tidy method of circumventing parochial state restrictions. The trust was not the only method of achieving monopoly power; the railroad and other holding companies were in time an even more powerful method of business growth and control, ultimately supplanting the trust. But the trust was the earliest successful method of economic consolidation and the word has remained with us today in the name of the type of law that was designed to control it—antitrust.

The disputatious nature of the American people insured that the introduction of business on the grand scale would not be greeted quietly. As early as 1867, with the formation of the Grange movement, farmers and others who were aggrieved by monopolistic practices agitated for governmental regulation of corporate power. By 1873 opposition groups forced Congress to abandon the outright grant of land and money to the railroads. Both political parties were on record the year before as against such grants. In 1880 the Greenbackers and in 1884 the Anti-Monopolists called for positive laws to control monopoly. By 1890, twenty-seven states (including territories) enacted antimonopoly legislation. The Michigan Supreme Court said in the *Diamond Match Company* case: It is doubtful if free government can long exist in a country where such enormous amounts of money are allowed to be accumulated in the vaults of corporations, to be used at discretion in controlling the property and business of the country against the interest of the public and that of the people for the personal gain and aggrandizement of a few individuals.

Big business was not merely insidious because of the enormous power it could legitimately exercise: it was hated and feared because much of it had been built through stealth and outright fraud by the "robber barons," as Matthew Josephson named them. Thus, four promoters of the Central Pacific railroad during the 1860's—Leland Stanford, Collis P. Huntington, Charles Crocker, and Mark Hopkins—personally received, courtesy of the public treasury, at least $63 million which they managed to siphon from their construction company via dummy firms.

By 1880 the Democrats recognized the political signs and included antitrust pledges in their campaign platforms. By 1888 the Republicans, having been branded the party of monopolists, avowed the need for such legislation, and upon assuming office their candidate, Benjamin Harrison, told Congress the next spring that the trusts were "dangerous conspiracies." Charles Francis Adams, historian, grandson and greatgrandson of presidents, expressed a common view in impassioned exaggeration when he wrote in 1871 that the corporations:

> have declared war, negotiated peace, reduced courts, legislatures and sovereign states to an unqualified obedience to their will, disturbed trade, agitated currency, imposed taxes, and, boldly setting both laws and public opinion at defiance, have freely exercised many other attributes of sovereignty. . . . All this they wielded in practical independence of the control both of government and of individuals.

Legislation against the trusts became as inevitable as law can be. Senator John Sherman, ranking Republican on the Senate Finance Committee, introduced a bill in 1888. After nearly two years of political maneuvering in the Senate, a substitute bill, not written by Sherman but shortly to bear his name, was passed by the Senate, agreed to by the House, and signed by President Harrison in July 1890.

The Sherman Act is simply worded: its prohibitions against contracts, combinations, or conspiracies in restraint of trade were aimed at what Senator Sherman characterized as the "kingly prerogative," saying that because the people "would not submit to an emperor . . . [they] should not submit to an autocrat of trade."

There was considerable irony in the passage of the first antitrust law in 1890, for in the years immediately preceding, the ideas of social Darwinism loomed large among some of the keenest minds in America. It was taken for granted by many economists, legislators, and social thinkers that the grand struggle for survival resulted in the best possible social ordering through the ultimate victory of the "fittest." In the *laissez-faire* scheme of things, nothing was more disastrous than for some reformist act of the political organs of society to alter the course of the natural economy, to redirect the struggle, or to attempt to redistribute the gains of its outcome. Despite appeals to the natural order, however, the Sherman Act became law. Because there is still left in our thought a residue of the social Darwinist distrust for legislative tinkering with the American economy, it is important to realize that antitrust laws were prompted by twin fears: that the corporation was becoming both politically and economically too powerful. For the granger and populist movements were not merely economic; they were based on a broad political appeal—one that still holds today—springing from the fear of concentrated power of any sort in the United States. Of course, it was not merely political fear that resulted in the Sherman Act, though political fear may have been a factor in the minds of many members of Congress. More importantly, the Sherman Act was a response to the very specific abuses of which trusts and corporations were capable as they grew larger and larger, encompassing ever more of the United States in their machinations. It had become plain that the trusts had outgrown that size which contemporary economic theory suggested was proper, the Darwinists to the contrary notwithstanding.

At bottom, the Sherman Act is rooted in the belief that for a modern economy to function at all responsively to the people who comprise it, producers must be subject to some degree of control by an impersonal market. As the Supreme Court has said:

> The Sherman Act was designed to be a comprehensive charter of economic liberty aimed at preserving free and unfettered competition as the rule of trade. It rests on the premise that the unrestrained interaction of competitive forces will yield the best allocation of our economic resources, the lowest prices, the highest quality and the greatest material progress, while at the same time providing an environment conducive to the preservation of our democratic political and social institutions.

Talk of "free and unfettered competition" may mean different things in different situations. Not always would a strict application of the principle of competition ultimately result in a better allocation of resources or lowest prices, highest quality or greatest material progress. For sizable companies may act aggressively and competitively, lowering prices to a point which smaller companies might be hard-pressed to meet. And if large corporations were able to put enough small enterprises out of business, through any number of legitimate or illegitimate means, whether through bankruptcy or through absorption, something very vital would be removed from the American economy.

During the course of the eighty years since the passage of the Sherman Act, a broad lace of statutes has been added to that original antitrust law. At every addition, the principle was inherent in the law that the abstract notion of "competition" was to be interpreted as a process that worked best through the operation of many businesses in the marketplace, not a competition among a few, but a competition among the many. Thus, in a precedent-setting case in 1962, the Supreme Court said in interpreting the basic antimerger law: "We cannot fail to recognize Congress' desire to promote competition through the protection of viable, small, locally owned business. Congress appreciated that occasional higher costs and prices might result from the maintenance of fragmented industries and markets. It resolved these competing considerations in favor of decentralization."

The passage of the Sherman Act did not bring immediate relief to those who suffered at the hands of the large industrial corporations. Indeed, the Act fell into disuse almost as soon as it became law. Not until the presidency of Theodore Roosevelt did the federal government begin to exert any concerted effort to enforce the law. For some years a serious dispute raged as to whether the Sherman Act prohibited all restraints or merely unreasonable ones; the Supreme Court finally settled the matter in 1911 (in a most inconclusive way) by deciding in the famous *Standard Oil* case that only unreasonable restraints were prohibited. Of course, this merely substituted one difficulty for another; henceforth, what was "unreasonable" would be grist in the judicial mill.

Still, even as judicial underbrush was cleared, it became clear that the existing antitrust law did not go far enough to prevent dangers to competition. One problem, inherent in the original impetus for the Sherman Act, was the increasing tendency of companies to acquire each other or, as we often say in general terms today, to merge. Though the Sherman Act prohibited conduct that restrained or attempted to monopolize trade, it was not clear that merely because the two companies ceased operating as independent units a restraint or monopolization had occurred. Ironically, the Supreme Court did hold in 1904 that a merger of the Great Northern and the Northern Pacific railroads was a violation of the Act, but the decision was based on the notion, later discredited, that any restraint, no matter how reasonable, was per se a violation. The Court did not inquire into the degree of competition that existed between the railroads nor did the Court analyze what effect the merger would have on competition among railroads. That was in 1904, and though subsequent railroad decisions were often treated similarly, by 1911 the Court had moved to the previously described position—that restraints must be unreasonable to be proscribed. That reading of the Sherman Act shifted the ground rules and made a finding of illegality much more difficult in the case of companies which desired to affiliate formally by acquisition rather than to achieve anticompetitive effects by formal contracts or more tacit agreements.

Antitrust remained a political as well as a legal issue. As the Court softened the seeming strictness of the Sherman Act, the argument for positive governmental *regulation* of business (as distinguished from pure antitrust, which relies on a competitive market to police itself) gained ground. In 1911, more than a year before the Bull Moose party made its voice heard in the national campaign, Theodore Roosevelt argued vigorously for recognition of the fact that some degree of monopoly is inevitable and that "any such effort" to strengthen "the Anti-Trust Law to restore business to the competitive conditions of the middle of the last century . . . is foredoomed to end in failure." He argued, therefore, for federal supervision and control of monopolistic industries:

> Business cannot be successfully conducted in accordance with the practices and theories of sixty years ago unless we abolish steam, electricity, big cities, and, in short, not only all modern business and modern industrial conditions, but all the modern conditions of our civilization. The effort to restore com-

petition as it was sixty years ago, and to trust for justice solely to this proposed restoration of competition, is just as foolish as if we should go back to the flintlocks of Washington's Continentals as a substitute for modern weapons of precision. The effort to prohibit all combinations, good or bad, is bound to fail, and ought to fail; when made, it merely means that some of the worst combinations are not checked and that honest business is checked. Our purpose should be, not to strangle business as an incident of strangling combinations, but to regulate big corporations in thoroughgoing and effective fashion, so as to help legitimate business as an incident to thoroughly and completely safeguarding the interests of the people as a whole.

Roosevelt did not, however, advocate breaking up giant companies merely because they were large:

But nothing of importance is gained by breaking up a huge inter-state and international industrial organization which has not offended otherwise than by its size, into a number of small concerns without any attempt to regulate the way in which those concerns as a whole shall do business. Nothing is gained by depriving the American Nation of good weapons wherewith to fight in the great field of international industrial competition. Those who would seek to restore the days of unlimited and uncontrolled competition, and who believe that a panacea for our industrial and economic ills is to be found in the mere breaking up of all big corporations, simply because they are big, are attempting not only the impossible, but what, if possible, would be undesirable. They are acting as we should act if we tried to dam the Mississippi, to stop its flow outright. The effort would be certain to result in failure and disaster; we would have attempted the impossible, and so would have achieved nothing, or worse than nothing. But by building levees along the Mississippi, not seeking to dam the stream, but to control it, we are able to achieve our object and to confer inestimable good in the course of so doing. . . .

Our aim should be a policy of construction and not one of destruction. Our aim should not be to punish the men who have made a big corporation successful merely because they have made it big and successful, but to exercise such thoroughgoing supervision and control over them as to insure their business skill being exercised in the interest of the public and not against the public interest.

To Roosevelt's argument, Woodrow Wilson, a stated opponent of the industrial giant, responded:

I have been told by a great many men that the idea I have that by restoring competition you can restore industrial freedom, is based upon a failure to observe the actual happenings of the last decades in this country; because, they say, it is just free competition that has made it possible for the big to crush the little.

I reply, it is not free competition that has done that; it is illicit competition. It is competition of the kind that the law ought to stop, and can stop—this crushing of the little man.

You know, of course, how the little man is crushed by the trusts. He gets a local market. The big concerns come in and undersell him in his local market, and that is the only market he has; if he cannot make a profit there he is killed. They can make a profit all through the rest of the Union, while they are underselling him in his locality, and recouping themselves by what they can earn elsewhere. Thus their competitors can be put out of business, one by one, wherever they dare to show a head. Inasmuch as they rise up only one by one, these big concerns can see to it that new competitors never come into the larger field.

At Congressional hearings before the Committee on Investigation of the United States Steel Corporation in 1912, Elbert H. Gary, chairman of U.S. Steel, proposed that through an exchange of information among the competitors in each industry, prices could be stabilized and economic regularity, if enforced by government supervision, would be achieved. He said:

[T]he only way we could lawfully prevent such demoralization and maintain a reasonable steadiness in business . . . was for the steel people to come together and to tell one to the others exactly what his business was. . . .

THE CHAIRMAN. If I apprehend you there . . . you believe that prices should be subject to change not through the external exigencies of trade or through natural or unnatural conditions, such as panics and the like, that they ought not to absolutely control prices, but that prices should change through the common consent and the kindly concurrence of the men most interested in those prices?

MR. GARY. No; your statement is all right until you come to the last part.

THE CHAIRMAN. I may have misunderstood you.

MR. GARY. I do not believe in the change by common consent. I do not believe you have a right to do that, but I do believe that if one individual is possessed of information concerning the conditions surrounding the other's business that it prevents many times, and perhaps in most cases, the extreme, the unreasonable, the bitter, and destructive competition which used to exist. Not only that, I believe it prevents the increases of prices. . . .

Stability, so far as it is practicable, is a thing often needed.

THE CHAIRMAN. I do not wish to interrupt the witness, but there is one statement that is surprising to me, and that is this obstinate hostility of the consumer to a reduction in prices.

MR. GARY. You have stated it perhaps different.

THE CHAIRMAN. Too strong?

MR. GARY. I think you have.

THE CHAIRMAN. I was surprised, although I may have misunderstood you. You spoke of the consumer objecting to fluctuations in prices, in which event he would have to object to a fall as well as a rise?

MR. GARY. I think any of us would rather have the prices of our tailor or our grocer substantially uniform, assuming they are fair and reasonable, year in and year out, than to have the prices very low in the time of panic and depression and then in other times very high and unreasonable. I think what the customer prefers is to have reasonable stability of prices. For instance, a man is desirous of putting up a steel building, and he finds the price of steel $30 a ton. If he thinks that is a reasonable price, he is perfectly willing to pay it unless he knows by experience or fear that next week another man can go to the same producer or some other producer and buy the same material 30 per cent cheaper, which would enable his competitor to put up a cheaper building and unduly compete with him in renting the building.

When the business is conducted in the way it used to be conducted, very frequently some of the men engaged in trade take advantage of the necessities of a competitor and suddenly and unduly drop the prices and drive him out of business. That has been resorted to. The customer does not like that, as a rule. He wants to know what he can depend upon.

I do not hesitate to say, Mr. Chairman, in connection with your suggestion, what I said two or three years before in appearing before a congressional committee. I realize as fully, I think, as this committee that it is very important to consider how the people shall be protected against imposition or oppression as the possible result of great aggregations of capital, whether in the possession of corporations or individuals. I believe that is a very important question, and personally I believe that the Sherman Act does not meet and will never fully prevent that. I believe we must come to enforced publicity and governmental control.

MR. YOUNG. You mean governmental control of prices?

MR. GARY. I do; even as to prices, and so far as I am concerned, speaking for our company, so far as I have the right, I would be very glad if we knew exactly where we stand, if we could be freed from danger, trouble, and criticism by the public, and if we had some place where we could go, to a responsible governmental authority, and say to them, "Here are our facts and figures, here is our property, here our cost of production, now you tell us what we have the right to do and what prices we have the right to charge." I know that is a very extreme view, and I know that the railroads objected to it for a long time; but whether the mere standpoint of making the most money is concerned or not, whether it is the wise thing, I believe it is the necessary thing, and it seems to me corporations have no right to disregard these public questions and these public interests.

MR. LITTLETON. Is it your position that cooperation is bound to take the place of competition?

MR. GARY. It is my position.

MR. LITTLETON. And that cooperation therefore requires strict governmental supervision?

MR. GARY. That is a very good statement of the case. I believe that thoroughly.

Against these sentiments Wilson countered with an affirmation that the government could not intercede at every point in the operation of business or the truth would be that businessmen would be running the government:

The third party says that the present system of our industry and trade has come to stay. Mind you, these artificially built up things, these things that can't maintain themselves in the market without monopoly, have come to stay, and the only thing that the third party proposes should be done, is to set up a commission to regulate them. It accepts them. It says: "We will not undertake . . . to prevent monopoly, but we will go into an arrangement by which we will make these monopolies kind to you. We will guarantee that they shall pay the right wages. We will guarantee that they shall do everything kind and public-spirited, which they have never heretofore shown the least inclination to do."

> Don't you realize that that is a blind alley? You can't find your way to liberty that way. You can't find your way to social reform through the forces that have made social reform necessary.
>
> The fundamental part of such a program is that the trusts shall be recognized as a permanent part of our economic order, and that the government shall try to make trusts the ministers, the instruments, through which the life of this country shall be justly and happily developed on its industrial side.

What evolved from the prolonged debate on the size of monopolies, the ease by which they could grow, and sharp business practices which prevailed throughout the country, was new legislation that built on the philosophy of the Sherman Act, labeling more types of conduct unlawful, but not making the federal government a partner in the conduct of business.

In 1914 the Clayton Act was enacted by Congress to plug many loopholes in antitrust law and enforcement. Among the provisions of the new law of particular concern here was Section 7, which prohibited the acquisition by one company of the stock of another where the effect of the acquisition might be "to substantially lessen competition between the corporation whose stock is so acquired and the corporation making the acquisition, or to restrain such commerce in any section or community, or to tend to create a monopoly of any line of commerce."

The danger that mergers pose to a competitive economy should be obvious. The horizontal merger, defined as the acquisition by one competitor of another, simply eliminates one element of competition from the marketplace. It thus may have the same effect as any price-fixing agreement or territorial allocation among competitors could have. The vertical merger, so called because it results from the acquisition by the supplier of his buyer or vice versa, may have more subtle effects, but nonetheless real ones, as, for instance, the foreclosure of part of the market for the supply, thus forcing competing purchasers of the product to pay higher prices and thus to bear heavier costs.

Even with the passage of the Clayton Act, and the Federal Trade Commission Act, which gave enforcement teeth to a new federal agency, the record of government prosecution of corporate acquisitions was not impressive. In 1920, for example, the Supreme Court ruled that the United States Steel Company, an enormous manufacturing corporation formed of numerous steel companies which had some 85 per cent of American steel manufacturing capacity when the consolidation was complete, was not guilty of restraining trade or attempting to monopolize the industry. Prosecution under the Clayton Act was not attempted, because of a large loophole that would not be plugged until 1950: acquisition of assets was not prohibited by Section 7; only the acquisition of stock was unlawful. Moreover, until 1957 it was the general belief, reinforced by the absence of any decision by the Supreme Court to the contrary, that Section 7 did not prohibit vertical-type mergers, because the law seemed to talk about acquisitions by and of competitors. In 1948 the Supreme Court, by a five-to-four vote, declined to rule unlawful the acquisition by United States Steel, still the largest steel company in America, of a sizable competitor and supplier which owned plants in California, Arizona, and Texas, following its acquisition of a government-owned steel plant in Utah.

By 1950 Congress concluded that the original Section 7 was ineffective in achieving its purposes. Consequently in that year Congress amended the section to read as follows:

> That no corporation engaged in commerce shall acquire, directly or indirectly, the whole or any part of the stock or other share capital and no corporation subject to the jurisdiction of the Federal Trade Commission shall acquire the whole or any part of the assets of another corporation engaged also in commerce, where in any line of commerce in any section of the country, the effect of such acquisition may be substantially to lessen competition or to tend to create a monopoly.

Not merely acquisitions of stock, but also acquisitions of assets were now prohibited where the requisite economic effects were found to exist. But that was not the only change, nor even perhaps the most important change, given the merger movement that was then thought to be in full tide. Congress feared "what was considered to be a rising tide of economic concentration in the American economy." The 1950 amendments made it evident, the Supreme Court said twelve years later in *Brown Shoe,* that Congress "hoped to make plain that §7 applied not only to mergers between actual competitors, but also to vertical and conglomerate mergers whose effect may tend to lessen competition in any line of commerce in any section of the Country." No longer was it sufficient to consider the effect of the merger on competition between the acquiring and acquired companies; now the test related to competition "in any line of commerce in any section of the country." This means, the Supreme Court has said, that "only in an economically significant 'section' of the country" are the effects of the merger to be measured. "Taken as a whole," said the Court, "the legislative history illuminates congressional concern with the protection of *competition,* not *competitors,* and its desire to restrain mergers only to the extent that such combinations may tend to lessen competition." Furthermore, noting the increasing trend in economic concentration, Congress emphasized by its continued use of the words *may be substantially to lessen competition* the desire to curb the trend in a given industry in its incipiency: "Congress saw the process of concentration in American business as a dynamic force; it sought to assure the Federal Trade Commission and the courts the power to brake this force at its outset and before it gathered momentum." To effectuate this policy, the courts need not demand proof that competition will be substantially lessened: Congress' "concern was with probabilities, not certainties." No trend could be arrested in its incipiency if one had to await its ultimate results to see whether in fact it was a trend.

Despite these general guides to an understanding of the amended Section 7 of the Clayton Act, the language remains tantalizingly vague. The reinvigorated section, like the Sherman Act which still plays a useful role in controlling mergers, is a broad-brush Congressional delegation to the courts of a power to influence the direction of the national economy. But as Mr. Justice Holmes said more than sixty-five years ago, "general propositions do not decide concrete cases." To these concrete cases—the situations which have given rise to antitrust attack—we must turn to determine the present ambit of Section 7.

11 Mergers Under the Original Clayton Act

EARLY LEGISLATIVE HISTORY

As we have noted previously, merger activity in the United States historically has been an important part of the rise of industrialization and corporate growth and has been distinctly noted by high points of corporate activity, or "waves" in which there has been a relatively large number of corporate mergers or acquisitions. The first of these is often termed the turn-of-the-century merger wave, which extended from about 1897 to 1903. The increased activity in mergers, acquisitions, and consolidations during this period produced an alarming number of corporate giants and trusts. The Sherman Act, which had been enacted in 1890, failed to halt the increased degree of economic concentration. Consequently, public pressure mounted for the Congress to enact legislation which would better stem the rising tide of corporate growth and thereby keep alive a large number of small competitors in business.

In 1914 a second antitrust law, the Clayton Act, was entered on the books. Section 7 of the Act had as its purpose the control and regulation of the merger movement. According to the legislative history, the Act sought "to prohibit and make unlawful certain trade practices, which . . . [were] not covered by the Sherman Act . . . and thus, by making these practices illegal, to arrest the creation of trusts, conspiracies, and monopolies in their incipiency and before consummation." Thus, the thrust of the Act was to provide the legal machinery to kill monopoly and economic concentration in the seed by prohibiting corporations from merging through the acquisition of the stock of their competitors. Optimistically, the legislators had hoped that the Act's effect would be to maintain reasonably competitive conditions. The essential provisions of Section 7 of the original Clayton Act were as follows:

> That no corporation engaged in commerce shall acquire, directly or indirectly, the whole or any part of the stock . . . of another corporation engaged also in commerce, where the effect of such acquisition may be to substantially lessen competition between the corporation whose stock is so acquired and the corporation making the acquisition or to restrain such commerce in any section or community or to tend to create a monopoly of any line of commerce.

A second paragraph similarly proscribed the acquisition by one company of two or more corporations if the effect of the acquisition "may be to substantially lessen competition between such corporations." This second paragraph might apply, for example, to a situation in which a large steel manufacturing company would acquire the stock of two competing pastry companies. Acquisitions of stocks of two or more competitors by holding companies might also be restricted by this portion of original Section 7.

The original Clayton Act also carved exemptions for activities in which a corporation purchased stock solely for investment, as long as it did not result in a substantial lessening of competition, or formed a subsidiary corporation for the actual execution of its lawful business.

The scope of the original act was very limited, as the later amendment confirmed. To sustain a violation of the Act, it was necessary to establish that the effect of the acquisition may be

1. To lessen substantially competition between the acquired corporation and the acquiring corporation.
2. To restrain interstate commerce in any section or community.
3. To tend to create a monopoly of any line of commerce.

By using the words *may be,* Section 7 predicated the legality of acquisitions on *probabilities.* The emphasis on *probable* effect meant that a merger need not in itself *actually* substantially lessen competition, restrain commerce, or create a monopoly. It was sufficient that the effect of the merger *may* produce one of those effects in the future. Because the substantive provisions of the original Clayton Act were premised on *probable consequences,* by their very terms, the standards of legality were unclear. Indirectly confirming charges that the Act was "inadequate in scope and vague in content," the task of administrative application and judicial interpretation proved to be a long process of legal evolution, disappointment, and frustration.

LITIGATION UNDER ORIGINAL SECTION 7

In enforcing the original Clayton Act, the government had to proceed on a case-by-case basis in order to ascertain the outer limits of the newest addition to the antitrust laws. The judicial development of each phrase within Section 7 had an important effect on the development of antitrust law in general and on the future application of the original Clayton Act in particular.

Section 7 forbade mergers where the effect *may be* to lessen competition substantially. Determining the meaning of *may be* required a considerable length of time in which the judicial system cast and recast its definition. In 1922 in the *Standard Fashion Co., Magrane-Houston Co.*

case, the Supreme Court construed the term to mean a probability, that is, more than a mere possibility:

> [W]e do not think that the purpose in using the word "may" was to prohibit the mere possibility of the consequences described. It was intended to prevent such agreements as would under the circumstances disclosed probably lessen competition or create an actual tendency to a monopoly. That it was not intended to reach every remote lessening of competition is shown in the requirement that such lessening must be substantial.

The concept of the reasonableness of the probability was continued in subsequent cases. The standard of a "reasonable probability" that the effect would be to lessen competition substantially also became a part of the *Corn Products Refining* case. The Supreme Court confused the issue in 1948 when it reshaped the standard and spoke in terms of a reasonable *possibility* in the *Morton Salt* case. The result of these divergent precepts caused concern and confusion in the legal and corporate worlds. Consequently, the thrust of later decisions was somewhat clouded by the different meanings which were given to the *may be* clause of Section 7. Perhaps the best resolution of the question is found in the opinion in which the judge held that there was no violation because the effect did not cause "any reasonable probability or even possibility" that competition would be injured substantially.

Another important phrase in the original Clayton Act which instigated academic discussion and protracted judicial litigation was the requirement that the acquisition *substantially lessen competition* between the acquiring and the acquired corporations. The phrase applied only to competition between the corporations involved; it apparently acted independent of any effect that it might have on competition within the industry. To illustrate, suppose Acme Corporation, a manufacturer whose sales are composed of toys (60 per cent) and sports equipment (40 per cent) acquires all the stock of Mini-Play, Inc., a manufacturer whose sales are composed of toys (75 per cent) and infant furniture (25 per cent). In the toy industry, however, the combined output of Acme and Mini-Play constituted only 5 per cent of the total industry output. Thus, the acquisition of these two firms would clearly eliminate a substantial amount of competition between the two companies, but it would have a *de minimis* effect on competition within the whole industry or on the public interest in enforcing open competition.

The question posed by the preceding example is whether the proscription of the Clayton Act would apply solely to the effect between the acquiring corporation and the acquired corporation or whether it would also require a substantial lessening of competition within the industry, that is, an injury to the public interest. The early cases upheld the literal words of the statute and held that if there was a substantial lessening of competition between the two corporations, the reasonableness of the transaction within the context of industry competition, or the effect, if any, on the public interest, would not be considered in determining the validity of the acquisition. The converse was also true: if the acquisition tended to create a monopoly or otherwise injured the public interest, the fact that no competition would be eliminated between the two companies would be of no consequence.

In 1930 the issue was resolved by the Supreme Court in the *International Shoe* case. In May of 1921 International Shoe Co. had acquired all of the stock of W. H. McElwain Company, a direct competitor in the marketing of dress shoes in a particular area. In spite of this the Supreme Court found that there was no actual competition between the two companies and that, therefore, there was no public injury. The Court's reasoning was based on the fact that International specialized in small community dealers and that 95 per cent of its products were sold in towns of less than 6,000 population. On the other hand, McElwain concentrated on city and fashionable retailers and sold 95 per cent of its products in towns of more than 10,000 population. The effect of the *International Shoe* decision was to subsume the Sherman Act standard of reasonableness, or the prejudice-to-public-interest standard, into the Clayton Act so as to emasculate the *substantially lessen* phrase of any real import. In making this transposition, the Court stated:

> Mere acquisition by one corporation of the stock of a competitor, even though it results in some lessening of competition, is not forbidden; the act deals only with such acquisitions as probably will result in lessening competition to a substantial degree . . . that is to say, to such a degree as will injuriously affect the public. Obviously, such acquisition will not produce the forbidden results if there be no pre-existing substantial competition to be affected; for the public is not concerned in the lessening of competition, which . . . is itself without real substance.

Later cases embellished the rule that it is not a question of eliminating substantial competition between two corporations; instead, it is a question of whether substantial competition was eliminated in the whole marketplace, that is, a public injury. In fact, the courts finally openly declared that the same public injury standard in determining Sherman Act violations also applied in determining Clayton Act violations. In the *V. Vivaudou* case, the court outrightly approved this amalgamation of standards:

> In determining whether given acts . . . substantially lessen competition . . . within the meaning of the Clayton Act the only standard of legality with which we are acquainted is the standard established by the Sherman Act in the words "restraint of trade or commerce" and "monopolize or attempt to monopolize" and by the courts in construing the Sherman Act with reference to acts "which operate to the prejudice of the public interest by unduly restricting competition or unduly obstructing the due course of trade," and "restrict the common liberty to engage therein."

Thus, the final effect of the *International Shoe* case and its progeny on the *substantially lessen competition between the acquiring and acquired corporations* phrase in the original Clayton Act was to erode any concepts of competition between the two corporations and supplant it with the prejudice-to-public-interest standard.

The same *prejudice to the public interest* which pervaded the *substantially lessen* phrase also permeated the *restrain commerce in any section or community* phrase. The cases seem to indicate that market dominance by a corporation, as a result of an acquisition or merger, is sufficient to support a finding that the public interest was injured and, consequently, that the Clayton Act was violated. In 1949 the Supreme Court shifted a little away from its earlier market-dominance pronouncements and moved toward approval of a violation if "competition has been foreclosed in a substantial share of the line of commerce affected." This was stated in the *Standard Oil of California* decision and demonstrates the extent to which the Court shifted—requiring less of a public interest injury in determining Clayton Act violations and relying more on the significant effect on the market in the line of commerce.

Another important phrase which required judicial scrutiny is the *tend to create a monopoly in any line of commerce* qualification. Generally the decisions subsumed the *tend to create a monopoly* phrase into the *substantially lessen* phrase. Perhaps the words *line of commerce* were initially thought to mean a coast-to-coast market. But the cases soon restricted it. In the *Standard Oil of California* case the Court made it clear that "the 'line of commerce' affected need not be nationwide, at least where the purchasers cannot, as a practical matter, turn to suppliers outside their area."

The preceding cases added initial meaning to the bare words of the statute. The early litigation demonstrated that the antitrust laws could stop economic concentration of power while it was in the incipiency stage. Unfortunately, other litigation under the original Clayton Act also bared certain deficiencies in the Act which significantly weakened the Act's authority.

DEFICIENCIES OF THE ORIGINAL CLAYTON ACT

Although the Clayton Act was put into effect amid high hopes of halting detrimental economic concentrations in their incipiency stage, it soon became clear that there were serious deficiencies in the Act which significantly weakened, if not abrogated, the entire thrust and spirit of the original Clayton Act. Consequently, the enthusiasm for enforcement of the Act soon degenerated, caused in large part by the frustration of having so many loopholes in the statute. Initially, there was a deficiency in the judicial implementation of the Act, that is, the courts were obliterating the spirit of the Clayton Act by masking it with the Sherman Act judicial standards. Even more indicative of the inadequacy of the Act were the three devices which, during the 1914–1950 period, were generally considered to be loopholes in the statute's language: (1) vertical acquisitions, (2) asset acquisitions, and (3) procedural evasions via the asset loophole.

The original Clayton Act made no express mention of vertical mergers. Its language spoke only of acquisitions, the effect of which would "substantially lessen competition," "restrain such commerce," or "tend to create a monopoly." The statute's apparent silence on vertical effects, combined with the context of the statute's legislative history, led most people to believe that the Clayton Act was meant to apply only to horizontal economic activity. Consequently, the FTC made no effort to apply original Section 7 to vertical acquisitions.

But it was the Department of Justice which dramatically and unexpectedly initiated a suit which resulted in the full-fledged application of the Act to vertical mergers and acquisitions. In 1949, one year before the Act was amended, the Justice Department filed a complaint alleging in part that E. I. du Pont violated Section 7 by its acquisition of 23 per cent of the outstanding stock of General Motors Corporation. Despite the absence of any significant vertical merger litigation in Section 7's history, the Supreme Court in 1957 in the *Du Pont* case found no trouble in construing the Act to apply to vertical mergers. Its approach was based on a reading of the statute which denoted that mergers are proscribed when their effect is to lessen competition substantially *or* tend to create a monopoly. The meaning of this disjunctive phraseology was clear: it was meant "to cover those situations in which a merger was effected which did not lessen competition, but did tend to create a monopoly—a vertical merger would fit that category, but a horizontal would not." Thus, forty years after it was enacted and seven years after it was amended, the original Clayton Act was revitalized by the *Du Pont* case. An old myth that the Act did not apply to vertical mergers and acquisitions was displaced by the new reality of the *Du Pont* decision.

Clearly missing from the Act's coverage was *asset acquisitions.* The statute spoke only of stock acquisitions. Apparently, the reason for this original grave omission was because, at the time of the enactment, almost all acquisitions were accomplished by stock purchases; the asset purchases were relatively unimportant. The Congress clearly viewed the problem with narrow spectacles, for once the stock acquisition route was closed, corporations and their counsel readily switched to acquisitions by purchase of assets. In spite of this gaping hole in the Act's penumbra, almost forty years passed before it was repaired.

The third deficiency in the Act was a corollary to the asset loophole. The statute clearly covered stock acquisitions, and just as clearly failed to cover asset acquisitions. But in between these areas lay another trouble spot which, upon exploitation by cunning corporate counsel, widened the asset loophole. Suppose corporation A buys all the stock of corporation B. Thereafter, the FTC commences an investigation to see if corporation A violated Section 7 of the Clayton Act, or corporation A fears that the FTC will investigate. To avoid governmental condemnation, corporation A buys all the *assets* of corporation B—which is then liquidated—and then argues that the FTC has no jurisdiction because (1) it no longer holds the stock and (2) it has effected a purchase of assets. The inability of the original Clayton Act to cope with the different stages of development in this area was the crowning blow which completely emaciated the Act of any meaningful vitality.

The first area is the only one in which the FTC was able to maintain the integrity of the Clayton Act. In this category is a case in which the Western Meat Company had acquired all the stock of Nevada Packing Company, a direct competitor. The FTC investigated, filed a complaint, and then issued a cease and desist order for Western Meat to divest itself of all its unlawfully acquired stock. To circumvent the FTC, Western Meat attempted to purchase all the *assets* of Nevada Packing. The Supreme Court held that this ruse would violate the cease and desist order. Clearly the result was just and necessary to effectuate the FTC's inherent power. But this was the last victory for the FTC in this area.

In the second area, the acquiring corporation, Thatcher Manufacturing Company, had purchased all the stock of four corporations and then effected a purchase of their assets, all before the FTC filed its formal complaint against it. Because Thatcher had acquired all the assets of the acquired corporations before the FTC had taken any formal action—even though the purchase of assets had been achieved through the unlawfully held stock—it was not amenable to sanction by the FTC.

In the preceding cases, the Supreme Court ruled on situations in which a corporation—after unlawfully acquiring a competitor's stock—effected a purchase of assets either before the FTC filed its complaint or after it issued its cease and desist order. But what of the intermediate situation? Suppose corporation A acquires all the stock of corporation B, a competitor. The FTC filed a complaint alleging a violation of the Clayton Act. But before the FTC was able to issue a cease and desist order, corporation A effected a purchase of the assets of corporation B. Did this deprive the FTC of the power to issue a binding order to A to divest itself of B's assets? Yes, the Supreme Court held in the *Arrow-Hart & Hegeman Electric Company* case, stating that because the FTC had not issued the order, it lacked authority to order divestiture. This decision significantly widened the jurisdictional loophole. It now became a legal race between the FTC and corporate counsel to see if the commission could issue a cease and desist order before the corporation used its unlawfully held stock to effectuate an asset acquisition. Quick action on the part of the acquiring corporation would avoid any governmental proscription, even though the stock had originally been acquired unlawfully. Certainly the original draftsmen had not envisioned this brash exploitation of the law; its resulting inadequacy to combat economic concentration was of consolation to no one.

CONCLUSION

The setbacks suffered by the Federal Trade Commission during the first twenty years of the Clayton Act made painfully clear that there could be no effective enforcement of the antimerger laws as long as the asset loophole remained unmended. After its defeat in the *Arrow-Hart & Hegeman* case, the FTC continually recommended that the Clayton Act be amended, but fifteen years would pass before those recommendations would become a reality. The utter frustration experienced by the FTC is demonstrated by the fact that after the *Arrow-Hart & Hegeman* decision, it issued no cease and desist orders under Section 7 of the original Clayton Act. In pressing for a proper amendment, the FTC frankly admitted, referring to original Section 7, that "the effectiveness of this section has been completely emasculated as a result of court decisions."

The enforcement web of the original Clayton Act was only partially complete and, hence, grossly ineffective in containing the swarm of mergers which swept across the nation during the late 1920's and years following. It was only with the enactment of the Celler–Kefauver Amendment to the Clayton Act that Section 7 had an appreciable import on the rising tide of economic concentration.

12 Mergers Under the Sherman Act

Because the original Clayton Act applied only to mergers in which there had been a stock acquisition, the government had to rely on the Sherman Act to block many of the early mergers produced by acquisition of assets. The Clayton Act had had some popularity because it had been able to stop mergers in their incipiency stage; the reason for this is that it prohibited acquisitions the effect of which "may be substantially to lessen competition, or to tend to create a monopoly." It was more difficult, however, to halt asset acquisitions and consolidations under the Sherman Act, because the government could only succeed in breaking up an acquisition if it proved an *actual restraint* on commerce. Section 1 of the Sherman Act contained the following: "Every contract, combination in the form of trust or otherwise, or conspiracy, in restraint of trade or commerce among the several States, or with foreign nations, is hereby declared to be illegal." Thus, to succeed under the Sherman Act in an asset acquisition or consolidation case, it was necessary for the government to demonstrate an "actual restraint" on interstate commerce. It would be insufficient if there was merely a showing of a tendency to lessen competition or a tendency to create a monopoly; proof of an actual restraint was necessary.

RAILROAD CASES

The first important application of the Sherman Act to mergers came in the four famous railroad cases during the period 1904–1922. In the *Northern Securities* case a holding company was formed by the combination of the Great Northern Railway and the Northern Pacific Railway Company. These two large railroads were deeply involved in the post-Civil War railroad expansion to the West Coast. Their railroad lines ran a parallel course across the upper tier of states from Minnesota to Washington and Oregon. When the validity of the acquisition was litigated by the government, the Supreme Court determined that the combination of these great railway carriers was an actual restraint on interstate commerce. The Court's emphasis was on the railroad lines' inherent horizontal competitive nature and on the fact that the consolidation of these two great competing railroads would disrupt the free competition among the carriers providing transportation to the West Coast: "The mere existence of such a combination, and the power acquired by the holding company as its trustee, constitute a menace to, and a restriction upon, that freedom of commerce which Congress intended to recognize and protect. . . ."

Although that particular merger was invalidated, the continued thrust of the westward expansion germinated new problems. Eight years later, the Supreme Court was again called upon to shatter another railroad's plan for a consolidated operation. The Union Pacific Railroad Company, with a line running from Omaha to Ogden, Utah, was in the process of purchasing a controlling interest in the Southern Pacific Railroad Company, a line running from New Orleans to California. Because of the great public interest in having free and unrestricted competition in the west-bound transportation and because of the large size of the two companies involved, the merger was disapproved as being in violation of the Sherman Act. Quoting from an earlier ruling, Mr. Justice Day said:

> It is the combination of these large and powerful corporations, covering vast sections of territory, and influencing trade throughout the whole extent thereof, and acting as one body in all matters over which the combination extends, that constitutes the alleged evil, and in regard to which, so far as the combination operates upon and restrains interstate commerce, Congress has power to legislate and to prohibit.

As it did in all the railroad cases, the Court in this case placed strong emphasis on the sheer size of the two companies involved in the consolidation. Throughout these opinions, the reader is reminded continually that these are "great competing systems of railroads" and that the combination of these systems would destroy or greatly abridge the free operation of competition on railroad rates. "It is the scope of such combinations and their power to suppress or stifle competition or create a monopoly which determines the applicability of the act."

The third railroad case, however, did not involve the western expansion. It was conceived with a holding company in Pennsylvania in which the parent company held control over one coal company and two railroad companies, one of which also had a coal company as its subsidiary:

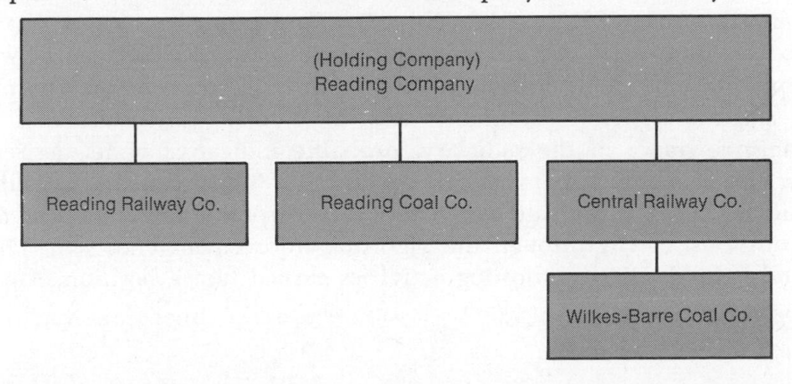

These railroads' economic livelihood depended upon freight charges for carrying anthracite coal from the mines to the market centers. The powerful and dominating position of the holding company in the industry strongly influenced the Court.

> This acquisition placed the Holding Company in a position of dominating control over two great competing interstate railroad carriers, but also over two great competing coal companies engaged extensively in mining and selling anthracite coal, which must be transported to interstate markets over the controlled interstate lines of railway.

With little discussion this combination was held to violate the Sherman Act by the very fact that two great competing railroad systems and two great competing coal companies were all merged into one holding company. *Ipso facto,* the Court held that this was sufficient to conclude that it was an illegal restraint of trade.

The final railroad case again involved the expanding railroad construction from the Midwest to the Pacific. The Southern Pacific, a railroad line extending from New Orleans to California, was acquiring the stock of the Central Pacific Railway Company, a line running from Ogden, Utah, to San Francisco. The same Justice Day who had rejected the Union Pacific's acquisition of Southern Pacific in 1912, also rejected the Southern Pacific's attempted acquisition of the Central Pacific Railway in 1922. Like the other railway cases, the motivating reason for disapproving this consolidation was that it involved "two great systems [who] are normally competitive."

The effect of these four early twentieth-century railroad cases in antitrust law was to establish a judicial principle that two large dominating companies would not be permitted to consolidate. The essential thrust of the four opinions was that such mergers and consolidations inherently suppressed, or materially reduced, the normal flow of free competition in interstate commerce. Accordingly, such consolidations were violative of the Sherman Act.

Merger litigation under Section 1 of the Sherman Act witnessed little development in the next twenty years—from the early 1920's to the middle 1940's. The executive and judicial inaction were in large part engendered initially by the economy's undisciplined expansion in the 1920's. This apathetic attitude toward mergers and acquisitions remained during the early 1930's as the "New Deal" attempted to inject vitality into the *Blue Eagle* reform and recovery measures. The courts were adopting a more lenient approach to the interpretation of the Sherman Act and the corporate community was finally being made aware of the permissive stance of the judiciary, probably indicative of its desire to start the economy moving again. As the 1930's progressed, the public again began to investigate and attack the corporate combinations and acquisitions, chiefly through the vigorous enforcement efforts of Thurmond Arnold. His trust-busting activities earned him a position of high honor in the minds of the public in general and the antitrust enforcement field in particular.

In the industrial transition period following World War II, many corporations were expanding, but many also were having some difficulty in converting from the production of war goods to an essentially civilian economy. Consequently, there was a substantial amount of acquiring, consolidating, and restructuring of existing corporations.

COLUMBIA STEEL

It was in this context that the next important merger case, based upon alleged violations of the Sherman Act, was litigated. The *Columbia Steel Company* case involved the attempted acquisition of Consolidated Steel Corporation by the United States Steel Corporation. The steel industry involves two essential production stages: (1) production of rolled steel products and (2) fabrication (structural or plate) of these products into finished steel products. U.S. Steel and its two subsidiaries were involved in both stages of production. Consolidated Steel was involved only in the second stage. Thus, Consolidated was functionally related, both vertically and horizontally, to United States Steel in the production of steel. Before the merger, as a purchaser of rolled steel products (the raw materials for the steel fabrication stage), Consolidated could buy from either U.S. Steel or any other company which produced rolled steel products. Approval of the acquisition would mean that Consolidated Steel would buy its products only from United States Steel. The vertical relationship would thereby deprive other producers of rolled steel products of an important prospective customer. Before the merger, as a fabricator of finished steel products, Consolidated Steel was competing with United States Steel as well as with all other steel fabricators. If the acquisition were approved, the horizontal competition between Consolidated and U.S. Steel would be eliminated, thereby depriving their customers of any meaningful choice between them.

Initially, the Court had to determine the relevant geographic market. The defendant argued that the steel industry constituted a nationwide market area. The Court rejected this argument, correctly stating that a restraint in commerce need not cover the entire United States before it violates the Sherman Act. "[W]e have consistently held that where the relevant competitive market covers only a small area the Sherman Act may be invoked to prevent unreasonable restraints within that area." Accordingly, the Court concluded that the eleven-state area, Consolidated's market sphere, was the proper geographic relevant market because it would be the area most affected by the acquisition. The Court held that U.S. Steel's acquisition of Consolidated Steel did not violate the Sherman Act. In so holding, the Court gave almost no consideration to the four previously discussed railroad cases, ostensibly because of their extremely dissimilar factual situations. There was no language bespeaking "great competing systems." The thrust of the opinion was to bring the standard for Sherman Act merger litigation more closely aligned to the "reasonable restraint" standard normally applied to Sherman Act litigation. In deciding the case, the Court established a new guide to determine whether a merger or an acquisition was an unreasonable restraint and therefore violative of the Sherman Act:

> In determining what constitutes unreasonable restraint, we do not think the dollar volume is in itself of compelling significance; we look rather to the percentage of business controlled, the strength of the remaining competition, whether the action springs from business requirements or purpose to monopolize, the probable development of the industry, consumer demands, and other characteristics of the market. We do not undertake to prescribe any set of percentage figures by which to measure the reasonableness of a corporation's enlargement of its activities by the purchase of the assets of a competitor. The relative effect of percentage command of a market varies with the setting in which that factor is placed.

Permeating the application of the preceding standard to the specific facts in *Columbia Steel* was the Court's belief that the gigantic size of the steel industry required some acquisitions to insure a viable, geographic expansion. Thus, the latent thrust of the case indicates that the acquisition was upheld, in part, because the "welcome westward extension" of the steel industry was in accord with the policy of the Court. Any other result would subject the country to the substantial risk that the geographic expansion of the steel industry would be aborted, to the detriment of the public interest. To avoid that result the Court concluded that the acquisition did not constitute an unreasonable restraint.

But the effect of the opinion in *Columbia Steel* went beyond its approval of that particular acquisition. The Court's new guide would, presumably, significantly affect future merger litigation under the Sherman Act. No longer would mergers be condemned solely because the companies involved were great competing systems in the industry. Now the validity of mergers and acquisitions involving large and small corporations would be judged in the light of all the factors enumerated previously.

It was generally believed that the *Columbia Steel* series of tests would become a long-standing merger law standard. However, the composition of the Supreme Court was changing and such personnel changes sometimes produce different results. This proved to be true in this area of merger law. In *Columbia Steel,* Mr. Justice Douglas had written a dissenting opinion in which he declared his strong disapproval of the merger. His dissent was based on the "Curse of Bigness" which he opined could become a social and industrial menace. Fifteen years later, in 1964, Mr. Justice Douglas' damnation of bigness again came to life when he became the spokesman for the majority of the Supreme Court in the

Lexington Bank case, another landmark case in merger litigation under Section 1 of the Sherman Act.

The First National Bank and Trust Company of Lexington, Kentucky, planned to consolidate with the Security Trust Company of Lexington to form the First Security National Bank and Trust Co. The comptroller of the currency had previously approved the consolidation, even though he believed that the consolidation would have an adverse effect on competition among the commercial banks in Fayette County, Kentucky.

Although mergers and acquisitions are normally attacked through Section 7 of the Clayton Act, the Justice Department had grave doubts that Section 7 applied to bank mergers. It therefore brought this antitrust action under the Sherman Act, alleging violations of Sections 1 and 2. The government's theory for not bringing the action under the Clayton Act was based upon language in that statute which restricted its application, as to *asset* acquisitions, to those corporations who were "subject to the jurisdiction of the Federal Trade Commission." Because banks were statutorily removed from the FTC's penumbra of jurisdiction, they felt insulated from Clayton Act attacks on any asset acquisitions by them. This background was the underlying reason why the Justice Department filed under the Sherman Act in *Lexington Bank*. It should be remembered, however, that by the time this case progressed from its filing stage to its final review in 1964 in the Supreme Court, the law was radically changed as to the application of Section 7 of the Clayton Act to bank mergers. In *Philadelphia National Bank,* decided in 1963, the Court concluded that the intent of Congress, in amending the Clayton Act in 1950, was to close all the loopholes and if bank mergers were exempted from its application, the Court would be thwarting the clear intent of Congress.

RELEVANT MARKET

All merger litigation requires the Court initially to define the relevant product market and the relevant geographic market in order to provide a frame of reference upon which to decide the merits of the merger or acquisition. In *Lexington Bank* there was little dispute as to the relevant product market: commercial banking. The thrust of earlier arguments that banks and other financial institutions were within the same competitive product market was blunted by the Supreme Court's prior holding to the contrary in the *Philadelphia National Bank* case. That holding was based on factors which differentiated commercial banks from other financial institutions—for example, the distinctive feature of checking accounts, the lower cost of small loans, and a marked consumer preference toward savings deposits with commercial banks. These distinctions in commercial banking products or services were sufficient to insulate *commercial banking* into a market which was "sufficiently inclusive to be meaningful in terms of trade realities."

The determination of the relevant geographic market also posed no difficulty for the Court in *Lexington Bank*. Just as *Philadelphia National Bank* had established a basis for the determination of relevant product market, so also did it provide a specific guideline for determining the relevant geographic market in mergers or acquisitions of commercial banks. The earlier case in formulating the guideline had discussed the geographic structure of the supplier–customer relationship:

> In banking, as in most service industries, convenience of location is essential to effective competition. Individuals and corporations typically confer the bulk of their patronage on banks in their local community; they find it impractical to conduct their banking business at a distance. The *factor of inconvenience* localizes banking competition as effectively as high transportation costs in other industries. [Emphasis added.]

Thus, the Court in *Lexington Bank* placed high reliance on the *factor of inconvenience*. Since over 95 per cent of the business of First National and Security Trust originated within Fayette County, Kentucky, that county was determined to be the relevant geographic market.

Prior to the consolidation, First National ranked first in assets among the six largest banks in the county. Security Trust was the fourth largest. Approval of the consolidation would mean not only that the new bank would be the largest in the county, but also that it would have more assets, more deposits, and more loans than the next four remaining banks combined.

With little discussion of the preceding facts, Mr. Justice Douglas stated it was clear that the elimination of significant competition between the two banks constituted an unreasonable restraint of trade, in violation of Section 1 of the Sherman Act. The Court based its decision on the *Northern Securities* case and the other three early railroad cases:

> The four railroad cases at least stand for the proposition that where merging companies are major competitive factors in a relevant market, the elimination of significant competition between them, by merger, itself constitutes a violation of §1 of the Sherman Act. This standard was met in the present case in view of the fact that the two banks in question had such a large share of the relevant market.

As the quoted excerpt indicates, the Court came close to a per se doctrine originally expounded in the railroad cases. The reasonable-restraint standard that had been announced in *Columbia Steel* was given only token consideration and that case was "confined to its special facts." Instead, the emphasis in *Lexington Bank* was on the "bigness" of the consolidated company and the significance of the eliminated competition in the relevant market. The unmentioned difference between this case and the earlier railroad cases was that the definition of *relevant market* had particularized itself into meaning smaller and smaller areas. In the railroad cases, the implication was that the relevant market area was the entire nation, or at least everything west of the Mississippi River. The judicial development of antitrust law resulted in more refined and localized market definitions. Thus, in *Lexington Bank,* the relevant market was Fayette County, Kentucky. It was one thing to hold that the per se consolidation of giant railroads, which served the needs of the entire country, would eliminate competition among great competing systems. It was another thing for the Court to conclude that the elimination of one bank, serving the needs of the people of Fayette County, Kentucky, constituted an elimination of such significant competition that the consolidation was held to be a per se violation of Section 1 of the Sherman Act. The clear result of the *Lexington Bank* case was to warn merging companies that their merger was susceptible to challenge if the companies were "major competitive forces" *in any relevant geographic market.*

PER SE OR PRESUMPTION OF INVALIDITY

The traditional view of the antitrust laws has always been that the Sherman Act requires proof of an actual restraint, whereas the Clayton Act requires showing only a probability of lessening of competition or tendency to create a monopoly. Normally, because of the differences in proof, one would suspect that the government would be more likely to block mergers with the Clayton Act than the Sherman Act. However, the *Philadelphia National Bank* case, decided by the Supreme Court just prior to *Lexington Bank,* caused the experts to reassess their thinking. In that earlier case, the Court had concluded that a merger resulting in a company controlling 30 per cent of the relevant market was violative of Section 7 of the Clayton Act. But it stated that such a merger would not be enjoined if there was "evidence clearly showing that the merger [was] not likely to have such anti-competitive effects." In the *Lexington Bank* case, however, the Court allowed no possible opening for the defendant to establish that no anticompetitive effect would result, or that it was a "reasonable restraint." Instead, in Sherman Act cases, the Court held that a merger was an unreasonable restraint, *ipso facto,* if there was an "elimination of significant competition."

The two bank cases, on superficial review, seemed to support a proposition that it would now be easier to attack mergers and acquisitions by alleging violations of the Sherman Act. The reason is that the *Lexington Bank* case proscribes mergers based on a per se test of market shares, whereas the *Philadelphia National Bank* case holds only a merger of two companies—which produces a company with an aggregate market share of 30 per cent, and which produces a 33 per cent increase in concentration of control between the two largest postmerger banks—would raise a presumption of illegality. This Sherman Act preference of a per se violation over a presumption of illegality would be valid at least when relatively large percentage shares of the market were involved. As the relevant shares of the market decreased in size, the government would be more apt to allege violations of the Clayton Act.

Although it was generally assumed that the actual restraint standard under the Sherman Act, vis-à-vis the incipiency standard under the Clayton Act, imposed a more strict burden of proof in order to sustain a violation, the results of recent litigation have cast a penumbra of uncertainty over that rule. In *Lexington Bank* the Court's holding of a per se violation precludes any defense to a merger attacked under the Sherman Act. In *Philadelphia National Bank,* the Court's discussion of a presumptive violation effectively precludes market performance defenses to a merger attacked under the Clayton Act:

> We are clear . . . that a merger the effect of which "may be substantially to lessen competition" is not saved because, on some ultimate reckoning of social or economic debits and credits, it may be deemed beneficial. A value of choice of such magnitude is beyond the ordinary limits of judicial competence, and in any event has been made for us already, by Congress when it enacted the amended §7. Congress determined to preserve our traditionally competitive economy. It therefore proscribed anticompetitive mergers, the benign and the malignant alike, fully aware, we must assume, that some price might have to be paid.

With this broad condemnation of the beneficial aspects of any merger, as a practical matter, in many cases, it will be of little practical import for a company to argue market performance defenses where it is faced with a per se violation or a presumptive violation. Thus, the practical effect of these cases is to align more closely the Clayton Act standards with the Sherman Act standards. Mr. Justice Harlan, in dissenting in *Lexington Bank,* argued that the government had not sustained the traditional, stricter, Sherman Act standards and that the effect of the Court's holding was to create "a Clayton Act case masquerading in the garb of the Sherman Act." More recent litigation seems to continue the trend of having the standards of the respective acts mesmerized into one judicial policy in which—no matter what statutory predicate is used—the "government always wins." The net result is that although *Lexington Bank*'s per se rule would seem to favor the Sherman Act as a trustbuster, the restriction of available defenses in Clayton Act litigation coupled with later decisions which have upheld violations in mergers involving minimal shares of the market enhance the conclusion that the Clayton Act will continue to be the major weapon in the government's antitrust arsenal—except, perhaps, in those cases in which there might be some technical obstacle to its application.

13 Mergers Under Section 5 of the FTC Act

Previous chapters have touched upon the role of the Federal Trade Commission in enforcing the antitrust laws as they apply to mergers. At this time, consideration will be given in detail to the method the FTC uses in approaching these problems. Because of the broad scope of the FTC powers in this area, mention will be made briefly of material already covered and of material to be discussed in later portions of the book, but the focus will be on Section 5 of the Federal Trade Commission Act.

The relevant portions of that Section provide that, "Unfair methods of competition in commerce . . . are declared unlawful." The Constitutional basis of the statute, passed in 1914, was the interstate commerce clause. Section 5 was amended in 1938 to include as unlawful "unfair or deceptive acts or practices in commerce," but this portion of the statute is not significant in the area of mergers. The definition of one of the key words in this section, *commerce,* is provided by Section 4 of the FTC Act which includes "[c]ommerce among the several states . . . or in any territory of the United States or in the District of Columbia, or between any such territory and any state or foreign nation. . . ." It is now apparent, though it has not always been so, that the outer limits of FTC power under this section coincides with the outer limits of the power of Congress to legislate under the Commerce Clause.

Thus, the requirement that the activity sought to be regulated must be "in commerce" is not presently a very limiting factor. The interstate commerce, for the purposes of Section 5, is not required to be substantial, although wholly intrastate commerce is excluded from the section's coverage. If the commission attempts to regulate some aspect of interstate commerce, it is no defense for the individual or firm involved to prove that the rest of his business activities are purely intrastate. The scope of Section 5 has broadened concurrently with that of the Commerce Clause, so now this section is a formidable weapon indeed.

Although the Federal Trade Commission Act has been held not to be one of the "antitrust laws" of the United States for purposes of private treble-damage actions, it is clear that the condemnation of unfair methods of competition is the broadest language in the trade regulation laws.

The scope of the statute was read very narrowly in *FTC* v. *Gratz,* the first case involving Section 5 to reach the Supreme Court. The restrictive approach, however, was set aside two years later in *FTC* v. *Beech Nut Packing Co.,* when the Supreme Court stated that:

> What shall constitute unfair methods of competition denounced by the Act, is left without specific definition. Congress deemed it better to leave the subject without precise definition, and to have each case determined upon its own facts, owing to the multifarious means by which it is sought to effectuate such schemes.

This reasoning has been refined through the years to the point where it has been settled by the Supreme Court that a violation of Section 5 can be predicated on activity that falls short of either a Sherman or Clayton Act violation.

The role of Section 5 of the FTC Act has not always been very well defined in the merger area, however. A review of the complaints filed in the merger area by the FTC based on either Section 5 of the FTC Act alone or Section 5 and Section 7 of the Clayton Act indicates that out of the first twelve complaints filed, only one led to a divestiture order. The one divestiture order was affirmed by the Supreme Court on the basis of a Clayton 7 violation, with the Court noting that "[t]his section [§5] is not presently important; the challenged orders sought to enforce obedience to Section 7 of the Clayton Act." Most of these first twelve complaints involved acquisitions by packing companies of stock and assets of competitors. The cases were usually dismissed after the answer without any reasons being given by the commission. In one case, however, the acquisition involved the assets of a competitor and the divestiture was denied under Section 7 of Clayton because at that time the section did not cover asset acquisitions, and the complaint also failed under Section 5 of the FTC Act because the commission decided that the "evidence is not sufficient to constitute a violation of the Federal Trade Commission Act."

If the FTC refused to test the strength of Section 5, and the merger involved assets before 1950, the private citizen or aggrieved party could be afforded no relief. The Federal Trade Commission Act could not be the basis of a private suit under Section 4 of Clayton because it was not an "antitrust law" within the meaning of that section. The Justice Department was foreclosed from attacking the merger because the FTC had sole authority to invoke Section 5 when a violation seemed probable. The loophole involving acquisition of assets under Clayton 7 had been remedied—by the Celler–Kefauver amendment of 1950—but the commission still has sole authority to sue in the case of an acquisition of a partnership or any other merger that falls short of a Section 7 violation.

CLAYTON ACT

The implementation strategy used by the commission in Section 5 cases cannot be fully appreciated without at least brief mention of the role of Section 7 of Clayton in the area. The Clayton Act, passed the same year as the FTC Act, was meant to serve the purpose of explicitly forbidding certain practices that were found to be against the public interest. Section 7 of that Act dealt with mergers and declared unlawful, acquisitions by one company of stock of another if the effect might be "to substantially lessen competition." The acquisition of assets was made unlawful in 1950 by amendment. The power exercised by Congress in passing that statute was similarly based on the Commerce Clause, but the section was intentionally meant to apply only to corporations. The use of the word *may* in the statute indicated that it was to be an incipiency statute—that is, to forbid activities that would violate the Sherman Act if allowed to become full-blown.

The power of the FTC to use Clayton 7 is found in a subsequent section of that Act. As a practical matter, the commission often alleges violations of both sections when attacking a merger. This is because a conviction under Section 7 can be used by private parties as prima facie evidence in a treble-damage suit, thereby encouraging consent decrees, and also because Section 5 covers some violations that might fail to meet Clayton 7 criteria. This practice was followed by complaint counsel in eleven out of the first twelve merger complaints filed by the FTC, but fell into disfavor soon afterward when it became apparent that the commission did not view Section 5 as pertinent to mergers. Now, however, the commission and the Supreme Court both acknowledge the applicability of Section 5 in all merger cases. In *FTC* v. *Beatrice Foods,* the commission noted that, "It is well established that section 5 reaches transactions which violate the standards of the Clayton Act though for technical reasons are not subject to that Act, unless such application of section 5 would be an attempt to 'supply what Congress has studiously omitted. . . .' " Clayton 7 and Section 5 of the FTC Act are also compatible because they are both incipiency statutes. Although Section 5 can be termed somewhat broader than Section 7, both statutes are utilized in the merger area to halt acquisitions that have a probability of becoming a restraint of trade. Section 5 is the most useful in cases involving acquisitions of noncorporate entities. As mentioned earlier, Clayton 7 cannot be used to invalidate the acquisition of a partnership, so this can be a real problem in a line of commerce that has most of the competition provided by small businessmen. The dairy industry and concrete manufacturers are cases in point. It is quite evident that the combination of Sections 5 and 7 have been very useful in these two areas.

SHERMAN ACT

Mention must also be made of Sections 1 and 2 of the Sherman Act and their application to the enforcement process under Section 5 of the FTC Act. Though the FTC cannot enforce the Sherman Act as such, it may do so indirectly, because anything that is a violation of the Sherman Act is "an unfair method of competition." The starting point is the fact that the test of illegality of a merger under both Section 5 of the FTC and Clayton 7 is that the acquisition has a *probability* of being a restraint of trade or monopoly under the Sherman Act. If the merger, given the worst possible outcome, could never amount to monopolization or a restraint of trade, then the merger will pass the test of both Clayton 7 and FTC 5. It is important to keep in perspective the rationale behind the incipiency-type statute, or soon it becomes questionable whether any merger can be legal. In *Procter & Gamble,* the commission stated, "Congress declared neither that all mergers, nor that mergers of a particular size or type, are per se *unlawful.* In every case the determination of illegality, if made, must rest upon specific facts."

Once a merger has been completed and it becomes apparent that there exists a monopoly situation or that an unreasonable restraint of trade has resulted from the merger, it could be attacked under the Sherman Act sections, as well as the Clayton and FTC acts. However, if the Sherman Act were relied on alone, the burden of proof would be harder to meet, because it would require proof of actual monopolization or of the unreasonable restraint. In view of these facts, it is easy to see why the Clayton and FTC acts dominate the merger field.

FTC PROCEDURES

The procedures followed by the FTC in the enforcement of Section 5 of the FTC Act and Section 7 of the Clayton Act will be covered in more detail in a subsequent chapter, but several of its more important aspects should be noted here. The commission occupies, within its own complaint structure, the roles of prosecutor, trial judge, and appellate judge. Of course, these roles are separate from each other to eliminate any misuse of influence. The complaint counsel within the commission, on commission authorization, recommends the complaint and prosecutes it before the administrative judge, who issues the preliminary findings of fact and law in the case and issues the initial order, if one is determined to be necessary. The commission itself can then hear the case on appeal and affirm, dismiss, or modify the findings or order in any way deemed necessary. The Supreme Court upheld this tripartite division of authority in the commission in the 1929 case of *FTC* v. *Klesner,* so it is settled that there is no violation of any due process requirements in such multiple agency roles at the FTC.

The concurrent jurisdiction of the commission and the Justice Department over different aspects of the antimerger statutes has prompted these agencies to develop expertise in the economies of various selected industries and to defer activity in the other's area unless some compelling reason overcomes the reluctance to interfere. In any event, whenever a complaint is filed or an investigation is initiated by one agency, the other is promptly notified so that alleged violators will not be subjected to dual enforcement.

The actual complaint filed with the FTC could have its genesis from several sources. The proposed merger could become known through the merger notification program or reporting requirements initiated in an outstanding cease and desist order, because of either the Justice Department's or the FTC's familiarity with a particular industry, by notification by the Securities and Exchange Commission, by a complaint filed by a private citizen, or from a variety of other sources such as business publications. Even before a complaint is filed, the FTC has broad investigatory powers to satisfy itself that competition in any line of commerce is not being lessened by any consummated merger. If the forbidden results manifest themselves years after the merger is completed, the merger is still subject to attack by the FTC. The commission may also use its subpoena powers to determine whether or not a prior cease and desist order is being followed. All of these methods combine to make the FTC very well informed on a variety of business practices.

After a complaint has gone through the various stages and the merger has been declared to be in violation of the law, the FTC has the authority to seek injunctions pending appeal in order to assure the effectiveness of the decree if it is affirmed. The powers of the commission have been expanded in the injunction area with the decision of the Supreme Court in *FTC* v. *Dean Foods*. The Court, after a complaint was filed by the complaint counsel under Section 5, held that the commission could petition the court of appeals to prevent consummation of the merger until the merits of the case could be decided by the hearing examiner and the full commission. The power was found in the Federal All Writs Act.

The role the courts of appeal play in merger cases brought under Section 5 is the same as if the complaint were based on Clayton 7. After the commission has reviewed the decision of the administrative judge and issued its opinion finding the merger illegal in at least one respect, the respondent to the complaint has sixty days to file a petition seeking review of the order in the circuit where he resides or carries on business. If no petition is filed, the order becomes final on its own. Assuming a petition for review has been filed, the court of appeals is rather limited in its power of review. According to the Supreme Court in *Eastman Kodak* v. *FTC*, the appellate court can only determine if the FTC properly exercised its authority; there is no original jurisdiction in the court of appeals, so the court may not award relief beyond the powers of the FTC. Within this area, however, the court may affirm, enforce, modify, reverse, or remand the order.

The test employed by the court of appeals is whether the findings of the commission are supported by substantial evidence. The Supreme Court, in *FTC* v. *Procter & Gamble Co.*, made it clear that all mergers attacked by the FTC under Clayton 7 "must be tested by the same standard, whether they are classified as horizontal, vertical, conglomerate or other." Because Section 5 embraces all that Clayton 7 does, the tests used in both are essentially the same.

Once an order has become final, either by failure to file an appeal or through the dismissal of the petition or affirmance of the order, the order is enforced by a civil suit for up to $5,000 per day for each violation. The court in this case only determines if the order has been violated; a review of the facts found by the FTC in the original proceeding is outside the jurisdiction of the court. Once the order has been issued under Section 5 by the commission and a petition for review has been filed, the court of appeals has the power under both the FTC Act and the Clayton Act to issue an injunction to restrain illegal activities pending the outcome of the appeal.

Whether the litigation initiated by the FTC under Section 5 is terminated by a consent order or by a final cease and desist order, it often has been the practice of the commission to include in the final order a provision directing the respondent to refrain from any future acquisitions for a period of years, usually ten, without first obtaining permission from the commission. This provision, as part of the final order, can result in a fine for violation. This type of an arrangement also makes it easier for the commission to keep track of proposed mergers and to refuse permission where a lessening of competition may be substantial.

Several industries, in the past prone to a great deal of merger activity, have become the subject of FTC rule-making power. Reports are required from the firms as to future plans in the merger area. Standards have been set for the cement, food distribution, grocery products manufacturing, and textile mill industries. These standards are discussed in Chapter 21.

FTC MERGER CASES

The early history of enforcement of Section 5 as it applied to mergers leaves the impression that it was of little or no use to the FTC. Complaint counsel soon learned to rely on Section 7 of Clayton if he wanted to succeed before either the commission or the courts. This restrictive reading can be justified partially by the failure of the Clayton Act to cover one gaping hole in the legal defenses against mergers. Because the only acquisitions forbidden by the Clayton Act before 1950 were those of another corporation's stock, the courts refused to read into Section 5 coverage of acquisitions of assets that might result in a lessening of competition. As early as 1926 the commission ruled in the *Armour Company* case that Section 5 could not be used to invalidate a merger effectuated between competitors if it came about by the acquisition of assets rather than of capital stock. The reasoning seemed to be that if such acquisitions were legal under Clayton and could have easily been made illegal by Congress, then the FTC Act should not be used to eliminate the exemption. Not only did the Supreme Court agree with this reasoning in two cases decided in the same year, but it went on to hold that mergers effectuated by purchases of stock that were subsequently converted into asset holdings could not be ruled illegal under Section 7, even though the stock acquisitions were originally illegal.

This narrow approach to the use of Section 5 stayed with the commission until well after the 1950 amendment to the Clayton Act that plugged up the loophole as it relates to the acquisition of assets that tend to lessen competition. However, the commission started to show signs of recovering from its shortsightedness around 1960, and the movement to involve Section 5 in every phase of merger control has gained momentum every year. Perhaps the best way to get an appreciation for the growth of the utility of Section 5 in the merger area is by analyzing the cases based on it in the three principal functional categories of mergers—horizontal, vertical, and conglomerate.

Horizontal Mergers

The horizontal merger—a merger between competitors—is perhaps the easiest merger to find illegal. An example would be the acquisition of one grocery store in a small town by another grocery store in the same town. The competition between the two stores is eliminated, and the adverse effects of monopoly are more likely to be present than they were before. Some of the tests used by the commission and the courts in reviewing horizontal mergers are (1) the competitive situation in the industry (how many competitors control what share of the market); (2) the elimination of substantial competition; (3) the market share of the acquiring and acquired concern; (4) the threat of defensive mergers from remaining competitors; and (5) the enhancement of the competitive position of the resulting firm.

All of the early complaints filed by the commission under Section 5 involved horizontal acquisitions of stock or assets. It was not at all clear to the commission that vertical integrations could be challenged under the Clayton Act or the FTC Act; indeed, as we have noted before, Section 5 of the FTC Act was not even deemed to apply to all horizontal mergers. The first complaints brought under Section 5 after 1950, the year that the assets acquisition loophole was plugged up in the Clayton Act, again involved mergers with mainly horizontal aspects.

The complaint in *Fruehauf Trailer Co.* in 1956 alleged violations of Clayton Section 7 and FTC Section 5 based on the acquisition of competitors and attempts to monopolize by offering special financing arrangements. A cease and desist order was entered nine years later, but the basis was not Section 5. According to the commission, Section 5 did not have to be relied on because "[O]n its facts, the case presents a clear violation of Section 7."

The next complaint involving an acquisition under Section 5 was *Crane Co.,* filed in 1960. The allegations charged a violation of Sections 5 and 7 because of the acquisition of all or part of the stock and assets of five competitors within two years time. The proceedings continued for two years until the complaint was dismissed by the hearing examiner on motion of the complaint counsel.

In a complaint filed in 1960 the commission contested the acquisition by *Continental Baking Co.* of several individual bakeries under Clayton 7, and then went on to allege a violation of Section 5 "by its continuous practice of acquiring various baking concerns throughout the United States." The merger activity complained of here can actually be defined as both horizontal and market extension. This latter category will be discussed under conglomerate mergers. A consent decree was entered into in 1962 whereby Continental agreed to divest itself of one of the concerns it had acquired and also to refrain from acquiring "any concern, corporate or noncorporate, engaged in any state of the United States in the production and sale of bread and bread type rolls" unless the commission granted permission.

In *Campbell Taggert Associated Bakeries* the charge was the same as in *Continental Baking Co.* just discussed. The complaint was issued in 1960 and the cease and desist order was entered in 1966. The acquired interests were all over the country, so the merger had both horizontal and market extension aspects to it.

The next FTC merger case under Section 5 supplied a large boost both in supplementary powers in the merger area and in staff morale. The case was *Dean Foods* and the complaint was entered on the acquisition by Dean of a competing diary company, Bowman Dairy. The complaint alleged violations of both Clayton 7 and FTC Section 5. The case went to the Supreme Court on the issue of whether the commission would request a temporary injunction from the court of appeals "to maintain the *status quo* until the commission determined the legality of the merger." When the Court determined that such relief was available to the commission under the All Writs Act, the hearing examiner heard the case on the merits. He dismissed the complaint: "[S]ince the acquisition neither had nor is 'likely to have any adverse effect on actual or potential competition in any line of commerce in any section of the country, it did not violate either Section 7 of the Clayton Act or Section 5 of the FTCA.' " On appeal from that adverse decision, the commission reversed and found the merger illegal. In an opinion by Commissioner

Jones, both Section 7 and Section 5 were found to have been violated. In that part of the complaint detailing the violation of Section 5, the allegation was that, "[T]he contract and combination by which Dean and Bowman undertook to eliminate the independent competition of Bowman is an unreasonable restraint of trade in commerce and may hinder, or have a dangerous tendency to hinder, competition unduly, thereby constituting an unfair act and practice in commerce, in violation of Section 5 of the Federal Trade Commission Act." The opinion noted that Dean had merely asserted "that Section 5 of the Federal Trade Commission Act cannot be used to 'outlaw mergers not condemned by Section 7.' " Bowman answered the charge by denying any authority of the FTC "to proceed against a company whose assets have been acquired by another. . . ." The commission, however, found both Dean and Bowman guilty of a violation of Section 5:

> We have found no case holding that a transaction which violates one statute cannot at the same time violate another statute. Indeed, it is settled that a contract may be in violation of both Section 1 of the Sherman Act and Section 3 of the Clayton Act. . . .
>
> Section 5 of the Federal Trade Commission Act has specifically been held to encompass any act which may violate Section 1 of the Sherman Act as well as activities which might not have developed into the magnitude of Sherman Act violations. . . .

The Supreme Court stated in *Federal Trade Commission* v. *Brown:*

> Since mergers which have the requisite effect upon competition are in violation of Section 7, it necessarily follows that an agreement to effect such a merger must conflict with the basic policies of the Clayton Act and therefore is in violation of Section 5 of the Federal Trade Commission Act. We have found that the acquisition does in fact violate Section 7 and we are unaware of any case that holds that such a ruling prevents the same act from violating Section 5 of the Federal Trade Commission Act.

The commission discussed the effect that *Foremost Dairies, Inc.* and *Beatrice Foods Company* had on this holding. The commission indicated in both of these cases that a series of acquisitions may violate Section 5 whether or not the individual violations are covered by Clayton 7. This was not the holding of either case, however. *Beatrice* did hold that a violation of Section 5 could be found in the case of a merger prohibited by Section 7, but where the company was not covered by the statute.

> Thus, for example, Section 7 speaks only of corporations and does not extend to persons and partnerships. Concluding that the failure to include persons and partnership was not deliberate on the part of Congress, the Commission stated: "Applying Section 5 to noncorporate acquisitions effectuates, rather than circumvents or conflicts with, Congress' policy with respect to the prevention of anticompetitive acquisitions." The reasoning behind this decision is directly relevant to the case at hand. There is no evidence that Congress deliberately omitted the acquired corporation from the reach of Section 7 of the Clayton Act. It is also clear that in proper circumstances the application of the law to the acquired corporation would effectuate

> rather than circumvent or conflict with the public policy sought to be effectuated by Congress in enacting the Section. Accordingly, we believe that Section 5 is the proper statute under which to charge an acquired corporation where the acquisition substantially lessens competition.

It was this case, as determined in both the Supreme Court and the commission, that gave the FTC new prestige in the merger area. This enunciation of the ability of Section 5 to plug the loophole of noncorporate acquisitions present in Clayton 7 gave Section 5 a real meaning to the commission no matter what the classification of the merger.

Vertical Mergers

A vertical merger is the acquisition by one firm of its customers, suppliers, or both. If company A is a ready-mix concrete dealer and he uses Portland cement in the mixing of the concrete, the acquisition of A by company B, a Portland cement dealer, is known as a vertical merger. The tests used in this type of merger vary slightly from those tests we have noted before. Here the important factors are (1) substantial lessening of competition or tendency toward a monopoly in some horizontal lines, (2) market shares of both parties in light of economic realities, (3) ease of entry into the competitive market, (4) amount of competition foreclosed on either level, (5) ability of the new combination to absorb losses temporarily, and (6) increase in production available over what would be available if the expansion had been accomplished by the construction of new facilities. Again, these are only some of the factors considered in each case, albeit very important ones. None of these factors individually is controlling or even universally considered.

The first three mergers challenged by the Federal Trade Commission under Section 5 after 1950 all involved the tendency toward vertical integration in the Portland cement industry. In *Ideal Cement Company* the Federal Trade Commission challenged the acquisition by Ideal Cement of Builders Supply Company of Houston, the fifth-largest ready-mix concrete producer in that area. The complaint was grounded on Section 5 only. The complaint noted that there was already a significant trend toward concentration in a ready-mix concrete area in major metropolitan markets in the United States. There had been at least thirty-five such acquisitions since 1959. It also noted that the Houston area was well advanced in this type of integration, with three of the five largest Portland cement consumers becoming integrated with Portland cement companies since 1961. It noted that the foreclosure percentage in this market amounted to almost 40 per cent at this time. In discussing one of the other tests we have mentioned, the complaint also noted that such substantial foreclosure places great pressure on competing manufacturers to acquire their own consumers also. Thus, such acquisitions form an integral part of the chain reaction of acquisitions which could eventually foreclose the market entirely. Other important factors were also considered by the complaint, but it was noted that the ability of nonintegrated competitors of Builders Supply Company to compete had already been or might be substantially impaired, and also that the entry of new Portland cement or ready-mix concrete dealers had been inhibited, or actually prevented. The final point made by the complaint was that now a market that had once been dominated by decentralized, locally controlled small businesses had become concentrated in the hands of a relatively few manufacturers of Portland cement. Some three months later the commission entered a consent order requiring Ideal Cement to sell within two years Builders Supply Company. In this consent order Ideal was given the option of retaining the ownership of the real property on which the ready-mix concrete plant was situated, but if such option was exercised, Ideal was required to lease as much of the real property as was necessary for the purchaser of the plant to operate efficiently for the next ten years. In the commission's view this solved the problem of at least one more market for Portland cement being foreclosed in the Houston area, and also took off some of the pressure from other competitors in the ready-mix concrete industry to become vertically integrated with other Portland cement manufacturers.

A second case challenging a vertical integration in the cement industry was *Lehigh Portland Cement Company,* filed in 1966. The company challenged the FTC's action in this case by asking for a dismissal of the complaint because of a concurrent industry investigation being conducted by the commission. This was denied by the commission. The commission similarly denied another attempt to avoid the FTC's jurisdiction in this case when the company moved for a transfer of the proceedings to the Department of Justice. In 1971 the commission issued an order denying Lehigh's motion for summary judgment, but granted in part complaint counsel's cross-motion for summary judgment and set a date for a preconference hearing. The basis for Lehigh's motion for a summary judgment was that the companies acquired were not in interstate commerce within the meaning of Section 7 of the Clayton Act. Lehigh contended that because no purchases or sales were made across state lines, the acquisitions do not fall within the prescriptions of either Section 7 or Section 5. The commission answered this contention by citing the Supreme Court case of *Standard Oil Company* v. *Federal Trade Commission* and noted that the flow-of-commerce theory discussed in that case was clearly analogous to the interstate transportation of the cement in this case. The commission also relied on the fact that the *Standard Oil* case was based on Section 2(a) of the Clayton Act which required "purchases in commerce." The commission decided that there could be no question but that purchases can be made in intrastate commerce and conform to the required jurisdictional basis. The other contention relied on by Lehigh was that because Clayton 7 did not apply in this case, the commission could not substitute a Section 5 action to accomplish what Congress did not intend to do under Section 7. The commission had merely to cite *FTC* v. *Brown Shoe Company,* to the effect that "our cases hold that the Commission had the power under Section 5 to arrest trade restraints in their incipiency without proof that they amount to an outright violation . . . of the Clayton Act, or other provisions of the antitrust laws."

In *Marquette Cement Manufacturing Company,* similar activities to those already mentioned were challenged. The commission also refused to dismiss on the basis of Marquette's claim that the industrywide survey was prejudicial to respondent's interests. In this case the commission found a violation and ordered divestiture of the acquired company.

The commission filed a complaint in 1968 against Allied Chemical Corporation, alleging that the acquisition by Allied and Jim Robbins Seat Belt Company of J. R. Company violated Section 7 of the Clayton Act and Section 5 of the FTC Act because "the acts and practices of Allied and Robbins in connection with their program of acquisition and expansion . . . have restrained competition in the domestic manufacture and sale of automobile seatbelt webbing and seatbelt yarn, and may restrain competition in the manufacture and sale of automotive seatbelts." In his opinion, the hearing examiner discussed several of the tests of vertical integration and decided that (1) an integrated manufacturer of seatbelts had a decisive competitive advantage over nonintegrated producers, (2) nonintegrated producers have been deprived of a substantial customer or potential customer, (3) additional mergers may possibly be precipitated by other firms in the seatbelt webbing industry, and (4) substantial barriers have been raised to other firms entering the automobile seatbelt webbing industry. Another factor discussed by the hearing examiner was that the concentration levels in the industry, which were already high, had the possibility of being increased substantially or, in other words, the possibility of decentralization being lessened substantially. After reviewing all of these factors, the hearing examiner decided that divestiture would be in order in this case and, upon review, the commission concurred in his opinion.

In *OKC Corporation* the FTC again attacked an acquisition by a cement manufacturer of a ready-mix concrete producer. The complaint was filed in 1969. The complaint counsel in this case requested an injunction under the All Writs Act, mentioned previously in *Dean Foods,* to maintain the status quo until the commission could determine the legality of the merger. The commission denied permission for this relief to be sought. However, a cease and desist order was entered by the commission and divestiture was ordered.

One of the more interesting acquisitions challenged by the Federal Trade Commission was in the 1970 *Beatrice Food Company* case. This merger involved the acquisition by Beatrice Foods of John Sexton & Company, an institutional dry grocery wholesaler from Chicago. The hearing examiner issued a cease and desist order in 1971 and ordered divestiture by Beatrice. The merger can be classified as both a vertical merger, because Beatrice Foods was already one of the largest food sup-

pliers to retail grocery stores, and a product-extension merger, because Beatrice had been thinking about entering into the institutional dry grocery sales industry. In the opinion, however, the hearing examiner seemed to place the greatest emphasis on the fact that Beatrice was actually a potential entrant into the field, and therefore, potential competition had been eliminated because of this merger. This area of the merger law under Section 5 will be discussed in the following section. The hearing examiner concluded his opinion with the statement that "as charged in the complaint, the acquisition likewise violates Section 5 of the Federal Trade Commission Act."

The commission has filed two recent complaints, alleging vertical merger activity in violation of Section 5 of the Federal Trade Commission Act and Section 7 of the Clayton Act. They are *United Brands Company* and *Georgia-Pacific Corporation*. The United Brands merger involved a purchase by United Fruit of nine small growers of fresh produce. The complaint alleged monopolistic and anticompetitive effects because (1) potential competition was reduced; (2) concentration in the industry was increased; (3) competitive advantage was achieved by United Fruit because of the subsidization of financial losses selling through national advertising, sources of credit, dominant market shares, and opportunities for reciprocity; (4) structure in the industry was changed from small and independent concerns to large conglomerate companies; and (5) barriers to entry into the industry were erected because of United Fruit's substantial financial resources, advertising capabilities, nationwide selling organizations, ability to borrow money at lower interest rates, reciprocity, and the large market share already owned by United Fruit. The complaint in *Georgia-Pacific* challenged the acquisition by Georgia-Pacific of sixteen firms owning over 600,000 acres of pine trees used to make plywood. Section 7 of Clayton and Section 5 were the basis for the complaint. The violations that the complaint alleged were (1) elimination of potential competition; (2) the enhancement of Georgia-Pacific's already dominant position; (3) the accelerated trend toward concentration in the industry; (4) the barriers to entry into the field; and (5) the foreclosure of land available to other producers of plywood. Although as of the time of this writing there has been no decision in the first of these cases, the commission has provisionally accepted a consent order in *Georgia-Pacific* whereby respondent will divest itself of 20 per cent of its assets and create a new independent company to operate the plants divested. Thus, Section 5 will apparently continue to play a large part in the challenging of vertical mergers in any already concentrated industry.

Conglomerate Mergers

The third category is necessarily the last because of its very nature; it serves as the catch-all category for all mergers that are not precisely horizontal or vertical. Listed as conglomerate are such mergers as the product-extension merger, the market-extension merger, and the true conglomerate

merger—the acquisition of a wholly unrelated business enterprise, such as the acquisition of a bakery by an automobile manufacturer. There is very little case law in the merger area on the legality of various modifications of the conglomerate merger. This is true because until the antitrust laws were enforced very vigorously, it made sense for a company in an acquiring mood to look for some related business so that by combining, both could benefit. This by definition is the vertical or horizontal merger. When this type of acquisition became less appealing, companies looking for a way to grow turned to profitable industries in other lines of manufacture or commerce. The popularity of this new merger caused the government to redefine its objectives and pursue those mergers that might "tend to lessen competition," no matter what the name given them.

From the discussion so far, it should seem quite likely that Section 5 of the FTC Act should be the most effective statute in discouraging the conglomerate merger. This is so not only because of the broad, new reading being given it by the commission and the courts, but because Clayton 7 can be read as being severely limited in enforcement powers because it talks in terms of "any line of commerce in any section of the country. . . ." As noted, those mergers known as conglomerate are so entitled because they encompass the acquisition of a business entity in a different but related line of commerce (the product-extension merger), a different section of the country (the market-extension merger), or neither (the true conglomerate merger).

The clearest statement of the commission's intention in the conglomerate merger area can be found in *Procter & Gamble Co.*, a relevant case to this discussion even though based upon Clayton 7. The commission sought the divestiture of Clorox, a manufacturer of liquid bleach, by Procter & Gamble. The commission described the purchase of Clorox as a product-extension merger, a variant of the horizontal merger. In the opinion ordering divestiture, the first point made was that Section 7 had not previously been used very often against this type of merger, although "businessmen were resorting to it increasingly as a mode of corporation expansion." The opinion then went on to analyze the principles of Section 7 in order to obtain some guidance in this case. This approach was necessary in the commission's view because of "[t]he absence of authoritative, specific precedents in this area. . . ." The principles distilled by the commission can be summarized briefly:

1. Section 7 was meant to apply to all mergers and they were all to be tested by the same standard. The differences in definition "import no legal distinctions under Section 7."
2. Competition is to be the main concern under Section 7. The "probability of a substantial anticompetitive effect," if shown, will make the merger illegal, save for but one defense.
3. Excessive concentration in an industry with high entry barriers impairs competition. Entry can be retarded by a dominant firm possess-

ing cost advantages, consumer identification, and financial strength and dominant size.

4. The effect of a merger on small business competition must also be gauged before the merger can be allowed. Congress was concerned with the vitality of small-scale competitors when Section 7 was enacted.
5. The Clayton Act was meant to be a preventive tool—"to be able to arrest the anti-competitive effects of market power in their incipiency." The Commission cannot afford to adopt a wait-and-see approach to these types of mergers.

After verbalizing these policy considerations, the commission discussed the reasons why this merger should not be allowed. The barriers to entry had been heightened because of P & G's size in relation to other possible competing firms. Clorox obtained substantial benefits in advertising discounts. Promotional advantages would accrue to Clorox if P & G used this sales force to help stimulate sales. P & G possessed the financial strength to sustain economic losses on Clorox's behalf that would put any competitor out of business. The opinion went on to detail how these anticompetitive effects were in fact substantial. Included in this consideration was the discrepancy in size between P & G and the rest of the bleach industry, the fact that an unhealthy market situation demanded more relief than a healthy market, the elimination of P & G as a potential competitor in the liquid bleach field, the fact that P & G was already dominant in related fields, and the rejection of the idea that economies accruing from this sort of a merger outweigh the need to protect inefficient competitors. Divestiture was ordered because the effects could not be enjoined; they were inherent in the merger itself.

On review the court of appeals reversed the commission determination of illegality, and the Supreme Court then reversed and reinstated the order. The Supreme Court relied on the same type of evidence as the commission did, and in this evidence found support for the possible lessening of competition. The observation of the commission on the applicability of the same standards was followed when the Court stated that "[a]ll mergers are within the reach of §7, and all must be tested by the same standard, whether they are classified as horizontal, vertical, conglomerate or other."

This opinion clearly indicates what the courts and commission will consider relevant when a merger is challenged under Section 7 of Clayton as an illegal conglomerate merger. It is also helpful when Section 5 is being employed because we have been told by both the commission and the reviewing courts that Section 5 is now understood to cover all that Clayton 7 covers, plus that which violates its spirit, if not its letter.

The FTC has challenged mergers under Section 5 and Clayton 7, *Continental Baking Company* and *Campbell Taggert Associated Bakeries,* as being both market extension and horizontal. In the former, divestiture was ordered in one of the three challenged acquisitions, and in the latter a consent order was entered. The philosophy behind the allegations charging Section 5 violations seemed to be that although each merger could be adjudged illegal under Clayton 7, the plan or scheme of acquiring these firms was itself a violation of Section 5. The logic complaint counsel used can be seen in two earlier cases involving a series of acquisitions—*Scott Paper Co.* v. *FTC* and *Foremost Dairies*. In *Scott* the Third Circuit dismissed as not supported the claim by the FTC that continuous acquisitions in the paper industry violated Section 5. The court held that even though the companies had sold some of their assets, they continued to produce paper in most cases, so the anticompetitive effects were minimal. In *Foremost,* the commission ruled that the cumulative effect of acquisitions is an element in determining legality of an acquisition, but is not proof that prior mergers are illegal. Because this was the case, the scheme or plan could not be a violation of Section 5. Since these cases, however, the breadth of Section 5 has expanded and it can now support a charge of illegality on its own.

A recent example of the type of conglomerate merger being challenged by the FTC is that involved in *Beatrice Foods*. Although the acquisition of an institutional dry grocery wholesaler by Beatrice, a large food supplier to retail grocery stores, had some vertical aspects, noted earlier, it was mainly a product-extension merger. Although the principal basis used by the examiner in finding the merger illegal was the fact that Beatrice was a potential entrant, he also relied on the fact that the industry was already concentrated, that the merged firm was a leader in the market, and that Beatrice was the most likely entrant.

In the future it can be expected that the new life given to Section 5 by allowing it to be the basis of a merger challenge will be increasingly implemented in an area of merger law where the standard of proof is by definition more difficult when Clayton 7 is relied on.

REMEDIES FOR ILLEGALITY UNDER SECTION 5

The type of relief the commission can grant in the case of a merger held to be illegal under Section 5 is much the same as that allowed in a complaint under Clayton 7. The commission's inquiry is focused on "[w]hat kind of order, within the broad range of an equity court's remedial powers, would, in the particular circumstances, be most effective to cure the ill effects of the illegal conduct, and assure the public freedom from its continuance." Once the commission affirms a finding of a violation, a cease and desist order is entered. This order becomes final unless a petition for review is filed. If appealed it becomes final after it is affirmed and no petition for certiorari is filed. The cease and desist order is just the formal name given to the decision of the commission. The order itself can take a variety of forms.

As in a violation of Section 7 of the Clayton Act, where divestiture is "peculiarly appropriate," the commission in a Section 5 proceeding may order divestiture of the acquired assets or stock. As a practical matter divestiture is almost always ordered because the anticompetitive effects cannot be easily enjoined. In a Section 7 action the power of divestiture is found in Section 11 of the Clayton Act. A similar power under Section 5 has been reasoned by analogy. The considerations in a divestment decision include the necessity for giving effect to the prohibitions of the law, the need to minimize the injury to the public interest, and the effect on private property.

Divestiture was held to be the proper remedy in *Crown Zellerbach Corp.* v. *FTC* even though property had been added to the acquired facilities and the value had increased. The court did allow the company to keep the added property if the operating condition of the acquired plant would not be destroyed once it was divested. A corollary of this premise is the order of divestiture that requires the acquiring company to divest the acquired company as a going concern. This is an expression of the commission's concern that not only should the acquiring company not be as dominant, but the acquired firm should be a capable competitor. The commission held that it had the power to order divestiture of the acquired property as a going concern under Section 7 in *Erie Sand & Gravel Co.,* and although the United States Third Circuit Court of Appeals remanded the case for re-evaluation of the line of commerce used, the court did not take issue with the commission's power to fashion an effective divestiture remedy.

The same remedy may be employed by the FTC in a case that is settled by consent decree. In *Lone Star Cement Corporation* the nation's largest Portland cement manufacturer was ordered to divest the W. D. Hayden Company of Houston, including its ready-mixed concrete plants and related equipment. The charge was brought under Section 5 on an allegation of a vertical foreclosure of competition. The consent decree was entered in 1967.

Although it will be noted in more detail later, mention should be made at this time of one of the more widely used enforcement remedies available under Section 5. This particular weapon is the ban on future acquisitions without commission consent. This can be included in a cease and desist order or a consent decree, and it gives the commission added flexibility when used in conjunction with an order of divestiture.

It is now undisputed that the commission can order a ban on acquisitions for a reasonable number of years when a company has violated Section 7 of the Clayton Act. It has also been accepted that Section 5 covers all that is illegal under Clayton 7 and more. For this reason the courts have been willing to find the power in the FTC to ban future acquisitions, and the commission has been more than willing to exercise that power.

The discussion of a few examples will demonstrate how Section 5 can serve as the basis for such an order. In *Continental Baking Co.,* discussed under both the horizontal and conglomerate merger sections of this chapter, the commission, after the entry of a consent decree to charges of violating Section 5 by its "continuous practice of acquiring various baking concerns," ordered that Continental cease and desist from acquiring "directly or indirectly . . . the whole or any part of the stock, share capital, or assets of any concern, corporate or noncorporate, engaged in . . . the production and sale of bread. . . ." The period during which such acquisitions were prohibited was to be ten years in duration, the usual term.

The commission ordered a ten-year ban on acquisitions in the dairy industry in the *Dean Foods* case. The violations found there were based on both Clayton 7 and Section 5. In ordering the ban, the commission noted that similar bans had been included in orders issued against other leading companies in the dairy industry. They include *Beatrice Foods Company, Foremost Dairies, Inc., Borden Company,* and *National Dairy Products Corporation.* The purpose of such a ban came to light in *Dean Foods* when the opinion noted that "it appears clear to us that, unless restrained Dean will continue to acquire dairy firms, in violation of Section 7 and its basic policy and purpose." In a second action against Beatrice Foods some six years later, an FTC hearing examiner entered an order that "would forbid Beatrice to acquire any institutional dry grocery business for ten years without the FTC's prior approval." Once these orders are entered, the FTC has the advantage of prior notice of a pending merger, where only notice is required, and where permission to acquire is made necessary, the commission can prevent mergers with possible illegal effects by merely refusing permission. The failure to observe this condition contained in a consent decree or cease and desist order is punishable by a civil suit for not more than $5,000 for each violation.

DEFENSES

Much has been said thus far in this chapter about the activities that are illegal and how the FTC makes use of Section 5 to end them. No space has yet been devoted to the types of defenses available to those against whom a complaint is brought. This can be explained rather simply, however. There just are not many defenses that will convince the commission that a Section 5 complaint is not well founded. If Mr. Justice Stewart thought that the government always won in a suit founded on Clayton 7, there is every indication that the trend in Section 5 cases would cause him to forecast even less hope for respondent's counsel in a case brought under that statute. This result seems naturally to follow acceptance of the argument that Section 5 can be used to invalidate everything illegal under Clayton 7, as well as those mergers that violate the spirit of Clayton 7. This type of coverage, when included with Section 5's jurisdiction over noncorporate acquisitions, seems to give the commission, under Section 5, all of Clayton 7's advantages with none of the disadvantages.

There still are some limits on the scope of the commission's powers under both the Clayton Act and the Federal Trade Commission Act that can be used to defeat the objectives of divestiture. The limits are similar for both statutes, although possibly construed more liberally in an action under Section 5. The starting point is the commission's statement in *Dean Foods* that an action under Section 5 cannot be dismissed because the activity falls short of the standard of illegality set in Clayton 7. Had the contention by respondents in that case—that Section 5 cannot be used to "outlaw mergers not condemned by Section 7"—been adopted, Section 5 would add nothing to the relief available under Clayton 7. But the commission did not agree with that statement. Section 5 can be employed where a merger involves an element not covered in Section 7 (for example, the acquisition of a noncorporate business firm).

The commission and the courts will readily acknowledge the lack of jurisdiction of the FTC if the respondent can prove that there was no interstate commerce involved. A federal court of appeals ruled in 1921 in *Canfield Oil Co.* v. *FTC* that a wholesaler could not be prosecuted by the FTC where the practices complained of were intrastate and not related interstate activities, even though the firm was involved in other commerce that was interstate. Sixteen years later another court of appeals noted that purely intrastate commerce was outside the scope of the FTC powers. Although these generalizations are still good law in theory, one cannot help but wonder what their practical effect is when some later holdings are considered along with the expansion of the number and kind of activities that the Supreme Court has held to be in interstate commerce for the purposes of a great variety of federal statutes. The Sixth Circuit discussed the flow-of-commerce theory as it applies to the FTC in *Ford Motor Co.* v. *FTC*. The court stated that anything that stimulates or decreases the flow of interstate commerce is reached by the Federal Trade Commission Act. That case was decided in 1941. A different circuit court noted in 1958 that the sales in interstate commerce did not have to be substantial to bring the activities within the Act. In 1959 still another circuit held in *Royal Oil Co.* v. *FTC* that the FTC had jurisdiction over interstate activities even though the company involved competes with intrastate companies which are exempt from FTC control. In *American News Co.* v. *FTC,* the FTC's authority over the respondent was confirmed even though most of the business was not interstate, the fact that the challenged activities were was enough. Another example of the liberal reading given the necessity of interstate commerce was demonstrated by the partial summary judgment granted to the complaint counsel in *Lehigh Portland Cement Co.* early in 1971. The finding of interstate commerce was based on purchases the acquired corporation made from Lehigh and other Florida cement firms. The fact that the supplier was in interstate commerce and brought the cement in from out of state made the subsequent purchases from the supplier enough to involve the buyer in interstate commerce. There does not seem to be much that cannot be classified in the "flow of commerce." The very fact that the FTC has filed the complaint seems *ipso facto* to make the activity interstate. The chances of getting a complaint dismissed because the acts or practices do not measure up to the standard of being "unfair" seems even more remote. The Congress acknowledged in the Senate report issued with the FTC Act that the commission was alone to determine what is unfair.

Other possible defenses can be discussed quickly because they will be discussed in more detail in Chapter 18. They include the failing-company doctrine (no injury to competition because of impending failure), the lack of injury to the public because of the acquired firm's small size, or the need to merge to meet already existing competition. These can all be advocated in cases brought under Section 5, and in an appealing case (a small company in a market dominated by large, integrated competitors) they will convince the commission to give its *imprimatur* to an acquisition that might otherwise be questionable. The Supreme Court, in *FTC* v. *Procter & Gamble,* made clear the fact that economies of scale would not be a defense in a government merger suit. Obviously a merger would not take place if there weren't some economic advantage involved. The argument that a series of acquisitions would benefit the industry as a whole has also fallen on deaf ears.

14 The Celler-Kefauver Amendment

As we have seen in previous chapters, Congress' plan that Section 7 of the Clayton Act be used to halt unhealthy concentrations of economic power in their incipiency was thwarted by a combination of poor legislative draftsmanship and restrictive judicial interpretation. In this chapter we will analyze the events which culminated in the 1950 Cellar–Kefauver Amendment to Section 7 of the Clayton Act, the amendment itself, and the first Supreme Court case interpreting the amendment.

HISTORICAL PERSPECTIVE

Four major loopholes developed in Section 7 as it was originally drafted. First, it applied only to acquisitions effected through the purchase of stock. Corporations could merge without fear of the Clayton Act merely by purchasing the assets of other corporations. Consequently, the majority of mergers consummated between 1914 and 1950 were asset acquisitions. Second, the Federal Trade Commission and the Antitrust Division of the Justice Department, which have concurrent jurisdiction over violations of Section 7, believed that the section applied only to horizontal acquisitions (the acquisition by one company of all or part of a competitor—a company offering the same goods or services in the same market area) and not to vertical (acquisition by one corporation of a customer or supplier corporation) or conglomerate acquisitions (acquisition of a company engaged in a business unrelated to that of the acquiring company). Third, the Supreme Court applied the more difficult to prove Sherman Act standards in evaluating whether a merger tended to "substantially lessen competition." A showing of mere diminution of competition between corporations in the transaction was not sufficient proof of a violation. Rather, the government had to prove that competition in the industry as a whole had been affected "to such a degree as will injuriously affect the public." Finally, the Supreme Court effectively emasculated Section 7 by holding that the Federal Trade Commission could order divestiture of stock acquired in violation of Section 7 only if the wrongfully acquired stock was held by the acquiring corporation at the time the commission's order was promulgated. Thus, the commission was deprived of jurisdiction if the acquiring corporation exchanged the stock for the assets of the acquired corporation at any time before the issuance of an order. Because considerable time lapses between the initial inquiry into the legality of a merger and the completion of the case, the Federal Trade Commission and the Justice Department came to believe that attempts to enforce Section 7 were futile, or as one member of the commission put it, like "chasing a vanishing will-o'-the wisp."

As early as 1921, bills were introduced in Congress to close the loopholes in Section 7. These proposals and the Federal Trade Commission's annual recommendations that Section 7 be amended were consistently ignored by Congress throughout the 1920's. Congress' reluctance to strengthen Section 7 is attributable to a marked shift in public attitude toward mergers. Unlike the generation that supported the trust-busting of Teddy Roosevelt and Woodrow Wilson, the new generation of the "roaring twenties" believed that economic concentration brought higher wages, greater returns on investments, and increased efficiency. During this period of relative prolonged prosperity and a buoyant stock market the nation idolized Henry Ford as the consummate businessman and made no demands on Congress to strengthen the antitrust laws.

As a result of the public's favorable attitude toward the concentration of economic power and of unfavorable Supreme Court decisions in 1926, the Federal Trade Commission and the Justice Department sharply curtailed their attempts to enforce Section 7. Between 1927 and 1950 the commission issued thirty-one complaints alleging violations of Section 7, only four of which culminated in cease and desist orders. No orders were issued after 1934. A small number of Justice Department suits issued under the Sherman Act were supplemented by Section 7 complaints. The department procured a divestment order in only one of these cases.

By taking full advantage of the loopholes in Section 7 and the low level of enforcement activity, businessmen and investment bankers created a wave of mergers between 1919 and 1930 that surpassed the great wave of the 1890's. In this second merger wave, 8,055 mining and manufacturing firms disappeared; so did 2,757 public utilities, 1,060 member banks of the Federal Reserve System, and 10,519 stores which were absorbed by various chains.

According to one commentator:

> By 1929 the 200 largest corporations controlled nearly half the nation's corporate assets. About one percent of the public utility companies accounted for over 80 percent of production. General Motors, Ford and Chrysler turned out nearly 90 percent of all American cars and trucks. Four tobacco companies produced over 90 percent of the cigarettes. While banking capital doubled, the number of banks actually declined: one percent of all financial institutions controlled 46 percent of the nation's banking business. Even retail merchandising, traditionally the domain of the small shopkeeper, re-

flected the trend. The A & P food chain expanded from 400 stores in 1912 to 5,000 in 1922 and 17,500 in 1928.

As these statistics illustrate, unlike the wave of the 1890's, the movement of the 1920's did not create a large group of single-dominant-firm industries. Often the single dominant firm that had been created in the 1890's remained static while firms on the second and lower levels launched merger programs, eventually creating oligopolies. However, large increases in concentration did take place in public utilities and in various newer industries that had not participated in the earlier wave of combinations, such as automobiles, chemicals, foods, metals, and petroleum refining.

The stock market crash of 1929 and the Great Depression brought a halt to the merger movement of the 1920's. The entire nation became preoccupied with relieving the millions who had lost their jobs and savings. Faith in government regulation replaced faith in free competition. The remedy proposed by Franklin Roosevelt's New Deal was national economic planning which necessitated governmental control and some restraint of free competition. Raymond Moley, chief of Roosevelt's Brain Trust in the early 1930's, wrote that the New Deal rejected the Jeffersonian philosophy

> that America could once more become a nation of small proprietors, of corner grocers and smithies under spreading chestnut trees. We believed that any attempt to atomize big business must destroy America's greatest contribution to a higher standard of living for the body of its citizenry—the development of mass production. We recognized that competition, as such, was not inherently virtuous; that competition created as many abuses as it prevented.

President Roosevelt and big business considered themselves partners in an attempt to rescue business from insolvency. Measures enacted by Congress to cure the Depression sought to circumscribe rather than strengthen competition. The most famous of these measures was the National Industrial Recovery Act (NIRA), which created the National Recovery Administration (NRA) to establish industrial codes designed to raise prices and restrict production, thereby protecting investors and business. Other measures included the Agricultural Adjustment Act and the Bituminous Coal Conservation Act.

The public's reaction to the Depression was not to call for a change in the antitrust laws to curtail merger activity, because this was accomplished automatically with the decline of prosperous times. Instead the frenzied promotional efforts of professional promoters were identified as the principal villain of the merger movement of the 1920's and legislation, such as the Securities Act of 1933 and the Securities Exchange Act of 1934, was enacted to cure the abuses of the promoters rather than to curtail merger activity. The Federal Trade Commission's annual request for the amendment of Section 7 went unanswered.

By 1935 the partnership between the president and big business had disintegrated. Roosevelt had become irritated when some businessmen openly flouted provisions of the NRA codes and when right-wing elements conducted campaigns to prevent his re-election by charging that he was an egomaniacal communist who sought to destroy the American system of free competition. Moreover, Senator Huey Long was rapidly building political strength to challenge Roosevelt for the presidency by claiming that Roosevelt was a puppet of big business and that Long knew "how to handle them moguls" to prevent the continued oppression of the poor by rich big businessmen.

To demonstrate his independence of big business Roosevelt successfully pushed for enactment of the Public Utility Holding Company Act in 1935, which was designed to undo the concentration that mergers had produced in public utilities. In addition, he began to speak out against wealth and power that were "built upon other people's money, other people's business, other people's labor." During the 1936 presidential campaign Roosevelt denounced businessmen as economic royalists, called for the return of economic democracy, and condemned the hands-off business attitude of the preceding Republican administrations. One commentator wrote:

> During those years of false prosperity and during the more recent years of exhausting depression, one business after another, one small corporation after another, their resources depleted, had failed or had fallen into the lap of a bigger competitor.
>
> A dangerous thing was happening. Half of the industrial corporate wealth of the country had come under the control of less than two hundred corporations. That is not all. These huge corporations in some cases did not even try to compete with each other. They themselves were tied together by interlocking directors, interlocking bankers, interlocking lawyers.
>
> Under this concentration independent business was allowed to exist only by sufferance. It has been a menace to the social system as well as to the economic system which we call American democracy.

After his overwhelming re-election Roosevelt and many of his new advisers, especially Thomas Corcoran and Thurman Arnold, became convinced that the entire New Deal was threatened by selfish and shortsighted big business. The recession of 1937–1938 was attributed to greedy price-fixing by monopolists and oligopolists. The public, and particularly small businessmen, began to demand an end to the policy of national economic planning and a return to the economic democracy which Roosevelt had promised in his campaign. In response to this public pressure Roosevelt sought to reinvigorate his antitrust program by naming Thurman Arnold as chief of the Justice Department's Antitrust Division and by sending a strongly worded message to Congress recommending a "thorough study of the concentration of economic power in American industry and the effect of that concentration upon the decline of competition."

Congress responded to his recommendation in 1939 by creating the

Temporary National Economic Committee (TNEC), which was composed of members from both houses of Congress supplemented by representatives from the Departments of Commerce, Justice, and Labor and from the Treasury, as well as from the FTC and the SEC. Between 1939 and 1941 TNEC held extensive hearings on the status of competition and commissioned many expert studies on various phases of the problem. TNEC issued its Final Report and Recommendations in March 1941. It recommended that Congress amend Section 7 to empower the FTC to establish a prior approval program under which both stock and asset acquisitions could not proceed unless the parties persuaded the commission that the merger would be "consistent with the public interest." Acquisitions of less than a size to be determined by Congress would have been exempted from this prior approval requirement.

World War II, however, diverted Congress' attention from these recommendations until 1945, when the first Congressional hearings were held on proposed amendments to Section 7. There was a great deal of controversy surrounding the proposed amendments. Each Congress from 1945 to 1950 held hearings, commissioned expert studies, and attempted to draft an amendment that was acceptable to a majority of both houses. The Truman administration supported a strong amendment especially after research studies began to reveal that a third wave of mergers had begun in 1940 and had expanded greatly after the war. In 1948 the FTC made public its statistical findings on mergers occurring in the 1940–1947 period. The report declared that corporate acquisitions from 1940 to 1947 had caused the disappearance of nearly 2,500 firms with total assets of $5 billion, representing 5.5 per cent of all manufacturing assets in the United States. The commission announced that the concentration of economic control was reaching the point where,

> like Alexander the Great, the modern monopolist may have to bring his merger activities to a halt, owing simply to the imminent absence of "New Worlds to Conquer." No great stretch of the imagination is required to foresee that if nothing is done to check the growth in concentration, either the giant corporations will ultimately take over the country, or the Government will be impelled to step in and impose some form of direct regulation in the public interest. In either event, collectivism will have triumphed over free enterprise, and the theory of competition will have been relegated to the limbo of well-intentioned but ineffective ideals.

The FTC's conclusions were disputed by several economists—especially John Lintner and J. Keith Butters. These economists noted that despite the large number of acquisitions that occurred between 1940 and 1947, the pre-eminent characteristic of this third merger wave was the small size of the corporations acquired. Thus, the effect of this third merger movement on concentration was minimal. In fact, because the largest firms made fewer acquisitions than the less large, the relative concentration of assets among both the 500 and the 1,000 largest manufacturing firms was actually diminished. Senator Paul Douglas of Illinois attempted to rebut these economists by attacking their statistical techniques; the majority of Congress dismissed their contentions rather summarily.

As the debates, hearings, and expert studies continued, two opposing philosophies emerged as the center of the controversy. Those who opposed any strengthening of the antimerger law argued that the basic problem was the most efficient allocation and use of the nation's limited resources. Many efficiencies can be realized through mergers, such as economies of scale, cost saving by eliminating middlemen through vertical mergers, and protection of investors by risk spreading through conglomerate acquisitions. The antimerger proposals, they continued, are designed to protect small, inefficient competitors from mergers which are a natural step in the pursuit of efficiency which characterizes a truly free competitive system. If these inefficient competitors are protected, there is no incentive to seek greater efficiency because there is no competitive advantage to be gained. Thus, they concluded, the United States would become a nation of small inefficient competitors and would be dominated in the world marketplace by large, highly efficient European cartels. Furthermore, because the Sherman Act is available to check abuses of economic power, amendment of the Clayton Act is unnecessary.

The proponents of an antimerger amendment responded to these arguments with a combination of economic and political theory. They were concerned not only about the efficient allocation of resources but with the preservation of democracy and a particular way of life. They argued that the task of government is to insure free and fair competition. Vigorous competition will keep prices at a fair level and will guarantee that commercial success is obtained by efficiency rather than by market control. The most important determinant of competitive vigor is the number and size of independent firms in the market. Up to a point, the more independent competitors there are competing with each other the more vigorous competition is likely to be. Mergers reduce the number of independent enterprises and lead to an unhealthy accumulation of market power. Furthermore, there is less competition where there are few market participants because each competitor is conscious that its attempts to gain competitive advantage will be duplicated by its rivals, thus nullifying the gain expected from the contemplated activity. An oligopolist, for example, will not lower his prices or increase his services, because the price cut or service increase will immediately be put into effect by the other oligopolists and the relative market share of each will remain constant.

Generally the proponents of new antimerger legislation favored business growth through internal expansion rather than by acquisitions that eliminate competition. The emphasis was on the long-run benefits to the economy and to the public of competitive free markets. Progress would be assured through invention, innovation, and free enterprise. More and better services would be made available through each independent businessman pursuing intelligently his own self-interest. As Representative Celler put it:

> We, in this country, for many years, have recognized the absolute necessity of a competitive economic system. We have turned our back on the easy way of cartels and monopolies, on price-fixing, on allocation of markets. We believe in the right of men to be free of artificial restraints upon their liberty to engage in business and to practice a calling. We believe that competition gives the most for the least, that it permits one to be relatively free from government regulation, and obviates the pressures that have led to nationalization of industries in other countries; and we believe that it has contributed to the expansion of a mobile social structure in the sense that equality of opportunity is a reality denied to other countries which deny competition as part of their economic structure.

Thurman Arnold added:

> There are two principal evils of concentrated economic power in a democracy. The first is the power of concentrated industry to charge administered prices rather than prices based on competitive demand. As a result, resources are not efficiently allocated; production is restricted and consumer wants go unfulfilled; and there is no incentive to reduce costs and to make innovation. A second evil is the tendency of such empires to swallow up local businesses and drain away local capital. Prior to the Depression this condition had advanced so far that our concentrated industrial groups had helped destroy their own markets by siphoning off the dollars that could have been a source of local purchasing power.

The supporters of an antimerger amendment also feared that the disappearance of local business through mergers would lead to a perilous accumulation of political power in the hands of a few corporate managers. These managers could manipulate their control over employees and economic resources so as to obtain decisions from political bodies that were based on the corporate rather than public interest. Thus small business and the consequent dispersion of economic power should be encouraged in order to protect political liberty.

THE CELLER–KEFAUVER AMENDMENT

The debate ended in December 1950 with the enactment of what has become known as the Celler–Kefauver Amendment. Three basic Congressional conclusions underlay the passage of this amendment to Sections 7 and 11 of the Clayton Act. First, Congress believed that there is a definite relationship between decentralized economic power and the preservation of democracy. Therefore, small business and the dispersion of economic power are salutary and should be encouraged. The free-enterprise, competitive system was being jeopardized by an increasing concentration of economic power which resulted in the elimination of small independent companies in industries which traditionally had been characterized by numerous small competitors. Second, experience had shown that the original Clayton Act was ineffective and that the Sherman Act alone was not capable of halting increasing concentration. Third, a complete ban on all mergers was not appropriate because some mergers are neutral with respect to competition and others might promote efficiency or increase competition or both. Furthermore, a complete prohibition of mergers would hinder free entry into and exit from various industries as well as the corollary freedom to buy and sell capital goods, thereby allocating capital to its most productive uses.

The substantive revisions contained in the Celler–Kefauver Amendment were changes in the wording of the first paragraph of Section 7. This paragraph follows. The words deleted from the original Section 7 are in brackets; the words added are italicized.

> No corporation engaged in commerce shall acquire, directly, or indirectly, the whole or any part of the stock or other share capital *and no corporation subject to the jurisdiction of the Federal Trade Commission shall acquire the whole or any part of the assets* of another corporation engaged also in commerce, where *in any line of commerce in any section of the country,* the effect of such acquisition may be [to] substantially *to* lessen competition [between the corporation whose stock is so acquired and the corporation making the acquisition or to restrain such commerce in any section or community,] or *to* tend to create a monopoly [of any line of commerce].

Congress intended that these additions and deletions change the original Section 7 in three ways. First, the addition of the words *the whole or any part of the assets* was intended to broaden the reach of Section 7 to include asset acquisitions, and thereby plug the loophole which had permitted circumvention of the original Section 7. The word *assets* is not defined in the statute. However, court decisions have made it clear that the word should be given broad and liberal interpretation. Thus, assets have been found to include intangible as well as tangible property. For example, acquisitions or transfers of copyrights, patents, trademarks, and trade names are considered assets for the purposes of Section 7.

The second major change was the deletion of the words *between the corporation whose stock is so acquired and the corporation making the acquisition.* This deletion was intended to make Section 7 clearly applicable to all types of mergers and acquisitions which have the effect of substantially lessening competition or tending to create a monopoly. Congress made this change in response to the belief expressed by the Federal Trade Commission that Section 7, as originally worded, applied only to horizontal mergers and not to vertical or conglomerate mergers, even if they substantially lessened competition. In addition, this deletion was intended to protect small business and to foster the retention of local control over industry. A literal application of the acquired–acquiring language would bar all mergers between competitors, regardless of their size, because the merger of two competing corporations always eliminates whatever degree of competition had existed between them. On the other hand, larger outside interests that were not competing in the local market could merge with a local company without violating the original Section 7. Thus the small independent business would disappear and control would shift outside of the community. According to Representative Celler:

> By striking this language [acquired–acquiring] small corporations with a relatively unimportant role in their respective lines of commerce will be able to merge with each other without raising legal doubts. At the same time, essential legal safeguards against large corporations making acquisitions are preserved and reenforced.

A few years later Representative Celler expanded this explanation:

> This new law does not prohibit all mergers; nor does it prohibit mergers between competitors where the effect on competition is not substantial. Imbedded in the legislative history is the principle that consolidations which enable smaller concerns in an industry to compete more effectively are in the public interest. At the same time the Act does not legalize mergers which were illegal under old section 7. Changes made by the new law were intended to enlarge the coverage of that section to apply to all types of corporate mergers and acquisitions—horizontal, vertical and conglomerate—which have the specified effects on competition.

The final major change was a modification of the standards for determining what constitutes an illegal merger. As passed in 1914, Section 7 contained three tests of illegality. Stock acquisitions were unlawful if their effect might be (1) to lessen competition substantially between the acquiring and acquired companies; (2) to restrain commerce in any section or community; or (3) to tend to create a monopoly of any line of commerce. Under the Celler–Kefauver Amendment an acquisition of stock or assets is illegal if "in any line of commerce in any section of the country, the effect of such acquisition may be substantially to lessen competition or to tend to create a monopoly." Congress neither adopted nor rejected any specific tests for determining the relevant product market (*line of commerce*) or the appropriate geographic market (*section of the county*) within which the anticompetitive effects of a merger are to be judged. Nor did it define the word *substantially*. However, Congress did set forth certain broad standards reflecting its general intent to guide subsequent interpretations by the FTC and the courts.

"MAY BE SUBSTANTIALLY TO LESSEN COMPETITION"

It was repeatedly emphasized that the amendment was intended to "arrest in their incipiency practices and acts which, if allowed to develop, would constitute unreasonable restraints of trade and monopolies." Thus, the emphasis is on reasonable *probability*. A merger need not in itself *actually* substantially lessen competition or create a monopoly. It is sufficient that the merger may produce one of those effects in the future. This rationale was intended to cope with the problem of a large concern that grows through a series of small acquisitions each of which is so minute as not to meet the Sherman Act's test of an unreasonable restraint of trade. If the cumulative effect of the series of acquisitions may be substantially to lessen competition or to tend to create a monopoly,

Section 7 is violated and the anticompetitive tendency can be stopped in its incipiency.

Representative Celler later pointed out that the law may be violated in other ways:

> by eliminating in whole or material part the competitive activity of an enterprise which has been a substantial factor in competition; by increasing the relative size of the enterprise making the acquisition to such a point that its advantage over its competitors threatens to be decisive; by unduly reducing the number of competing enterprises; or by establishing relationships between buyers and sellers which deprive their rivals of a fair opportunity to compete.

"ANY LINE OF COMMERCE"

On the subject of the definition of the relevant product market the report of the Senate Judiciary Committee stated, "It is intended that acquisitions which substantially lessen competition, as well as those which tend to create a monopoly, will be unlawful if they have the specified effect in any line of commerce, whether or not that line of commerce is a large part of the business of any of the corporations involved in the acquisition." The House committee report added, "the test . . . is not intended to be applicable only where the specified effect may appear on a Nation-wide or industry-wide scale. The purpose of the bill is to protect competition in each line of commerce in each section of the country." The House committee gave the following illustration:

> If, for example, one or a number of raw-material producers purchases firms in a fabricating field (a "forward vertical" acquisition), and if as a result thereof competition in that fabricating field is substantially lessened in any section of the country, the law would be violated, even though there did not exist any competition between the acquiring (raw material) and the acquired (fabricating) firms. The same principles would, of course, apply to backward vertical and conglomerate acquisitions and mergers.

"ANY SECTION OF THE COUNTRY"

The Senate Judiciary Committee offered the following standard to guide interpretation of what constitutes the relevant geographic market or "section of the country."

> What constitutes a section will vary with the nature of the product. Owing to the differences in the size and character of markets, it would be meaningless, from an economic point of view, to attempt to apply for all products a uniform definition of section, whether such a definition were based upon miles, population, income, or any other unit of measurement. A section which would be economically significant for a heavy, durable product, such as large machine tools, might well be meaningless for a light product, such as milk.
>
> As the Supreme Court stated in *Standard Oil Co.* v. *U.S.* (337 U.S. 293), "Since it is the preservation of competition which is at stake, the significant proportion of coverage is that within the area of effective competition."

> In determining the area of effective competition for a given product, it will be necessary to decide what comprises an appreciable segment of the market. An appreciable segment of the market may not only be a segment which is largely segregated from, independent of, or not affected by the trade in that product in other parts of the country.
>
> It should be noted that although the section of the country in which there may be a lessening of competition will normally be one in which the acquired company or the acquiring company may do business, the bill is broad enough to cope with a substantial lessening of competition in any other section of the country as well.

Thus, the geographic market in each case is not to be determined by geographical boundaries but rather by the realities of competition.

SUMMARY CHECKLIST

If we synthesize these guidelines with the language of the first paragraph of Section 7 as it was amended by the Celler–Kefauver Act, the following checklist emerges to assist in determining whether a particular acquisition violates Section 7.

At the outset four jurisdictional prerequisites must be satisfied. First, the requirement is clear that both the acquiring and acquired firms must be corporations. Acquisitions by individuals or partnerships may be attacked under other antitrust provisions, but not under Section 7. A corporation cannot, however, avoid the proscription of Section 7 by use of a noncorporate dummy. As in other fields of the law, courts and commissions have looked through form to substance. Thus, in one early case, the Federal Trade Commission held that an acquisition of a corporation by another corporation was illegal even though initially the acquired company was purchased by the president of the acquiring company in his capacity as an individual.

Second, Section 7 requires as a condition of its applicability that both corporations be engaged in interstate commerce. This restriction is more apparent than real, however, because almost any activity across state borders—for example, two or three sales over a two-year period—forms the basis for finding a company so engaged. Also, it is only requisite that the corporations be engaged in commerce, not that anticompetitive effects be demonstrated in interstate commerce.

Third, though the phrase *acquisition of assets* would appear to require a company to obtain title to the assets involved, it has been held to the contrary. Thus, a twenty-year lease of an oil refinery has been held to be an *acquisition of assets,* as has a contract for the exclusive right to license the film inventory of a major motion picture studio to local television stations.

Finally, the phrase *no corporation subject to the jurisdiction of the Federal Trade Commission shall acquire the whole or any part of the assets of another corporation. . . .* presents problems of dual jurisdiction between administrative agencies. The question of whether, if a regulatory agency approves an acquisition of companies operating within its jurisdiction, the FTC or the Justice Department are powerless to challenge the possible anticompetitive effects of the merger, has been examined in several recent Supreme Court cases. These cases will be discussed in a subsequent chapter. Suffice it to say that a merger between firms in a regulated industry presents special problems of jurisdiction which should be carefully analyzed before commitments are made.

If all of these prerequisites have been satisfied the next step in determining the legality of a merger is to delineate the relevant markets within which the probability of a substantial lessening of competition or a tendency to monopoly is to be judged. There will be both a product market (*line of commerce*) and a geographic market (*section of the country*). The product market may consist of one or a number of products or services offered by either the acquired or the acquiring company. The geographic market is determined by ascertaining the area in which the acquired company, the acquiring company, or both companies conduct operations.

The definition of the relevant product and geographic markets is normally the major issue in a merger case. Because the character of these markets often determines the extent of the competitive effects by which the merger will be judged, tremendous amounts of time and money have frequently been expended to produce sophisticated economic analysis showing that these markets should be framed in terms favorable to the company attacked.

The importance of market definition to the testing of competitive effect can be demonstrated by a brief example. Suppose that two dairies which produce only fluid milk for sale only within the city limits of San Francisco have merged. Suppose also that together they account for 40 per cent of the sales in that city. If the two dairies were to prevail in their argument that the product market should be defined as all dairy products, including ice cream, butter, and cheese, their market share might drop to 15 per cent, because they are engaged only in the sale of fluid milk. Similarly, if they were also to prevail in their argument that the geographic market should be the Bay area rather than the ctiy of San Francisco, their market share might drop even further, to 5 per cent. No economic training is necessary to conclude that a merger affecting only 5 per cent of the market is far less likely to have adverse competitive effects than one affecting 40 per cent of the market.

Unfortunately, the preceding example is deceptive in its definition of the product market. Naturally, the government is interested in framing the market narrowly, and because Section 7 speaks in terms of "any line of commerce in any section of the country," the government is frequently able to prevail. In the horizontal merger of the two dairies described, the product market probably would be defined as the sale of fluid milk. Of course, a company should, in most cases, argue for a broader market definition, but it should be recognized that the chance of success is limited.

Once the relevant product and geographic markets have been established, the legality of the merger can be measured against its probable effect of substantially lessening competition or tending to create a monopoly. The factors to be considered include the proportion of the relevant market held by the acquiring and the acquired companies, the economic size and strength of the particular market involved, the trend in the industry with respect to concentration, the ease with which new companies may enter the market, and the probable cumulative effects if the merger being examined is one of a series of mergers. Finally, the possible presence of a defense to a charge of Section 7 illegality should be examined. These defenses will be discussed in a subsequent chapter.

THE DU PONT–G.M. CASE

The Supreme Court's first decision involving Section 7 after enactment of the Celler–Kefauver Amendment came in the case of *United States* v. *E. I. du Pont de Nemours & Co.* The Justice Department had filed suit in 1949 against the Du Pont Company, General Motors, United Rubber Company, certain holding companies and members of the Du Pont family under Section 1 and 2 of the Sherman Act and Section 7 of the Clayton Act. Among other things the suit charged Du Pont with acquiring a 23 per cent stock interest in General Motors and using that interest to obtain an illegal preference over its competition in the sale to General Motors of its products—especially fabrics, finishes, and chemicals—and a further illegal preference in the development of chemical discoveries made by General Motors. The Supreme Court held that the purchase by Du Pont in 1917–1919 of a 23 per cent stock interest in General Motors constituted a violation of Section 7 as originally enacted because the stock acquisition gave Du Pont a preferred position as a supplier of General Motors.

Although the Court's decision was based on Section 7 as it stood before the passage of the 1950 amendment, it is significant today for two reasons. First, the Court ruled that, because there is no statute of limitations for violations of Section 7, an action can be instituted at any time the incipient danger becomes apparent, when the acquisition is first made or years later when the use that is made of an acquisition reveals incipient dangers. Mr. Justice Brennan, speaking for the Court, wrote:

> To accomplish the congressional aim, the Government may proceed *at any time* that an acquisition may be said with reasonable probability to contain a threat that it may lead to a restraint of commerce or tend to create a monopoly of a line of commerce. Even when the purchase is solely for investment, the plain language of §7 contemplates an action at any time the stock is used to bring about or in attempting to bring about the substantial lessening of competition.

Although such an attack on a merger that occurred years earlier is a rarity, the so-called backward-sweep doctrine has been reaffirmed, at least in dictum, in a case arising under the amended Section 7. Thus, its possible use should be considered seriously, particularly by large companies that have grown through successive acquisitions. As Mr. Justice Burton warned in his dissent from the court's opinion:

> It now becomes apparent for the first time that §7 has been a sleeping giant all along. Every corporation which has acquired a stock interest in another corporation after the enactment of the Clayton Act in 1914, and which has had business dealings with that corporation is exposed, retroactively, to the bite of the newly discovered teeth of §7.

The *Du Pont–G.M.* suit was also the first case that presented the Supreme Court with the question of whether the original Section 7 applied only to horizontal acquisitions or whether it also applied to vertical acquisitions. The government had not invoked Section 7 against vertical acquisitions during the thirty-five years before this suit was filed, and the FTC had stated that Section 7 did not apply to vertical acquisitions until the passage of the Celler–Kefauver Amendment. Nevertheless, the Court rejected the commission position and held that the original Section 7 does apply to vertical as well as horizontal acquisitions. Thus, vertical acquisitions which were completed before 1950 were subject to challenge under the original Section 7.

THE BROWN SHOE CASE

The case of *Brown Shoe Company* v. *United States* provided the Supreme Court with its first opportunity to render a detailed analysis of the scope and purposes of the Celler–Kefauver amendment. In 1956 Brown Shoe Company, the fourth-largest shoe manufacturer and retailer, acquired the G. R. Kinney Company, one of the largest independent retail shoe store chains and manufacturers of shoes. The government charged that the merger violated Section 7 in three ways, (1) through the vertical combination of Brown's manufacturing facilities with Kinney's retail stores, (2) through the horizontal merger of the retail outlets of both companies, and (3) through the horizontal merger of the manufacturing facilities of both companies.

The Supreme Court began its analysis of the case with an extensive review of the legislative history of the Celler–Kefauver Amendment. It concluded that although Congress had not provided precise standards for courts to apply in judging the legality of particular mergers, it had expressed a consistent point of view. "The dominant theme pervading Congressional consideration of the 1950 amendments was a fear of what was considered to be a rising tide of economic concentration in the American economy." Furthermore, Congress clearly had rejected, as inappropriate to the problem it sought to remedy, the application to Section 7 cases of standards for judging the legality of mergers adopted by the courts in cases arising under the Sherman Act. Thus, the problem under the Celler–Kefauver Amendment was to develop standards applicable to cases, such as *Brown Shoe,* where the effect on competition was "neither of monopoly nor de minimis proportions." These new standards should implement the Congressional desire to arrest in their incipiency mergers which "may" lessen competition. In other words, as Mr. Chief Justice Warren stated, the amendment was concerned "with probabilities not certainties."

After gleaning this Congressional guidance from the amendment's legislative history, the Court considered the vertical and horizontal aspects of the Brown–Kinney merger separately. Mr. Chief Justice Warren noted that in evaluating both aspects of the acquisitions, a necessary predicate to a finding of a violation of the amended Clayton Act is the determination of the relevant product and geographic markets within which the merger's effects are to be appraised.

The Court enunciated the following guidelines for determining the boundaries of the relevant product market under amended Section 7. "The outer boundaries of a product market," it said, are determined by "the reasonable interchangeability of use or the cross-elasticity of demand between the product itself and substitutes for it." The Court quickly added, however, that "within this broad market, well-defined submarkets may exist which, in themselves, constitute product markets for antitrust purposes." The boundaries of these submarkets were to be defined by certain "practical indicia," including industry or public recognition of the submarket as a separate economic entity, peculiar characteristics and uses, unique production facilities, distinct customers, distinct prices, sensitivity to price changes, and specialized vendors. It is necessary to examine the effects of a merger in connection with every economically significant product submarket, for if there is a reasonable probability that the merger will lessen competition substantially in any one submarket, the merger is unlawful.

Applying these principles, men's, women's, and children's shoes were found to constitute submarkets, because each had separate manufacturing facilities, a distinct class of customers, and public recognition as separate entities. The Court refused to refine further the product market to create submarkets for lower- and higher-priced shoes because it believed that shoes of different prices were in effective competition with each other for the purchaser's dollar. However, the Court was careful to point out that, in other cases, price–quality differences "may be of importance in determining the likely effect of a merger. But the boundaries of the relevant market must be drawn with sufficient breadth to include the competing products of each of the merging companies and to recognize competition where, in fact, competition exist." Brown Shoe's contentions that further age and sex distinctions should have been recognized in defining the product market were also rejected as inappropriate.

The approach used in *Brown Shoe* to determine the appropriate geographic market was essentially the same as that used to determine the relevant product market. Just as a product submarket was to be considered the appropriate "line of commerce," a geographic submarket was to be considered the appropriate "section of the country." A "pragmatic, factual approach" is to be applied in defining the relevant market, not a "formal, legalistic one." Thus, the geographic market must "correspond to the commercial realities of the industry and be economically significant." Consequently, the geographic market may vary from the entire nation to a single metropolitan area. Moreover, because Section 7 speaks of "*any* section of the country":

> The fact that two merging firms have competed directly on the horizontal level in but a fraction of the geographic markets in which either has operated does not, in itself, place their merger outside the scope of Section 7. . . . If anti-competitive effects of a merger are probable in any significant market, the merger—at least to that extent—is proscribed.

The Court gave the following illustration:

> If two retailers, one operating primarily in the eastern half of the Nation, and the other operating largely in the West, competed in but two mid-Western cities, the fact that the latter outlets represented but a small share of each company's business would not immunize the merger in those markets in which competition might be adversely affected.

The Court agreed with the parties that insofar as the vertical aspect of the merger was concerned, the relevant geographic market was the entire nation because the relationships of product value, bulk, weight, and consumer demand enable manufacturers to distribute their shoes on a nationwide basis. With regard to the horizontal aspect of the merger, the Court found the relevant product markets to be metropolitan areas with populations exceeding 10,000 in which both Brown and Kinney had retail stores because: "Such markets are large enough to include the downtown shops and suburban shopping centers in areas contiguous to the city, which are the important competitive factors, and yet are small enough to exclude stores beyond the immediate environs of the city, which are of little competitive significance."

Once the product and geographic markets have been delineated, an analysis must be made to determine if the effect of the merger "may be substantially to lessen competition, or to tend to create a monopoly" in the relevant markets. Mr. Chief Justice Warren defined the factors to be considered when the possible competitive effects of a merger are examined:

> Congress indicated plainly that a merger had to be functionally viewed, in the context of its particular industry. That is, whether the consolidation was to take place in an industry that was fragmented rather than concentrated, that had seen a recent trend toward domination by a few leaders or had remained fairly consistent in its distribution of market shares among the participating companies, that had experienced easy access to markets by

> suppliers and easy access to suppliers by buyers or had witnessed foreclosure of business, that had witnessed the ready entry of new competition or the erection of barriers to prospective entrants, all were aspects, varying in importance with the merger under consideration, which would properly be taken into account.

Applying these considerations to the vertical merger between Brown's manufacturing facilities and Kinney's retail stores, the Court noted that vertical arrangements foreclose a share of the market otherwise open to competitors and result in a "diminution of the vigor of competition." Thus, the size of the share of the market foreclosed—here 1.2 per cent of the final retail market by dollar volume—is "an important consideration" in determining the probable anticompetitive effect of the merger. Another important factor, the Court continued, is the "very nature and purpose of the arrangement." Brown's acquisition of Kinney was a consolidation between the fourth-largest manufacturer of shoes and the largest chain of family shoe stores in the nation. "Thus, in this industry, no merger between a manufacturer and an independent retailer could involve a larger potential market foreclosure." Moreover, it was apparent to the Court both from Brown's past history of vigorously pursuing vertical integration and from the testimony of Brown's president, that Brown would use its ownership of Kinney to force Brown shoes into the Kinney stores. Thus, the Court concluded that the merger was "quite analogous" to a contract involving a tying clause (a tie-in sale occurs when a party refuses to sell one item—the tying product—unless the purchaser also agrees to take another distinct item—the tied product) and noted that the Court had already held that because such tying contracts are inherently anticompetitive "its use by an established company is likely substantially to lessen competition although only a relatively small amount of commerce is affected."

The final factor considered by the Court was the existence of a "definite trend" toward vertical integration by large shoe manufacturers which was the result of deliberate policies of Brown and other leading shoe manufacturers. The result of this trend was the foreclosure of independent manufacturers from markets otherwise open to them. Brown argued that the merger did not violate Section 7 because the shoe industry was presently composed of a large number of manufacturers and retailers who were highly competitive despite the trend toward vertical integration. The Court rejected this argument for two reasons. First, because "remaining vigor cannot immunize a merger if the trend in that industry is toward oligopoly." Moreover, the Court believed that Section 7 requires not only an examination of the probable effects of the merger upon the economics of the particular markets affected but also an examination of "its probable effects upon the economic way of life sought to be preserved by Congress. Congress was desirous of preventing the formation of further oligopolies with their attendant adverse effects upon local control of industry and upon smaller businesses. Where an industry was composed of numerous independent units, Congress appeared anxious to preserve this structure." Brown's acquisition of Kinney would exacerbate the trend toward integration and destroy the fragmented character of the shoe industry.

Thus, the Court held that the vertical aspect of the merger violated Section 7 because the probable effect of the cumulative series of vertical mergers in the shoe industry, if left unchecked, would be "substantially to lessen competition." The Court noted, "We reach this conclusion because the trend toward vertical integration in the shoe industry, when combined with Brown's avowed policy of forcing its own shoes upon its retail subsidiaries, may foreclose competition from a substantial share of the markets for men's, women's, and children's shoes, without producing any counteracting, competitive, economic, or social advantages."

The acquisition of Kinney by Brown also resulted in a horizontal combination at both the manufacturing and retailing levels in their businesses. However, the Supreme Court did not consider the merger of manufacturing facilities because the government did not appeal the lower court's finding that the combination of Brown's 5 per cent share of the nationwide manufacturing market with Kinney's 0.5 per cent share was economically too insignificant to come within the prohibitions of Section 7. On the other hand, the Court did examine the merger of Brown's 1,230 retail outlets with Kinney's 350 stores.

As mentioned earlier, the relevant product markets were found to be men's, women's, and children's shoes. The geographic market was defined as metropolitan areas having populations in excess of 10,000 in which both firms had retail outlets. A statistical survey showed that in the 118 such metropolitan areas, the combined market shares of Brown and Kinney in the sale of one of the relevant products exceeded 5 per cent. In forty-seven cities, their share exceeded 5 per cent in all three products.

As a preliminary procedural matter, the Court stated that although the 118 relevant geographic markets varied in size, climate, and wealth, a detailed analysis of each market is not required if, as in this case, the "basic issues . . . may be determined through study of a fair sample" because Section 7 speaks of probable anticompetitive effects in "*any* section of the country." Moreover, "there is no reason to protract already complex antitrust litigation by detailed analysis of peripheral economic facts."

Chief Justice Warren began his discussion of the horizontal probable effect by announcing that the market share which companies may control by merging is "one of the most important factors" to be considered in determining the effects of the merger. Shoe retailing is a fragmented industry. Therefore, a merger giving 5 per cent control to Brown would be substantial. Furthermore, the Court expressed the fear that if it approved this merger it might be forced to approve all subsequent mergers in which the resulting market share did not exceed 5 per cent, thereby fostering the oligopoly which Congress sought to prevent.

As a second objection to the horizontal merger, the Chief Justice pointed out that a large national chain has the potential to drive smaller competitors out of business. It can insulate selected stores from competition in particular locations, and it can, through its ability rapidly to change styles in footwear, render independents incapable of maintaining a competitive inventory.

The Court further objected to the competitive advantages that a large chain of retailers integrated with manufacturers would possess. By eliminating wholesalers and increasing volume, the chain retail outlets could sell at lower prices than competing independent businesses. After admitting that such a chain operation might be beneficial to consumers and that the Clayton Act was designed to protect competition, and not competitors, the Court concluded, "But we cannot fail to recognize Congress' desire to promote competition through the protection of viable, small, locally owned businesses. Congress appreciated that occasional higher costs and prices might result from the maintenance of fragmented industries and markets. It resolved these competing considerations in favor of decentralization. We must give effect to that decision."

Finally, as in the vertical aspect of the merger, the Court stressed the trend toward concentration in the retail shoe industry and the Congressional mandate to stop concentration in its incipiency. The merger of Brown and Kinney joined the largest single group of retail stores which were still independent of a large manufacturer, with an already substantial aggregation of retail outlets controlled by Brown. As a result of the merger, Brown moved into second place nationally in terms of retail shoe stores, with 1,600 outlets under its control, or about 7.2 per cent of the nation's retail shoe stores. In the light of this trend toward concentration, the Court held that the horizontal aspect of the merger violated Section 7 and that this case was "an appropriate place at which to call a halt." Consequently, Brown Shoe was ordered to divest itself of Kinney as soon as possible.

All seven Justices who participated in the case (Justices Frankfurter and White took no part in its consideration) agreed that the Brown–Kinney merger violated Section 7 because there was a reasonable probability that it might lessen competition substantially. However, Justices Clark and Harlan disagreed with the majority's delineation of the relevant product and geographic markets.

Mr. Justice Clark felt that the Court should avoid "splintering the product line" by defining it as "shoes of all types" because after the merger Kinney stores would handle the full line of shoes manufactured by Brown. He also believed that the proper geographic market for the horizontal aspects of the merger should have been defined as the "entire country" because Brown's business was on a national scale and its policy of integrating manufacturing and retailing was also on a nationwide basis.

Mr. Justice Harlan found it necessary to review only the vertical aspects of the merger and agreed with the majority that the relevant geographic market was the entire country. However, on the issue of the proper product market with respect to the merger between Brown's manufacturing facilities and Kinney's retail outlets, he argued that the relevant market "might more accurately be defined as the complete wearing-apparel shoe market" because shoe manufacturers had the ability to adapt or convert their plants and machines so as to manufacture varying goods and types of shoes.

The *Brown Shoe* decision was quickly hailed as a landmark development in the field of antimerger enforcement. Most commentators saw the opinion as a strong precedent for the proposition that the Supreme Court would evaluate the competitive significance of a merger by analyzing a complex of facts rather than by developing statistical standards of illegality. The emphasis was on the reasonable inferences to be drawn from market structure, market behavior, and market performance in the context of the patterns of competition prevailing in the relevant industries and markets. An examination of market structure would include consideration of market shares, market ranks, concentration ratios, merger trends, and ease of entry into the market. Market behavior is comprised principally of the techniques, methods, and dimensions of competition in the market; and market performance concerns the contributions of the merging firms and the industry at large to the economy in terms of employment, growth, and innovation.

Other commentators criticized the decision on two grounds. First, they objected to the Court's equating "incipiency" with a "trend" in the industry because they believed this equation caused the Court's ultimate conclusion of illegality to rest not on the facts of the Brown acquisition, but on the general trend toward concentration in the shoe industry. Although Brown's prior acquisitions and its purchase of Kinney were a part of this trend, the commentators saw an implication that lacking history of mergers in the industry generally and on the part of Brown in particular, an acquisition of such relatively small dimensions might not violate Section 7. Thus, Brown had suffered not so much because of its own wrongdoing but because of a trend in the industry over which Brown had no control.

The other major criticism of the *Brown Shoe* decision was that the Court was not concerned with the preservation of competition, but rather with the preservation of competitors. It was pointed out that the Court itself recognized that the horizontal merger of Brown's and Kinney's retail stores led to efficiencies which benefited consumers. Despite these efficiencies, the Court felt compelled to void the merger in order to protect small, less efficient businesses. Thus, rather than protecting and encouraging free competition—including the achievement of efficient use of all of our resources through merger—the Court was stifling competition to protect inefficiency.

15 Classification of Mergers

Whereas corporate law treats a corporate acquisition or merger in the light of the method of reaching its new form and its resulting tax consequence, if any, antitrust law, in its merger policies, tends to treat a corporate acquisition or merger in the light of its functional effect on competition. The purpose of governmental enforcement under Section 7 of the Clayton Act is to preserve and promote market structures conducive to competition. In determining the antitrust effect of a given merger or acquisition, one must look at the merger in the context of the particular market structure affected by that merger or acquisition. The type of merger determines the likelihood of a finding of illegality, as well as the method by which illegality will be determined.

Almost all economists and lawyers classify the different types of mergers into three broad categories: horizontal, vertical, and conglomerate. As will be seen, vertical mergers are subclassified into backward vertical integration and forward vertical integration. In addition, conglomerate mergers are generally classified in three subcategories: geographic market-extension, product-extension, and the "pure" conglomerate merger, that is, a merger in which there is no functional economic relationship between the acquiring firm and the acquired firm. The definition and the legal standard applicable to each of these categories will be discussed more fully later.

HORIZONTAL MERGERS

A horizontal merger is a merger in which one company acquires all or part of the stock or assets of another company which is a direct competitor in the same product line and in the same geographic area. Thus, suppose one auto parts retailing company located in the Detroit area were to acquire all the stock or all the assets of another auto parts retailing company also located in the Detroit area. The effect of this merger would eliminate the competition between these two companies in the Detroit area. The legality of the merger would depend on the market structure in the retail auto parts industry and on the relative market shares previously held by each of the companies.

The United States Supreme Court thoroughly discussed the problems attending a horizontal merger in *Brown Shoe Co.* v. *United States.* The Brown Shoe Company, a manufacturer and retailer of shoes, and the G. R. Kinney Company, also a manufacturer and retailer, attempted to merge through an exchange of stock. Because of the market structure of the industry and the relative market shares of the two companies involved, the Court ruled that the merger violated Section 7 of the Clayton Act. Chief Justice Warren analyzed the problem as follows:

> An economic arrangement between companies performing similar functions in the production or sale of comparable goods or services is characterized as "horizontal." The effect on competition of such an arrangement depends, of course, upon its character and scope. Thus, its validity in the face of antitrust laws will depend upon such factors as: the relative size and number of the parties to the arrangement; whether it allocates shares of the market among the parties; whether it fixes prices at which the parties will sell their product; or whether it absorbs or insulates competitors.

The Brown Shoe Company, with over 1,230 owned, operated, or controlled outlets, was the third-largest seller of shoes in dollar volume in the nation. Kinney, with over 350 retail outlets, was the eighth-largest seller by dollar volume. The Court noted three additional factors which significantly contributed to the determination of an illegal merger: (1) the shoe retailing industry was very fragmented, with many sellers; (2) there was a tendency of concentration in the industry, with an increasing number of retail outlets merging or being purchased by a larger company; and (3) the result of the merger would create a large national retailing chain with an integrated manufacturing operation.

The development of horizontal merger law continued in 1963 with the Court's decision in *United States* v. *Philadelphia National Bank,* in which that bank had attempted to merge with the Girard & Trust Corn Exchange Bank, both of which were located in the Philadelphia area. The combination of these two banks would have produced a market share of 36 per cent of the total assets and 34 per cent of the total deposits, creating the largest bank in the four-county area. The Court took a stern look at this horizontal merger which would have so strongly affected the market structure and the amount of competition in the banking industry. In its view, the effect of the merger was "inherently likely to lessen competition substantially. . . . The merger . . . will result in a single bank's controlling at least 30% of the commercial banking business. . . . Without attempting to specify the smallest market share which would still be considered to threaten undue concentration, we are clear that 30% presents that threat." Thus, the effect of this decision is to raise an inference that any horizontal merger which creates a combined market share of 30 per cent or more is illegal.

The emphasis on the market structure and on the relative shares of [illegible] *Brewing* case. In an industry [illegible] concentration and a decrease [illegible] Company attempted to [illegible] combination of these com- [illegible] beer in the nation and the [illegible]. Because of the marked thirty-year [illegible] brewers and the sharp rise in the share of the [illegible] brewers, the Court concluded that the merger was [illegible]

[illegible] toward concentration in an industry was also a very signifi- [illegible] factor in *United States* v. *Von's Grocery Company,* a horizontal merger case in which Von's had acquired Shopping Boy Food Store, a direct competitor of Von's in the Los Angeles area. The merger of these two local retail stores created the second-largest grocery chain in Los Angeles, with a market share of 7.5 per cent. In spite of this low market share percentage, the evidence showed that before the merger both companies had been expanding aggressively through internal growth. Moreover, the number of independent grocery store owners had been decreasing rapidly. The Court held that the trend toward concentration in this industry was sufficiently steadfast so that the Von's merger could not be given judicial approval.

The effect of these decisions has been to inject extreme caution and reluctance in any merger plans involving direct competitors. In light of the government's strong emphasis on market structure, industry trends, and relative shares of the market, most businessmen and lawyers were legitimately anxious about the legality of any merger proposals they were contemplating. Even assuming that the merger might be upheld eventually the cost and time consumed by the necessary litigation was an additional factor to consider.

To add clarity to the situation, the Department of Justice, in May of 1968, issued its Merger Guidelines, in which it outlined its standards for determining whether to oppose corporate acquisitions or mergers under Section 7 of the Clayton Act. With respect to horizontal mergers, the government vowed to uphold the following purposes:

(i) preventing elimination as an independent business entity of any company likely to have been a substantial competitive influence in a market;

(ii) preventing any company or small group of companies from obtaining a position of dominance in a market;

(iii) preventing significant increases in concentration in a market; and

(iv) preserving significant possibilities for eventual deconcentration in a concentrated market.

Businessmen and lawyers can find the particular guidelines described in the three categories of the merging firms' market shares, grouped by size. In a highly concentrated market—that is, in which the four largest firms have 75 per cent or more of the market—the government ordinarily will challenge any merger in which the companies possess the following percentages of the market:

Acquiring Firm	Acquired Firm
4%	4% or more
10%	2% or more
15% or more	1% or more

In a less highly concentrated market—that is, in which the four largest firms have less than 75 per cent—the government will ordinarily challenge any merger if it falls within the following percentages:

Acquiring Firm	Acquired Firm
5%	5% or more
10%	4% or more
15%	3% or more
20%	2% or more
25% or more	1% or more

In a market characterized by a trend toward concentration, an additional, stricter standard than the preceding percentages rule will be applied. If the aggregate market share of any grouping of the eight largest companies in the market (or a grouping of a lesser number), is determined to have increased its aggregate market share by 7 per cent or more in the past five to ten years, then the industry comes under this category. If one of those eight largest companies acquires a company who has 2 per cent or more of the market, the government ordinarily will challenge the acquisition. For example, if Acme Corporation, one of a group of the eight largest companies in the toy manufacturing industry whose aggregate sales have increased 7.5 per cent over the past ten years, attempts to acquire ToyCo, a company with 2.3 per cent of the toy market, the government ordinarily will challenge that acquisition.

The net effect of the judicial decisions and the administrative guidelines in respect to horizontal mergers is to give the lawyer and the businessman a meaningful standard from which they can consider intelligently the pros and cons of merging and, with some knowledgeability, try to predict whether or not any merger will be challenged by the government.

VERTICAL MERGERS

A vertical merger is a merger in which one company acquires all or part of the stock or assets of another company who is a customer or supplier of the acquired company. If the acquiring company integrates *vertical integration,* that is, within the line of production from raw material to final customer purchase, the manufacturer is integrating his operations forward, or toward the final customer.

On the other hand, if the auto parts manufacturer were to acquire a metal fabricating plant which normally supplies him with the basic material for the manufacture of mufflers, it would be called a backward vertical integration. The result of this acquisition could eliminate all competition as to which fabricating plant would supply the manufacturer with his basic materials. In addition, the presence of this integrated company might present barriers to entry into the market for other companies who might reasonably believe that they must also have a fully integrated business in order to compete. Lacking the financial resources for the entire integrated operation, they stay out of the market entirely.

Whether or not a particular vertical, forward or backward, acquisition will violate Section 7 of the Clayton Act will ultimately depend upon market shares of the merging companies and upon the conditions of entry into the market which already exists.

Chief Justice Earl Warren, in discussing the vertical aspects of the *Brown Shoe* case, described a vertical merger as follows:

> Economic arrangements between companies in a supplier-customer relationship are characterized as "vertical." The primary vice of a vertical merger or other arrangement tying a customer to a supplier is that, by foreclosing the competitors of either party from a segment of the market otherwise open to them, the arrangement may act as a "clog on competition" . . . which deprive[s] . . . rivals of a fair opportunity to compete.

The thrust of Section 7 and the *Brown* case is to preclude any vertical merger in which "foreclosure of the market" is sufficient to lessen competition substantially or tend to create a monopoly. Given this end result, the important determination, of course, is to resolve what types of vertical mergers violate that standard.

In *Brown* the Court emphasized the nature of the economic arrangement, that is, whether it would eliminate all competition in purchases of the two firms, or perhaps, whether it would only restrict it. As was also true in horizontal mergers, any trend toward concentration in the industry is a very important factor in determining the legality of a vertical merger. The facts of *Brown* were that Brown Shoe Company was the fourth-largest manufacturer and that Kinney, with over 350 retail outlets, owned and operated the largest independent chain of family shoe stores in the nation. Thus, the Court held, "[I]n this industry, no merger between a manufacturer and an independent retailer could involve a larger potential market foreclosure."

Perhaps one of the most surprising vertical merger cases was that of *United States* v. *E. I. du Pont de Nemours & Co.,* in which the government challenged that company's acquisition of 23 per cent of General Motors' stock thirty years after it has acquired it. "The fire that was kindled in 1917 continues to smolder." This time lapse did not preclude the suit because, in the Court's view, the important determination is whether the acquisition tended substantially to lessen competition *at the time the lawsuit is brought.* The Supreme Court determined that Du Pont's acquisition of the General Motors' stock was unlawful because it gave Du Pont an unfair and anticompetitive advantage in being the leading supplier of automotive finishes and fabrics to General Motors. The end result was a court order requiring Du Pont to divest itself of all its holdings of G.M.'s stock.

In a forward vertical integration acquisition, *Reynolds Aluminum,* the U.S. Court of Appeals for the District of Columbia concentrated on the factor that the assimilation of capital structures of the two companies created a substantial elimination of competition and established barriers to entry because of their integrated operation. Reynolds Aluminum, the largest producer of aluminum foil, had acquired Arrow Brands, Inc., one of the eight aluminum converters who transformed the aluminum foil into decorative foil used essentially in the florist trade. Immediately eliminated was all competition as to which manufacturer would sell its foil to the Arrow converting plant, a company which already had 33.3 per cent of the florist trade. Even more important was the court's fear that the combined large capital structure opened the possibility that the merged company would be able to sell at or below cost and thereby drive out all competition.

The Justice Department, in its Merger Guidelines, announced that it would challenge those vertical mergers that were likely to raise barriers to entry in the market. The government used a market share analysis, applied to both the supplying and the purchasing firms' markets to establish its standard. If the supplying firm has 10 per cent or more of the market and the purchasing firm makes up 6 per cent or more of that supplier's market, the government ordinarily will challenge it.

In addition, in mergers not subject to challenge under the preceding standard, the government will challenge the acquisition if it raises entry barriers in the purchasing firm's market by conferring on him a significant advantage over unintegrated or partly integrated existing competitors or potential competitors. Also, if there is a significant trend of concentration in the industry, almost every merger would be suspect to the government.

Again, by its preventive guidelines, the Justice Department seeks to forewarn lawyers and businessmen as to those vertical mergers which will be challenged by judicial prosecution.

CONGLOMERATE MERGERS

A conglomerate merger is a merger in which one company acquires all or part of the stock or assets of another company which is not in a competitive relation and which does not have a customer–supplier relationship with the acquiring company. There are three subcategories of conglomerate mergers: pure, geographic market extension and product extension. Prior to 1950 there was little discussion and almost no law on conglomerate mergers. At that time the Clayton Act was generally believed to apply to horizontal stock acquisitions. Section 7 only proscribed stock acquisitions which would "lessen competition between the corporation whose stock is so acquired and the corporation making the acquisition." To help curb the rising number of mergers and acquisitions, Congress sought to pass a law which would apply "to all types of mergers and acquisitions, vertical and conglomerate as well as horizontal, which have the specified effects of substantially lessening competition . . . or tending to create a monopoly." Implementation of this purpose came in 1950 in the Celler–Kefauver Amendment to the Section 7 of the Clayton Act. This amendment sought to preserve the American ideal that "[c]ompetition is likely to be greatest when there are many sellers, none of which has any significant market share." It was only after this amendment had been in law for several years that the validity of conglomerate mergers was litigated and the different judicial concepts of conglomerates emerged. In formulating the applicable legal standards the courts developed several subdivisions within the concept of conglomerate mergers.

If the products of the two firms are totally, functionally and economically, unrelated, the merger is termed a pure conglomerate merger. Thus, the acquisition of an electronics company by a soap distributor would come under this category. This is, perhaps, the true conglomerate. By the merger, the larger company diversifies into a multimarket enterprise. Yet it may be difficult to charge a lessening of competition because the two companies are not in a buyer–seller relationship, nor are their products functionally related. An attack may be based on the diversified company's inherent economic power with which it can substantially affect competition through a shift in its marketing techniques—for example, channeling all advertising to the promotion of one product. Or competition may be affected unlawfully by price cutting of one product line while at the same time, covering any deficits by profits in the other product lines. Ascertaining prospective standards for pure conglomerate mergers is most difficult. Of course, there is always the broad standard given in Section 7. In addition, the businessman and the lawyer can project the legal standards created for the other two types of conglomerates, a discussion of which follows, and, with the advice of expert antitrust counsel, project those standards to their own particular situation.

If two merging companies produce or sell the same products, but do so in different geographic areas, the resulting merger is a geographic market

le, if Tom Thumb Co., a frozen food distributor in
nd Indiana, acquires FreezCo., a frozen food dis-
it area, the resulting combination would be a
erger.

c-extension case, *United States* v. *El Paso Natu-*
he sole out-of-state supplier of natural gas to
assets of Pacific Northwest Pipeline Company,
ans-Rocky Mountain states, who had never been in
ia market. Emphasizing the strong potential for competition
was eliminated—the likelihood that Pacific Northwest would
enter the California market—the Court ruled that this acquisition violated Section 7 because, if permitted to exist, it would tend to create or maintain a monopoly for El Paso in the California market.

In 1966 the Federal Trade Commission ruled that National Tea Company violated Section 7 by its acquisition of 485 retail grocery stores, some 450 of which were located in areas in which National Tea had not previously operated. As was also noted in *Von's Grocery,* a very significant factor was the trend of a declining number of independently owned grocery stores. In addition, National Tea's expansion might effect higher prices, discriminating promotional allowances, and subsidization of price-cutting ventures at some of the stores. The commission repeated an oft-quoted axiom: "[c]ompetition is likely to be greatest where there are many sellers, none of which has any significant market share." The FTC did not require divestiture of the completed acquisitions; it did, however, prohibit any future acquisition by National Tea.

Significant factors already have been noted in judging geographic market-extension situations, that is, potential for future entry, barriers to entry, and anticompetitive effects created by a large conglomeration which can push its economic power to the fullest extent, leaving smaller companies to flounder in their attempts to remain competitive and at the same time earn a reasonable rate of return on their invested capital. These factors must be thoroughly re-examined and applied to any particular factual situation which may arise.

If two merging companies manufacture or distribute products that are functionally related to each other, in production and/or in distribution, the result is a product-extension type of conglomerate merger. To illustrate, if United Typewriter Company, an electric typewriter manufacturer, acquired AddCo, an electric adding machine manufacturer, the result would be a product-extension type of conglomerate merger. Whether or not this type of merger is challenged by the government will depend on market shares, industry trends, entry barriers, potential competition, and the potential for reciprocal buying.

The term *product-extension merger* was first coined by the Federal Trade Commission in the *Procter & Gamble* case. Procter & Gamble was a large, diversified manufacturer of low-priced household products. Thereafter it acquired Clorox, maker of a household bleach, a product that Procter & Gamble had previously not manufactured. The Court, noting that all liquid bleach was chemically identical, concentrated on the power of advertising and sales promotion which were available through the resources of Procter & Gamble. In addition, the Court believed that there was a strong possibility that Procter & Gamble, had it not acquired Clorox, would have itself entered the bleach market with a product of its own. Because the products were complementary and because the integration of distribution, promotion, and advertising was likely to discourage possible entrants into the market, the Court concluded that the acquisition violated Section 7 of the Clayton Act.

In a similar type of case, the Federal Trade Commission found that General Foods violated Section 7 when it acquired S.O.S. Company, a manufacturer of household steel wool pads. The anticompetitive effect was found in the integration of S.O.S.'s advertising budget into the vastly larger General Foods budget, thereby creating huge savings through volume discounts, to the strong economic detriment of Brillo, its chief competitor.

Reciprocal-buying ability, resulting from a conglomerate merger, was disapproved as violative of Section 7 in the *Consolidated Foods* case. Consolidated, a food distributor, acquired Gentry, Inc., a manufacturer of dehydrated onion and garlic. One of the two major producers of dehydrated onions and garlic, Gentry would sell to food processors who would use those items in preparing and packaging the food items. The food processors in turn would sell to the distributors, one of whom was Consolidated. The danger was that as the processors would seek orders from Consolidated, the distributor, they would attempt to reciprocate and place orders with Consolidated's subsidiary, Gentry. The effect was almost a tying relationship, that is, "I'll buy your processed food, if you will purchase my dehydrated onions." The Supreme Court clearly stated that once the probability of substantial reciprocal buying is created, the arrangement definitely violates Section 7 of the Clayton Act. The Justice Department, pursuant to its guideline, ordinarily will challenge an arrangement if it creates a significant danger of reciprocal buying. The department also will challenge any acquisition where it has been shown that actual reciprocal buying has occurred after the acquisition.

A relatively new field in conglomerates is that of the implications of joint ventures. In *United States* v. *Penn-Olin,* Pennsalt Chemicals Corporation and Olin Mathieson Chemical Corporation launched a joint venture, each contributing one half of the capital, to form the Penn-Olin Chemical Corporation to produce and sell sodium chlorate in the Southeastern United States. Neither of these two companies were in the sodium chlorate market prior to the joint venture. The Supreme Court ruled that Section 7 applied to joint ventures in general and to this one in particular in that it created barriers to entry by other companies and in that it foreclosed the likely possibility that the two parent companies would enter that same market. Of course, criteria must be set up for joint ventures that are different from those that exist for other types of mergers. A merger eliminates one of the two companies, whereas a joint venture creates a new competitive force. However, the traditional principles of raising entry barriers and foreclosing potential competition are especially applicable to this type of arrangement.

The classification of mergers is a very important determination. As we have seen, there are different standards and criteria to be applied in judging the lawfulness of the different types of mergers. An understanding of these different classifications and subcategories is essential to the development of the businessman's knowledge of mergers.

16 Relevant Market

Crucial to the outcome of any merger litigation is definition of the relevant market. Indeed, that determination may be the most critical factor, because it is within the context of a particular market that the courts will judge the effects of the merger on competition. Unless we know where to look, in other words, we cannot know what effect the merger will have or how substantial that effect will be. Moreover, until the extent of the market is defined, considerations which bear on the lawfulness of a merger, such as the degree of or trend toward concentration within an industry, cannot be measured. Because the merger of two firms in a larger market will seem to have less impact than the same merger in a smaller market, where the line is drawn may make all the difference to an ultimate verdict in favor of the merger.

Section 7 of the Clayton Act, as amended in 1950, prohibits those mergers which have certain specified illegal effects "in any line of commerce in any section of the country." Although the words *relevant market* never appear in the antitrust statutes themselves, it is clear that the words *line of commerce* and *section of the country* denote product and geographic markets whose boundaries must be determined prior to further antitrust analysis. As the Supreme Court has said, "determination of the relevant market is a necessary predicate to a finding of a violation of the Clayton Act because the threatened monopoly must be one which will substantially lessen competition 'within the area of effective competition.' Substantiality can be determined only in terms of the market affected."

The determination of both the product and geographic markets are often extremely difficult to make. The Attorney General's National Committee to Study the Antitrust Laws said in its 1955 report, "the 'market' is the sphere of competitive rivalry in which the crucial transfer of buyers' patronage from one supplier of goods or services to another can take place freely. The boundaries of an 'industry' or 'market' will often be uncertain and controversial, and a definition appropriate in one case may be inappropriate in another." Although the attorney general's committee was speaking of market definition for the purpose of measuring monopoly power, the same general statement still holds in analyzing market definition under Section 7 of the Clayton Act.

There is no single or simple test which will clearly demonstrate the existence of a particularly defined market upon which both the merging companies and the government will agree. For instance, if the merging companies produce the same or similar products, they may want to argue that their markets did not exist in the same geographic regions. The government will argue that the geographic area is broader than that contended for by the defendants in order to show that they were in fact competing. On the other hand, the merging companies may argue, depending on the nature of the industry, that the geographic market is national, because by having a large market in which to measure the effects of the merger it may prove to be inconsequential against an industrial backdrop of the entire United States. As in most aspects of antitrust law, therefore, the courts will look for some reasonable tests which will provide a fair basis for determining the actual effects the merger might have on competition. What these tests are and how they have been employed by the courts is the subject of this chapter.

PRODUCT MARKET

In its most concise definition of the product market, the Supreme Court said in the 1962 *Brown Shoe* case:

> The outer boundaries of the product market are determined by the reasonable interchangeability of use or the cross-elasticity of demand between the product itself and substitutes for it. However, within this broad market, well-defined submarkets may exist which, in themselves, constitute product markets for antitrust purposes. . . . The boundaries of such a submarket may be determined by examining such practical indicia as industry or public recognition of the submarket as a separate economic entity, the product's peculiar characteristics and uses, unique production facilities, distinct customers, distinct prices, sensitivity to price changes, and specialized vendors.

Following the 1950 amendment to Section 7 of the Clayton Act, the first case in which the Supreme Court examined the product market of two merging companies was *United States* v. *E. I. du Pont de Nemours & Co.* The issue in the case was "whether Du Pont's commanding position as General Motors' supplier of automotive finishes and fabrics was achieved on competitive merit alone, or because its acquisition of the General Motors' stock, and the consequent close intercompany relationship, led to the insulation of most of the General Motors market from free competition. . . ." Before a conclusion could be drawn, it was necessary to determine whether automotive finishes and fabrics as opposed to all finishes and fabrics, constitute a distinct line of commerce. The Supreme Court concluded they did:

> The record shows that automotive finishes and fabrics have sufficient peculiar characteristics and uses to constitute them products sufficiently distinct from

all other finishes and fabrics to make them a "line of commerce" within the meaning of the Clayton Act. . . . Thus, the bounds of the relevant market for the purposes of this case, are not coextensive with the total market for finishes and fabrics, but are coextensive with the automobile industry, the relevant market for automotive finishes and fabrics.

In judging that automotive fabrics and finishes constitute a separate line of commerce—a distinct relevant product market—the Court looked to Du Pont's own statement that its "largest single finish item" sold to G.M. "is a low-viscosity nitrocellulose lacquer, discovered and patented by Du Pont . . . , the invention and development of [which] represented a truly significant advance in the art of paint making and in the production of automobiles . . . [and] without [which] mass production of automobiles would not have been possible." With respect to fabrics, the Supreme Court noted Du Pont's testimony at trial that automotive fabrics differed, among others, from furniture fabrics. The director of sales said: "You see, in the automobile industry, each manufacturer uses a different construction. They all have their own peculiar ideas of what they want about these fabrics. Some want dyed backs, and some want different finishes, so you don't have any standard prices in the automobile industry."

The district court in its opinion following the original trial noted an extensive discussion of the technical problems of automobile finishes, that such finishes were required to last for the life of the automobile, have high gloss, adhere to metal undercoats, and be capable of application to the metal undercoats "on the assembly line in a matter of hours." The court went so far as to note that Du Pont's invention and development of automobile finishes "was one of the factors that made possible mass production of automobiles." Similarly, in its discussion of automobile fabrics, the district court suggested that a considerable amount of effort went into the dvelopment of fabrics with special properties specifically for the use of automobile manufacturers.

Statistics available for the years in question showed Du Pont had captured a large share of the relevant market in its sales to General Motors. Thus, in 1946 Du Pont supplied General Motors with 67 per cent of its requirements for finishes. In that year General Motors accounted for 50 per cent of the market for such finishes. From such figures as these the court was able to conclude that Du Pont's acquisition of some 23 per cent of General Motors stock during the years 1917 to 1919 was unlawful because of the substantial competitive effect the merger had in subsequent decades.

The peculiar-characteristics-and-usages test is not confined to cases involving products which have a particular function such as automobile finishes and fabrics. Sometimes the entire output of an industry may constitute a separate line of commerce. In the federal suit against the Bethlehem Steel Corporation and the Youngstown Sheet and Tube Company merger a federal district court in New York concluded that the relevant market in which to measure the effects of the merger was the iron and steel industry as a whole. The merging companies had argued that the broad line of commerce should be "common finished steel products." In reaching its conclusion, the court said:

> The products of the iron and steel industry as a group are generally standardized, are not subject to the vagaries of style appeal, and have peculiar characteristics and usages for which there are no effective substitutes. The manufacture of such products require special know how and experience, huge capital investment and a trained labor force. The products of the iron and steel industry are generally distinct one from the other and as a group distinct from the product of other industries. They are sold in a recognized market with its own competitive standards. The iron and steel industry is commonly recognized by its members as well as the community at large as a separate industry. It has its own trade association, treating the industry as separate and distinct.

Within this broad market the court found numerous submarkets, such as hot-rolled sheets, cold-rolled sheets, hot-rolled bars, and so on. The court rejected the companies' argument that the flexibility of the manufacturing process required these individual products to be lumped together in somewhat broader submarkets. The court noted that "in practice steel producers have not been quick to shift from product to product in response to the demand." Moreover, the court emphasized that "competition is not just rivalry among sellers. It is rivalry for the custom of buyers. . . . Any definition of line of commerce which ignores the buyers and focuses on what the sellers do, or theoretically can do, is not meaningful."

In view of the court's ultimate conclusion in the *Bethlehem Steel* case—namely, that the merger would violate Section 7 of the Clayton Act in each and every relevant market defined by the court—the businessman may well question whether the lengthy analysis of each of the product markets is necessary in view of the fact that a probable lessening of competition in any of the markets would be sufficient to render the merger illegal. The answer is simply that the courts do not initiate lawsuits. When the government brings a complex antitrust case a court will usually consider, for the sake of completeness, all aspects of the effect of the merger on competition.

It has been said that the peculiar-characteristics-and-uses test and the test of reasonable interchangeability are "different verbalizations of the same criterion." That is, if a product is or can be substituted for another product they should be considered in the same product market.

Traditionally, the question has been whether a slight change in price in one item, for example, an increase in the price of cigarettes, will shift demand to cigars or pipe tobacco. If so, the items are price elastic to demand and they will be in the same product market. If not, demand is inelastic and the items are in different product markets. Though the reasonable-interchangeability test may be a simpler one, unfortunately it probably is not a substitute for the peculiar-characteristics test.

In the *Cellophane* case, the Supreme Court held in a monopolization suit under Section 2 of the Sherman Act that cellophane was reasonably interchangeable with a number of other packaging materials. The Court limited its analysis of the interchangeability test in this case, however, to Section 2 of the Sherman Act; because it was concerned there only with monopoly power, the Court's concern with "cross-elasticity of demand between products" called for a broader definition of market than that necessarily called for in Clayton Act, Section 7 cases. In other words, monopoly power and the probability of substantial lessening of competition are two different things: a firm may not have monopoly power over a particular product because the existence of substitutes may keep the power over prices in check, but the same substitutes do not necessarily mean that competition would not be diminished if the company manufacturing the product in question were to merge with a company manufacturing one of the substitutes.

Peculiarity of the characteristics or uses can be only a rough approximation at best. In the *Brown Shoe* case, involving a merger between *Brown* (the fourth-largest shoe manufacturer in the United States) and Kinney (the largest family-style shoe store and twelfth-largest shoe manufacturer), the Supreme Court found that the relevant lines of commerce were three—men's, women's, and children's shoes: "These product lines are recognized by the public; each line is manufactured in separate plants; each has characteristics peculiar to itself rendering it generally noncompetitive with the other; and each is, of course, directed toward a distinct class of customers." Brown contended that this delineation of markets did not sufficiently recognize the peculiarity of the shoe market; thus, Brown argued that a "little boy does not wear a little girl's black patent leather pump" nor can a "male baby wear a growing boy's shoes." Although the defendant's argument may be logically correct, the Court concluded that further fractionalization of the markets for purposes of analysis would not be helpful. Specifically, the Court pointed out that Brown "can point to no advantage it would enjoy were finer divisions than those chosen by the District Court employed."

Thus, the peculiar-characteristics-and-uses test is primarily a pragmatic one, as are all tests in antitrust: not what is mathematically precise, but what picture can be drawn to permit a not unreasonable assessment of the competitive impact of the merger. As the Court put it in the first important bank merger case following the 1950 amendment: "It is clear that commercial banking is a market 'sufficiently inclusive to be meaningful in terms of trade realities.' " In the *Philadelphia National Bank* case, the Court held that the "cluster of products (various kinds of credit) and services (such as checking accounts and trust administration) denoted by the term 'commercial banking,' comprises a distinct line of commerce."

As the Supreme Court indicated in *Brown Shoe,* the peculiar-characteristics-and-uses test is not the only criterion for determining relevant market. In the *Rome Cable* case, the Court weighted heavily sensitivity to price in defining the product market. The case concerned the merger of Alcoa and Rome Cable; Alcoa produced bare and insulated aluminum conductor but no copper conductor; Rome manufactured both copper and aluminum conductor. Though it was agreed that bare aluminum conductor is a sufficient line of commerce, the lower court refused to join bare and insulated aluminum conductor together in a broad line of commerce. The court reasoned that insulated aluminum conductor could not be separated from insulated copper conductor in a line of commerce and that because it could not be separated, insulated aluminum conductor could not be added by itself to bare aluminum conductor. The Supreme Court reversed, finding that bare and insulated aluminum conductor could be aggregated as a line of commerce separate and apart from copper. This seemingly overtechnical argument was raised because of the industry's statistics: Alcoa produced 32.5 per cent of bare aluminum conductor, a product all agreed would constitute a line of commerce; but Rome Cable produced only 0.3 per cent of bare aluminum conductor, and that small fraction of total industry production might well have been too small to allow any finding of substantial lessening of competition. Rome Cable did, however, produce 4.7 per cent of insulated aluminum conductor—a figure which if added to Alcoa's production of 11.6 per cent of the industry's insulated aluminum conductor would be sufficient to sustain the finding of an unlawful lessening of competition. What was to be included within the product market was, therefore, crucial. The Supreme Court reasoned that the evidence indicated that aluminum conductor "dominates" in aboveground transmission lines, whereas copper cable "remains virtually unrivaled in all other conductor applications." The Court admitted that copper and aluminum cable do compete in overhead distribution lines and that they could thus be grouped together in a single product market. Yet, said the Court, that they can be grouped together in a product market does not preclude the existence of two separate submarkets for purposes of Section 7 of the Clayton Act. And here the separate submarkets are founded on price differentials. The price of insulated aluminum cable ranges between one third and one half that of insulated copper cable; between 1950 and 1959, aluminum's share of annual installation rose from 6.5 to 77.2 per cent. The difference between the two products was not quality but price: "here, where insulated aluminum conductor pricewise stands so distinctly apart, to ignore price in determining relevant line of commerce is to ignore the single, most important, practical factor in the business." Thus, the Supreme Court concluded that aluminum conductor could be separated from copper conductor in determining the relevant market.

With copper and aluminum cable separated it remained to put insulated and bare aluminum conductor together in a single product market. At this point, a use test and customer test were employed to fuse the two together: "Both types [bare and insulated aluminum] are used for the purpose of conducting electricity and are sold to the same customers, electrical utilities."

The relevant product market need not be confined exclusively to one industry; interindustry competition may be intense enough to warrant a finding that products of different industries with different characteristics but similar uses may be aggregated in a common line of commerce. In the *Continental Can* case, the second-largest metal container manufacturer (Continental Can Company) bought the third-largest glass container manufacturer (Hazel-Atlas Glass Company). The lower court had held that both cans and glass containers constituted separate lines of commerce; except for competition among various types of beer containers, the lower court did not agree with the government's contention that both metal and glass containers were in sufficient competition to be lumped together in one product market. The Supreme Court reversed. In analyzing the historical competition among glass, metal, and plastic as used in containers for consumer products the Supreme Court specifically rejected the argument that the "reasonable interchangeability of use or the cross-elasticity of demand" tests as used in *Brown Shoe* "were intended to limit the competition protected by Section 7 to competition between identical products, the kind of competition which exists, for example, between the metal containers of one company and those of another, or between the several manufacturers of glass containers." Thus, what might have been a conglomerate merger became, by holding of the Court, an ordinary horizontal merger.

The application of the tests spelled out in *Brown Shoe* cannot be classified easily. To achieve a sense of reality in product market definition, the Supreme Court recognized that the existence of a broad product market does not exclude the possibility of narrower submarkets within which to measure the effects of the merger on competition. In using the *Brown Shoe* tests to define submarkets the courts have been reluctant to recognize anything but narrow submarkets. Thus, household liquid bleach has been held to be a "distinctive product with no close substitutes." Similarly, sanitary paper products, florist aluminum foil, household steel wool, paper-insulated power cable, and Penn-grade crude oil have each been held to be separate and distinct lines of commerce.

GEOGRAPHIC MARKET

The search for the relevant geographic market is closely analogous to that for the product market. As the Supreme Court said in *Brown Shoe:*

> Just as a product market may have Section 7 significance as the proper "line of commerce," so may a geographic submarket be considered the appropriate "section of the country." . . . Congress prescribed a pragmatic, factual ap-

> proach to the definition of the relevant market and not a formal, legalistic one. The Geographic market selected must, therefore, both "correspond to the commercial realities" of the industry and be economically significant. Thus, although the geographic market in some instances may encompass the entire Nation, under other circumstances it may be as small as a single metropolitan area. . . . The fact that two merging firms have competed directly on the horizontal level in but a fraction of the geographic market in which either has operated, does not, in itself, place their merger out of the scope of Section 7. That section speaks of ". . . any section of the country," and if anticompetitive effects of a merger are probable in "any" significant market, the merger—at least to that extent—is proscribed.

In *Brown Shoe* itself the determination of the geographic market was complicated by the existence of vertical and horizontal aspects to the merger. Because Brown and Kinney were both manufacturers and retailers their competition for sales at the manufacturing and retail level comprised the horizontal aspects of the merger; the vertical aspect resulted from the fact that a manufacturer was acquiring a large chain of retail stores through which shoes could be sold to the consumer. The lower court found, and the parties did not disagree, that the relevant geographic market for both the vertical aspects and the manufacturing part of the horizontal aspect was the nation as a whole. The companies disagreed with the lower court's finding that the relevant geographic market for the retail aspect of the merger consisted of those cities with a population in excess of 10,000 and their "immediate contiguous surrounding territory in which both Brown and Kinney sold shoes at retail through stores they either owned or controlled." This test limited consideration of the effects of the merger to less than half the number of cities in which Brown Shoe marketed its product at the retail level. Brown Shoe argued that the geographic market should be limited in some instances to the central metropolitan area of the city and that in other instances the geographic area should be broadened so as to include the standard metropolitan area surrounding the city. The Supreme Court agreed with the lower court's findings that downtown shoe stores effectively compete with those in outlying areas "and that while there is undoubtedly some commercial intercourse between smaller communities within a single 'standard metropolitan area,' the most intense and important competition in retail sales will be confined to stores within the particular communities in such an area and their immediate environs." Said the higher court of the geographic area carved out by its definition: "Such markets are large enough to include the downtown shops and suburban shopping centers in areas contiguous to the city, which are the important competitive factors, and yet are small enough to include stores beyond the immediate environs of the city, which are of little competitive significance."

The Supreme Court followed its *Brown Shoe* decision one year later in *United States* v. *Philadelphia National Bank*. Again, the Court emphasized that the search for relevant market is a pragmatic search for an area in which the effects of the merger can be measured: "The proper question to be asked in this case is not where the parties to the merger do business or even where they compete, but where, within the area of competitive overlap, the effect of the merger on competition will be direct and immediate." The Court found that in banking "convenience of location is essential to effective competition. . . . The factor of inconvenience localizes banking competition as effectively as high transportation costs in other industries." Thus, in circumscribing the area of effective competition the customers as well as the suppliers or producers must be taken into account. As the Court had earlier said, the "area of effective competition in the known line of commerce must be charted by careful selection of the market area in which the seller operates, and to which the purchaser can practicably turn for supplies." Of course, in banking, large customers may find it necessary to borrow or apply for other banking services in communities that are different from their own; likewise, small customers may find it impossible to avail themselves of banking services in any bank but that closest to them. The Court recognized

> that a workable compromise must be found: some fair intermediate delineation which avoids the indefensible extremes of drawing the market either so expensively as to make the effect of the merger upon competition seem insignificant, because only the very largest of banks' customers are taken into account in defining the market, or so narrowly as to place [the banks] in different markets, because only the smallest customers are considered.

In the *Philadelphia National Bank* case, the Court held that the four-county Philadelphia metropolitan area was the relevant geographic market for purposes of the case.

More recent language from the Supreme Court may indicate that the search for the relevant geographic market is less important than for product market, at least as an initial matter, in analyzing a merger case. In *United States* v. *Pabst Brewing Co.,* the lower court dismissed the case following the government's presentation of evidence, holding, among other reasons, that the government had not shown that Wisconsin and the three-state area of Wisconsin, Michigan, and Illinois constituted relevant geographic markets. The Supreme Court reversed. The Clayton Act, according to the Court

> requires merely that the Government prove the merger may have a substantial anticompetitive effect somewhere in the United States—"in *any* section" of the United States. This phrase does not call for the delineation of a "section of the country" by metes and bounds as a surveyor would lay off a plot of ground. . . . Congress did not seem to be troubled about the exact spot where competition might be lessened; it simply intended to outlaw mergers which threatened competition in any or all parts of the country. Proof of the section of the country where the anticompetitive effect exists is entirely subsidiary to the crucial question in this and every Section 7 case which is

whether a merger may substantially lessen competition anywhere in the United States.

Of course, the *Pabst* case does not mean that there is always necessarily a relevant geographic market in which to measure the effects of a merger, nor does it mean that defendants in a government prosecution may not introduce evidence to prove that the geographic market contended for by the government is not the market in which the case should be considered. *Pabst,* after all, was simply a holding that a lower court cannot dismiss the government's complaint once the government had introduced some evidence that the effects of a merger could be tested in a particular market area. Indeed, facts in the *Pabst* case suggest that there was significance to the selection of Wisconsin and the three-state area as relevant geographic markets. In 1961, three years after the merger, Pabst was the third-largest brewer in the United States with but 5.83 per cent share of the market. In Wisconsin, however, Pabst then had nearly a quarter of the market, making it the largest retailer of beer there, and it had more than 11 per cent of sales in the three-state area.

Because the determination of geographic market rests on the peculiarities of each case no general classification of geographic markets by product or industry can be made. It should be sufficient to point out that at various times national, regional, and local markets (whether single states or metropolitan areas) have been held to be relevant geographic markets. Thus, the markets for glass and can containers, for aluminum conductor, and for manufacture of shoes have all been held to be the nation as a whole. Regional markets have been found in contiguous areas overlapping state lines and also in combinations of various states; for example, the southeastern part of the United States has been held to be a relevant geographic market. In an important steel case, the northeastern part of the United States; Michigan, Ohio, Pennsylvania, and New York, as a four-state area; and collectively, the states of Michigan and Ohio have likewise been held to be relevant geographic markets. Sometimes a single state has been held to be the market area to be considered; thus California was the market area to be considered in a gas merger case. And, of course, a single metropolitan area can be a relevant geographic market; for example, the Los Angeles area was the market for a retail grocery chain merger, and noncontiguous cities of more than 10,000 population and their immediately surrounding environs were the market considered in the merger of retail shoe stores.

As has been emphasized throughout this chapter, the determination of relevant market, whether it be product or geographic, is a threshold question. Though it can be dispositive of a case because the market boundaries may control the use of all statistics to be introduced to show the effect of the merger on competition, the determination of market in and of itself is not an end to the merger case. The Supreme Court has noted on many occasions that the determination of relevant market is not one that calls for mathematical or economic precision. Because mergers of any sort can have economic effects that ripple throughout the economy the ultimate question in a merger case is what the effect of that merger will be. In order thus to reach that question courts will necessarily select the markets through a process of compromise and judgment that eludes rigorous, black-letter rules.

17 Tests of Unlawfulness

When a corporation is considering the pros and cons of a merger or acquisition, it is helpful to have at least some familiarity with the statutes directly governing this phase of corporate law. To put the statutes into some kind of perspective, it is necessary that they be read in conjunction with the cases interpreting them. This has been the aim of this book up to this point. However, this is still not enough. In order for the businessman to acquire some insight into the actual functioning of the antitrust laws as they relate to mergers, the cases must be remembered for more than just the result finally reached by the court. The most important reason for studying the prior cases dealing with mergers is so that once the reader is familiar with them he will be able to predict the probable conclusion a court would arrive at when faced with a question involving different facts. This ability to predict results is important and can be arrived at only when the cases are studied with the emphasis on the reasons why the court made the decision it did.

For that reason this chapter will be concerned with the tests used by the courts in determining whether a merger is unlawful or not. Because the tests vary, depending on the type of merger involved and the statute employed, it is important to decide on some kind of organization within which to discuss the tests. For our purposes the clearest presentation will be made possible by discussing the several different types of mergers in sequence—horizontal, vertical, and conglomerate. Within each category the tests will be explained, including the practical indicia the courts have deemed to be relevant. Because Section 7 of the Clayton Act is the most important section in the merger area, the tests mentioned in each case will be applicable to Section 7 unless stated otherwise. Other statutes included in the area of concern—Section 5 of the Federal Trade Commission Act and Sections 1 and 2 of the Sherman Act—will be mentioned where necessary. However, before specific tests applied in each type of merger are discussed, it will be necessary to define two key concepts presented by Section 7. The two all-important phrases are the *line of commerce* and *section of the country*.

LINE OF COMMERCE

The courts have dealt frequently with the problem of singling out a line of commerce in order to determine actual anticompetitive effects, and realizing its importance, the Supreme Court has set down the guidelines for drawing the outer boundaries of a line of commerce. This task was necessary in view of the Congressional failure to define *line of commerce* in either the statute or the Congressional reports accompanying the bill. This failure was due directly to the fact that the phrase was added to the bill in conference. An early finding of a distinct line of commerce was made in 1930 by the Supreme Court in *International Shoe Co.* v. *FTC,* where it was stated:

> It is plain . . . that the product of the two companies here in question, because of the differences in appearance and workmanship, appealed to the tastes of entirely different classes of customers; that while a portion of the product of both companies went into the same states, in the main the product of each was sold to a different class of dealers and found its way into distinctly separate markets.

This "distinct customer" definition was a workable one for almost two decades even though the Court had not attempted to define the concept until as late as 1929. It was inevitable that the Court would find it necessary to supplement this formula and it was accomplished with the "interchangeability of product" test set down in *United States* v. *Columbia Steel Co.* A refinement of this test was forthcoming in 1956 when the Supreme Court decided the *Cellophane* case (*United States* v. *E. I. du Pont de Nemours & Co.*). In this case, brought under Section 2 of the Sherman Act, the Court concluded, "Determination of the competitive market for commodities depends on how different from one another are the offered commodities in character use, how far buyers will go to substitute one commodity for another." The test is based on the economic theory of crosselasticity of demand and today the interchangeability-of-use test is the primary test for determining a Section 7 line of commerce. The test was formulated in a case requiring an actual restraint, but it has not been changed even though it is acknowledged that such a test could be less strict under the Clayton Act. In a case involving Du Pont a year later, the Court stressed the need to delineate the line of commerce by noting that the

> determination of the relevant market [line of commerce and section of the country] is a necessary predicate to a finding of a violation of the Clayton Act because the threatened monopoly must be one which will substantially lessen competition "within the area of effective competition." Substantiality can be determined only in terms of the market affected.

Although it has been noted that the tests are economic in origin, it must always be remembered that when employed by courts in cases such as these, they also become legal concepts subject to analysis in light of the Congressional purposes in passing Section 7. If this thought is kept in mind, it is easier to reconcile some later modifications of the test that have already been discussed. Although it has always been admitted that the line of commerce finally decided on need not be a large part of the company's business to subject it to liability, in *A. G. Spalding & Co.* v. *FTC,* the United States Court of Appeals for the Third Circuit agreed with the commission that even a market's own recognition of a separate line of commerce was enough to meet the peculiar-use test. The same court noted that distinct prices for products could also establish a separate line. The Supreme Court, in *Brown Shoe Co.* v. *United States,* ruled that anticompetitive effects could be analyzed in a submarket if it was "meaningful in terms of trade realities." The test for a submarket that can be so employed was defined by "practical indicia" such as (1) industry or public recognition, (2) peculiar characteristics or uses, (3) unique production facilities, (4) distinct customers, (5) distinct prices, (6) sensitivity to price changes, and (7) specialized vendors. However, a later case that attempted to apply the practical indicia enunciated in *Brown Shoe* was reversed by the Court because the "interindustry competition" justified treating the two products as one line.

> Since the purpose of delineating a line of commerce is to provide an adequate basis for measuring the effects of a given acquisition, its contours must, as nearly as possible, conform to competitive reality. Where the area of effective competition cuts across industry lines, so must the relevant line of commerce, otherwise an adequate determination of the merger's true impact cannot be made.

At least one writer on the subject feels that the use of the submarket to define a narrow line of commerce when a broad line of commerce cannot be found makes the rule a per se test. No less an authority than Mr. Justice Harlan declared in a dissent in *United States* v. *Continental Can Co.* that the failure to include a competing product in the line of commerce "reads the 'line of commerce' element out of Section 7, and destroys its usefulness as an aid to analysis." The test really seems to be that if a line of commerce can be isolated and used to find a merger illegal, then the practical-indicia test of *Brown Shoe* is not to be used to try to avoid such a finding. However, if no broad line can be found, the practical-indicia test can and should be employed to find a submarket on which to base the relief requested. This conclusion is buttressed by the 1964 Supreme Court decision in the *Alcoa* case that used practical indicia to find a submarket that the lower court had found not to exist. In justifying the use of the *Brown Shoe* test here the Court stated that "to ignore price in determining the relevant line of commerce is to ignore the single, most important, practical factor in business." The conclusion seems to be that the Supreme Court has sanctioned the use of a series of tests that makes it much more probable that the necessary "line of commerce" will be found than that it will be overlooked.

SECTION OF THE COUNTRY

The other determination that must be made by the court or the Federal Trade Commission consists in whether there may be a substantial lessening of competition in any section of the country. Although the underlying approach to this part of the problem seems to have changed drastically since the *Pabst Brewing* case, to appreciate exactly what changes have resulted mention should be made of the previous judicial rulings on the meaning of the phrase *section of the country*.

The early theory that made the finding of a "section of the country" necessary was that a determination of whether competition has been or may be lessened was impossible without knowing exactly where the competition was that might be lessened. Without knowing the boundaries, courts realized it was futile to try to assess the effect of any amalgamation. The need for a geographic market determination was recognized in *Transamerica Corp.* v. *Board of Governors,* but no citation of authority was given by the court of appeals. The court explained by saying, "The application of this clause [§7] obviously requires a preliminary determination of the area of effective competition between the companies involved before the question of competition between them may be considered." The Supreme Court agreed with this conclusion in 1962 in *Brown Shoe*. This is not to say, however, that the area had to be contiguous. As early as 1948 the Supreme Court allowed a finding of monopolization under Section 2 of the Sherman Act where the "section of the country" consisted of all cities in the country over a certain size. The fact that this "section" could not be defined by any particular metes and bounds did not foreclose the use of this category. The important thing was that the area was definable and identifiable as such; with these requirements met, the effect on competition could be gauged. Fourteen years later the Court went even further and stated, in *Brown Shoe,* that "just as a product submarket may have §7 significance as the proper 'line of commerce,' so may a geographic submarket be considered the appropriate 'section of the country.' " The same observations about the use of the submarket approach to find a merger illegal in the line-of-commerce requirement apply to the section-of-the-country requirement. The Court, in *Brown Shoe,* also observed that "Congress prescribed a pragmatic, factual approach to the definition of the relevant market. . . ." The application of this approach to the geographic market should result in a market that would " 'correspond to the commercial realities' of the industry and be economically significant." The local convenience of some businesses, such as banking and amusements, should be given special weight in some cases; in others, weight should be given to the role of transportation and freight costs.

This steady stream of cases that resulted in a defining and redefining of the approach to be used in determining the significant geographic market or "section of the country" seemed to be heading toward two inevitable goals: (1) predictability for the businessman who had to anticipate the courts' reaction if his company merged with some other company and (2) easy administration of the rules by the district courts called on to interpret them on a somewhat consistent fashion. This heading was abruptly changed in 1966 by two decisions, one by the FTC and one by the Supreme Court, that have left the state of the law concerning the necessity of defining a "section of the country" for merger purposes in confusion.

In *National Tea Co.* the commission, in a complaint challenging mergers under both Clayton Section 7 and FTC Section 5, ruled that it was not necessary to focus on any particular market to determine illegality. Rather, it found justification for the finding of illegality in the fact that there was a trend toward concentration that made acquisitions by a big company like National prima facie illegal. As a result of the ruling, the commission did not find it necessary to consider whether competition was actually lessened in a "section of the country" because of each acquisition. This decision made it uncertain when the commission would abandon the traditional section-of-the-country approach in favor of the concentration argument, especially because the concentration element had not been clearly defined by the commission in the opinion.

The second case, and by far the more important, was *United States* v. *Pabst Brewing Co.* In this decision the Supreme Court reversed a district court dismissal of a merger suit based on the government's failure to prove a specific "section of the country." In holding that the government was not required to prove a particular section affected by the merger, the Court stated:

> The language of the section [§7] requires merely that the Government prove the merger has a substantial anti-competitive effect somewhere in the United States—"in *any* section" of the United States. This phrase does not call for the delineation of a "section of the country" by metes and bounds as a survey would lay off a plot of ground.

Although a dissent sought to defend the "complicated and elaborate" search for a specific section as being "necessary," the majority effected a major shift in the burden of proof in the government's suits. Although several writers have concluded that this decision indicates just how concerned the Court is with concentration rather than competition, other authorities feel that this decision should be read as attempting to eliminate complex economic analysis.

Whatever the correct conclusion about the reasons for the *Pabst* decision, it will not be difficult to see that it will have a real impact on merger law from now on. This brief look at the first two requirements in proving a violation of the antitrust laws will, we hope, make the tests employed by the courts in each case that much more understandable. For in a real way the tests are all the same, the differences being only verbalizations to make their application more predictable and uniform.

HORIZONTAL MERGERS

The first type of merger that Congress was concerned about was the horizontal merger or acquisition—a merger between two companies in actual competition with each other. That this was the first concern of Congress seems understandable when one realizes that at the outset competition was to be the protected commodity and that the horizontal merger was its greatest threat. Although many will argue that the focus has shifted from the promotion of competition as the main concern of the antitrust laws, it still is of enormous importance. For this reason it seems appropriate to look at the various tests formulated by the courts through the years to aid them in determining whether or not a horizontal merger is illegal, and at some of the cases that employ the tests so recognized. It must always be kept in mind that the "line of commerce" and "section of the country" must be determined before the court can move on to the application of these tests.

Elimination of Substantial Competition

Where one of the results of the merger will be that the relevant market as defined earlier will have one less substantial competitor, the merger will almost always be held illegal. In *United States* v. *Bethlehem Steel Corporation* a United States district court held illegal the proposed merger of the second- and sixth-largest steel corporations in the country. The entire nation was the "section" and the government relied on several "lines of commerce." In the case presented, the court concluded that the merger "eliminates a substantial factor in competition," and, therefore, was proscribed.

The situation has become so changed since the first cases decided under this test that some commentators believe that it would be more accurate to substitute the word *any* for the word *substantial* in the name of the test. For support they point to the case of *United States* v. *Aluminum Company of America,* where the Supreme Court found illegal a merger between the largest aluminum cable producer and one of the smallest producers. Alcoa's percentage of the market was raised from 27.8 to 29.1 per cent, but the Court noted that "[i]t is a basic premise of that law [Section 7] that competition will be most vital when there are many sellers, none of which has any significant market shares." From this analysis, it does seem that the acquisition of a direct competitor, whether "substantial" or not would raise the question of illegality under Section 7.

Concentration

The courts have become more interested in the concentration in an industry when faced with a merger question than with any other single factor. Although some consider the concern with concentration just another way of preventing the elimination of a competitor, it is actually more than that. In effect, it makes the effect of mergers previously unchallenged and consummated important in each new merger or acquisition in the same relevant market. It may be considered a way to make up for past mistakes in allowing other mergers to be completed. To appreciate the importance of concentration, one need only read the most recent Supreme Court decisions and it will become quite clear.

The starting point is always the Congressional concern with the increasing tide of concentration and what its eventual result will be if left unchecked. Although there is some question as to whether the declaration should be taken at face value, the Supreme Court has glossed over this trouble spot. In *United States* v. *Von's Grocery Company,* the Court held illegal the acquisition of the sixth-largest grocery store chain in Los Angeles by the third-largest chain. The Court first discussed the increase in concentration in the market in the past and then stated that "[w]hat we have . . . is simply the case of two already powerful companies merging in a way which makes them even more powerful than they were before." Such an increase in concentration could not be allowed even though together they only controlled 7.5 per cent of the market.

In *Philadelphia National Bank* the merger of two large banks in Philadelphia was held illegal. After the merger the two largest banks would have had 60 per cent of the market and the Court could not sanction such a substantial increase in concentration.

> Specifically, we think that a merger which produces a firm controlling an undue percentage share of the relevant market [30 per cent], and results in a significant increase in the concentration of firms in that market [33 per cent], is so inherently likely to lessen competition substantially that it must be enjoined in the absence of evidence showing that the merger is not likely to have such anticompetitive effects.

Some writers have gone so far as to say that *Philadelphia National Bank* has reduced the tests of the effect on market power to just one—concentration.

The result of these decisions and others following them, notably *United States* v. *Continental Can Co.* and *Alcoa–Rome,* has been to help assure competition by having small competitors around to prevent collusion. Because the Court feels this is a justifiable goal, even slight increases in concentration have been stopped when concentration is already high. Whether the theory of concentration and competition as endorsed by the Supreme Court will be found valid in the long run is still an open question, but the concentration present in the relevant market will be undoubtedly of immense importance in the future.

Market Share

The market share a company possesses is measured by the company's dollar amount of sales and volume of sales divided by the total dollar and volume sales, respectively. Observers indicate that a high market share standing by itself is not necessarily significant, but when it is coupled with a merger or acquisition in a highly concentrated market, it takes on more importance. The closer the market approaches an oligopoly or monopoly, the less proof of market share dominance is needed for the merger to be found illegal. There is no doubt that the significance of market power has increased since the Celler–Kefauver Amendment of 1950.

The Court in *Philadelphia National Bank* found the possession by the combined bank of 30 per cent of the market a threat to the market; the result was not a per se finding of illegality because of the market share, but the burden was on the advocate of the merger to justify the allowance of such a large percentage. In *United States* v. *Brown Shoe* the market share in different cities varied from 5 to 57 per cent. When combined with the concentration in the industry, the Court had no trouble finding the merger illegal. The district court found the merger, in *United States* v. *Bethlehem Steel Corporation,* illegal when it appeared that the combined company would have over 20 per cent of the relevant market. This, combined with several other factors also present, forced the court to conclude that competition would be lessened.

Ease of Entry

Ease of entry into the relevant market is one of the most important characteristics of the market for purposes of antitrust analysis. The logic of this statement is compelling when one realizes that even the most concentrated and oligopolistic market will probably not remain static if entry conditions are such that anyone willing to make a small capital expenditure can compete with the existing companies and make a profit. The only excuse a potential competitor would need to enter a market like this would be price, quality, or quantity abuses by the existing powers, thus making entry attractive. Once the entry was accomplished, the previous manufacturers would soon be forced to meet the competition or lose their market share.

The importance of the doctrine can be thought of as emerging in *American Crystal Sugar Co.* v. *Cuban-American Sugar Company,* where a United States district court noted that "it is important to determine the opportunity for new firms to enter the industry. For if there is reasonable access to an industry, amelioration of market structure conditions is possible." This reasoning was supported by the Supreme Court in *Brown Shoe.* The effect ease of entry should have on the enforcement of Section 7 was one of the subjects of Congressional hearings published in 1949. The attorney general's report also considered the relative ease of entry into a market to be extremely important. The consensus seems to be that where ease of entry into the market is not a reality (barriers to entry exist), then the standard in the relevant market should be stricter. Although the converse is not always true, the Justice Department has noted that ease of entry into a market might keep an action from being brought. However, this is not the case with the FTC. As far as the commission is concerned, ease of entry is no justification for a merger. This was made clear in a ruling in Ekco Products Company where a merger was disallowed even though entry into the market was relatively easy. The commission decision was affirmed by the United States Court of Appeals for the Seventh Circuit.

The tests used to measure the ease of entry have been listed by both the writers and the cases. Of foremost importance is the actual number of new entrants, followed by considerations of whether the capital investment needed is large, whether the supply of raw materials is limited, and whether there are any government restrictions on entry. Also significant is the relative size of the firms already competing, the existence of patents, integrated advantages possessed by existing firms, and free access to suppliers. Some factors not considered are economics of scale and the existence of unused capacity.

Possibility of Future Mergers

Although this test is actually employed much more often in the vertical merger situation, the Court has been aware of the possibility of more mergers resulting in the same market if the one under consideration is allowed. This is an extremely subjective test and does not lend itself to quantification. Nevertheless, the Supreme Court did mention it as a factor in deciding the *Brown Shoe* case, and in view of the prominence of that case it deserves some mention. The rationale used by the Court was summarized when the Court hypothesized that "[i]f a merger achieving 5 per cent control were now approved, we might be required to approve future merger efforts by Brown's competitors seeking similar market shares."

It is possible to view this type of test as just being another step in an inevitable approach to a per se rule, but such a conclusion is not necessary. The theory that it is serving as a makeweight is just as plausible. However, it should be kept in mind in the case involving an industry with a strong inclination toward merger.

Advantages of Bigness

Observers of merger activity for the last two decades have made one not too surprising observation—mergers between big companies are usually challenged. Because this observation does not shock too many people, can it be said that a separate test is employed by the courts to determine whether a merger between big companies is illegal, or is it just that by their very size the inherently bad aspects of mergers are just that much more abundant and easy to find? There is some support for the conclusion that there is a separate test and it is simply that in mergers "bigness is badness." Look, for example, at *Philadelphia National Bank,* where the Court noted a presumption of illegality in a merger that would give the resulting bank 30 per cent of the relevant market. The burden shifted to the proponent of the merger because of the size of the two banks involved. In two subsequent cases, *United States* v. *First National Bank and Trust Co.* and *United States* v. *Continental Can Co.,* the same reasoning was followed. It was the majority opinion in *Continental Can* that prompted Mr. Justice Harlan, in a dissent, to complain that the majority was "laying down a 'per se' rule that mergers between two large companies in related industries are presumptively unlawful under Section 7." The Court also noted in *Brown Shoe* some of the anticompetitive effects that result from having a big firm get even bigger. Brown's size alone gave it advantages in style trends and the ability to insulate selected outlets from competition.

The conclusion seems to be that a separate test is being formulated to judge the legality of mergers of large companies and it is available for use. As such it should be given special attention, whether in reality its indicators are nothing more than the sum of the other tests already mentioned.

Reduction in Number of Independent Businessmen

Actually this test is a corollary to the first two tests discussed in this section. Obviously, when a competitor is eliminated or concentration is increased, there has to be a reduction in the number of independent businessmen. There is a special significance in phrasing the test this way, however, and because of this a separate test is not as repetitious as it might seem. Congress and the Supreme Court have always been concerned with the ability of the small firm to compete in this day of industrial giants. It is this concern that would prompt the Court to deal especially harshly with an attempted take-over of a small business by a giant in the same field. Aside from the concentration and competition aspects, the Court is also trying to recognize the value of the small businessman—an ideal that seems to be slipping away from us.

It is clear that although the Court might have based part of the decision in *Von's Grocery* on this ground because of the swallowing of a competitor in the metropolitan grocery business, it seems much more appropriate for the Court to use the test in a case like *United States* v. *Aluminum Company of America* where the industry giant attempted to acquire one of its smallest competitors. The test, whether phrased in this way or in its more recognizable form, is important because it exists to give some protection to the small businessman and recognition apart from his significance as a statistic of some percentage increase in concentration.

History of Acquisition in Firm or Industry

A test that is more often differentiated as such in the vertical merger area, the history of acquisition plays a small part in horizontal merger cases too. Actually another corollary of the concentration test, it is the method by which courts track down the reason for a high concentration in any relevant market. The courts will be more strict if the industry has become increasingly concentrated in recent years, as they were in *Brown Shoe, Philadelphia National Bank,* and *Von's Grocery*. The tendency will become even more pronounced if the reason for the concentration in the industry is the company before them at the moment. For this reason consideration must be given to previous acquisitions and mergers in related areas, as well as to the acquisitions made by the businessman's own company.

VERTICAL MERGERS

When a suit is filed by the Justice Department or the FTC challenging the consummation or continuance of a vertical merger, the considerations are different from those in the horizontal-merger area. For this reason a completely separate group of tests has been developed by the courts to determine the anticompetitive effects of each individual merger. A vertical integration is the acquisition of or merger with either a supplier of the company's raw materials, in which case it is called a backward vertical merger, or a purchaser of the company's finished product, known as a forward vertical merger. To summarize the potential evils in a vertical merger is actually to list the various tests developed to measure its legality. They will be discussed in the following paragraphs, although the order does not necessarily indicate importance or frequency of use. Again it must be remembered that these tests are applied only after the court or commission is satisfied that the relevant market has been correctly drawn.

Foreclosure

A particularly dangerous result of a vertical merger when viewed by a competitor, especially from the point of view of an independent businessman, is the threat of being foreclosed from some part of the market that he relied on to function as a competitor. In a backward vertical merger the company or individual foreclosed might be a competitor of the acquiring concern—supplies from the merged company could be kept from the competitor and a lessening of competition would result. However, in a forward vertical merger the party who could be potentially harmed would be a competitor of the acquired firm. The manufactured items which before the acquisition were equally available to all distributors would or could be sold exclusively to the distributorships acquired, thereby lessening competition.

A leading case on the question of foreclosure is the *United States* v. *E. I. du Pont de Nemours,* otherwise known as the *Du Pont–G.M.* case. Involved in that case was a challenge under Section 7 to the continued holding of General Motors stock by Du Pont with the resulting tendency of G.M. to purchase more of Du Pont's automotive supplies to the exclusion of other suppliers. The proof of foreclosure came from the substantial percentages of finishes (68 per cent) and fabrics (38.5 per cent) purchased by G.M. from Du Pont in 1947, and the proof of substantiality from the fact that G.M. was the largest car maker in the country. That the stock ownership was the cause of this foreclosure could not be proved, but the Court noted that "[t]he inference is overwhelming that Du Pont's commanding position was promoted by its stock interest and was not gained solely on competitive merit." Even the intent to so use the power "to overreach . . . competitors" was not necessary to the case.

The Supreme Court again dealt with the problem of foreclosure in *Brown Shoe* some five years later. The suit was brought under amended Section 7 seeking to prevent the acquisition of Kinney, a large shoe retailer, by Brown, a large shoe manufacturer. As to the vertical aspects of the merger, the test of unlawfulness relied on was the foreclosure of other shoe manufacturers from selling shoes to Kinney for resale to the public. Even though the actual percentage of foreclosure would amount to about 1.2 per cent, the Court noted that "in this industry, no merger between a manufacturer and an independent retailer could involve a larger potential market foreclosure." Also persuasive to the Court was the fact that by the time of the trial, Brown's share of Kinney's purchases rose from 0 to 7.9 per cent, indicating that any potential foreclosure would probably become actual.

As is usually the case, writers on this area of merger law do not necessarily agree with the Court's emphasis on foreclosure. One author argued that the foreclosure test should not be used unless there is proof that competitors will not be able to purchase what they need from another source or sell what they make to another buyer. Evidently, the type of proof that would be considered satisfactory would be the testimony of the competitors themselves indicating that they felt a market would be foreclosed. This was the proof relied on by the FTC in *Crown-Zellerbach Corp.* v. *FTC,* holding illegal an acquisition of a paper company because jobbers indicated that no other comparable source of supply existed.

Two other writers feel that the absolute size of the acquiring and acquired firm should be the most important factor in vertical mergers, rather than percentage foreclosure. This harks back to *Du Pont–G.M.,* the only case relying on quantitative foreclosure. However, there is no argument that foreclosure as a test should not be used. Although discussion may continue on the relative merits of one type of measurement over another, foreclosure will remain uppermost in the minds of reviewing courts in vertical mergers.

This conclusion is borne out in the Supreme Court's recent decision in

Ford Motor Company v. *United States,* which struck down Ford's acquisition of The Electric Autolite Co. (Autolite), a leading independent manufacturer of spark plugs. At the time that Ford acquired Autolite in 1961, there were only three major domestic producers of spark plugs. These three firms had a 95 per cent share of the domestic spark plug market. General Motors, which produced the AC brand, accounted for 30 per cent of the overall market. Autolite's market share was 15 per cent, and the lone remaining major independent—Champion Spark Plug Company—had a market share of approximately 50 per cent. The few other brand names of spark plugs—Eltra's Prestolite, Standard Oil's Atlas, and Montgomery Ward's Riverside—had very small market shares, individually and collectively, and were all manufactured by "the only [three other] producers of any stature at all after the 'Big Three.' "

The existence within the domestic spark plug market of two submarkets and the relationship between those submarkets formed much of the basis for the Court's decision. The original equipment (or OE) market involves spark plugs sold to automobile producers for use as original equipment in new cars. The market for spark plugs used in the replacement of original equipment spark plugs is called the aftermarket. There is a strong tie between the OE market and the aftermarket, which arises, in the Court's own words, because the "custom and practice among mechanics . . . [is that] the *aftermarket* plug is usually the same brand as the OE plug." This OE tie, the Court found, caused spark plug manufacturers, such as Autolite, who were independent of automobile manufacturers, to furnish "the auto manufacturers with OE plugs at cost or less . . . and they continued to sell at that price even though their cost increased three-fold. The independents sought to recover their losses on OE sales by profitable sales in the *aftermarket* where the requirement of each vehicle during its lifetime is about five replacement plug sets." Although Autolite and Champion were the only two major "independent" producers, they were each paired with a major automobile producer in their sales of OE plugs—Autolite with Chrysler and Champion with Ford.

Section 7 of the Clayton Act, the provision which the Court held was violated by the merger, proscribes mergers or acquisitions the effect of which in any section of the country "may be substantially to lessen competition." It is well to keep in mind that proof of a violation of Section 7 requires demonstration only that the merger *may* substantially lessen competition. The words *may be* connote the concept of reasonable probability and are intended to apply in arresting: "restraints of trade in their incipiency and before they develop into full-fledged restraints violative of the Sherman Act. A requirement of certainty and actuality of injury to competition is incompatible with any effort to supplement the Sherman Act by reaching incipient restraints [such as where] . . . a large concern grows through a series of . . . small acquisitions." Despite this lower standard of proof, Ford's acquisitions of Autolite's assets ten years before the decision in this case afforded the Court a greater opportunity to observe the actual effects of the merger than Section 7 contemplates.

The spark plug industry, which the Court found to be the competitive setting in which the merger was to be examined, was characterized by high concentration (95 per cent of the market shared by just a few very large producers), a substantial tie between the submarkets for OE and replacement plugs, and a high degree of interdependency between the manufacturers of spark plugs and automobile makers, the latter also comprising a highly concentrated industry.

Against this background the Court determined that the merger would be likely to reduce competition substantially in two major ways. First, it would eliminate Ford as a potential competitor of the spark plug producers and as a prime candidate for entry into the manufacture of spark plugs by means of internal expansion. Quoting the decision of the lower court, the Supreme Court explained this effect: "An interested firm on the outside is of twofold significance. It may someday go in and set the stage for noticeable deconcentration. While it merely stays at the edge, it is a deterrent to current competitors."

The second major anticompetitive effect was that the "acquisition marked 'the foreclosure of Ford as a purchaser of about ten percent of total industry output.' " Prior to the acquisition, Ford was the major OE customer of Champion. The acquisition, therefore, not only removed the independent producer Autolite from the market, but also deprived the only other major independent producer, Champion, of its major OE customer.

Ease of Entry

As was mentioned in the section on horizontal mergers, the importance of the entry conditions into any market is the most widely accepted doctrine under Section 7. Consideration of entry conditions not only permeates the actual determination of the relevant market, but also is the major premise for the test applied once the market is defined. In *United States* v. *Pabst Brewing Company,* Mr. Justice Harlan wrote a concurring opinion where he defined the relevant market as the "area in which the parties to the merger or acquisition compete, and around which there exists *economic barriers* that significantly impede the entry of new competitors. . . ." (Emphasis added.)

Once the market is agreed on, the presence or absence of barriers to entry might stiffen or relax the opposition to the merger, as the case may be. If the key point against the merger is potential foreclosure of markets, and those markets have no real economic barriers to keep other buyers or sellers out, the foreclosure has a poor chance of ever materializing. The other tests to be listed will also be recognized as involving the entry conditions into the market as a key factor. Classifying the entry considerations themselves as a test merely gives the courts the option of referring to the phenomenon directly instead of having to approach the issue indirectly by discussing the foundation of the other tests.

In the *Ford* case, discussed earlier in this chapter, the Court found entry barriers to constitute an additional reason to invalidate the merger. With two of the major automobile producers (General Motors and Ford) manufacturing their own plugs for both the OE market and aftermarket, the single remaining major automobile manufacturer which did not produce its own spark plugs (Chrysler) would be the only likely customer of the single major producer remaining in the spark plug industry, or of possible future spark plug producers. The lower court and the Supreme Court both noted that the likely effect of this would be not only to lessen substantially existing competition in the spark plug industry, but also to raise drastically the barriers to entry into the spark plug market. Specifically, the existence of only one major customer (Chrysler) and the existence of a well-established spark plug producer which was economically dependent upon serving that single customer would have the very likely effect of discouraging any new business from trying to compete in such a limited market.

In discussing this last point, the following observation of the lower court was quoted by the Supreme Court:

> It will also be noted that the number of competitors in the spark plug manufacturing industry closely parallels the number of competitors in the automobile manufacturing industry and the barriers to entry into the auto industry are virtually insurmountable at present and will remain so for the foreseeable future. Ford's acquisition of the Autolite assets, particularly when viewed in the context of the original equipment (OE) tie and of GM's ownership of AC, has the result of transmitting the rigidity of the oligopolistic structure of the automobile industry to the spark plug industry, thus reducing the chances of future deconcentration of the spark plug market by forces at work within that market.

Although it has already been noted that the absence of barriers to entry may not have the effect of condoning what would otherwise be a questionable merger (for example, the opinion of the FTC in *Scott Paper Co.* v. *FTC*), the presence of such barriers will give the courts the chance to impose stricter standards than otherwise might be applied. The actual statistics employed by the courts in deciding whether barriers exist are listed under the ease-of-entry test in horizontal mergers.

The Nature and Purpose of the Merger

The test is taken directly from the Supreme Court decision in *Brown Shoe Co.* v. *United States,* where the court stated emphatically, "A most important [economic and historical] factor to examine is the very nature and purpose of the arrangement." Analogizing the test to be applied in a Section 7 case to that of Section 3 of the Clayton Act, the Court noted that the purpose for an arrangement can have an effect on the government's burden of proof. An example of this would be an arrangement meant to be a limited-term exclusive dealing contract instead of a tying contract. In *Brown Shoe* the Court determined the purpose of the acquiring firm to be illegal—seeking an arrangement whereby Brown's shoes could be forced on Kinney.

There is little more elaboration on the test than this and there do not seem to be many cases following *Brown Shoe* that have utilized it as such. In appearance it seems to be the verbalization of a rather subjective factor that is present in all merger cases. However, one commentator has included it as one of the factors that should be considered in a vertical-merger analysis.

History in the Industry

Concerned with essentially the same statistics as the concentration test discussed under horizontal mergers, but listed separately in *Brown Shoe,* the test requires the courts to make a "prognosis of the probable *future* effect of the merger." The Supreme Court has learned that the past history, especially if it indicated a trend toward concentration, can be a valuable indication of what the future holds in store in the market. The Court in *Brown Shoe* qualified the test by admitting, "It is true, of course, that the statute prohibits a given merger only if the effect of that merger may be substantially to lessen competition."

Concentration vertically does not have the same effects as it does horizontally, so it is not clear that the criticisms of the Supreme Court's logic are equally applicable here. There just have not been enough cases relying on it as a test in the vertical-merger area. The most that can be said is that one writer listed it as a miscellaneous factor in vertical merger cases without much comment.

Expectations of the Acquiring Company

This standard of illegality, when used in conjunction with the foreclosure test, served to make the continued holding of stock a violation of Section 7 in the *Du Pont–G.M.* case. There is a question as to whether this serves as an actual test of unlawful activity, or merely as a countering tactic when the company being sued tries to qualify questionable stock holding as within the exception of being held "solely for investment." This seemed to be the posture of the case in *Du Pont–G.M.,* but its striking resemblance to the test of the nature and purpose of the arrangement creates some doubt as to whether its use is so limited. The expectations of the acquiring company were also considered relevant in *Brown Shoe Co.* v. *United States,* as well as being denominated a miscellaneous factor by one writer.

Other Tests

Although it is difficult to categorize some of the other considerations that enter into the analysis of a vertical merger as tests along with "foreclosure" and "ease of entry," the considerations should nevertheless be mentioned and remembered.

The courts will consider carefully a merger or acquisition that will have the effect of forcing remaining competitors into defensive mergers. Such would be the case if an area had two rock quarries and several concrete producers, and one concrete producer acquired one of the two quarries. The foreclosure effects not only would be felt immediately but the remaining concrete producers might feel compelled to acquire a rock quarry in order to protect themselves. This is exactly the type of merger psychology that the courts seek to prevent.

A problem of vertical mergers between manufacturers and distribution outlets that the courts have noted in addition to foreclosure has been the elimination of potential competition. In a market containing two distributors of a product and several manufacturers, the acquisition of a distributor by a manufacturer not only foreclosed some of the market, but it also eliminated any possibility of that manufacturer organizing his own distribution chain and thereby stimulating competition on the distributor level.

CONGLOMERATE MERGERS

Within the last ten years the government has become increasingly interested in challenging the one type of merger that had heretofore been left alone—the conglomerate merger. The reason for this interest is perhaps because of its dramatic increase in popularity. The shift of corporate emphasis to the conglomerate-type merger can most probably be explained by the vigorous enforcement activity of the Antitrust Division and the FTC in the other two categories of mergers previously discussed. Whatever the reason, during the three-year period following 1948 conglomerate mergers accounted for 30 per cent of all mergers, whereas in 1968, 91 per cent of the mergers could be classified as conglomerate. At least one result of the startling increase in the number of suits brought against conglomerate mergers has been the rapid formation of a variety of tests for the courts to use when measuring the substantiality of the anticompetitive effects of a merger. These tests will be discussed separately, but one must be aware of the artificiality of the divisions, for in some cases one test will appear to be nothing more than a restatement of a preceding test. It is also worth noting here that some tests will be more relevant in product-extension mergers, one variety of the conglomerate, than in a pure conglomerate merger. This is also true for the market-extension merger. Briefly, the conglomerate merger or acquisition is one involving two businesses that have no relation with each other in any way, whereas the product-extension merger involves a company prominent in one line of products which acquires another company in a related line. The market-extension merger, as the name suggests, is the combination of two companies making the same or similar products, but in two different and separated areas of the country.

Reciprocity

One of the most feared and most discussed anticompetitive possibilities resulting from a conglomerate merger is the practice of reciprocal buying. Essentially, this is the name given to that aspect of a merger that encourages one company to purchase its requirements, where possible, from the other company, and vice versa. The Supreme Court in *FTC* v. *Consolidated Foods Corporation* discussed one of its evils when it stated that reciprocity " 'results in an irrelevant and a lien factor' . . . intruding into the choice among competing products, creating at least 'a priority on the business at equal prices.' "

This broad statement does little to clarify the matter. It is necessary to inquire further why the "priority" created is evil. One writer lists the disadvantages resulting from reciprocity as (1) a false impression of stability; (2) a lessening of selling efforts with a corresponding loss of selling ability; (3) inordinate expenditure of executive time to ensure the continuation of reciprocal buying programs; and (4) a distinct possibility of both parties paying higher prices for lower-quality merchandise than is available on the open market. Other adverse effects of a diligent practice of reciprocity include deterring the entry of new competitors and fostering rigidity.

The next step is to find out how the courts determine whether reciprocity exists and whether or not its existence is dangerous. All that is necessary for the possibility of reciprocal dealing to be proved is evidence tending to show that both companies involved have something the other wants. Obviously, if neither party manufactured anything the other could use, by definition there could not be any reciprocal dealing. Of course, there is always the possibility of a reciprocal buying ring being established, but in essence it is the same as the two-party arrangement and just as easily proved. Once the possibility of such reciprocity has been proved through the companies' own supply needs, not much else has to be proved. As early as 1963 in *United States* v. *Ingersoll-Rand Co.,* the United States Third Circuit Court of Appeals stated that, "The mere existence of this purchasing power might make its conscious employment toward this end unnecessary; the possession of the power is frequently sufficient, as sophisticated businessmen are quick to see the advantages in securing the good will of the possessor." This reasoning of the Court has been labeled "psychological reciprocity" because of its power to create the unwanted effect by psychological rather than overt means.

Two years later the Supreme Court reversed a Seventh Circuit dismissal of an FTC finding of illegality in *FTC* v. *Consolidated Food Corporation,* and held that Section 7 had been violated because (1) the merger altered the market to create a situation conducive to reciprocity, and (2) there was a reasonable probability that competition would be substantially lessened. The case involved the acquisition by Consolidated of a leading competitor in the manufacture of dried onions and similar products. Although the Court did not define what a substantial share was, or decide whether the relevant market was the buying or selling market, or even mention whether the acquiring firm's share of the market was important, the qualification was made that:

> We do not go so far as to say that any acquisition, no matter how small, violates §7 if there is a probability of reciprocal buying. Some may amount only to *de minimis*. But where, as here, the acquisition is of a company that commands a substantial share of a market, a finding of probability of reciprocal buying by the Commission . . . should be honored, if there is substantial evidence to support it.

The tests that one can derive from these two cases seem to indicate that the required probability of substantially lessened competition will be presumed if a company with a substantial market share is involved and if a probability of reciprocal buying is the result, whether that probability is substantial or not. This conclusion is buttressed by the concurring opinion of Mr. Justice Stewart in *Consolidated Food,* where he stated that the "opportunity for reciprocity is not alone enough to invalidate a merger under §7." Without a substantial market share, the substantiality of the anticompetitive effect cannot be presumed.

A more recent case has shed some light on this area of confusion. In *Allis-Chalmers Mfg. Co.* v. *White Consolidated Industries, Inc.,* the Third Circuit ruled that there was no need to show a history of reciprocal dealing either before or after the merger or acquisition in question. The burden of proof is satisfied if the challenging party is able to show a potential market conducive to reciprocity. When the Supreme Court denied certiorari in this case, the theory of "structural reciprocity" advanced by this decision became even more significant.

The increasingly lax standard of proof allowed by the courts in those conglomerate mergers exhibiting a potential for reciprocity has been criticized. Some experts in the area feel that the use of the reciprocity test for illegality should be reserved for those mergers that actually result in reciprocal dealing in goods or services. The psychological reciprocity discussed in *United States* v. *Ingersoll-Rand Co.* seems to be more than just a little subjective. Even the Supreme Court has admitted that possession of reciprocity power is not illegal itself. Its view seems to be that only if the power is used, and its effect is substantial, should it become illegal under Section 7.

The arguments countering this criticism are the facts that (1) Section 7 was meant to fulfill an incipiency role, (2) no actual agreement is needed for the reciprocal dealing to occur, (3) the proof is difficult, (4) postacquisition evidence is not needed to find a merger unlawful, and (5) divestiture is much more difficult later. After assessing the trend of the few cases since reciprocity became important, it appears that the arguments for use of reciprocity as a test will continue to prevail.

Potential Competition

Another of the more significant indications used by the courts in determining the legality of a merger is the elimination of potential competition. We have already seen how important the elimination of even one competitor has become in the horizontal merger area. The elimination of potential competition is held in almost the same reverence in the conglomerate merger area because in essence it is the same test. If courts were forced to rely on the test that requires the lessening or elimination of actual competition, it would be almost impossible to prove a conglomerate merger illegal, because by its very definition a conglomerate merger includes mergers between companies not actually competitors. To get around this stumbling block, the courts have theorized that potential competition—those companies waiting in the wings for the present competitors to step out of line—serves to keep competition at an acceptable level in the same way that actual competition does. Logically it must be accepted that if company X and company Y are the only two actual competitors in a given market and they decide to fix prices at an artificially high profit margin, company Z, a company with the capacity of becoming a competitor if the venture appears to offer an acceptable return, will step in and eventually force the prices down to their former level. In view of this theoretical competitive picture, the courts have refused to allow mergers between either X or Y and company Z.

This is precisely the basis relied on by the Supreme Court in *United States* v. *El Paso Natural Gas Company,* decided in 1964. Challenged in that case was the acquisition of the only other interstate supplier of natural gas on the West Coast, Pacific Northwest, by El Paso. Although Pacific did not supply gas to California, it would have been able to once it built the necessary pipeline. The Court considered the potential competition factor extremely important: "We would have to wear blinders not to see that the mere efforts of Pacific Northwest to get into the California market, though unsuccessful, had a powerful influence on El Paso's business attitudes within the State." The Court measured the actual "potentiality" of the competition by referring to the "nature and extent of the market and by the nearness of the absorbed company to it, that company's eagerness to enter that market, its resourcefulness, and so on." When these factors were considered, they were held to be met and the divestiture was ordered "without delay."

In the same year the Supreme Court held that Section 7 applied to joint ventures, and in that case the test relied on was the elimination of potential competition. The considerations relevant to the question presented were clarified by the Court. In the joint venture it was not necessary to show that both companies, or even one, would have entered. The Court would be satisfied if the joint venture "eliminated the potential competition of the corporation that might have remained at the edge of the market, continually threatening to enter." The Court also noted that potential competition could not "be put to a subjective test," but did reiterate the "potentiality" factors announced in *El Paso.*

The Federal Trade Commission had been relying on the elimination of potential competition as one of its grounds for attacking conglomerate mergers and acquisitions, but there were some doubts concerning the FTC's authority to apply such a test. These doubts were laid to rest by the Supreme Court in *Federal Trade Commission* v. *The Procter & Gamble Company.* The case involved the FTC ruling that Procter & Gamble's acquisition of Clorox was illegal under Section 7 because of its elimination of potential competition. The commission had decided that Procter was the most likely entrant into the field of liquid bleach, so the competition was definitely "potential." The Court agreed with the commission, observing that "[i]t is clear that the existence of Procter at the edge of the industry exerted considerable influence on the market." That influence was substantial because (1) the market behavior in the industry was affected by predictions of actual and potential competition; (2) the barriers to Procter's entry were small when compared with its resources; (3) only a few firms could be considered potential competitors of Clorox; (4) Procter was the most likely of these competitors. The commission's order of divestment was ordered enforced.

The commission's rationale in *Procter & Gamble* has been criticized since the decision was announced. The premise that competition would be better off if Procter challenged Clorox in the liquid bleach industry might be fallacious, because the end results might be that all the smaller competitors had been forced out by a price war, with the only two survivors being Clorox and Procter. If this reasoning is correct, it has not been followed or even mentioned in such recent cases as *Allis-Chalmers Mfg. Co.* v. *White Consolidated Industries, Inc.,* and *United States* v. *LTV, Inc.,* where the elimination of potential competition was a significant part of the challenge.

Deep Pocket

The theory behind the deep-pocket or rich-parent test is that a company that has been acquired by a large, well-funded company will be allowed to make use of the parent's reserve capital in order to wage a price war. A price war in an industry that had previously been made up of medium- to small-sized companies could be disastrous. Although the acquired company could remain solvent even though selling at or below cost, his competitors could easily be forced out of business. Once the competition had been eliminated, the remaining company would control the market and the price. The fear brought on by a merger between a small company and a large, well-funded company was expressed by Judge (now Mr. Chief Justice) Burger in *Reynolds Metal Company* v. *Federal Trade Commission.*

> Arrow's assimilation into Reynolds' enormous capital structure and resources gave Arrow an immediate advantage over its competitors who were contend-

> ing for a share of the market for florist foil. The power of the "deep pocket" or "rich parent" for one of the florist foil suppliers in a competitive group where previously no company was very large . . . opened the possibility and power to sell at prices approximating cost or below and *thus to undercut and ravage* the least affluent competition. [Emphasis supplied]

This was the court's feeling in *Reynolds,* a vertical merger case, so the importance of this consideration is multiplied when considered in the conglomerate sphere.

The Supreme Court in *Procter & Gamble* relied on this view when it listed one of the anticompetitive effects as the "substitution of the powerful acquiring firm for the smaller, but already dominant firm [that] may substantially reduce the competitive structure of the industry . . . by dissuading the smaller firms from aggressively competing. . . ." The threat that Procter would conduct a drastic price war that no one else could survive would keep the other competition in line. The effectiveness of such a price cut was discussed by the Court in a footnote detailing Clorox's major competitor's problems ten years earlier. "There is every reason to assume that the smaller firms would become more cautious in competing due to their fear of retaliation by Procter."

When history teaches us over and over again that we should learn to expect the worst that is possible, it is clear that the temptation to strike back against competitors is a strong one and that the courts should think twice before allowing the acquisition of that power by anyone.

Ease of Entry

When applied in the field of conglomerate mergers, this test requires the courts to look at the same types of indicators as in the horizontal and vertical mergers, but the perspective is somewhat different. The statistics that the courts review in both the horizontal and vertical area, such as actual number of new entries and availability of raw materials, have been thoroughly discussed earlier in the chapter. In conglomerate mergers the courts look not so much at the actual barriers that already keep out competitors, but rather at the change in the size of the barriers that will result if a conglomerate merger is allowed to be consummated. This is in line with the potential-competition test previously explained —the court does not look to see if a competitor already in business has been eliminated, but does notice whether a business previously considering moving into the market has now been discouraged from entering. Here we are concerned not so much with the absolute size of the barriers to entry, although that is important, as with the relative change in the barriers.

Again the *Procter & Gamble* case illustrates the application and importance of this consideration when a conglomerate merger is involved. Although the bleach industry preceding the acquisition had been characterized as an industry known for its ease of entry, the acquisition had changed that. The success of any marketing scheme depended heavily on advertising, because chemically there was little or no difference in the quality of the various bleaches available. Prior to the merger Clorox had a relatively small budget, and because of this was unable to obtain substantial discounts in advertising rates.

However, Procter spent more than $80 million on advertising and received substantial discounts. After the Clorox time was included in Procter's advertising set-up, Clorox could obtain almost one third more advertising coverage with the same expenditure. The Court concluded that "Procter would be able to use its volume discounts to advantage in advertising Clorox. Thus, a new entrant would be much more reluctant to face the giant Procter than it would have been to the smaller Clorox."

The barriers to entry either created or heightened by a conglomerate merger can result from several causes. The practice of reciprocity raises barriers by making it that much more difficult for a firm with a better product to take business away from competitors. The acquisition of a small firm in an industry characterized by small competitors raises barriers because of the "deep pocket" provided by the acquired firm. Barriers can be increased when a company capable of providing economies of scale acquires a small firm and puts those abilities to good use. Thus, heightened barriers to entry will continue to be an important consideration in conglomerate mergers.

Size

Although it has never been held that a conglomerate merger or acquisition is illegal merely because one of the companies involved is large, the disadvantages possessed by a large company in merger litigation must be commented on. Without even including the fact that mergers involving large companies are more often challenged, each of the tests of illegality used by the courts is more apt to be the basis for an order of divestiture because size compounds the undesirable results. In *Procter & Gamble* the forbidden effects of raising the barriers to entry and eliminating potential competition were the more prominent because of Procter's size. The deep-pocket test was made all the more persuasive because of Procter's big discounts, the result of huge advertising expenditures. The reciprocity fears were that much more convincing in *Allis-Chalmers* and *Ingersoll-Rand,* because of the purchasing power of these industrial behemoths.

So even though the judges continue to recite the magic words that "bigness in conglomerate mergers is not enough," as long as the adverse effect on competition remains the test of validity, mergers between large companies will always be more likely to be ruled illegal.

Other Tests

The major criteria used by the courts and the commission in judging mergers have already been detailed. To be complete, however, some attention should be given to miscellaneous factors mentioned in various cases that seem relevant. As always, these may just be the reformulation of another test, or merely a separate classification for some of the by-products resulting from the presence of a more important forbidden effect. In *Procter & Gamble* the Court noted that if the acquisition of Clorox was allowed the market would become more rigid, an undesirable change. By rigidity the Court meant that the market would not be as open to changes in market leadership as would be a market with vigorous competition and opportunities to capitalize on improvements in methods and processes. Market rigidity can be considered one of the manifestations of an accomplished oligopoly, but its presence can also be one more reason to deny an application to effect a merger.

Another test that could be classified as a variation of the deep-pocket theory is the concern with entrenchment. For entrenchment to be a factor, one of the merging companies must be of significant size in a concentrated market and the merger or acquisition must result in further concentration. This test has generally been employed in product-extension mergers. The Third Circuit mentioned this as one of its considerations in *Allis-Chalmers.* One of White's subsidiaries was a leader in the metal rolling mill market, and because Allis-Chalmers provided the electrical drive system for such mills, the subsidiary would be the only fully integrated supplier, thereby enhancing its position and entrenching itself even further in its dominant role. Because these considerations are also taken care of in the deep-pocket and ease-of-entry tests, it is not necessary to dwell on them further.

The final warning that should be kept in mind is that even if the merger is not attacked at the outset as being violative of Section 7 in light of the standards already discussed, it may be the subject of litigation if postmerger abuses emerge. *Reynolds Metals, Procter & Gamble,* and *Continental Can* have made this clear. This position derives from the incipiency theory itself. Because a merger may be challenged on the basis of potential anticompetitive effects, the government has the option of allowing the merger to be completed and waiting to see whether the potential becomes actual. Were it any other way, the government would feel compelled to challenge all mergers at the start or the successful masking of adverse effects at the start would preclude the filing of a suit once the merger was completed.

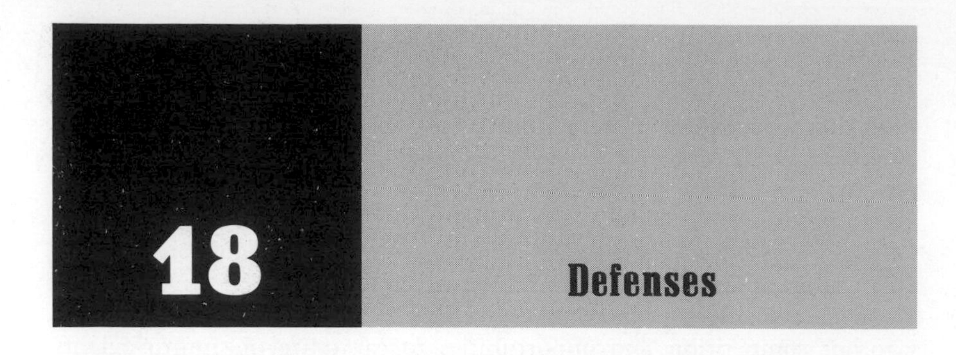

18 Defenses

As noted in earlier chapters, the principal issue usually involved in Section 7 litigation is whether the probable effects of a merger will be "substantially to lessen competition" in the relevant product and geographic markets. Accordingly, a defendant's case usually consists of challenging the plaintiff's determination as to what are the relevant product and geographic markets involved and in arguing that competition is not likely to be substantially lessened in any relevant market. There are, however, specific affirmative defenses which may be available under limited circumstances. These defenses are the subject of this chapter.

PURPOSE OF THE MERGER

The United States Supreme Court, in its 1962 *Brown Shoe* decision, took its first full look at a case brought under Section 7 as amended in 1950. The Court explored in some detail the history and purpose behind Section 7, and in so doing suggested some possible defenses available to those accused of its violation.

The case of *Brown Shoe* involved the acquisition of the Kinney Company by the Brown Shoe Company. In 1955, the year before the merger, Brown was the fourth-largest shoe manufacturer in the country, accounting for 4 per cent of the total national output. Kinney accounted for 1.6 per cent of total shoe sales in the nation, in addition to manufacturing 0.5 per cent of the total shoe product. The government brought a civil action under Section 15 of the Clayton Act, seeking an injunction to restrain consummation of the proposed merger. The injunction was denied, and the companies were allowed to merge as long as the businesses were operated separately and the assets were kept separately identifiable.

In discussing the vertical aspects of the merger, the Court offered a detailed examination of the factors that enter into its decision of whether or not Section 7 has been violated. It noted that once the relevant product and geographic markets have been established, it must consider whether the probable effect of the merger would be substantially to lessen competition in those markets. The share of the relevant market foreclosed to competitors is an "important factor" in this consideration, but it "will seldom be determinative." Unless the market share foreclosed is so great that a monopoly is created, or so small that it is clearly *de minimis,* it "becomes necessary to undertake an examination of various economic and historical factors in order to determine whether the arrangement is of the type Congress sought to proscribe." A most important factor is the very nature and purpose of the arrangement.

The Court cited the House Report of the 1950 amendment to Section 7 as an indication that Congress intended that similar judicial tests be applied in Section 7 actions as were applied with respect to other sections of the Act. The Court observed that Congress had used "virtually identical" language in Section 7 as it had in Section 3. Basically, Section 3 prohibits the sale of an item with the condition that the purchaser not buy anything from the seller's competitors, where the effect of such condition "may be to substantially lessen competition or to tend to create a monopoly in any line of commerce."

The Court in *Brown Shoe* noted that it had interpreted Section 3 to require an "examination of the interdependence of the market share foreclosed by, and the economic purpose of, the vertical arrangement." For example, if there were a tying contract involved (where in order to purchase item A from the seller, the buyer must also agree to purchase item B), such an arrangement would be so inherently anticompetitive in nature and purpose that it would likely be held unlawful even if only a relatively small percentage of the relevant market were involved. On the other hand, if a requirements contract were involved (where the customer has decided to purchase all that he needs of a particular item from a supplier selected on the basis of his competitive merit), the Court would view such an arrangement as less anticompetitive than the tying agreement. The requirements contract "may escape censure if only a small share of the market is involved, if the purpose of the agreement is to insure to the customer a sufficient supply of a commodity vital to the customer's trade or to insure to the supplier a market for his output and if there is no trend toward concentration in the industry."

Thus, with a given percentage of the relevant market foreclosed to competitors, a court may be moved to approve or disapprove a merger depending on some subjective consideration of the nature and purpose behind the merger. The Sixth Circuit Court of Appeals looked to the purpose behind a vertical acquisition in the case of *United States Steel Corp.* v. *Federal Trade Commission* (which is discussed in some detail later in connection with the failing-company doctrine). In that case the court found that the acquiring company had purchased the acquired firm, its customer, for the purpose of ensuring its own participation in the acquired firm's market. The court regarded this purpose as "obnoxious."

An example of a purpose acceptable to a court can be found in the landmark decision in *International Shoe,* which formulated and sustained the failing-company defense (discussed at length later in this chapter). According to the Supreme Court, the purpose of the acquisition in *International Shoe* was "clearly" not to "thereby affect competition"; rather the "controlling purpose" was "to secure additional factories which it (the acquiring company) could not itself build with sufficient speed to meet the pressing requirements of its business."

Although it appears that a court may be influenced in its treatment of a merger by the nature and purpose behind it, there is little likelihood that a valid business purpose would ever by itself save a merger which blatantly offends Section 7. According to *Brown Shoe,* purpose is only one factor, albeit an important one, which a court may consider in determining whether there has been a violation of Section 7. In 1968 a United States district court took a more guarded view, suggesting that the "mere existence of a valid business purpose for the merger, with possible limited exceptions inapplicable here, will not rescue the merger from the Clayton Act if it has a probably anti-competitive effect." The court went on to say that where it finds "no anti-competitive effects, then the existence of a valid business purpose for the merger allays the inherent suspicion cast upon mergers by the Clayton Act."

To be distinguished from the kind of purpose talked about in *Brown Shoe* is the purpose defense supplied by the Clayton Act itself where the stock of another firm is acquired for investment purposes only. Section 7, according to the language contained therein, does not "apply to corporations purchasing such stock solely for investment and not using the same by voting or otherwise to bring about, or in attempting to bring about, the substantial lessening of competition."

The Supreme Court took note of this language in its 1957 decision in the *E. I. du Pont de Nemours* case. According to the Court, "Even when the purchase is solely for investment, the plain language of Section 7 contemplates an action at any time the stock is used to bring about, or in attempting to bring about, the substantial lessening of competition." The evidence in the *Du Pont* case showed that the main reason Du Pont had purchased 23 per cent of General Motors' stock was to secure a customer for its line of automotive finishes and fabrics. The Court easily dismissed Du Pont's contention that the acquisition was for investment purposes only. A stricter interpretation of the investment defense was offered in a recent United States district court decision which suggested that a "merger cannot be defended as a mere 'investment' once it appears that the acquiring company *intends* to vote its stock and exercise control." (Italics added.)

A second distinction to be made is one between purpose and intent. Although a court, according to *Brown Shoe,* may consider the purpose behind a merger as a factor in determining whether Section 7 has been violated, the absence of an intent to violate the section does not, according to *Du Pont,* serve as a defense. The Court said in *Du Pont* that Section 7 "is violated whether or not actual restraints or monopolies, or the substantial lessening of competition, have occurred *or are intended.*" (Italics added.) It went on to note that the "fact that all concerned in high executive posts in both companies acted honorably and fairly, each in the honest conviction that his actions were in the best interests of his own company and without any design to overreach anyone, including Du Pont's competitors, does not defeat the Government's right to relief. It is not requisite to the proof of a violation of Section 7 to show that restraint or monopoly was intended."

TWO SMALL COMPANIES

The Court in *Brown Shoe* offered a second possible defense which it regarded as also related to the notion of economic purpose. This defense covers the situation of two small firms that merge in order to compete more effectively with larger firms. According to the Court, "Congress foresaw that the merger of two large companies or a large and a small company might violate the Clayton Act while the merger of two small companies might not, although the share of the market foreclosed be identical, if the purpose of the small companies is to enable them to compete with larger corporations dominating the market."

The House Report on the 1950 amendment indicated that this issue of two small companies merging was raised by those who feared that such mergers would be prohibited by Section 7 as amended. The report asserted that such fears were unfounded according to the following analysis. The language of Section 7 prior to the amendment (which spoke of lessening competition between the acquiring and the acquired firms) had been theoretically a far greater threat to small-firm mergers than would be the language of the amended Section 7 (which speaks of substantially lessening competition in a line of commerce). Small companies that had merged in order to become a more effective competitor had not been attacked under the old law, and it was not intended that they be attacked under the law as amended.

One suspects that the two-small-company argument would rarely appear in litigation under Section 7. Rather, it would be a factor weighed by the Justice Department or the Federal Trade Commission in determining whether or not to bring an action in the first place. For example, the Justice Department's Merger Guidelines indicate that in the case of horizontal mergers the fact that the acquisition will produce economies will not ordinarily be a defense. However, the guidelines note, as one of the reasons for this general rule, that the department would not ordinarily challenge the merger of "companies operating significantly below the size necessary to achieve significant economies of scale."

The point of the two-small-company situation was put well (if perhaps too metaphorically) by a United States district court judge in Hawaii. He suggested in the following passage that Congress was not concerned with small-company mergers:

> It was not concerned with the mating of ordinary cats, but only the matings or the acquisitions by the big tigers, lions and leopards in the business world. As the cases indicate, both the Department of Justice and the FTC have concerned themselves with acquisitions by the "big cats." No complaints were issued by the FTC against approximately 180,000 manufacturing corporations with assets of less than $5 million involved in mergers in 1950–1966, and less than .5% of merging companies with less than $25 million had any of their acquisitions challenged by the Commission during that period.

The court went on to warn in a footnote that it must not be inferred from the preceding passage that a "Clayton Section 7 violation cannot be committed by a tabby cat."

In concluding its analysis of possible Section 7 defenses, the Court in *Brown Shoe* noted that none of the defenses discussed would be available to the defendant in the case before it. Neither Brown nor Kinney, both leading firms in their industries, could be considered a small company. Similarly, neither was in a failing financial condition. As for purpose, the Court found evidence that Brown intended to use the merger to force the sale of its shoes in Kinney's stores. The Court regarded this as analogous to the tying arrangement, which had met with its disapproval under Section 3 of the Clayton Act.

Although the Court discussed these possible defenses while it was examining the vertical aspects of the merger, there was nothing to indicate that they would not be equally relevant in the case of horizontal mergers. In fact, when the Court went on to discuss the horizontal aspects of the merger, it remarked that the defendant had failed to offer in mitigation any evidence to support a finding of two small companies or a failing firm.

TOEHOLD ACQUISITIONS

The Court in *Brown Shoe* did not examine conglomerate mergers. There is a possible defense peculiar to the conglomerate situation, and it involves the so-called toehold acquisition. A toehold acquisition describes the case of one company acquiring a very small company in another industry, presumably with the thought of expanding that small company into a more substantial competitive force. Such acquisitions are not ordinarily challenged.

A firm sitting outside a given market as a potential entrant has a beneficial effect on competition within that market by the very threat of its entry. Two ways in which that firm can become an actual entrant without destroying that beneficial effect are through internal expansion or a toehold acquisition (followed theoretically by internal expansion of the acquired firm). In taking either route, the threatened potential competition will have been replaced by increased actual competition. If, on the other hand, the potential entrant merges with a sizable member of the market, then actual competition within the market will not be enhanced, and the beneficial effects stemming from the existence of a potential entrant will have ceased.

The Justice Department Merger Guidelines define the limits of the toehold acquisition by stating that the department will ordinarily challenge acquisitions by a potential entrant of a market member which falls within one of the following categories: (1) it has a 25 per cent or larger share of the market; (2) it is one of the two largest firms in the market, where the two firms have a 50 per cent or larger share of the market; (3) it has more than 10 per cent of the market and is one of the four largest firms in a market where the eight largest firms have a 75 per cent or larger share; or (4) it is one of the eight largest firms having a 75 per cent or larger share and its share "is not insubstantial" (where there are no more than one or two likely entrants into the market) or it is a rapidly growing firm.

The role of the toehold theory has been tentatively enhanced by a recent FTC decision involving the Bendix Corporation. Prior to the *Bendix* decision, a firm was considered to be a potential entrant only if it had the interest and capacity to enter into a given market by means of internal expansion. The *Bendix* decision broadened the definition of a potential entrant to include a firm having the possibility of entering the market by means of a toehold acquisition. Thus, as the result of *Bendix,* the "pure conglomerate merger might now be treated as causing an anticompetitive elimination of potential competition when leading firm acquisition is chosen instead of the toehold acquisition."

FAILING COMPANIES

A doctrine which has achieved limited success is the failing-company defense. This doctrine has since 1930 provided a legal defense to actions brought under Section 7 where one or more parties to a merger has been in a failing financial condition. The basic rationale underlying the failing-company doctrine is the following: because a failing company in any event is destined, as a result of its financial condition, to cease to be a competitive factor in the relevant market, its merger with another firm cannot be regarded as an event the effect of which "may be substantially to lessen competition, or to tend to create a monopoly" as required under Section 7.

The failing-company doctrine was formulated by the Supreme Court in the 1930 *International Shoe* case. The International Shoe Company manufactured and sold throughout the country all varieties of shoes. It gave rise to the 1930 Supreme Court case by purchasing all the stock of the McElwain Company, which manufactured men and boys shoes and sold them in several states. The Court first found that International and McElwain had appealed to a very different class of customers, and that for the most part there was really no competition between them. The Court then noted that the "financial condition of the (McElwain) Company became such that its officers . . . concluded that the Company was faced with financial ruin, and that the only alternatives presented were liquidation through a receiver or outright sale." At the time of acquisition McElwain had been experiencing a decline in the shoe market in general and in the demand for its products in particular, losing almost $6 million in little more than a year. It had ceased paying dividends, and its asset portion was such that it would have been declared insolvent under the laws of Massachusetts, where it was incorporated. McElwain had actively sought out other potential buyers and concluded that International was the only available purchaser.

Given this set of circumstances the Court held the following, which remains today the basic formulation of the failing-company doctrine:

> In the light of the case thus disclosed of a corporation with resources so depleted and the prospect of rehabilitation so remote that it faced the grave probability of a business failure with resulting loss to its stockholders and injury to the communities where its plants were operated, we hold that the purchase of its capital stock by a competitor (there being no other prospective purchaser) not with a purpose to lessen competition, but to facilitate the accumulated business of the purchaser and with the effect of mitigating seriously injurious consequences otherwise probable, is not in the contemplation of law prejudicial to the public and does not substantially lessen competition or restrain commerce within the interest of the Clayton Act.

Section 7 underwent substantial amendment in 1950. There is ample evidence in the legislative history of the amendment that Congress wished to preserve the failing-company doctrine that the Supreme Court fashioned in *International Shoe*. For example, the report on the amendment by the Senate Judiciary Committee revealed the following:

> The argument has been made that the proposed bill, if passed, would have the effect of preventing a company which is in a failing or bankrupt condition from selling out. The Committee are in full accord with the proposition that any firm in such a condition should be free to dispose of its stock or assets. The Committee, however, do not believe that the proposed bill will prevent sales of this type. The judicial interpretation on this point goes back many years and is abundantly clear.

Since 1950 the failing-company defense has been raised in numerous court cases. Although the doctrine has grown to be recognized as theoretically one of the strongest defenses to a Section 7 action, it has in a practical sense been of little aid to defendants once the matter has reached the stage of litigation. There have in fact been only two cases since *International Shoe* in which the defense has been sustained by the courts.

The first of the two cases sustaining the defense was a 1958 United

States district court decision, *United States* v. *Maryland and Virginia Milk Producers Association, Inc.* The association had purchased the stock of the Richfield and Wakefield Dairies. The Richfield company was no longer operating its dairy at the time of acquisition, but it did own and control the stock of the Wakefield Dairy. According to the court, the "evidence establishes without contradiction that at the time when the capital stock of those two corporations was purchased by the defendant the two companies were hopelessly insolvent and were deeply in debt. The defendant was a very large creditor, for an amount exceeding $300,000, for unpaid milk bills. The Wakefield Dairy was in fact on the brink of bankruptcy."

The other case to sustain the failing-company defense was the 1967 decision in *Grandaer* v. *Public Bank.* A county judge had declared Public Bank to be insolvent and appointed the F.D.I.C. as receiver. Subsequently, the Bank of the Commonwealth purchased Public's assets. The court found that Public "was on the brink of bankruptcy with no chance of rehabilitation"; that the Bank of the Commonwealth "provided the best offer in the light of the circumstances"; and that "therefore the acquisition of Public Bank's assets did not violate Section 7" because of the failing-company doctrine.

The United States Supreme Court has intimated its approval of the failing-company doctrine on several occasions, although it has not since *International Shoe* allowed the defense in a case before it. In its 1962 *Brown Shoe* decision, the Court suggested that parts of the legislative history of the 1950 amendment to Section 7 "evince an intention to preserve the 'failing company' doctrine of Intnatl. Shoe. . . ." It noted that "when concern for the Act's breadth was expressed, supportees of the amendment indicated that it would not impede, for example, . . . a merger between a corporation which is financially healthy and a failing one which no longer can be a vital competitive factor in the market."

Also in 1962, the Court in *United States* v. *Diebold* reviewed, *per curiam,* a United States district court decision granting a summary judgment against the government based on the failing-company doctrine.

The district court in *Diebold* had concluded that the acquired company "was hopelessly insolvent and faced with imminent receivership" and that the acquiring company was the "only bona fide prospective purchaser." The Supreme Court remanded the case on the grounds that the facts presented below, viewed in a light most favorable to the government, might have led to another conclusion; thus it had been improper for the district court to grant summary judgment. However, the Supreme Court did not challenge, and therefore by implication approved, the principles of the failing-company defense as set forth by the district court.

In its 1968 decision in *Citizen Publishing* v. *United States* the Supreme Court offered its most explicit and restrictive formulation of the failing-company defense. The *Citizen Publishing* case involved a pooling agreement between two Tucson newspapers, the Star and the Citizen. Under the agreement, the two papers were in effect merged into one business entity while maintaining separate and independent editorial and news departments. The Citizen had been a losing operation prior to the agreement (it had been suffering losses of about $23,000 per year whereas the Star had been enjoying annual profits of about $25,000); and the failing-company doctrine was offered as a defense to an action brought for violation of Section 7.

The Court, in disallowing the failing-company contention, sustained the district court's finding that the Citizen was not on the verge of going out of business prior to its entering into the joint agreement. The Court noted that there was "no indication that the owners of the Citizen were contemplating liquidation. They never sought to sell the Citizen, and there is no evidence that the joint operating agreement was the last straw at which the Citizen grasped."

In disallowing the failing-company defense, the Court set forth three elements necessary for a successful defense under the doctrine. First, it reiterated the requirement in the *International Shoe* holding that the financial condition of the allegedly failing company must be so distressed that "it faced the grave possibility of a business failure." Second, the Court made an express requirement out of what had been noted parenthetically in *International Shoe*— that the acquiring company had been the only available bona fide purchaser. This requirement, like the first, had been given implied approval by the Court in the *Diebold* decision discussed earlier.

By its third requirement the Court in *Citizen Publishing* broke new ground and narrowed the scope of protection offered by the failing-company doctrine. The Court noted that failing companies often emerge strong after they have been reorganized through receivership or bankruptcy proceedings. Thus, in order for the failing-company doctrine to be available to the defendant, it had to be shown that the prospects of the acquired company surviving by means of reorganization were "dim or nonexistent."

The Supreme Court has looked at the failing-company doctrine one more time since *Citizen Publishing*. In its 1971 decision in the case of *United States* v. *Greater Buffalo Press,* the Supreme Court made no mention of the third requirement in *Citizen Publishing,* but it found the first two sufficient to reverse a United States district court decision sustaining the failing-company defense.

The Greater Buffalo Company, commercial printers of color comics and supplements for newspapers, had acquired the outstanding stock of the International Color Printing Corporation, whose sole business was printing color comics for the King Syndicate. The evidence showed that International had a working-capital deficit of $100,000 prior to the acquisition and that it was unable to finance necessary improvements or to persuade King to enter into a long-term contract with it. The district court concluded that International's "resources were so depleted and the prospect of its rehabilitation was so remote, that it faced the grave probability of a business failure. No other person or corporation was interested in purchasing International which was a failing company."

On appeal, the Supreme Court found that the defense had met neither the test of the "grave probability of a business failure" nor that of the "only prospective purchaser" of the failing-company doctrine. The Court observed that in the year of the sale International had shown a substantial increase in profits, that it was paying dividends, and that it was actively pursuing expansion plans. Although International was unable to secure a long-term contract with the King Syndicate, King had neither revoked nor threatened to revoke the six-month cancellation provision in the existing contract. The Court noted finally that International had never approached anyone other than Greater Buffalo or King as prospective purchasers.

Along with the trend toward narrowing the scope of the failing-company defense, there has also been a tendency in the courts to place an ever-increasing burden on defendants to prove that they come within the narrowing scope. The Supreme Court in *Citizen's Publishing* placed squarely the "burden of proving the conditions of the failing company doctrine . . . on those who seek refuge under it."

Illustrative of this strenuous burden of proof is the 1969 United States district court decision in *United States* v. *Pabst Brewing Company*. This case concerned the acquisition by Pabst of the Blatz Brewing Company in 1958. Pabst's sales had been declining an average of 15 per cent annually from 1952 to 1958. Its profit and loss standing had fallen from an after-tax profit of $7.7 million in 1952 to a net loss of $2.9 million in 1957. The court conceded that Pabst was in a "very serious, even precarious financial position at the time of merger." However, the court insisted that Pabst needed to show, in order for the failing-company defense to be sustained, that "it had made every reasonable effort to explore alternative management and merger possibilities, either as a prospective acquiring firm or as a firm to be acquired." It found that Pabst had failed to prove the following conditions necessary for the defense: "that the firm was heading inevitably in the direction of bankruptcy, with the grave probability that failure would ensue—that is, that the trend was irreversible"; and that except for the merger "there were no reasonable, possible, or feasible alternatives which would have permitted the acquiring firm to remain an independent, competitive factor within the brewing industry."

The Federal Trade Commission has been even more reluctant than the courts to allow the failing-company doctrine as a defense. One startling example of its reluctance to allow the defense is its recent decision involving the United States Steel Corporation. The FTC there ruled that the failing-company doctrine is not an absolute defense, that it does not automatically grant every merger antitrust immunity. The commission noted that substantial lessening of competition could result even where one firm to a merger meets every test of a failing company. Where such lessening of competition *could* occur, the merger is unlawful, notwithstanding the failing condition of one of the firms, unless disallowing the merger would result in "probable harm to innocent individuals so serious and substantial that the public interest requires that the acquisition nevertheless be permitted."

The case involved the acquisition of the Certified Company by United States Steel. Prior to the acquisition, United States Steel (through its subsidiary, U.A.C.) was one of the nation's four largest producers of portland cement and was the sixth-largest supplier of portland cement in the New York metropolitan area. The Certified Company, one of the nation's four largest producers of ready-mixed concrete, was the second-largest consumer of portland cement in the New York metropolitan area. In 1961, the last year in which Certified was financially independent from United States Steel, Certified purchased 8.4 per cent of its cement from U.A.C. Beginning that year United States Steel became the creditor and guarantor with respect to increasingly large sums of money lent to Certified. By 1964, the year of the acquisition, Certified was purchasing 88.4 per cent of its cement requirement from U.A.C.

During the last six months of 1963 Certified suffered a loss of almost $930,000. By January 1, 1964, it had a deficit in net working capital of $279,000. The Federal Trade Commission hearing examiner found that Certified was a failing company at the time of the acquisition, and the commission agreed. The Federal Trade Commission, however, went on to state that the presence of a failing firm does not necessarily create a presumption "conclusive or otherwise" that the merger in question will not cause a substantial lessening of competition.

The implication of this last statement by the Federal Trade Commission is that in some cases it might be better for competition within an industry if the failing firm did, in fact, fail instead of being acquired. For example, in the case of a horizontal merger the acquiring firm may receive from the failing company a particular patent or access to some scarce resource that would give it a special advantage over the other competing firms in the industry. Also, simply acquiring the production capacity of the failing company may give the acquiring firm an unfair edge over the others. Similarly, if the firm had been allowed to fail, the decreased production capacity of the industry, given a steady or increasing demand for its product, would have made the industry more attractive to potential entrants.

In the case of the vertical merger involved in *United States Steel,* the Federal Trade Commission indicated that competition in both the portland cement and the ready-mixed concrete industries in the New York area would have been better served had Certified gone out of business. Certified's customers would have satisfied their need for concrete from Certified's competitors, who in turn would have satisfied their increased need for portland cement by purchasing from United States Steel as well as from its competitors. The Federal Trade Commission observed further that there had been quite a bit of price competition among ready-made concrete producers in the New York metropolitan area. It suggested that United States Steel would be able to withstand that rigorous competition and would eventually bring about a concrete industry characterized by more conservative and rigid pricing policies.

The legislative history of the 1950 amendment to Section 7 might indicate that the Federal Trade Commission's treatment of the failing-company doctrine in the *United States Steel* decision was unfounded. There is language in the history which indicates that the amended section was not intended to apply in the case of a failing company; that, in other words, a failing company provided an absolute defense. However, Congress seemed to have based this intent mainly on the *International Shoe* decision, which, as commentators have noted, provides no clear answer as to whether the failing-company defense is an absolute one.

On the one hand, it is possible to argue that the Court's holding in *International Shoe* was apparently based on that part of the original Section 7 prohibiting stock acquisitions that substantially lessened competition between the acquiring and acquired firm. It follows that if the acquired firm were failing anyway, it would have been logically impossible to say that the merger lessened competition between it and the acquiring firm. On this theory, the Court must have regarded the failing-company defense as an absolute one. On the other hand, there was in the original Section 7 facing the Court language prohibiting stock acquisitions that would "restrain . . . commerce in any section or community, or tend to create a monopoly of any line of commerce." It would not be logically impossible for an acquisition of a failing company to violate this language along the lines of the Federal Trade Commission's *United States Steel* theory based on the language in the current Section 7. Also, the Court in its *International Shoe* holding did note that a business failure of the acquired company would have resulted in "loss to its stockholders and injury to the communities where its plants were operated." This at least hints at the sort of balancing of interests that the Federal Trade Commission alluded to in its *United States Steel* decision.

The Federal Trade Commission's interpretation of the failing-company doctrine has yet to be squarely faced by a court. The Federal Trade Commission's decision in *United States Steel* was appealed to the Sixth Circuit in 1970. The court found "substantial evidence to support the Commission's finding that the anticompetitive consequences in Certified's continued existence as a giant vertically integrated concern would deteriorate competitive conditions in the concrete and cement industry more than its elimination by business failure." However, it did not address the issue of whether the failing-company doctrine would automatically permit a merger that threatened competition. Instead, the court found that United States Steel had failed to meet the burden of proving the third requirement set forth in *Citizen Publishing*—that the prospects of Certified surviving by means of reorganization had been dim or nonexistent. (The Federal Trade Commission's decision in *United States Steel* had been made prior to *Citizen Publishing*.) The Court, therefore, remanded the case to the Federal Trade Commission for reconsideration in light of *Citizen Publishing*.

There is an interesting twist to the Federal Trade Commission's theory in *United States Steel* found today in the area of bank mergers. Whereas the public interest, according to the Federal Trade Commission, might require precluding an acquisition that is unlawful notwithstanding the existence of a failing company, in the case of a bank merger the public interest may allow an acquisition in violation of Section 7 even where neither firm involved meets the failing-company criteria. The Bank Merger Act of 1966 has created a new Section 7 defense. It allows the comptroller of the currency to approve a merger that would otherwise violate Section 7 if he finds "that the anticompetitive effects of the proposed transaction are clearly outweighed in the public interest by the probable effect of the transaction in meeting the convenience and needs of the community to be served." The Supreme Court has recognized this new defense. In suggesting that the courts would continue to make the ultimate determination of Section 7 violation in bank merger cases, the Court made the following observation: "The area of 'the convenience and needs of the community to be served,' now in focus as part of the defense under the 1966 Act, is related, though perhaps remotely, to the failing company doctrine, long known to the courts in antitrust merger cases." The foregoing analysis of the failing-company doctrine may lead one to believe that it is of little practical use to a defendant in a Section 7 action. Indeed, in light of the trend of recent cases the defense has been characterized as a "slim reed" once the government decides to prosecute.

The failing-company defense, however, does appear to be of significant value in initially warding off prosecution. The Justice Department has indicated in its Merger Guidelines, published in 1968, that it will not ordinarily challenge a merger if "(1) the resources of one of the merging firms are so depleted and its prospects for rehabilitation so remote that the firm faces the clear probability of a business failure, and (2) good-faith efforts by the failing firm have failed to elicit a reasonable offer of acquisition more consistent with the purposes of Section 7 by a firm which intends to keep the failing firm in the market." The guidelines say further that the Justice Department "regards as failing only those firms with no reasonable prospect of remaining viable; it does not regard a firm as failing merely because the firm has been unprofitable for a period of time, has lost market position or failed to maintain its competitive position in some other respect, has poor management, or has not fully explored the possibility of overcoming its difficulty through self-help."

Similarly, the Federal Trade Commission has indicated on several occasions that it too pays some heed to the failing-company defense in determining not to oppose a given acquisition. These indications are found in the commission's premerger advisory program, which was substantially changed in 1962 so that requests for premerger clearance were to be made to one of two places. Ordinary requests were to go to the Division of Advisory Opinions; requests where one party to the proposed merger is subject to a commission order prohibiting further acquisitions without prior approval were to be made to the Bureau of Restraint of Trade.

In 1967 the Federal Trade Commission issued a report on the first five years of the revised premerger advisory program. During that period the Division of Advisory Opinions had received twenty-one applications for merger approval, of which ten were granted. In eight of the ten approvals the commission found that the "proposed acquired company was experiencing financial difficulties." During the same period the Bureau of Restraint of Trade granted its approval in thirteen of twenty applications it received (of which four were still pending as of 1967). In eight of those thirteen approvals the Federal Trade Commission noted the poor financial condition of the proposed acquired company.

There have also been more recent cases where the Federal Trade Commission has offered the presence of a failing company as reason for approving a merger. Early in 1970 it announced that it would have no objection to the acquisition of Pacific Western Industries by the General Portland Cement Company. It noted that "Pacific Western is in critical financial straits and its owners need relief promptly to continue operations."

Later in 1970 the Federal Trade Commission approved the acquisition of the Golden West Dairies by the Beatrice Foods Company. Beatrice had been under a Federal Trade Commission order to divest several dairy operations and not to acquire any others without prior commission approval. The Federal Trade Commission noted that Golden West had been losing money for the past five years and that its owner's age and ill health made it impossible to continue operating.

Also in 1970 the Federal Trade Commission approved the acquisition of the Pay Less grocery store in Dixon, Illinois, by the National Tea Company. The Federal Trade Commission noted that the Pay Less store had been in "failing financial circumstances"; that no other purchaser could be found; that operating the Dixon store was increasing the burden on the other stores in the Pay Less chain; and that after the merger the Pay Less company would be able better to devote its efforts to making its other stores stronger competitors.

There is some indication that the Federal Trade Commission, even in its advisory opinions, will not automatically allow the failing-company doctrine without making some determination, independent of the doctrine, that the proposed merger does not threaten competition. Prior to the Pay Less acquisition, the National Tea Company had requested an amendment to the restraining order it was under that prohibited it from acquiring more food stores without prior approval. The requested amendment would have allowed National Tea to acquire without prior approval up to two stores that had already initiated bankruptcy proceedings. It argued the failing-company doctrine in support of its request. The Federal Trade Commission refused to grant the amendment. It echoed the theme of its *United States Steel* decision by arguing that the sole fact that the stores had initiated bankruptcy proceedings would not be sufficient to guarantee that their acquisition by National Tea would not have the probable effect of substantially lessening competition.

OVERALL PROCOMPETITIVE EFFECTS

In *Ford Motor Company* v. *United States,* discussed in detail in the preceding chapter, the Supreme Court held that Ford's acquisition of The Electric Autolite Co. (Autolite), a leading independent manufacturer of spark plugs, violated Section 7 of the Clayton Act. Ford's defense was not to deny certain negative effects on competition found by the Court, but to assert that in other ways the acquisition produced procompetitive effects, so that overall there was no injury to competition. Ford claimed benefits to competition resulted from Ford's having made Autolite a "more vigorous and effective competitor against Champion and General Motors" than before, and from the increase in the number of competitors in the domestic spark plug market produced by the acquisition. The latter argument was premised on the fact that Ford had acquired only part of the assets of The Electric Autolite Company and that the remaining unacquired assets were still used by Eltra Corp. to produce spark plugs which in 1964 comprised 1.6 per cent of the domestic business. In response to these assertions of defense, the Court made its most important declaration, borrowed from the *Philadelphia National Bank* case, that illegality under Section 7 of the Clayton Act is not to be avoided on the basis of some "ultimate reckoning of social or economic debits and credits" which involves a value choice "beyond the ordinary limits of judicial competence." There follows the expression of the view that anticompetitive mergers, whether benign or malignant, are proscribed by Section 7.

Although this declaration, on its face, would suggest that the Court should not analyze the merits of Ford's allegations of counterbalancing benefits, the Court did, in fact, proceed to engage in such an examination and balancing process. This gives rise to the question of whether the Court really meant what it said about avoiding a balancing process under

Section 7 of the Clayton Act. Further, the perceptive comments of Mr. Justice Stewart in his concurring opinion note that the facts upon which the language from *Philadelphia National Bank* was based differ significantly from those in the *Ford* case.

In the *Philadelphia National Bank* case, the countervailing benefits raised in defense of the challenged bank merger only related to community development and general economic well-being, so-called convenience and needs, which the merged bank could supply, and not specifically to the state or nature of competition. In contrast, Ford asserted that the acquisition produced effects directly beneficial to competition itself. Thus, Ford argued, the net effect of the acquisition upon competition could not be determined until the negative competitive effects asserted by the government were weighed against the positive competitive effects which Ford raised as a matter of defense. General economic benefits, such as those raised in the *Philadelphia National Bank* case, relate to competition as do apples to oranges. But in the *Ford* case, both the government and Ford were talking about effects on competition. Both were talking about oranges. Mr. Justice Stewart described this situation as follows:

> Ford argues that the acquisition allowed Autolite to compete more effectively against the two larger brands, Champion and AC. Since this argument is addressed to the effect of the acquisition upon *competition,* the Court obviously provides no answer to the argument when it quotes *Philadelphia National Bank* for the proposition that arguments unrelated to the merger's effect upon *competition* are irrelevant in a §7 case.

Although the majority opinion in *Ford* does not explicitly recognize that the defensive matters raised by Ford related directly to competition, the Court's subsequent determination that even though the "acquisition left the market place with a greater number of competitors," the acquisition still "aggravated an already oligopolistic market," implicitly recognized the competitive nature of the benefits claimed by Ford. By determining that the competitive injury resulting from the foreclosure of Ford as a customer for spark plugs outweighed the benefits resulting from increasing the number of competitors, the Court, in fact, did balance the competitive injury against the competitive benefits. This would appear inconsistent with the Court's citation of *Philadelphia National Bank.*

The result is confusing. If one must hazard a guess as to the Court's meaning, as a large firm currently contemplating a vertical acquisition might have to do, it would be that the Court would not interpret Section 7 of the Clayton Act to allow the offsetting of competitive injury by showing of benefits, whether they relate to competition or not. In *Topco,* a nonmerger case decided the same day as *Ford,* the Court again manifested a very clear disposition not to become involved in complicated economic analyses or balancing processes in applying the antitrust laws. In this case the Court specifically cited *Philadelphia National Bank,* by analogy, for the proposition that the alleged promotion of competition in one market is no defense for the production of competitive injury in another market. The Court's actual performance of a balancing test in *Ford* could be described as mere surplusage. Although possibly a form of "overkill," the Court may have been saying to Ford that even though it did not accept Ford's position that the good and bad effects on competition should be balanced, its adoption of such a legal standard would not have changed the results of the case, because the benefits to competition alleged by Ford did not, in fact, offset the injury to competition found by the Court. This is the interpretation of Ford that the antitrust enforcement agencies will most likely adopt in their evaluation of injury to competition and in determining whether or not to file suit challenging mergers and acquisitions.

An important (and perhaps unintended) sidelight of the Court's ruling on the illegality of this acquisition is that it could be interpreted by some to affect adversely a novel merger theory which was expounded by the former assistant attorney general for antitrust, Richard W. McLaren, and is now being relied upon in litigation by the Federal Trade Commission. The theory relates to toehold acquisitions, described earlier. It states that where a potential entrant seeks to enter a market by acquisition of a leading producer in that market instead of by acquisition of a smaller or toehold firm or by internal expansion, the acquisition of the leading producer violates Section 7 of the Clayton Act.

It is not believed that the Court's reference to Ford's foothold in the aftermarket was intended to cast doubt upon the toehold acquisition theory. The adverse effects of Ford's acquisition upon competition in the domestic spark plug market were aggravated because of high concentration in both the producer and customer markets for spark plugs and because of the interrelationship of the submarkets for spark plugs. Thus, on the facts of this case alone, Ford's gaining of even a foothold in the aftermarket was likely to lessen competition substantially. This is entirely distinguishable from the legal assertion that in a market which is not suffering from such aggravated competitive conditions, the acquisition of a leading producer by a potential entrant, when entry could have been achieved through acquisition of a small toehold producer or by internal expansion, is a violation of Section 7 of the Clayton Act. The *Ford* decision should not influence subsequent determination of the legality of the toehold theory on its own merits.

19 Miscellaneous Corporate Amalgamations

Although technically Section 7 of the Clayton Act applies only to stock and asset acquisitions, the Supreme Court's 1963 decision in *Philadelphia National Bank* expanded its ambit to all "corporate amalgamations" the probable effect of which is to lessen competition substantially. As we shall see in this chapter the practical effect of the quoted language has been to interpose antitrust considerations into many types of business activities not traditionally viewed as within the antimerger laws.

JOINT VENTURES

The penumbra of Section 7 of the Clayton Act has continued to be enlarged as a result of legislative and judicial action. In the last decade a unique species of corporate activity has been construed to be within the proscriptions of the antimerger law. Appropriately termed a *joint venture,* this species involves the organizing and conducting of a separate business by two or more corporations. In its simplest form, corporation A and corporation B form corporation C, each parent owning 50 per cent of C's stock. Until recently, the courts and the academicians gave little treatment to the antitrust laws' effect on the joint venture. But the 1950's and 1960's spawned an alarming increase in the size and number of this type of interlock mergers, reflecting the surging desire of American corporations to expand their business activities. For example, in the period 1960–1968, the 200 largest manufacturing corporations established over 700 joint ventures. The intercorporate ties created by these joint ventures tended to amplify the pre-existing trend toward a concentration of industrial resources and economic policy-making. Corporations were achieving product and geographic extensions at one half the cost and without fear of competition from their coventurers. Economic studies have demonstrated that a majority of the joint ventures formed in 1965 by the 500 largest corporations involved products functionally related to those of the parents. In other words, the parents of the joint-venture corporation were either direct competitors or competitors within closely related product markets. This concentration of power, policy, and industrial resources magnified as an increasing number of large firms engaged in joint ventures. The net result, of course, was an enhancement of market power for the participants at the expense of reducing or eliminating actual or potential competition from other firms.

As the overall scope of a corporation's activities becomes more diversified, the effect of a particular joint venture, in terms of enhancing its market power, is an assumption of a more anticompetitive posture. As one commentator has indicated:

> Creation of the joint venture itself changes the structural dimensions of the industry. Firms having no market power before formation of the joint venture may gain market power in either . . . [market] as a result of cooperation between the parents and the joint venture and between the parents themselves. Where either parent enjoyed a market power position prior to creation of the joint venture, such market power would be enhanced with the expected cooperative behavior.

The increasing number of corporate interlockings arising from joint ventures during the late 1950's and 1960's jeopardized the Justice Department and Federal Trade Commission policies to curb the merger mania in the areas of horizontal, vertical, and conglomerate mergers. This initial frustration in public policy developed because the joint ventures did not easily fit within the usual merger concepts. Consequently, the legality of a joint venture was never resolved vis-à-vis Section 7's aim of promoting competition by proscribing acquisitions which have probable monopolistic or anticompetitive effects. The need for a judicial examination and exposition of Section 7's effect on a joint venture was satisfied in 1964 in the Supreme Court's opinion in *United States* v. *Penn-Olin Chemical Co.*

Essentially, Mr. Justice Clark, speaking for a majority of the Supreme Court, held that Section 7 applies to the formation of a joint venture and the acquisition of its stock by its parents. More specifically, the Court ruled that the formation of Penn-Olin by Pennsalt and Olin-Mathieson, each holding 50 per cent of the stock of Penn-Olin, could constitute a violation of Section 7. To understand more fully the *Penn-Olin* holding and its implications, it is necessary to place it in its factual setting.

The focal product in *Penn-Olin* was sodium chlorate, an acidified solution of sodium chloride produced by electrolysis and used primarily (64 per cent) in the pulp and paper industry as a bleaching agent. Pennsalt, a manufacturer of various chemicals and chemical products, with assets of about $100 million, controlled a 57.8 per cent market share of the sales of sodium chlorate west of the Rocky Mountains. This market advantage was primarily due to the location of its production plant at Portland, Oregon, thereby saving substantial amounts of transportation costs. Nationally, Pennsalt was the third largest producer of sodium chlorate, behind both Hooker Chemical Corporation and American Potash & Chemical Corporation. In the southeastern area of the United States, the Hooker and American Potash corporations controlled over 90 per cent of the sodium chlorate market. The southeastern market expanded considerably in the 1950's, and by 1960 the heaviest concentration of sodium chlorate purchasers was located in the southeastern market. However, in spite of the increased demand in that market, Pennsalt had some difficulty in increasing sales because it could effectively compete only if it absorbed substantial marketing costs in transporting the sodium chlorate from Oregon to the Southeast.

Consequently, Pennsalt was continually looking for methods to increase its southeastern market share and its profit margins. Throughout the prior ten years Pennsalt had considered constructing a sodium chlorate plant in the Southeast, specifically contemplating Calvert City, Kentucky. Four different new plant proposals were considered by the Pennsalt management, but all were rejected because of unattractive estimated rates of return. Pennsalt did not, however, rule out a joint venture; and the logical partner for a joint venture was Olin-Mathieson Chemical Corporation, a large diversified corporation which, at this same time, was also exploring the possibility of entering the sodium chlorate industry. Already a producer of a number of functionally related chemical products, Olin-Mathieson considered at least one proposal which recommended entry into the market as an "attractive venture" and as a logical expansion of its existing chemical product lines. Olin-Mathieson's management was dubious about the proposal and shelved it without a final acceptance or rejection.

In the meantime, in order to test its ability to penetrate the southeastern market, Pennsalt initially entered into a sales arrangement with Olin-Mathieson by which Olin-Mathieson became its exclusive seller for sodium chlorate in the Southeast. Through this agreement, Pennsalt marketed over 4,000 tons of sodium chlorate, accounting for 8.9 per cent of the sales in the southeastern markets in 1960. The exclusive sales agreement entered into by Pennsalt and Olin-Mathieson provided in part that neither of the parties "should move in the chlorate or perchlorate field without keeping the other party informed." The sales agreement was superseded in 1960 by the joint-venture agreement providing for the formation of Penn-Olin Chemical Company, with its plant operations located at Calvert City, Kentucky. Each parent owned 50 per cent of the outstanding stock of the joint subsidiary. Production commenced in 1961, and by 1962 Penn-Olin had captured about 27.6 per cent of the southeastern market.

It was in this factual setting that the Justice Department charged that the acquisition and ownership of Penn-Olin's stock by Pennsalt and Olin-Mathieson violated Section 7 of the Clayton Act. The federal district court, after hearing all the evidence and arguments, dismissed the government's complaint, concluding that the government had failed to prove that *both* Pennsalt and Olin-Mathieson would have entered the sodium chlorate market in the Southeast. This conclusion was based in part on the proposition that the creation of Penn-Olin injected a new competitor into the market, implying thereby that competition would not be lessened unless it was probable that *both* of the joint venturers would have otherwise become a competitor. The trial court found it impossible to conclude that both Pennsalt and Olin-Mathieson probably would have invested in a sodium chlorate plant. On appeal of the district court's ruling, the Supreme Court vacated the judgment, remanded the case, and, in doing so, established some landmark rules for applying the antitrust laws to joint ventures.

In deciding the case, the Supreme Court used a two-step approach. First, is Section 7 applicable to joint ventures? And if that question was answered affirmatively, second, did this particular joint venture violate Section 7? Although admittedly plowing new ground, the Court had no difficulty concluding that joint ventures, because they foreclose competition between the organizers, are subject to Clayton Section 7. The defendants' argument, that Penn-Olin, the acquired joint-venture company, was not engaged in "commerce" at the time of the acquisition and therefore not subject to Section 7, fell on deaf ears. In the Court's view, because Penn-Olin was engaged in commerce at the time the suit was brought, any contrary conclusion "would create a large loophole in a statute designed to close a loophole."

In applying the existing body of merger law to joint ventures, the Court posited that, generally, the same considerations apply to joint ventures as apply to more traditional mergers and acquisitions in that the pre-existing aim is to expound a "national policy enunciated by the Congress to preserve and promote a free competitive economy." The key to the effectiveness of this legislative intent has been the government's ability to arrest threats of concentration in their incipiency. The net result, of course, is that almost all judicial Section 7 determinations must be based on probabilities, not certainties.

Even though traditional merger concepts were readily held applicable to joint ventures, they still had to be translated into more specific terms to fit the peculiar attributes of joint ventures; then these specific guides had to be applied to Penn-Olin. As noted earlier, the trial court had concluded that there was no violation of Section 7 because it determined that it was not probable that *both* Pennsalt and Olin-Mathieson would have entered the sodium chlorate market in the Southeast in the absence of their entry in the joint venture. This conclusion was reached in the face of substantial evidence that both Pennsalt and Olin-Mathieson had the capacity, in terms of technical knowhow, to enter the market and that both had substantial interest, that is, each had actively considered formal reports recommending entry into the southeastern market. Essentially asserting that the joint venture, Penn-Olin, was just as effective a competitor as either Pennsalt or Olin-Mathieson would have been, the lower court concluded that there was no substantial lessening of competition. The Supreme Court disagreed and, by shifting the emphasis from a lessening of *actual* competition to a lessening of *potential* competition, ruled that the real test of a violation of Section 7 should *not* be whether *both* Pennsalt and Olin-Mathieson would have entered the market. Instead, the Supreme Court concluded that another alternative remained, that is, the possibility that *either* Pennsalt or Olin would enter the market and that the presence of the other, remaining at the edge of the market as a potential competitor, might restrain the market entrant from overcharging its customers and underpaying its suppliers. In other words, the potential competitor remaining at the edge of the market would be a key competitive factor in evaluating the impact on the market. But the creation of the joint venture between Olin and Pennsalt eliminated more than the possibility that both would enter the market; in addition, it eliminated the possibility that either corporation would ever act as a potential competitor to the corporation that had entered the market. The fact that the joint venture eliminated the prospect that the nonmarket entrant would have remained aloof watching market developments, waiting anxiously to enter an oligopolistic market, played a very heavy role in the Court's decision.

At first glance, the Supreme Court's argument seems to be contrary to the traditional lenient approach applied to joint ventures—an approach usually justified because a joint venture creates a new competitor that otherwise might not have existed. But the facts presented in *Penn-Olin* hardly justified an application of that benign approach. The evidence established that both Pennsalt and Olin previously had independently and actively contemplated sodium chlorate production in the southeastern market. As the Court noted: "[R]ight up to the creation of Penn-Olin, each had evidenced a long-sustained and strong interest in entering the relevant market; each enjoyed good reputation and business connections with the major consumers of sodium chlorate in the relevant market, i.e., the pulp and paper mills; and, finally, each had the know-how and the capacity to enter that market and could have done so individually at a reasonable profit." Based on this evidence, a very reasonable probability existed that the creation of Penn-Olin did not augment competition because it was a new entrant in the market; rather its creation lessened competition because what may have been two independent competitors actually became a single joint enterprise.

One last point in the *Penn-Olin* case must be examined—the mode of proof. Should the courts use a subjective or objective test in determining the probability that if one corporation entered the market by building a plant, the other corporation would have remained a significant potential competitor? In remanding the case, the Supreme Court, after setting out the many factors that provided strong incentives for both Pennsalt and Olin to enter the market independently, noted that "[u]nless we are going to require subjective evidence, this array of probability certainly reaches the prima facie stage." This would seem to be an indication by the Supreme Court that it would be appropriate to use an *objective* test, that is, what reasonable corporate executives would have done if confronted with the alternatives of (1) a joint-venture proposal and (2) an independent internal expansion proposal. Yet, on remand, the district court utilized a subjective standard in concluding that the government failed to prove that either Pennsalt or Olin would have constructed a sodium chlorate plant in the southeast if Penn-Olin had not been formed. The use of a *subjective* test has been criticized as being unreliable, unrealistic, and in some instances, inaccurate. It is anticipated that the development of joint venture law will include an inclination toward the objective test. In other words, the courts will not necessarily be swayed by a signed report retrieved from the corporate files showing that the board of directors had "formally" rejected independent internal expansion into the market. Instead, the courts will examine the joint venture parent's (1) capability of entry (for example, its accumulation of trade secrets, patents, manufacturing knowhow, existing production of functionally related products, and so on, (2) interest in market entry (normally satisfied by the mere participation in the joint venture), and (3) estimated rate of return on the independent investment based on an examination of market structure, money-market conditions, and other expansion data.

The Supreme Court in *Penn-Olin,* without expressly dictating either a subjective or an objective test, did delineate a number of criteria which might be considered in determining whether a particular joint venture violated Section 7. The criteria are as follows:

> the number and power of the competitors in the relevant market; the background of their growth; the power of the joint venturers; the relationship of their lines of commerce; the competition existing between them and the power of each in dealing with the competitors of the other; the setting in which the joint venture was created; the reasons and necessities for its existence; the joint venture's line of commerce and the relationship thereof to that of its parents; the adaptability of its line of commerce to noncompetitive practices; the potential power of the joint venture in the relevant market; an appraisal of what the competition in the relevant market would have been if one of the joint venturers had entered it alone instead of through Penn-Olin; the effect, in the event of this occurrence, of the other joint venturer's potential competition; and such other factors as might indicate potential risk to competition in the relevant market.

These factors expand on the three factors mentioned previously and indicate to the lawyer and to the businessman the length and breadth of a court's examination of a particular joint venture.

Little case law has been germinated by the *Penn-Olin* decision. Because of this paucity of litigation, constructing prospective rules for joint ventures is more difficult. To date, neither the Justice Department nor the Federal Trade Commission has issued any guidelines on joint ventures. A careful examination of the *Penn-Olin* decision does, however, point out some joint ventures which would definitely be suspect under that holding. The first type would be the situation in which but for the joint venture, both of the parent corporations would have entered the market. The formation of the joint venture would clearly reduce the number of competitors in the relevant product market. It would be the clearest violation of Section 7. The second type would be the situation in which but for the joint venture, one parent would have entered the market and the other would have remained on the edge of the market as a potential competitor to the market entrant. This example conforms entirely to the posited facts in *Penn-Olin* and, presumably, would dictate the same result. The third type would be the situation in which the parents of the joint venture are direct competitors in an oligopolistic market in which they are recognized leaders in the market or markets directly related to the joint venture. This situation would also present a substantial risk if the products of the parents were functionally related. A fourth type would be the situation in which the parents create the joint venture in order to complete a vital vertical link in their manufacturing structure. To illustrate this last example, suppose the prejoint-venture manufacturing structure was as follows:

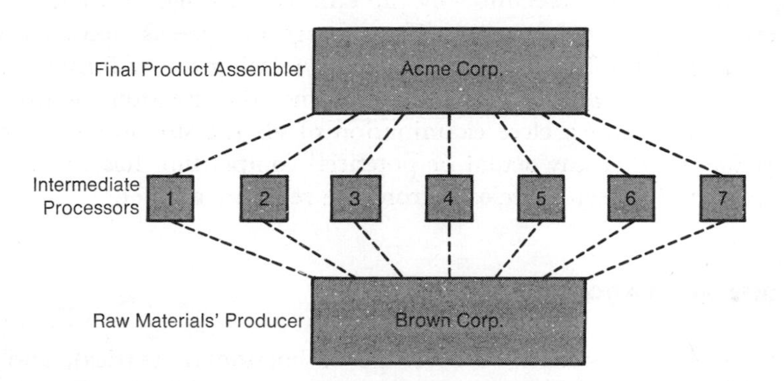

Brown Corporation sells its raw materials to any of the seven independent, intermediary corporations who process the raw materials into component parts for sale to numerous final manufacturers, one of which is Acme Corporation. After independent studies to increase sales and decrease costs, Acme and Brown agree to form a joint venture, Co-op, Inc., which will perform the intermediary processing. Being jointly owned by Acme and Brown, Co-op will be a captive buyer for Brown's raw materials and a captive seller to Acme Corporation. Thus, the vertical manufacturing structure is radically changed. The previous seven independent processors are now foreclosed from either buying from Brown or selling to Acme. There is little doubt that the courts would rule this joint venture a violation of Section 7. Of course, the same risk of violation would be posed if both parents occupied the manufacturing level of Brown, that is, each would then be selling to the joint venture; the parents' control of the joint venture's supply would create grave risks under Section 7 as interpreted by existing case law. Conversely, if both parents to the joint venture occupied the manufacturing level of Acme, that is, each would be buying from the joint venture, the risks would remain. The parents would have complete control over a vital link in the vertical chain and the elimination of existing competition for their business.

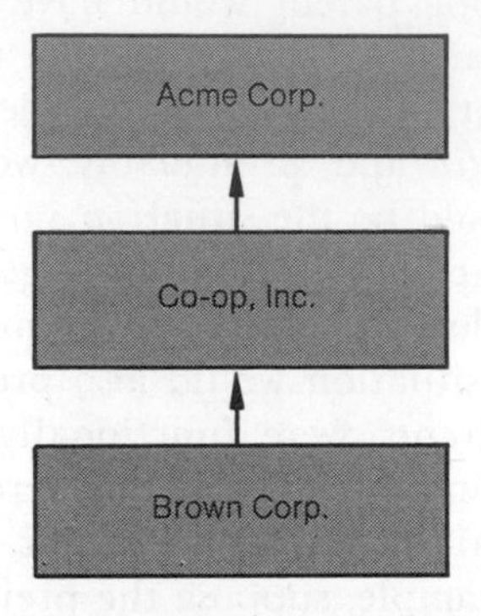

These examples point out some types of joint ventures that would be subjected to likely prosecution by the enforcement agencies and to careful examination by the courts. The passage of time is necessary for a more precise formulation of the guidelines relating to the formation and holding of joint ventures. In the meantime, the creation of any joint venture is cause for a close examination of all the surrounding facts to determine whether any actual or potential competition has with reasonable probability been foreclosed from the relevant market.

OTHER APPLICATIONS OF SECTION 7

In addition to Section 7's coverage of horizontal, vertical, and conglomerate mergers, as well as joint ventures, Section 7 has also been extended beyond those transactions. The government has long attacked acquisitions of partial amounts of stock as within Section 7. However, in spite of the clear and express language in the statute which proscribes the acquisition of the "whole or any part of the assets," acquisitions of partial amounts of assets were completely ignored for the first five years after the Celler–Kefauver amendment. The legislative history of the Clayton Act amendment fully depicted Congress' intent in enacting the law: "[The bill] covers not only the purchase of assets or stock but also any other method of acquisition, such as, for example, lease of assets. It forbids not only direct acquisitions but also indirect acquisitions, whether through a subsidiary or affiliate or otherwise." The legislative history emphasized the statute's intent to proscribe more than acquisitions of the entire assets of an enterprise, that is, a simple merger disguised as an asset acquisition. Relying in part on the well-settled rule that "immunity from the antitrust laws is not lightly implied," the Supreme Court approvingly quoted the excerpt from the legislative history already noted and stated that a broad coverage was necessary "to ensure against the blunting of the antimerger thrust of the section [Section 7] by evasive transactions such as had rendered the original section ineffectual."

Pursuant to the announced legislative and judicial policy, Section 7's prohibitions have been extended to acquisitions of individual assets, including patents, trademarks, copyrights, and exclusive licenses. For example, in *United States* v. *Columbia Pictures Corp.*, Universal Pictures sold to Screen Gems, a subsidiary distributor of Columbia Pictures, an "exclusive license" to distribute its pre-1948 feature films for television exhibition. Based upon its legally supported hypothesis that " 'assets' may mean anything of value," the Court asserted that the term had a broad, but pragmatic meaning, depending on the effect of the transaction. Rejecting arguments that "acquisition of assets" presumes transfers of property of significant magnitude, the Court concluded "that by entering into and performing the exclusive long-term, license-distribution arrangement, Screen Gems acquired a part of Universal's assets within the meaning of Section 7 of the Clayton Act." The judicial recognition of the expansive scope of Section 7 is readily seen in this case. Although Screen Gems did not acquire title to an ownership of the pre-1948 feature films, they did acquire an intangible "exclusive license" to distribute those films. Presumably, if the effect of the transaction would substantially tend to lessen competition or tend toward a monopoly, the application of this case would also condemn an exclusive license for use of customer, subscriber, or other similar lists.

The flexibility of Section 7 in the meaning of *assets* can be wielded as a very effective tool in antitrust enforcement. On the other hand, the broadly drawn language of the statute provides little certitude for businessmen. Perhaps the best approach is to look at the final result of the transaction and determine whether the acquiring corporation has received legal and economic rights and privileges which support a reasonable probability that competition will be lessened or that there is a tendency toward a monopoly.

The scope of Section 7 has also been extended into the areas of patents, trademarks, and copyrights. Although it is well settled that the mere accumulation of patents by grant does not violate the antitrust laws, the same cannot be said for accumulation of patents by purchase or by acquisition or, possibly, by grant-back. Ever since the Celler–Kefauver Amendment in 1950, Section 7 has proscribed the acquisition of *assets* if the transaction triggers the necessary adverse competitive effects. The initial problem is to determine whether *asset,* as used in Section 7, includes patents, trademarks, and copyrights. The legislative history of the Celler–Kefauver amendment makes no mention of including those items within the meaning of Section 7. Conversely, Section 7 contains nothing to indicate that they were not to be included. Although the issue has not often been litigated, there is a definite judicial authority interpreting that section and asserting that patents, trademarks, and copyrights are assets the acquisition of which may violate Section 7 if it produces anticompetitive effects. In *United States* v. *Lever Brothers Company,* a federal district court was called upon to rule on an agreement by which Monsanto conveyed to Lever Brothers its entire trademarks, copyrights, and patents relating to a detergent named *All.* Recognizing the dearth of litigation on the issue, the court, nevertheless, faced the issue squarely and concluded that patents, trademarks, and copyrights were indeed "very valuable assets of a company," and, hence, assets within the meaning of Section 7. Although the court concluded that in that particular case there was no substantial lessening of competition, it still established a viable precedent to the effect that the acquisition of patents, trademarks, or copyrights, if accompanied by the necessary anticompetitive effects, will violate Section 7. Consequently, *Lever Brothers* has been consistently cited for the proposition that a corporation which has already achieved a dominant position in an industry by the accumulation of patents runs a substantial risk of violating Section 7 if it continues to acquire future patent rights.

Although it seems reasonable to conclude that a nonexclusive patent license is an asset within the meaning of Section 7, the difficult question is determining whether an acquisition of a nonexclusive license would cause a substantial lessening of competition or tendency toward a monopoly. A nonexclusive license does not give its holder complete rights to the patent, but merely permits its holder to share with other nonexclusive license holders the right to utilize the patent technology. Ostensibly, the nonexclusive license should promote competition. However, it is possible that a corporation's acquisition of a nonexclusive patent license might produce a substantial lessening of competition. For example, suppose Acme Corporation achieved a dominant position in a particular industry essentially through its structure of funneling patents and patent licenses into its own portfolio of technology. If Acme then acquired a nonexclusive patent license that would improve its relative market position, it is reasonable to conclude that that acquisition would violate Section 7.

Depending on the structure of the market and the terms of the agreements, patent pools and cross-licensing compacts may or may not be subject to attack under Section 7. Patent pooling and cross-licensing agreements permit each member of the pact to utilize the technological improvements contained in the patents of all the participating members. If the arrangement is as simple as that, it is presumed that no antitrust law is violated because the effect is to improve technology among the participants and, hence, promote competition. But what if several smaller competitors were excluded from the arrangement? This has not yet been condemned, but it seems reasonable to suggest that Section 7 may be extended in the future to these compacts if the dominant firms in the industry continue to acquire new patent rights which cause the company to become entrenched in its dominant position within the industry.

Acquisition of patents pursuant to *grant-back* agreements may also come under the scrutiny of Section 7. Suppose Electube Corporation, a manufacturer of electronic components, has a vast accumulation of technical patents and has established itself as a leader in the electronic components industry. It subsequently conveys nonexclusive licenses to several corporations but only on the condition that those corporations *grant back* to Electube Corporation any patents or patent rights which may thereafter be owned or controlled by them. It can reasonably be argued that any patents or patent rights subsequently received by Electube Corporation pursuant to this grant-back agreement may be an "acquisition" as in Section 7. Once that hurdle is cleared—that it is an acquisition—it is a short step to conclude that a dominant corporation which agglomerates a superiority in patent technology through this funneling device has made an acquisition the effect of which "may be substantially to lessen competition, or tend to create a monopoly." Although this issue has yet to be litigated the businessman should be aware of it because the future of Section 7 may very well include this extension.

The newspaper industry has also felt the brunt of Section 7's embracive application. Faced with rising labor costs and the high cost of newsprint, newspapers in recent years have increasingly sought new methods and business arrangements to cut costs and increase efficiency. To this end some newspapers have engaged in sharing certain facilities or even departments to improve their efficiencies. The more sophisticated sharing arrangements are generally referred to as joint-operating agreements. However, depending upon the scope of joint operation and upon the structure of the relevant market, these agreements run the risk of violation of Section 7 of the Clayton Act, as well as Sections 1 and 2 of the Sherman Act. Although a joint-operating agreement is something less than the traditional concept of a merger, it still may come within the ambit of Section 7 because of the prohibition of any corporate amalgamation which accomplishes the proscribed results. The typical joint-operating agreement provides for a joint printing department, but maintains the individual publishing and editorializing departments. The natural effect, of course, is a termination of competition between the two papers for advertising. This is especially true if the agreement provides for uniform advertising rates or combination rates for the two newspapers, for example, $15 per square inch for placement in one paper and $20 per square inch for placement in both papers. This type of arrangement has recently received the Supreme Court's attention and illustrates another area in which businessmen must be aware of the antitrust laws in general and the merger laws in particular.

In 1940 two Tucson, Arizona, newspapers, the Citizen Publishing Company and the Star Publishing Company, entered into a joint-operating agreement by which an agency corporation, Tucson Newspapers, Inc. (TNI), was formed to manage and operate all the publishing departments of both newspapers. Excluded from this integration were the news and editorial departments which retained their independent functions. Thus, the advertising, production, and circulation departments of both newspapers were joined under the control of the agency corporation, TNI.

Although there were definite aspects of the agreement which came under the Sherman Act, a "stock agreement" provision incurred the condemnation of Section 7 of the Clayton Act. Under this provision if the stock owners of either newspaper ever desired to sell their stock, the owners of the other corporation had the first option to purchase. In 1964 the owners of the Star Publishing Company were willing to sell their stock and soon received an offer from an outside corporation. At this point the owners of the other corporation, Citizen Publishing Company, decided to exercise their option and organized a separate corporation, Arden, to carry out the acquisition. The result was that the previously independent news and editorial departments of the Star were now controlled by the owners of the Citizen. All phases of competition between the Star and the Citizen were virtually eliminated. Under these circumstances the district court found that the acquisition of Star stock by the Citizen shareholders violated Section 7 because it substantially lessened competition and tended to create a monopoly in the Tucson daily newspaper business. On an expedited appeal the Supreme Court affirmed, reiterating the lower court's finding that the acquisition of Star stock made permanent the elimination of commercial competition that had resulted from the operating agreement.

The Court was careful not to condemn all forms of joint operation. But there is no doubt that the Citizen Publishing Co. case warns that a stock agreement provision would violate Section 7 in almost all cases. However, certain forms of joint operations are still permitted, as long as there are no acquisitions of a competitor's stock, price-fixing, market control, or profit-pooling provisions that would violate the antitrust laws.

The full extent of Section 7's coverage has not yet been determined. Its scope continues to be enlarged in order to meet the demands caused by the effects of particular business transactions. The government enforcement agencies and the judiciary can be expected to take full advantage of the section's flexibility to achieve the law's purpose of curbing the rising tide of economic concentration by blocking all acquisitions or amalgamations that substantially lessen competition or tend toward a monopoly.

20 Mergers Involving Foreign Commerce

Man's journeys to the moon reflect in part the continual shrinking of the world. This is no less true in the commercial sphere. Expanding activities of United States corporations have injected substantial amounts of American commerce into the international arena. The creation of the European Common Market has fed fuel to the fires of international business growth. Sophisticated and complex international business transactions are now commonplace. In fact, it has been predicted that by 1984, the third-ranking economic power behind the United States and Russia will be not the Common Market but American industry abroad. This cumulative onslaught of international corporate expansion has sparked numerous antitrust repercussions. Indeed, the third great merger wave has left significant antitrust effects in its wake. Caused in part by the catapulting of the United States into the position of a world industrial power in the post-World War II era, this burgeoning of American corporate activity into international trade has produced new depths of investment in extraterritorial expansion. For example, during the period 1946–1967, American corporate investment abroad soared from $12 billion to $55 billion. Through different types of business creations—mergers, foreign acquisitions, and international joint ventures—American industry, aided by the compatible world political and economic climate, has been restructured into a dominant factor in foreign commerce. As alluded to earlier, this phenomenon has not gone unnoticed by vigilant antitrust enforcers. The problem of applying the antitrust laws to these transnational business ventures has been complicated by international political implications; countries are unwilling to challenge economic enterprises when the diplomatic damage will outweigh any gain in domestic competition. The net result of this reticence has been the escape from antitrust enforcement of a number of international business enterprises which otherwise might have been subjected to scrutiny by the courts of the United States. Recently, however, antitrust enforcement activity by the United States has accelerated sharply, and it is anticipated that more antitrust suits attacking mergers or joint ventures involving foreign companies and foreign commerce will be forthcoming. For these reasons it is important that issues in the area of foreign amalgamations be surveyed and analyzed in order to pinpoint the potential pitfalls and outline for the international businessman and lawyer the possible American antitrust risks that might beset any international enterprise.

RELEVANT LAWS

Any discussion of the U.S. antitrust impact of foreign amalgamations must commence with a survey of the relevant statutes. Generally aimed at trade restraints in domestic interstate commerce, these statutes, either by their very words or by their analogous meaning through judicial decisions, have been applied, in limited degree, to international transactions. The legislative history of these statutes—the Sherman Act, the Clayton Act, the Federal Trade Commission, and the Webb–Pomerene Act—reveals little about the Congress' intent or desire to affect foreign mergers and acquisitions. There are few reported decisions which specifically explore the law's impact on mergers or acquisitions which are unconnected to any conspiracy, monopoly, price fixing, or other restraint of trade. It has been only in recent years that the enforcement agencies have filed antitrust suits aimed at mergers and acquisitions embracing foreign and domestic companies.

Sherman Act

Since 1890 the oldest antitrust law, the Sherman Act, has prohibited contracts, combinations, and conspiracies which restrain trade or commerce among the states or with foreign nations. Section 1 of the Sherman Act proscribes "[e]very contract, combination . . . or conspiracy, in restraint of trade or commerce among the several States, or with foreign nations." Section 2 forbids every person from monopolizing, attempting to monopolize, or combining or conspiring to monopolize "any part of the trade or commerce among the several States or with foreign nations." The applicability of the Sherman Act to contracts, combinations, and conspiracies which restrain trade and which involve foreign commerce is clear from the statute itself. Despite this clear Congressional mandate for the statute's enforcement, notwithstanding the involvement of foreign commerce, the impact of the Sherman Act on foreign acquisitions and mergers has been diminished significantly, if not abrogated, by the statute's own inadequacies as interpreted by the courts in its attempted application to domestic mergers and acquisitions. As noted in the earlier chapter on mergers and acquisitions under the Sherman Act, the traditional, more lenient standard of reasonableness under the Sherman Act, vis-à-vis the Clayton Act standard, provided little deterrence during the domestic wave of mergers, and, presumably, even less deterrence in the field of foreign acquisitions and mergers. The Supreme Court's 1948 pronouncement in the *Columbia Steel Co.* case of a multifactor test to determine the reasonableness of a merger or acquisition added more confusion and less deterrence to the Sherman Act's merger enforcement theory. That case was the only pronouncement on the Sherman Act's application to mergers until the 1964 Supreme Court decision in *United States* v. *First National Bank & Trust Co. of Lexington* which held that the elimination of substantial competitive factors in the relevant market was a restraint of trade in violation of Section 1 of the Sherman Act. But the effectiveness of even this standard in the foreign commerce area is minimized because it is doubted by many whether the test of elimination of significant competition between competing firms can withstand the special considerations present in the foreign amalgamations area.

Clayton Act

Although the implications of the Sherman Act always should be considered, its use as a tool against mergers and acquisitions, both foreign and domestic, has been extremely diminished since the passage of the Celler–Kefauver amendment to the Clayton Act. Instead of the Sherman Act's stringent requirement of proof of unreasonable restraint of trade, antitrust enforcement authorities since 1951 have availed themselves of the Clayton Act's more liberal test of proscribing mergers and acquisitions the effect of which "may be substantially to lessen competition or tend to create a monopoly." The more stringent substantive tests of the Clayton Act were legislatively created to help stem the rising tide of economic concentration. Section 7 of the Act establishes the statutory tests for the validity of mergers, both foreign and domestic.

> [N]o corporation engaged in commerce shall acquire, directly or indirectly, the whole or any part of the stock or . . . the whole or any part of the assets of another corporation engaged also in commerce, where in any line of commerce in any section of the country, the effect of such acquisition may be substantially to lessen competition, or to tend to create a monopoly.

There are some difficult and unsettled problems in applying the Clayton Act to foreign acquisitions and mergers. Section 7 applies to acquisitions if the acquiring or acquired corporation is engaged "in commerce." Because *commerce* is defined in Section 1 of the Clayton Act as "trade or commerce among the several states and with foreign nations," and because Section 7 imposes no other territorial restrictions, one might assume that Section 7 would extend to foreign mergers. Unfortunately, the paucity of relevant cases makes a definite answer difficult. Presumably, the conclusion would be affirmative and, thereby, in accord with the pervasive domestic penumbras already given Section 7 by the judiciary. Moreover, the emphasis in the Section 7 cases has not been on the nationality or situs of the corporations involved; instead, it has been on the effects of the merger or acquisition in the United States. (Other problems encountered in applying the Clayton Act will be discussed in the following paragraphs.)

Federal Trade Commission Act

In the area of antitrust enforcement respecting mergers and acquisitions, the Federal Trade Commission Act has proved to be a powerful supplement to the Sherman and Clayton acts. Unlike the Clayton Act, the FTC Act does not require that the acquiring and acquired corporations be "engaged in commerce" to trigger its jurisdiction. Moreover, its definition of *commerce* includes "commerce . . . with foreign nations." This pervasive definition provides a wide spectrum of subject-matter jurisdiction. Unlike the Clayton Act, the FTC Act covers "persons," not simply the "corporations" covered by the Clayton Act. It is at least conceivable that an individual might make a foreign acquisition which might have a detrimental effect on commerce in the United States. Under those facts, Section 7 could not reach the individual because it applies only to corporations; yet the FTC Act would reach him because it applies to "persons." Although the Sherman Act also covers "persons," its effect would be limited in those facts because of the requirement of proof of an unreasonable restraint; on the other hand, the FTC Act is generally considered to apply to mergers and acquisitions which threaten to eliminate competition or which eliminate actual or potential competition, that is, a test similar to that under Section 7 of the Clayton Act.

One source of authority for using the FTC Act in the area of foreign amalgamations comes from Section 4 of the Webb–Pomerene Act, which expressly provides that the FTC Act's substantive tests and remedies are extended to "unfair methods of competition used in export trade against competitors engaged in export trade, even though the acts constituting such unfair methods are done without the territorial jurisdiction of the United States." Thus, corporations relying on the limited exemptions of the Webb–Pomerene Act are not exempted from "unfair methods of competition" as enforced by the Federal Trade Commission.

Webb–Pomerene Act

A carefully constructed exemption from the antitrust laws, the Webb–Pomerene Act permits domestic corporations to join in an association formed for the purpose of exporting goods to other countries on at least as favorable a basis as competing local or foreign firms. Essentially, the Act allows American firms to take part in cooperative export associations. The Act was passed in part because of the difficulties small American exporters were having in competing with foreign cartels. The heart of the Act is found in Section 2 which provides that nothing in the Sherman Act

> shall be construed as declaring to be illegal an association entered for the sole purpose of engaging in export trade, and actually engaged in such export trade, or an agreement made, or act done in the course of export trade by such association, provided such association, agreement, or act is not in restraint of trade within the United States, and is not in restraint of the export trade or any domestic competitor of such association. . . .

Although the Act permits voluntary associations for exporting of trade, it does not permit the voluntary association of domestic companies for the establishing and financing of manufacturing plants in foreign countries. As Judge Wyzanski stated in *United States* v. *Minnesota, Mining & Manufacturing Co.,* "Export of capital is not export of trade." The same reasoning would preclude any arguments that a merger acquisition, or joint venture between domestic and foreign companies would be exempted under the Webb–Pomerene Act. One readily recognizable basis for this conclusion is that the Webb–Pomerene Act only provides for exemptions from the Sherman Act, not from the Clayton Act. Thus, although the Act is relevant to any discussion of American business interests abroad, it neither authorizes nor expressly condemns (except insofar as it condemns unfair methods of competition in export trade), amalgamations of foreign and domestic corporations. Accordingly, any antitrust enforcement action against mergers, acquisitions, or joint ventures must be premised under one of the other antitrust laws previously discussed, that is the Sherman Act, the Clayton Act, or the Federal Trade Commission Act.

JURISDICTION

Article 1, Section 8 of the United States Constitution empowers the Congress to "regulate commerce with foreign nations." Implemented by, *inter alia,* the Sherman Act, the Clayton Act, and the Federal Trade Commission Act, this Constitutional grant of power is held in check by the exercise of international comity which insures that any exercise of this power would be to this country's political or economic benefit in its global affairs. It is this broad, overriding interest that requires a discussion of the reach of the U.S. antitrust laws to foreign transactions and, hence, the extent of the exercise of our courts' *jurisdiction* over foreign mergers, acquisitions, and other amalgamations. Of course, the concept of *jurisdiction* is generally divided into two areas: personal jurisdiction and subject-matter jurisdiction. It is generally understood that any action brought in the area of foreign acquisitions or mergers would involve at least one domestic participant; it is extremely unlikely that the Justice Department would attempt to break up a merger between two foreign corporations which have no base of operations in the United States. Accordingly, in any international action reasonably contemplated under the antitrust laws, it will be assumed that one of the participants in the merger or acquisition is a domestic entity or has agents within the United States. The necessary result of this assumption is that the problems of personal jurisdiction are significantly diminished, if not abrogated. In other words, the requirements for personal jurisdiction are no different for foreign mergers, acquisitions, or amalgamations than they are for any civil suit. Thus, the long-settled *International Shoe* doctrine is fully applicable, that is, that due process requires only that the defendant have some "minimum contacts" within the jurisdiction so that the maintenance of the proceeding does not offend traditional notions of fair play and substantive justice. Of course, there still remains the practical problem of actually getting service of process on a foreign party. Often the foreign corporation will have in the United States an agent or officer who can validly accept service of process.

The second aspect of the jurisdictional issue, subject-matter jurisdiction, requires special consideration because of the international aspects of the transactions. Any exposition of the subject-matter jurisdictional reach of the antitrust laws must have at its initial focal point Judge Learned Hand's opinion in *United States* v. *Aluminum Company of America.* Heralded as the "highwater mark of extraterritorial antitrust enforcement," the *Alcoa* case, as it is commonly called, is the pivotal and most pervasive discussion of the extraterritorial reach of the antitrust laws. Alcoa had created Aluminum Limited, a Canadian corporation, for the purpose of taking over "those properties of 'Alcoa' which were outside the United States." Because Alcoa had Aluminum Limited's stock issued to its (Alcoa's) shareholders, Limited was not a subsidiary, but, more appropriately termed, an Alcoa affiliate. Independent of the charges of Alcoa's monopolization of the domestic aluminum ingot market, the government also charged that Alcoa, through Aluminum Limited, had taken part in an international cartel which resulted in the protection of Alcoa's domestic monopolistic market position. Aluminum Limited had joined with corporations and business entities from Great Britain, France, Switzerland, and Germany to form a Swiss corporation, Alliance, to administer their international cartel agreement. Alcoa was not a party to the cartel and the court did not hold Alcoa responsible for Aluminum Limited's cartel participation. Despite this lack of specific participation by Alcoa, because the cartel was meant to and did affect foreign and domestic commerce adversely, and because the court had personal jurisdiction over Aluminum Limited (via its New York offices), it enjoined Aluminum Limited from further active participation in the international alliance.

Apart from the specific relief granted in the *Alcoa* case, its importance lies in Judge Learned Hand's discussion of what types of agreements were subject to the enforcement of the antitrust laws of the United States. Restricting himself, as indeed he was required, to only the laws of the United States, Judge Learned Hand started with the accepted proposition that "any state may impose liabilities, even upon persons not within its allegiance, for conduct outside its borders that has consequences within its borders which the state reprehends." In spite of this hypothesis, he was quick to point out that Congress should not be imputed with an intent to make liable everyone whom the courts can reach even though their conduct had no adverse consequences within the United States. Judge Hand then set out two possible situations in which the antitrust laws would not apply; complementing those situations were instances in which, in Judge Hand's opinion, the antitrust laws would be directly applicable.

Where Agreement Made	Agreement Intended to Affect U.S. Imports	Affect U.S. Imports	U.S. Antitrust Laws Apply
Outside U.S.	No	Yes	No
Outside U.S.	Yes	No	No
Outside U.S.	Yes	Yes	Yes
Inside U.S.	Yes	Yes	Yes

The first example put forth was an agreement made abroad which had no intent to affect imports into the United States but which, in operation, did affect imports. Although Judge Hand believed that any limitation on supply abroad would have some effect on U.S. trade, he concluded that the international complications "which would accompany any attempt to declare those agreements unlawful necessarily required the conclusion that Congress did not intend for the antitrust laws to apply to those agreements." The second situation was one in which the agreement made abroad was made with the intent to affect imports into the United States but which, in operation, had no effect upon imports, it also was thought by Judge Hand to be outside the pale of the United States antitrust laws. Acts done abroad with no consequences in the United States certainly should not be within the penumbra of Congress' antitrust proscriptions. Unfulfilled intent was no substitute for performance of restraints on United States trade. Therefore, Judge Hand concluded that the antitrust laws did not apply to the second example.

But, obviously, if the agreement made abroad was intended to affect U.S. imports and did, in fact, affect those imports, then, Judge Hand readily concluded, the United States antitrust laws were appropriately applicable to those agreements. Although Judge Hand made only passing reference to the fourth situation, it is elementary that that type of agreement would be subject to the applicability of the antitrust laws of the United States.

Under Judge Learned Hand's view, in order for an agreement made outside the United States to come under the American antitrust laws, the participants must have intended to affect United States imports or exports adversely and the operation of the foreign agreement must actually affect that commerce. The interesting and important aspect of Judge Hand's opinion is his conclusion that once the government proves that the participants acted with the "intent to affect imports," the burden of proof then shifts to the defendants to establish that there was no actual adverse affect upon United States imports or exports. In effect, this conclusion creates a rebuttable presumption that a wrongful intent will be deemed to be accompanied by actual adverse effects upon United States commerce. It is readily apparent that this rule is highly advantageous to the enforcement of the antitrust laws; indeed, this very rule was decisive in the *Alcoa* case. Because of the lack of evidence in the record to establish that the cartel operation did not affect imports into the United States, the presumption remained that imports were affected adversely; accordingly, the cartel was declared violative of the antitrust laws.

Notwithstanding its allure, Judge Hand's formula of intent plus presumed territorial effects equals an antitrust violation has been criticized as being insufficient to provide a proper basis for attachment of jurisdiction. One writer has criticized Hand's formula as being unrealistic in a situation in which the intent plus the presumed territorial effects are present but all participants in the transaction are foreigners or foreign corporations entirely owned abroad. Because of that writer's conclusion that it is most unlikely that jurisdiction would be exercised in that situation, he believes that Learned Hand's formula has utility only if coupled with an "additional territorial nexus" upon which legitimate jurisdiction can be exercised. And on close examination, the additional "territorial nexus" appears to be nothing more than a test similar to the "minimum contacts" used to determine if personal jurisdiction can properly attach. Viewed in this light, Judge Hand's thesis still retains substantial validity if used as a guide in determining subject-matter jurisdiction, subject, perhaps, to an additional requirement that the merger's effects have some territorial nexus to United States commerce.

Jurisdiction as an obstacle to attacking mergers, acquisitions, or other corporate amalgamations involving foreign corporations or persons is significantly minimized when analyzed under existing statutes and case law. Almost any commercial connection is sufficient to trigger both the minimum contacts and territorial nexus that are necessary to sustain personal and subject-matter jurisdiction. Thus, any merger, acquisition, or similar corporate purchase which is intended to and which does affect United States imports or exports is subject to the scrutiny of the antitrust enforcement agencies. Further, there is some reasonable speculation that the *Alcoa* rationale will be applied in reverse. In other words, if the government establishes that the merger or acquisition has had a substantial effect on United States imports or exports, it will then permit an inference that the defendants intended to affect the commerce of the United States. With the double applicability of the basic *Alcoa* rationale, the jurisdictional issues are somewhat minimized and attention can be turned toward the substantive tests of legality of foreign mergers, acquisitions, and amalgamations.

APPLICATION OF THE ANTITRUST LAWS

The scope of American corporate interests in international commerce is enlarging continually. Indeed, the encouragement of our export market is explicitly recognized as an American objective. In part, this has resulted from a reasonable and practical national objective of providing a legal basis by which corporations can compete meaningfully in the international market. Conflicting with this policy is the pre-existing national policy of promoting free competition and proscribing monopolies and restraints of trade. Nevertheless, in balancing these countervailing policies, the full force and effect of Clayton Section 7 and, to a lesser extent, the Sherman Act, upon these mergers, acquisitions, joint ventures, and other foreign amalgamations must be applied to these international transactions. The essential difficulty in doing so is determining the standards of illegality to be applied to these international transactions.

HORIZONTAL MERGERS

This segment will discuss mergers, acquisitions, joint ventures, or other foreign amalgamations having "horizontal" implications. The very few reported cases in this area provide minimal solid precedent; however, a combination of economic analysis and the existing case law does permit a reasonable discussion of the probable application of the merger laws to the various combinations and amalgamations involving foreign commerce and/or foreign corporations. In the area of horizontal amalgamations there are a number of slightly different combinations possible. The particular facts and circumstances present in each possibility must be weighed against the legal standards promulgated by the merger laws.

The situation which is most closely related to the domestic merger setting is that in which a domestic corporation acquires a foreign corporation which already has existing American plant facilities in competition with the acquiring corporation. Economically, the effects of this acquisition are not different from the effects of a purely domestic acquisition. The ramifications of the merger will be felt in those portions of the country in which the participating companies were competing previously. Therefore, the same substantive merger rules should be applied to this "international" example as have been applied to purely domestic acquisitions and mergers. Further, economically and legally, it should make no difference if the foreign corporation is operating its own production facilities in the United States or is doing so through a wholly owned subsidiary. In either event the economic results are indistinguishable; the same legal result should also follow. Therefore, the application of the merger cases should depend, as in purely domestic mergers or acquisitions, on the dominance of the participants in the relevant line of commerce and section of the country, the risk of precluding potential competition, and the tendency toward a monopoly.

This type of economic situation and its resulting legal consequences are depicted in the *Schlitz* case. The Jos. Schlitz Brewing Company, a Wisconsin corporation, acquired 39.3 per cent (a controlling interest) of

John Labatt Limited, a Canadian corporation, which in turn controlled a majority interest of the General Brewing Company, a California corporation. Thus, on the surface, an American corporation acquired a foreign corporation. But, analytically, and economically, *Schlitz,* a domestic corporation, acquired General Brewing, another domestic corporation. Hence, the thrust of the opinion was directed at the economically real acquisition of General Brewing. Using beer as the relevant line of commerce and California and the eight western states as the relevant sections of the country, the court concluded Schlitz's acquisition of General Brewing lessened competition and tended to create a monopoly in violation of Section 7 of the Clayton Act. This conclusion was bolstered significantly by *Schlitz'* almost simultaneous acquisition of all the assets of Burgermeister Brewing Corporation, also a California corporation, with its principal place of business in San Francisco. This asset acquisition facilitated the court's conclusion as to a violation of Section 7.

> The acquisition by Schlitz of the assets of Burgermeister, in connection with Schlitz' subsequent acquisition of Labatt stock and thereby control of General Brewing, is further evidence of the continuing trend toward concentration in the brewing industry in general and of the attempts by Schlitz in particular, to increase its sales and market share by the acquisition of competition.

Although the court gave negligible discussion to the jurisdictional aspects, it did provide a basis for some comments. Defendants, Jos. Schlitz and General Brewing were, of course, domestic corporations. Because it was an acquisition by a domestic corporation of a Canadian corporation, the court did not necessarily need personal jurisdiction over John Labatt Limited because the divestiture actions would be taken by Jos. Schlitz, which was within the personal jurisdiction of the court. Further, although unnecessary because John Labatt was not a party, the court did make findings which would have been sufficient to sustain its jurisdiction. For example, although John Labatt Limited was a Canadian corporation, its marketing structure included a "continuous flow of beer from Canada to Labatt's distributors in the United States," and constituted an "engagement in foreign and interstate commerce." In addition, there was a specific finding that John Labatt Limited engaged in United States commerce "through its control of, and close business relationship with and assistance to, General Brewing Corporation," its California subsidiary. Thus, although the court omitted any judicial discussion on the important jurisdictional issues, a close examination of the case reveals that the court made sufficient specific findings to sustain jurisdiction of the subject matter and personal jurisdiction of the relevant corporation. Except for these specific findings, the court treated Schlitz' acquisition of General Brewing like any other domestic merger case. Logically and legally this was the correct approach. Because the scope of the foreign corporation's activities was in the United States and because the chief situs of the acquisition's effect was in the United States, the traditional

Section 7 standards of legality were directly applicable; there was no reason for unique treatment merely because the acquired corporation's parent was a Canadian corporation.

Another horizontal merger involving foreign corporations was settled in 1970 by a consent order. The controversy centered over the proposed merger of Standard Oil Company, an Ohio corporation (SOHIO) and British Petroleum Company, Limited, a British corporation (BP). The Justice Department had opposed the merger because of alleged elimination of competition between the two companies, particularly in Ohio and western Pennsylvania. To safeguard competition the consent decree required that SOHIO divest itself of retail Ohio outlets accounting for taxable motor fuel volume in Ohio of not less than 400 million gallons, and that either SOHIO or BP divest itself of all its retail motor fuel outlets in western Pennsylvania. The resolution of this is squarely within traditional domestic merger guidelines, even though some of the parties were foreign corporations. (Of course, it should be noted that the foreign corporations denied jurisdiction over them in the absence of their voluntary submission for the purposes of the consent order.)

A slightly different factual basis will not necessarily affect the applicable legal standard. Suppose USA Corporation, operating in the northeast section of the United States, acquires International Ltd., a foreign corporation operating in the Midwest. Both corporations are engaged in the same line of commerce. Readers will readily recognize this example, except for the foreign nature and origin of the corporate charger, as a simple geographic market-extension merger. Economically and legally, the thrust of the acquisition's impact will be identical to the situation where all participating corporations were domestically chartered. Hence, there is no sound reason why this acquisition (or merger) should be treated differently from a purely domestic, geographic market-extension case. Therefore, it is entirely reasonable to expect that courts, confronted with a geographic market-extension case involving foreign corporations, would, after the jurisdictional hurdles are cleared, merely apply the existing Section 7 standards initially set out in the *El Paso Natural Gas* case. Under these standards the courts, in determining the legality of the acquisition (or merger), essentially will be deciding whether the two participants were potential entrants into each other's market area or whether both were potential entrants into a different market area. In addition, courts will analyze the market structure in each geographic area, that is, how many competitors there are and whether one participant is dominant in that industry and area. The end result, of course, is the conclusion that the foreign nature of a participant's corporate charter is ignored for purposes of economic and legal effect under the antitrust laws.

The preceding discussion on geographic market-extension mergers or acquisitions is directly applicable to the product-extension case. For example, a German electric typewriter corporation operating in the United States through wholly owned distributors merges with a domestic adding machine corporation. Both corporations market their products in the same section of the country. Further, because the products are complementary, assuming appropriate market shares and barriers to entry, the merger participants can well expect an attack upon the merger by the antitrust enforcement agencies. The *Procter & Gamble* case had announced the doctrine that the acquisition of a corporation which marketed a product complementary to one of the acquiring company's (in *Procter & Gamble,* the acquiring corporation, a diversified maker of household products, including cleansers, acquired Clorox, maker of a household bleach) violated Section 7 because it foreclosed Procter & Gamble from being a potential, independent entrant into the household bleach market. Again, once the jurisdiction obstacles are resolved—as, indeed, they will be in any case in which the foreign corporation operates manufacturing plants or distributors in the United States either by itself or through wholly owned subsidiaries—the courts can be expected to disregard the participant's foreign status. Treating it essentially as a domestic corporation, the court will analyze the merger or acquisition, considering primarily market shares, potential for entry, industry trends, and potential for reciprocal buying. In short, the tests for the validity of a product-extension merger on an acquisition involving a foreign corporation which has a base of operations in the United States is essentially identical to the result reached if that foreign company were a domestic corporation.

Of course, the permutation of types of essentially horizontal mergers is magnified in the international arena. For example, a foreign corporation, although not owning American subsidiaries or operating American manufacturing plants or distributorships, may, nevertheless, conduct a substantial business of exporting to the United States. These imports compete with domestic products within the same line of commerce and within the same section of the country. Consequently, if a domestic manufacturer were to acquire a foreign corporation whose imports competed with the products of the acquiring corporation, the basic economic effects of the acquisitions are not significantly different than they would be if the participants were exclusively American corporations. The potential for a lessening of competition or a tendency toward a monopoly within the relevant market is certainly no less merely because one of the participants is a foreign corporation whose American imports merely compete in the domestic markets. It is true that the foreign importing corporation, because it may be subject to tariffs and in some instances import quotas, may demand special consideration because of the political implications and effects of foreign trade policies; but although that fact may influence the enforcement policies in certain circumstances, it should not denigrate the basic conclusion that sound economic analysis of the effects of the merger or acquisition, under the existing horizontal doctrines and guidelines, may run afoul of Section 7. Nor should domestic corporations contemplating a foreign acquisition or merger expect that "foreign trade considerations" will necessarily support their exemption from antitrust enforcement.

Although there are not yet any reported cases in this precise area, the Federal Trade Commission has challenged Litton Industries' acquisition of Triumph-Adler, a German manufacturer whose electric typewriters are a major American import. Consequently, those imports are in direct competition with the Royal electric typewriters produced by a Litton subsidiary. This government challenge is a strong indication that the enforcement agencies will not permit mergers or acquisitions involving foreign corporations to go unchecked merely because the foreign corporation has no domestic base of operations.

To carry this latest type of example one step further, suppose that two foreign corporations, neither of whom have American manufacturing or distributing facilities but both of whom are major exporters to the United States, merge when, theretofore, their imported products were competing against each other in the American market. Despite sound economic analysis which may indicate a probable violation of Section 7, it is generally believed, and rightly so, that the foreign policy and international commerce considerations would overrule any thought of challenging that type of merger in the American courts.

The Clayton Act, Section 7, condemns a lessening of both actual competition and potential competition. Applying these concepts, as enunciated in the *El Paso* and *Penn-Olin* cases, to our present discussion, if the merger or acquisition eliminates potential competition—that is, those corporations who are sitting at the edge of the market, continually threatening to enter—it has violated Section 7. Recent events support the conclusion that this concept is fully applicable to the international merger arena. The Justice Department also has challenged recently the acquisition by Gilette Company, American manufacturer of safety razors, of Braun Aktiengesellschaft, a German manufacturer of electrical appliances, including electric shavers. Although Braun electric razors were not sold directly in the United States, its basic type was marketed in the United States by Ronson, pursuant to a license agreement between Braun and Ronson which expires in 1976. The apparent contention of the government is that upon the expiration of the license agreement, Braun will be a potential entrant into the American shaving market. Hence, Braun's electric shavers are a potential competitor of Gilette's safety razors. The government is seeking a direct application of the *El Paso* and *Penn-Olin* doctrines to this international acquisition.

The trend is quite clear at this point. Once the jurisdictional requirements are met, both personal and subject-matter, the result generally has been a disregard of the corporation's nationality and a direct application of the existing, well-developed, domestic merger doctrine.

Heretofore, the general thrust of discussion has been aimed at the economic marriage of domestic and foreign firms who have been competing in the domestic marketplace. But what if the merger is essentially export oriented—an American corporation, essentially an exporting company, merges with a foreign corporation which had been competing with the foreign corporation in the relevant international market. For example, suppose Exporco is an American manufacturer of Euro-Widgets, an item which it exports to Europe exclusively, with a heavy concentration of its sales in Germany. In the German market Exporco competes with Ruhrco Ltd., three other German corporations, and two other American major exporting companies. Assume further that the Euro-Widget market is an oligopolistic, highly concentrated industry. Suppose Exporco acquires Ruhrco Ltd. Obviously, in the highly concentrated Euro-Widget market in German, there has been a drastic anticompetitive effect caused by the amalgamation of two dominant companies in the oligopolistic industry. But does that violate Section 7 of the Clayton Act? That statute proscribes mergers and acquisitions only if they have the requisite anticompetitive effect in any "section in the country." In this example, the merger's effects are centered in Germany. In spite of what appears to be an area beyond the pale of Section 7, it has been argued that the combination may enable the American corporation to dominate the foreign market, which would have the concomitant effect of weakening the economic position of other American corporations competing in the same foreign market. The basis for that argument is the belief that Section 7 is aimed at protecting competitors as well as consumers. Thus, in our example, even though no American consumers are affected by the merger, so the argument goes, the fact that it affects adversely the competitive potential of competing American exports is sufficient to trigger Section 7's effects.

Although it may be true that Section 7 seeks to protect competitors as well as consumers, the unspoken assumption of the legislative policy is that it presupposes a market condition of American consumers and suppliers. The key point is the meaning of *lessening of competition.* From a definitional standpoint, it is quite apparent that the competition encompasses an economic condition involving both buyers and sellers. In the preceding example that condition is present only in Germany, not in the United States.

Again, like much of the earlier discussions in this chapter, the paucity of reported cases makes it very difficult to set out with absolute certainty an appropriate legal doctrine. Yet in light of the preceding contention that "competition" will be unaffected, it seems reasonable to suggest that it is extremely unlikely that any United States court, given the preceding hypothetical, would order Exporco to divest itself of Ruhrco.

VERTICAL MERGERS

Generally speaking, the same basic concepts apply to vertical mergers involving foreign corporations or facilities as apply to wholly domestic vertical mergers. Consequently, courts will be examining increased entry barriers because a supplier was eliminated, the number of suppliers whose competition was precluded by the merger, and any trend toward concentration in the industry.

An instance in which a vertical merger produced an economic analysis similar to that of the *Schlitz* case in the horizontal merger area is the *Dresser* case before the Federal Trade Commission. Dresser, a Delaware corporation, through its wholly owned subsidiary, Magnet Cove Barium Corporation, an Arkansas corporation, had acquired all the assets of Canadian Industrial Minerals, Ltd. (CIM), a Canadian corporation. Thus, the economic reality was a domestic corporation acquiring a foreign corporation. The relevant product market and geographic market was the sale of ground barite to end users for oil well drilling purposes in the Gulf Coast area. Prior to the acquisition, Magnet Cove was the chief purchaser of crude barite from CIM, Ltd. The second major purchaser was Milwhite, a competitor of Magnet Cove. The hearing examiner dismissed the complaint for lack of evidence establishing that the acquisition tended to lessen competition. The evidence revealed that after the acquisition, Milwhite had found other adequate sources of crude barite and continued to compete as before, including a substantial increase in its share of the relevant market. Without adopting the hearing examiner's opinion, the commission affirmed the dismissal, but accompanied it with a stern caveat aimed at future acquisitions in this highly concentrated industry. Significantly, neither the hearing examiner nor the commission based its decision on any foreign acquisition issue. But as was true in the *Schlitz* case, in *Dresser* there was a sufficient factual basis to satisfy the jurisdictional requirements. There was a finding that all the relevant product produced by CIM, Ltd., both before and after the acquisition, was shipped to the Gulf Coast area. Therefore, the Canadian corporation, CIM, Ltd., had substantial operations within the United States. Thus, as in the *Schlitz* case, disregarding the corporate charter's origin, the economic realities resulting from the acquisition were indistinguishable from those of a domestic acquisition. It logically follows that the legal result should also be indistinguishable. In *Dresser* this rule was adhered to silently. The complaint was dismissed pursuant to existing applicable standards for domestic acquisitions. No deviation in the standards of legality were pronounced merely because one of the participants was incorporated in a foreign country. Again, the dearth of relevant legal authority litigation in this area makes a clear and certain exposition of all the ramifications of the law on vertical mergers difficult. However, there is no reason to suspect that the substantive standards of legality for foreign-oriented vertical mergers will be appreciably different from those for domestic vertical mergers. For example, suppose Amtro Co., a Pennsylvania manufacturer of titanium rotors, operating in a highly concentrated industry, acquires Titan, a foreign corporation selling raw materials. Amtro imports its raw materials from

Europe; up until the merger 60 per cent of its raw materials were purchased from Titan; the remaining 40 per cent were purchased from competing American suppliers. Section 7 clearly would be applicable here. Definite entry barriers have been erected to impede other corporations from entering the titanium rotor market because Amtro now has exclusive control over a major titanium supplier. Further, American suppliers of titanium have been foreclosed from competing for Amtro's business. Because Titan can supply its entire requirements, Amtro has no need to bid in the open market for titanium. Further, the amalgamation of Amtro and Titan reflects a clear tendency toward concentration in an industry which is already oligopolistic. Thus, the anticompetitive effects in the preceding example are obvious and a Section 7 violation is readily apparent. The fact that Titan is a European corporation will not affect the result at all.

The result would probably not be different if the suppliers foreclosed from competing for Amtro's business were foreign corporations instead of domestic corporations. The barriers to market entry would stand just as high and be just as foreboding. The rising tide of concentration in the industry would not be changed. The same number of competing suppliers would be foreclosed from Amtro's business. The only difference is that these suppliers are foreign corporations rather than American corporations. Should this lone factor be sufficient to dissipate Section 7's penumbra? Courts probably would not diffuse Section 7's coverage on the basis of this factor alone. The argument against coverage by Section 7 is that the Act itself restricts its application to effects "in any section of the country"; therefore, because the suppliers foreclosed are located in foreign countries, Section 7 has no application. There are several methods, however, by which courts might conclude differently and hold that Section 7 is applicable. First, the courts might concentrate on the initial two factors—that is, the barriers to entry and the industry concentration—and conclude that these alone are sufficient to sustain Section 7's application. Second, they may posit that although the companies are located in a foreign country, the precluded sales are American imports; thus, the merger has precluded competition from American imports. In that light, the merger's effects are clearly "in any section of the country," that is, that section in which imports are marketed. Third, the courts may take a broader approach and view the relevant market in terms of its international dimensions. For example, the true structure of competition may be fully appreciated only in the context of the worldwide market. Thus, in economic reality, many mergers involve worldwide markets of which the American arena is really but a submarket. Although this is unprecedented in American law, it would give a more accurate picture of the effects in the whole industry, and it would be in accord with Section 7's increasingly expansive interpretation.

So far our discussion of vertical mergers has been import oriented. But it is also possible to have an export-oriented vertical merger, that is, an American raw-materials-exporting company might acquire its chief customer, a foreign processing corporation. If previous to the acquisition other American corporations had been competing for the foreign corporation's business, then, obviously, the effect of the acquisition has been to foreclose those American corporations from competition. In this situation, whether Section 7 has been violated will depend primarily on concentration in the industry (assuming, of course, there is a relevant market in any section of the country which, in turn, would depend on the effects of the merger and on barriers to entry into the market). Secondarily, it will depend on the foreclosure of competition for the foreign company's purchases of American exports. The importance of this secondary consideration will increase if the merger or acquisition has the effect of raising barriers to the export business itself, as opposed to merely raising barriers to the worldwide market or foreclosing competition from one foreign purchaser.

CONGLOMERATE MERGERS

We have already discussed product-extension mergers and market-extension mergers in the context of the standards applicable to horizontal mergers. Those mergers are, in general, a hybrid of the pure conglomerate merger and the traditional horizontal merger and are amenable to treatment in either context. Remaining to be examined, therefore, is only the "pure" conglomerate merger, that is, a merger in which the products of the acquiring and acquired corporations are not related. In the domestic arena, enforcement agencies and the courts have condemned those mergers when they eliminate potential competition, provide incentives and opportunities for business reciprocity, or entrench the company's market position. In light of the recent numerous attacks on domestic conglomerate mergers, it is safe to assume that conglomerate mergers involving foreign corporations are certainly not immune from close examination. No reported cases have yet emerged on pure conglomerate foreign mergers. But the application of Section 7 to other types of mergers makes it quite clear that once the jurisdictional obstacles are hurdled, the courts will apply the existing legal standards, taking into account the foreign corporate aspects only insofar as they affect the legal analysis of relevant products, relevant market area, trends in the industry, and probable effect on competition.

JOINT VENTURES

An increasingly popular business entity is the joint venture, both in United States commerce and, even more so, in international trade. A joint venture, as has been noted in an earlier chapter, is an entity organized and conducted as a separate business by two or more corporations. Its utility in the international market can be readily appreciated. A foreign corporation with a sufficient amount of capital may be willing to expand its business if it can have a domestic co-venture which can supply local knowhow and its share of the cost. In addition, in a political sense, the use of joint ventures is very advantageous in countries which either demand or encourage locally owned, at least in part, businesses. Freely conceding the utility of the international joint venture, its legality still must be examined. In the *Penn-Olin* case, the Supreme Court concluded that joint ventures were subject to Section 7, and that, generally, the same doctrines applicable to mergers also apply to joint ventures. Moreover, it is generally believed that the legal standards for foreign joint ventures will be the same as those for domestic joint ventures. (Those standards are set out in detail in Chapter 19.) Briefly noted, this will necessitate an examination of such factors as the likelihood of individual entry by a co-venturer if there had been no joint venture, the trend toward concentration in the industry, the barriers raised to entry by potential competitors, and the foreclosure of competition between the co-venturers.

The international joint venture most susceptible to challenge is a domestic joint venture formed by a domestic corporation and a foreign corporation. This combination places the venture's effects directly in the United States. For example, the Justice Department successfully negotiated a consent decree involving a joint venture of this type. Monsanto, a Delaware corporation, entered into a joint venture agreement with Farbenfabriken Bayer A. G., a German corporation, to form and operate Mobay Chemical Co., a Delaware corporation. Both parents were diversified chemical companies. Mobay was formed to produce and market flexible urethane foam, a polyurethane product manufactured from isocyanates. Monsanto was one of the four largest chemical companies in both the United States and the world. Bayer, the German parent, was alleged to be the largest chemical company in West Germany and the fifth-largest in the world. The allegation was that both parents had been producers of isocyanates and competing sellers in both the United States and the world; the formation of the joint venture eliminated the potential entry of each parent into the urethane foam market. In neither the complaint allegations nor the consent decree provisions was any exception taken or expansion given to existing standards on the legality of joint ventures. The resolution of the case appears to be a pure and simple application of the *Penn-Olin* principles.

On the other end of the international joint-venture spectrum, a domestic parent and a foreign parent forming a foreign joint venture, or two or more domestic parents forming a foreign joint venture—are less susceptible, but nevertheless not immune from challenge. The factor militating against application of the Clayton Act is that there is no probability of competitive injury. Of course, this argument has validity only if the foreign joint venture competes solely in foreign markets, for then it can be urged that there were no adverse competitive effects "in any section of the country." On the other hand, if the foreign joint venture turns around and competes in domestic markets through imports, it then will run a substantial risk of challenge, assuming the applicable market factors are present. This same type of joint venture might raise barriers to entry into the particular market by other domestic companies.

As indicated, a foreign joint venture formed by two or more domestic corporations may violate the antitrust laws, but it will depend on all the surrounding circumstances. For example, to the extent the foreign joint venture does not compete in the American import market, its risks are diminished but not extinguished. And, conversely, although no similar cases have been brought under Section 7, a somewhat similar case was brought under Section 1 of the Sherman Act. In the *Minnesota Mining* case, four fifths of the American abrasives manufacturers combined, ostensibly in a Webb-Pomerene export association, and established and financed factories in foreign countries. Finding the Webb–Pomerene exemption to be no defense to the export of *capital* to a foreign company, Judge Wyzanski found a violation of the Sherman Act because the foreign joint venture restrained competition both among the co-ventures and between the joint ventures and other domestic competitors. Further, *in dicta,* the court issued this ominous warning:

> [T]he reasonableness of the foreign conduct would . . . be irrelevant. Joint foreign factories like domestic price fixing would be invalid *per se* because they eliminate or restrain competitors in the American domestic market. That suppression of domestic competition is in each case the fundamental evil, and the good or evil nature of the immediate manifestations of the producers' joint action is a superficial consideration. [Citations omitted.]

Thus, this latest type of potential co-venture is faced with the specter of Judge Wyzanski's ominous dicta. Since that time, no similar cases have arisen; it is suspected that he may have frightened off some potential co-ventures.

The per se condemnation in *Minnesota Mining* appears to be limited to the joint establishment and operation of foreign factories. In other instances, courts have applied a rule of reason to international joint ventures. For example, in *United States* v. *Pan American World Airways, Inc.,* the government attacked Pan American Grace Airways, Inc. (Panagra), an air transport joint venture formed by Pan American, an important airline, and W. R. Grace & Co., an important shipper. Panagra's purpose was to provide air transport service to countries on the west coast of South America. Because prior to the venture, Pan American's activities were focused on the east coast of South America and Grace's shipping activities were focused on the west coast, the court concluded that they were not actual competitors. Moreover, the court reasoned, the extremely heavy capital investment required for the venture and the governmental policy of letting only one airmail contract for each route made it extremely unlikely that more than one airline could ever operate efficiently in the same market. Hence, an analysis of the joint venture's formation supported a belief that its creation was not unreasonable in light of market conditions. "The union of their [Pan American and W. R. Grace] physical and technical resources assured the maximum possibilities of success in instituting and carrying on a pioneering venture, useful to the community which did not theretofore exist."

Thus, when the courts have examined foreign ventures, they have used the same standards applicable to domestic joint ventures. In general, therefore, the international joint venture will be scrutinized in light of market conditions, likelihood of independent entry, foreclosure of potential competition, and in some instances, reasonableness. Overriding these factors, in a very rare case, will be international policy implications of a challenge to a particular joint venture. But this will be the rare exception and lawyers and businessmen should not rely upon it.

21 Recent Developments in the Antimerger Laws

In Chapters 15–20 we have detailed the development of the antitrust laws as they apply to mergers since adoption of the Celler–Kefauver Act of 1950. The approach has been primarily case analysis, because this is the means by which general laws achieve substance and permit predictability as to which mergers may be attacked and how their anticompetitive effects are to be analyzed. Additional predictability has been afforded by certain rules promulgated by the Department of Justice and the Federal Trade Commission, the texts of which are reprinted in the appendixes. It is to an analysis of these rules that this chapter is directed.

JUSTICE DEPARTMENT GUIDELINES

The guidelines of the Justice Department set out its policy of enforcing Section 7 of the Clayton Act against corporate acquisitions and mergers. Because the guidelines purport to cover the entire economy, they are of necessity stated in general terms. The primary focus of the guidelines is on "market structure," which is described as those market conditions that are fairly permanent or subject only to slow change—for example, the number of firms selling in the market, the relative sizes of their respective market shares, and the substantiality of barriers to the entry of new firms into the market.

To put the guidelines in proper perspective, the Justice Department stated that *market* would be defined in terms of its "product dimension" (line of commerce) and its "geographic dimension" (section of the country). *Line of commerce* is described as the "sales of any product or service which is distinguishable as a matter of commercial practice from other products or services." A section of the country is constituted by the "total sales of a product or service in any commercially significant section of the country (even as small as a single community), or aggregate of such sections." As defined, the standards are merely a restatement of existing case law. However, there is one later addition which suggests that the proposed enforcement policy is an extension of the case law:

> Because data limitations or other intrinsic difficulties will often make precise delineation of geographic markets impossible, there may often be two or more groupings of sales which may reasonably be treated as constituting a relevant geographic market. In such circumstances, the Department believes it to be ordinarily most consistent with the purposes of Section 7 to challenge any merger which appears to be illegal in any reasonable geographic market, even though in another reasonable market it would not appear to be illegal.

The import of this qualification is that if there are two reasonable geographic market alternatives, the Justice Department will determine its enforcement policy on the basis of the geographic market which places the merger or acquisition in the more disadvantageous position.

Horizontal Mergers

The Justice Department's guidelines set out different policies for enforcing Section 7 for horizontal, vertical, and conglomerate mergers and acquisitions. For horizontal mergers the department's aim is to prevent elimination of independent businesses, to prevent a company from obtaining position, to prevent significant increases in concentration, and to preserve the possibilities for eventual deconcentration in concentrated markets. In promulgating the guides for horizontal mergers, the primary emphasis is on the "market shares" of acquiring and acquired companies. This is in keeping with its overall reliance on market structure in assessing and predicting its enforcement policy.

For a highly concentrated market—that is the four largest firms constitute approximately 75 per cent or more of the market—the Justice Department ordinarily will challenge any horizontal merger in a range from which the acquiring firm has 4 per cent and the acquired firm has 4 per cent or more, to a situation in which the acquiring firm has 15 per cent or more and the acquired firm has 1 per cent or more. In a less highly concentrated market—that is the four largest firms have less than 75 per cent of the relevant market—the Justice Department will ordinarily challenge mergers according to the following table:

Acquiring Firm	*Acquired Firm*
5%	5% or more
10%	4% or more
15%	3% or more
20%	2% or more
25% or more	1% or more

In addition to the percentage tests applied in highly concentrated and less highly concentrated markets, the Justice Department utilizes an additional, more strict standard in determining whether to challenge mergers in any market in which there is a significant trend toward increased concentration, that is, a "trend" exists when the aggregate market share of any grouping of the two largest to the eight largest companies has increased by approximately 7 per cent or more in any time frame from five to ten years. Assuming that this "trend market" exists, the Justice Department will challenge any acquisition by any company in the above-noted grouping of any company whose market share is at least 2 per cent.

Although market share standards constitute the bulk of the guidelines for horizontal mergers, the Justice Department also will challenge the following mergers: (1) a company's acquisition of a competitor which is a particularly "disturbing" or "disruptive" competitive factor in the market, and (2) a merger of a substantial company and a company that, though it has a negligible market share, has a unique potential, for example, a company that holds a significant new patent.

There are two additional clarifications to the horizontal standards. The first is that mergers otherwise suspect will not be challenged if one of the parties is a "failing company"—that is, one who has no reasonable prospect of remaining viable. The second clarification is that any proffered arguments that the merger has resulted in economies of production or distribution will not justify an otherwise subject merger.

Vertical Mergers

The primary reliance on market structure and market shares is continued in the vertical merger guidelines. The basic goal of the department is to prevent changes in market structure which have long run anticompetitive consequences. This goal is implemented by challenging those vertical acquisitions which tend to raise barriers to entry or tend to disadvantage existing nonintegrated competitors.

In the "supplying firm's" market the department will determine whether to challenge a particular merger by analyzing the market share of the supplying firm, the market share of the purchasing firm, and the conditions of entry into the market. Those mergers will be challenged in which the supplying firm accounts for at least 10 per cent of the sales in its market and the purchasing firm accounts for approximately 6 per cent or more. The only qualification is that mergers otherwise subject to challenge will not be if there are no significant market entry barriers.

Looking at mergers in the context of the "purchasing firm's" market, initial guidelines for predictable challenges are found in the standards for the supplying firm's market set out earlier. But if the purchasing firm accounts for less than 6 per cent of its market, the department will focus upon whether the merger raises barriers to entry or whether it disadvantages the purchasing firm's nonintegrated competitors.

Although primary attention is given to market shares, the department will also determine its enforcement policy independent of market structure in instances in which there is a significant trend toward concentration or in which the acquisition will not result in economies other than advertising and promotion.

Conglomerate Mergers

Constructing proposed enforcement standards for conglomerate mergers is predictably difficult. Defined as those mergers which are neither horizontal nor vertical, conglomerate mergers specifically include market-extension mergers and, inferentially, product-extension mergers. The primary purpose of these guides is to prevent changes in market structure which would over the course of time cause a substantial lessening of competition.

The department invests two types of conglomerate mergers with specific structural guides: mergers involving potential entrants and mergers creating a danger of reciprocal buying. The first type focuses on the elimination of potential competition. Hence, a merger will be challenged if it is between a likely potential market entrant and (1) a firm with at least 25 per cent of the market, (2) one of the two largest firms in a market in which the two largest firms' total market share is approximately 50 per cent, (3) one of the four largest firms in the market in which the eight largest firms constitute 75 per cent of the total market share and the merging company's share equals approximately at least 10 per cent, or (4) one of the eight largest companies whose total market share constitutes 75 per cent of the relevant market, provided either the merging company's share is significant and there are only one or two potential entrants or the merging company is a rapidly growing company.

The second type focuses on the danger of reciprocal buying; that is, favoring one's customer when making purchases of a product that is sold by the customer. The department may challenge the merger on this basis. The significance of reciprocal buying will be determined by market shares; that is, any time 15 per cent or more of the total purchases in a market in which one of the merging firms sells are accounted for by firms which also make substantial sales in markets in which the other merging firm is both a substantial buyer and a more substantial buyer than all or most of the competitors of the selling firm.

Without using market share standards, the department additionally will challenge mergers which have the effect of entrenching or increasing market power, or raising entry barriers. The guidelines list several examples such as a merger which produces a very large disparity between the merged firm and the largest remaining company in the industry, or a merger of firms making related products which because of fear of leverage may induce purchasers to buy products of the merged firms rather than those of competitors, or a merger which enhances the ability of the merger company to increase its product differentiation.

The paucity of case law in the area necessarily limits the conglomerate guidelines to broad generalities. Further, the very concept of a conglomerate merger requires individual analysis of the peculiarities of the one or more markets involved.

FTC POLICY STATEMENTS AND RULES

The Federal Trade Commission has promulgated two sets of statements relevant to mergers. The first is a set of merger guidelines for particular industries. The second is a set of rules requiring that certain corporations must notify the Federal Trade Commission prior to a merger or acquisition in which the firms involved have combined assets of $250 million or more. The merger policy statements promulgated by the Federal Trade Commission do not have the force of law, but are statements based on the commission's interpretation of which types of mergers it will challenge in the cement industry, the food distribution industry, the grocery products manufacturing industry, and the textile mill products industry. Like the Justice Department's guidelines, those of the FTC are based primarily on the particular market industry's structure. Thus, prices and efficiency are ignored and market share, industry concentration, and market entry barriers are emphasized. The importance of the FTC policy statements lies in their business planning utility. If a merger of acquisition is within the guidelines, the parties can consummate the transaction with little risk of challenge by the Federal Trade Commission. Conversely, a merger or acquisition which violates the promulgated enforcement policies creates a severe risk of government challenge and, along with it, substantial business uncertainty for the corporations involved.

Cement Industry

Based on an industrywide investigation, including surveys, staff analysis, and, public hearings, the FTC formulated its cement industry guidelines. The FTC's critical concern was vertical mergers and acquisitions involving cement manufacturers and their customers, the ready-mixed concrete firms. This the FTC regards as a highly oligopolistic market, a relevant market frequently involving five or fewer competitors. Moreover, because of high transportation costs, almost all cement is sold and used near the site of production; consequently, the relevant geographic market typically is limited to one metropolitan area.

Because the ready-mixed concrete firms are the crucial link in cement distribution, the FTC's guides seek to maintain full and free competition in this market by preventing vertical integration in the industry. Specifically, the commission announced an intention to investigate with a view toward challenging an acquisition by a cement producer of any *substantial* ready-mixed concrete firm in any market in which the acquiring firm is an actual or potential supplier. These enforcement intentions are defined in terms of market structure:

> In general, the acquisition of any ready-mixed firm ranking among the leading four nonintegrated ready-mixed producers in any metropolitan market, or the acquisition of any ready-mixed concrete company, or other cement consumer, which regularly purchases 50,000 barrels of cement or more annually, will be considered to constitute a substantial acquisition.

In addition, the commission also normally will challenge an acquisition of smaller size if it is one of a series of acquisitions of small ready-mixed concrete producers.

To implement the cement industry guides, the FTC inserted a requirement that all cement companies notify the commission within at least sixty days of any merger or acquisition involving any ready-mixed concrete producers.

Food Distribution Industries

Ranging from the neighborhood independent grocery store to the large supermarket chains and wholesalers, the food distribution industries have been affected by significant structure changes in the past twenty years. The trend has been one of increased concentration on both the local and national level. The FTC's primary concern is aimed at horizontal mergers. The policy statements reflect in part the *Brown Shoe* and *Von's Grocery Store* opinions. Those cases lend support for preventing the elimination of small independent retailers which have significant effect on competition.

The commission focuses attention on horizontal mergers or acquisitions in which the parties have combined annual sales in excess of $100 million and particular attention on mergers by firms with sales in excess of $500 million. With these considerations in mind, the commission set out the following guidelines:

> I. Mergers and acquisitions by retail food chains which result in combined annual food store sales in excess of $500 million annually raise sufficient questions regarding their legal status to warrant attention and consideration by the Commission under the statutes administered by it.
>
> II. Mergers and acquisitions by voluntary and cooperative groups of food retailers creating a wholesale volume of sales comparable to those of food chains with sales in excess of $500 million annually also raise sufficient questions regarding their legal status to warrant attention and consideration by the Commission under the statutes administered by it.
>
> III. Mergers and acquisitions by food chains or wholesalers which result in combined annual food store sales of between $100 million and $500 million appear to warrant investigation by the Commission to determine whether there has been or may be a violation of any statutes administered by the Commission.

The commission did qualify its enforcement policy in one respect. Even though a merger or acquisition otherwise violates the guidelines, the Federal Trade Commission will not challenge it, if it satisfies *all* of the following criteria: (1) the merger or acquisition does not involve more than four food or grocery stores; (2) the merger or acquisition is of food or grocery stores or food wholesaling establishments which represent annual food or grocery product sales of not more than $5 million; *and* (3) it is a merger or acquisition of grocery store or food wholesaling establishments whose combined food store sales do not constitute more than 5 per cent of the total food stores sales in any city or county in the United States.

The guidelines implement two underlying policy considerations. The first is that firms who want to expand to increase efficiency should do so by internal growth, not by horizontal acquisitions. The second is the commission's determination that competition is best preserved, even in fragmented industries, if the elimination of small independent retailers can be prevented.

Like the cement industry guidelines, the guides for the food distribution industries require every good retailer and wholesaler with annual sales in excess of $100 million to notify the FTC within sixty days of any merger, acquisition, or consolidation involving any food retailer or wholesaler.

Grocery Products Manufacturing Industry

The FTC also has become very concerned about the grocery products manufacturing industry, which has been becoming increasingly concentrated and where small companies have been disappearing. Based on statistical reports indicating that the food manufacturing firms were growing beyond that required for full operating efficiencies and that this growth was chiefly the result of merger and acquisition, the FTC's concern is directed at the anticompetitive effects of the large firms' promotional and advertising activities and their product-extension mergers which have had the effect of eliminating potential and actual competition.

The principal cases relied upon by the FTC in formulating the guidelines were *FTC* v. *Procter & Gamble* and *FTC* v. *Consolidated Foods Corp.* In the former, Procter & Gamble, a large, diversified grocery products manufacturing company, acquired Clorox, a firm which controlled about 50 per cent of the liquid bleach market. The Supreme Court concluded that the acquisition violated Section 7 because it eliminated Procter & Gamble as a potential competitor in the liquid bleach market and, given the large advertising and promotional programs of Procter & Gamble, the acquisition would entrench its market power further. In *Consolidated Foods* a large food processor acquired Gentry, a producer of dehydrated onion and garlic. The fear of anticompetitive reciprocal buying was a major factor in the court's conclusion that the merger violated the merger laws.

Another significant concern of the FTC is the proliferation of product-extension mergers in the industry. The largest food manufacturers were a major part of the merger movement. In 1965 nearly one fourth of the total assets of the fifty largest food manufacturers were attributable to mergers made during the previous fifteen-year period. The FTC's fear was that the proliferation would continue. As of 1966, excluding the fifty largest food manufacturers, almost one half of the next-largest 170 food manufacturers had a significant degree of product differentiation. Unless enforcement activity was stepped up, the FTC feared that these seventy-five firms would be the chief targets of future acquisitions.

The FTC's premises are that competition is best effected by promoting internal growth and by prohibiting acquisitions which have the effect of eliminating potential competition and erecting barriers to entry by others into the market. The FTC, although acknowledging the presence of 30,000 food manufacturers, stressed that as few as fifty firms are either the leading actual competitors or the leading potential competitors in the most highly concentrated grocery product markets. To safeguard competition in these industries, the FTC concluded that enforcement policy statements were necessary to provide industry businessmen with guidance on which product-extension mergers were subject to probable challenge under Section 7. These concerns provided the underlying basis for the FTC's enforcement guidelines. The FTC listed four criteria it would use in determining whether to challenge particular acquisitions or mergers.

(1) Both the acquiring and acquired companies engage in the manufacture of grocery products. Grocery products include food and other consumer products customarily sold in food and grocery stores.

(2) The combined company has assets in excess of $250 million.

(3) The acquiring company engages in extensive promotion efforts, sells highly differentiated consumer products, and produces a number of products, in some of which it holds a strong market position. A strong market position is defined as being one of the top four producers of a product in which the top four companies hold 40 percent or more of the value of shipments.

(4) The *acquired* company is either among the top eight producers of any one important grocery product, or has more than a 5 percent share of a relevant market.

The criteria apparently would affect almost every acquisition by any of the fifty largest food manufacturers. The first three criteria presumably would apply to these firms. Given the narrow definition of the "relevant market"—for example, liquid bleach—almost every acquired company would have at least 5 per cent of a relevant market or be among the top eight producers of *any one* important grocery product. Although *important* is not further defined, given the general expansive interpretation in Section 7 litigation, that concept should not be considered restrictive. Although the guidelines are more strict than the supporting case law, they are consistent with the overall government antitrust enforcement policy, that is, to promote full and fair competition by preventing the elimination of independent competitors.

Textile Mill Products Industry

In the textile mill products industry the FTC relies again primarily on market structure. The textile mill products industry, which encompasses the intermediate production stage of the apparel trades as well as finished products in the carpeting and towel markets, has had a considerable increase in concentration—principally resulting from mergers—since the early 1950's. Although the textile industry generally had been considered highly fragmented, the recent proliferation of all types of mergers has increased concentration dramatically in the industry in general and in several submarkets in particular. Using a firm's total assets as the measure for indicating the increased concentration in the industry, the FTC's statistics revealed that during the period 1951–1967 the assets of the four largest firms almost doubled in relative size and that the share of the eight largest firms increased from 18 to 29 per cent of the total industry assets. Moreover, one half of these increases were a direct result of merger activity. Further, the four largest firms' percentage share of total market profits increased from 15 to 19 per cent. For the eight largest firms the increase was from 14 to 30 per cent.

The FTC statistics reveal that a substantial portion of the sales increases was a direct result of mergers and acquisitions, for example, for the eight largest firms, 52 per cent of increased sales resulted from mergers and acquisitions. Further, for the largest firm, 62 per cent of its sales increase was the result of its merger activity. Statistics of the increases of the large firms tell only half the story, said the FTC. They did not reflect the concurrent increasing disparity in size between the largest firms and the remaining industry firms. Moreover, there is no way to measure what the growth of the eliminated firms would have been if they had remained competitors.

In addition to the overall market share changes, denoting an increased concentration, the commission's concern also centered on some very basic industry structure changes. The "bigness" created by the horizontal, vertical, and product-extension mergers made entry into the industry increasingly difficult. The initial capital requirements created high entry barriers. The implication of these changes had reinforced anticompetitive effects. The larger firms' entry into different submarkets by merger or acquisition not only eliminated the acquired firm, but also eliminated the acquiring firm from entering the market through internal expansion. The cumulative effect was to heighten entry barriers for other small to medium-sized firms and for new firms which might otherwise enter the market. To avoid the danger of eliminating further competition, the commission set out enforcement policy guidelines that were designed to arrest the increasing concentration and to attempt to encourage internal expansion and to preserve competition.

The guides are aimed specifically at horizontal and vertical mergers in particular product submarkets and product-extension mergers within the entire industry. The primary focus of the promulgated guides is on merger activity by the eight largest companies in the industry; that is, those firms whose current assets or annual sales exceed $300 million. A secondary focus is on acquisitions by industry firms with assets or annual sales in excess of $100 million by nonindustry giant conglomerates.

The FTC set out four criteria which it will use to determine if industry mergers or acquisitions raise significant questions of law and policy under Section 7. The first guide proscribes almost all merger activity by any of the largest eight firms in the industry:

> 1. Any merger between textile mill product firms where the combined sales or assets of the firms exceeds $300 million and the sales or assets of the smaller firm in the merger exceeds $10 million.

The second guide is directed at anticompetitive effects in particular submarkets. It casts doubt on mergers when the surviving firm is among the top four in the submarket, or has at least 5 per cent in *any* oligopolistic submarket:

> 2. Any horizontal merger in a textile mill product submarket where (1) the combined firms rank among the top 4 or (2) have a combined market share of 5 percent or more of any submarket in which the four largest firms account for 35 percent or more of the market.

The third policy guide affects both forward and backward vertical mergers. Presumably, relying on the vertical-merger aspects of *Brown Shoe,* the FTC is attempting to arrest mergers which raise entry barriers that effectively exclude all but national firms with large promotion and advertising capacity.

> 3. Any vertical merger, either "backward" into the supplying market or "forward" into a purchasing market, where a particular acquisition or a series of acquisitions may involve market shares of 10 percent or more of the relevant market or where the acquisition or series of acquisitions may tend significantly to raise barriers to entry in either market or to disadvantage existing non-integrated or partially integrated firms in either market by denying them fair access to sources of supply or markets.

The fourth guide implements the FTC's secondary focus on acquisition of industry firms by nonindustry conglomerates. To the extent the guide purports to include "pure" conglomerate mergers, it has no support in relevant case law. But if the commission establishes that it creates such anticompetitive effects as reciprocal buying, leverage, elimination of potential competition, or other anticompetitive factors, the merger may be invalidated.

> 4. Any acquisition of a textile mill product firm with sales or assets of $100 million or more and ranking among the four largest producers of a textile mill product by a non-textile mill product firm with sales or assets in excess of $250 million and with a substantial market position in another industry.

A substantial market position is defined as being one of the top four sellers of a product or service in which the four largest companies account for 40 percent or more of the market.

Although the Justice Department's guidelines apply to all merger activity and reflect its policy for Section 7 enforcement, the FTC's policy statements give more particularized guidance for businessmen and lawyers operating within the specified industries.

FTC PREMERGER NOTIFICATION RULES

In addition to its guidelines for particular industries, the Federal Trade Commission has also promulgated rules for a premerger notification program. Mergers triggering the notification requirement are those in which the participating firms (1) are under the jurisdiction of the FTC, (2) have assets of $10 million or more, and (3) have *combined* assets of $250 million or more.

For those mergers the FTC imposes requirements of prior notification and, in certain instances, of filing a special report. For asset acquisitions, within ten days after any agreement principle is reached and not less than sixty days prior to consummation of the transaction, the parties must notify the commission. In addition, any party having assets of $250 million or more must file a special report setting out a substantial amount of information about the company's operations (see Appendix VII).

For stock acquisitions any corporation having assets (or sales under a new notification procedure) of at least $250 million which acquires 10 per cent or more of the voting stock of another corporation with assets of at least $10 million must within ten days notify the commission of such stock holdings; in addition, the acquiring corporation must file a special report. If the acquiring corporation's assets are less than $250 million, but the combined assets of the parties exceeds $250 million, the acquiring corporation must notify the FTC and may have to file a special report.

Further, a corporation having assets of at least $250 million which effects a stock acquisition resulting in its holding 50 per cent or more of the voting stock of another corporation having at least $10 million assets must notify the FTC at least sixty days prior to the acquisition and file a special report. If the acquiring corporation has less than $250 million of assets, but the combined assets of the participants exceed $250 million, the commission must be notified and a special report may be required.

The FTC's release stated that premerger notifications would become a part of the agency's public records, but that special reports would remain in the agency's confidential investigation records. In other words, the notification data are available to the general public, but the special reports are excluded from public dissemination based upon one of the exceptions of the Freedom of Information Act. Another aspect to be noted is that the FTC's premerger notification requirements were not promulgated with the intent of imposing a sixty-day "waiting period." In the event that business negotiations dictate that consummation of the merger be within less than sixty days of the agreement in principle, the prescribed notice need only be submitted as "promptly as possible."

The FTC also has a premerger clearance procedure which permits advance rulings on contemplated mergers and acquisitions. In May 1969, the FTC established a new procedure which will publicize the provisional approvals together with a statement of the supporting reasons. In addition, the application for approval will be made public except for those portions for which the applicant has justifiably demonstrated a need for confidentiality or which the FTC determines should not be made public because of statutory reasons, agency rules, or the public interest.

The commission will also make public those applications which are disapproved, except that the commission will delete the names of the applicant and the other company and any other confidential information contained in the opinion letter.

PART IV

Enforcement and Remedies

In Part III we were concerned with the substantive antitrust laws as they bear on mergers and amalgamations. Here we turn our attention to the remedies available to the principal enforcing agencies and to the procedures employed by those bodies in accomplishing the policy objectives of the antimerger laws of this country. Separate chapters treat Justice Department procedure, Federal Trade Commission procedure, and private actions.

22 Justice Department Procedure and Enforcement

The year 1903 provided the first significant milestone in antitrust enforcement after passage of the Sherman Act. In February of that year Congress first appropriated money for what is now known as the Antitrust Division of the Department of Justice. The Antitrust Division has since become the principal enforcer of the federal antitrust laws. Under Teddy Roosevelt, the "trust-buster," it had only five lawyers and four stenographers. Today it has well over 300 lawyers and 230 nonlegal employees.

The Antitrust Division is one of eight divisions in the Department of Justice and is run by an assistant attorney general (AAG). It is structured along two lines: (1) federal court litigation and (2) consumer and agency regulation. The director of operations is in charge of the trial sections and field offices and directs most of the federal court litigation. The director of policy planning directs several sections whose principal activities also include such functions as appellate work, policy review, and interagency activities.

The litigation side of the division is made up of four trial sections and seven field offices. The four trial sections are Trial, Special Trial, General Litigation, and Special Litigation. There is no particular significance to their names and each has the same function: to investigate complaints, conduct preliminary investigations, conduct grand jury inquiries, issue Civil Investigative Demands, and request FBI investigations. They also prepare and try both the civil and criminal antitrust cases brought by the Division. Assignments are allotted among the Washington trial sections on the basis of the experience of each section with particular industries, commodities, and services.

The Judgments and Judgment Enforcement Section, in conjunction with the relevant trial section or field office, is active in negotiating and preparing the consent judgments. Of all the "nontrial" sections defendants will have the most contact with this one. The procedure for negotiating a consent judgment will be discussed later in the chapter. This section also handles the modification, interpretation, and enforcement of both litigated and consent judgments. The Patent Section is also located in the Operations division.

The field offices have the same functions as the trial sections. Because of their ties with particular communities the field offices frequently handle regional offenses. However, they also handle matters of national concern. For example, a merger with possible nationwide implications might be investigated and challenged by the Cleveland field office, if one of the parties has significant ties to that office's field operations.

The rest of the division consists of six sections, each of which has large areas of responsibility not directed to federal district court litigation. Some of these sections do, however, conduct investigations and try district court cases. The Appellate Section naturally enough handles all the appellate work for the division. Its attorneys usually work with one or more of the attorneys who tried the case and if the case goes to the Supreme Court, will also work with the solicitor general's office. (The division step-by-step appellate procedure is discussed later in this chapter.) The Foreign Commerce Section is the liaison with the State Department and foreign agencies in connection with all matters relating to foreign commerce, foreign nationals, or governments. It may become involved in merger litigation if foreign corporations are involved.

The Economic Section is responsible for any professional economic research required by the division either in its investigation or litigation. It will supply the expert witnesses for the analysis and interpretation of economic data for the division at trial. For instance, in a merger trial they will testify as to the market structure before and after the proposed acquisition. Many times, however, the division will go outside for its expert witnesses in order to take advantage of the prestige of nationally known economists. In these cases the division economists will work closely with the outside experts.

The Evaluation Section has several attorneys who prepare studies on antitrust policy, perform a review function, and make recommendations to the assistant attorney general on how to implement the basic policy objectives of the division. In recent years members of the section have been active in the Antitrust Division's bank merger program and stock exchange activities. The Public Counsel Section is responsible for the Antitrust Division's representation before various regulatory agencies and in court concerning regulatory matters involving antitrust policy. It is also the division's liaison with Congressional committees on antitrust matters and will usually be instrumental in drafting new antitrust legislation.

The Consumer Affairs Section is a newly formed unit. It is a response to the upsurge in consumer-minded public opinion. It is also a possible precursor to what some hope will be a separate Consumer Division in the Department of Justice. It has no responsibility for antitrust enforcement and therefore would not become involved in a merger case.

In addition to this permanent staff, the division has the assistance of the Federal Bureau of Investigation and the ninety-three United States Attorneys around the country. In the early 1960's the Department of

Justice initiated a program to have the U.S. Attorneys handle antitrust cases. This program has had limited success. The principal reason is that the U.S. Attorney offices lack both the expertise and the staff necessary to conduct long, complex antitrust investigations and litigations. In any case, as of this writing there have been only four antitrust suits litigated by the U.S. Attorney's office. Whatever the future success of this program, however, it will have no effect on mergers and acquisitions because its scope has been limited to price-fixing enforcement.

The Antitrust Division views competition as the "fundamental national economic policy." And in the words of one AAG, "to preserve and protect it [competition] is the reason for the Antitrust Division's existence." The division's efforts to enforce competition are divided into three main areas: (1) seeking out and prosecuting anticompetitive practices, (2) attempting to maintain a competitive economic structure, and (3) acting as an advocate for competition wherever administrative regulation is not essential in the regulated industries.

We are concerned primarily with the second area, which includes merger and monopolization questions. Although the division has filed very few monopolization cases, it is now spending a large percentage of its time on mergers. This has occurred principally as a result of the conglomerate merger phenomenon which hit its peak in the late 1960's but which is still evident throughout the economy.

A DEPARTMENT OF JUSTICE MERGER SUIT

We shall now examine the Department of Justice's procedure and enforcement policies as they arise in the litigation process from the initial investigation to the final appeal. The emphasis, of course, will be on the process as it applies to mergers.

In merger litigation the question of whether to litigate should be considered at the same time the merger itself is considered. This means an early appraisal of the antitrust problems. To accomplish this the company's attorneys should evaluate the proposed acquisition in light of the Department of Justice or the Federal Trade Commission merger guidelines and the applicable case law. If this is done properly, the businessman will be in a better position than usual, for very often his first indication of an antitrust violation (or at least a detection of an antitrust violation) is a letter of inquiry from an Antitrust Division staff attorney or a rumor of an FBI investigation.

There are two Antitrust Division aids to a company's initial consideration of its merger problems: the merger guidelines and the business review procedure. The first is substantive and is often helpful in evaluating the vulnerability of a proposed merger. The second is procedural and may under certain circumstances reduce an acquiring company's exposure.

Merger Guidelines

The merger guidelines, released in May of 1968, outline the division's standards for determining whether to oppose corporate acquisitions or mergers under Section 7 of the Clayton Act. Although mergers can be challenged under Section 1 of the Sherman Act, it is most likely that challenges will be made under Section 7 and it was to this section that the guidelines were directed.

The Federal Trade Commission also has merger guidelines. The FTC's guidelines are aimed at specific industries, but the Justice Department's are broad and all-inclusive, covering vertical, horizontal, and conglomerate mergers in all industries. Necessarily the Justice Department guidelines lack the helpful detail which the FTC guidelines can provide. Both guidelines are basically similar, however, in that they are concerned with market structure and the effect an acquisition will have, presently and prospectively, on that market structure.

Although the department's guidelines do not have the force of law, the courts have relied on them in their determinations. The United States Third Circuit Court of Appeals in *Allis-Chalmers* v. *White Consolidated Industries* was an example of this:

> I recognize that the primary purpose of the guidelines is to indicate the standards being applied by the Department of Justice in determining whether to challenge corporate acquisitions and mergers under Section 7 and that the guidelines do not purport to be a concise statement of the present status of the law which the Courts are bound to follow. But, because the Justice Department is obviously one of the principal Government agencies charged with the duty of enforcing the antitrust laws, I think its position is entitled to some consideration, particularly when elements of the guidelines find support in the developing case law.

When releasing the guidelines, the Department of Justice was careful to indicate that they were a statement of current department policy and were subject to change at any time without prior notice. Furthermore, it stressed that because the guidelines were necessarily framed in general terms and because the critical factors in any particular guideline formulation might be evaluated differently by the department than by the parties, the guidelines were not to be treated as a substitute for the Antitrust Division's business review procedure. This disclaimer has been reinforced by the courts. In *United States* v. *Atlantic Richfield Co.,* a federal district court rejected the defense that the government's suit went beyond its merger guidelines and stated that the guidelines:

> [a]re in no way binding on the Department in a particular case and the Department is entitled to evaluate each case on the basis of its own facts and the varied factors that must be taken into consideration. Indeed, the Department has available a business review procedure. . . . The defendants did not avail themselves of the review procedure here.

The court concluded by noting that "in any event, of course, the guidelines are in no way binding on the courts." The moral of all this is that the guidelines, while providing a helpful hint to the government's enforcement intentions, will provide no solid assurances one way or the other.

Business Review Procedure

The business review procedure, on the other hand, does provide substantial assurance. Although the Department of Justice is not authorized to give advisory opinions to private parties, there are circumstances when it will indicate its enforcement intentions as to proposed business practices or conduct. Originally this procedure was known as a railroad release and applied only to whether the division intended to initiate criminal proceedings. Merger clearances have since been added and now both are combined in the business review procedure.

Many antitrust lawyers advise their clients not to seek out the intentions of the Antitrust Division. This is primarily because it will subject the acquisition to a scrutiny it might not otherwise have received. One's own antitrust counsel, so the argument goes, should be able to determine, with the aid of the merger guidelines and his own experience, the lawfulness of the merger under the antitrust laws. Another argument is that the division uses a tougher standard in reviewing mergers through the business review procedure than it does when it is investigating a merger with an eye toward litigation. The division denies this. Such a policy they claim would force them to litigate weak cases because they usually sue if the company goes ahead after being informed that the division would oppose the merger. These litigations would waste manpower, probably produce a bad court track record, and consequently hurt their enforcement program.

Another drawback to the business review procedure is that it produces a written document that might be used by private litigants. In at least one instance the division has given oral advice about its intentions, although it issued a press release concurrently with the oral advice.

The fact is that today the business review procedure is being used less than ever. However, because businessmen have used and are still using it in some circumstances, it is important to understand how it works and what you actually receive when you do use it.

The first step in the procedure is to submit a written request to the assistant attorney general in charge of the Antitrust Division. The request must concern only *proposed* business conduct. Naturally enough, the conduct must involve either interstate or foreign commerce, for otherwise the Department of Justice would not have jurisdiction over it. Once a request has been submitted, there is an obligation to make full disclosure with respect to the proposed conduct. The division may also conduct any investigation on its own that it considers appropriate.

The division will refuse to review a merger that is subject to approval by a regulatory agency (unless there are special emergency circumstances) until the agency has approved it. It will never review a proposed bank merger before it has been cleared by the appropriate banking agency.

After submitting the documents and information, and replying to further requests of the division, the requesting party still might not receive an answer as to the division's enforcement intentions. This is because the division reserves the right to decline to pass on the request. Usually, however, it will take a position one way or the other. Ordinarily it is only with respect to mergers, acquisitions, or similar arrangements that the division will state its present intention not to bring a civil action.

If and when a business review letter is received, it will be noted that it only states the enforcement intentions of the division as of the date of the letter. The division remains completely free to bring whatever action or proceeding it subsequently comes to believe is required by the public interest. If there has been a good-faith disclosure, the division's present intentions are usually its permanent intentions. There has never been a case when the division has exercised its right to bring a *criminal* action where there has been such a disclosure.

It should be kept in mind that any document submitted to the division can be used for any and all antitrust investigatory purposes. This includes a grand jury. During the investigation, the request may be withdrawn; however, this does not stop the division from continuing the investigation and it might have the effect of stirring more interest in the acquisition than if it had not been withdrawn.

INVESTIGATIONS

If the business review procedure is not used, how does the division learn about the merger? The answer is, in the same way as the rest of the financial community. Two thirds of the merger investigations in the Antitrust Division start when an attorney or staff member reads of the merger in a trade or financial publication. As one antitrust observer has remarked, the division attorneys, "[h]ave available to them one of the best intelligence networks in the country. It has agents all over the country. They are experienced in gathering economic data, preparing it, analyzing it and presenting it in final form every morning. And I am not referring to the FBI or the CIA, I am referring to the *Wall Street Journal.*"

The other third of the merger investigations are similar to any other Sherman Act or Clayton Act investigation which usually starts when a competitor makes a complaint to the division directly or through some member of Congress or another government agency. Sometimes the division learns of a proposed merger from the company that is going to be acquired. In this situation the company is usually fighting a take-over and is looking for help from wherever it can get it.

There are two staff workers in the office of the director of operations who record each merger that has been reported in business publications. They are responsible for sending around the merger information to the appropriate trial section for an initial opinion as to its anticompetitive interest. If the section chief feels that it merits further study, he sends a recommendation for a preliminary inquiry back to the director of operations. By this time clearance has been made with the Federal Trade Commission to ensure that the two agencies do not duplicate investigations. If approved, the package is sent back to the original trial section or field office for the preliminary investigation.

A preliminary investigation (PI) merely determines if the situation warrants a more thorough investigation. It is conducted by one staff attorney, who studies trade manuals, department files, or reports from other agencies for industry data. He might request information from the merging companies through an informal letter, but at this stage will not use the FBI or compulsory discovery measures, such as the civil investigative demand (CID). It is usually considered wise to cooperate with the informal inquiry, because the division can always resort to compulsory measures. It is important to note that even at this early stage in a government action, one should have the full assistance of legal counsel.

If the staff attorney feels that more information is needed (and the process will require more than five man-days of work), he sends a request for a full investigation back up the ladder to the director of operations. This recommendation might also go to the director of policy planning or the chief of the economic section for a balanced enforcement appraisal. If approved, a full investigation is conducted back in the original trial section or field office. At this stage a number of attorneys may be working on the investigation. They may use CID's or have the FBI assist them. They also may themselves interview officials and employees of the company under investigation, its competitors, or other members of the industry. It should be noted that the division takes the position that the attorneys for the corporation are not automatically the attorneys for all the employees of the company and that in some cases it would be a conflict of interest for them to represent both. Therefore, it does not consider itself obligated to give notice to the company or its attorneys that it is going to interview the company's employees during an investigation. Because some attorney should be present during any government interview, it is important to be aware of this government policy.

The division attorneys conducting a full merger investigation cannot use a grand jury because Section 7 of the Clayton Act has no criminal provisions, but they will use any precomplaint discovery tools available to the division in order to determine whether the merger will violate the antitrust laws. In the past there was extensive use of civil investigative demands.

Civil Investigative Demands

The civil investigative demand is a compulsory investigative tool that resembles a grand jury subpoena *duces tecum.* The principal distinctions are that a CID is civil in nature and may only be issued to a company that is itself under investigation. The Antitrust Civil Process Act permits the attorney general or the assistant attorney general in charge of the Antitrust Division, whenever either has reason to believe that a person under investigation has documents relevant to an antitrust inquiry, to issue and serve upon such a person a CID requiring production of the documents for examination. The demand must (1) state the nature of the conduct being investigated and the statute which it is alleged to violate, (2) describe the documents to be produced with sufficient "definiteness and certainty as to permit such material to be fairly identified," (3) prescribe a reasonable return date (the average is thirty days), and (4) must identify the custodian to whom the material should be made available.

CID's can be served in person either upon an executive officer, partner, and so on, or at the company's principal place of business. However, the most common method is by registered or certified mail. If a CID is received, the documents requested must be produced at the company's principal place of business. This is more convenient than a grand jury subpoena *duces tecum* which requires transportation of the documents to wherever the grand jury is sitting. Many times a company will reproduce the documents requested at its own expense and ship them to the Antitrust Division. This has the advantage of keeping government investigators from personally searching the company's files. However, the wording of the statute indicates all that is rquired is that the company make the documents available for inspection and copying. Although the government might dispute who is to pay for copying, it has never litigated the point. If there are voluminous documents, it is not unusual for the government to inspect them at the company's place of business. In any case, it is never a good idea to part with original documents. The division recognizes this, but if copies are produced it will request that the originals be kept intact in case they are later required.

Information produced pursuant to CID's is kept confidential by the Antitrust Division before a complaint is filed. The documents may be used in a court case or grand jury proceeding and may become part of the record of those proceedings. There are, however, some limitations on their use. In *Upjohn* v. *Bernstein,* Judge Holtzoff refused to allow documents containing Upjohn's trade secrets to be used in the suit against its competitors. The investigation of Upjohn had been completed and no action, civil or criminal, was contemplated against the company. The documents were being used by different attorneys from those who investigated Upjohn. The court ordered that the documents containing the trade secrets be returned to Upjohn within a reasonable time. The division has not accepted this as a bar on similar future use of CID documents. In discussing this case, the director of operations for the division stated that "the Division did not feel that the issue was then significant enough to be reviewed by an appellate court," and that the position of the division remained "that documents lawfully obtained through CID's may be made available by the custodian to every staff and division for enforcement activities."

Any company receiving a CID has the right to object to it. Within twenty days after the receipt of the CID or any time before the return date, the company can file a petition to modify or set aside the demand in the judicial district of its principal place of business. If the company fails to either comply or object to the demand in that time, the government will file a petition for an order of enforcement. During the litigation of either the defendant's or government's petition, the compliance requirement of the CID is stayed. There are times when objections to the CID's can be met short of court action. Negotiations with the staff attorneys from the trial section that issued the CID can accomplish this. The problem might be that the division attorney was not familiar with the filing systems of the company or that the documents were not kept in the exact form sought. In these situations it is more than likely that a simple conference will solve the problems.

Criminal penalties have been drafted into the CID Act. Any willful obstruction of the antitrust civil process done with "intent to avoid, evade, prevent, or obstruct compliance" with a demand is punishable by a fine of $5,000 or five years in jail or both. In this regard it would be wise for a company to notify all personnel not to destroy any records, even if it is a routine procedure, while the company is the subject of an Antitrust Division investigation.

The courts have generally adopted liberal standards for the drafting of CIDs. For instance the Act requires that both the nature of conduct constituting the alleged violation and the applicable provision of the antitrust laws be stated in the CID. In the *Gold Bond* case, a federal court stated the standard as follows: "[W]hether the statement in the demand as to the nature of conduct under investigation is sufficient to inform adequately the person being investigated and sufficicent to determine the relevancy of the documents demanded for inspection."

It is noted that "great specificity would defeat the purposes of the Act by breeding litigation by persons being investigated." In merger investigations the standard has never been a problem because the obvious conduct under investigation is the merger between the two companies and Section 7 of the Clayton Act is the applicable antitrust provision.

On questions of whether (1) the documents sought are relevant to the inquiry, (2) adequately specified, (3) privileged, or whether (4) compliance would be unduly burdensome and oppressive, the courts have adopted standards similar to those for grand jury subpoenas. On the question of whether a demand has to state that the addressee is "under investigation," the courts in *Hyster Co.* v. *United States* and *Lightning Road Manufacturers Association* v. *Staal* held that there is a presumption that the attorney general met the requirements of the Antitrust Civil Process Act that demands only be served on persons under investigation.

Constitutional challenges to CID's have been uniformly denied. The first was in the *Gold Bond* case. In a "pioneer" opinion which the United States Eighth Circuit Court of Appeals unanimously affirmed and called an "excellent and comprehensive analysis of the Act," a federal court rejected the argument that the power given to the attorney general was overly broad in violation of the Fourth Amendment. It reviewed the Congressional purpose of the Act and held that the power was within the "guideposts erected by the Supreme Court in the Oklahoma Press Publishing Co. and Morton Salt Company cases." Two other challenges were made in the *Hyster* case. There the court held that a CID was not an unreasonable search and seizure because it was only enforceable by a court order and federal Rules 37 and 30(b) were available to the recipients for protection. It rejected a Fifth Amendment challenge noting that a CID could only be served on corporations or other nonnatural persons who do not have Fifth Amendment rights.

As seen in the *Upjohn* decision, all the case law has not been favorable to the government. In *United States* v. *Union Oil Co. of California,* the majority opinion held a CID could not be issued against a merger that had not yet been consummated. The court based its opinion on the fact that the "section clearly imposes the requirement that the Demand be for material relevant to a 'civil antitrust investigation' "; and that an "antitrust investigation" is defined in the Act as "Any inquiry conducted by any antitrust investigator for the purpose of ascertaining whether any person *is or has been engaged in any antitrust violation.*" (Emphasis added.) Therefore, since the merger is only proposed no person "is or has been engaged in any antitrust violation." The concurring opinion of Circuit Judge Merril agreed that if the merger was merely contemplated by the companies a CID could not be issued. But "If companies are engaged in activities leading to that end which they can under the antitrust laws be halted from pursuing I would say that they are presently engaged in the process of acquiring and accordingly are presently in the process of violating the anti-trust laws." Therefore, in that situation he felt a CID could be issued. It should be noted that the Antitrust Division follows this standard and will issue CID's in investigations in which the merger has not yet been consummated. This practice has not been challenged subsequently. One reason might be the fact that in merger investigations informal letters of inquiry now predominate, and in consequence there has been no occasion to challenge it.

In another case, *Chattanooga Pharmaceutical Ass'n.,* the Court quashed the CID's on the basis of the petitioners' allegations that the government was harrassing the association in order to stop its private suit against a large "cut-rate" drug company, which was allegedly selling drug store items below the Tennessee fair trade laws. The key to the decision was the failure of the government to introduce an affidavit denying the petitioner's allegations. The division based its refusal on the position "that the burden rested on the petitioner to prove that the investigation had no lawful purpose." The Department of Justice did not appeal the decision and has since filed affidavits when its CID's are similarly attacked. The wisdom of this change can be seen in a recent decision in *American Pharmaceutical Assn.* v. *United States Department of Justice.* The pharmaceutical associations claimed that CID's were issued by the division for fraudulent and improper motives—one of which was to aid two "cut-rate" drug companies in their suits against the associations. Assistant Attorney General McLaren filed an affidavit in which he denied the allegations and stated that he authorized the CID's because he had reason to believe, as a result of preliminary investigations, that these associations might have been parties to a conspiracy to suppress price competition in the retail medicine market.

The court granted the government's petition for enforcement. It distinguished *Chattanooga* on the basis of the McLaren affidavit and on the fact that the associations were not the accusers in the pending state litigations, as in *Chattanooga,* but rather were the accused who were charged with fixing prices in the prescription drug market. It seems safe to say that *Chattanooga* is no longer of much benefit to CID recipients unless the government fails to file an affidavit or there is overwhelming proof of improper motives for the investigation.

One of the first impetus' for CID legislation came from the Attorney General's National Committee to Study the Antitrust Laws. In summing up its discussion of the need for a bill, the committee stated:

> We recognize that the Department has been handicapped and accept the Judicial Conference conclusion that the present civil investigative machinery is inadequate for effective antitrust enforcement. The problem is, therefore, to devise a pre-complaint civil discovery process for use when civil proceedings are initially contemplated and voluntary cooperation by those under investigation fails.

The situation was further aggravated when in 1958 the Supreme Court in *United States* v. *Procter & Gamble* held that it was an abuse of the grand jury process to conduct a grand jury investigation where no criminal proceedings were contemplated. This left the Antitrust Division with the alternative of seeking voluntary compliance from those under investigation or filing a suit on a skeleton set of facts and then using the Federal Rules of Civil Procedure to obtain the necessary discovery. This was unsatisfactory on both counts. As to voluntary compliance the attorney general's committee stated: "Voluntary cooperation of parties under investigation has often been sufficient but compulsory process is required in some cases. Moreover a Government agency should not be in a position of sole dependence upon voluntary cooperation for discharge of its responsibilities." This is especially true for merger investigations, because they are conducted under Section 7 of the Clayton Act, which has no criminal provisions. Therefore, the division can never consider using a grand jury even under the *Procter & Gamble* standard. The second alternative of filing a suit and then using the Federal Rules for discovery is an unsound enforcement technique. The division must go forward on insufficient evidence and possibly waste time and money (both its own and the defendant's) in litigation that might have been avoided if compulsory investigative procedures had been available.

In 1955, the year the attorney general committee's report came out, a bill was introduced to carry out its recommendations. Seven years later the Antitrust Civil Process Act was finally passed. The CID at that time was not a novel antitrust concept. Fourteen states had already given similar power to their attorney generals to enforce state antitrust laws and various other federal agencies had similar investigative authority in their respective jurisdictions. After the Act was first passed, CID's were used extensively. However, since then they have been used less often. Today informal letters of inquiry from staff attorneys predominate in the division's investigations. Contrary to what some had envisioned, the CID has not revolutionized antitrust investigations. One of the reasons for this may be that companies are willing to comply informally, knowing full well that the CID's are available if they do not. Another is that it is easier for the staff attorneys to send an informal letter than to draft and have approved a CID that must be able to withstand attack in the courts.

The greatest drop in the use of CID's has been in merger investigation. This is true even though the CID is well suited to the extensive document searches that are necessary to analyze market structure. There are perhaps two reasons for this. One is the fact that the companies usually want the investigation to be completed as quickly as possible, because time and the current condition of the stock market are often factors in merger deals, thus inducing cooperation. A second is the knowledge that informal compliance, even if it does reveal a Section 7 violation, will rarely if ever subject the companies to future treble-damage suits.

The Antitrust Division's merger investigatory role, therefore, can be characterized as speaking softly with letters of inquiry, while carrying a big CID stick. There are still some situations, however, when a company will resist both letters of inquiry and CID's. The principal reason is the protection of trade secrets. Usually a protective order can be worked out through negotiations between the staff attorneys and the company. If this cannot be done informally, the department will file a CID for those specific documents containing the trade secrets. The defendant then would go to court for a protective order and the two parties would litigate the scope of the order.

There are no current bills that seek to amend the Antitrust Civil Process Act. However the Department of Justice has expressed some interest in expanding CID's to include compulsory depositions of company officers and employees. CID's would then resemble the FTC's subpoena power. There is little or no activity on this proposal now and there does not appear to be any likely in the near future. This might be because the government knows that in the precarious legislative process there is always the possibility that if it seeks more, it might lose some of what it already has.

AFTER THE COMPLAINT

Once the investigation has been completed the attorneys handling the matter, if they feel that the merger will violate or has violated the antitrust laws, will prepare a complaint in a form suitable for filing in the various district courts. They will also prepare a fact memorandum setting forth in considerable detail the evidence that will be used at trial to support the charge. This memo will also discuss the case in terms of overall antitrust policy and will describe why certain relief has been sought. These two documents, along with a shorter memorandum that summarizes the fact memorandum for the attorney general, are sent through the section chief, director of operations, director of policy planning, and chief of the Economic Section, and finally to the deputy assistant and assistant attorney general. The assistant attorney general will usually hold a briefing conference with most of the preceding to discuss their recommendations. If he gives approval, the complaint and short memorandum are sent to the attorney general for final authorization.

A government complaint should never catch merging companies by surprise. As already mentioned both companies should have considered the antitrust problems and the basic question of whether or not to litigate if the merger is challenged when each was deciding whether or not to merge. These initial considerations, it should be pointed out, involve more than legal questions of antitrust law. There are basic business considerations involved. Although it is not within the scope of this chapter to go into them in depth, it is worthwhile to name a few. For instance could the acquisition and litigation money be better spent on internal expansion or smaller acquisitions? Will the merger, however short its existence, be justified on the basis of gained knowhow or new management personnel? Is it more important to litigate and possibly lose than to give a competitor a chance to acquire the company? Is there any chance of favorable Congressional legislation if the government wins the suit? Another important consideration is whether the company that is to be acquired, in fact, wants to be acquired. As one antitrust observer noted:

> If *Northwest Industries* teaches anything, it teaches the difficulties of litigating when the object of your attention is unwilling. In these days of potential competition, a non-cooperating defendant may have no problems producing some evidence that it is a potential competitor. Moreover, as a practical matter, obtaining the necessary information to defend is difficult if your codefendant is cooperating with the Government. [Footnotes omitted.]

Finally, can the two companies live with a preliminary injunction or a severe hold-separate order? These questions do not exhaust the considerations, but they do point to the fact that at the point the company receives the complaint it should have already considered whether a long government litigation is worth it.

Once the complaint is filed there will follow a long period of discovery, involving large numbers of depositions and interrogatories. In order to speed its case at trial the government might seek to introduce its depositions to establish such things as business volume and market structure. As can be seen, depositions are a very important part of the litigation process. Before taking a deposition, the government attorneys may want to interview the witness. This is so they can extract a complete and coherent record at the deposition in case it is later necessary to introduce it at trial. Whether you are the party or a non-party witness it is important to have an attorney at both the interview and deposition.

The government interrogatories are usually concerned with the important facts of the case, leaving the minor evidentiary points to be picked up at the deposition. These interrogatories usually avoid what might be considered harassing document searches. The reasons for this are simple. Aside from the question of professional propriety, such interrogatories would delay the pretrial stage and put into question the validity of the division's objections if it felt that defendant was using such harassing interrogatories. This type of defendant interrogatory can add years to the litigation, something that the government naturally wants to avoid.

APPEAL

Most government antitrust suits are litigated with the Supreme Court in mind. This is especially true in civil cases because under the Expediting Act, an appeal bypasses the court of appeals. Initially in a merger case the overriding concern is with the preliminary injunction motion. However, once this is past the counsel becomes just as concerned with making a record for appeal. Of course, not all judgments are appealed. If the government wins, a decision on whether to appeal is made only by the defendant and his counsel. If the defendant wins, the government's decision goes through many lawyers before a final determination is made.

There is a Department of Justice rule that requires a recommendation on whether to appeal for every government loss. In the case of the Antitrust Division, the initial recommendation is made by the trial section or field office that handled the case. This recommendation either goes through the office of the director of operations for his views or goes straight to the Appellate Section. The Appellate Section then sends it to the director of policy planning, who passes it on to the AAG for his decision.

If the AAG is in favor of an appeal, this decision along with all the papers in the case would be reviewed by staff attorneys in the solicitor general's office. At this stage, these attorneys might send it back to the division for further research or development of facts. Once they have completed their review, they give the case with their recommendation to the solicitor, who has the final decision.

If the AAG had recommended that the case not be appealed, the solicitor's office would have assigned only one attorney to review the case and the tendency has been to support the division's recommendations in these situations.

Can or should a defense attorney try to affect the government's determination somewhere along the decision-making process? This is a difficult question. Some attorneys have tried. Some have gone to the division's Trial Section first and then followed the case up. Others have gone straight to the solicitor general's office. The department claims that these efforts have generally been unsuccessful, but admits that sometimes they have affected its decision. This stage in the appellate process is important and should not be ignored. One reason is that the solicitor or division (for one reason or another) may be more reluctant to challenge the findings of a district court than the Supreme Court. This is fortunate for defendants because it has been suggested that the "clearly erroneous" rule on reviewing findings of fact is less evident in Supreme Court antitrust (and also civil rights) cases than in other types of cases.

CONSENT DECREES

Not all government complaints are litigated. Most in fact never get to trial. They are settled by consent decrees. These are a very important part of the Antitrust Division's enforcement program. Between 75 and 85 per cent of the government's civil suits are disposed of in this manner. Although the federal antitrust laws do not directly authorize them, they have been an effective enforcement tool since 1906. In 1928 their constitutionality and statutory validity was established in *Swift & Co.* v. *United States.* The Supreme Court in the same opinion held that the only grounds for appeal from a decree are (1) clerical errors, (2) lack of consent, (3) fraud, and (4) lack of subject-matter jurisdiction. If the decree has other flaws, such as erroneous factual or legal conclusions or provisions that go beyond the scope of the antitrust laws, the defendant cannot challenge it once he has given his consent.

The government, the defendant, and the courts each benefit from the use of these decrees. Let us first look at the advantages to the government. The Antitrust Division has limited resources. The budget for the division has never exceeded $12 million. Consequently, it is limited in the number of cases and investigations it can conduct. It is easy to understand how a decree that releases manpower and at the same time produces inexpensive and rapid relief is of benefit to the division. Sometimes the division can also obtain broader and more radical relief in a consent decree than it could after a trial on the merits. It thereby gets an opportunity to expand the reach of substantive antitrust law and experiment with new forms of relief. This is why when one is attempting to judge the future direction of the division's enforcement policy, he should study its consent judgments.

Consent judgments also give the government the opportunity to supervise a particular industry's activities, and if future violations occur in that industry, the burden of proving the legality of the activity may shift to the defendants. In the past these decrees have given the government a chance to settle a whole range of issues besides the basic antitrust complaint away from public and judicial scrutiny. This, though, is changing, as will be seen later in the chapter.

Antitrust defendants' interest in consent decrees grew rapidly after the passage of the Clayton Act in 1914. Section 4 of the Act allowed private treble-damage actions for violations of the antitrust laws, and Section 5 made successful government-litigated judgments prima facie proof of a violation in later private suits. The important section for defendant(s), however, is 5(a), which exempted consent judgments from this provision. Avoidance of this prima facie proof in subsequent private suits is still the main incentive for defendants to enter into consent decrees. This is especially true after Rule 23 of the Federal Rules of Civil Procedure, amended in 1966, expanded class-action opportunities.

Another reason for defendants to seek consent decrees is the expense and notoriety of protracted litigation. The long-drawn-out discovery with numerous depositions and interrogatories places a heavy burden on the time of the company's officers and employees. If the case goes to trial they might be further occupied for weeks. Furthermore, a trial can produce a lot of publicity. Because many companies desire an antitrust-pure reputation, they sincerely wish to avoid headlines that contain finger-pointing allegations.

An advantage of lesser immediate importance to the defendant is that a consent decree ensures that no damaging legal precedent will be set. This is often more important in areas where the government has been making new law, such as in mergers, than in the price-fixing area, where usually the only question is whether the defendant did what the government claims it did.

In the past it was claimed that once the consent decree had been entered, the defendant's future conduct stood a good chance of being ignored by the Antitrust Division. Whether this view was true or not, however, the decree did and still does instruct the defendant as to what conduct will keep him clear of future government suits and this is always an advantage.

Consent decrees are helpful to the courts. Overcrowded dockets are a fact of life in the present judicial system. An antitrust suit perhaps more than any other type of suit adds to this problem. What judge would not be delighted to have a complex and time-consuming litigation that could occupy his attention for months, and even years, removed from his calendar? Also, the decree saves the judge from the possibility of a reversal on the many antitrust, procedural, and evidentiary rulings that would arise during discovery and trial. The judge, in fact, probably appreciates more than anyone else the value of a consent decree.

Consent negotiations are not initiated by the Antitrust Division, but it will usually negotiate if the defendant requests it. Although there is no general rule on when to start negotiations, it is advisable to make sure that they are completed before the case reaches the Supreme Court. The *El Paso Natural Gas* case is a good example of what can happen to negotiations after an adverse decision in the Supreme Court. On remand from a Supreme Court divestiture opinion the government, defendant, and district court after considerable time and energy agreed on a consent judgment. Third parties attempted to intervene in order to object to the judgment. The district court denied the applications for intervention and the parties appealed. The Supreme Court in a blistering opinion, *Cascade Natural Gas,* granted the intervention, vacated the judgment, rebuked the Department of Justice, and removed the trial judge from the case. The Court declared that the parties below had no authority to change its mandate for a complete divestiture. *Cascade* is now considered *sui generis* on the question of intervention, but it is still good law as to the latitude of settlement negotiations once there has been a mandate from the Supreme Court.

A company need not wait until a complaint is filed to start negotiations. *Prefiling negotiations* can be initiated during the government's investigation. The advantage to the defendant is that these negotiations, if successful, will result in the complaint and the consent judgment being filed at the same time. The adverse publicity surrounding the filing of an antitrust case is thereby considerably reduced.

The Antitrust Division's attitude toward these negotiations has varied through the years and to a large degree depends on who you talk to in the division. It has expressed the fear that if the practice became widespread a tendency might develop to tailor the complaint to fit the relief that was being negotiated. This would set a bad precedent and take the deterrent sting out of government investigations and complaints. Another disadvantage is that the suit may be delayed considerably while negotiations, which later prove fruitless, drag on. The anticompetitive practices would then continue unchecked and the impact of an antitrust complaint on the rest of the industry would be delayed. It is also possible that a prolonged delay might weaken the government's case if for any reason its witnesses become unavailable. To combat these problems in 1970 the division instituted a sixty-day time limit for prefiling negotiations. Extensions are limited to only exceptional cases. The government's reasoning is that if the defendants are sincere in seeking a consent decree, sixty days is more than enough time to reach a settlement. Extensions are given, however, and if a company feels that it needs more time it should submit a request to the staff attorney who is handling the investigation and he will forward it to the assistant attorney general for a decision. Whatever the problems with prefiling negotiations, the trend is to more settlements of this type. Because consumers are becoming more sophisticated and aware of trade-practice violations, businessmen would do well to consider this alternative whenever they are faced with a government investigation.

Negotiations, whenever they are begun, start with the staff attorneys in the field office or Trial Section that is handling the case. If defendants offer a consent decree in writing that is satisfactory to the trial staff and the respective section chief or field office chief, negotiations are shifted to the Judgment and Judgment Enforcement Section in Washington. The negotiations then become more detailed and formalized. If the defendant had been negotiating several consent judgments in interrelated cases, the negotiations would now be consolidated. This occurred in both the recent ITT merger cases and in the electrical conspiracy cases against General Electric in 1961. In the latter case one consent judgment resulted in seventeen separate suits against General Electric being dismissed.

The government takes the position that the consent decree should give much the same relief that it would have received after litigation. It cites a number of reasons for this. One is that the advantage of releasing manpower and resources for other matters would be of little value if the result was less than adequate relief in the cases the division was filing. Another is that the continued acceptance of less than full relief might leave the impression that cases are being brought lightly in the anticipation of a hard game of bargaining. Finally if the practice was regularly followed, this impression might become a reality. There is still another possibility—if the division did gain a reputation for this practice, the courts might take a more active role in the entry of consent decrees to protect the public interest both through its own efforts and by allowing more interventions by third parties. This is something neither the government nor defendants want.

The foregoing discussion should not lead anyone to think that the bargaining element is not involved in consent-decree negotiations. As a practical matter when two sides sit down to discuss a settlement there is usually a willingness to make the negotiations work. As one assistant attorney general put it: "I would suppose that, inevitably, the process of attempting mutually to work out the details of appropriate relief before the strains and tensions of litigation have crystallized judgments and opinions, probably results in a greater appreciation of the other fellow's problem or a greater tolerance of the other fellow's views of debatable facts."

The division readily admits that there are times when it will compromise on relief. These can be summarized as follows: (1) when the theory under which a complaint was brought, although still tenable, is not as convincing as it was at the time of filing; (2) when the problems of proof of critical facts are far harder than anticipated, therefore making the trial effort of debatable value; and (3) when the expenses of litigation would far outweigh the benefits to be obtained by minor improvements in the relief already offered. If the division feels that it was plainly in the wrong in its initial assumptions, it claims it will be prepared to dismiss the suit altogether. This, however, should not give anyone false hope. In the adversary system it is often very hard for an attorney to be objective about the merits of the case; it would perhaps be overly optimistic to expect him to dismiss his whole litigation as a mistake.

Precedent does not carry very much weight in consent-decree negotiations. Unlike other areas of the law, it can hardly be argued that people conduct their business in a possibly unlawful manner with an eye to what someone else was required to do in a consent decree and expect that if challenged by the government they will be entitled to the same provisions. Consent-decree relief is tailored to current business conditions and the peculiarities of the situation of the defendant. Therefore, it would be rare to find a completely parallel situation. Even if there were such a situation, however, there is no reason why the government should be held to provisions it considers to be past mistakes.

The government concedes that there might be one situation in which it would look to precedent and that would be in the case of competing companies in the same market engaged in the same unlawful practices. But generally it takes the position of the assistant attorney general who remarked, "[D]ecree watching, like girl watching, is good clean fun. But it does not necessarily mean that a company is entitled to the prettiest decree it has seen."

The relief given in a consent decree may be broader than the mere cessation of the particular violation and may even prevent acts that are in themselves legal. For instance, if there were a resale-price-maintenance violation, the decree might prohibit the manufacturer from using its otherwise legal fair-trade rights, and the restriction might cover a broader geographic area and a larger group of products than did the price-maintenance program. Similarly, in a merger decree there might be a divestiture of companies other than those named in the original complaint or a prohibition on certain types of future mergers. There might also be a "trigger device," requiring a divestiture of a subsidiary when the company obtains or goes over a certain market share in that industry.

Consent decrees might also require affirmative relief. For example, a company subject to divestiture might be required to take steps to guarantee the short-term viability of the operation to be divested. Or, in lieu of divestiture, a company might be required to supply companies that might otherwise be threatened with a "supply squeeze." In a group boycott case the decree might require compulsory sales to any buyer. One thing that is no longer found is an "upset-price" provision in a divestiture decree. This allows the company to back out of the forced sale if it cannot receive a certain price. The *Kaiser* case was the only one that in fact contained it. The division now refuses to allow these because it does not want to give the defendants any excuse not to divest. The closest one might get to it today is a provision requiring a sale on "reasonable terms." This was used in the *Lucky Lager Brewing* case but is also not favored, and it is doubtful that such a provision will be agreed to in the future.

The entry of a consent decree was once a very simple matter. The decree was filed with the court and that was that. Today entry can be a very difficult part of the consent-decree process. This development started in 1961 when in response to some public and Congressional pressure, the division initiated a thirty-day waiting period after the filing of the decree. The public was invited to submit its views, either directly to the division or in the form of *amici curiae* briefs with the court. The division reserved the right to withdraw its consent if it was persuaded that the decree was not in the public interest. The number of decrees initially dropped until defendants became accustomed to the new publicity. The courts' attitude changed and they began to take a more active role in the entry of a consent decree. The first indication of this came in the Supreme Court opinion in *Cascade Natural Gas Corp.* v. *El Paso Natural Gas,* which was discussed earlier. In this Section 7 case, the Supreme Court had ordered a divestiture in an earlier opinion. On remand a consent decree was agreed upon that did not include divestiture. The Court in another appeal allowed the state of California and a large industrial user of natural gas (as consumers desirous of retaining competition in California) to intervene as of right under the old Rule 23(a)(3) of the Federal Rules of Civil Procedure because they would be "adversely affected" by a disposition of property in control of the court. There was a strong dissent by Justice Stewart (joined by Justice Harlan) to this expansion of the right to intervene. After the decision the number of applicants for intervention increased. There were many critics of the opinion who like Milton Handler feared that "this procedural development if judicially encouraged, could easily undermine the efficacy of anti-trust enforcement." Both defendants and the Department of Justice have consistently opposed such applicants for intervention. The major reason for this is that if allowed to intervene, a third party can appeal, adding years to the final filing of a decree. The government's view is that "once the Attorney General has weighed all the considerations in determining that a particular consent decree is in the public interest, and the court after exposure of the issue, has concurred by entering that judgment, antitrust litigation should terminate." Many courts have now denied motions for interventions, distinguishing *Cascade* on its reliance on the protection of a Supreme Court mandate. Every such denial that has been appealed to the Supreme Court has been affirmed without argument or briefing. It can be safely said that *Cascade* is now considered *sui generis.* Judge Frankel of the Southern District of New York, when entering a recent merger-consent decree in *Ciba-Geigy,* enunciated a standard for intervention derived from these cases: "[T]he interest justifying the intervention as of right in an antitrust suit brought by the United States must be substantial, must lie at the center of the controversy, and must be shown clearly, in the language of the Rule to be less than 'adequately represented' by the Department of Justice." This standard will normally deny intervention as of right as well as permissive intervention. This is because the typical applicant for intervention has a purely private grievance that can be resolved in a private suit without hamstringing the enforcement attempts of the Department of Justice.

Once a decree is entered, it is very difficult to modify it. The landmark case on this point is *United States* v. *Swift & Co.* It laid down a very strict standard: "Nothing less than a clear showing of grievous wrong evoked by new and unforeseen conditions should lead us to change what was decreed after years of litigation with the consent of all concerned." This test was reaffirmed in the second *Swift* decision in 1961. The fact is that only three times since the Sherman Act was passed has a decree been modified without the consent of both parties. There have been arguments that there should be a different modification standard for the government than for defendants. The theory is that to require the government to produce proof under the *Swift* ruling would force it to enter decrees more cautiously, taking every future circumstance into consideration and thereby requiring greater relief in decrees. This, so the argument goes, would reduce the number of decrees and negate the value of the consent-decree program.

Perhaps recognizing some of these problems, government has demonstrated some flexibility in fashioning its consent decrees. More and more the decrees are limited for a period of years. For instance, consent decrees in both the reciprocity cases and the ITT merger cases had provisions which limited their effect to ten years. In other words, the government is willing to recognize that an industry can significantly change over the years, and that a decree that binds companies for many years can sometimes produce anticompetitive results. Another factor in the government's willingness to include time limits is the realization that defendants will be more willing to enter into decrees and will accept more controls.

It is unlikely the government would be willing to limit decrees that merely enjoin illegal activity. This is because a prohibition on price-fixing is not likely to produce anticompetitive effects—no matter how long it lasts. However, as mentioned, decrees of this type are giving way to those containing regulation and affirmative relief even in the per se cases.

COMPLIANCE AND ENFORCEMENT OF DECREES

The Antitrust Division's enforcement program for judgments—both litigated and consent—has not been very effective. In the past it became interested in a judgment in only one of two ways: (1) if it received a complaint or other information that the decree was being violated, and (2) if the defense counsel asked for an interpretation or modification of the decree. As one report noted, the division's surveillance mechanism has been a mailbag. This program has not been without criticism. A 1959 House Antitrust Subcommittee Report concluded that it was ineffective and cited as the cause:

> The complete absence of procedures to bring automatically to the attention of the Antitrust Division instances where defendants fail to comply with the requirements of a judgment. . . . The Antitrust Division relies upon the same surveillance procedures for an industry that is subject to the terms of an Antitrust Consent Decree that it used in an industry which has no history of antitrust litigation.

Recently a Nader study has also criticized the program. In fact the title of its chapter on consent-decree enforcement was "when winning is losing."

The Division has heeded these criticisms and has attempted to revamp its program. It established a new Judgment Enforcement Section, taking this function away from the old Judgment and Judgment Enforcement Section. This new section was to do nothing but check compliance with past decrees. Division consent decrees also started to require annual reports of defendants' compliance efforts. This had been done in the past in divestiture decrees but now was to be included in decrees requiring all types of relief. The goal of the division is to review each decree once, either preliminarily or thoroughly every ten years. Even if this is achieved, one wonders whether it will provide adequate enforcement. The Judgment and Judgment Enforcement sections have recently been recombined in order that the attorneys who negotiate the consent decree can also follow up and do the compliance checks. Some reports have suggested that the attorneys who litigated the case should also enforce the decrees because they are familiar with the industry. So far this practice has not been adopted by the division. Whether this new compliance effort will be sustained or in the long run be successful is uncertain. As yet there are only a handful of men assigned to the task; they do not have nor can they expect to acquire an expertise in all the various industries; and as of 1970, they had approximately 1,200 outstanding decrees to monitor.

THE EXPEDITING ACT

The Antitrust Division was not the only new arrival of 1903. That year also saw the passage of the Expediting Act. Senator Hoar, the oft-proclaimed expert on monopoly problems, introduced the bill in January and a little over a month later it was signed by President Roosevelt. The bill had been prepared upon recommendations of the attorney general that were contained in a reply to a Congressional invitation to submit the Department of Justice's views on needed reforms in the field of antitrust legislation.

Section 1 of the Act gives the attorney general the option to call a three-judge district court when in his opinion the "case is of general public importance." This section also provides that the hearing of the case should be expedited. Section 2 provides for a direct appeal to the Supreme Court within sixty days from the final judgment in a government civil antitrust case. Interlocutory appeals are not available since the Act bypasses the Court of Appeals and therefore the interlocutory appeals statute, 28 U.S.C. §1292, does not apply. Criminal cases are not affected by the Act. They are rarely filed to set standards, establish standards, or make law; their main function is deterrence and punishment for the more gross antitrust violations. Private civil suits, likewise, are not vehicles for developing the law in any uniform manner, but are merely methods of righting private wrongs. Therefore, it was not considered necessary to expedite the hearing of these two types of cases.

Today it appears that everyone from members of the Supreme Court to the American Bar Association and the Department of Justice is in favor of amending the Act. Before we look at the proposals for change, however, let us review the reasons why the Act was passed in 1903.

In that year antitrust law was still new and the type of cases that were being filed, such as *Northern Securities, Addyston Pipe,* and *Standard Oil,* presented novel questions whose impact on the economy was as yet untested. Although today it is not uncommon to find a judge who is unfamiliar with the complexities of antitrust law, in that period every judge was unfamiliar with them. Therefore, it was deemed a good idea to have three judges with their combined wisdom and experience plow through this virgin territory when it appeared to the attorney general that the case was of general public importance. It is interesting to note that this was the first time that the three-judge district court panel was established. It has since been adopted in a number of other statutes.

The concept of a direct appeal to the Supreme Court was not at all novel in 1903. The Act simply indicated that government antitrust cases were in the same category as other important cases that were already being directly appealed to the Court. Few people objected to bypassing the court of appeals, since at that time it had been in existence only twelve years and there were doubts as to both its usefulness and competence. Furthermore, there was the advantage that direct appeals would allow the Supreme Court quickly and uniformly to apply the growing antitrust law throughout the land.

Today conditions have changed and these reasons no longer exist. For instance antitrust law is no longer novel. Present-day trial judges who have yet to be exposed to antitrust cases have abundant case law and sophisticated counsel to guide them if and when they need it. (Although economic expertise remains a problem, a three-judge court would not necessarily add any expertise.) Therefore, these panels no longer serve their initial purpose. Professor Donald Turner expressed a widely held view when he was an AAG in charge of the Antitrust Division:

> The use of three judges to hear long hours of testimony, read and digest sizable quantities of documentary evidence, and prepare detailed and complicated findings of fact and conclusions of law is an inappropriate luxury in an era of progressively expanding court dockets. Indeed, with the venue of most antitrust cases in district courts located in our principal metropolitan centers where their problem of mounting caseloads is particularly acute, the extra judicial effort caused by convening a three-judge court to hear such lengthy and protracted cases might well substantially disrupt the administration of justice in that district.

Since 1940 the attorney general has filed only about seven three-judge expediting certificates, and there has only been one in the last fourteen years. The only two possible advantages to using this procedure today are that: (1) it puts a case in a priority position on the court's docket, and (2) there is the theoretical possibility that a direct appeal from the grant or denial of a preliminary injunction can be taken from a three-judge district court pursuant to 28 U.S.C. §1253, whereas it cannot be from a one-judge district court. This question was expressly left open by Justice Goldberg in *United States* v. *F.M.C. Corp*. However these two possible advantages do not warrant retention of the three-judge court procedure considering the burden it puts on the court system.

The reasons for Section 2 of the Act are also no longer present. The court of appeals has certainly been accepted as a competent and worthwhile institution. Furthermore, the Supreme Court's role has changed drastically since 1903. At that time after an intermediate appeal all cases involving more than $1,000 and not falling within certain statutory exemptions were appealable as of right to the Supreme Court. Today the Court is no longer merely a court of last resort to individual litigants. It concerns itself only with issues of wide public or governmental interest. Although in 1903 the Act did not force the Court to hear cases that it would not eventually have to hear anyway, it does have that effect today. For instance, when dealing with small antitrust suits such as the *Phillipsburg National Bank* merger case, the attorney general is faced with the choice of burdening the Supreme Court with a possible full record review if the suit is lost in the district court or abandoning the case.

The Supreme Court has sought to protect its discretion in hearing appeals by establishing a summary as well as plenary review of cases. If the Court decides that it does not want to hear oral arguments or have the issues fully briefed, it decides the case on a summary review. The value of such a review is, of course, limited. Justice Harlan and Justice Goldberg recognized this in their dissent in *Kennecott Copper Corp.* v. *United States*. Noting that it was the appellant's first and only appeal under the Expediting Act and that the questions presented were not insubstantial, they concluded that "so long as this statute remains on the books and Congress provides no intermediate review [citation omitted], it is our view that the policy of the Act is, in general, best served by plenary rather than summary dispositions of such appeals." It is ironic that if these cases were appealed first to the court of appeals, nearly all would receive an initial plenary review. This certainly must have been the intention of the drafters of the Expediting Act.

The Supreme Court on a number of other occasions has expressed a negative view toward the Expediting Act. Justice Harlan, particularly, was vocal in his disapproval. In his dissent in *Brown Shoe* he stated his position at length:

> At this period of mounting dockets there is certainly much to be said in favor of relieving this Court of the often arduous task of searching through the voluminous trial testimony and exhibits to determine whether a single district judge's findings of fact are supportable. The legal issues in most civil antitrust cases are no longer so novel or unsettled as to make them especially appropriate for initial appellate consideration by this Court, as compared with those in a variety of other areas of federal law. And under modern conditions it may well be doubted whether direct review of such cases by this Court truly serves the purpose of expedition which underlay the original passage of the Expediting Act. I venture to predict that a critical reappraisal of the problem would lead to the conclusion that "expedition" and also, over-all, more satisfactory appellate review would be achieved in these cases were primary appellate jurisdiction returned to the Court of Appeals. . . . As things now stand this Court must deal with *all* government civil antitrust cases, often either at the unnecessary expenditure of its own time or at the risk of inadequate appellate review if a summary disposition of the appeal is made.

In *United States* v. *Singer Mfg. Co.* Justice Clark in a footnote in the majority opinion expressed a similar view: "Whatever may have been the wisdom of the Expediting Act in providing direct appeals in antitrust cases at the time of its enactment in 1903, time has proven it unsatisfactory. [Citation omitted.] Direct appeals not only place a great burden on the Court but also deprive us of the valuable assistance of the Court of Appeals."

At least one Justice has not concurred in this view. Justice White, in the *Singer* case, without stating his reasons, noted his disagreement with the footnote in the majority opinion. Justice Harlan, on the other hand, in the same case went so far as to predict that the final outcome might have been different had the Expediting Act not prevented the assistance of the court of appeals.

Both the American Bar Association and the Department of Justice also are in favor of amending the Expediting Act. One may question, therefore, why the Act to this date has not been amended. If we look at the proposals for change we may see why.

One proposal that presents no problem is that the provision in Section 1 for the empaneling of a three-judge district court be eliminated. There is general agreement that this would be a good idea. The second proposal is that the direct appeal in Section 2 of the Act be eliminated and that the initial appeal be in the court of appeals. The Department of Justice does not object to this amendment but strongly believes that the possibility of immediate review by the Supreme Court should be preserved for cases of general importance. The question remains who is to decide what cases are of general importance? The department thinks that the attorney general should be given this decision. Others believe that it should be given to the district court. Whether the attorney general or the court, or both, receive this power should not be a tremendously difficult question to resolve.

The third group of proposals which concern interlocutory appeals is the most troublesome. The Department of Justice would like to see interlocutory appeals from decrees granting, modifying, or denying injunctions. This is presently provided in most other civil litigation by 28 U.S.C. §1292(a). On the other hand, the department does not want appeals to be allowed from other interlocutory orders such as those under 28 U.S.C. §1292(b) that involve "controlling questions of law."

The first proposal for interlocutory appeals from injunction decrees strikes at the heart of merger litigation. Many times a merger case is won or lost at the preliminary injunction hearing. If the government loses its motion, the companies will merge. Rare is the government victory on the merits that brings a complete divestiture decree. Even if there is such a decree, the merged company can do business freely for the years it will take to litigate the case. (Hold-separate orders, however, might prevent this.) If the government wins the motion, this will often kill the merger. The company that is being acquired usually is interested in receiving money quickly. If it has to wait years for the outcome of the case, it will not only not receive any money but its options will be closed for that period. So these companies very often will back out at this stage. If they do not back out, years later they still might not be able to merge if the case is lost on the merits. This is significant because in the past if the case reached the Supreme Court, defendants would almost always lose on the merits. As Justice Stewart remarked in his dissent in the *Von's Grocery* case, "the Government always wins." Because of this characteristic of Supreme Court merger opinions, defense lawyers have liked the idea of no right of appeal from district court injunction orders. They rightfully felt that their clients would stand a better chance in the district court. The government for the same reasons wanted appeals from these orders. This is why, in the past at least, there has been a strong split on this proposal.

On the other hand, many nongovernment lawyers would like to see the availability of interlocutory appeals from orders on controlling questions of law. Delay always has been a viable defense tactic in antitrust cases. This proposal would aid that tactic because appeals could be taken from more orders than before. The government realizes this and the fact that its cases are already often too long and complex (especially for juries). In its opinion there are plenty of delaying obstacles available now to defendants without opening an appellate Pandora's box. For these reasons it is uncertain when the Expediting Act will be amended. Bills have been introduced regularly without success. It seems that the proponents would, at least for now, prefer no changes rather than risk the passage of provisions which would present more problems than they already have.

REMEDIES AND RELIEF

We have discussed the types of remedies available to the government once a merger has been held to be illegal in preceding chapters and in this chapter in the section on negotiated settlements. Suffice it to say that in addition to the remedies of dissolution, divestiture, and divorcement provided for in Section 4 of the Sherman Act, district courts have great discretion in fashioning appropriate relief under the circumstances, that is, to preserve or reconstitute a competitive market situation. The Supreme Court, in its recent decision in *Ford Motor Company* v. *United States* (discussed in detail in previous chapters) provides an excellent insight into this discretion. The Supreme Court stated that the "main controversy here has been over the nature and degree of the relief to be afforded." The district court ordered that Ford divest itself of the Autolite assets it had acquired. The majority opinion concluded with dispatch that the lower court had been correct in ordering divestiture as the only means to "correct the condition caused by the unlawful acquisition." It reasoned, "To permit Ford to retain the Autolite plant and name and to continue manufacturing spark plugs would perpetuate the anticompetitive effects of the acquisition."

> [I]t would be a novel, not to say absurd, interpretation of the antitrust act to hold that after an unlawful combination is formed and has acquired the power which it has no right to acquire—namely, to restrain commerce by suppressing competition—and is proceeding to use it and execute the purpose for which the combination was formed, it must be left in possession of the power it has acquired, with full freedom to exercise it. [*Northern Securities Co.* v. *United States,* 193 U.S. 197, 347.]

In addition to divestiture the lower court ordered ancillary relief that was designed to effectuate divestiture and restore competition by guaranteeing the ability of the divested plant to compete effectively for a period of time after divestiture in both the OE market and aftermarket. This additional relief included three provisions that were without litigated precedent and were vigorously opposed by Ford. These contested provisions, as described by the Supreme Court,

> (1) enjoined Ford for 10 years from manufacturing spark plugs,
> (2) ordered Ford for five years to purchase one-half of its total annual requirement of spark plugs from the divested plant under the "Autolite" name,
> (3) prohibited Ford for the same period from using its own tradenames on plugs.

In holding that these provisions were a reasonable and necessary form of relief, the Court explained, "they are designed to give the divested plant an opportunity to establish its competitive position."

The ten-year prohibition upon Ford's manufacturing its own plugs was not specifically related by the Court to the following finding, but seems to be critical to it: "[T]he private brand sector of the spark plug market will grow substantially in the next decade because mass merchandisers are entering this market in force. They not only sell all brands over the counter but have service bays where many carry only spark plugs of their own proprietary brand. It is anticipated that by 1980 the total private brand portion of the spark plug market may then represent 17% of the total aftermarket." The Court also adopted the lower court's findings that spark plug manufacturers, such as the divested plant, which are not owned by the auto makers would seek to supply spark plugs under private brands to mass merchandisers as a way of improving their competitive position in the aftermarket.

Were Ford to produce its own plugs during the ten years preceding the time when the private label portion of the aftermarket had grown to such an extent that it could afford the divested plant at least a toehold in the aftermarket, mechanics and owners of Ford automobiles, because of the undiminished OE tie during the ten years, would be lost to the divested plant as customers in the aftermarket. This result would be in addition to foreclosing Ford to the divested plant as an OE customer. The ten-year restriction against Ford's manufacturing plugs, therefore, has the effect of insuring that Autolite will have the opportunity to re-establish itself in the replacement market as competition among private brands in that market begins to sever the OE tie and open up opportunities for greater competition in manufacturing and selling replacement plugs.

The second provision in the decree requiring Ford to purchase one half of its total annual spark plug requirements from the divested plant for five years under the Autolite name was designed "to give the divested enterprise an assured customer while it struggles to be re-established as an effective, independent competitor," and to give it "at least a foothold in the lucrative *aftermarket* . . . ."

The third provision prohibiting Ford from using or marketing plugs bearing the Ford trade name during the initial five-year period was for the stated purpose of avoiding foreclosure of the replacement parts market from Autolite before it had time to enter that market in which its ultimate competitive prospects were the brightest. The Court reasoned, "In view of the importance of the OE tie, if Ford were permitted to use its own brand name during the initial five-year period, there would be a tendency to impose the oligopolistic structure of the automotive industry on the replacement parts market and the divested enterprise might well be unable to become a strong competitor."

These ancillary provisions in the lower court's decree were attacked for their undue harshness not only by Ford but by Chief Justice Burger in his dissenting opinion. The most important area of criticism was that the restrictions placed upon Ford were not related to Ford's illegal conduct, but were said by the majority to be necessary to overcome the strong tie between the OE market and the aftermarket. Chief Justice Burger recognized the existence of the strong tie but reasoned that it was not something for which Ford should, in effect, be punished. The majority opinion did not specifically answer this contention. Its likely answer is found in two portions of the opinion:

> As a result of the acquisition of Autolite, the structure of the spark plug industry changed drastically, as already noted, . . . The result was to foreclose to the remaining independent spark plug manufacturers the substantial segment of the market previously open to competitive selling and to remove the significant procompetitive effects in the concentrated spark plug market that resulted from Ford's position on the edge of the market as a potential entrant.
>
> * * *
>
> The District Court concluded that the forces of competition must be nurtured to correct for Ford's illegal acquisition. We view its decree as a means to that end.

Given the choice of possibly failing to re-establish Autolite as an effective competitor or imposing restrictions upon Ford's competitive activities which in and of themselves were not part of the illegal acquisition, the Court chose to foster new competition by Autolite even if it involved some sacrifice on the part of Ford as a potential entrant by legal means into the spark plug market.

23 Federal Trade Commission–Practice and Procedure

The Federal Trade Commission was established by Congress in 1914 as an independent regulatory agency. Among its other duties is the enforcement of the Clayton Act and Section 5 of the Federal Trade Commission Act as they pertain to mergers. It is composed of five commissioners, appointed by the president and confirmed by the Senate for terms of seven years. No more than three commissioners may be members of the same political party. Since 1950 the president has by law designated one of the commissioners to serve as chairman. The chairman has broad authority over commission personnel, including appointments and promotions. The chairman, subject to the policy guidance of his four colleagues, also has broad authority over the use and expenditure of funds and the distribution of business within the commission. Under the direction of the chairman, the executive director is the chief administrative officer, who exercises supervisory authority over the various offices within the commission and over the staff of the commission. The secretary of the commission has responsibility for the commission's correspondence and records. The general counsel is the commission's chief legal expert. His office is responsible for representing the commission in the federal courts. An economic adviser, the Office of Congressional Relations, and the Office of Public Information report directly to the chairman. There also is an Office of Policy Planning and Evaluation and an Office of Administrative Law Judges. The latter office provides the FTC's independent administrative judges for the formal proceedings.

Effective July 1, 1970, the work of the commission was divided into two main areas, that of antitrust and restraint of trade matters, under the title of the Bureau of Competition, and that of consumer protection, under the name of the Bureau of Consumer Protection, which is an expanded version of the former Bureau of Deceptive Practices. The Bureau of Competition, which largely includes the work done by the former Bureau of Restraint of Trade, is headed by a director and seven assistants who supervise the following divisions: Accounting, Compliance, Evaluation, General Litigation, Industry Guidance, Small Business, and Special Projects. A third operating bureau, the Bureau of Economics, performs the same work as in the past was allocated to the three divisions of Economic Evidence, Financial Statistics, and Industry Analysis.

The commission's employees total over 1,200, of which nearly 500 are attorneys and 125 are other professional personnel. The FTC's headquarters is in Washington, D.C., but more than 300 employees are located in eleven field offices throughout the country, in the following places: Atlanta, Boston, Chicago, Cleveland, Kansas City, Los Angeles, New Orleans, New York, San Francisco, Seattle, and the Washington, D.C., area. In addition to their traditional investigative role, these field offices also may handle the trial of some formal cases. They also coordinate local consumer protection work, including active participation in consumer councils.

Violations of the law are brought to the commission's attention in a variety of ways. Letters are received from consumers, business competitors, suppliers, and customers, sometimes directly, sometimes from other agencies of the government. The procedure for filing a complaint is informal. All that is necessary is a letter to the commission detailing the facts believed to constitute a violation of the law. Most merger law proceedings, however, do not stem from complaints but from information gathered from trade journals, periodicals, and other similar sources. The commission possesses extremely broad investigative powers under the Federal Trade Commission Act. This Act provides the commission with the power of access to documentary evidence, the authority to require annual and special reports from any firm, access to information in the hands of other government agencies, including the Internal Revenue Service, and the power to issue subpoenas. The power to require special reports from corporations has been exercised in several ways during the history of the commission. Reports have been used to gather information for the *Quarterly Financial Report for Manufacturing Corporations,* prepared jointly by the Federal Trade Commission and the Securities and Exchange Commission. Extensive use of this power has been made in connection with general economic surveys conducted by the commission, including several dealing with trends of concentration in particular industries. Special reports also have been used to gather data in the trial of specific cases, as well as to investigate compliance with outstanding cease and desist orders under Section 5 of the Federal Trade Commission Act. In recent years the commission has used its special report power to conduct general legal investigations of alleged widespread violations of the laws throughout an entire industry.

In the merger area a recent innovation has been the use of this authority to require information in advance of certain types of mergers. In 1969 the commission began requiring premerger notification both for mergers or asset acquisitions greater than $10 million where the combined assets (or sales, by a 1972 resolution) exceed $250 million and for stock acquisitions of firms with assets greater than $10 million where the combined size exceeds $250 million and either the 10 or 50 per cent ownership plateau is reached. Additionally, some parties to these transactions are specifically required to file detailed special reports, and others similarly may be ordered to file by the commission. Notification also must be given of all vertical mergers and acquisitions in the Portland cement industry and all acquisitions by food retailers or wholesalers with sales exceeding $100 million annually. It is emphasized that none of these procedures imply that commission approval is required before any transaction. There have, however, been some questions raised concerning this use of the Section 6(b) reporting power. Preliminarily there is a practical problem of enforcement. Section 10 of the Federal Trade Commission Act does not impose any penalties for failure to comply with a report order until thirty days after notice of default on that order. Under the current guidelines, notification must be given within ten days after the merger has been agreed to in principle and at least sixty days before consummation. If there is not sixty days between agreement and consummation, then the report is required "as soon as possible" after the agreement. Additional reports are also due at least sixty days prior to the consummation. If the deadline cannot be met, an explanatory letter must be filed with the commission. But if no penalty can be imposed until thirty days after the FTC becomes aware of the merger and gives notice of default, it is hard to see how the commission can benefit by this procedure except in the case of voluntary compliance.

Furthermore there has been some doubt expressed as to the authority for this use of Section 6(b). Its provisions were held specifically applicable to merger proceedings in *United States* v. *St. Regis Paper Co.*, but the question is whether it can be used to gain premerger information. The FTC lobbied for the authority to require premerger notification for years before it decided it already had that power in some cases. The Justice Department has been held not to have similar power under the wording of its civil investigative demand section which allows such demands only in the context of any inquiry to determine if there "is or has been . . . any antitrust violation. . . ." In one case a court said that because a proposed acquisition "is not, and quite obviously has not been a violation," the use of compulsory reporting powers was unauthorized. Both the language of Section 6(b) itself and its broad interpretation in *United States* v. *Morton Salt* suggest that FTC's authority is more extensive than that of the Justice Department, but there is Supreme Court language in *American Tobacco* strongly suggesting that there must be at least a basis for believing that there has been some wrongdoing before Section 6(b) investigative powers may be used constitutionally. The Court, in *Morton Salt,* however, seems to read this case as only prohibiting inquiries "of such a sweeping nature and so unrelated to the matter properly under inquiry as to exceed the investigatory power." Although the narrower issue in *Morton Salt* was the propriety of report orders to determine compliance with previous judgments, there is broad dicta arguing for a very far-reaching power on the part of the commission. The Court said, "Even if we regard the request for information in this case as caused by nothing more than official curiosity, nevertheless, law enforcing agencies have a legitimate right to satisfy themselves that corporate behavior, is consistent with the law and public interest." At any rate, as long as the premerger notification requirements are limited to mergers of very large corporations or of corporations in industries where there is a history of serious concentration problems, it can be argued strongly that these procedures are within bounds of their authority even as seen by the *American Tobacco* Court. The mere fact of a merger of a certain size or in a certain industry may so strongly suggest a merger law violation as to warrant investigation.

When a possible violation of the law comes to the commission's attention, either through its own investigation or through one of the media mentioned earlier, the procedures for enforcement are varied and flexible. The Federal Trade Commission Act provides that if it appears a formal proceeding would be in the interest of the public, the commission may issue a complaint against the alleged offender and set a hearing date. Such hearings are conducted publicly before hearing judges, who serve as administrative trial judges, and the proceedings are similar to those employed in federal courts. The rules of evidence are somewhat relaxed in such hearings, yet they remain subject to due process requirements of fairness. The respondent is given compulsory means of acquiring evidence and an opportunity to present it as well as to cross-examine witnesses. Postmerger evidence is admissible when relevant. There is also a procedure for summary judgment when the trial judge finds no real issue of fact. After the hearings are completed and evidence has been received from the commission's lawyers and the lawyer representing the respondent, the administrative judge makes an initial decision. This decision becomes final if not appealed or modified by the commission. If the initial decision is appealed to the full commission for review, or if the commission reviews the matter of its own volition, it may modify the order in any way it sees fit. If the decision is against the respondent, the commission may issue an order to cease and desist. Such an order is like an injunction and remains in effect indefinitely, unless later modified or dismissed for reasons of changes in the circumstances of fact or law. If the order is violated, the respondent may be prosecuted in a federal district court for civil penalties, which may run as high as $5,000 for each violation, with each day of a continuing violation counting as a separate offense. A cease and desist order does not become final until sixty days after it has been served on the respondent. During this period the respondent may appeal to a federal court of appeals. Before such courts the commission's finding regarding the facts are conclusive if supported by substantial evidence on the whole record. Cease and desist orders include a provision that respondents file, within sixty days from the date of the service of the order, a report of compliance setting forth the manner of compliance.

There is a remedial tool which the commission can bring into play even before a cease and desist order has been issued. It may seek and the United States court of appeals may grant a temporary injunction to prevent consummation of a merger. The court's authority to grant such an injunction is based not on statute but on the All Writs Act, which permits it to issue such writs as are necessary to preserve its appellate jurisdiction. Thus when subsequent divestiture would be an ineffective remedy, because, for example, the merging firms have scrambled the assets, the court may issue an injunction to block the merger pending adjudication by the FTC in order to insure that practical remedies remain available. The decision to petition for injunction is with the commissioners and *not* complaint counsel. FTC practice under this statute is extremely limited so it is not yet clear what standards the court will require before granting this relief. Similar injunctive relief is allowed the Justice Department under Section 15 of the Clayton Act on a showing in district court of a reasonable probability of success in the adjudication on the merits. In addition, the courts usually weigh the harm done to respondents and the adequacy of divestiture to prevent public harm. Sometimes they require expedited trial proceedings also. So-called hold-separate orders are occasionally used in place of outright prohibitions to mitigate the harm to the parties. Which remedy to employ is within the discretion of the court. In *Dean Foods* the Supreme Court said jurisdiction was shown if the court of appeals found "that an effective remedial order, once the merger was implemented, would otherwise be virtually impossible." On remand the Seventh Circuit, in a brief order, found only that it was "reasonably probable that the agreement . . . [might] ultimately be determined by the Federal Trade Commission . . . to be a violation of . . . the Clayton Act." This language seems to imply that probable success at the agency level instead of the appellate level is all that need be demonstrated, but the thrust of the Supreme Court opinion toward insuring that the court of appeals has available the remedies it needs implies that the commission must make a stronger showing. The Seventh Circuit made no finding on the feasibility of divestiture on these facts, an issue which the Supreme Court left open. The Fifth Circuit, in *FTC* v. *OKC Corp.*, granted a preliminary injunction prohibiting restructuring of an acquired corporation. It adopted the precise language of the Supreme Court in *Dean Foods* requiring a showing that divestiture will be impractical and also the Seventh Circuit's language requiring a demonstration that the commission is likely to find the merger illegal. None of these courts shows any signs of considering the potential harm to the merging parties. In light of the near certain death that injunction and subsequent administrative delays promise for what may be a wholly legal merger, general equitable principles might seem to require a weighing of the public injury against the injury to the merging parties, but if the courts view the action strictly in terms of protecting their jurisdiction, they may not consider that factor at all.

Once a violation has been found, the commission has broad discretion to tailor a cease and desist order that will prevent the evils it seeks to control. Such an order may be based either on Section 11(b) of the Clayton Act or Section 5 of the FTC Act, depending on which statute's provisions were found to have been violated. The Clayton Act authorizes the FTC to issue orders "to cease and desist from . . . violations, and divest . . . stock . . . or assets. . . ." Until the *Luria Bros & Co.* case in 1963, commission orders (other than consent orders) under this section required only divestiture. In *Luria* and many subsequent cases, the commission also has claimed the authority to prohibit specified types of future acquisitions without prior approval, usually for a specified period. In the case which put this practice most directly in question, the Sixth Circuit allowed the order with little comment over arguments that such a provision, designed to promote competition over the long run, was not within the bounds of statutory authority. Section 11(b) Clayton Act orders also have required that divestiture be done in such a manner and with sufficient technical assistance as to create a "viable competitor."

Section 5 of the FTC Act authorizes orders to "cease and desist the unfair practices." The commission was held to have a wide latitude in fashioning orders under this section so long as the remedy bears a reasonable relationship to the unfair practices in *Jacob Siegal Co.* v. *FTC*. Older cases held that the commission's discretion falls short of the powers of a court of equity, but at least one recent case compares its powers with those of a court fashioning a Sherman Act decree. The courts will look only to see if the commission has abused its discretion in choosing a remedy. The order may bar repetition of similar conduct with parties other than those involved in the proceedings as well as related but different activities. In *Atlantic Richfield Co.* v. *FTC,* the Supreme Court found that Atlantic had abused its coercive power over its station owners to its own advantage and to that of Goodyear Tire Company, with whom it had a dealership contract. Therefore it prohibited either party from entering into a similar contract with anyone where even a potential of such an abuse could arise. This order was upheld over dissents by Justices Stewart and Harlan, who argued that the commission had overextended its authority when it tried to prohibit contracts not actually in violation of the law. The Court apparently has not tried to read any defenses into these orders as was done in the *Rubberoid* case. Both acts have supported detailed provisions insuring effective separation upon divestiture such as prohibitions of purchases from specific suppliers or sales to specific consumers.

FTC cease and desist orders under the Clayton Act have a special bite in merger cases because of Sections 5(a) and (b) of the Act. Section 5(a) makes a "final judgment or decree . . . in any civil or criminal proceeding brought by or on behalf of the United States under the antitrust laws" prima facie evidence against the same defendant in any private antitrust treble-damage suit to the extent the judgment would be an estoppel between the original parties. Section 5(b) tolls the statute of limitations during the pendancy of such a government proceeding and for one year thereafter. The identity of parties and issues need only be "substantial." The Supreme Court has held Section 5(b) applicable to FTC Clayton Act proceedings in *Minnesota Mining and Mfg. Co.* v. *New Jersey Wood Finishing Co.* Although the Supreme Court has never ruled directly on the applicability of Section 5(a), recent lower-court cases generally hold that it is also applicable. The older cases denying Section 5(a)'s applicability, though not overruled directly by *Minnesota Mining,* had whatever was left of their rationale after the 1959 Clayton Act amendments cut from beneath them. Those cases had reasoned that the results of FTC proceedings were not (1) final judgments or decrees, (2) in civil or criminal proceedings, (3) on behalf of the United States. The second and third requirements are also part of Section 5(b), which the Court found applicable in *Minnesota Mining.* It would be difficult to argue that their meaning varied in those two clauses. That left only the question whether it is a "final judgment or decree." After the Finality Act of 1959 there could be little question about the first part of the phrase. According to the court in *Farmington Dowel,* the question whether it was a "judgment or decree" under the statutory language depended on whether the procedural safeguards in FTC proceedings were sufficient to provide the defendant his day in court on the issues on which he was to be estopped. It found that they were. Therefore in light of the "spirit" of *Minnesota Mining,* which favored giving the private litigant as much of the benefit of government litigation as possible, the court found Section 5(a) applicable also.

A question remaining open is whether Section 5(a) and Section 5(b) are applicable to proceedings under Section 5 of the FTC Act. The general teaching has been that they are not because the FTC Act is not enumerated as an "antitrust law" in Section 4. But at least one court has held Section 5(b) applicable. Section 5(b) is activated by a proceeding "to prevent, restrain, or punish violations of any of the antitrust laws." The court, in *Lippa & Co.* v. *Lenox, Inc.,* noted that although the FTC Act is not an antitrust law per se, Section 5 may be used to reach Sherman Act violations, and generally to reach antitrust violations in their incipiency. Therefore, although Section 5 proceedings are not based on an antitrust law, the court reasoned, to the extent that FTC Act violations are actual or incipient antitrust violations, the proceeding is, in fact, a proceeding "to prevent . . . or punish violations . . . of antitrust laws." This reasoning, however, could not be applied as easily to Section 5(a). That section requires that the proceeding be "under the antitrust laws." The *Lippa* court itself read *Nashville Milk Co.* v. *Carnation Co.,* to foreclose that possibility. But that case is pre-

Minnesota Mining and might need to be reviewed in light of the latter case's philosophy, its reading of legislative history, and its desire to prevent arbitrary differences, depending on the form and forum in which the government action is brought. It may be that the Supreme Court would now recognize Section 5 of the FTC Act to the extent it deals with antitrust matters as being in fact, if not in theory, an antitrust law. To the extent that any decree does fall under Section 5(a), its use as evidence is governed by the general rules of estoppel, "giving the suitor as large an advantage as . . . [that] doctrine would afford had the government brought suit." It provides rebuttable prima facie evidence only on ultimate facts put "distinctly in conflict and directly determined." The manner of a decree's use at trial is within the discretion of the trial judge.

The commission seeks to encourage compliance with the requirements of the laws it administers by a number of means other than the formal proceedings just outlined, as informal techniques may be quicker, cheaper, and equally effective. These methods include administrative treatment, trade practice conferences, trade regulation rules, issuance of guides, advisory opinions, and consent settlement procedures. It is important to note that there is a commission policy of effecting industry-wide compliance, whenever possible or practicable, if alleged violations of law are extensive. This policy is a most important one in the agency's current program.

Administrative treatment is the simplest and one of the newest of the informal methods and is used by the commission chiefly in the area of misrepresentation through advertising. Letters of discontinuance or affidavits signed by responsible officials of the offending concern, accompanied by evidence of compliance with the law and assurance that the questioned practices will not be resumed, are accepted in settlement of many smaller infractions. In this connection it is important to note that currently the commission's eleven field offices have authority in proper instances to accept administrative settlements of alleged violations. However, the field office must obtain enough facts to disclose a probable violation and may not accept a settlement tendered by a businessman seeking to avoid further government involvement without regard to whether or not the facts indicate that a violation has occurred. The rules state, "In determining whether the public interest will be fully safeguarded through such informal administrative treatment, the Commission will consider (1) the nature and gravity of the alleged violation; (2) the prior record of good faith of the parties involved; and (3) other factors, including, where appropriate, adequate assurance that the practice has been discontinued and will not be resumed."

In 1962 provision was made for issuance of trade regulation rules applicable to unlawful trade practices. These rules are designed to express the judgment of the commission, based on facts of which it has knowledge derived from its past experience, regarding practices clearly violative of the law. Such rules may be sharply limited to particular areas of industries or to particular products or geographic areas, as appropriate. Provision is made for reliance upon these rules in litigated cases if the respondent is given a fair hearing on the legality and propriety of applying a particular rule to a particular case. Also, there is the usual provision for formal due process procedures prior to the final issuance of the rules. Rules of this nature increasingly are being used by the commission to solve industrywide problems, but no such binding rules have been issued in the merger area, although such a program has been suggested.

For many years the commission has provided procedures for trade practice conferences upon the application of businessmen and their trade associations in a particular industry or upon the commission's own motion. If the commission concludes that such a conference would be useful and proper, notice is given to members of the industry concerned. They and other interested parties appear and freely express their views regarding practices that are prevalent in the industry, practices that perhaps should be eliminated. Such conferences may, where appropriate, voluntarily repudiate widespread illegal practices in a particular industry. Conferences often involve formal trade practice rules with which members of a given industry may signify their willingness to comply. Compliance with such rules is not permissive, because they express what the law already prohibits. Recently such trade conference procedures have merged into the industry guides program also. Other rules, which the members of an industry may agree voluntarily to follow, condemn practices that the particular industry deems to be harmful or unethical even though such practices are not illegal. Trade practice rules upon adoption, on occasion have become the basis for settlement of investigative matters pending against members of the industry concerned. The commission has held such conferences to evaluate merger policies in particular industries for which it later issued guidelines.

In recent years the commission has published a series of guides in an effort to make clear to businessmen which practices are prohibited and thus to be avoided. Guides, unlike the trade practice rules, may deal with practices common to many industries. Although preparation of guides which are both informative and accurate is not an overnight task, there is no necessity for hearings or conferences concerning them. The guides are not intended to cover gaps in the law by dealing with factual situations that have not yet come before the commission in any form. Rather, they set forth in easily understood language the principles already established by the courts and the commission in decided cases. Their purpose is to give the businessman some knowledge of what the law requires of him. Additionally, the guides, by delineating areas of potential trouble, should alert the businessman to consult the lawyer when a problem arises and before a violation of law occurs. The commission has sought the greatest publicity for its guides in an effort to reach as many businessmen as possible. Copies are available without charge upon request to the commission. In the merger area this type of effort has taken the form of "Enforcement Policy Statements" in which the commission does not purport to state the law but merely to indicate under what circumstances and for what reasons the commission is likely to give particularly close scrutiny to any merger or acquisition in the given industry. They also may state explicitly that complaints will be issued in specific situations. Examples are the *FTC Enforcement Policy with Regard to Vertical Mergers in the Cement Industry,* and the *FTC Enforcement Policy with Regard to Mergers in the Food Distribution Industry,* which were published after industrywide conferences aimed at exploring problems and trends in those business communities.

In this age of increasing corporate complexity it is often extremely difficult for businessmen and their legal counsel to determine accurately the legality of proposed business actions. Some assistance may be obtained by seeking an advisory opinion from the commission. Although such advice is not binding on the commission in regard to future activity of the requesting party, the recipient will not be penalized for acting in good faith reliance on an advisory opinion based on his accurate statement of the circumstances so long as he discontinues the practice on notification of any change in FTC position. Clayton Act prosecutions have occurred and have been upheld after advisory-opinion letters had given preliminary approval. A special procedure has been provided for premerger clearance when requested by the parties or required by a previous order. As originally announced the commission would make a provisional decision based on the information submitted by the parties. If that decision were positive, it was to be published together with the reasons for the result, the application itself, and all supporting material except for that classified as confidential either by the commission itself or by request. There then would be a thirty-day period for written objections or comments by any interested member of the public as well as further factual investigation by the commission before a final decision was reached. If the provisional decision was negative, it was to be published with supporting reasoning but without the names of the parties or any confidential information. The purpose of these procedures is to allow the public to raise any matters overlooked by the commission and to allow a more thorough investigation by the commission. Apparently in response to criticism from Commissioner Elman that the effective decision still remained secret and ex parte, this procedure was revised so that the application and other information is now released on receipt with press release announcing its availability. This is followed by the same thirty-day waiting period. The commission's disposition of the application and statement of supporting reasons are made public in a press release.

In connection with the advisory-opinion procedure it is important to note the circumstances in which the commission will not give advice:

(1) where the course of action is being followed already by the requesting party; (2) where the same or substantially the same course of action is under investigation or is or has been the subject of a proceeding, order, or decree initiated or obtained by the commission or government agency against the requesting party; or (3) where the proposed course of action is such that an informed decision thereon could be made only after extensive investigation, clinical study, testing, or collateral inquiry.

Finally, the commission may employ the consent decree procedure to halt illegal practices. Following notification by the commission of its determination to issue a complaint, a party may indicate to the commission its willingness to have the proceedings disposed of by the entry or an order. The consent decree, by which the objectionable practices may be prohibited effectively is negotiated concurrently with the trial and investigative staff, advised in this connection by the general counsel. If an agreement is approved by the commission, the complaint and proposed order will be issued. If the proposed consent settlement is rejected, the complaint is issued and the matter set down for adjudication in regular course. It is possible to obtain a consent decree after adjudicatory proceedings have begun, but only in exceptional cases [Rule 2.34(d)]. In merger proceedings the consent-decree method of settlement has a particular attraction because such a decree cannot be used as prima facie evidence in a private treble-damage suit. It may be considered an admission against interests under evidentiary rules, but a consent decree entered before any testimony is taken is specifically exempted from Section 5(a). A consent decree negotiated after testimony, however, may be admissible.

The Commission shares with the Justice Department and other agencies the task of enforcing the Clayton Act. Many practices at the same time violate the Federal Trade Commission Act and statutes for which other agencies are responsible. In such cases the practice in question could be attacked by either enforcement agency. Although many have criticized this dual enforcement, the intersection of regulatory activity by two or more government agencies need not cause overlapping of effort, undue harassment of the industries regulated, or constant jurisdictional quarrels. The Federal Trade Commission and other agencies responsible for preventing certain practices have long worked to eliminate all of these possible dangers. Thus, since the World War II working agreements setting forth the primary responsibilities of each agency, the areas of sole jurisdiction, the policies governing duplication of proceedings, and the nature of liaison between the agencies have been concluded with these other agencies.

Exemplary of these working relationships is the one prevailing between the commission and the Antitrust Division of the Department of Justice in the antitrust area. This relationship has been characterized by willing interchange of information, avoidance of the duplication of effort, and the careful assignment of cases to the agency whose action will be likely to do the most good. Both agencies have certain industries in which they have developed an expertise in merger matters, and in these industries they take prime responsibility. The FTC, for example, handles almost all questions concerning acquisitions in the cement, food distribution, and textile mills products industries. At the same time, in recognition of their mutual and separate responsibilities, each agency has preserved its individual freedom to take independent action whenever it believes it to be necessary.

To avoid duplication of enforcement efforts, an elaborate system of notification and negotiation has been worked out. If either agency begins an investigation, the other agency is promptly notified. If the commission schedules a trade practice conference, the division is immediately informed. If the agency notified has any objections, a conference is held to effect a workable compromise. Although each agency retains its right to initiate separate proceedings, in practice their working agreement has prevented wasteful duplication entirely. Similarly, only rarely will either the division or the commission institute action when a private suit has been brought against the same conduct.

This working relationship obviously is tailored to avoid duplication of enforcement effort, and all means of increasing the effectiveness of both agencies are readily embraced. The system has been remarkably effective in practice, and this alone is a tribute to the practical bent of those charged with the enforcement of the antitrust and unfair trade practice laws. Similar working arrangements between the commission and the Food and Drug Administration, the Federal Communications Commission, and the Post Office Department have been equally successful. It would appear, therefore, that there is little to fear from multiple enforcement, and a great deal to be gained.

24 Private Enforcement

A rising tide of economic concentration has become an increasing cause of concern during the past two decades. The full impact of this wave of merger activity has not yet been ascertained. It is clear, however, that there has been a significant decrease in the number of firms and, at the same time, a significant increase in the size of the presently existing companies, an economic phenomenon which has not gone unnoticed in either the public or the private sectors. The government has maintained an increasingly effective enforcement of the antitrust laws relating to mergers, an enforcement program that has been amplified by what sometimes seems to be the universal rule that the government always wins.

In addition to governmental actions, either criminal or civil, to enforce the antitrust laws, the Congress has also enacted legislation which permits—indeed, encourages—private litigants to enforce the antitrust laws.

Section 4 of the Clayton Act provides, in part, that:

> any person who shall be injured in his business or property by reason of anything forbidden in the antitrust laws may sue therefor in any district court of the United States in the district in which the defendant resides, or is found, or has an agent, without respect to the amount of controversy, and shall recover threefold the damages by him sustained, and the cost of suit, including a reasonable attorney's fee.

The prospect of a treble-damage recovery can certainly be a sufficient incentive for a private plaintiff to institute an action to enforce the antitrust laws. Thus, private treble-damage actions have aided the enforcement of antitrust laws significantly. The great majority of these actions have been premised upon violations of Sections 1 and 2 of the Sherman Act and Sections 2 and 3 of the Clayton Act. Although it is sometimes overshadowed by the statutes upon which other private actions are premised, Section 7 of the Clayton Act—the merger law—is also an antitrust law. Section 1 of the Clayton Act specifically so provides; Section 7 also, therefore, can be enforced by a private litigant. In exercising his right to enforce Section 7, the private litigant can seek either an equitable remedy (injunction or divestiture) or a legal remedy (money damages). The former remedy is governed by Section 16; the latter is governed by Section 4.

EQUITABLE REMEDIES

A very important enforcement tool for the private litigant is authorized specifically by Section 16 of the Clayton Act. This provision states in relevant part:

> That any person, firm, corporation, or association shall be entitled to sue for and have injunctive relief . . . as against threatened loss or damage by a violation of the antitrust laws, including sections two, three, seven and eight of this Act, when and under the same conditions and principles as injunctive relief against threatened conduct that will cause loss or damage is granted by courts of equity, under the rules governing such proceedings. . . .

The effectiveness of this provision was given full force in *American Crystal Sugar Co.* v. *Cuban-American Sugar Co.* In this case the defendant had acquired a substantial block of stock in the plaintiff corporation. The parties were competitors in the same product market (refined sugar) and in the same geographic market (a ten-state area spreading over the Mississippi River valley). The plaintiff was granted an injunction whereby the defendant was prohibited from voting the stock it held in the plaintiff corporation, from acquiring representation on the plaintiff's board of directors, and from acquiring additional stock of plaintiff corporation. Before the court granted the injunction, it, of necessity, first had to determine that the evidence established a violation of Section 7. Even though the plaintiff had not established any elimination of competition, proof that the defendant's program was designed to bring a "closer association" between the two corporations was sufficient to show that the acquisition of stock by the defendant tended to lessen competition. This conclusion was necessary to implement fully the Clayton Act's legislative intent to "arrest restraints of trade in their incipiency." Therefore, there was no requirement that the plaintiff prove that competition actually was lessened. It was only necessary to prove that the acquisition *might* lessen competition and that the plaintiff was threatened with loss or damage thereby.

Moreover, the importance of the *American Crystal Sugar Co.* case lies in its affirmance of the private party's right to enforce the merger law —Clayton Act, Section 7—through actions for injunctions. This is in accord with the congressional intent that this private right of action provides a necessary and vigilant enforcement of the Clayton Act. Although probably not as economically enticing to the private litigant as a treble-damage action, the equitable right under Section 16 of the Clayton Act does indeed provide a definite remedy. An injunction issued by a court can prevent the incipient evil from maturing into an actual restraint. In order to invoke the Section 16 equitable remedy, the plaintiff need only show a *threatened loss or damage* by a merger or acquisition. In *American Crystal Sugar Co.*, the threatened loss was the expense the plaintiff could expect if the Justice Department instituted enforcement proceedings against it. Section 16 as a tool in the field of private enforcement of the antitrust laws is particularly effective in the area of mergers. If private parties had to establish *actual injury* to their property before an injunction could be granted, the effectiveness of the cause of action would be nullified, or at least significantly decreased. But the courts consistently have upheld the express language of Section 16. Only a violation and threatened harm need be demonstrated; actual injury is not necessary. The Supreme Court reaffirmed this doctrine in 1969: "That remedy [injunction] is characteristically available even though the plaintiff has not yet suffered actual injury . . . he need only demonstrate a significant threat of injury from a contemporary violation likely to continue or recur."

Although Section 16 speaks only of injunctions, with no specific delineation of other equitable relief, it seems reasonable to conclude that it also encompasses divestiture of stock as an appropriate remedy. In the *American Crystal Sugar Co.* case, the court noted, without disapproval, that divestiture was requested in addition to the permanent injunction. The court's reason for not granting divestiture was that the injunction was a sufficient remedy "so that divestiture is not necessary." Although divestiture is certainly a harsh remedy, its use is necessary in certain instances to give any meaningful effect to a court's injunction. Otherwise it might be of little import if a company was enjoined from acquiring additional stock of X company when, in fact, it already had sufficient stock to control X company's business plans and policies. The practical effect of that injunction would be meaningless; it would be no remedy at all for the private plaintiff.

Moreover, the idea of divestiture as a proper tool to remedy a Section 7 violation is inherent in the nature of the evil proscribed by that statute. If the acquisition of a particular stock is the violation of Section 7, the divestiture of that same stock necessarily should be the appropriate remedy. In spite of the logic of the position, the judicial formulation of the rule has been one of confusion and difficulty. For example, in *American Commercial Barge Line* v. *Eastern Gas and Fuel Associates,* a federal district court, with no discussion or citation of authority, concluded that an "action cannot properly be brought by a private litigant under Section 16 of the Clayton Act for divestiture of assets allegedly acquired in violation of the antitrust laws." The straightforward and unsupported erroneous conclusion of the ruling has not been followed elsewhere. Other courts, although not granting divestiture, have suggested that it would be a proper remedy in an appropriate case. For example, in the *Bostitch* case, a federal district court judge concluded that divestiture was within the meaning of Section 16 of the Clayton Act. In *Burkhead* v. *Phillips Petroleum Company,* the court, although acknowledging that the issue was not settled fully, stated that it concurred in the opinion expressed in the *Bostitch* case that divestiture was a proper remedy under Section 16:

> We are inclined to agree with this conclusion that divestiture *may* be an appropriate form of relief under Clayton Act Section 16 and that we should not rule out the possibility of such relief at this point. While the divestiture would appear to be appropriate only in a limited number of cases where no other form of preventative would suffice, one such case where divestiture might be the only adequate and complete remedy would be where, as here, plaintiff alleges a monopoly and restraint of trade which is injuring the plaintiff.

Although courts have indicated, for example, in the *Bostitch* and *Burkhead* decisions, that divestiture is a proper remedy under Section 16, they also are very reluctant to order it in a particular case. For example, in *Schrader* v. *National Screen Service Corp.,* the court pointed out that policy considerations are against granting divestiture when it would effect the complete destruction of a nationwide business. Other decisions have implied that divestiture is an appropriate remedy, have expressly so stated in *dicta,* or have outright held that divestiture was the only effective remedy.

Although opponents of divestiture may argue that the remedy is too severe and that it may destroy a corporation's business, their argument is weakened significantly, if not negated, by the inherent attributes of an equitable remedy. Foremost of these factors is the judge's discretion in deciding whether or not to grant divestiture. The existence of a Section 7 violation does not, *ipso facto,* require divestiture; the Supreme Court rejected that argument in the *Du Pont* case. Instead, the decision whether or not to grant divestiture rests with the judge. This alone will avoid wholesale divestiture orders. Moreover, even if divestiture is granted, it is subject to appellate review to determine whether such discretion was abused.

The defendant in a private antitrust suit also has a definite interest in whether divestiture should be ordered. If it appears that divestiture will be an appropriate remedy, the defendant can take steps to minimize its impact. For example, he might be able to negotiate a settlement which would accomplish the same objective without his immediate abandonment of the stock. For example, an injunction might be entered prohibiting the defendant from voting the stock, the stock might be converted to nonvoting stock, or the stock might be transferred to a trustee. Partial divestiture or gradual divestiture are other alternatives which might be agreed to in a particular case.

The use of divestiture as a means of enforcing Section 7 has not yet been developed fully. Additional judicial development is required to construct guidelines for its applicability as an appropriate remedy. Divestiture is an equitable remedy which can be an extremely effective antitrust enforcement weapon; its only limiting factor is that it makes no recompense to the plaintiff for his damages suffered or for his litigation expenses.

LEGAL REMEDIES

The counterpart to the equitable remedies of injunction and divestiture is, of course, the legal remedy of money damages. In the area of antitrust law, this is particularly attractive to the private litigant because Section 4 of the Clayton Act authorizes treble damages, that is, a recovery of three times the amount of litigant's actual injury. Everyone is aware of treble-damage actions based upon such notorious Sherman Act violations as price fixing and market division. It is also well settled that treble-damage recoveries can be predicated upon violations of Section 2 (price discrimination) and Section 3 (tie-in arrangements) of the Clayton Act. Does a violation of Section 7 of the Clayton Act also support a Section 4 treble-damage action? Logically, there should be no escape from an affirmative conclusion. Section 4 authorizes recovery of treble damages for "anything forbidden in the antitrust laws." Section 1 of the Clayton Act makes clear that Section 7 is one of the antitrust laws. Reading those two provisions together—as indeed, it appears they must be read—it seems unmistakably clear that a violation of Section 7 of the Clayton Act would support a treble-damage recovery.

Despite the logical ease in reaching this conclusion, the judicial route has been long and replete with obstacles. In 1957, immediately after the Supreme Court's decision in *United States* v. *E. I. du Pont de Nemours & Co.,* minority stockholders of General Motors brought a treble-damage derivative suit, *Gottesman* v. *General Motors,* alleging that Du Pont violated Section 7 of the Clayton Act and that it breached its common-law fiduciary duty by selling its products to General Motors at excessive prices. Despite the fact that this was the first case that litigated the issue of whether treble damages could be recovered for a violation of Section 7 of the Clayton Act, the district court gave short shrift to the issue: "The test is whether 'there is a reasonable probability that the acquisition is likely to result in the condemned restraints.' Plaintiffs cannot be damaged by a *potential* restraint of trade or monopolization. There can be no claim for money damages for a violation of section 7." Because this was a pretrial ruling, appellate review was not automatic and, in this instance, did not occur for over five years. The pretrial ruling in *Gottesman* was, however, followed in two subsequent decisions. In *Bailey's Bakery,* a district court also refused to litigate a complaint asking for money damages resulting from violation of Section. 7. "Since Clayton §7 is concerned with the future monopolistic and restraining tendencies of corporate acquisition, that is probable (and hence not certain) future restraints on commerce, any damages claimed for prospective restraint of trade would be purely speculative." In *Highland Supply*

Corporation v. *Reynolds Metals Company,* the District Court for the Eastern District of Missouri, confronted with the *Gottesman* and the *Bailey's Bakery* decisions and with an indication by the Eighth Circuit in a related proceeding to the effect that there was no private right of action, begrudgingly concluded that the cause of action for money damages based on Section 7 had to be dismissed.

The apparent trend toward complete denial of any consideration of treble-damage actions for Section 7 violations was partially aborted in *Julius M. Ames Co.* v. *Bostitch, Inc.* Factually distinguishing the three earlier cases, the district judge in *Bostitch* concluded that the nature of the injury in the case *sub judice* permitted a monetary recovery. The facts of this case were as follows: Pursuant to a pre-existing agreement, the plaintiff was a distributor of metal fasteners from Calnail who, in turn, was the exclusive agent for Calwire, the manufacturer. The defendant, Bostitch, was the principal competitor in this metal fastener product market. In 1961 Bostitch entered into an agreement by which Calwire would be merged into Calnail and Bostitch then would acquire all the stock of Calnail. Another integral part of the acquisition agreement was that all "pre-existing arrangements" for the distribution of Calwire products were to be eliminated. Thus, the effect of the acquisition was to cancel the plaintiff's distributorship agreement with Calnail. It was this important fact which distinguished the earlier cases from *Bostitch.* In the former, at the moment of acquisition, there was, optimistically, only a *probability* that the plaintiffs actually would be harmed. In the latter case, at the very moment of the acquisition, the plaintiff could point to a specific injury, i.e., the loss of his distributorship agreement. Moreover, the plaintiff's loss of the distributorship agreement was caused by an acquisition that had been conceded, for the purposes of that proceeding, to be violative of Clayton Section 7. There was no escape from the logical conclusion that the plaintiffs were entitled to seek money damages and the court accordingly held that the complaint did state a claim upon which relief could be granted. Two years later, the Fifth Circuit, in *Dailey* v. *Quality School Plan, Inc.,* agreed and held that a treble-damage action could be predicated upon a Section 7 violation. In spite of the number of courts which had rejected the argument that money damages could be based upon an illegal acquisition, the courts in the *Bostitch* and *Quality School Plan* decisions concluded that, as a matter of law, a plaintiff was entitled at least to bring a treble-damage action for violations of Clayton Section 7. Naturally, these diverse cases caused the law in the area to become very unsettled. The hodgepodge of decisions left most of the legal world in confusion, if not in outright disbelief. At a minimum, it resulted in forum shopping by plaintiffs attempting to find a district or circuit which was amenable to their position. At a maximum, the confusion, the ambiguity, and the judicial inconsistencies spawned a genuine need to clarify and resolve this split in the law.

This need was satisfied when the Second Circuit finally directly considered the original *Gottesman* pretrial ruling in 1969—six years after the district judge, in a pretrial proceeding, had ruled that Section 7 of the Clayton Act did not permit a cause of action for money damages. After extensive discovery and pretrial proceedings, the parties finally had come to trial in 1966, limited only to the causes of action relating to Du Pont's sale of automotive finishes and fabrics to General Motors for use in its passenger cars. Even on these issues the trial was limited solely on the question of liability of Du Pont and injury to General Motors. The issue of the amount of damages, if any, was not to be litigated at this stage. After hearing all the evidence, the district court judge dismissed those causes of action and found that Du Pont had not used its stock to control General Motors' purchases and that Du Pont had not abused any fiduciary duty owed to General Motors. Because these causes of action were separate claims and there was no just reason for delay, the findings of the district court were ripe for appellate review. The Second Circuit gave little treatment to the issues resolved at the trial; instead, it reviewed and then reversed the district court's 1963 pretrial ruling in which it had held that Section 7 of the Clayton Act could not support a private cause of action for money damages. After reviewing the cases which had denied the cause of action, those which had upheld it, and the legal commentary which had supported it, the Second Circuit concluded that it was in agreement with those authorities who had concluded that Section 7 *did* furnish a basis for money damages in a private action. Even though Section 7 speaks of reasonable *probabilities* of restraint of trade or monopolization, if, in fact, actual restraint occurs as a proximate result of the illegal merger or acquisition, then, the court ruled, compensable injury has been incurred. The court further stated that even though Section 7 connotes violations based on threatened harm, it does not preclude money damage recoveries if actual harm can be proved:

> But if the threat ripens into reality we do not see why there can never be a private cause of action for damages. If Section 7 is designed to prevent acquisitions that "may" or "tend to" cause specified harm, such an acquisition may either itself directly bring about the harm, or make possible acts that do. We do not say that a section 7 violation must or even probably will, have that result; but that it may and that plaintiffs should have a chance to prove injury "by reason of" the violation are persuasive propositions.

The Second Circuit decision in *Gottesman* was quickly followed by the District Court of Hawaii in *Kirihara* v. *Bendix Corporation*. Reversing the position that it had taken in *Bailey's Bakery*, the same district court concluded that it had thrown "too wide a loop" when it stated in *Bailey's Bakery* that no private action accrued from a violation of Section 7. Admitting that at the time of the *Bailey's Bakery* decision it was but a "novitiate in the antitrust sect of the judicial priesthood," the court concluded that a treble-damage action could be premised on a Clayton Section 7 violation and that a contrary holding would negate the clear inference that Congress intended Clayton Section 4 (treble-damage action) to apply to all the antitrust laws, including Section 7.

The authoritative statement from the Second Circuit in *Gottesman,* coupled with the *Kirihara* decision in which a district court completely reversed its position on the issue, seems clearly to indicate that the issue of whether a private cause of action for money damages can be predicated upon a violation of Clayton Section 7 is finally and fully resolved in favor of permitting the suit.

VIOLATION, FACT, AND AMOUNT OF DAMAGES

The courts have been confused sometimes by the distinction between the *right* of the litigant to sue, and his *burden of proof* to win. In other words, he must establish that a certain amount of damages have befallen him and that this injury was caused directly or proximately by the illegal acquisition or merger. This perhaps was a major cause of the *Gottesman*-type of litigation. Once the plaintiff has been accorded his right to bring a treble-damage action based on an alleged violation of Section 7, he still has some very important hurdles to jump before he can consider his quest for treble damages a complete success. The *Gottesman* and *Kirihara* decisions, and their progeny, only give the right to sue. *He still must sustain his burden of proof to win his case.* Implicit in the preceding statement is the requirement that the plaintiff must prove by a preponderance of the evidence (1) a violation of Section 7; (2) the fact of damage to his person or property (which includes injury and causation); and (3) a reasonably certain amount of damages flowing from that injury.

Violation

First and foremost for the plaintiff to prove is that the defendant violated one of the antitrust laws—in this instance, Section 7 of the Clayton Act, which proscribes mergers and acquisitions the effect of which "may be substantially to lessen competition, or tend to create a monopoly." Unlike the Sherman Act, which proscribes actual restraints, Section 7 outlaws potential restraints based upon factors which are admittedly probabilities. This of course is an advantage to the plaintiff in establishing a violation of the antitrust laws because he can rely on a more lenient standard than provided for in the Sherman Act. Moreover, if recent decisions in cases brought by the government are indicative of the judicial requirement for upholding a violation of Section 7, the private plaintiff can be reasonably optimistic about his ability to prove a violation.

In addition, private parties frequently can use a prior judgment in a government suit as prima facie evidence of an antitrust violation. This is specifically permitted under Section 5(a) of the Clayton Act. The only limitation upon its use is that, by express provision, Section 5(a) does not apply to consent judgments which, in turn, have been interpreted judicially to include *nolo contendere* pleas. However, if a private plaintiff is able to use a prior government judgment as prima facie evidence of a violation, his suit is invaluably enhanced. Moreover, even if the government action resulted in a consent judgment and, consequently, was inadmissible, the government's earlier case might disclose other sources of evidence from which further investigation and discovery might produce additional admissible evidence. Finally, the four-year statute of limitations for bringing private actions is not in effect while the government suit is pending.

One question that has not been resolved completely in this area is whether a violation for one period of time can be proven by a government judgment which establishes a violation for a different period. This issue arose in the *Gottesman–General Motors* litigation. The judgment in the government suit was made as of June 1949, the time at which the government suit was brought. The plaintiffs, minority stockholders of General Motors, were seeking damages for injury incurred by General Motors after May 4, 1950. Because the two cases covered different time frames, the trial judge ruled that the government judgment could not be used against the defendants. The Second Circuit disagreed. Acknowledging that some decisions took a strict view and did not permit the admission of a government judgment unless it covered all or a part of the same period alleged in the private action, the court rejected this rigid rule in favor of a more flexible one which would determine the admissibility of a government judgment (covering a different time period) after evaluating the relevancy and materiality of that judgment to the pending litigation. In the *Gottesman* litigation, although the government judgment found a violation as of June 1949, no relief was decreed until 1961. Hence, it was reasonable to conclude that because there was a probability of lessening of competition in 1949, that probability continued throughout the 1950's; therefore, the government judgment was relevant and material, and entitled to substantial evidentiary weight in the trial court's determination of whether there was a violation of Section 7 after May 4, 1950. If this case is followed by other circuits and district courts, the result will be a somewhat less restrictive use of a government judgment and another factor which will encourage private enforcement of the antitrust laws. This flexible standard also will be more reasonable in that the admissibility of a particular judgment is to be determined by relevance and materiality. This should go far in avoiding needless injustices to private plaintiffs.

The private plaintiff must prove a violation of Section 7. Whether or not he can use a prior government judgment, the proof of a Section 7 violation is a *sine qua non* to a successful prosecution of a private treble-damage suit. The probability standard of the Clayton Act—compared to the actual restraint standard of the Sherman Act—should alleviate the plaintiff's burden substantially. Indeed, it should make the proof of a violation the easiest of the three hurdles to a money damages recovery.

Fact of Damage

The second hurdle in the private treble-damage action based upon a violation of Clayton Section 7 is that the plaintiff must show that he was *in fact* damaged by the illegal acquisition. This point distinguishes the private plaintiff from the government, which only has to establish a violation in order to obtain relief. In a treble-damage action the private litigant must establish that he was injured and that this injury was caused directly by the illegal acquisition. This is perhaps the most difficult aspect of a treble-damage action. In addition, his proof is probably more difficult than his proof in an action based on, for example, price fixing or price discrimination. In the latter type of situation, the plaintiff can establish that his competitors paid price $\$x$ and he was forced to pay price $\$x + 1$. In an action based on Section 7, the plaintiff has to establish that the illegal acquisition directly injured his business. The difficulty is increased because numerous variables and economic factors must be evaluated even though they either did not matrialize or were merely a small part of the overall national economic pattern. The quantum and quality of these numerous economic and legal variables sometimes makes the determination of legal injury appear to be little more than informed speculation.

Failure to prove *injury* was the demise of the plaintiffs' case in the *Gottesman* litigation. In initially permitting the plaintiff to bring the treble-damage action, the Second Circuit stated that the plaintiffs, in addition to proving a violation, must "prove that they have been injured by the violation." Because it was a stockholders' derivative suit, the plaintiffs were required to prove injury to General Motors. Although they had alleged that Du Pont had used its ownership of G.M. stock to cause G.M. to purchase its automobile finishes and fabrics from them, they failed to prove that G.M. could have purchased the materials from someone other than Du Pont at lower prices with equal service and quality. In addition, the small percentage of G.M.'s fabric requirements that was allocated to Du Pont also significantly deflated the plaintiff's allegations. The trial judge concluded that G.M.'s decision to purchase Du Pont's products was one of "considered business judgments" and not legally susceptible to allegations that the purchases were due to Du Pont's ownership of 23 per cent of G.M.'s stock.

The result in the *Gottesman* litigation is some indication of the difficulty a plaintiff encounters in proving that an acquisition directly caused economic injury to his person or property. In some cases, however, the injury element might not be at all speculative. For example, in the *Bostitch* case the plaintiff, a distributor of Calnail's products, had his distributorship agreement terminated upon Calnail's being acquired by Bostitch, Inc., which, in turn, already had its own marketing distribution structure. A specific provision of the acquisition agreement was that all distributorship agreements were to be canceled; thus, the plaintiff had no difficulty establishing a specific injury directly caused by the acquisition. That having been proved, the plaintiff had sustained his burden as to the fact of damage.

Consider another example, however. Suppose A Corporation acquires B Corporation, which is a competitor of C and D Corporations. Assuming that in the year following the acquisition, the sales of C and D are down, is it reasonably possible to conclude that the decrease in sales was an *injury* caused by A's acquisition of B (assuming the acquisition was a violation of Section 7)? Probably not! As can be readily seen, the spectrum of difficulty in proving "injury" and "causation" in a private action is vast indeed. The lack of absolute standards in this area of antitrust litigation compounds the difficulty. It is no wonder that proving the *fact of damage* is one area upon which the private plaintiff must tread most carefully in order to keep his suit successfully afloat.

Amount of Damages

In addition to proving that the defendant's merger or acquisition violated Section 7 and that that violation directly injured his person or property, the plaintiff must prove a reasonably certain amount of damages flowing from that injury. This is one of the most difficult problems for the private plaintiff; it frequently requires the consultation and expert testimony of economists and certified public accountants. Because in most instances the plaintiff is seeking recovery for lost profits or for decreased business, his efforts reasonably to ascertain and estimate his damages may border on being speculative and conjectural. This has never been permitted because guesses and speculations of witnesses "form no better basis of recovery than the speculations of the jury themselves." In spite of the difficulties of demonstrating the amount of damages, courts have permitted the awarding of damages if the plaintiff has established a factual basis from which they can be reasonably determined. In other words, although guessing is not permitted, courts do not require a mathematical certainty in proving the amount of damages.

A guideline for the resolution between the two extremes of mathematical certainty and sheer speculation was issued by the Supreme Court in 1946 in *Bigelow* v. *RKO Radio Pictures, Inc.* In spite of the inherent difficulty in proving damages to a precise certainty in an antitrust case, the Court ruled that, as between the victim-plaintiff and the wrongdoer-defendant, the plaintiff should be awarded the damages if he can provide a factual basis from which the jury can reasonably estimate the amount:

> [T]he jury may not render a verdict based on speculation or guesswork. But the jury may make just and reasonable estimate of the damage based on

relevant data, and render its verdict accordingly. In such circumstances, "juries are allowed to act on probable and inferential as well as upon direct and positive proof. . . ." Any other rule would enable the wrongdoer to profit by his wrongdoing at the expense of his victim. It would be an inducement to make wrongdoing so effective and complete in every case as to preclude any recovery by rendering the measure of damages uncertain. Failure to apply it would mean that the more grievous the wrong done, the less likelihood there would be of a recovery.

The most elementary conceptions of justice and public policy require that the wrongdoer shall bear the risk of uncertainty which his own wrong has created. . . .

"The constant tendency of the courts is to find some way in which damages can be awarded where a wrong has been done. Difficulty of ascertainment is no longer confused with right of recovery" for a proven invasion of the plaintiff's rights.

Thus, if the defendant has caused the plaintiff harm, he has no reason to complain if the plaintiff encounters difficulty proving the amount of damages to a precise certainty. In spite of the *Bigelow* doctrine, the determination of what is speculation and conjecture and what are reasonable estimates based on furnished facts continues to be a perplexing problem for litigants and judges. This determination must of necessity be made on a case-by-case basis. The Ninth Circuit attempted to state a general rule as follows: "Under all the facts in the case, the damages must have a reasonable and fair relationship to the type, extent and period of the restraint and the kind of product, its price and saleability, the profit made on sales, and an estimate of the amount of profit lost by reason of the illegal activities by the defendant."

Frequently proof of the amount of damage is intertwined with proof of the fact of damage. In a treble-damage action, based on Clayton Section 7, the problem may be further compounded because of that statute's proscription of mergers and acquisitions the effect of which may be substantially to lessen competition or tend to create a monopoly. The original *Gottesman* decision alluded to the difficulty of proving the fact or amount of damages caused by *potential* restraint of trade or monopolization. *Bailey's Bakery* espoused the same difficulty, that is, Clayton Section 7 is concerned with future, anticipated but unimplemented acts of restraint. However, the better theory seems to be that uttered by the Second Circuit in *Gottesman:* "The basis of the pre-trial ruling [denying the money claim cause of action] was that a section 7 violation can cause no damage because it establishes only that harm was threatened, not that it occurred. *But if the threat ripens into reality we do not see why there can never be a private cause of action for damages.*" (Emphasis added.) It becomes readily apparent that if the plaintiff has to establish that the threatened harm (probable restraint or monopolization) has ripened into reality, he, in effect, has the burden of establishing an actual restraint or actual monopolization. Thus, the practical effect might be a Sherman suit (Sections 1, 2) disguised as a Clayton Section 7 suit. The Second Circuit queried whether the practical result would be concomitant proof of a Sherman Act claim, or if it would, perhaps, result in a holding that a "section 7 violation proximately caused damage which might not in itself constitute a cause of action under the Sherman Act."

Proving the amount of damages directly resulting from an illegal merger or acquisition is as difficult, if not more so, as proving the amount of damages due to other antitrust violations. For example, in a horizontal merger situation, X corporation, plaintiff, may argue that the merger forced him to lower his prices to try to remain competitive and that, in spite of this, his sales volume decreased. If the merger is illegal, he would seek damages to cover diminished profits on sales made and lost profits on sales which were lost due to the merger; in addition, the plaintiff may argue that his decreased amount of earnings caused an additional amount of injury in the form of a decreased return on his capital investment. In order to furnish a sufficient factual basis upon which the amount of damages can be reasonably inferred, the plaintiff must produce credible witnesses who can construct an economic-analysis model that is both simple enough for the jury to comprehend and sophisticated enough to convey the facts and figures necessary to compute the requested amount of damages.

The method by which the amount of damages is proved can be one of several alternatives. Most common is the "before and after," or "temporal," method, in which the plaintiff brings in facts and figures of his economic picture both before and after the illegal merger or acquisition. This theory can be a very effective way of portraying the amount of damages inuring to the plaintiff. This theory has substantial validity as long as the effect of the illegal merger or acquisition can be isolated and other economic variables—for example, general recession, inflation, strikes—can be extracted before the evidence is presented at trial. The courts have accepted this method as one which presents a sufficient factual basis and one which will withstand any argument that damages were based on speculation and conjecture.

Another method of proving the amount of damages is by the "cross-sectional," "yardstick theory," by which evidence is presented as to the economic picture of the plaintiff and then is compared to evidence which depicts the economic picture of a competitor. The corporation used as the yardstick must be a comparable business, which means that, for a private action predicated on a violation of Clayton Section 7, it must be in the same product market and same geographic market. In addition, the extraneous variables must be extracted from the testimony so that there is a minimal amount of variance resulting from unrelated and uncontrollable collateral factors and the verdict will be an amount reflective of the damages resulting solely from the illegal merger or acquisition. If constructed correctly this presentation can be very effective and sufficiently factual to permit a reasonable computation of damages.

A third method suggested for providing a factual basis from which damages can be reasonably estimated is the use of expert witnesses. A highly qualified economist or management consultant will present his expert opinion as to what would have happened had the illegal merger or acquisition not occurred. His answers to these hypothetical questions will enable the jury to compute reasonably the amount of damages. Expert testimony alone is not sufficient, however. The plaintiff must present actual facts relating to his business so that the expert's opinion can be applied to the particular facts of the plaintiff's business. This factual basis must be introduced to avoid or negate arguments that the verdict was a result of speculation based only on hypothetical situations. If the plaintiff has actual evidence of the injury to his business, the expert testimony merely fills in the gaps that are unavailable because the illegal merger made them unavailable. The defendant cannot complain because his antitrust violation created the risk of uncertainty.

Measuring the amount of damages caused by a merger or acquisition which violated Clayton Section 7 is very important indeed. It is one of the most difficult obstacles for the private litigant to hurdle. Although the *Bigelow* decision relaxed the standard of proof in favor of the plaintiff, the nature of the problem—proving what would have happened if the merger had not taken place—always subjects the verdict to attacks of speculation and conjecture. But if the plaintiff has utilized an accepted procedure of measuring his damages, he will be certain that he has furnished a factual basis from which the amount of damages can be reasonably inferred and computed. The quantum of damages will always depend on the operating and financial data of the plaintiff's business. Proper presentation of these facts will insure the private plaintiff that his verdict has a sufficient factual basis to be upheld on appeal.

PROPER PLAINTIFFS

In a private action seeking redress for an illegal merger or acquisition, as in any private antitrust action, the plaintiff must have standing to bring the action, that is, he must be a proper plaintiff. In general, antitrust law takes a more restrictive view than tort law in defining those plaintiffs who have standing to bring actions for recovery for their injuries. The plaintiff must, of course, have suffered injury. An injury to the public interest is insufficient; it must be an injury to his business. The difficulty is in determining how directly the plaintiff must be injured before he can properly bring an action. Compounding, or perhaps causing, the problem is that any recovery is automatically trebled. Thus, the potential liability of a defendant would become astronomical if too wide a scope of plaintiffs were permitted. Judge Wyzanski alluded to this in an early case: "In effect, businessmen would be subject to liabilities of indefinable scope for conduct already subject to drastic private remedies. Courts aware of these considerations have been reluctant to allow those who were not in direct competition with the defendant to have a private action. . . ." The problem continually arises and should demand consideration in every case. Whether an injury is direct and proximate or whether it is remote and incidental is a question which by its very nature is susceptible of no definitive rule. Although no general rule has yet been formulated, some rather consistent guidelines have evolved which delineate certain categories of persons who can and cannot institute private antitrust actions.

If one corporation makes an acquisition or merger which results in a substantial lessening of competition and tendency toward a monopoly, any corporation that has suffered a direct injury from that illegal merger or acquisition has standing to sue the violator. But the right to sue belongs only to the corporation. The corporation's right can be exercised by the corporation itself, or it can be exercised by a shareholder's derivative suit. Although there had been a very early holding that stockholders could not bring a derivative action for treble damages because that remedy was essentially an equitable remedy, that obstacle presumably has been eliminated with the abolition of the distinction between law and equity.

Although standing to sue inures to the corporation, either directly or derivatively, it does not extend to private shareholders who seek recovery for damages incurred by them, not necessarily the corporation. Courts have uniformly rejected private stockholders' contentions that they have the requisite standing. The rationale for the rejection is that any injury to the shareholders is too incidental and remote to support a cause of action. More importantly, stockholders' private suits are not permitted because of the very nature of their claim. In a stockholder's private suit the plaintiff is essentially seeking recompense for the injury to his stock caused by the diminution in value; he is not seeking any recovery for the corporation. But the target of the illegal merger or acquisition was the corporation, not the stockholders. As one expert commentator observed, the rule is predicated on sound policy reasons by requiring a single corporate action rather than multiple private stockholder actions.

For the same reasons, courts have consistently held that any injury to officers, directors, and employees are too peripheral to support a private, independent action for recovery for an injury suffered essentially by the corporation. Even if an officer or an employee has his employment relationship severed as a result of the illegal merger or acquisition, his injury is, as a matter of law, too remote to merit standing. Although most employment terminations resulting from antitrust violations are probably a result of conspiracies proscribed by Sherman Section 1, it is possible that in a Clayton Section 7 situation a lessening of competition would force residuary firms to pare their employment rosters in order to stay economically alive. But the former employee would have no cause of action because of the well-settled rule that individual injuries sustained by corporate employees by monopolistic practices are too remote and incidental.

Like shareholders and employees, creditors of an injured corporation are also incapable of suing the antitrust violator even if the infraction has rendered the injured corporation unable to pay its outstanding debts to the creditor. This rule has solidified to deny standing to any creditor wishing to enforce the antitrust laws. Included within this class are suppliers who are also denied standing; it has been well established by the courts that a supplier is too remote and too far removed from the target area to recover damages resulting from a violation of the antitrust laws directed against the supplier's customers.

In spite of the broad and enthusiastic encouragement given for private enforcement of the antitrust laws, the number of potential plaintiffs has been restricted because of the rules on standing. Although the injured corporation has standing, either on its own or by a derivative suit, to bring the action, "shareholders, creditors, directors, and officers of corporations injured by monopolistic practices of competitors cannot recover their individual losses" because they have no standing.

CONCLUSION

A significant evolution in the area of private litigation predicated on violations of Section 7 of the Clayton Act has occurred within recent years. Recent litigation, most notably the *Gottesman* and *Kirihara* cases, has solidified the private plaintiffs' right to seek treble damages based on illegal mergers or acquisitions. Attempts to procure equitable remedies—injunction or divestiture—have been few; however, the right to injunctive relief has been steadfastly upheld and the right to divestiture has been headed in an affirmative direction.

If the government has obtained a prior judgment of a Section 7 violation, the plaintiff's burden is eased significantly. But in view of the less restrictive standards necessary to prove a violation of the Clayton Act, vis-à-vis the standards for Sherman Act violations, the burden of proving the Section 7 violation is the least oppressive of the necessary elements. More burdensome—if not, in fact, the most difficult element—is proof of the *fact of injury*. Once the fact of injury is proved, proof of the amount of damages has been subject to a less onerous standard.

The issue of probabilities that is inherent in a private Section 7 action continues to plague the private litigants. Although courts have directed equitable relief pursuant to Section 16, they have not yet actually awarded treble damages in a particular case. Thus, the road for a private plaintiff seeking treble damages is, indeed, little traveled; it is replete with chuckholes and other obstacles; and it has yet to be successfully completed. But the prize of treble damages awaits the successful litigant and it can be reasonably assumed that that goal will soon be attained.

PART V

Special Industry Mergers

The antitrust laws apply in general to all mergers, the effect of which may be to lessen competition substantially. These laws are, in effect, ground rules to govern competition and monopoly and to prevent our free enterprise system from destroying itself.

In certain areas of business activity, however, special rules have developed. These rules have come about through legislative enactment and by rules and/or decisions of specialized administrative agencies established to promote and/or regulate the industry involved. Examples include Interstate Commerce Commission regulation of railroad and truck line mergers. In some instances such activities are exempted from the application of the antitrust laws. In others, they are not. In some instances, the specialized industry has primary jurisdiction—the initial (but not final) responsibility for balancing anticompetitive effects against the needs and convenience of the community. This complex area of overlapping governmental jurisdiction is the subject of this part of the book.

25 Mergers in the Regulated Industries

The merger policies, statutes, and cases discussed to this point in the book have been concerned almost exclusively with that part of our economy that is theoretically in open and free competition; indeed, the whole emphasis of merger law seems to be the protection of competitors and competition in the marketplace. However, in this chapter it will be necessary to readjust and re-examine the policies defined earlier, because by definition the regulated industries are not solely concerned with competition. Many other considerations come into play when a proposal to increase concentration is acted on. It is estimated that about one ninth of this country's gross national product is produced by those parts of our economy under pervasive governmental control, but this segment evokes more than its share of Congressional and judicial concern. Since the first major regulatory statute was passed by Congress in 1888, the complaints of abuse and cries for reform have continued and increased. An examination of the merger histories of these industries will give the reader a chance to judge whether the criticism is deserved or not.

THE ROLE OF COMPETITION

When a merger, acquisition, or amalgamation of some sort is proposed within a regulated industry, the effects of the combination on competition will be considered by the agency. The influence that resulting anticompetitive effects will have on the eventual outcome is anything but a constant. Not too long ago the Supreme Court, in a case involving the Federal Maritime Commission, declared that anticompetitive effects "alone will normally constitute substantial evidence that the [proposal] is 'contrary to the public interest' unless other evidence in the record fairly detracts from the weight of this factor." Because the public interest is most often the standard to be used by the regulatory body in deciding whether to approve a merger or not, this seems to be an extremely forceful statement regarding the emphasis to be put on the presence or absence of anticompetitive effects. It has been noted, however, that the reconciliation of the antitrust laws and the goals of the regulatory scheme are the most difficult in the merger area, because of a lack of real concern with competition. One author, with a little more critical outlook as to the effect of the judiciary's policies, summarized: "In industry after industry, regulatory rule-making and adjudication, operating within a broad discretion and reinforced by Congressional tolerance or support, have resulted in the elimination of both actual and potential competition." The true role that competition has played in the legality of mergers when tested under the public-interest criteria is probably somewhere in between.

The courts have been generally consistent in their opinion that competition is one of the factors that the agencies must consider when deciding whether or not to allow a merger or acquisition. Competition is not consistent with the idea of direct economic regulation. Although it has been facetiously suggested that no competition is needed where an industry is pervasively regulated, because one firm would be easier to control than many, most commentators agree that competition can provide benefits to an industry that no amount of regulation can equal. Too often it seems that the regulations issued have as their primary goal the protection of the existing regulated companies, and that is not justifiable. This should be no surprise to even the casual observer of regulated industries, because the threat of increased competition in their market always evokes predictions of disaster from the monopolist or oligopolist. It is conceded that broad regulatory powers do not have to result in overly oppressive regulations, so it is often suggested that the most beneficial results would be accomplished by encouraging the agencies to rely on competition heavily, with the goals sought to be achieved being specified at the outset. With this framework, it should then be up to the advocates of regulation to convince the agency that regulation is needed.

There are few who doubt that establishing viable competition and encouraging its growth in the regulated sphere would be more expensive in the short run. This does not necessarily mean that such a policy should not be followed. On the contrary, the beneficial effects of increased efficiency and innovation would more than compensate for this initial increased expenditure. Although it is true that resources may have to be allocated in a way that will reflect a benefit to society—a benefit not attainable if regulated competition is relied on—there is no real consensus on how this reallocation should be accomplished. Those who see the antitrust laws as reflecting a general policy, a policy that can be adopted to meet new challenges as they arise, argue that what adjustments that are necessary can be arrived at without direct interference with the economy. Other experts feel that there are some areas of our economy that must be controlled in the interests of securing our population from the unbridled power of natural monopolies, or protecting the existing competitors from ruinous competition. While the controversy over the merits of regulation rages on, even those who accept the government's role in the economy as desirable or inevitable, still have not agreed on how extensive the government's interference should be. As we shall see later, each major agency involved in decisions relating to mergers has answered the question of how far to rely on competition in a slightly different way.

The markets that the various agencies, boards, and commissions deal with are, in many respects, different from the ordinary markets protected from excessive concentration by Section 7 of the Clayton Act. For a variety of reasons these differences made it necessary, in the opinion of Congress, for some external forces to come into play to counteract the absence of competition or the excesses of competition. In the case of a natural monopoly, like the Bell telephone system, some controls had to be placed on the rates and services to protect the country from overpricing and substandard services. In the case of overly vigorous competition, as in the railroad system at the turn of the century, some protection had to be given to the competitors to assure them that irresponsible price wars would not bankrupt the companies and thereby harm the economy. Once the controls were put on, other secondary protections had to be provided to assure that the primary system would work—as in the necessity to prevent diversification to avoid the brunt of fixed rates. When the whole system had been set up with all its ramifications, the courts found it necessary to bend the provisions of the antitrust law to avoid doing harm to the goal of regulation. These adoptions in the regulated industry, whether statutory or judicial in origin, have made it fruitless to talk about mergers between competitors in a regulated industry in terms of a relevant market or substantial lessening of competition. New tests have had to be devised and changed when necessary to arrive at the goal set out in the regulating statutes. The standards arrived at by each agency will be discussed, but first it will be helpful to discuss one of the judicial adaptations made in the light of ever-broadening regulatory schemes, although there is often a good deal of controversy over whether it is really a justifiable policy.

PRIMARY JURISDICTION

The doctrine of primary jurisdiction was first announced by the Supreme Court in 1907 in a case challenging rates approved by the ICC as unreasonable. The Court summarized the components of the doctrine in 1956 in *United States* v. *Western Pacific Railway* when it said; "Primary jurisdiction applies where a claim is originally cognizable in the courts, and comes into play whenever enforcement of the claim requires the resolution of issues which, under a regulatory scheme, have been placed within the special competence of an administrative body; in such a case, the judicial process is suspended pending referral of such issues to the administrative body for its views." The reasons stated for this discretionary referral process have been the need for uniformity of action in the administrative process, the fact that the decision requires the expertise of a body of specialists thoroughly familiar with all of the ramifications, and the fact that the regulatory statute supersedes the antitrust laws so the agency must be consulted first. The underlying purpose for staying of judicial action has been recognized as an attempt to promote the proper relationship between the courts and the agencies involved.

The conflict between the courts and the administrative agencies came about in the first place because the Congress gave the agencies the power to consider the antitrust laws when they were required to decide whether some proposal was "in the public interest." Several of the agencies, after being given the power to enforce some of the antitrust laws, were also given the authority to exempt the approved transaction from any subsequent antitrust suit. This was deemed necessary because of the impossibility of defining precisely the boundaries of the antitrust laws' applicability, and the possibility of a Justice Department or Federal Trade Commission suit after the proposal had been carried out. There are conflicting views concerning the doctrine of primary jurisdiction, with one side advocating it as a convenient method of obtaining the opinions of both the agency responsible and ultimately the courts and the other side viewing it as little more than a judicial attempt "not to get involved" with difficult questions for which they share the responsibility. The latter view holds that the regulatory statutes and the antitrust laws are in essence complementary but that the antitrust laws rate priority in the case of a conflict.

Primary jurisdiction becomes an important consideration in the merger area when the agency in charge has the authority to approve a proposed merger and exempt it from the antitrust laws. In this situation the actual merger is truly cognizable in both the agency and the courts. The Interstate Commerce Commission and the Civil Aeronautics Board are examples of agencies that have had merger questions referred to them by the courts because of their statutory authority to grant exemptions. This deference is not accorded equally to all similar agencies. For example, in *California* v. *Federal Power Commission* the Supreme Court held that the FPC should have stayed its proceedings on the acquisition of Pacific Northwest Pipeline Corporation's assets by El Paso Natural Gas because an antitrust suit challenging the stock acquisition was pending in federal court. The Court refused to imply the power to grant immunity from the regulatory scheme taken as a whole because such "[i]mmunity from the antitrust laws is not lightly implied." The Court summarized the primary jurisdiction considerations when it stated, "Where the primary jurisdiction is in the agency, courts withhold action until the agency has acted. . . . The converse should also be true, lest the antitrust policy whose enforcement Congress in this situation has entrusted to the courts is in practical effect taken over by the Federal Power Commission." The conclusion seems to be that if the regulatory body has no power to consider the anticompetitive effects when a merger or acquisition has been proposed, it would amount to nothing more than a waste of time for the courts to wait for the agency's decision. A judicial determination of illegality under Section 7 of the Clayton Act renders the prior proceeding moot. However, if the agency is instructed to consider the anticompetitive effects, and to allow the merger if they are outweighed by other public-interest factors, then the judicial determination of illegality could be subsequently reversed by commission approval, as was the case in several railroad mergers in the early 1920's.

STATUTORY PROVISIONS

The authority of each board or commission to deal with merger proposals within its sphere of influence depends on the statutory formulation of the Clayton Act and the regulatory statute. Section 7 of the Clayton Act, the main provision forbidding mergers, after detailing the test of illegality, states, "Nothing contained in this section shall apply to transactions duly consummated pursuant to authority given by the Civil Aeronautics Board, Federal Communications Commission, Federal Power Commission, Interstate Commerce Commission, . . . [or the] United States Maritime Commission. . . ." This is the section granting immunity to those transactions sanctioned by the agency involved when it has such authority. That all of the agencies listed did not have the power was made clear by the Supreme Court in 1962 when it noted that "by this provision in §7 of the Clayton Act . . . 'it is not intended that . . . any . . . agency' mentioned 'shall be granted any authority or powers it does not already possess.' " The agencies that have the authority to so immunize transactions against the antitrust laws will be mentioned shortly.

Section 11 of the Clayton Act gives the authority to enforce several of its sections, including Section 7, to the ICC where applicable to common carriers; the FCC where applicable to common carriers (telephone and telegraph); the CAB where applicable to air carriers; and the Federal Reserve Board where applicable to banks. This means that the agencies mentioned do not have to rely on the Department of Justice to file a complaint under the Clayton Act when some illegal activity is going on. The agency is empowered to determine whether or not the activity should be forbidden through its own hearing procedures.

The Interstate Commerce Commission is mentioned in both Sections 7 and 11, but its authority to immunize the approved merger or acquisition comes from the Transportation Act of 1920. As revised, it now reads, "The authority conferred by this section shall be exclusive and plenary . . . and any carriers . . . participating in a transaction approved or authorized under the provisions of this section shall be and they are relieved from the operation of the antitrust laws. . . ." The Court has made it clear that the anticompetitive effects of a merger are to be considered by the ICC when passing upon its merits under Section 5 of the Transportation Act, but it has become clear that the commission uses a different test when measuring anticompetitive effects before approving or disapproving a merger than is used when challenging a merger under Section 7 of the Clayton Act. The commission sees this as the natural by-product of its concern under Section 5 with more than just the anti-competitive effects of a merger. Before approving a consolidation of two interstate carriers, the commission is required to find that it "will be consistent with the public interest," and the commission may order such modification and impose such terms and conditions as will be found to be "just and reasonable."

Mergers between air carriers must be approved by the Civil Aeronautics Board, and if approved they are beyond the reach of the antitrust laws. Besides being mentioned in the last part of Section 7 and being authorized to enforce that provision by Section 11, the Federal Aviation Act provides that a merger or consolidation between "two or more air carriers, . . . any air carrier and any other common carrier or any person engaged in any phase of aeronautics" "shall be unlawful unless approved by order of the Board. . . ." Also forbidden in this section is the purchase, lease or acquisition of control of any air carrier without the board's approval. The test to be employed by the Board when it is judging whether or not a merger is illegal is the public interest. Unless the board finds it inconsistent with the public interest, it is to be approved, except that a merger giving the combined firm a monopoly cannot be permitted. The Supreme Court in *Pan American World Airways* v. *United States* ruled that the antitrust laws were displaced only to the extent necessary to effectuate the purposes of the Act, but that the "Clayton Act, insofar as it is applicable to air carriers, is enforceable by the Board." The regulatory schemes of the ICC and CAB as they affect mergers have been described as "pervasive," so even without the statutory immunization, some believe that their decisions should be left alone lest the purpose of the regulatory statute be frustrated. Whatever the rationale, these two agencies enjoy extensive discretion in the field of merger policy as it applies to the common carriers under their jurisdiction.

The Federal Communications Commission operates a dual system of regulation under its statutory directives. As was the case with the previous two regulatory bodies mentioned, the FCC is mentioned in Clayton Act Sections 7 and 11, although Section 11 refers to the FCC's power to enforce the antitrust laws only as they apply to common carriers within its jurisdiction; that is, to telephone and telegraph companies. Mergers between the telephone companies are governed by the section of the United States Code that provides for notice to the governors and state regulatory commissions of the states affected and any others deemed advisable. A hearing is held and if the merger "will be of advantage to the persons to whom service is to be rendered and in the public interest," the commission is to certify it. After such certification, "any Act or Acts of Congress making the proposed transaction unlawful shall not apply." The section governing telegraph company mergers or consolidations has many of the same procedures, with notification also directed to various government bodies. It is apparent, then, that the FCC has virtually the same powers in the field of telephone and telegraph consolidations as the ICC and CAB have in their fields. The immunity provisions are not granted to those mergers or acquisitions in the broadcast industry. Although the FCC must give its consent to the transfer, assignment or disposal of a broadcast license, and that consent is based on a "finding by the Commission that the public interest, convenience, and necessity will be served thereby," the antitrust laws remain in effect and the consolidation may be attacked by the Justice Department or FTC.

In the shipping industry there is a notable lack of the classical merger activity that has been the characteristic of the other regulated industries. This is not a result of a less volatile competitive situation within the industry itself, but rather a different way of approaching the problem of too much competition with a concomitantly different solution. Under Section 15 of the Shipping Act, the shipping lines are permitted to enter into agreements "fixing or regulating transportation rates or fares" when the agreements have been submitted to and approved by the Federal Maritime Commission. Once the participating shipping lines, or conferences as they are more commonly called, have had the conference rate agreements approved, they are exempt from antitrust enforcement or regulation. The Justice Department still retains the authority to prosecute those rate agreements that have not been approved by the FMC, or have had their approval withdrawn. In the House committee report (Merchant Marine and Fisheries) that was published two years previous to the enactment of the original Shipping Act, that the existence of the conferences obviated the need for extensive merger activity in the shipping industry was made clear when the report discussed the possibility of a failure to sanction existing conferences. To terminate agreements would necessarily bring about one of two results: the lines would either engage in rate wars which would mean the elimination of the weak and the survival of the strong, or, to avoid a costly struggle, they would consolidate through common ownership.

In view of the fact that the shipping conferences provide the same beneficial relief from the antitrust laws to the shipping lines involved that mergers provide in some of the other regulated areas, mention will be made later of the actual workings of the conferences and the role of the antitrust laws on the periphery. The question of whether or not the FMC has jurisdiction to approve an actual merger in the shipping industry under the authority of Section 15 is in a state of flux, but the two opposing cases will be reviewed to gain an appreciation of the statutory framework. The powers of the Justice Department in shipping mergers will depend on the outcome of a case docketed before the Supreme Court now.

The position occupied by the Antitrust Division of the Department of Justice is much more prominent in the remaining agencies who have the power to pass on the requests for consolidation but not to immunize them if approved. Although it is true that the division has been extremely active in rule-making procedures and merger hearings before the ICC, CAB, and FCC, if the agency chooses to disregard the advice offered, it is free to do so. This is not true in the remaining regulatory agencies. The Federal Power Commission has control of pipeline acquisitions under the Natural Gas Act and public utility mergers under the Federal Power Act, but because approval in neither means immunity, the Justice Department is free to challenge the merger. As to pipeline companies, if the commission finds a possible violation of the antitrust laws, the information is to be relayed to the attorney general for possible suit. "Other administrative agencies are authorized to enforce Section 7 of the Clayton Act when it comes to certain classes of companies or persons; but the Federal Power Commission is not included in the list."

The regulation of the electric utilities is accomplished by the complementary work of two agencies. The Securities and Exchange Commission is responsible for the approval of acquisitions by holding company systems in the utility area, whereas the Federal Power Commission is responsible for the regulation of interstate power transmission and interstate sales of electricity. The Public Utility Holding Company Act of 1935, the source of the SEC's power, provides in part:

> Unless the acquisition has been approved by the Commission under Section 10, it shall be unlawful—
>
> (1) for any registered holding company or any subsidiary company thereof . . . to acquire, directly or indirectly, any securities or utility assets or any other interest in any business. . . .

The authority of the FPC is found in the Federal Power Act, Part II, where it states that:

> No public utility shall sell, lease, or otherwise dispose of the whole of its facilities subject to the jurisdiction of the Commission, . . . or by any means whatsoever, directly or indirectly, merge or consolidate such facilities or any part thereof with those of any other person, or purchase, acquire, or take any security of any other public utility, without first having secured an order of the Commission authorizing it to do so. . . .

Cases dealing with the authority of both agencies in this area will be focused on later in this chapter. The last important regulated field with significant merger activity—the area of banking—will be covered in depth in the following chapter.

Keeping in mind the statutory sections involved, we will now analyze mergers in each of the regulated industries in order to understand better the statutory schemes and their effectiveness.

MERGERS AND THE AGENCIES

Interstate Commerce Commission

Although some authorities view the Interstate Commerce Commission's regulation of motor carriers as almost inseparable from the regulation of railroads, the merger activity in each area will be discussed separately. The Interstate Commerce Act as passed in 1888 had no provisions regulating mergers by railroads. When the Sherman Act was enacted in 1890, it was construed to cover railroad price fixing and consolidations, with the result being that such activity was prosecuted vigorously. The passage of the Clayton Act in 1914 did not provide any relief for the railroads; instead, Section 7 provided a more stringent test for mergers and Section 11 gave the ICC the authority to enforce it concurrently with the courts. It was not until the Transportation Act of 1920 that the ICC was given the authority to pass on the merits of a proposed railroad merger and grant it immunity from the antitrust laws if it was in the public interest.

The 1920 Act suggested for the first time that the commission develop a long-range plan for consolidation in the railroad industry, suggesting a Congressional acceptance of the inevitability of mergers in this gigantic industry. Mergers were more apt to be approved by the ICC if they could be harmonized with the overall plan, although it was not adopted until nearly ten years after the Act. Another important factor was the attempt to include weak rail lines into the merger; indeed, the commission conditioned the consummation of several mergers on the inclusion of short-line railroads. The Emergency Railroad Transportation Act of 1933 made several changes in the statutory formula, including the elimination of the different standards applicable to consolidations and acquisitions of control. In 1935 motor carriers were brought within the ICC's jurisdiction, and Section 5 of the ICC Act was made applicable to mergers of all common carriers under the ICC by the Transportation Act of 1940. This latter Act also dropped the requirement of an overall plan in the rail merger area.

The railroads were the targets of many antitrust suits before the passage of the first Transportation Act. In 1904 the Supreme Court ruled that a merger between two competing railroads (their lines paralleled each other across the Pacific Northwest) was violative of the Sherman Act. The reversal of the situation is highlighted by the fact that the ICC subsequently gave conditional approval to those same two rail lines to effectuate a merger in *Great Northern Pacific Railway Co. Acquisition*. The decision by the commission that the merger should be allowed was based on the economies of scale that would result; the fact that other competition was available; the fact that in a substantial percentage of the total areas served, the two lines were not actually competitive; and the further consideration that the proposal fit in with the overall plan recently proposed. The merger never came about at that time, however, because one of the conditions set down by the ICC—that the control of the Burlington line be divested—was unacceptable. This case was a forecast of the commission's willingness to forego the old antitrust tests in judging the merits of a merger proposal. Two years later, in *New York Central Securities Co.* v. *United States,* the Supreme Court ruled that the commission's authority to allow a merger was not an unconstitutional delegation of power. The power of Congress to improve competition by imposing regulations against mergers also allowed it to give the power of relaxation of the regulations to the ICC. The Court held that the term *public interest* was "not a concept without ascertainable criteria, but has a direct relation to adequacy of transportation service, to its essential conditions of economy and efficiency, and to appropriate provision and best use of transportation facilities. . . ."

Despite these two cases there was a dearth of major railroad consolidations between 1920 and 1940. The Transportation Act of 1940 brought an enunciation of the factors to be considered by the commission when a merger proposal was brought before it. The considerations were listed under Section 5 as:

> (1) The effect of the proposed transaction upon adequate transportation service to the public;
> (2) The effect upon the public interest of the inclusion or failure to include, other railroads in the territory involved in the proposed transaction;
> (3) The total fixed charges resulting from the proposed transaction; and
> (4) The interest of the carrier employees affected.

This listing by Congress of the important considerations in the railroad merger area was significant. Although the commission did not approve every proposal that came before it, the investigation into the effect on the competitors—the relevant market inquiry, if you will—made the approval or disapproval more structured and easier to justify on other than an arbitrary-decision basis. In 1948 the ICC was able to deny the application to consolidate by two of the strongest lines in one section of the country because competing lines would be adversely affected by the resulting single line capability. The Supreme Court, in *Minneapolis & St. Louis Railway* v. *United States,* allowed the acquisition of joint control of another railroad as long as the following conditions were met: (1) the railroad, although jointly owned, would be kept separate; (2) the properties of the acquired line would be improved and maintained; (3) the line would be allowed to solicit traffic on its own; and (4) the tract would be available to all without discrimination. To the charge that the acquisition was illegal under Section 7 of the Clayton Act and that the commission had abused its discretion, the Court answered that the "diversion would not jeopardize the maintenance of adequate transportation service by the objecting intervening carriers."

The merger movement of the railroads that blossomed in the 1960's can be argued to be the result of any one, or combination, of a number of reasons. However these factors interacted, many observers believe that the beginning of the movement was in 1959, when the commission allowed the merger in the *Norfolk & Western Railway* case. In that decision the ICC allowed the acquisition of the Virginian Railway. A year later the commission allowed the Erie Railroad to merge with the Delaware, Lackawanna & Western Railroad. After the Chesapeake & Ohio was allowed to acquire the Baltimore & Ohio, the Erie Lackawanna, the result of the previously mentioned merger, petitioned to be included in the acquisition of the New York, Chicago & St. Louis Railway by the Norfolk & Western Railway. The petition was subsequently withdrawn and the merger allowed with one of the conditions being the later possibility of a petition for inclusion by Erie.

One of the most complicated merger proposals to be handled by the commission was the merger of the Pennsylvania Railroad and the New York Central. The case went to the Supreme Court several times and was finally approved in 1968. As finally allowed, the merger included the New Haven Railroad along with the New York Central. Three smaller railroads that also requested inclusion were joined with the Norfolk & Western Railway instead. This was the first use of a subsection in the Act that allowed the forced inclusion of weaker railroads in this manner.

The commission, and eventually the Supreme Court, agreed that a merger would be in the public interest in the *Seaboard Air Line Railroad* case. The merger between the two competing lines on the eastern coast was allowed even though both lines were in good financial shape. The ICC found that the reduction in competition (the combined line would have 54 per cent of the mileage in six states and 81 per cent in Florida) was outweighed by more effective competition resulting from economies of scale and improved service. In the decision the commission also noted that it did not have to enforce Section 7 of the Clayton Act, because Section 5 of the Transportation Act made it redundant. The dissent in the opinion argued for a relevant market determination under Section 7 in order to determine anticompetitive effects. On appeal, the court reversed on the grounds advanced by the dissenting commissioner, but the Supreme Court held that this test was not the proper one. The Court noted that the anticompetitive effects could be outweighed by the improvements in service, and if this were the case, then the commission approval could be "consistent with the public interest."

The Supreme Court, in a direct appeal from a three-judge district court decision in 1969, was called on to review one of the larger railroad mergers of the last few years, and in *United States* v. *Interstate Commerce Commission,* the Court affirmed the commission's allowance of the merger. Briefly, the merger involved the consolidation of the Great Northern Railway and the Northern Pacific Railway and their subsidiary railroads —the same two companies whose consolidation was declared illegal in the *Northern Securities* case and later allowed by the commission, but never consummated because of unacceptable conditions attached. The negotiations between the two railroads began in 1955, with the proposal for merger filed with the ICC in 1961. Hearings were held for several years with many parties submitting evidence pro and con; the hearing examiner reported the merger with favorable recommendations in 1964, but the commission rejected the recommendation by a vote of 6 to 5. Reconsideration was granted when the two companies notified the commission that protective conditions would be acceptable and that employee attrition agreements had been reached. The commission reopened the hearings and the amount of savings resulting from the merger was questioned again. Based on the finding of more substantial savings and the fact that protective agreements had been entered into, the commission, in a second report, approved the merger.

After the approval was received, the Department of Justice filed suit, and several parties intervened. The district court panel upheld the commission decision, but issued a further stay pending appeal. The Supreme Court, in affirming the district court, noted that the review was to "determine whether the Commission has proceeded in accordance with law and whether its findings and conclusion accord with the statutory standards and are supported by substantial evidence," quoting the *Penn-Central* merger case. The Court reiterated the factors to be given weight under Section 5, and then answered the Justice Department complaint that they had not been properly applied by stating, "Thus, a rail merger that furthers the development of a more efficient transportation unit and one that results in the joining of a 'sick' with a strong carrier serve equally to promote the long-range objectives of Congress and, upon approval by the Commission, both are immunized from the operation of the antitrust laws." When the Court concluded that the application of the standards had been correct, it went on to discuss the weight to be given to antitrust policy in the commission proceedings. This task required only extensive quoting from *McLean Trucking Co.* v. *United States,* with the result being the reiteration of the holding that "the Commission is not bound . . . to accede to the policies of the anti-trust laws. . . ." "Striking the balance is for the Commission and [the Court] cannot properly say that it did so improperly." The Court then traced the benefits of the merger and noted the scope of the protective conditions. The rest of the opinion was devoted to rejecting the grounds for reversal advanced by the various intervenor-petitioners, including the following allegations: (1) that the commission abused its discretion and failed to provide substantial evidence for approving the exchange ratios for stock agreed on in negotiations; (2) that the assessment of the merger's impact on the affected communities was incorrect and that the approval was ineffective because of the failure to explain why the benefits outweighed the adverse consequences of the merger; and (3) that the ICC had no authority to approve a merger because one of the railroads did not own the franchise and, even if it did, no merger would be allowed under the terms of the sale of the franchise without Congressional approval. All of these contentions were met by the Court and answered in order.

By using this case as a vehicle for extended discussion of the standards to be employed by the commission, the Supreme Court has reaffirmed its faith in the ICC's ability to wade through these complex problems and arrive at a result that is "consistent with the public interest." Because almost every major railroad has been in some type of merger litigation in the last ten years, this is a reliance on the commission's judgment that has affected or will affect every phase of the railroad industry. Under the authority of Section 5, the commission also regulates the trucking industry, so at this point it is appropriate to review some of the more important decisions in the truck merger area.

Although many authors have criticized the existence of the ICC's authority over motor carriers as serving only one purpose—the protection of the railroads from competition—the fact is that the regulatory scheme exists, has been allowed by the Supreme Court, and must be contended with if any type of consolidation is attempted in the interstate trucking field.

As was mentioned in the first part of this section, the motor carriers were brought under the wing of the ICC in the Transportation Act of 1940, and Section 5 of the Act was made applicable to all common carriers within the commission's amended jurisdiction. The premier case in the area was decided four years after that Act and *McLean Trucking* v. *United States* has been extensively cited ever since then. The merger in dispute there involved seven large carriers with combined coverage ranging from Massachusetts to Florida, making it the largest carrier of its kind in the country. The commission allowed the merger and the Supreme Court affirmed its holding. The opinion issued by the Court mentioned the contention by the Justice Department that the commission's authority over motor carrier mergers was not "exclusive and plenary," but rather that a merger could only be allowed "when the existing service is inadequate and consolidation is necessary to bring adequate service to the public. . . ." However, the Court noted that railroads and motor carriers were governed by identical provisions: "On its face the contention would seem to run in the teeth of the language and the purpose of Section 5(11)." The antitrust laws were not the only standards to be used by the commission, but the policy was to be considered as one factor. The resolution of the conflicting policy considerations was left to the commission. The findings of the ICC that the merger would result in improved service, increased efficiency, and substantial operating economies were recognized, along with its determination that railroads would provide sufficient competition for the merged line. The majority held that, keeping in mind the commission's judgment, experience, and expertise, the standards used could not be said to be contrary to those meant by Congress to be applied.

The ICC has not allowed all requests for mergers or consolidations in the trucking industry, however. In 1950 the commission denied the request of Pacific Intermountain Express to acquire the assets of Keeshin, a firm in reorganization at the time. The policy of the commission in these cases was enunciated:

> We think that under [§5] it . . . is our duty to consider the effect which a proposed new unified service will have on the continuance, efficiency, and economy of existing carrier services, and, if such proposed new unified service would adversely affect to any substantial extent the continuance, efficiency and economy of existing carrier services, to the detriment of the public, whether it would result in offsetting advantages to the public and whether approval or disapproval would more nearly conform with the policy of Congress declared in the national transportation policy.

The commission, following these tests, decided that there would bc no offsetting advantage to the substantial harm caused to competitors by the unified system. The result of the new longer-range hauling capacity would be a diversion of higher-rate traffic from the railroads, endangering their ability to survive. For these reasons and other considerations, the commission denied the application.

The *McLean* case made it clear that the antitrust laws were not to be the only statutes referred to in order to determine the will of Congress, but the policies espoused therein still loomed large in the commission's determinations. A proposed acquisition of a number of motor carriers by a large holding company involved in carriage through subsidiaries was considered by the ICC in 1960. Objections were voiced by the Antitrust Division, the railroads affected, and other trucking firms. The commission allowed two of the acquisitions because the consolidations would be more of the end-to-end than competing variety and because the existence of other competition at all points obviated the claims of monopoly power. The complaints of the railroad were dismissed by the ICC because of the failure to show actual loss of freight, and also because the motor carriers had to be allowed to grow. The three acquisitions rejected were felt to possess anticompetitive aspects because of the very real possibility that multiple-line operations then existing would be changed because of consolidation into single-line capacity. In other words, where competition and service would not be lowered substantially, the acquisitions were permitted in order to allow needed growth and expansion, but further growth would not be allowed at the expense of customers and competitors who would be materially affected. This result bears a striking resemblance to the reasoning of the courts in some of the merger cases under Clayton 7.

The exact interplay between Section 5 of the Transportation Act and Section 7 of the Clayton Act was the subject of a Supreme Court case in 1967. The issues involved in *Denver and Rio Grande Western Railroad* v. *United States* concerned the approval by the commission, without a hearing, of the acquisition of 500,000 shares of Railway Express Agency by Greyhound. The agreement as put before the commission included the continuing offer of Greyhound, for a duration of sixty days, to purchase another 1 million shares at the same price if REA so desired. The transfer of stock came within the commission's jurisdiction under Section

20a of the Interstate Commerce Act, which had no statutory exemption from the antitrust laws. In approving the transaction, the commission decided to delay a possible hearing on the control and anticompetitive issues under Clayton 7 because such an investigation "would not be appropriate at this time." The district court agreed with the ICC in its assessment of the situation—because control was conjectural and might never occur without the later acquisition, a hearing would be premature.

The Supreme Court reversed and remanded the case to the ICC for further proceedings. The Court noted that antitrust considerations are more often encountered in proceedings under Section 5, but explained that the "foundations of the ICC's obligation under §5 are largely applicable to §20a as well." The Court reminded the commission of other cases where it had refused permission to acquire stock under Section 20a where it would be a violation of Section 5, and observed that the principles espoused there would be "equally applicable here." After holding that the ICC had a duty "to consider the control and anticompetitive consequences before approving stock issuances under §20a(2)," the Court held that the considerations of control consequences could be put off until the end of the sixty-day option period. However, the anticompetitive aspects under Clayton 7 were not limited by the threshhold question of actual acquisition of control, so the ICC was under a duty to consider Section 7 issues. The arguments advanced by the commission to justify the deferral of the anticompetitive considerations, including no harm to the contestants or public interest and the administrative inconvenience of tackling the problem at this stage, were rejected by the Court. A hearing was required because there existed "serious questions under Section 7 of the Clayton Act" before the commission.

The commission's decision to allow a merger between two intercity bus companies has been affirmed several times, the latest of which was by a federal district court dismissing a private suit challenging the merger in *Interstate Investors, Inc.* v. *Transcontinental Bus System, Inc.* The complaint alleged violation of the antitrust laws that could not be immunized by the commission's approval of a merger—namely, conspiratorial acts performed in pursuance of the merger itself. The summary judgment motion of the defendant was granted on the basis of the immunity given to mergers under Section 5 of the Interstate Commerce Act. The contention that Section 5 could not act retroactively to forgive such alleged conspiratorial acts was based on a Federal Maritime Commission approved agreement, but the court rejected it as inapposite in this case. In conclusion the court stated, "The foregoing analysis demonstrates that Section 5(11) confers antitrust immunity on the defendants, notwithstanding plaintiff's contentions as to the inapplicability of that provision when conspiracies or conduct that preceded I.C.C. approval are involved."

It can be safely predicted that the Interstate Commerce Commission will continue to be involved in controversy in the merger area. This is to be expected when the policies of the antitrust laws can be overridden by the commission in order to achieve a more important goal. As long as commentators contend that surface transportation would be more efficient without regulation by the ICC or argue that the regulation of motor carriers is solely aimed at protecting railroads, someone will be on hand to challenge the decisions made by the commission and thereby serve to define further the scope of the ICC's authority.

Civil Aeronautics Board

The statutory authority of the CAB to regulate merger activity in the field of air carriers is found in Section 408 of the Federal Aviation Act. Mergers are forbidden between air carriers and other common carriers or persons engaged in any phase of aeronautics without the board's approval. Acquisitions or consolidations of this type are to be sanctioned by the CAB unless it would not be "consistent with the public interest." This mandate is limited, however, by the caveat that a merger cannot be allowed if it would result in a monopoly and restrain competition. The authority of the board has been described as "pervasive" in the air carrier field, and the board takes its job seriously. "It has properly concluded, in light of the immunity from the antitrust laws conferred by §414 [of the Federal Aviation Act], that it must consider anticompetitive effects less extreme than those [considered] in the provision determining whether the transaction will 'be consistent with the public interest' as defined in §102. . . ."

In an important decision by the CAB in 1946, permission to acquire an air carrier was denied because of the lack of any real benefit resulting from the acquisition. American Airlines, the largest air carrier in America, with a coast-to-coast route, sought to acquire Mid-Continent Airlines, a carrier with an overall north–south route. Before the board a bleak picture of the future of Mid-Continent was painted by American, but the members felt that the problems of Mid-Continent could be overcome in other ways. The advantages pressed on the board by the applicant were discounted: (1) the new services claimed to be possible were relatively insignificant because of the low amount of traffic involved; (2) allegations of availability of new equipment did not stand up—such equipment was available without American; (3) economies of scale were not proved to the board; (4) reduced fares were probably possible by Mid-Continent alone; and (5) reductions in mail expenditures made as subsidies were not really important—competition was more critical.

The disadvantages of the consolidation were then discussed by the board. The good will created by American would carry over to the routes now serviced by Mid-Continent, giving American a competitive advantage over other airlines that would be difficult to calculate or overcome, a more circuitous route might be chosen by the passenger because of this carryover of good will. The diversion of traffic would undoubtedly hurt the other airlines. The board also feared that the connecting services would be precluded from "reaching and retaining their necessary level of adequacy and efficiency, and thus would obstruct the application of the statutory directive set forth in section 2(b) to improve the relations between, and coordinate transportation by, air carriers." All facts considered, the board felt that the benefits, although tangible, were relatively slight and were outweighed by the substantial injuries to competition that would result.

The CAB exhibited its concern for competition in two later cases by allowing the proposed merger. However, both of the acquired carriers were found to be in danger of collapse and the board felt that mergers, allowed under a modified failing-company test, were the only course of action available to preserve the service offered. The acquisition of Colonial Airlines by Eastern was judged to be necessary because internal difficulties made efficient use of equipment impossible. The two contenders for Colonial were Eastern and National; the conclusion that less traffic would be diverted from National made Eastern the choice. Also significant was the fact that an agreement between the two airlines had already been hammered out, whereas such an agreement with National was only speculative. Oddly enough, the board also felt that a savings in subsidies of around $850,000 was an important factor in this case, even though a similar savings was dismissed as unimportant in the *American–Mid-Continent* case.

Seven years later, in 1961, the board allowed a merger between United Air Lines and Capital Airlines for substantially the same reasons. The collapse of Capital was felt to be imminent, and the board refused to sustain the objections to possible monopoly power being obtained by United simply because all other potential remedies were too remote and uncertain. After noting that older precedents established by the board were not influential because of the different facts involved, the discussion then turned to the financial confidence that would result from the allowance of the merger. "Although lenders are primarily concerned with the economic potential of the particular company with which they are dealing, the prospects of an individual company can never be divorced from the prospects of the industry of which it is a part." The public interest requirement was found to be satisfied by the integration potential between the routes operated by the two lines, evaluated by including cost savings and improved use of facilities. The most important complaint—that of diversion of traffic—was found to be outweighed by the improved service potential. The board refused to impose conditions on some of the routes to protect other lines from excessive diversion lest the agreement be jeopardized. Other conditions were allowed to protect smaller carriers who were already dependent on subsidies in the form of mail contracts. The focus of the CAB in these cases seemed to be to try to preserve the status quo—forbid mergers between companies if the resulting company would be too large, but allow mergers with already large airlines if the only other choice was the failure of the weak company, with the consequent loss of service.

The Court of Appeals for the Second Circuit, in a 1968 case, reviewed most of the factors to be considered in an acquisition by an air carrier. The case was *Butler Aviation Company* v. *CAB,* and it concerned the acquisition by Eastern Airlines of Remmert-Werner, Inc., a sales agent for an executive jet aircraft and also a leading aviation service, or "fixed-base," operator. The CAB had jurisdiction because Remmert-Werner was "engaged in any phase of aeronautics otherwise than as an air carrier." The acquisition was allowed by the board and that decision was upheld by the court. The meaning of Section 408 was stated to be that "the Board cannot approve a transaction if its effects will be so extreme as to violate the proviso [against monopoly and restraint on competition] but must approve others if, but only if, it finds the disadvantage of any curtailment of competition to be outweighed by 'the advantages of improved service.' " The advantages of improved service were contended to be minimal, "[b]ut the Board was warranted in finding that any disadvantages were equally small." The court, when considering the entry of Eastern into the market of executive jet sales, found the argument of market dominance relied on in *FTC* v. *Procter & Gamble* to be inappropriate. Since R-W was already a strong competitor, and also because other big companies were unable to achieve a higher market share at the expense of the smaller competitors, the court found little danger of the "deep-pocket" syndrome. The market did not lend itself to cutthroat competition in one area of the country, subsidized in effect by higher prices in the remaining sections.

As to the aircraft servicing portion of R-W's operation, the board and the court found the competition "limited to operators having facilities at a particular airport." The fear seemed to be more than that R-W would be able to secure service locations at new airports more easily, and this could not be considered a major obstacle. As to the test in *Procter & Gamble,* the examiner did not find Eastern to be a potential entrant into the fixed-base operation, nor did it find advertising to be a key point in the sale of services in this business: "It is rather hard to imagine a television commercial devoted to extolling the charms of Florida palms and sands including a plug for R-W's fueling operations." The one problem the court had trouble with was the examiner's, and consequently the board's, rejection of a suggestion that Eastern agree not to claim antitrust immunity under Section 414, and this despite the fact that Eastern was willing to waive the immunity. However, when considering the facts that Congress wanted the decision to be final, subject to judicial review, and also that such an out might tempt the board "to neglect thorough assessment of anticompetitive considerations on the basis that the transaction would remain open to later attack . . . ," the court found the decision to keep the immunity provision in force was justifiable. The *Butler* case was followed in the District of Columbia Circuit Court's opinion in *National Aviation Trades Association* v. *CAB* a year later.

Although the CAB has been criticized by one commentator for employing different standards in some cases—in some cases allowing merger because of competition from without, and in others denying merger approval because of the creation of a monopoly—the board reviews the evidence and hears comments from interveners in an attempt to determine what action in each case will result in the greatest good.

Federal Communications Commission

The merger activity within the jurisdiction of the FCC is difficult to analyze in a clear but comprehensive fashion. The duties of the commission are complicated because it has two distinct types of communication media under its authority: (1) telegraph and telephone companies, along with Communications Satellite Corporation—the common carriers; and (2) radio and television stations. Title 47 of the United States Code provides a different regulatory scheme for both groups, the former being governed by Sections 221 and 222 and the latter by Section 310. If a consolidation under Section 221 is approved by the commission in the manner provided, "any Act or Acts of Congress making the proposed transaction unlawful shall not apply." Likewise, Section 222 governing telegraph companies, provides that after approval "any law or laws making consolidations and mergers unlawful shall not apply to the proposed consolidation or merger." However, there is no corresponding immunity under Section 310 if the FCC approves the acquisition of a radio or television station. The transaction is open to attack by the Antitrust Division.

The steps the commission has taken in the broadcasting industry to try and deal with the problem of concentration have usually been by rule making; the commission has defined and redefined its conception of its license-granting role to obtain diversification in broadcasting. When the problem is attacked in this manner, the commission eliminates the need to inquire whether the grant of a license might be inconsistent with Section 7 of the Clayton Act and therefore possibly against the public interest. The rule draws a clear line between those licenses that are legal and those that are illegal, without going into other considerations. The placement of the line is the only relevant factor, at least according to the rule. Whether this should be the case when all of the commission's responsibilities are considered will be left to the legal writers and analysts to discuss. The determination of whether or not the commission has actually followed this philosophy and left the Section 7 enforcement, if inconsistent, to another agent of the government can only be made by looking at the actual proceedings themselves. If the commission has refused to become involved in this enforcement, it will be necessary to make note of the Justice Department's role subsequent to the granting of a license or approval of an acquisition that might be anticompetitive in light of Section 7's standards. Unfortunately, there has not been the clarification of the responsibilities of the parties and agencies involved that litigation has produced in other regulated areas.

These problems must be resolved by application of principles laid down in judicial and commission decisions of analogous issues.

The Supreme Court reviewed the commission decision to grant a radio license to a newspaper company in *FCC* v. *Sanders Brothers Radio Station,* decided in 1940. The decision was alleged to be "arbitrary and capricious" by Sanders Brothers because they operated a radio station in the same area and they had offered testimony that only one station could survive in that area. The Court was asked to decide whether economic injury to an existing station was a sufficient reason to require rejection of the newspaper's application. In holding that it was not, the Court observed that the broadcasting field was still one of free competition: "The sections dealing with broadcasting demonstrate that Congress has not, in its regulatory scheme, abandoned the principle of free competition. . . ." The commission had to consider several facets of inter-station competition when it was called on to pass on an application for a new station, but for the Court to hold the "economic injury" could not be allowed would mean that "the Commission's function is to grant a monopoly in the field of broadcasting, a result which the Act itself expressly negatives. . . ." This much was settled—the commission did not regulate broadcasting to the extent that competition was not important. How competition would interrelate with the statutory considerations was not at all settled.

Three years later the Court was called on to decide whether the FCC had the authority to issue regulations proscribing certain practices in "chain" or network broadcasting. In affirming the lower court dismissal of the injunction request against the FCC, the Supreme Court held that "[t]he Act itself establishes that the Commission's powers are not limited to the engineering and technical aspects of regulation of radio communication." However, another ground of attack was that the commission was attempting to administer the antitrust laws in the regulations and that the attempt was *ultra vires.* This contention was answered by quoting the commission's opinion: "It is not our function to apply the anti-trust laws as such. It is our duty, however, to refuse licenses or renewals to any person who engages or proposes to engage in practices which will prevent either himself or other licensees or both from making the fullest use of radio facilities." Although the opinion was not predicated on the enforcement of the Sherman Act, it was clear that conduct illegal under the Sherman Act is not unfettered merely because the commission is not given explicit jurisdiction over the Sherman Act. Such conduct is also, or may be, against the public interest and is thereby prohibited.

The Sherman Act was evoked again in a case involving the FCC, but in *United States* v. *Radio Corporation of America* the Justice Department was challenging the approval of the commission given to a plan to exchange radio stations between RCA and Westinghouse. The complaint alleged a conspiracy to violate the Sherman Act, but the district court dismissed the complaint. In holding that government was entitled to the relief it requested—divestitive among other things—the Court reached several conclusions. First, after a review of the history of the FCC Act it was agreed that the commission was not meant to pass on the merits of alleged antitrust violations and that the courts "retained jurisdiction to pass on [them] irrespective of Commission action." Obviously, then, "Commission action was not intended to prevent enforcement of the antitrust laws in federal courts." Secondly, the invocation of primary jurisdiction was not proper in this case because there was no pervasive regulatory scheme "to throw out of balance." The Court reiterated its findings, however, that antitrust considerations should play a part in determining what is in the public interest. Finally, the decision dismissed out of hand the defenses of *res judicata* and *laches* because the attempt by the commission to pass on the merits of the antitrust claims was not proper and could not bind the government. It appears, then, that by 1959 the role of the Sherman Act in FCC proceedings had been set out. It is to be a factor in the decision to license a new station or to approve the transfer of an existing license. But it is to be only one factor and not of controlling importance, and the courts will be free to judge the application of the Sherman Act to the specific facts if anticompetitive activity has been allowed that should not have been. Is it then settled that the provisions of Section 7 of the Clayton Act are to be treated in the same manner?

The commission has had more than a decade to demonstrate how it will implement the policies of Section 7, but as yet the only arguments in the commission proceedings relating to Clayton 7 have been raised by intervening parties—chiefly the Antitrust Division. In the consideration of the International Telephone & Telegraph Corporation's application to acquire American Broadcasting Company, the commission did not discuss the application of Clayton Section 7 to the facts until the Justice Department moved to intervene in the proceedings and have the approval set aside. When the Clayton Act arguments were placed squarely before the commission, the outcome was the same, although the merger was never completed. After the decision against it, the Justice Department appealed; while the appeal was pending, the contract between ITT and ABC expired and ITT decided not to go through with the merger. The treatment given to the allegations by the Antitrust Division was thorough, although the antitrust concepts were only considered by the commission to be relevant and not controlling. The relevant market was agreed to be national television networks. The issues brought up by the department were (1) ITT as a potential entrant into network broadcasting, rejected because ITT realized it could only succeed by acquisition; (2) possible retardation of technological innovations, rejected because ABC would be better able to conduct such research after merger; (3) elimination of independent ABC in regulatory proceedings, rejected in view of merger arrangements to keep it separate; (4) foreclosure of advertising from other networks, viewed as insignificant even if possible; and (5) reciprocal dealing potential, rejected because not practiced by ITT. The abandonment of the merger after the appeal by the Antitrust Division has prevented the courts from passing on the merits of these commission determinations.

A more recent chance to clarify further the Section 7 application in the transfer of a broadcasting license was lost when the application was withdrawn following the submission of a memorandum by the Antitrust Division arguing a violation of Section 7. The loss of these opportunities to litigate the questions to a final determination has been regretted. Even though the FCC is not given the power to immunize transactions in the broadcasting field, many commentators feel that the FCC should be required to consider the Section 7 tests. The tests have been made so easy to apply, especially with all the information available to the commission, that the avoidance of this enforcement task should not be allowed. The remedies are available to the FCC, and the inclusion of Clayton Act standards would be no hardship or waste of time. It must be admitted that without the help of the FCC in this matter, only a very few of the transfers allowed will be able to be tested by the competitive standards of Section 7. What the commission will consider beyond its clear-cut rules on multiple ownership is not decided yet, but the precedent for a thorough analysis of Section 7's application has been established in the ITT–ABC merger.

Federal Maritime Commission

One of the older regulatory agencies, established by the Shipping Act of 1916, the Federal Maritime Commission has had its performance subjected to extreme criticism almost since its inception. The commission's job is to regulate international merchant carriers, and the primary system relied on for this purpose was the shipping conference set up to fix the rates for services. The conference was decided upon as the optimal solution to a difficult problem; the monopoly that would result by prohibiting shipping lines from entering into agreements on the rates to be offered was not wanted, but neither was extensive merger activity within the industry in order to reduce competition. The conferences enabled the rates to be set without the finality of an actual merger. The language of Section 15 of the Shipping Act goes into great detail about the agreements that can be immunized from the antitrust laws: a memorandum of any agreement fixing rates, giving special rates, controlling competition, allotting parts, limiting volume of freight, and so on, is to be filed with the commission and kept up to date; the Commission can disapprove any agreement that it finds "unjustly discriminatory"; independent action must be allowed and admission must be open to qualified carriers; the agreements are unlawful unless approved by the commission; approved conferences are exempt from the antitrust laws; and a violation can be punished by a fine of up to $1,000 per day. The extent of the word *agreement* has been in dispute recently. Cases construing it will be discussed. It is undisputed that Section 15 does give the commission the authority to approve a rate conference and thereby exempt it from the antitrust laws, and this will be the first area of the FMC's jurisdiction discussed.

The conference approach to the shipping problems prior to 1916 was clearly a compromise. After an investigation of the industry that was published in 1914 indicated that the already existing practice of conference rate making had resulted in stable prices in the trade, and because Congress feared a rate war would result if they were ordered disbanded, the conferences were allowed to continue. This way the carriers could be relatively sure about the amount of traffic they would be carrying, because the discounts were only given to shippers who patronized one conference. When the conferences were filed, the commission was ordered to approve them unless they were found "to be unjustly discriminatory or unfair as between carriers, shippers, exporters, importers, or ports. . . ." If later found to violate these criteria, the conference could be disbanded. As a practical matter, however, there was little threat of such disbanding, because the FMC considered agreements filed pursuant to the already discussed section to be prima facie valid, unless a defect was discovered later. The latter possibility was remote too because the commission failed to inquire into the validity of agreements once approved. By a process of omission the agreements, or conferences, were assumed valid and out of reach of the antitrust laws.

This cavalier exemption from the antitrust laws, granted in many cases without even a review of the merits of the rates, was found to be a source of irritation and demanded some correction. Such corrective action was late in coming though, because it was not until 1954 that it was decided that liquidated damages specified for a breach of conference agreements would not be collected if the conference had not been formally approved by the commission. The court of appeals for the District of Columbia also held, in *Isbrandtsen Co.* v. *United States,* "that such agreements or modifications 'shall be lawful only *when* and as long as *approved*' by the [Commission]." This made it quite clear that the conferences then existing that had not been formally approved (according to some sources most of the conferences fell into this category) were not exempt from prosecution under the antitrust laws. However, instead of embarking on a comprehensive plan to review the conferences, and to approve those whose rates were not "unjustly discriminatory," the commission reiterated its opinion that express approval was not needed. This unwarranted assumption allowed the exemption to continue without any support in statute or case law.

That an antitrust cause of action could be predicated on activities performed pursuant to a conference whose approval had been withdrawn, or never granted originally, was the effect of the Supreme Court holding in *Carnation Company* v. *Pacific Westbound Conference.* A treble-damage action against the conference, based on the per se violation of price fixing, was allowed because the express exemption did "not apply to the implementation of unapproved agreements, which [was] specifically prohibited by §15." The Court distinguished two earlier cases because a decision in them might cause a conflict with later commission action, whereas here the commission could not "validate pre-approval implementation of such agreements," so no conflict could arise. The relief in the two earlier cases differed also, because the plaintiff had requested injunctive, as opposed to treble-damage, relief. Action has been taken by both the commission and private parties since the *Carnation* decision; the commission has disbanded conferences which have refused to comply with its discovery attempts to determine whether the conference should be approved or remain approved, and private parties have begun pressing treble-damage claims where the commission approval has been revoked. It appears that the conference will no longer be the easy method to enjoy the benefits of a merger without permanent consolidation or approval by the commission. The function of the conference should now more closely parallel the original intent of Congress when conferences were first allowed.

As was alluded to earlier, there is some disagreement over the authority of the Federal Maritime Commission in an actual merger between a shipping carrier and some other company. Although the conference procedure seems to obviate the need for most mergers between carriers, there have been at least three consolidations lately that have been litigated and different conclusions have been reached. The problem arises from the statutory definition of the word *agreement* in Section 15 that "includes understandings, conferences, and other arrangements."

The first case to consider is *Matson Navigation Co.* v. *Federal Maritime Commission,* wherein the Ninth Circuit Court of Appeals held that the commission could not approve an agreement to merge between three shipping carriers. The holding rested, however, on the ground that the merger plan was not final as approved because it was to be accomplished "in the form and by the procedures as the directors and the stockholders of the three companies shall approve." In the court's view, the parties had "simply agreed to agree" on the merger, and the approval therefore was "not a sufficient discharge of the Commission's responsibilities." On the question of the FMC's authority over mergers generally, the Ninth Circuit ruled that such authority could be derived from Section 15, quoting extensively from *Volkswagenwerk* v. *Federal Maritime Commission.* Declining the invitation to read Section 15 narrowly, the court preferred to follow its reading of the Alexander Report and its purposes: "The direct and destructive impact upon competition which may result from a merger renders it the kind of arrangement as to which expert scrutiny most clearly is to be desired. . . . [T]o leave enforcement . . . to the FTC, the Department of Justice and the courts would apply the full and unconditional force of the antitrust laws to such agreements contrary to the intent of the Shipping Act. . . ." Although this particular merger agreement was sent back to the commission, this case seemed to be a clear enunciation of the FMC's authority to allow the merger once the plans were finalized.

A more recent case has taken issue with this ruling in holding that the FMC has no authority to pass on the legality of actual mergers, as opposed to rate conferences, and cannot immunize them from further antitrust actions. A United States district court in New Jersey ruled in *United States* v. *R. J. Reynolds Tobacco Co.* that "Congress did not intend to subject merger agreements to the supervision of the FMC." The merger was to be between RJI Corporation, a subsidiary of R. J. Reynolds Tobacco, and U.S. Lines, a subsidiary of Walter Kidde & Company. The agreement was filed with the FMC and the ICC, but before the hearings by the FMC were completed the Antitrust Division filed the suit to have the agreement enjoined. Noting that Section 15 was derived from the Alexander Report, the court analyzed the phrase relied on (every agreement . . . controlling, regulating, preventing or destroying competition) in light of that report. Concluding that the "Alexander Committee distinguished conceptually between agreements in the sense of ongoing, cooperative agreements and agreements of 'consolidation' or 'acquisition,'" the court found the use of the word *agreement* to be a "term of art" and thereby incapable of being read to include mergers within its scope. When confronted with the *Matson* decision already discussed, the opinion answered that the decision had relied on *Volkswagenwerk* heavily, a case that did not involve a merger and that therefore could not be controlling. The finding of Congressional interest favoring FMC authority in the merger area was also held to be misconceived, in view of the *Philadelphia National Bank* case and the reluctance to imply immunity from the antitrust laws.

One argument advanced in *Reynolds* that was not covered in *Matson* was that the filing with the ICC, necessary because of a small amount of intercoastal trade by U.S. Lines, could result in approval and antitrust immunity derived from the ICC's admitted authority over mergers under Section 5 of the ICC Act. This was rejected because the "nature and complexities of marine transportation of freight in foreign commerce would clearly be beyond the scope of the ICC expertise." The lack of expertise in the area plus the small amount of intercoastal traffic involved (5 per cent) made total immunity inappropriate. The court allowed the intervention of the FMC into the proceedings but denied the requested dismissal of the complaint or stay of the proceedings. The decision has been appealed to the Supreme Court.

The *Reynolds* decision was relied on heavily in a decision by the United States Circuit Court for the District of Columbia that denied the FMC the power to approve mergers and thereby bestow immunity. The case, *Seatrain Lines, Inc.* v. *FMC,* was on review from the commission after it had allowed the acquisition of Oceanic Steamship Company's assets by Pacific Far East Line, Inc. The question posed by the case was "whether this agreement falls within the scope of the Commission's jurisdiction as defined by the Shipping Act of 1916." The decision was that it did not. In a carefully drafted and well-organized opinion the court set down the factors it relied on: (1) the wording of the statute indicated that the commission was only to have authority over "working" agreements and the catchall clause of Section 15 was to be limited to the specific areas enunciated earlier; (2) the Shipping Act was to be construed in a way that would not interfere with the antitrust laws unless such a construction was unavoidable; (3) other statutes enacted contemporaneously dealt specifically with acquisitions of control, indicating that if Congress had intended that type of coverage, it would have provided for it; (4) the report on which the Act was based distinguished between control of competition by acquisition and by agreement, intending only the latter to be covered by legislation; (5) no authority to approve mergers can be discovered based on Congressional inaction since the passage of the Act; (6) the previous commission decisions in this area have involved covenants not to compete, over which the commission does have authority, so such precedent cannot be relied on by the commission to bootstrap its own jurisdiction; and (7) the more realistic of the two recent opinions on this question decided that the legislative history of the Act precludes the FMC's contentions. Also important in the court's opinion was that, in approving this acquisition of assets, the commission had not held a public hearing or developed a record. Judicial review of this action would have been impossible even if the commission had the requisite authority. For all of these reasons the decision of the commission was vacated and the agreement ordered removed from the docket.

The decision of the Supreme Court, whether granting certiorari in *Seatrain* and deciding on the merits or denying review at this stage, will just further point up the fact that this area of merger law is in a constant state of flux. Despite the fact that the FMC appeared dormant twenty years ago, the commission has come to life and the industry can no longer take for granted its ability to avoid the antitrust laws at will.

Federal Power Commission

Two different statutory enactments govern the authority of the Federal Power Commission over mergers in separate regulated fields. The Natural Gas Act, passed in 1938, sets forth the commission's duty in the area of natural gas transmission and distribution, with Section 7 covering its jurisdiction over mergers and acquisitions. The Federal Power Act, enacted eighteen years earlier, dealt with the generation and transmission of electric energy; Section 203 provides the merger criteria in this field. The two different utility responsibilities are quite unrelated and lend themselves to separate examinations, so the natural gas merger will be analyzed first, with electric utility mergers mentioned afterward.

Natural Gas

The regulatory provisions of the Natural Gas Act are not pervasive enough for the courts to construe any immunity from the antitrust laws. Section 7 of the Act forbids abandonment of facilities by any company subject to the FPC's jurisdiction without approval; the transportation and sale of gas is forbidden without a "certificate of public convenience and necessity issued by the Commission. . . ." A hearing is provided for, and approval is required if the applicant is willing to perform the service and if the "sale . . . or acquisition . . . is or will be required by present or future public convenience or necessity."

The scope of the commission's authority came into issue in *California v. Federal Power Commission,* a Supreme Court decision on appeal from the approval by the commission of a merger between El Paso Natural Gas and Pacific Northwest Pipeline Corporation. The merger had been challenged in the courts before the commission's permission to acquire the assets of Pacific had been sought, but the FPC refused to stay its proceedings while the courts decided the legality of the merger. California had intervened before the commission, and when the merger was allowed, it appealed. Although the Court found that "[e]vidence of antitrust violations is plainly relevant in merger applications" as part of the "public convenience and necessity," the majority refused to imply immunity from the antitrust laws once the merger had been passed on by the commission. The regulatory scheme was not pervasive, and although some agencies were given statutory authority to relieve approved transactions from the operation of the antitrust laws, "there [was] no comparable provision under the Natural Gas Act." The mention of the Federal Power Commission in the proviso to Section 7 of the Clayton Act did not grant any additional power not already possessed. Although the Court did not decide if the Clayton Act had been violated, it noted that a decision by a federal court that the merger was illegal would close the question, whereas the commission decision allowing the merger was necessary but not sufficient for legality. The merger was subsequently found violative of Clayton 7 and divestiture was ordered.

Much of the activity before the commission in the last decade has been concerned with competition between pipelines. As a direct result of these decisions, most major metropolitan areas have more than one supplier of natural gas via pipeline. The decisions have not always been on the side of admitting new competitors, as in the commission denial of entry to a third pipeline in the Los Angeles area. Among some of the other decisions, however, was the approval of a second pipeline for the metropolitan Washington area. For the first time in its history, the commission exercised its authority to order connection of gas transportation facilities under Section 7(a) of the Act. In *Algonquin Gas Transmission Company,* the FPC rejected Algonquin's application to serve the Hartford Gas Company and ordered the Tennessee Gas Transmission Company to serve it instead. However, the commission saw this action as extraordinary and suited to only a "few occasions."

While the decision in *California* v. *FPC* settled the question of the commission's immunity power under the Natural Gas Act, it did not seem to resolve the extent to which the antitrust laws were to be considered by the commission as defining the "public convenience and necessity." The FPC was given further instruction on this point in *Northern Natural Gas Company* v. *FPC,* a lengthy decision remanding to the commission the approval of an application for a jointly owned pipeline for the purpose of considering competitive issues. The Court of Appeals for the District of Columbia, in finding that the "Commission gave inadequate consideration to the antitrust policy of the United States," noted that direct regulation, through governmental agencies, and indirect regulations through the antitrust laws were meant to be complementary—the combination of the two helping to arrive at an efficient allocation of resources while stimulating better service at lower cost. Although noting that the commission could not determine violations of the antitrust laws or be bound by the dictates of these laws, the court nevertheless stated, "But because competitive considerations are an important element of the 'public interest,' we believe that . . . the Commission was obliged to make findings related to the pertinent antitrust policies, draw conclusions from the findings, and weigh these conclusions along with other important public interest considerations." After reviewing the standards under Clayton 7 for joint ventures, the court found one of the parties to the joint venture to be a likely potential entrant into the area dominated by the other party. Recounting the importance of potential competition as set forth in *El Paso* and *Penn-Olin,* the invitable decision was that "[t]he joint venture approved in this case had the effect of foreclosing this new development [new competition] and, therfore, tended to lessen competition substantially among suppliers in the Wisconsin and Michigan markets." Before concluding, the court mentioned two other anticompetitive effects to consider: (1) the distortion of the regulatory process because of market division deals agreed on before submitting proposals to the FPC; and (2) the increased risk of future joint endeavors by the two participants here. An immunity defense was raised by the two parties because of the prior approval of the SEC given to the stock acquisition, but this was rejected by the court because the SEC's decision was made without a hearing and was not directed at the same type of determinations that were to be made by the FPC.

The conclusion in the area of natural gas pipeline mergers is that the commission, although not allowed to decide whether a proposed merger or acquisition violates the antitrust laws, must take into consideration the same type of anticompetitive effects that will result from the merger that the court would consider in a suit brought by the government. Because the antitrust laws form the basis of the competitive policies of this country, they are necessarily part of the public interest and should be so considered. The FPC's position to acquire the necessary data also makes inappropriate any complaint that these determinations present an unreasonable workload.

Electric Utility Mergers

Section 203 of the Federal Power Act, the FPC's statutory authority over electric utility facilities, provides, subject to an exception for facilities under $50,000, that, "No public utility shall sell, lease or otherwise dispose of the whole of its facilities subject to the jurisdiction of the Commission . . . or by any means whatsoever, directly or indirectly, merge or consolidate such facilities or any part thereof with those of any person, or purchase, acquire, or take any security of any other public utility, without first having secured an order of the Commission authorizing it to do so." In the more than thirty-five years since the enactment of this statute the commission has developed some guidelines in analyzing applications for mergers and acquisitions, although the amount of litigation challenging the commission's decisions has been less than in other regulated fields.

An early case under this Act, *Pacific Power & Light Co.* v. *FPC,* decided in 1940, came to a rather unusual decision—unusual especially when one remembers the traditional importance of competition and also the deference given to the administrative body. Pacific had sought FPC approval of the acquisition of Inland Power & Light Company's assets; Pacific already owned all of Inland's stock. The commission refused to grant its approval, even though the two state regulatory agencies had agreed, on the ground that it was unable to find that "any substantial advantage or benefits to the public will result therefrom." The commission held that the proponent of the merger must show more than the absence of harm; he was required to show that a benefit to the public would result from the merger. The decision to forbid the merger was reversed and sent back to the commission for reconsideration. The court of appeals did not agree with the commission's reading of the section: "We see no more in the prohibition than the purpose of insuring against public disadvantage through the requirement of a showing that mergers of this sort will not result in detriment to consumers or investors or to other legitimate national interests." The continuing validity of this statement has been brought into question in recent cases, and it is not settled that the court was correct in this early case. In a decision allowing a merger between two electric utilities who were not physically connected, the commission noted, "Whatever validity the ninth circuit's opinion in Pacific Power & Light Co. v. Federal Power Commission . . . may otherwise have, it is clear that in such a situation a showing of positive benefit to counteract the detrimental consequence of one-company ownership of two unconnected utility systems is essential." The benefit found was the heightened attempts to achieve connection between the two utilities in a sparsely settled part of the country, and the merger was expressly conditioned on continued connection attempts.

A more thorough enunciation of the type of factors the FPC will consider when confronted with an electric utility merger was made in the decision of *Commonwealth Edison Co.* and *Central Illinois Electricity & Gas Co.* Because of the variety of issues raised in the application, the commission used the decision as a vehicle to set down merger criteria. In the application, Commonwealth proposed a merger with Central, a company selling electricity and gas to five noncontiguous areas in Illinois. Central's largest area, Rockford, was bounded on three sides by one of the Commonwealth service areas. The factors discussed in the opinion were (1) the reasonableness of the purchase price, making sure that stockholders of neither company suffer from an offer that is either too high or too low; (2) the accounting treatment given to the transaction insuring no increase in capitalization in the remaining company over the sum of its parts; (3) the economic effect on the consumer to avoid unnecessary rate increases, and to encourage rate reductions made possible by economies of scale; (4) whether the merger had been coerced through boycotts by the acquiring company that made a merger necessary to the acquired company's survival; (5) the effect on the competitive situation—avoiding concentration, elimination of potential competition, and adverse impact on competing energy sources; (6) the resulting effectiveness of regulation to prevent the home state from losing control because of an acquisition across state lines; and (7) whether the merger will include noncontiguous properties, lest the mandate of the Public Utility Holding Company Act discouraging noncontiguous utilities be violated. The commission found the merger to meet the first six requirements and decided to allow the merger while waiting for connection between the noncontiguous areas. The decision was upheld by the court of appeals, but mainly on the ground that the appellant, a group of Edison customers, had no standing to complain of anticompetitive effects.

Securities and Exchange Commission

The Public Utility Holding Company Act of 1935, passed at the same time as the Federal Power Act noted previously, gave the Securities and Exchange Commission broad powers over holding companies that controlled, or owned over 10 per cent of the stock of, gas or electric operating utilities. The Act sets forth detailed instructions on the administrative controls and restrictions, with Sections 8, 9, and 10 covering the acquisition of securities, utility assets, or other business interests. There are several standards and qualifications enunciated that cover specific problems, but one part of Section 10 does state that the commission shall not approve "(2) the acquisition of securities or utility assets of a public-utility or holding company unless the Commission finds that such acquisition will serve the public interest by tending towards the economical and efficient development of an integrated public utility system. . . ." The importance of the SEC's authority in this area has dwindled considerably since the passage of the Act mainly because of the reduction in numbers of the companies subject to the SEC's jurisdiction. Between 1938 and 1962, over 2,400 companies were subject to the provisions of the Act at one time or another, and by 1962 only 184 companies comprising twenty-two holding company systems were still subject to the Act. The commission succeeded in reducing the number by divesting those nonintegrated parts of the systems that made the company subject to the Act; mergers, consolidations, and dissolutions also took their toll.

A series of proceedings conducted by the SEC during 1945 and 1946 are illustrative of the procedures of the commission under this Act. The holding company involved was American Gas & Electric Company; more specifically, the commission dealt with its three systems—the Central, Northeast Pennsylvania, and South Jersey. The first system, Central, was held to be retainable by American even though it served 1,706 communities and had a network encompassing 90,000 square miles. The entire system was interconnected, there was substantial interchange of electricity, and the system was highly coordinated. Also significant was the fact that the size of the system did not impair the effectiveness of regulation. The other two systems mentioned were not held to be retainable. They were not interconnected or related in an operating capacity; the commission held them to be separate integrated systems that would not be damaged by a severance from the central system. In a later report the SEC denied American's request to allow it to acquire Columbus and Southern Ohio Electric Company. Considered important was the size of the resulting system, identified as an independent factor, and the fact that the acquisition would be a major extension into new territory.

The commission did approve American's acquisition of Indiana Service Corporation, based on the existing interconnection between the two, the purchase by Indiana of 75 per cent of its energy from American, and the fact that the two systems were contiguous. Also mentioned was the fact that Indiana's generating plant was obsolete and incapable of being replaced within the service area.

Almost ten years later the SEC issued a decision allowing twelve companies to organize Yankee Atomic Electric Company to construct and operate a commercial atomic power plant. The commission construed the stock acquisition to be within the permissible limits of Section 10, noting that the interlocking relationship was no more than what was required under the circumstances. When the SEC reviewed the operating data, it found that the plant's capacity would be only 5.8 per cent of the total kilowatt hours sold. All the participants were reasonably close and capable of interconnection with the plant, and they agreed to use all the power generated. When the SEC considered the necessity for the experiment, the inability of one company to go it alone, and the potential reductions in fuel cost and increases in efficiency, it found the project legal under the standards set down by Congress.

The Supreme Court was called on to interpret that section of the Act that allowed divestment of "integrated public utility systems" in 1966. The case was *SEC* v. *New England Electric System.* The divestiture ordered was that of a gas utility held by NEES. The commission found no substantial loss of economies arising from divestiture, but the court of appeals disagreed and reversed. The court agreed with the commission and went on to clarify the meaning of the phrase *without the loss of substantial economies.* After noting that the Congressional report on the statute stated that it meant to allow inclusion of additional systems where they "were in the same region as the principal system and were so small that they were incapable of independent economical operation," the court found the commission's construction as meaning "inability to stand by itself" to be well within the permissible range given to those who are charged with the task of giving an intricate statutory scheme practical sense and application." The decision of the court of appeals that the clause "called for a business judgment of what would be a significant loss, not for a finding of total loss of economy or efficiency" was rejected. The expertise of the SEC in this area was relied on instead.

Bank Mergers

Former Supreme Court Justice Abe Fortas once said that "antitrust is as deeply embedded in the American scene as baseball, bourbon whiskey, and aspirin." Although many people would agree with this statement, it is perhaps the least true when applied to banking. This is evidenced by the bitter reaction to the application of the antitrust laws to bank mergers. This chapter will explore that reaction as well as the rather unusual development of bank-merger regulation and its effect on both bank mergers and bank-holding-company mergers. First we shall take a brief look at the relationship of banks and competition, for this might help explain the policy struggle that came to a climax in the 1960's.

BANKING AND COMPETITION

There has always been a dichotomy of views on the value of competition in banking. This was evidenced in the struggles of Jefferson and Hamilton, Jackson and Biddle, and much later Carter Glass and Huey Long.

After the defeat of the Second Bank of the United States, the proponents of free competition dominated the scene. Andrew Jackson expressed the view of many when in vetoing the renewal of the Second Bank of the United States he stated, "it is easy to conceive, that great evils to our country and its institutions might flow from such a concentration of power in the hands of a few men." President Tyler vetoed the charter for a Third Bank for much the same reasons. On the local level many states in order to restrict banking concentration imposed strict branching regulations, and both federal and state laws allowed easy entry into banking.

This permitted the growth of many local banks and reflected the desire that banking should not be limited to the privileged and rich. However, there can be too much of a good thing, and "free banking" led to situations in some states where anyone could open his own bank without any form of security or supervision and even issue his own bank notes. A compromise to resolve the differences between the monopolistic National Bank and the financial insecurity of free banking was introduced by Senator Sherman in 1863. It was in the form of a bill to create a "National Bank System." The subsequent creation of this national bank system and the strengthening of the state bank system resulted in the dual banking system we have today.

The Depression had a strong effect on the banking industry. In the early 1930's there were over 9,000 bank failures, and 2,300 more banks were absorbed by mergers. This bank instability led to the bank holiday of March 1933, the Emergency Banking Act of 1933, and the Banking Act of 1935. As a result of these and other laws entry into banking became much more difficult. However, even without the impact of the Depression the banking industry had been undergoing changes. The improvement of transportation facilities meant fewer local banks were needed because customers had more mobility and could travel to town. Industrial growth meant that larger, more centralized banks with greater assets were needed. More banks merged and some others failed from natural causes as the banking market became more concentrated. From 1921 to 1933 over 15,000 banks failed and the total number of banking offices decreased from 31,000 to 17,000. In the middle 1930's, as a result of the federal legislation, the banking situation stabilized, and for the next fifteen years banking concentration even slowly declined. However, those traumatic years were not forgotten; many remembered with horror the bank failures and bankruptcies. An important lesson can often be learned from experience and many would have agreed that such a lesson was in the Senate report that found the banking failures the "result of too much competition."

In the 1950's there was a tremendous resurgence in mergers, resulting in further banking concentration. This brought into conflict once again the two opposing philosophies. The question this time was whether the antitrust laws should be applicable to bank mergers. One side felt in the words of the attorney general that "because of the central role of banks in relation to other businesses, the traditional antitrust goal of prevention of undue concentration is as important in banking as in any other field." The other side countered that to permit unregulated and unrestricted competition to become the business philosophy of banking could only have dire consequences for the general public, which prefers a stable financial structure. Increased concentration lends strength to the resulting institutions which serves as a safeguard against failures.

For five years bills were introduced that sought to check banking concentration. Finally in 1960 the Bank Merger Act was passed. This Act can be viewed as something of a compromise between the two philosophies because it recognized the unique nature of banking and also (though maybe less so) the need for competition. Yet it did not resolve the conflict. In fact it marked only the first round in a policy struggle that was to match Congress and the Supreme Court and one government agency against another. Some observers characterized this struggle as a breakdown in the separation-of-powers doctrine between the legislature and the judiciary. Whether this is true or not, these events did cast doubt on the ability of Congress to regulate economic activity and at the same time provided one of the most interesting chapters in American antitrust history.

WHY DO BANKS MERGE?

Before we discuss the substantive development of bank-merger regulation it would be wise to examine some of the reasons that motivate banks to merge. The principal motivation is the desire to expand the capital assets of the bank. There are federal limitations on the amount a bank can lend based upon a percentage of capital stock and surplus. A bank might fear that with its present assets it would be unable to service its growing industrial clients or to compete for larger industrial clients. This was one of the reasons for the Philadelphia Bank merger and was one of the reasons frequently noted by the comptroller of the currency in his approval of mergers.

Another motivation is the desire to realize economies of scale. Such economies can be realized, even though not to the same extent as in some other industries. For instance, many banks suffer a lack of depth in management. When two banks merge, the best personnel of the banks can be used to manage and develop the larger assets of the combined bank. Furthermore, the larger size of the bank and larger salaries that it can afford can be used to attract new talent. Banks compete with the glamour conglomerates for management personnel; therefore they cannot afford to be considered small backwaters or retirement farms. This was an important factor in the Phillipsburg Bank merger and is another reason the comptroller of the currency has often cited in his approval of mergers.

A third reason is the desire for competitive diversification of deposits and services. By merging, a bank can increase its number of branches or its ability to branch in the future. In the same way a bank can combine its specialty with that of another bank. For example, one bank might have abundant trust funds while the other has a good investment-counseling service. A merger would allow for the maximum efficient use of both.

Sometimes the sheer size of a large bank will force potential competitors to merge in order to meet the challenge. This was the case in the Crocker-Anglo National Bank merger, which was part of an effort to compete with the mammoth Bank of America in California. Although these are not the only motivations for banks to merge, they are certainly the dominant ones. And in almost any merger one can see a variation of them. Yet although there may be justification enough for the stockholders and comptroller, as we shall see, they may not be justification for the courts.

BANK MERGERS AND THE ANTITRUST LAWS

Bank mergers for many years were considered out of the reach of the antitrust laws. Section 7 of the Clayton Act, as discussed in Chapter 14, had a large loophole in that it did not reach asset acquisitions. Historically, banks have almost always combined through such asset acquisitions, with assumption of liabilities or exchanges of stock. One of the reasons for this is that federal law generally prohibits member banks of the Federal Reserve System from directly purchasing corporate stock. Consequently, the Clayton Act did not have much effect on bank mergers in the same way that it had little effect on other industrial mergers.

The Sherman Act applied to bank mergers, but in over seventy years only one case had been filed and that not until 1959. The problem with the Sherman Act was that the government had to prove that the merger had, in fact, already restrained trade unreasonably. This burden of proof was very difficult. This was especially true after the *Columbia Steel* decision in which the Supreme Court established a broad rule-of-reason test for mergers.

There are two other statutes that could have applied antitrust principles to bank mergers: the National Bank Consolidation Act of 1918 and the Federal Deposit Insurance Act. Although each provided banking-agency review of mergers, neither established standards as to the competitive nature or results of the combinations. Furthermore because neither the comptroller of the currency nor the FDIC had much experience in this area, and had not been particularly equipped to give adequate consideration to it, competition was never a strong factor in the public-interest standard applied by these agencies.

Finally, the Federal Reserve Board in Section 11 of the Clayton Act was given authority to enforce compliance with those sections of the Act that were "applicable to banks, banking associations and trust companies." The first time the board used that power in connection with mergers was in 1948 when it filed a complaint that charged Transamerica Corporation with a violation of Section 7 for its systematic acquisition of independent banks for many years over a five-state area. The board entered an order in 1952 requiring substantial divestiture. On appeal, the board was reversed. However, an important point of the decision was that the court of appeals rejected Transamerica's argument that Section 7 was not applicable to banks. Transamerica argued that Congress had always used special banking legislation to regulate banks and that it did not mean to depart from this practice with the Clayton Act. The court held that Section 7 did apply even though it was "doubtless true that the members of Congress in enacting Section 7 of the Clayton

Act in 1914 did not specifically contemplate that 'corporations engaged in commerce' would include banks." Although Transamerica's bank acquisitions were upheld, the court's reasoning on this point was an omen of things to come.

The Effect of the Celler–Kefauver Amendment

As discussed in Chapter 14, Congress became concerned about the growing trend toward industrial concentration and amended the Clayton Act in 1950 to read:

> No Corporation engaged in commerce shall acquire, directly, or indirectly, the whole or any part of the stock or other share capital, and no Corporation *subject to the jurisdiction of the Federal Trade Commission* shall acquire the whole or any part of the assets of another Corporation engaged also in commerce, where in any line of commerce in any section of the country the effect of such acquisition may be substantially to lessen competition or to tend to create a monopoly. [Emphasis supplied.]

At the time it was generally thought that the phrase "subject to the jurisdiction of the Federal Trade Commission" exempted banks from the asset provision because Section 11 of the Act specifically gave jurisdiction over banks to the Federal Reserve Board. Legislators, the banking agencies, and even the heads of the Antitrust Division of the Department of Justice subscribed to this theory. The well-known Kaysen and Turner book *Antitrust Policy,* written in 1959, included banks in its list of industries exempt from the antitrust laws. Furthermore, the *Report of the Attorney General's Committee to Study the Antitrust Laws* gave no special attention to bank mergers. This was later attributed to the lack of case law, legislation, or legal writing connecting bank mergers to the antitrust laws. The position of most observers before 1960 was summarized by the assistant attorney general in charge of the Antitrust Division, Stanley Barnes, in his testimony on a proposal before Congress to amend Section 7 of the Clayton Act to apply to banks:

> The pending proposal would close a loop hole left by present Section 7's failure to cover asset acquisitions by banks. On the one hand, that provision's stock acquisition bar applies to all Corporations, "engaged in commerce." Section 7's acquisition portion, in sharp contrast, covers only Corporations "subject to the jurisdiction of the Federal Trade Commission." Further, Section 11 of the Clayton Act exempts banks from Federal Trade Commission jurisdiction by specifying that "authority to enforce compliance" with Section 7 "is hereby vested . . . in the Federal Reserve Board where applicable to banks, banking associations and trust companies." On the basis of these provisions this Department has concluded that asset acquisition by banks is not covered by Section 7 as amended in 1950.

Bank-Merger Trend

As mentioned earlier, a strong bank-merger trend developed in the early 1950's and became especially strong after 1954. From 1950 to 1958, 1,300 bank combinations occurred involving over $26 billion. Yet even more alarming than the total number of mergers was the dramatic combinations of nationally known banks. In 1955 the Chase National Bank with assets of $5.7 billion merged with both the Bank of Manhattan Company, with assets of $1.6 billion, and the Bronx County Trust Company, with assets of $76 million. The Antitrust Division had made an investigation of this merger and afterward told the banks "we have concluded that this Department would not have jurisdiction to proceed under Section 7 of the Clayton Act." Then Bankers Trust with $2.3 billion in assets acquired Public National with over $500 million in assets, and National City Bank with over $6 billion in assets acquired First National with $715 million in assets. In 1956 the West Coast picked up the trend and the Crocker National Bank with $1.5 billion in assets acquired the Anglo National Bank with $1 billion in assets. By 1960 the four largest banks in the sixteen most important financial centers of the country controlled 60 per cent of all bank assets in those centers. The most startling fact to Congress was that most of these mergers needed no federal approval whatsoever. It was possible for banks to avoid review by all three banking agencies. For instance, the Federal Reserve Board could review a merger only if the merger would produce a member bank with a smaller capital or surplus than the combined capital or surplus of the banks involved in the transaction. It is unusual that the resulting bank could not be provided with capital and surplus to match those of the merging banks. Likewise, the FDIC could not review mergers of FDIC-insured state banks (not members of the Federal Reserve System) when the total capital stock or surplus of the resulting or assuming bank was not less than the aggregate capital stock or aggregate surplus, respectively, of all the merging or consolidating banks or all the parties to the assumptions of the liabilities. Finally, if a national bank purchased assets and assumed liabilities of another bank, the comptroller's approval was not directly acquired unless the capital stock or surplus of the assuming bank would be less than the aggregate capital stock or surplus of the combining banks. It became apparent to everybody that something had to be done.

BANK MERGER ACT OF 1960

Legislative History

Legislation was introduced in Congress throughout the 1950's. In 1956 seven different proposals were introduced to deal with these combinations. Four sought to bring acquisitions of businesses not subject to the jurisdiction of the FTC (which everyone at that time thought included banks) within the scope of Section 7; two would prevent bank acquisitions that would "reduce competition substantially"; and one would have set up standards for judging whether the merger was in the public interest. This last bill was introduced by Senator Robertson who is considered the father of the Bank Merger Act of 1960. It required the banking agencies to consider six noncompetitive or banking factors as well as "whether the effect thereof (of the merger) may be to lessen competition unduly or to tend unduly to create a monopoly. . . ." The "unduly" qualification was criticized because some thought it would allow the banking agencies too much discretion, and as Senator Douglas explained, there is a "tendency for regulatory agencies to be more or less taken over by . . . industries that they are supposed to regulate." Senator Robertson's bill died along with the others but was reintroduced in 1957 and passed the Senate but never reached the floor of the House. In 1959 the bill with a provision for a Department of Justice opinion on the competitive effects of the proposed merger again passed the Senate. The next year the House passed a similar version and it eventually became the Bank Merger Act of 1960.

The Provisions of the BMA of 1960

The Bank Merger Act of 1960 gave the three banking agencies approval rights over mergers among banks in their jurisdiction: the Federal Reserve Board over the state member banks, the FDIC over state nonmember banks, and the comptroller of the currency over national banks. This meant that approximately 95 per cent of the banks in the United States were required to have federal approval for their mergers. The agencies had to consider two sets of factors—competitive and banking. The banking factors were (1) the financial history and condition of each of the banks involved, (2) the adequacy of its structure, (3) its future earning prospects, (4) the general character of its management, (5) the convenience and needs of the community to be served, and (6) whether or not its corporate powers are consistent with the purpose of this Act. The competitive factor was simply defined as the "effect of the transaction on competition (including any tendency toward monopoly)." The term *unduly* had been dropped along the way. The agency was not to approve the transaction "unless, considering all of such factors, it finds a transaction to be in the public interest." Although this was more guidance than had ever been given the banking agencies concerning merger approval, it still did not spell out the weight that was to be given to each factor or set of facts. The legislative history is confused and not very instructive on this point. However, it can be safely said that most legislators agreed with the sentiment of the House report that concluded "some bank mergers are in the public interest, even though they lessen competition to a degree."

As a result of this ambiguity the three banking agencies developed different policies in applying the criteria set up in the statute. The comptroller of the currency followed a "balanced banking structure" policy. This stressed the range of bank size. It was thought that each market should have a range of small, medium, and large banks. The FDIC stressed a "strengthening of competition" concept. According to this, disparity in bank sizes was to be avoided. Finally, the Federal Reserve Board followed a variety-of-banking-services doctrine. The board felt it was important that there be a broad range of banking services available to the public and was less concerned about the particular size of the banks in the market.

It is interesting to note that although the agencies differed in their criteria for approval, they reached the same result: overwhelming approval of bank mergers. In the five-year period from 1960 to 1965 almost 900 bank-merger applications were reviewed by the three banking agencies and only thirty-one were denied. A survey of the applications for 1963 revealed that two thirds of the proposed mergers were deemed to have anticompetitive effects by the Department of Justice. It became obvious that the Department of Justice and the banking agencies were talking two different languages. The department was using straight antitrust principles which emphasized the protection of competition over the protection of competitors, whereas the banking agencies were concerned with and attuned to the problems of the banks or the "competitors." Although it is no wonder that they reached different results, one might ask whether the extraordinary rate of bank-merger approval was the result Congress intended when it passed the Bank Merger Act of 1960. The impetus for the Act had been Congressional concern over the reduction in the number of banks, which caused an increase in the concentration of banking assets in numerous markets. There was also fear that financing would become unavailable to small businesses because it was felt that larger banks would be less inclined to deal sympathetically with small borrowers, many of whom rely on reputation in the community for credit. It is doubtful that anyone in Congress had anticipated this wholesale approval of bank-merger applications. As one critic from within the industry put it, "in the years since the Bank Merger Act of 1960 became operative the bank supervisory agencies, especially the Comptroller of the Currency, have demonstrated that they are merger happy. They almost never see a bad merger." He was not the only one concerned with the bank-agency situation. President Johnson in 1964, citing "a lack of coordination of action and procedures among the Federal agencies charged with responsibility for the regulation of banks," directed the secretary of the treasury "to establish procedures which will insure that every effort is made by these agencies to act in concert and compose their differences." The comptroller himself complained that "with the administrative approach to bank mergers in such a state of conflict, it is virtually impossible for a reasonably prudent banker to plan intelligently for future expansion." As a result, the secretary of the treasury and the attorney general created an Interdepartmental Committee on Bank Mergers in which all four agencies were represented. By this time though the Department of Justice had filed its own suits to enjoin mergers that had been approved by the banking agencies and the comptroller in turn was seeking to intervene to oppose the Department of Justice. It was apparent that the system was not healthy.

The Justice Department suits brought many questions concerning the Bank Merger Act of 1960 before the courts. The first was whether the Act precluded Justice from suing under the antitrust laws. There had been references in both Houses to the fact that the bill "would not affect in anyway the applicability of the Sherman Act to bank mergers." This was not much of a concession, though, because in 1948 the Supreme Court decision in *Columbia Steel* was considered to have greatly emasculated the ability of the Sherman Act to deal with mergers. Furthermore, as noted earlier, most people felt that the Clayton Act was of little significance in dealing with bank mergers, for it was thought to apply only to stock acquisitions which could be easily avoided. In fact the idea of the Justice Department attacking bank mergers was probably not seriously considered by any of the drafters of the Act and, as noted earlier, the idea was rejected by the Justice Department itself for a long time.

The unscrambling of the regulatory scheme, therefore, was left to the courts. This is not an unusual occurrence. Many times the legislative process produces ambiguities that force the courts to define the law. In these circumstances there may not be any "true intent" of a bill and the court will be forced to make a choice out of a number of practical alternatives. The result may be that the effect of the Act is something other than most of the legislators had imagined. The court, unlike the legislature, cannot duck hard questions by drafting ambigious phrases. No matter how difficult the choice, it must reach a conclusion. It is interesting to note, however, that in the Supreme Court opinions which were to follow, it did not appear that the choices were as difficult for the Court to make as they were for Congress and bankers to accept.

THE COURT AND BANK MERGERS: ROUND ONE

Although the decision in *Transamerica Corporation,* discussed earlier, gave notice that Section 7 of the Clayton Act applied to banks, the decision in the first Justice Department bank-merger suit, *Firstamerica Corp.,* gave notice that the Department of Justice and the courts were not going to defer to the jurisdiction of banking agencies in approval of bank mergers. Justice filed suit in March of 1959 charging that the acquisition of California Bank by the bank-holding company Firstamerica was a violation of both Section 1 of the Sherman Act and Section 7 of the Clayton Act. The defendants moved to dismiss on the grounds that the Federal Reserve Board had already approved the merger and under Section 11 of the Clayton Act it had exclusive jurisdiction. The court denied the motion and the Supreme Court denied a petition for *certiorari*. This rejection of the concept that banking agencies had exclusive or primary jurisdiction over bank mergers was to set the tone for the government suits and subsequent court decisions that were to follow the passage of the Bank Merger Act of 1960 in the next year.

Philadelphia National Bank

After the BMA of 1960 was signed into law, the Justice Department quickly dispelled any doubt about its intentions to continue to sue under the antitrust laws. It filed four bank suits in 1961, the first of which was *United States* v. *Philadelphia National Bank*.

The comptroller of the currency had approved this merger after receiving the three reports required by the Bank Merger Act of 1960 from the FDIC, the Federal Reserve Board, and the Department of Justice. All three reports found that the merger would have anticompetitive effects. The purpose of these reports was to give uniformity to the judgments of the banking agencies. However, as discussed earlier, this rarely occurred. In this case the comptroller reasoned that "[s]ince there will remain an adequate number of alternative sources of banking services in Philadelphia, and in view of the beneficial effects of this consolidation upon international and national competition it was concluded that the overall effect upon competition would not be unfavorable." Furthermore, he concluded that the new bank "would be far better able to serve the convenience and needs of its community by being of material assistance to this city and state in their efforts to attract new industry and to retain existing industry." The day after the comptroller had approved the merger the Justice Department filed suit in the Eastern District of Pennsylvania charging violations of Section 1 of the Sherman Act and Section 7 of the Clayton Act.

The district court agreed with the Justice Department that it was entitled to sue under the antitrust laws, holding the BMA of 1960 did not repeal by implication the antitrust laws insofar as they applied to bank mergers. It is also agreed that the product market or "line of commerce" was "commercial banking." However, after that, the court and the Justice Department parted company. It held Section 7 was inapplicable to bank mergers accomplished through acquisition of assets because banks are not "subject to the jurisdiction of the Federal Trade Commission." But even assuming that Section 7 was applicable, the court found that the government's delineation of the four-county Philadelphia metropolitan area was not the proper geographic market; yet even assuming that it was, there still was no reasonable probability that competition among commercial banks in the area would be substantially lessened as a result of the merger. As to the Sherman Act charge the court found that because the merger did not violate the Clayton Act, a fortiori, it did not violate Section 1 of the Sherman Act.

On appeal the defendants did not contest the adverse findings of the district court (line of commerce, right of Justice to sue under antitrust laws), but concentrated on supporting those rulings favorable to it. Both parties emphasized the alleged Sherman Act violation in their briefs and paid little attention to the Section 7 case. The government did not even discuss this charge in its reply brief. Ironically, the Supreme Court did not reach the question of violation of the Sherman Act, for in a decision that stunned the banking community, it found that the "merger of appellees is forbidden by §7 of the Clayton Act and so must be enjoined. . . ." Justice Brennan's opinion was a tour de force for which very few lawyers or congressmen, or, for that matter, anyone else, were prepared. The opinion dealt with several issues. Following are the main points of the decision, with a summary of the Court's reasoning for each point:

1. *Bank mergers through asset acquisitions are subject to Section 7 of the Clayton Act.* The Court found a Congressional desire to embrace bank mergers in the legislative history of the statute. It reasoned that the Celler–Kefauver amendment was designed to close loopholes that had allowed mergers. In order to close loopholes, Congress contemplated that the 1950 amendment would give Section 7 a reach that would bring the entire range of corporate amalgamations, from pure stock acquisitions to pure asset acquisitions within the scope of Section 7. To reach this conclusion the Court read together the stock-acquisition and asset-acquisition portions of Section 7. Approached in this manner, Section 7 would apply to mergers "which fit neither category perfectly but lie somewhere between the two ends of the spectrum." This then limited the qualifying phrase "subject to the jurisdiction of the Federal Trade Commission," which had previously been thought to exclude bank mergers, to straight asset acquisitions when not accomplished by merger. The Court went on to cite reasons why this was the only possible interpretation of the section: (1) any other interpretation would create a large loophole in a statute designed to close a loophole; (2) Congress was aware of the difference between a merger and a pure purchase of assets, and its intent was to cover mergers; (3) the phrase *subject to the jurisdiction of the Federal Trade Commission* was meant to make explicit the role of the FTC in administering the section and was not meant to undercut the dominant purpose of eliminating the difference in treatment accorded stock acquisitions and mergers by the original Section 7 as construed; and (4) immunity from the antitrust laws is not lightly to be implied.

The Court realized that its construction of amended Section 7 was different from that voiced by members of Congress and, for a time, the Justice Department. Yet it noted that the "views of a subsequent Congress form a hazardous basis for inferring the intent on an earlier one." It stressed also that there were no Supreme Court opinions upon which these other views were based and which therefore might bind the Court in this opinion. It concluded: "[t]he design fashioned in the Bank Merger Act was predicated upon uncertainties to the scope of §7 and we do no violence to that design by dispelling the uncertainty."

2. *The Bank Merger Act of 1960 did not preclude application of the*

antitrust laws. The Court noted that no express immunity was conferred by the Act and as mentioned earlier repeals of the antitrust laws by implications are strongly disfavored. Furthermore, it found that Congress did not embrace the view that the banking regulation was so pervasive that the enforcement of the antitrust laws would be unnecessary or disruptive. It noted that the primary jurisdiction of the banking agency, if there was any, would not bar jurisdiction of the courts but would only postpone it. But here primary jurisdiction was not a problem because the agency had already acted. The Court went on to state that it would be anomalous to conclude that Congress, while intending that the Sherman Act remain fully applicable to bank mergers and Section 7 be applicable to pure stock acquisitions by banks, nevertheless intended Section 7 to be completely inapplicable to bank mergers.

3. *The merger is in violation of Section 7 of the Clayton Act.* The Court had "no difficulty" in finding that the "line of commerce" or product market was the "cluster of products and services" or "commercial banking"; or that the "section of the country" or geographic market was the four-county area advocated by the Justice Department. It declared that the standard for determining a geographic market was "where within the area of competitive overlap, the effect of the merger on competition will be direct and immediate." The Court noted that the four-county area was a market "which state law apparently recognizes as a meaningful banking community . . . and which would seem roughly to delineate the area in which bank customers that are neither very large nor very small find it practical to do their banking business. . . ." As to the standard for determining the probable competitive effects of a bank merger, the Court stated, "we think that a merger which produces a firm controlling an undue percentage share of the relevant market, and results in the significant increase in the concentration of firms in that market, is so inherently likely to lessen competition substantially that it must be enjoined in the absence of evidence clearly showing that the merger is not likely to have such anti-competitive effects." Philadelphia National Bank's market share of 30 percent clearly presented to the Court a threat of undue concentration. It also noted that the increase of 33 percent in the concentration of the market as a result of the merger was significant. Finally it defended its conclusion that Philadelphia National Bank's percentage share raised an inference of anticompetitive effects even though neither the terms of Section 7 nor the legislative history of the Act suggested that any particular percentage share was deemed critical by Congress.

4. *Affirmative defenses.* The Court rejected all three of defendants' affirmative defenses:

a. *The only way to follow customers to the suburbs is by branching through mergers.* The Court made short shrift of this by indicating the alternative is *de novo* branching and that "surely one premise of an antimerger statute such as §7 is that corporate growth by internal expansion is socially preferable to growth by acquisition."

b. *Enlarged lending limits as a result of the merger would allow the bank to compete with large out-of-state banks.* The Court rejected this "application of 'countervailing power'" saying that "if anti-competitive effects in one market could be justified by pro-competitive consequences in another, the logical upshot would be that every firm in an industry could, without violating §7, embark on a series of mergers that would make it in the end as large as the industry leader." And in the city of Philadelphia the result would be that only one bank would remain, because all the banks combined would still be smaller that the largest bank in New York City.

c. *Philadelphia needs a bank larger than it has now in order to bring industry to the area and to stimulate economic development.* The Court responded with a straight antitrust analysis:

> we are clear, however, that a merger the effect of which "may be substantially to lessen competition" is not saved because, on some ultimate reckoning of social or economic debits or credits, it may be deemed beneficial. . . . Congress determined to preserve our traditionally competitive economy. It therefore prescribed anticompetitive mergers, the benign and the malignant alike, fully aware, we must assume, that some price might have to be paid.

This argument disturbed critics and the banking industry the most because it had been thought that the BMA of 1960 if nothing else provided the modest concession that some mergers were to be allowed even if they had anticompetitive effects.

There is no doubt that Justice Brennan's opinion was an example of ingenious and skillful judicial reasoning. Yet as two critics observed, "the Court's legal analysis was designed to justify an overriding policy decision, not to aid in determining the appropriate result." Of this there can be little doubt.

After the initial shock, there followed a virtual flood of criticism attacking this opinion. One of the most well reasoned was Justice Harlan's dissenting opinion. However, there is no need to go into those criticisms here. The point to remember is that the Supreme Court served notice that the antitrust laws were to be applied to bank mergers and that this industry was not going to be treated differently from any other, not withstanding the BMA of 1960. Justice Harlan was not exaggerating when he said that the result of *Philadelphia Bank* was "that the Bank Merger Act is almost completely nullified."

Lexington Bank

The *Lexington Bank* case was filed one month after the *Philadelphia Bank* case. For some reason the Justice Department did not include a Section 7 count, but relied solely on the Sherman Act in its complaint. If it had been otherwise, the Supreme Court would never have decided the applicability of the Sherman Act because this case like *Philadelphia Bank* would have been won or lost on the easier Section 7 standard.

This merger was a consolidation of two commercial banks whose principal places of business were in Lexington, Kentucky. The two banks were ranked first and fourth in total assets, deposits, and loans among the commercial banks in the geographic market which was determined to be Fayette County in Tennessee. The two banks also held 94 per cent of all trust assets, 92 per cent of all trust earnings, and 79 per cent of all trust accounts in that county. After the consolidation the bank was bigger than all the remaining commercial banks in a market where the five largest banks held 99 per cent of the total deposits. The comptroller of the currency, as in *Philadelphia National Bank,* received adverse reports on the competitive effect from the FDIC, the Federal Reserve Board, and the Justice Department. Nevertheless, he approved the merger. The Justice Department filed suit two days after the comptroller's approval, on the same day the merger was effected.

The district court, after a trial on the matter, dismissed the government's suit holding that no violation of either Section 1 or Section 2 of the Sherman Act had been shown. The Supreme Court reversed the lower court on the Section 1 count and never reached the Section 2 monopolization charge.

The principal significance of the case was that the Court brushed aside the *Columbia Steel* criteria and relied on a "major competitive factor" theory. In *Columbia Steel* the Court had said:

> In determining what constitutes unreasonable restraint, we do not think the dollar value is in itself of compelling significance; we look rather to the percentage of business controlled, the strength of the remaining competition, whether the action springs from business requirements or purpose to monopolize, the probable development of the industry, consumer demands, and other characteristics of the market. We do not undertake to prescribe any set of percentage figures by which to measure the reasonableness of a corporation's enlargement of its activities by the purchase of the assets of a competitor. The relative effect of percentage command of a market varies with the setting in which that factor is placed.

Justice Douglas, speaking for the Court in *Lexington Bank,* declared "[t]he Columbia Steel case must be confined to its special facts." However, he noted that even if the factors in *Columbia Steel* were considered they pointed against the merger. But "where, as here, the merging companies are *major competitive factors in a relevant market, the elimination of significant competition between them constitutes a violation of §1 of the Sherman Act.*" (Emphasis supplied.) In support of this proposition Justice Douglas did not provide any independent reasoning or analysis, but relied solely upon four railroad-merger cases decided at the turn of the century. He found that the "major competitive factor" standard derived from those cases was met in the present case in view of the fact that the two banks in question had such a large share of the relevant market.

Justice Brennan and Justice White concurred in the result but would have relied solely on the conclusion that the factors relied on in *Columbia Steel* clearly compelled the reversal. Justice Harlan, joined by Justice Stewart, dissented, declaring that the opinion amounted "to an invocation of formulas of antitrust numerology and a presumption that in the antitrust field good things come usually, if not always, in small packages." As a result of this opinion, it was now almost as easy to enjoin a merger under the Sherman Act as under Section 7 of Clayton. Although it is true, quoting Justice Harlan again, that this case was "doomed to be a novelty in the reports" (because of the effect of the *Philadelphia Bank* decision on Section 7 the year before), it was still significant because as one observer noted, it demonstrated "not merely that the Court does not accept, but that apparently it is actually hostile to, any attempted construction of banking statutes which would tend to inhibit the application of the anti-trust laws to banking."

CONGRESS AND BANK MERGERS: ROUND TWO—BANK MERGER ACT OF 1966

Legislative History

The *Philadelphia Bank* decision as mentioned earlier caused considerable concern both in Congress and in the banking industry. Senator Robertson, chairman of the Senate Banking and Currency Committee, who had been one of the principal authors of the Bank Merger Act of 1960, was among the first to complain that the decision did not come close to reflecting Congress' intent. Bankers were upset because it not only presented problems for future bank mergers but also threatened the legality of approximately 2,000 bank mergers that had occurred since the 1950 amendment of the Clayton Act. (The threat to these mergers was not imaginary for the Justice Department in the *Du Pont–General Motors* case filed suit thirty years after the particular stock acquisition was made.) Furthermore two bank-merger litigations, which started before *Philadelphia Bank* decision, were going to be affected seriously by its result. They were *Manufacturers-Hanover* in New York and *Continental-Illinois* in Chicago. Needless to say they also had lobbyists pushing for legislative relief.

To resolve these problems Senator Robertson introduced a bill to amend the Bank Merger Act of 1960 and alter radically the *Philadelphia Bank* result. It (1) would have given the banking agencies "exclusive and plenary authority to approve mergers, consolidations, acquisitions of stock or assets and assumptions of liabilities" and would have immunized approved transactions from suits under the antitrust laws; and (2) would have given immunity to insured banks which had merged before the passage of the Bank Merger Act of 1960 from future prosecution under the antitrust laws. This bill was supported by the American Bankers Association and the majority of state banking associations. The banking agencies also appeared to be in favor of it. However, the Independent Bankers Association, which did not believe in the proposal that all bank mergers were for the good, wanted a provision inserted that would allow the Justice Department to sue within a certain period of time after the merger was approved by a federal banking agency. To gain further support for the Robertson bill, Senator Proxmire introduced this "now or never" amendment which, although a major compromise, was accepted.

When the bill went over to the House it ran into a formidable roadblock in the person of Congressman Wright Patman, the chairman of the House Banking and Currency Committee. An indication of the fight the banking interests would face was his first reaction to the bill: "if you exempt banks from antitrust, you might as well also shoot the policeman on the corner." He sought to delay hearings on the bill in order to drum up opposition to it. Meanwhile, Congressman Ashley introduced another measure that would require bank-agency hearings with court of appeals review. This was objected to by the Department of Justice as being unnecessary because in the vast majority of applications there were no serious antitrust problems, and when there were serious problems, the public disclosure of pertinent financial data would not be appropriate for review of bank mergers. Congressman Ashley with Congressman Ottinger then revised the bill, allowing for suits by the Justice Department. However, it also provided that a merger which would violate the antitrust laws was to be approved if the adverse competitive effect would be clearly outweighed by the transaction's meeting the convenience and needs of the community to be served.

Although compromises were being made to gain support for the bill, Chairman Patman was not interested. He did not envision a need for any bank-merger bill and was not interested in furthering the progress of the two before him. He delayed so long in holding hearings that Congressman Ashley with a majority of the Banking Committee convened a session of the committee without informing him. He was furious when he learned of the meeting and ordered it disbanded. The majority rebuffed him and reported out the Ashley–Ottinger bill. Immediately both Congressman Patman and Congressman Reuss took the position that the meeting was a rump session held without sanction and that therefore the bill was defective. Congressman Reuss then requested both the attorney general and the secretary of the treasury to comment on proposals he was going to submit. He adopted these comments into his amendment and it appeared that a floor fight might result between the Reuss and Ashley–Ottinger proposals. To avoid this, the proponents of the Ashley–Ottinger bill agreed to further compromises, and Congressman Patman, who was against the bill "as a matter of principle," agreed to introduce it. It was passed in the House and the Senate *in toto* and was signed by the president.

BMA of 1966—Main Provisions

The following is a summary of the important sections of the Act:

§1828(c):

(1) No insured bank could merge or consolidate in any manner without the approval of the banking agency with jurisdiction over it.

(4) Reports on the competitive factors had to be sought from the attorney general and the other two banking agencies unless the agency felt it must act immediately in order to prevent the probable failure of one of the banks.

(5) The standards for agency approval were as follows:

the agency shall not approve—
(A) any proposed merger or transaction which would result in a monopoly, or which would be in furtherance of any combination or conspiracy to monopolize or attempt to monopolize the business of banking in any part of the United States, or
(B) any other proposed merger transaction whose effect in any section of the country may be substantially to lessen competition, or to tend to create a monopoly, or which in any other manner would be in restraint of trade, unless it finds that the anticompetitive effects of the proposed transaction are clearly outweighed in the public interest by the probable effect of the transaction in meeting the convenience and needs of the community to be served.

(6) Except in emergencies, the merger could not be consummated before the thirtieth calendar day after the date of the approval by the agency.

(7) (A) A suit under the antitrust laws filed before the legal date for consummation of the merger would stay the effectiveness of the agency approval unless the court should otherwise specifically order. In a suit under the antitrust laws the court should "review *de novo*" the issues presented.

(7) (B) In antitrust suits other than under Section 2 of the Sherman Act, the standards applied by the court should be identical with those that the banking agencies were directed to apply under paragraph (5).

(7) (C) Upon termination of an antitrust suit, or the period in which antitrust suits could be filed, the merger was then exempt from further antitrust suits except those proceedings based on the theory that the merger alone and of itself constituted a violation of Section 2 of the Sherman Act.

(7) (D) Any state or federal banking agency that had jurisdiction over the bank had a right to appear as a party of its own motion and as of right in any antitrust suit that attacked a bank merger approved by a federal banking agency.

The Act raised almost as many questions as it answered. The *Wall Street Journal,* on February 8, 1966, two weeks before the Act became effective, remarked:

> And now, after months of comic parliamentary pratfalls and fishwifery invective, the bank merger bill is about to pass. Sure enough, it reasserts congressional authority over the subject. But that reassertion is so vaguely worded that the Supreme Court inevitably will be asked to define what Congress really meant, and the honorable Justices will have considerable leeway again to make their own law.
>
> The incredible history of the bank merger bill demonstrates again just how hard it is for Congress to shape business regulatory policy.

The following questions remained ultimately for the Supreme Court to decide after the passage of the Act.

(1) Were the standards in (5)(B) to be pleaded by the plaintiff to state a cause of action or did they establish an affirmative defense to a suit under the antitrust law?
(2) What was the effect of the omission of the phrase "in any line of commerce" in paragraph (5)(B)? Was this omitted in order to eliminate the "commercial banking" line of commerce established in *Philadelphia Bank?*
(3) Section (7)(A), which stated that an antitrust suit shall stay the approval of the merger "unless the court shall otherwise specifically order," raised the obvious question of what standard the court should use in determining whether to dissolve the stay.
(4) What did the phrase in Section (7)(A) "the court shall review *de novo* the issues presented" mean? "Review *de novo*" had no precedent in federal administrative statutes; the usual expression was "try *de novo*." Therefore, what was the scope of judicial review of federal banking-agency approval?
(5) How was the agency and the court to apply the standards set up in Section (5)(B) and what weight was to be given to the "convenience and needs of the community" in offsetting the anticompetitive effects of the merger?

The Act did resolve some points that had bothered both the banks and Congress. Mergers consummated prior to June 17, 1963 (the date of the *Philadelphia Bank* decision), were "conclusively presumed to have not been in violation of any antitrust laws other than Section 2 of (the Sherman Act)." This gave immunity to those 2,000 mergers as well as the Manufacturers-Hanover, Continental-Illinois, and Lexington Bank mergers. Mergers consummated after June 16, 1963, and not attacked by the time the Act went into effect, unless attacked on a Section 2 charge, were also immune. For mergers consummated after *Philadelphia Bank* but before the Act went into effect, the courts were to apply the standards set forth in the Act. There was also the Proxmire "now or never" provision, which would give banks immunity from suits thirty days after agency approval. Furthermore, it was now impossible for the courts to ignore the "convenience and needs" provisions of the Act; they could never say again, as Justice Brennan did in *Philadelphia Bank,* that Congress proscribed anticompetitive mergers, the "benign and the malignant alike."

In the series of compromises to gain support for the bill, the banks did lose significant benefits from Senator Robertson's bill. There was no longer a provision for exclusive jurisdiction in the banking agencies. Also, the banks because of the automatic-stay provision could not slip a merger by an overworked Justice Department. Finally, the competitive factor was elevated to being the prime factor rather than one among many, as in the BMA of 1960. However, this provision was still better than the *Philadelphia Bank* result of having competition as the only factor in determining the legality of the merger.

THE COURTS TAKE OVER: ROUND THREE

There were six lower-court opinions before the Supreme Court had an opportunity to rule on the BMA of 1966. These six are interesting for the fact that of the eight judges who heard these cases (a three-judge panel sat on the *Crocker-Anglo* case), not one came close to the Supreme Court's interpretation of the Act.

The Houston and Provident Decision

The first Supreme Court review decided two bank-merger cases in one opinion. Banks in Texas and Pennsylvania applied to the comptroller of the currency for approval of bank mergers. In what was a familiar scenario the Federal Reserve Board and the attorney general both submitted adverse reports and the comptroller went ahead and approved the mergers. The United States filed civil suits under Section 7 of the Clayton Act in both Texas and Pennsylvania and both district courts dismissed the suits. The comptroller intervened in the suit under the authority of the BMA of 1966.

The opinion discussed *four* major questions concerning the Act: (1) the burden of pleading, (2) the burden of proof, (3) the scope of review, and (4) the standards for determining whether to lift the statutory stay. It was a rare Supreme Court bank-merger opinion for two reasons. The first was that it was a unanimous decision. (In fact it has been the only unanimous Supreme Court bank-merger decision.) The second was that there was little criticism of it.

The five procedural issues are of sufficient importance that it would be worthwhile briefly to summarize the court's rulings:

Pleading. Defendants had contended that the complaints were defective because they did not mention the Bank Merger Act of 1966 but only cited Section 7 of the Clayton Act. The Justice Department left out reference to the Act in order to place the burden of pleading and proof of the "convenience and needs" issue on the defendants. Otherwise the initial government investigation would have to be much more thorough and the government would have to delay the filing of the suit or the trial date in order to prepare to plead and prove this issue in its case in chief. Quoting the language of the Act, the Supreme Court held that an action challenging a bank merger on the grounds of its anticompetitive effects was meant to be brought under the antitrust laws and not the BMA of 1966. The Court stated:

> There is no indication that an action challenging a merger . . . is bottomed on the Bank Merger Act of 1966 rather than on the antitrust laws. What is apparent is that Congress intended that a defense or justification be available once it had been determined that a transaction would have anticompetitive effects, as judged by the standards normally applied in antitrust actions.

Burden of Proof. As to the question of whether the burden of proof is on the defendant banks to establish that an anticompetitive merger is within the exception of 12 U.S.C. §1828(c)(5)(B) ("convenience and needs of the community") or whether it was on the government, the Court found it "plain that the banks carry the burden. That is the general rule where one claims the benefits of an exception to the prohibition of a statute." Justice Douglas went on to quote from a statement Congressman Patman made when he introduced the bill. This is, of course, questionable support, because it was acknowledged by everybody, including Congressman Patman, that he was a bitter enemy of the bill. Quoting individual legislators as to the meaning of an act is always tricky business, but at least the legislator chosen should have no axe to grind when he makes the remarks. In any case it is questionable whether putting this burden of proof on the banks is harmful to them. Any bank, having thoroughly prepared the bank-merger application, should be ready to go forward with this type of evidence, and only if the evidence is evenly divided (which is rare) will the banks lose because they have the burden of proof. Furthermore, this will speed up the trial because the banks will be ready quicker than the government would be. One might question whether a speedy trial helps an antitrust defendant. Normally not, but in a bank case there will probably be an automatic stay in effect; therefore any time saved will be of benefit to both the banks and the government.

Scope of Review. The Court found no intent in Congress to change the administrative procedure spelled out in *Philadelphia Bank.* In support of this the Court noted that Congress had traditionally put antitrust suits involving regulated industries on a different basis than was familiar in administrative procedure generally. Furthermore, the Act itself stated that the standards for the agency and the court review should be the same. This is not the conventional judicial administrative review standard, which is whether the agency's action is supported by the evidence.

It appears that the phrase *review de novo* was an example of unfortunate draftmanship. In any case the Court focused on the words *de novo* and *issues presented* rather than on the ambiguous term *review*. It found that these two phrases indicated that an independent court determination was desired by Congress. Furthermore, the Court noted that the comptroller's proceedings were informal and no hearings in the customary sense were held. Nor did the BMA of 1966 require the comptroller to hold formal hearings. Therefore to hold that there should be only an administrative review of the agency proceedings would force the Court "to assume that Congress made a revolutionary innovation by making administrative action well nigh conclusive, even though no hearing had been held and no record in the customary sense created."

Weight of the Comptroller's Decision. The Court rejected the constitutional arguments that to have the Court judge the factors enumerated in the BMA of 1966 would force the Court to perform nonjudicial tasks. It noted the long prevalent "rule-of-reason" approach in antitrust law in which appraisal of competitive factors had always been "grist for the antitrust mill." Consequently, it held that no special weight should be given to the agency approval and that "it is the court's judgment, not the Comptroller's, that finally determines whether the merger is legal."

Standards on Dissolving the Automatic Stay. The Court was very firm on the point that a stay should not be dissolved except in extraordinary conditions: ". . . absent a frivolous complaint by the United States, which we presume will be infrequent, a stay is essential until the judicial remedies have been exhausted." The Court noted that the caption of the Act stated that it was designed "to establish a procedure . . . to eliminate the necessity for the dissolution of merged banks." Furthermore, it found the legislative history was "replete with references to the difficulty of unscrambling two or more banks *after* their merger." Therefore, the "normal procedure should be maintenance of the status quo until the antitrust litigation has run its course, lest consummation take place and the unscrambling process that Congress abhorred *in the case of banks* be necessary." (Court's emphasis.)

There was little adverse reaction to the *Provident–Houston* decision and even some Congressional endorsement. One of the reasons may have been that after the *Philadelphia Bank* and *Lexington Bank,* most observers had prepared themselves for the worst or at least a reaffirmation of the policies behind those opinions. Although the decision differed dramatically from the six lower-court decisions, it was consistent with past Supreme Court opinions. The appeal had been concerned with procedural issues only; therefore the Court offered no views on the merits of the mergers or on the justifications that were urged in their support. Therefore the very important question concerning the meaning of the "convenience and needs" defense and when it would outweigh the anticompetitive effects of a merger was left for later opinions to spell out.

Nashville Bank

United States v. *Third National Bank in Nashville* was decided in the next Supreme Court term. The district court had upheld the merger on the grounds that it would not tend substantially to lessen competition, but even assuming there was an anticompetitive effect, it would be outweighed by the benefit to the convenience and needs of the community. It also ruled that as a result of the BMA of 1966, the *Philadelphia Bank* criteria for judging the anticompetitive effect of a merger was no longer applicable and it adopted a *Columbia Steel*-type standard.

The Supreme Court reversed. It reiterated that *Columbia Steel* had been confined to its facts in *Lexington Bank* and the BMA of 1966 did not change this. Therefore, the straight antitrust *Philadelphia Bank* standard was to be used in judging the anticompetitive effects of a merger. Judging the proposed merger by that standard, the Court unanimously concluded that the merger was anticompetitive. The larger bank had 40 per cent of the city's banking business and the smaller bank, which was not a failing concern, had previously been an important competitive element in certain facets of city banking.

The most important point of the decision concerned the "convenience-and-needs" defense. The Court set up a two-step process for establishing the defense. As usual the trial court would have to decide that the benefit to "convenience and needs of the community" clearly outweighed the anticompetitive effect, but first it must find that the banks made a reasonable effort to solve the problems they claimed justified the merger or at least find that such efforts would have been unlikely to succeed. In other words, the trial court in the first step must "sufficiently or reliably establish the unavailability of alternate solutions."

Finally, the Court determined that because the district court did not correctly analyze the anticompetitive effects of the merger, it could not have properly weighed the countervailing benefits to the community. Therefore, the case was remanded for a new balancing of the competitive and "convenience and needs" factors to determine whether the merger was in the public interest.

RESULT OF *PROVIDENT–HOUSTON* AND *NASHVILLE BANK*

After these two Supreme Court opinions there was not much left of the Bank Merger Act of 1966. Although Justice White in *Nashville Bank* had recognized that Congress "wished to alter both the procedures by which the Justice Department challenges bank mergers and the legal standard which courts apply in judging those mergers," the result of both opinions was that the straight antitrust standard was still king.

The end result of the years of legislative activity that produced the BMA of 1966 can be briefly summarized: (1) The 2,000 bank mergers consummated before *Philadelphia Bank* and after the Celler–Kefauver amendment were immunized; (2) three bank mergers attacked by the Justice Department were saved from divestiture; (3) the Justice Department was given a thirty-day period in which to decide whether to sue; (4) Justice was also given an automatic stay of the merger approval once it filed suit; and (5) the "convenience-and-needs-of-the-community" defense was established. In retrospect it appears that Justice and the three banks were the real winners because the convenience and needs defense was severely limited by *Nashville Bank* and the Justice Department had little objection to the immunization of those 2,000 or more consummated but unattacked mergers. The automatic stay was a substantial aid to the government, for preliminary injunctions are never easy to obtain and the denial of a preliminary injunction motion is not appealable to, what the government and others might consider, a more sympathetic Supreme Court.

An example of how valuable this stay provision can be was seen in the recent case of *United States* v. *United Banks of Colorado*. This was a bank-holding-company merger but the automatic stay language in the Bank Holding Company Act of 1966 is identical to that in BMA of 1966. The defendants argued that the stay should be lifted because (1) if it was not lifted the contractual arrangements to acquire the bank would expire and the government might defeat the merger without reaching the merits of the case; (2) there was substantial doubt that the government would prevail on the merits because the case presented a novel, experimental, and untried extension of antitrust theory; and (3) the government did not need a stay because the bank-holding company would maintain the bank as a separate entity and would agree to any reasonable hold-separate order. The district court concluded that although there may have been some equity to defendant's claim, it had failed to prove the narrow issue of whether the government's complaint was "frivolous" under the *Provident–Houston* standard. Therefore it had "failed to establish their burden to overturn the statutory stay." If more courts construe the standard as strictly as this one did, no defendant will be able to get the stay lifted, for whatever one might say about the Antitrust Division's complaints, they certainly are not "frivolous."

It is safe to assume that the opinions in *Provident–Houston* and *Nashville Bank* served to nip many prospective mergers in the bud. One can see that there is little point in banks going through the complicated preparation for a merger if it becomes obvious that there is more than an excellent chance the merger will be killed in the courts—even if it would be approved by the banking agencies. This prophylactic effect was greatly enhanced by the next Supreme Court opinion, *United States* v. *Phillipsburg National Bank*. This was a significant opinion for a number of reasons, one of which was that the banks involved were so small. Previously the government had attacked mergers that would have resulted in banks with total assets ranging from $6 billion to $389 million. The Phillipsburg merger, on the other hand, would have produced a bank with $41 million in assets. It was now time for the small banks to look up and pay attention to those opinions being handed down in Washington.

Phillipsburg National Bank

Phillipsburg involved the proposed merger of two of three small competing commercial banks located in the city of Phillipsburg, New Jersey. The district court, while recognizing "commercial banking" as a relevant product market, looked to certain submarkets that involved competition with other financial institutions. It rejected the geographic market that had been recognized by the FDIC, the Federal Reserve Board, and the Department of Justice in their determination that the merger "would have significantly harmful effect upon competition in that area." Finally the district court dismissed the complaint, holding that there was no showing of probable anticompetitive effect and if there was any possibility of anticompetitive effect in the geographic market suggested by the government, it would be outweighed by the benefit of the "convenience and needs" of Phillipsburg.

The Supreme Court reversed and found error in each of these holdings. From Justice Brennan's opinion we can derive certain guidelines that will be of assistance in the planning of future bank mergers—large and small. The first is that "commercial banking" is the product market in which every horizontal bank merger will be judged. If there are other submarkets, all well and good, but one should not rely on justifying his merger in terms of competition with other financial institutions in these submarkets. The second guideline is that the size of the bank is not going to deter the application of the antitrust laws. The Court had this to say about antitrust and small banks:

> Mergers of directly competing small commercial banks in small communities, no less than those of large banks in large communities, are subject to scrutiny under these standards. Indeed, competitive commercial banks, with their cluster of products and services, play a particularly significant role in a small community unable to support a large variety of alternative financial institutions. Thus, if anything it is even more true in the small town than in the large city that "if the businessman is denied credit because his banking alternatives have been eliminated by mergers, the whole edifice of an entrepreneurial system is threatened; if the costs of banking services and credit are allowed to become excessive by the absence of competitive pressures, virtually all costs, in our credit economy, will be affected. . . ." [Citation omitted.]

Nor would it be advisable to depend on the defense that the relevant geographic market is too small to be an "economically significant section of the country" under the *Brown Shoe* standard. Defendants argued this on appeal and the Court rejected it, noting that even in the *Brown Shoe* opinion it had recognized relevant geographic markets in cities "with a population exceeding 10,000, and their environs." Phillipsburg–Easton and its immediate environs had a population of almost 90,000. In fact only rarely will one find a market with a population less than 10,000, and even then the Court might find it to be an economically significant section of the county if enough banks compete for those 10,000 people. However, because the Justice Department can sue, this does not mean it will. In 1966 it failed to file a suit against a merger of two of the only three banks in the relevant market and those two banks had a 65 per cent share of market. Furthermore the banks were "nearly equal in size and competition between them [was] keen." On the other hand, they had deposits of only $9,327,000 and $8,993,000, respectively, and the population of the county was only 25,000 people. It must be remembered that this occurred over four years before *Phillipsburg* and it may no longer be indicative of Justice policy today. (Of course, it may have only been indicative of an overworked staff then.) However, in the same year the department did file suit against two banks which had deposits of $21,000,000 and $16,000,000, respectively. They also had a market share of 85 per cent of all deposits and 84 per cent of all loans. So if there is a Justice Department *de minimis* policy, it is inapplicable to all but the smallest banks.

The third guideline is that when estimating the anticompetitive effects of a proposed merger, one should use a narrow geographic market. This is especially true if the customers are small borrowers, depositors, or businessmen. On this point the Court said:

> The localization of business typical of the banking industry is particularly pronounced when small customers are involved. We stated in Philadelphia Bank . . . that in "banking the relevant geographical market is a function of each separate customer's economic scale"—that "the smaller the customer, the smaller is his banking market geographically." Small depositors have little reason to deal with a bank other than the one most geographically convenient to them.

The fourth guideline is that in balance the benefits to the convenience and needs of the community with the anticompetitive effects of the merger, the same geographical market must be used for both evaluations. Although this might seem elementary, the Supreme Court found, despite appellee's argument to the contrary, that the district court had judged the anticompetitive effect of the merger in Phillipsburg–Easton or the "one-town" market, while it had judged the benefit to the community only in Phillipsburg. The Court noted that the result of this kind of balancing would be "[a]pproval of a merger that, though it has anticompetitive effects throughout the market, has countervailing beneficial impact in only part of the market . . . [and] such a result would unfairly deny the benefits of the merger to some of those who sustain its direct and immediate anticompetitive effects."

Finally, the fifth lesson we can derive from *Phillipsburg* was the Court's guideline to the district court on remand that in judging the convenience and needs of the community, it must consider all the customers of the bank, large and small, not just those seeking larger loans or specialized services. And it reiterated its holding in *Nashville Bank* that before this is done, the first step is to see whether there were alternative solutions that could have solved the bank's problems and thus benefited the community without a merger.

Justice Harlan's dissent questioned the government's bringing of the case in the first place. "With tigers still at large in our competitive jungle why should the Department be taking aim at such small game?" From the Department of Justice's point of view though, as he acknowledged, the result of the decision fully justified the effort, because "after today's opinion the legality of every merger of two directly competing banks no matter how small is placed in doubt if a court, through what has become an exercise in 'antitrust numerology,' concludes that the merger 'produces a firm controlling an undue percentage share of the relevant market.' " (Citations omitted.) The department's effort did indeed save both it and the federal banking agencies much work, because it can be safely assumed that a considerable number of mergers between small- and medium-sized banks that might have been attempted before the opinion, after the opinion were not.

Was It Worth It?

We have already discussed the purpose of the Bank Merger Act of 1960. Congress intended to check the growing bank concentration resulting from mergers which among other things would be detrimental to the general economy and specifically to the small bank customer trying to obtain credit. Did the ten years of effort by the Justice Department, the federal banking agencies and the courts (and the additional effort of Congress in passing the Bank Merger Act of 1966) produce a result concomitant with that original Congressional purpose? A recent empirical study by Schull and Horvitz concluded that it did. They analyzed various "standard metropolitan statistical areas" and found that in the 1960's concentration had declined or leveled off from the concentration ratios of the 1950's. Furthermore the phenomenon that dramatized the need for legislation, the big bank merger, has disappeared: "Clearly, combinations of major banks in the same city appear now to be a thing of the past." The study also computed the concentration ratio of the three largest banks for several large cities and what the ratio would have been if some of the proposed mergers in those cities had not been denied. The results are represented in the following chart reprinted from that article:

SMSA	*Per Cent Three-Bank Concentration Ratio*	*Concentration Ratio If All Mergers Approved*
Atlanta	62.1	70.1
Baltimore	64.2	81.0
Houston	44.8	53.2
Louisville	69.1	82.1
New York	44.3	49.9
Philadelphia	46.3	61.6

However, as the authors pointed out, "it is clear that this is a minimal measure of the impact of the Bank Merger Act. Without application of antitrust standards to banking, it is certain that additional mergers would have been proposed."

Has the small bank customer benefited? As we saw in *Phillipsburg,* both the government and the Supreme Court were very concerned with guaranteeing the protection of the antitrust laws for the small customer. The Court had said, "The effect (of ruling in favor of defendants) would likely be to deny customers of small banks—and thus residents of many small towns—the antitrust protection to which they are no less entitled than customers of large city banks." And the recent case of *United States* v. *County National Bank of Bennington,* discussed later, indicates this rule is not being ignored by the district courts.

There has been another procompetitive change since the passage of the Act. The federal banking agencies, which at first seemed to resent the intrusion of competitive principles in merger approvals, have adjusted to the overriding purpose of the Act and are now applying antitrust standards as thoroughly as any court. The Federal Reserve Board has been a prime example of this and has in fact been complimented by the Justice Department for its efforts in this area. The FDIC has also been applying these standards. For instance, following the *Phillipsburg* decision the chairman of the FDIC announced that 15 per cent of the banking assets in a market would be the new critical point in weighing the antitrust aspects of a merger. On the other hand, the comptroller of the currency recently approved a merger that he conceded, if consummated, would tend substantially to lessen competition and to create a monopoly in commercial banking in the geographic market. Mr. Camp justified his decision on the basis that the market was simply too insignificant to be regarded as a "section of the country" within the meaning of the Act. The Justice Department filed suit and the comptroller intervened on behalf of the defendants (*United States* v. *County National Bank of Bennington*). This was over two years after *Phillipsburg,* in which it will be remembered Mr. Camp also intervened after approving the merger, and the same argument was rejected by the Supreme Court. The district court, in granting summary judgment for the government, cited *Phillipsburg* and concluded that the position of Mr. Camp was "contrary to that adopted in decisions by the Supreme Court and belies the manifestations of congressional intent indicating that the particular product involved is of substantial importance in determining an area constituting a section of the country for purpose of the Clayton Act."

Value of BMA of 1960

One might ask whether the Bank Merger Act of 1960 was very instrumental in achieving these competitive results, for it was apparent after *Firstamerica Corp.* that the Justice Department was going to sue under the antitrust laws with or without the Act. This may be true; yet the principal significance of the Bank Merger Act of 1960 is not the application of the antitrust laws to bank mergers (*Philadelphia Bank* did that) but the requirement of federal agency approval (with the advice of the Justice Department) for every proposed bank merger. This is significantly better than the hit-and-miss technique that results when the Antitrust Division is forced to discover and evaluate every merger in all industries and then prepare a case in time to file a preliminary injunction motion. The Antitrust Division obviously does not have the manpower to attack every merger, and without the notification and stay provisions of the Act it would not be able to prevent the consummation of those it did attack. Furthermore, its burden is further lightened by those banking agencies who, as was just discussed, are applying for the most part the same criteria in judging mergers that are used by the Antitrust Division.

The Act has also had an effect on related areas in banking. According to Shull and Horvitz,

> In a more general sense, the introduction of effective constraints on bank combinations in the 1960's may be viewed as part of the process of dismantling the pervasive controls which were erected in the early part of the 20th century to stabilize individual commercial banks, and which invariably suppressed competition. The Bank Merger Act of 1960 is a principal element in the reintroduction of competition and competitive ethics to an industry which had, since the mid-1930's, withdrawn into regulated and cooperative methods of doing business.

Finally, the ten years of enforcement of antitrust laws to bank mergers has had another procompetitive effect. The Justice Department has been so successful in blocking horizontal mergers, that there has been a shift in interest to market- and product-extension mergers. Both of these have potential for increasing competition and to that extent are more valuable than horizontal mergers, which have little or no hope of doing this. We shall spend the rest of the chapter exploring these two types of mergers, along with the bank-holding companies and the legislation that has been passed to regulate them.

MARKET-EXTENSION MERGERS

The Department of Justice has been very successful in its suits to enjoin horizontal bank mergers. However, in its attempt to block what are termed *market-extension* bank mergers, it has had very little success. Of all the mergers attacked by the department since 1963 (the year of *Philadelphia Bank*) only five were eventually effected. All five were market-extension mergers. They were *Crocker-Anglo National Bank, First National Bank of Jackson, Bank of Maryland, Bank of Jackson, Idaho First National,* and the *Bank of Greeley*. In its attempt to find a suitable case for the first Supreme Court review, the department passed by the first four and finally filed an appeal in the *Greeley* case to be heard in the October term of 1972.

A market-extension merger, as discussed in Chapter 15, is a form of conglomerate merger. It is the acquisition of a firm located in a different geographic market but engaged in the same line of commerce as the acquiring firm. In banking this would be accomplished by a bank or bank-holding company acquiring another bank in an area in which it did not complete. A market-extension bank merger is dealt with in similar manner as a conglomerate merger in any industry. The three principal theories used to attack such a merger are (1) potential competition, (2) entrenchment, and (3) reciprocity.

Potential Competition. The potential-competition theory is firmly entrenched in the antitrust laws and has been frequently used in suits in other industries. The anticompetitive-effect standard really involves double incipiency—a merger which *may tend* to eliminate *potential* competition in any line of commerce is unlawful.

Potential competition serves both as a supplement to and as a substitute for actual competition. If a firm is aware that there are other firms "on the periphery" of its market with the ability and interest to enter, it will be motivated in much the same manner as if they were already in the market competing with it. Potential competition plays its biggest role in concentrated markets which have what is termed *imperfect competition*. Therefore, it is particularly applicable to the banking industry.

Although the government has had little success in its market-extension bank cases, it has had quite a bit of success in similar suits in other industries. Furthermore, the Federal Reserve Board has blocked bank-holding-company mergers on the basis of a probable lessening of potential competition. What therefore is the reason for the government losses? It has been suggested that they can be attributed to the district courts' reliance on issues other than the potential competition issue. One of these has been the "convenience-and-needs" defense. Another possibility is simply that the government chose the wrong mergers to attack. Whether or not either of these alternatives is true, it is apparent that the department faces at least one potential competition problem that is peculiar to bank-merger cases. This is the fact that the banks need regulatory approval to enter new markets. In four out of the five government defeats, the court relied to some extent on the view that the federal banking agency would not allow *de novo* entry into the relevant market. The government will undoubtedly seek a Supreme Court ruling on the propriety of this reliance, but until that time it appears that the agency's determination will continue to carry weight.

There is no lack of guidance from the Supreme Court on the potential competition issue. Three of the more important opinions are *Procter & Gamble, Penn-Olin* (joint venture), and *El Paso Natural Gas*. They, among other things, have established the criteria for determining who are the potential competitors. Because it was established in *Philadelphia Bank* and re-established in *Provident–Houston* that the antitrust laws are applicable to bank mergers, it is important to understand the principles in these cases. (They are discussed in Chapter 15.) In this regard it is interesting to note that the Supreme Court scheduled the *Greeley* case to be argued in conjunction with the *Falstaff–Narragansett* beer merger case, which also involves the potential-competition issue. This is perhaps an indication that it plans to treat the application of the potential-competition issue to bank mergers no differently than other industries. This would of course be consistent with the horizontal bank-merger cases.

Once the potential entrants have been identified (using the principles established in the three cases just cited) one must be concerned, as in all merger cases, with the relevant product market or "line of commerce" and the geographic market or "section of the country." It appears from the emphasis in *Phillipsburg* that the product market in potential-competition cases will be the same as in the direct-competition cases, or in other words "commercial banking." Of the five market-extension cases, only *Greeley* used this product market exclusively. *Phillipsburg,* by the way, seems to have negated the three-judge panel ruling in *Crocker-Anglo* that the omission of the words *line of commerce* from the BMA of 1966 made it proper to consider the competitive effect of other financial institutions, thereby diluting the "commercial-banking" market.

Determination of the proper geographic market by its nature necessitates a case-by-case approach. Yet in banking it should be remembered there are the general guidelines of *Philadelphia Bank* that the market varies as to type of customer (small, medium, and large) and the lesson of *Phillipsburg* not to ignore the localized nature of banking markets and in particular the even smaller market for banks with small customers.

There are several criteria in determining whether a potential competitor is likely to enter the market. First, it should be remembered that this is an objective and not a subjective test. Some of the questions to be asked are the following:

1. What are the present and future growth prospects of the market?
2. What are the barriers to entry (the prospect of the comptroller's approval has been considered here)?
3. What is the financial and managerial capacity of the firm?
4. What is the bank's past history of mergers and branching?

Once it has been determined what the relevant market is and who the most likely entrants are, there is still the question of what factors will cause the Justice Department to challenge the merger. The Merger Guidelines, discussed in Chapter 27, are of some help in this matter. The appropriate section reads:

> . . . the Department will ordinarily challenge the merger between one of the most likely entrants into the market and:
> (i) any firm with approximately 25 percent or more of the market;
> (ii) one of the two largest firms in a market in which the shares of the two largest firms amount to approximately 50 percent or more;

(iii) one of the four largest firms in a market in which the shares of the eight largest firms amount to approximately 75 percent or more, provided the merging firm's share of the market amounts to approximately 10 percent or more; or

(iv) one of the eight largest firms in a market in which the shares of these firms amount to approximately 75 percent or more, provided either (A) the merging firm's share of the market is not insubstantial and there are no more than one or two likely entrants into the market or (B) the merging firm is a rapidly growing firm.

Because these guidelines are very general and there is an absence of controlling legal precedent (the district court opinions without Supreme Court consideration of the issues have little precedential weight), we will have to wait, as with horizontal bank mergers and antitrust law, for the Supreme Court to establish further guidelines.

Entrenchment. The *entrenchment theory* is used when a large firm or "giant" enters a market of smaller firms through a merger. The theory is that the large firm with its resources will scare off any potential entrants into the market and also intimidate the firms already there. The *Procter & Gamble* case cited in the discussion of potential competition is the principal authority for this theory. In only one of the five bank cases was this an issue. The court in *Bank of Jackson* found not only that the government did not prove the entrenchment claim but that the merger if allowed would have five procompetitive effects which it enumerated in the opinion.

The Department of Justice has also dealt with entrenchment in its Merger Guidelines:

20. Mergers Which Entrench Market Power And Other Conglomerate Mergers.

The Department will ordinarily investigate the possibility of anticompetitive consequences, and may in particular circumstances bring suit, where an acquisition of a leading firm in a relatively concentrated or rapidly concentrating market may serve to entrench or increase the market power of that firm or raise barriers to entry in that market. Examples of this type of merger include: (i) a merger which produces a very large disparity in absolute size between the merged firm and the largest remaining firms in the relevant markets, (ii) a merger of firms producing related products which may induce purchasers, concerned about the merged firm's possible use of leverage, to buy products of the merged firm rather than those of competitors, and (iii) a merger which may enhance the ability of the merged firm to increase product differentiation in the relevant markets. [*Merger Guidelines,* p. 25, ¶20.]

These guidelines are obviously very general and create more questions than they answer. For example, how large is a "very large disparity"? When are products sufficiently related to induce purchasers to be concerned about the possible use of leverage? And what are the criteria for judging the ability of a merged firm to "increase product differentiation in the relevant markets"? These and other questions will have to be answered by the courts and will probably require more than one opinion of the Supreme Court.

The entrenchment issue at this point is not as thoroughly established as others, such as potential competition. Furthermore it is likely to be successful only in suits against very large bank-holding companies and banks with vast resources and marketing know-how rather than in suits involving middle-sized and less-sophisticated banks.

Reciprocity. This third test was established originally in *FTC* v. *Consolidated Foods Corp.* in 1965. In effect the rule prohibits both coercive and mutual-trade practices of the "you scratch my back and I'll scratch yours" type. It is most applicable to the bank-holding companies where banking customers might be encouraged or coerced into using the nonbanking services of the bank-holding companies. As the word gets around, overt coercion and explicit mutual agreements will become less common, but this will not end the problem. There is still the possibility that customers of the acquired bank will seek these nonbanking services on their own in order to "score points" with the bank. This is called *reciprocity effect* (or tying effect) by the Antitrust Division, and is impossible to attack under the Sherman Act because there is no conspiracy in restraint of trade but merely the efforts of one actor who is looking out for what he considers his economic self-interest without any encouragement from the bank. It is therefore an inherent problem of the market structure and can be prevented only by blocking the merger. This will be discussed more fully later in the section on bank-holding companies. The competitive evil of both reciprocity and reciprocity effect is that they take the product or service out of the marketplace. The individual merits of the item are no longer at issue, merely what advantage can be gained in another transaction. The government has been successful in pressing this claim and has obtained a number of consent and litigated judgments in its favor. Only a "not insubstantial" amount of commerce need be involved, which can be less than $200,000. The reciprocity issue, however, was not used in any of the five market-extension bank mergers lost so far by the government.

The sister of reciprocity is the *tie-in.* This is proscribed in the *Fortner* case, which is discussed in a previous chapter. Therefore it will not be dealt with here except to note that it is another factor to consider when planning a market extension or, for that matter, any conglomerate merger.

PRODUCT-EXTENSION MERGERS

A product-extension merger is also a form of conglomerate merger. It consists of a firm acquiring another firm in a similar market but engaged in a different line of commerce. An example would be a bank-holding company acquiring a credit-card company. The Federal Trade Commission described this type of merger in *Procter & Gamble* as an entry into a "market which adjoins, as it were, those markets in which [a company] is already established, and which is virtually indistinguishable from them insofar as problems and techniques of marketing the product of the ultimate consumer are concerned." The same theories that are used against market-extension bank mergers can be used against product-extension bank mergers.

There have not been many product-extension bank-merger suits. In 1965 the Antitrust Division filed one against the First National City Bank for its acquisition of Carte Blanche. It was eventually settled by a consent decree in which First National City sold Carte Blanche and agreed not to reacquire it. In 1969 the division intended to file another suit against First National City for its proposed acquisition of Chubb & Sons, a large casualty insurance firm. The government feared it would create the classic opportunity for tying insurance to loans, and vice versa. When First National City learned of the government's opposition, it abandoned the transaction before the complaint was filed. Recently the department filed a suit against Wachovia Corporation, the parent of the largest commercial bank in the Southeast, for its proposed acquisition of American Credit, a $400 million institution operating in sales and consumer financing, factoring, and insurance. The complaint alleged elimination of actual and potential competition as well as the possibility of reciprocity, tying, and tying effect. This is presently being litigated.

The rules of the product-extension game were changed somewhat recently. New bank-holding legislation was passed which will restrict some of the freedom one-bank-holding companies have had in acquiring nonbanking firms and will give more leeway to multibank-holding companies, which have been subject to the Bank Holding Company Act of 1956. This legislation will be discussed later.

BANK-HOLDING COMPANIES

This country has had a traditional policy of separating commercial banking from other areas of economic activity. There are three principal considerations behind this policy: (1) the desire to ensure the solvency of the banks, (2) the fear that affiliation of banks and nonbanking businesses would create unfair competitive advantages, and (3) the general concern over economic concentration throughout the economy. This policy is represented in the Glass–Steagall Act of 1933, which prohibited banks from engaging in the securities business in order to avoid repetition of the abuses of the 1920's. One might also say that it is the antithesis of that policy in Japan and some other countries where the banks have become the centers of huge industrial-commercial groups.

The first and third considerations behind this policy have been discussed elsewhere in the book, so there is no need to discuss them here. It might be helpful, however, to explore briefly the second consideration —the fear that affiliation of banks and nonbanking business would create unfair competitive advantages.

As has been noted banks usually compete in concentrated markets of a local nature. Because the banking alternatives are few they have considerable market power. Furthermore the Supreme Court noted in *Philadelphia Bank* and *Phillipsburg* that bank customers (excluding the huge national ones) tend to patronize their local bank even if they could travel to another bank for a better interest rate. Unlike firms in other industries banks do not have to worry about banks freely coming in and deconcentrating their market because branch banking is closely regulated by banking agencies and even forbidden in one third of the states.

Where banks have the most power is in their control over credit. Bank–customer relationships are not of a quick, high-turnover type anyway, but the credit relationships tend to be even more continuous. Usually one does not shop around for credit. It can require the disclosure of highly personal or sensitive competitive information. Moreover some borrowers depend on reputation for credit and cannot afford to jeopardize good standing with the bank that has acknowledged this reputation. A long-term relationship, with a proper showing of loyalty by the customer, may help in times of tight money if the bank decides to look after its own, an informal method of credit rationing.

Add to all this the fact that many times the bank customer does not possess the same degree of financial sophistication (or at least feels he does not, which is just as important) as the bank officers. One can see that this gives more economic power to the banks even if, as one AAG of the Antitrust Division said, "it is the subconscious exercise of economic power."

When a bank expands into a nonbanking market, this economic power does not disappear; on the contrary it can severely influence the competitive make-up of the nonbanking market. There is the strong danger of reciprocity, tying, and reciprocity (or tying) effect. Most important from the Antitrust Division's point of view is the last of these. It cannot do anything to stop it. An example of reciprocity effect can be demonstrated if First National City Bank had acquired Chubb & Sons, a casualty insurance firm. A potential loan applicant of First National City might place all of his casualty insurance business with Chubb in the hopes, however unfounded, that this would help in securing a loan, perhaps on more favorable terms. Whether or not it has any effect on his loan, the damage is done to the competition in casualty insurance. This is a market-structure problem that can only be stopped by blocking the merger. This is what the Antitrust Division decided to do and, as mentioned earlier, First National City abandoned the transaction after it learned of the department's opposition.

It can be seen therefore that the fear that affiliation of banks with nonbanking businesses will create unfair competitive advantages is very real. This is especially true when one considers that the structure of financial markets tends to be an enduring one and divestitures tend to be difficult.

The Genesis of the Bank-Holding Company

After World War II there was tremendous economic growth. The banking public demanded more and new kinds of services. By the 1960's as a result of these demands and changes in technology (i.e., the computer), it was hard to discern the line between what was and what was not banking. Yet the industry was still regulated by laws based on the 1930's concept of banking. The banks resented these laws, which they considered anachronistic. Furthermore, they did not want to be left out of the mainstream of economic growth. (Already they were no longer the principal suppliers of money for the economy, as other institutions took over this function.) They sought ways to expand both geographically and functionally following the example of the conglomerates. In other words they were looking for a piece of the action. It was the bank-holding company and more specifically the one-bank-holding company which gave it to them.

The bank-holding company enabled banks to go into nonbanking fields and also enabled conglomerates to go into banking. This was a novel concept and Congress moved to impose the traditional banking limitations on them. In 1956 it passed the Bank Holding Company Act. This had two principal purposes: (1) to control the acquisition of banks by holding companies and (2) to restrict the nonbanking activities of the holding companies. It did this simply by limiting the kinds of nonbanking activities in which they could invest and by limiting the activities of the holding companies themselves. However, there was one important exception. The Act did not regulate the activities of one-bank-holding companies. In 1956 there was little concern with the one-bank-holding companies. They were for the most part small and local, formed for the convenience of small investors. They had no real effect on the national economy and although some conglomerates acquired banks, it was largely for investment purposes. Moreover the banks were usually kept separate from the other activities of the conglomerate.

The Growth of One-Bank-Holding Companies

In 1956 there were only 117 one-bank-holding companies that controlled $11.6 billion in commercial bank deposits. In 1965 the number grew to 550 and controlled $15 billion in deposits or 4.5 per cent of all the commercial bank deposits in the country. By the first part of 1968 the amount of bank deposits controlled grew to $18 billion. Then First National City Bank, on July 3, 1968, announced that it intended to take the one-bank-holding route to expand its activities outside the banking field. It was the gold rush all over again. By the end of 1969 there were 890 one-bank holding companies with $181 billion of commercial banking deposits or 43 per cent of all bank deposits in the country. This unbelievable growth and overnight concentration of the nation's banking assets caused considerable concern. The first to act was Congressman

Patman, who quickly introduced legislation to control one-bank-holding companies.

Bank-Holding-Company Legislation

This legislative history should be viewed with the understanding that in the background various industry lobbies were pushing to confine banking to its own backyard; the banking lobby was trying to break down the backyard fence; and others (that is, Antitrust Division, Treasury Department) sought to establish flexible boundaries that would do the most for competition regardless of the industry involved. Through it all ran the question, "What is banking?"

Congressman Patman's bill (H.R. 6778) was changed in the House Banking and Currency Committee and reported out through a parliamentary maneuver of the minority Republicans and five Democrats. When it reached the floor it was significantly changed as a result of much lobbying as well as considerable antibank sentiment. As a bank-holding-company representative remarked, "all of the venom and frustration against interest rates, banking conglomerates and all the rest of it came out and the Bill was completely rewritten." The stronger bill was passed and went to the Senate.

The Senate had three choices: the House bill, the administration bill, and Senator Proxmire's bill. All three would close the "one-bank-holding company" loophole in the Bank Holding Company Act of 1956. Both the administration bill and the House bill changed provisions of the 1956 Act dealing with nonbanking activities of bank-holding companies (Section 4(c)(8)). Although the language was different the concept was the same. The administration still gave supervision to the three banking agencies (shades of BMA of 1960) and the House bill relied solely on the Federal Reserve Board. Furthermore the House bill would have proscribed bank expansion into certain nonbanking activities completely. This was a testament to the strength of the lobbies in those industries. The Antitrust Division opposed this "negative laundry list" of proscribed industries because it had not been demonstrated that banking expansion would be harmful to competition in these industries and the absolute exclusion of banking would immediately wipe out the effect of banking as a potential competitor. Senator Proxmire's bill was essentially a stopgap measure that would have made the Bank Holding Company Act of 1956 applicable to one-bank-holding companies pending further study of a newly created Presidential Commission on Banking. All three bills would have left intact all previous antitrust remedies.

The Bank Holding Company Act of 1970

The 1970 Act has been called the "most important piece of banking legislation in at least a generation." It reflected the traditional policy toward banking discussed earlier, but also recognized that the distinction between banking and other financial activities had been blurred and that the entry of banking into other financial fields, although potentially dangerous, could be procompetitive.

Administration

The principal section for our concern is Section 4(c)(8), which deals with the affiliation of banks with nonbanking firms. The House version giving approval authority to the Federal Reserve Board alone was enacted. This is a preferable method for a number of reasons. For one it is simpler. Second, there is less chance of conflicting interpretation, as happened under the Bank Merger Act of 1960. Third, such interpretations create the possibility of "forum shopping," that is, holding companies altering the character of their bank affiliates to get the agency whose interpretation is most desirable for that particular transaction. The fact that the administration bill would have required unanimous approval of all three agencies would not have completely prevented this while at the same time making administration of the section more complex.

If one-agency approval is best, why the Federal Reserve Board? The board already had experience under the old Section 4(c)(8) under the Bank Holding Company Act of 1956 regulating multibank-holding-company expansion. Furthermore it has several distinguished professional economists who are well qualified to make these highly important decisions. And as a past head of the Antitrust Division testified in the hearings on the Act;

> in our view, the Board has done a generally sound and responsible job of handling bank acquisition under the competitive tests established under the Bank Holding Company Acts of 1956 and 1966 and the Bank Merger Acts of 1960 and 1966; there is no reason to believe it would not carry forward such experience and policy in applying the new competition tests for nonbank acquisitions. . . .

Finally the board under both bills had approval over subsequent *bank* acquisitions by all bank-holding companies. Therefore under the three-agency approval system the banking and nonbanking activities of a bank-holding company could be regulated by two different agencies. This would cause duplication and waste of agency expertise and create uncertainty in bank-holding-company planning and operations.

Substantive Standards

The Federal Reserve Board can permit bank-holding companies (both single and multibank) to acquire companies the "activities of which the Board after due notice and opportunity for hearing has determined (by order or regulation) to be so closely related to banking or managing or controlling banks as to be a proper incident thereto." Therefore in the first step—either through a regulation or a case-by-case approach—the board must determine whether the company's activity was "closely related to the banking." Consequently under no circumstances will a bank-holding company be engaged in making automobiles, refrigerators, or popcorn. The board has already issued regulations (Regulation Y) classifying certain activities as fitting the standard.

In the second step the Act requires the board to determine whether the acquisition will be in the "public interest" or more specifically:

> Whether performance of the activity proposed by the holding company, under the particular circumstances involved can reasonably be expected to produce benefits to the public, such as greater convenience, increased competition, or gains in efficiency, that outweigh possible adverse effects, such as undue concentration of resources, decreased or unfair competition, conflicts of interest, or unsound banking practices.

The Act authorized the board to distinguish between *de novo* activities and acquisitions. It has done this recognizing that *de novo* entry is prima facie procompetitive. Regulation Y provides that if the bank-holding-company engages in any of the listed activities *de novo* the acquisition will be deemed in the public interest and approved unless applicant is notified to the contrary within forty-five days. This reflects the board's concern with the effect on competition. As one veteran antitrust observer noted, although the Act sets out more banking factors than competitive factors," [i]t nevertheless seems clear that 'increased competition' and 'undue concentration of resources' will be the paramount standards to be applied."

After much hard fighting the "negative laundry list" was excluded from the Act. Although objected to by those industries who would have been protected from banking competition, it seems to be for the best. Although the exclusion does not mean that expansion will be allowed into all those industries, it does mean that the board has flexibility to allow some and not others and, after further experience under the Act, to change its mind if it appears banking expansion will serve the public interest. In other words Congress, recognizing there is little or no evidence justifying absolute exclusion of banking entry (with the exception of the securities industry), has wisely left the final decision to an expert banking agency while supplying the public-interest standards to be applied.

It should not be forgotten that even after board approval, the acquisition may still be attacked under the antitrust laws. A by-product of litigation attacking bank-holding company's acquisitions of nonbanking firms under the Act will be further guidelines on product-extension bank mergers discussed earlier.

The final success or failure of the Act will not be measured by how well the act was drafted but by its application. Bank-holding-company legislation is vitally important to the economic well-being of this country. The Bank Holding Company Act of 1970 is a good, equitable approach to the problem, but in the words of one Antitrust Division official, "the enactment of the statute is—in Churchill's phrase—'not the end. It is not even the beginning of the end. But it is perhaps, the end of the beginning.' "

27 Conclusion—A Final Word on the Conglomerate

Mergers have played an important part in the growth of our economy to its position as strongest in the world. But as the child grows to adulthood and then stops growing, there is a point at which mergers must diminish if our free enterprise economy is to survive. Competition is the lifeblood of our economic system, and it is the function of the antitrust laws to insure that competition in free markets continues to regulate the flow of goods and services therein. To this end the enforcing agencies of these laws—the Justice Department and the Federal Trade Commission—have increasingly devoted a substantial portion of their time and resources to merger law enforcement.

Of course, the law continues to develop in this area. What was lawful yesterday may be unlawful today or tomorrow. This is particularly true of the conglomerate, a relatively new form of merger whose procompetitive and anticompetitive effects are still being debated. The change in attitude is illustrated by the merger guidelines of the assistant attorneys general in 1954 and 1969.

In 1954, shortly after the Celler–Kefauver Amendment to Section 7 of the Clayton Act had been enacted, U.S. Attorney General Brownell described a delicately balanced set of guidelines to be considered and weighed before determining whether a proposed merger ran afoul of its provisions. Those guidelines directed attention to

- The locations, physical and financial size, past acquisitions, products, and activities of the merging companies, individually and in combination.
- The structure and size of the industry in terms of production and capacity.
- The relative position in the industry of the two companies individually and combined.
- The ease by which competitors may enter the industry.
- The number of companies active in the industry, their respective size, and their relative standing in sales and total assets.

- Sales, relative standing, and like factors of the two companies and their competitors in definable market areas, if relevant.
- The nature of the industry—that is, whether infant, dynamic, or declining.
- The effect the proposed merger may have on sources of raw materials and methods and patterns of distribution.
- Whether the acquisition may result in a significant reduction in competition.
- Whether the acquisition may increase the relative size of the purchasing company in such a fashion as to give it a substantial advantage over its competitors.
- Whether the relationships between the purchaser and other companies that may be brought about by the merger might result in a lessening of competition.

By June 1969, after several changes of administration, the Department of Justice made clear that it had abandoned the last vestige of this careful balancing approach. Attorney General Mitchell's own much-simplified guidelines revealed that

- The Department of Justice may very well oppose any merger among the top 200 manufacturing firms or firms of comparable size in other industries.
- The Department of Justice will probably oppose any merger by one of the top 200 manufacturing firms of any leading producer in any concentrated industry.
- And, of course, the department will continue to challenge mergers which may substantially lessen potential competition or develop a substantial potential for reciprocity.

This drastic change in enforcement philosophy well can be attributed to the rise of the conglomerate corporation.

In the mid-1960's an editor of *Fortune* hailed conglomerates as "really nothing more than the latest attempt to exploit all the potential of the corporate vehicle and its apparatus within the framework of 20th Century capitalism." Other spokesmen urged industries to join together to meet the challenge of "monolithic communism." More recently, the editor of *Mergers and Acquisitions,* a periodical devoted to merger-minded companies, stated:

> The staggering fact is [that] the conglomerate itself, standing ready to enter any market at a moment's notice, is probably the greatest force that has ever existed in all economic history to keep those in the marketplace continually competitive. And that's also why the Establishment is screaming. . . . [I]t is only a Litton or a Gulf and Western or a Ling-Temco that will someday

> challenge the present steel or auto or chemical oligarchies. . . . Certainly the conglomerate is the only answer to the oligopoly-triad of General Motors-Chrysler-Ford.

Not everyone agreed with these analyses.

First, it became increasingly clear that many conglomerates had been built on a foundation of financial manipulation that crumbled under the first serious wave of economic recession. Second, although certain "efficiencies" were realized as a result of these conglomerate mergers, the benefits of these efficiencies never seemed to trickle down to the consumer. Third, doubt was cast on several basic assumptions—namely, that modern technology necessitated bigness to sustain innovative research and development programs, and to produce goods most efficiently—that had earlier served to justify the merger trend. More and more observers concluded that the largest American corporations were less efficient and innovative than their smaller counterparts. Conglomerate corporations themselves realized that apples could not always be mixed with oranges, and began selling off unprofitable divisions on a massive scale. Fourth, serious doubts were raised as to the long-range financial value to a small firm of merging into a conglomerate. Besides the possibility of receiving "funny money" in return for ownership of a profitable enterprise, at least one study concluded that ownership by a conglomerate would actually hurt the competitive prospects of a smaller firm. Fifth, the submersion of local businesses into national concerns raised problems of a social and political nature. By increasing the size of national power groups and diminishing the importance of local participation, many argued, the political balance of our nation might be jeopardized.

These and other similar objections, however serious, are not the central concern of the federal antitrust laws. Section 7 of the Clayton Act prohibits only those mergers that "substantially . . . lessen competition." Considering the arguments of those who urge that conglomerate mergers increase competitive forces in our oligopolistic economy, more specific objections to conglomeration were needed before a broad-based attack could be justified.

Those objections were not long in coming, as experience with the performance of conglomerates began accumulating. It became apparent that "better" competition could easily lead to "unfair" competition if these corporations chose to exercise the prerogatives of their size and makeup. By lumping together unproductive units with units in protected markets, for example, cross-subsidization, reciprocal dealing arrangements, increased advertising expenditures having the effect of increasing entry barriers, an increased propensity for large conglomerate firms to behave interdependently in making market decisions, and other "deep-pocket" consequences of doing business were encouraged. Although these practices might have been "unfair," many argued that they could be dealt with as they surfaced, using traditional enforcement devises to separate the wheat from the chaff. A broad-based attack on conglomerates could not be justified simply because some conglomerate firms insisted on abusing their power.

Largely as a result of the work of Dr. Willard F. Mueller, at that time director of the Bureau of Economics of the Federal Trade Commission, this type of limited-enforcement policy, focusing on actual performance of firms, fell into disrepute. Dr. Mueller's philosophy emphasized instead the importance of market structure *in itself* as dictating the appropriate enforcement response. To him mergers played a significant role in creating that structure and therefore deserved careful scrutiny.

Dr. Mueller's brand of economics taught that "*market structure* plays a powerful role in determining or conditioning *business conduct* and business conduct in turn determines the ultimate quality of *industrial performance*." Thus, if the market structure was unduly concentrated, he argued, industrial performance was *bound* to suffer. Citing a growing body of empirical studies to support his thesis, he recommended a broad-based attack on further industrial concentration as the only effective way to preserve the strength of the American economy.

Needless to say, Dr. Mueller's views generated widespread opposition. For different reasons, critics as diverse as Professor Galbraith, Betty Bock, and *Fortune* magazine took issue with his thesis, urging once again that attention be directed solely at performance. These critics occasionally generated statistics of their own to attempt to disprove his hypothesis. With dogged persistence Dr. Mueller and his staff at the FTC rebutted these objections and held to their views.

Undoubtedly, more research needs to be done before the economic consequences of the current merger movement can be established beyond doubt. In the meantime, however, those who fashion public policy must choose a course of action. Should they act at once to slow the level of merger activity or should they await the final ballot?

The 1969 Presidential Task Force on Productivity and Competition (the Stigler Report) came down on the side of caution, recommending that the "Department [of Justice] decline to undertake a program of action against conglomerate mergers and conglomerate enterprises, pending a conference to gather information and opinion on the economic effects of the conglomerate phenomenon. More broadly, we urge the Department to resist the natural temptation to utilize the antitrust laws to combat social problems not related to the competitive functioning of markets."

Joel Davidow echoed these sentiments, if in more colorful language: "At the very least it can be argued that the experiment should be allowed to continue, since the economy is sufficiently dynamic and competitive to ensure that the laggards will fall by the wayside, the charlatans will be unmasked, and the dinosaurs with pea-sized brains will become extinct."

In the final analysis, however, what economists eventually conclude will not really answer these questions. As Professor Adelman observed in 1954, "So far as these broad policy questions are concerned, I sometimes doubt whether economists really have very much of importance to say. Decisions here seem to turn on what people want, what kind of a society they desire; the value judgments tend to be of a very deep and inarticulate kind. The economist's voice is and perhaps should be just one among many." Each administration will undoubtedly reach its own conclusions as to enforcement policy until such time as a Congressional mandate is formulated.

PART VI

Appendixes

Appendix I

Selected Bibliography

Chapter 1: Introduction

BIBLIOGRAPHY

Berle and Means, *The Modern Corporation and Private Property* (1933).

Blair and Houghton, *The Lintner-Butters Analysis of the effect of Mergers on Industrial Concentration, 1940–47,* 33 Rev. of Econ. & Statistics 63 (1951).

Bock, *Mergers and Markets* (1969).

Butters, Lintner, and Cary, "Effects of Taxation," *Corporate Mergers* (1951).

Davis, *Essays in the Earlier History of American Corporation* (1917) *The Merger Movements.*

Federal Trade Commission Reports.

Current Trends in Merger Activity, 1968 (1969).

Economics Report on Corporate Mergers (1969).

Report on Corporate Mergers and Acquisitions (1955).

Report of the Federal Trade Commission on the Merger Movement, A Summary Report (1948).

Foulke, *Diversification in Business Activity* (1956).

Hearings on Economic Concentration, Subcommittee on Antitrust and Monopoly, Committee on the Judiciary, U.S. Senate, 89th Cong., 1st Sess. (1964–65).

Hotchkiss, Thorp, and Farnham, "Mergers, Consolidations and Affiliations," American Management Association, New York (1929).

Lintner and Butters, *Effect of Mergers on Industrial Concentration, 1940–47,* 32 Rev. of Econ. & Statistics 30 (1950).

McCarthy, *Acquisitions and Mergers* (1963).

Nelson, *Merger Movements in American Industry 1895–1956* (1959).

Weston, *The Role of Mergers in the Growth of Large Firms* (1961).

Wilcox, *Public Policies Toward Business* (1966).

Chapter 2: Why Firms Merge

BIBLIOGRAPHY

Alberts and Segall, *The Corporate Merger,* Chap. 2, 3 (1966).

Berman, "Using Tax Laws to Help Finance Corporate Acquisitions," The Analysts Journal, May 1956.

Bossons, Cohen, and Reid, "Mergers for Whom—Managers or Stockholders?" Carnegie Institute of Technology, Working Paper #14.
"Clients and Conglomerates," Trial Magazine, April/May 1969.
"Day of Reckoning?" Barron's, April 3, 1967.
Federal Trade Commission, *Economics Report of Corporate Mergers* (1969).
Harris, "The Urge to Merge," Fortune, November 1954.
Hutchison, *The Business of Acquisitions and Mergers* (1968).
Linowes, *Managing Growth Through Acquisition,* Chap. 3 (1968).

Chapter 3: Choosing the Method of Purchase

BIBLIOGRAPHY

ABA-ALI Model Business Corporation Act §§65–74.
Alberts and Segall, *The Corporate Merger* (1966).
Arthur D. Little, Inc., *Mergers and Acquisitions: Planning and Action* (1963).
Burrus and Savarese, *Developments in Antitrust During the Past Year,* 37 ABA Antitrust L.J. 381, 384 (1968).
Choka, *Buying, Selling and Merging Businesses* (1969).
Comment, *The Short Merger Statute,* 32 U. Chi. L. Rev. 596 (1965).
Darrell, *The Use of Reorganization Techniques in Corporate Acquisitions,* 70 Harv. L. Rev. 1183 (1957).
Drayton, Emerson, and Griswold, *Mergers and Acquisitions* (1963).
Folk, *Corporation Law Developments—1969,* 56 U. Va. L. Rev. 755, 789–96 (1970).
Folk, *De Facto Mergers in Delaware: Hariton v. Arco Electronics, Inc.,* 49 U. Va. L. Rev. 1261 (1963).
Fox and Fox, *Corporate Acquisitions and Mergers* (1969–70).
Fuld, *Some Practical Aspects of a Merger,* 60 Harv. L. Rev. 1092 (1947).
Gross, *Make or Buy* (1966).
Handler, *Through the Anti-Trust Looking Glass—Twenty-first Annual Anti-trust Review,* 57 Cal. L. Rev. (1969).
Herwitz, *Business Planning,* Chap. 5 (1966).
Holmes, *Buyer's Counsel Looks at Acquisitions,* 18 Bus. Law. 755 (1963).
Hutchinson, *The Business of Acquisitions and Mergers* (1968).
Israels, *Corporate Practice,* Chaps. XIII, XIV (1968).
Kempf, *Bathtub Conspiracies, Has Seagram Distilled a More Potent Brew,* 24 Bus. Law. 173 (1958).
McCarthy, *Acquisitions and Mergers* (1963).
Mace and Montgomery, *Management Problems of Corporate Acquisitions* (1962).
Manning, *The Shareholder's Appraisal Remedy: An Essay for Frank Coker,* 72 Yale L.J. 223 (1962).
Note, *Effect of Merger and Consolidation on Property, Rights and Franchises of the Constituent Corporations,* 38 U. Va. L. Rev. 496 (1962).
Note, *The Right of Shareholders Dissenting from Corporate Combinations to Demand Cash Payments for Their Shares,* 72 Harv. L. Rev. 1132 (1959).
Note, *Valuation of Dissenters' Stock under Appraisal Statutes,* 79 Harv. L. Rev. 1453 (1966).
O'Neal and Derwin, *Expulsion or Oppression of Business Associates—"Squeeze-Outs" in Small Enterprises* (1961).
Practicing Law Institute, *Sales, Mergers and Acquisitions* (1969).
Rohrlich, *Organizing Corporate and Other Business Enterprises* (1967).
Sealy, *The 1963 Ohio Acquisition and Merger Amendments,* 5 Corp. Prac. Com. 366 (1964).
Sealy, *Acquisitions and Mergers,* 16 Bus. Law 209 (1960).

Sebring, *Statutory Mergers and Asset Acquisitions Check List,* 21 Bus. Law. 799 (1966).
Scharf, *Techniques for Buying, Selling and Merging Businesses* (1964).
Skolder, *Some Observations on the Scope of Appraisal Statutes,* 13 Bus. Law. 240 (1958).
Stephan, *Acquisition Trouble Spots,* 21 Bus. Law. 401 (1966).
Turner address before the American Bar Assoc. 10 Antitrust Bull. 685 (1965).
Vorenberg, *Exclusiveness of the Dissenting Stockholder's Appraisal Right,* 77 Harv. L. Rev. 1189 (1964).
Willis and Pitofsky, *Antitrust Consequences of Using Corporate Subsidiaries,* 43 N.Y.U.L. Rev. 20 (1968).

CASES

Abelow v. *Midstates Oil Corp.,* 189 A.2d 675 (Del. Sup. Ct. 1963).
Alcott v. *Hyman,* 184 A.2d 90 (Del. Ch. 1962).
Applestein v. *United Board & Carton Corp.,* 60 N.J. Super. 333, 159 A.2d 146, *aff'd per curiam,* 33 N.J. 72, 161 A.2d 474 (1960).
Beloff v. *Consolidated Edison Co.,* 300 N.Y. 11, 87 N.E.2d 561 (1949).
Coyne v. *Park & Tilford Distillers Corp.,* 38 Del. Ch. 514, 154 A.2d 893 (Sup. Ct. 1959).
Drug, Inc. v. *Hunt,* 35 Del (5 W. W. Harr.) 339, 168 A. 87 (1933).
Farris v. *Glen Alden Corp.,* 393 Pa. 427, 143 A.2d 25 (1958).
Finch v. *Warrior Cement Corp.,* 16 Del. Ch. 44, 141 A. 54 (1928).
Hariton v. *Arco Electronics, Inc.,* 188 A.2d 123 (Del. 1963), *aff'g* 182 A.2d 22 (Del. Ch. 1962).
Hawaiian Oke & Liquors, Ltd. v. *Joseph E. Seagram and Sons, Inc.,* 272 F. Supp. 915 (D. Hawaii 1967), *rev'd, Joseph E. Seagram and Sons, Inc.* v. *Hawaiian Oke and Liquors, Ltd.,* 416 F.2d 71 (9th Cir. 1969).
Heilbrunn v. *Sun Chem. Corp.,* 38 Del. Ch. 321, 150 A.2d 755 (Sup. Ct. 1959), *aff'g* 37 Del. Ch. 552, 146 A.2d 757 (Ch. 1958).
In Re San Joaquin Light & Power Corp., 52 Cal. App. 2d 814, 127 P.2d 29 (1942).
Kellogg v. *Georgia-Pacific Paper Corp.,* 227 F. Supp. 719 (W.D. Ark. 1964).
Kiefer-Stewart Co. v. *Joseph E. Seagram & Sons, Inc.,* 340 U.S. 211 (1951).
Mitchell Inv. Co. v. *Republic Steel Corp.,* 63 F. Supp. 323 (N.D. Ohio 1944), *aff'd per curiam,* 152 F.2d 105 (6th Cir. 1945).
Nelson Radio & Supply Co. v. *Motorola,* 200 F.2d 911 (5th Cir. 1952), *cert. denied,* 343 U.S. 925 (1953).
Orzeck v. *Englehart,* 192 A.2d 36 (Del. Ch. 1963).
Perma Life Mufflers, Inc. v. *International Parts Corporation,* 392 U.S. 134 (1968).
Rath v. *Rath Packing Co.,* 257 Iowa 1277, 136 N.W.2d 410 (1965).
Stauffer v. *Standard Brands, Inc.,* 187 A.2d 78 (Del.), *aff'g* 178 A.2d 311 (Del. Ch. 1962).
Sunkist Growers, Inc. v. *Winckler,* 370 U.S. 19 (1962).
United States v. *Arnold, Schwinn & Co.,* 388 U.S. 365 (1967).
Zimmerman v. *Tide Water Associated Oil Co.,* 61 Cal. App. 2d 585, 143 P.2d 409 (1943).

Chapter 4: Dealing in Securities

BIBLIOGRAPHY

Andrews, *The Stockholder's Rights to Equal Opportunity in the Sale of Shares,* 78 Harv. L. Rev. 505 (1965) (and articles cited therein).
Bayne, *The Sale of Corporate Control,* 33 Fordham L. Rev. 583 (1965).

Bayne, *A Legitimate Transfer of Control: The Weyenberg Shoe-Florsheim Case Study,* 18 Stan. L. Rev. 438 (1966).

Bayne, *The Sale of Corporate Control: The Definition,* 53 Minn. L. Rev. 485 (1969).

Bayne, *The Sale of Control Premium: The Intrinsic Illegitimacy,* 47 Texas L. Rev. 215 (1969).

Berle, *The Price of Power: Sale of Control,* 50 Corn. L.Q. 628 (1965).

Connolly, *Perlman* v. *Feldmann and the Sale of Control—A Brief Reconsideration,* 25 Bus. Law. 1259 (1971).

Hill, *The Sale of Controlling Shares,* 70 Harv. L. Rev. 986 (1957).

Kennedy, *The Case of the Scarlet Letter or the Easy Way Out on "Private Offerings,"* 23 Bus. Law. 23 (1967).

Leech, *Transactions in Corporate Control,* 104 U. Pa. L. Rev. 725 (1956).

Loss, *Securities Regulation,* Vol. I, (2d ed. 1961, Supp. 1969).

Note, *The Sale of Control: The Berle Theory and the Law,* 25 U. Pitt. L. Rev. 59 (1963).

PLI, *Texas Gulf Sulphur—Insider Disclosure Problems* (1968).

Posternak, *Restricted Securities: The Private Placement Exemption and Rule 144 of the Securities Act of 1933,* 57 Mass. L.Q. 11 (1972).

Schneider, *Acquisitions Under the Federal Securities Acts—A Program for Reform,* 116 U. Pa. L. Rev. 1323 (1968).

Securities Act Release No. 4552, November 6, 1962 [factors to be considered in determining the availability of the exemption from registration provided by Section 4 (2) of the 1933 Act].

Securities Act Release No. 4936, December 9, 1968 (concerning shelf registration).

Securities Act Release No. 5087, September 22, 1970 (containing proposed Rule 144).

Securities Act Release No. 5121, December 30, 1970 (use of restrictive legends and stop transfer instructions as factor in determining availability of private offering exemption).

Securities Act Release No. 5223, January 11, 1972 (containing adoption of Rule 144).

Securities Act Release No. 5316, October 6, 1972 (containing adoption of Rule 145).

Wheat, *Disclosure to Investors—A Reappraisal of Administrative Policies under the '33 and '34 Acts* (1969).

Whiting, *Personal Exposure of Officers and Directors in Mergers and Acquisitions,* 1 Mergers and Acquisitions 34 (Summer 1966).

CASES

Burke v. *Triple A Machine Shop, Inc.,* 438 F.2d 978 (9th Cir. 1971).

Cady, Roberts & Co., 40 S.E.C. 907 (1961).

Crowell-Collier Publishing Co., Securities Act Release No. 3825 (August 12, 1957), *aff'd sub nom. Gilligan, Will & Co.* v. *SEC,* 267 F.2d 461 (2d Cir.), *cert. denied,* 361 U.S. 896 (1959).

Great Sweet Grass Oils, Ltd., 37 S.E.C. 683 (1957), *aff'd per curiam,* 256 F.2d 893 (D.C. Cir. 1958).

Honigman v. *Green Giant Co.,* 208 F. Supp. 754 (D. Minn. 1961), *aff'd,* 309 F.2d 667 (6th Cir.), *cert. denied,* 372 U.S. 941 (1963).

Ingraffia v. *Belle Meade Hospital, Inc.,* CCH Fed. Sec. L. Rep. ¶ 92,896 (D.C. La. 1970).

Nathanson v. *Weis, Voisin, Canon, Inc.,* 325 F. Supp. 50 (S.D.N.Y. 1971).

Perlman v. *Feldmann,* 219 F.2d 173 (2d Cir.), *cert. denied,* 349 U.S. 952 (1955).

SEC v. *National Securities, Inc.,* 393 U.S. 453 (1969).

SEC v. *Ralston Purina Co.,* 346 U.S. 119 (1953).
SEC v. *Texas Gulf Sulphur Co.,* 401 F.2d 833 (2d Cir. 1968), *cert. denied,* 394 U.S. 976 (1969).
Speed v. *Transamerica Corp.,* 99 F. Supp. 808 (D. Del. 1951).

Chapter 5: Tender Offers and Take-overs

BIBLIOGRAPHY

Aranow and Einhorn, *Proxy Contests for Corporate Control* (1968).
Austin and Fishman, *Corporations in Conflict: The Tender Offer* (1970).
Bromberg, *The Securities Law of Tender Offers,* 15 N.Y.L.F. 459 (1969).
Brudney, *Note on Chilling Tender Solicitations,* 21 Rutgers L. Rev. 609 (1967).
Burck, *The Merger Movement Rides High,* Fortune, Feb. 1969, at 79.
Cary, *Corporate Devices used to Insulate Management from Attack,* 39 ABA Antitrust L.J. 318 (1970); 25 Bus. Law. 839 (1970).
Cohen, *Note on Takeover Bids and Corporate Purchases of Stock,* Address before American Society of Corporate Secretaries, Inc., Colorado Springs, Colo., June 28, 1966, reprinted at 22 Bus. Law. 149 (1966); 2 Mergers & Acquisitions 87 (Fall, 1966).
Comment, *Application of Margin Requirements to the Cash Tender Offer,* 116 U. Pa. L. Rev. 103 (1967).
Comment, *Corporate Defenses to Takeover Bids,* 44 Tul. L. Rev. 517 (1970).
Comment, *Eurodollar Financing of Cash Tender Offers: A New Challenge to the Margin Requirements,* 118 U. Pa. L. Rev. 767 (1970).
Comment, *Take-Over Bids in Virginia,* 26 Wash. & Lee L. Rev. 323 (1969).
Fleischer and Mundheim, *Corporate Acquisition by Tender Offer,* 115 U. Pa. L. Rev. 317 (1967).
Haack, *Take-Overs and Tenders: A Stock Exchange Viewpoint,* 44 St. John's L. Rev. 915 (Spring 1970, Special Edition); 25 Bus. Law. 931 (1970).
Hamilton, *Some Reflections on Cash Tender Offer Legislation,* 15 N.Y.L.F. 269 (1969).
Hayes and Taussig, *Tactics of Cash Takeover Bids,* 45 Harv. Bus. Rev. 135 (March–April 1967).
Hearings on H.R. 14475, S. 510, Before the Subcomm. on Commerce and Finance of the House Comm. on Interstate and Foreign Commerce, 90th Cong., 2d Sess., ser. 90–44 (1968).
Hearings on S. 510 Before the Subcomm. on Sec. of the Senate Comm. on Banking and Currency, 90th Cong., 1st Sess., at 3 (1967).
Herzel, *Strategy and Tactics in Stockholder Litigation,* 15 Prac. Law. 65 (May 1969).
How to Fend Off a Take-Over, Fortune, Feb. 1969, at 83.
Kelly, *Some Observations on Contested Take-Over Bids,* 15 N.Y.L.F. 619 (1969).
Kennedy, *Defensive Take-over Procedures since the Williams Act,* 19 Catholic U. L. Rev. 158 (1969).
Kennedy, *Tender Moment,* 23 Bus. Law. 1091 (1968).
Kennedy, *Corporation's Obligations When It Is Trading in Its Stock,* 50 Chi. B. Rec. 384 (1969).
Klink, *Management's Role in Recommending For or Against an Offer,* 39 ABA Antitrust L.J. 325 (1970).
Manne, *Cash Tender Offers for Shares—A Reply to Chairman Cohen,* 1967 Duke L.J. 231.
Mullaney, *Guarding Against Takeovers—Defensive Charter Provisions,* 25 Bus. Law. 1441 (1970).

Note, "*Proper Purpose*" *for Inspection of Corporate Stock Ledger,* 1970 Duke L.J. 393.
Note, *Cash Tender Offers,* 83 Harv. L. Rev. 377 (1969).
Note, *Closing the Disclosure Gap in Corporate Take-Overs: The Williams Amendments and the Wheat Report,* 44 St. John's L. Rev. 484 (1970).
Note, *Defensive Tactics Employed by Incumbent Managements in Contesting Tender Offers,* 21 Stan. L. Rev. 1104 (1969).
Note, *Williams Amendments: An Evaluation of the Early Returns,* 23 Vand. L. Rev. 700 (1970).
O'Boyle, *Changing Tactics in Tender Offers,* 39 ABA Antitrust L.J. 345 (1970).
O'Hanlon, *Goodrich's Four-Ply Defense,* Fortune, July 1969, at 110.
Rukeyser, *Getting Tough with Tenders,* Fortune, August 1967, at 108.
Schmults and Kelly, *Cash Take-over Bids—Defense Tactics,* 23 Bus. Law. 115 (1967).
Sen. Comm. on Banking and Currency, *Full Disclosure of Corporate Equity Ownership and in Corporate Takeover Bids,* S.Rep. No. 550, 90th Cong., 1st Sess. (1967).
Smith, *Conglomerates and Take-Overs,* 44 St. John's L. Rev. 905 (Spring 1970, Special Edition).
Taussig and Hayes, *Are Cash Take-Over Bids Unethical?* 23 Fin. Analysts J. 107 (Jan.–Feb. 1967).
Vance, *Is Your Company a Take-Over Target?* 47 Harv. Bus. Rev. 93 (May–June 1969).
Wetzel, *Defensive Tactics—Who Are the Goodies and Who Are the Baddies?* 25 Bus. Law. 545 (1970).

CASES

Bath Indus., Inc. v. *Blot,* 427 F.2d 97 (7th Cir. 1970).
Birnbaum v. *Newport Steel Corp.,* 193 F.2d 461 (2d Cir.), *cert. denied* 343 U.S. 956 (1952).
Broffe v. *Horton,* 172 F.2d 489 (2d Cir. 1949).
Cady, Roberts & Co., 40 S.E.C. 907 (1961).
Cheff v. *Mathes,* 41 Del. Ch. 494, 199 A.2d 548 (1964).
Chris-Craft Industries, Inc. v. *Bangor Punta Corp.,* 426 F.2d 569 (2d Cir. 1970).
Cockrane v. *Channing Corp.,* 211 F. Supp. 239 (S.D.N.Y. 1962).
Electronic Specialty Co. v. *International Controls Corp.,* 409 F.2d 937 (2d Cir. 1969).
Elgin National Industries, Inc. v. *Chemetron Corp.,* 299 F. Supp. 367 (D. Del. 1969).
Gerstle v. *Gamble-Skogmo, Inc.,* 298 F. Supp. 66 (E.D.N.Y. 1969).
Mills v. *Sarjem Corp.,* 133 F. Supp. 753 (D. N.J. 1955).
Pan American Sulphur Co. v. *Susquehanna Corp.,* 423 F.2d 1075 (5th Cir. 1970).
SEC v. *Georgia-Pacific Corp.,* 1964–1966 CCH Fed. Sec. L. Rep. ¶ 91,692 (S.D.N.Y. 1966).
SEC v. *Texas Gulf Sulphur Co.,* 401 F.2d 833 (2d Cir. 1968), *cert. denied,* 394 U.S. 976 (1969).
Sunray DX Oil Co. v. *Helmerich & Payne, Inc.,* 398 F.2d 447 (10th Cir. 1968).

Chapter 6: Accounting Aspects of Mergers

BIBLIOGRAPHY

American Institute of Certified Public Accountants:
Accounting for Convertible Debt and Debt Issued with Stock Purchase Warrants, APB Op. No. 14 (1969).

Business Combinations, APB Op. No. 16 (1970).
Business Combinations, ARB No. 48 (1957).
Business Combinations, ARB No. 40 (1950).
Consolidated Financial Statements, ARB No. 51 (1959).
Disclosure of Supplemental Financial Information by Diversified Companies, APB Stat. No. 2 (1967).
Earnings Per Share, APB Op. No. 15 (1969).
Earnings Per Share, ARB No. 49 (1968).
Intangible Assets, APB Op. No. 17 (1970).
Olson and Catlett, *Accounting for Goodwill,* Study No. 10 (1968).
Omnibus Opinion, APB Op. No. 10 (1966).
Reporting the Results of Operations, APB Op. No. 9 (1966).
Restatement and Revision of Accounting Research Bulletins, ARB No. 43 (1953).
Wyatt, *A Critical Study of Accounting for Business Combinations,* Study No. 5 (1963).

Backer and McFarland, *External Reporting for Segments of a Business* (1968).
Briloff, *Dirty Pooling,* 42 Accounting Rev. 489 (1967).
Briloff, *Distortions Arising from Pooling-of-Interests Accounting,* Fin. Analysts J., March–April, 1968, at 71.
Briloff, *Dirty Pooling: How to Succeed in Business Without Really Trying,* Barron's, July 15, 1968, at 1.
Briloff, *Much-Abused Goodwill,* Barron's, April 28, 1969, at 3.
Briloff, *Out of Focus,* Barron's, July 28, 1969, at 5.
Briloff, *The "Funny-Money" Game,* Fin. Analysts J., May–June, 1969, at 73.
Conglomerate Mergers and Acquisitions: Opinion and Analysis, 44 St. John's L. Rev. (Spring 1970) (Special Edition).
Gunther, *Part Purchase—Part Pooling: The Infusion of Confusion Into Fusion,* 39 N.Y.C.P.A. 241 (April 1969).
Harris, *The Need to Keep Growing by Acquisition and the Increasing Difficulty of Doing So,* 39 ABA Antitrust L.J. 282 (1969).
Hill, *Accounting Options and Conglomerates,* 39 ABA Antitrust L.J. 49 (1969).
Hobgood, *Voluntary Disclosure in 1968 Annual Reports,* Financial Executive, Aug. 1969, at 64.
Kripke, *Accounting for Corporate Acquisitions and the Treatment of Goodwill: An Alert Signal to All Business Lawyers,* 24 Bus. Law. 89 (1968).
Kripke, *Accounting Options Which Facilitate Conglomerate Growth,* 39 ABA Antitrust L.J. 35 (1969).
Kripke, *A Good Look at Goodwill in Corporate Acquisitions,* 78 Banking L.J. 1028 (1961).
Machinery and Allied Products Institute, *Top Management Looks at Product-Line Reporting* (1967).
Mautz, *Financial Reporting by Diversified Companies* (Fin. Exec. Inst. Study 1968).
Mosich, *Retroactive Poolings in Corporate Mergers,* 41 J. Bus. 352 (1968).
Pacter, *Conglomerate Reporting—The Debate Continues,* 127 J. Accountancy 24 (1969).
Rappaport and Lerner, *A Framework for Financial Reporting by Diversified Companies* (1969).
Rappaport, Firmin, and Zeff, *Public Reporting by Conglomerates* (1968).
Savoie, *Financial Communication: The Public's Right to Know,* 36 Financial Executive, Dec. 1968, at 21.
SEC, Accounting Series Release No. 50 (1945).
SEC, *Disclosure to Investors, A Reappraisal of Federal Administrative Policies Under the '33 and '34 Acts* (1969) (the Wheat Report).

Sommer, *Conglomerate Disclosure: Friend or Foe?* 23 Bus. Law. 317 (1967).
Taussig and Hayes, *Cash Takeovers and Accounting Valuations,* 43 Accounting Rev. 68 (1968).

Chapter 7: Tax Considerations

BIBLIOGRAPHY

Dailey, *The Voting Stock Requirement of B & C Reorganizations*, 26 Tax L. Rev. 725 (1971).
Flyer, *An Analysis of the New "A" Reorganization: Its Operation & Planning Potential,* 35 J. Taxation 30 (1971).
Hagendorf, *A Study of Tax-free Reorganizations,* 5 Mergers & Acquisitions 4 (1970).
Hagendorf, *Tax Primer for Buying or Selling an Operating Division,* 4 Mergers & Acquisitions 24 (1969).
Lowenstein, *"A" Reorganizations: Technical Requirements for Compliance Under the New Law,* 30 J. Taxation 169 (1969).
Shors, *Corporate Reorganizations: Some Current Developments Including The Tax Reform Act of 1969,* 44 St. John's L. Rev. 1128 (1970) (Special Edition).
Sinrich, *Tax Incentives and the Conglomerate Merger: An Introduction,* 44 St. John's L. Rev. 1009 (1971) (Special Edition).
Walsh and Gerard, *Planning Possibilities in Using Parent's Stock in a Corporate Reorganization,* 30 J. Taxation 168 (1969).

Chapter 8: Labor Aspects of Mergers

BIBLIOGRAPHY

Banta, *Labor Obligations of Successor Employers,* 36 Geo. Wash. L. Rev. 215 (1967).
Barbash, *Status of the Collective Bargaining Agreement under Wiley v. Livingston: A Management Counsel's View,* 18 N.Y.U. Conf. on Labor 259 (1966).
Bernstein, *Labor Problems on Acquisitions and Sale of Assets,* 22 N.Y.U. Conf. on Labor 81 (1970).
Bliss, *Labor's Plan Closure Pains,* 24 Sw. L.J. 259 (1970).
Comment, *Duty of Employer to Arbitrate with Union Representing Employees of Purchased Company,* 66 Colum. L. Rev. 967 (1966).
Comment, *Impact of John Wiley Revisited—From the Vindication of Policy to the Verge of Inequity,* 21 Syracuse L. Rev. 875 (1970).
Comment, *Successor Employer's Obligation Under Predecessor's Collective Bargaining Agreement After a Business Reorganization,* 36 Fordham L. Rev. 569 (1968).
Dunau, *Subcontracting and Unilateral Employer Action,* 18 N.Y.U. Conf. on Labor 219 (1966).
Feller, *Status of the Collective Bargaining Agreement Under Wiley v. Livingston: A Union Counsel's View,* 18 N.Y.U. Conf. on Labor 277 (1966).
Fuhrer, *Assumption by a Purchasing, Merging or Consolidation Corporation of Labor Contract Obligations of Its Predecessor,* 17 N.Y.U. Intra. L. Rev. 228 (1962).
Goldberg, *The Labor Law Obligations of a Successor Employer,* 63 Nw. U.L. Rev. 735 (1969).
Gordon, *Legal Questions of Successorship,* 3 Georgia L. Rev. 280 (1969).
Jay, *Change of Ownership and Representation Problems,* 18 N.Y.U. Conf. on Labor 293 (1966).

Laner, *A Buyer Views the Purchase of a Unionized Business,* 47 Chi. Bar Rec. 93 (1965).
Lanquist, *Successor Employer—Something Else to Consider,* 44 Fla. B.J. 590 (1970).
Lippman, *Changes of Ownership and Representation Problems: A Union View,* 18 N.Y.U. Conf. on Labor 315 (1966).
Maddux, *Labor Law Problems in Changed Business Operations,* 20 Bus. Law. 573 (1965).
Mermin, *The Impact of Darlington—Fibreboard,* 18 N.Y.U. Conf. on Labor 235 (1966).
Moss, *Labor Law Problems, Purchase of a Business,* 43 Calif. S.B.J. 387 (1968).
Nelson, *Through a Looking Glass Darkly; Fibreboard Five Years Later,* 21 Lab. L.J. 755 (1970).
Note, *Obligations of Successor Employers: Recent Variations on the John Wiley Theme,* 2 Georgia L. Rev. 574 (1968).
Note, *Obligations of the Purchasing Employer on a Pre-Existing Labor Contract,* 5 Santa Clara Law. 182 (1965).
Note, *Seniority Rights in Mergers,* 52 Iowa L. Rev. 95 (1966).
Note, *The Duties of Successor Employers Under John Wiley & Sons v. Livingston and Its Progeny,* 43 N.Y.U. L. Rev. 498 (1968).
Note, *The Successor Employer's Duty to Arbitrate: A Reconsideration of John Wiley & Sons, Inc. v. Livingston,* 82 Harv. L. Rev. 418 (1968).
O'Neill, *Collective Bargaining from Acquisition to Termination—The Law and Some Advice,* 19 Lab. L.J. 407 (1968).
Oviatt, *The Aftermath of Fibreboard: Some Unanswered Questions,* 19 N.Y.U. Conf. on Labor 397 (1967).
Oviatt, *Union Contracts, Sales and Mergers,* 41 Conn. B.J. 70 (1967).
Platt, *The Duty to Bargain as Applied to Management Decisions,* 19 Lab. L.J. 143 (1968).
Platt, *The NLRB and the Arbitrator in Sale and Merger Situations,* 19 N.Y.U. Conf. on Labor 375 (1967).
Sangerman, *The Labor Obligations of the Successor to a Unionized Business,* 19 Lab. L.J. 160 (1968).
Shaw and Carter, *Sales, Mergers and Union Contract Relations,* 19 N.Y.U. Conf. on Labor 357 (1967).
Spelfogel, *Labor Liabilities in Purchases, Acquisitions and Mergers: The NLRB's Successor and Accretion Doctrines,* 21 Lab. L.J. 577 (1970).
Sullivan, *The Sale of a Business—Seller's View,* 47 Chi. Bar Rec. 102 (1965).
Tockman, *Labor Law Considerations and Consequences of "Change" in Business Operations,* 59 Ill. B.J. 454 (1971).
Vernon, *Business Combinations and Collective Bargaining Agreements,* 19 Catholic U. L. Rev. 1 (1969).
Willard, *Labor Law Aspects of Corporate Acquisitions,* 36 U.M.K.C.L. Rev. 241 (1968).
Zeman, *The Aftermath of Fibreboard: The Cooling Off Period,* 19 N.Y.U. Conf. on Labor 413 (1967).

CASES

Chemrock Corp., 151 N.L.R.B. No. 111 (1965).
Emerald Maintenance, Inc., 188 N.L.R.B. No. 139 (1971).
Fibreboard Paper Prod. Corp. v. *N.L.R.B.,* 379 U.S. 203 (1964).
Garwin Corp., 153 N.L.R.B. No. 59 (1965).
Hackney Iron & Steel Co., 182 N.L.R.B. No. 53 (1970).
Interscience Encyclopedia, Inc., 55 L.A. 210, Aug. 7, 1970 (Benjamin C. Roberts, Arbitrator).

John Wiley & Sons, Inc. v. *Livingston,* 376 U.S. 543 (1964).
Kota Division of Dura Corp., 182 N.L.R.B. No. 51 (1970).
McGuire v. *Humble Oil & Refining Co.,* 355 F.2d 352 (2d Cir.), *cert. denied,* 384 U.S. 988 (1966).
Monroe Sander Corp. v. *Livingston,* 377 F.2d 6 (2d Cir.), *cert. denied,* 389 U.S. 831 (1967).
New York Mirror, Division of The Hearst Corp., 151 N.L.R.B. No. 110 (1965).
N.L.R.B. v. *Adams Dairy, Inc.,* 350 F.2d 108 (8th Cir. 1965).
N.L.R.B. v. *Dixie Ohio Express Co.,* 409 F.2d 10 (6th Cir. 1969).
N.L.R.B. v. *King Radio Corp.,* 416 F.2d 569 (10th Cir. 1969).
N.L.R.B. v. *Rapid Bindery, Inc.,* 293 F.2d 170 (2nd Cir. 1961).
N.L.R.B. v. *Transmarine Navigation Corp.,* 380 F.2d 933 (9th Cir. 1967).
Overnite Transportation Co. v. *N.L.R.B.,* 372 F.2d 765 (4th Cir.), *cert. denied,* 389 U.S. 838 (1967).
Pepsi-Cola Bottling Co. of Beckley, 145 N.L.R.B. No. 82 (1964).
Perma Vinyl Corp., Dade Plastics Co., and U.S. Pipe & Foundry Co., 164 N.L.R.B. No. 119 (1967), *aff'd,* 398 F.2d 544 (5th Cir. 1968).
Ramada Inns, Inc., 171 N.L.R.B. No. 115 (1968).
Renton News Record, 136 N.L.R.B. 1294 (1962).
Royal Plating and Polishing Co., 152 N.L.R.B. No. 76, *enforcement denied,* 350 F.2d 191 (3d Cir. 1965).
S. B. Penick & Co., 64–3 ARB ¶ 9102 (Burton Turkus, Arbitrator).
Simmons Engineering Co., 65 N.L.R.B. 1373 (1946).
Teamsters v. *Red Ball Motor Freight, Inc.,* 374 F.2d 932 (5th Cir. 1967).
Travelodge Corp., 182 N.L.R.B. No. 52 (1970).
United Steelworkers v. *Reliance Universal, Inc.,* 335 F.2d 891 (3rd Cir. 1964).
U.S. Gypsum Co. v. *United Steelworkers,* 384 F.2d 38 (5th Cir. 1967), *cert. denied,* 389 U.S. 1042 (1968).
Wackenhut Corp. v. *United Plant Guard Workers,* 332 F.2d 954 (9th Cir. 1964).
Webb Tractor & Equip. Co., 181 N.L.R.B. No. 39 (1970).
William J. Burns International Detective Agency, 182 N.L.R.B. No. 50 (1970), *enforced in part,* 441 F.2d 911 (2d Cir. 1971).

Chapter 10: Antitrust Theory

BIBLIOGRAPHY

Hacker, *The Triumph of American Capitalism* (1947).
Hamilton, *Report on Manufactures* (1791).
Hofstadter, *Social Darwinism in American Thought* (3rd. ed. 1965).
Kariel, *The Decline of American Pluralism* (1967).
Letwin, *A Documentary History of American Economic Policy Since 1789* (1962).
Rozwenc, *Roosevelt, Wilson and the Trusts* (1950).
Wilson, *The New Freedom* (1913).

CASES

Brown Shoe Co. v. *United States,* 370 U.S. 294 (1962).
Richardson v. *Buhl,* 77 Mich. 632, 43 N.W. 1102 (1889).
Standard Oil Co. v. *United States,* 193 U.S. 197 (1904).
United States v. *United States Steel Corp.,* 251 U.S. 417 (1920).
United States v. *United States Steel Corp.,* 334 U.S. 862 (1948).

Chapter 11: Mergers Under the Original Clayton Act

BIBLIOGRAPHY

Carter, *The Clayton Act, Original Section 7: Re-examination & Reappraisal,* 8 Antitrust Bull. 187 (1963).
Hernacki, *Mergerism & Section 7 of the Clayton Act,* 20 Geo. Wash. L. Rev. 659 (1952).
Martin, *Mergers and the Clayton Act* (1959).
Weston, *The Role of Mergers in the Growth of Large Firms* (1953).
Vuskasin, *The Anti-merger Law of the United States: Yesterday, Today, Tomorrow* (Part 1), 3 Antitrust Bull. 309 (1958).
The Celler-Kefauver Act: Sixteen Years of Enforcement, FTC Economic Papers 1966–69.

CASES

FTC v. *Western Meat Co.,* 272 U.S. 554 (1926).
International Shoe Co. v. *FTC,* 280 U.S. 291 (1930).
Swift & Co. v. *FTC,* 272 U.S. 554 (1926).
Standard Fashion Company v. *Magrane-Houston Co.,* 258 U.S. 346 (1922).
Thatcher Manufacturing Company v. *FTC,* 272 U.S. 554 (1926).
United States v. *E. I. du Pont de Nemours & Co.,* 353 U.S. 586 (1957).
V. Vivaudou, Inc. v. *FTC,* 54 F.2d 273 (2d Cir. 1931).

Chapter 12: Mergers Under the Sherman Act

BIBLIOGRAPHY

Arnold, *Fair Fights & Foul* (1960).
Bock, *Mergers & Markets* (1960).
Carter, *Commercial Banking and the Antitrust Laws,* 11 Antitrust Bull. 141 (1966).
Casson and Burrus, *Federal Regulation of Bank Mergers,* 18 Am. U. L. Rev. 677 (1969).
Fortas, *Thurman Arnold and the Theatre of the Law,* 79 Yale L.J. 988 (1970).
Hampton, *The Merger Movement in Historic Perspective—A Lawyer's View,* 39 ABA Antitrust L.J. 107 (1969–70).
Handler, *Industrial Mergers and the Antitrust Laws,* 32 Colum. L. Rev. 179 (1932).
Handler, *The Supreme Court and the Antitrust Laws* (From the Viewpoint of the Critic), 34 ABA Antitrust L.J. 21 (1969).
Hodges, *The Antitrust Act & The Supreme Court* (1941).
Kaysen and Turner, *Antitrust Policy* (1959).
Memorandum of Felix Frankfurter, Roosevelt & Frankfurter: Their Correspondence 1928–1945 (1967).
"Mergers Under the Sherman Act," *Antitrust & Trade Regulation Today* 124 (BNA 2d ed. 1966).
Note, *Merger Litigation Under the Sherman Act—Choice or Echo,* 18 Sw. L.J. 712 (1964).
Oppenheim and Weston, *Federal Antitrust Laws* (3rd ed. 1968).
Rostow, *Thurman Arnold,* 79 Yale L.J. 985 (1970).
Seely, *Banks & Antitrust,* 21 Bus. Law. 917 (1966).
Studies in Banking Competition & The Banking Structure (1966) (*Nat'l Banking Review* reprints).

Survey, *Economic Institutions & Value Survey: Legal Conflicts Within the Banking Industry,* 42 Notre Dame Law. 707 (1967).
Van Cise, *Understanding the Antitrust Laws* (1966).
Waxberg & Robinson, *Chaos in Federal Regulation of Bank Mergers: A Need for Legislative Revision,* 82 Banking L.J. 377 (1965).

CASES

American Crystal Sugar Co. v. *Cuban-American Sugar Co.,* 152 F. Supp. 387 (S.D.N.Y. 1957), *aff'd,* 259 F.2d 524 (2d Cir. 1958).
Crown Zellerbach Corp. v. *FTC,* 296 F.2d 800 (9th Cir. 1961).
International Shoe Co. v. *FTC,* 280 U.S. 291 (1930).
Northern Securities Co. v. *United States,* 193 U.S. 197 (1904).
Standard Oil Company v. *United States,* 221 U.S. 1 (1911).
Transamerica Corp. v. *Board of Governors,* 206 F.2d 163 (3rd Cir. 1953).
United States v. *American Tobacco Company,* 221 U.S. 106 (1911).
United States v. *Columbia Steel Company,* 334 U.S. 495 (1948).
United States v. *First National Bank of Maryland,* 1970 Trade Cas. ¶ 73,061 (D. Md. 1970).
United States v. *First National Bank & Trust Company of Lexington,* 376 U.S. 665 (1964).
United States v. *Joint Traffic Ass'n,* 171 U.S. 905 (1898).
United States v. *Philadelphia National Bank,* 374 U.S. 321 (1963).
United States v. *Reading Co.,* 253 U.S. 26 (1920).
United States v. *Southern Pacific Company,* 259 U.S. 214 (1922).
United States v. *Union Pacific Railroad,* 226 U.S. 61 (1912).
United States v. *Von's Grocery Co.,* 384 U.S. 270 (1966).

Chapter 13: Mergers Under Section 5 of the FTC Act

BIBLIOGRAPHY

Comment, *Per Se Rules and Section 5 of the Federal Trade Commission Act,* 54 Cal. L. Rev. 2049 (1966).
Oppenheim, *Guides to Harmonizing Section 5 of the Federal Trade Commission Act with the Sherman and Clayton Acts,* 59 Mich. L. Rev. 821 (1961).
Phillips and Hall, *Merger Litigation, 1951–1960,* 6 Antitrust Bull. 19 (1961).

CASES

Allied Chemical Corp., [1967–70 Transfer Binder] Trade Reg. Rep. ¶ 19,237 (FTC 1970).
American News Co. v. *FTC,* 300 F.2d 104 (2d Cir. 1962).
Armour Co., 10 F.T.C. 427 (1926).
Beatrice Foods Co., 1971 Trade Reg. Rep. ¶ 19,642 (FTC 1971).
Beatrice Foods Co., [1965–67 Transfer Binder] Trade Reg. Rep. ¶ 17,244 (FTC 1965).
Campbell Taggert Asso. Bakeries, Inc., [1967–70 Transfer Binder] Trade Reg. Rep. ¶ 17,912 (FTC 1967).
Canfield Oil Co. v. *FTC,* 224 F. 571 (6th Cir. 1921).
Continental Baking Co., 60 F.T.C. 1191 (1962).
Crane Co., 61 F.T.C. 1462 (1962).
Crown-Zellerbach Corp. v. *FTC,* 296 F.2d 800 (9th Cir. 1961).
Eastman Kodak v. *FTC,* 224 U.S. 619 (1927).

Erie Sand & Gravel Co., 56 F.T.C. 437 (1959), *remanded,* 291 F.2d 279 (3rd Cir. 1961).
Ford Motor Co. v. *FTC,* 274 F. 571 (6th Cir. 1921).
Foremost Dairies, Inc., 60 F.T.C. 944 (1962).
Fruehauf Trailer Co., 53 F.T.C. 1269 (1965).
FTC v. *Beechnut Packing Co.,* 257 U.S. 441 (1922).
FTC v. *Brown Shoe Co.,* 384 U.S. 316 (1966).
FTC v. *Dean Foods Co.,* 384 U.S. 597 (1966).
FTC v. *Gratz,* 253 U.S. 421 (1920).
FTC v. *Klesner,* 280 U.S. 19 (1929).
FTC v. *Procter & Gamble Co.,* 386 U.S. 568 (1967).
Georgia Pacific Corp., 1971 Trade Reg. Rep. ¶ 19,578 (FTC 1971).
Ideal Cement Co., [1965–67 Transfer Binder] Trade Reg. Rep. ¶ 17,547 (FTC 1966).
Lehigh Portland Cement Co., 1971 Trade Reg. Rep. ¶ 19,455 (FTC 1971).
Lone Star Cement Corp., [1965–67 Transfer Binder] Trade Reg. Rep. ¶ 17,823 (FTC 1967).
Marquette Cement Manufacturing Co., [1967–70 Transfer Binder] Trade Reg. Rep. ¶ 18,888 (FTC 1966).
OKC Corp., 1971 Trade Reg. Rep. ¶ 19,369 (FTC 1970).
Proctor & Gamble Co., 63 F.T.C. 1465 (1963).
Royal Oil Co. v. *FTC,* 262 F.2d 741 (4th Cir. 1959).
Scott Paper Co. v. *FTC,* 301 F.2d 579 (3rd Cir. 1962).
Standard Oil Co. v. *FTC,* 340 U.S. 231 (1950).
United Brands Co., 1971 Trade Reg. Rep. ¶ 19,485 (FTC 1971).

Chapter 14: The Celler-Kefauver Amendment

BIBLIOGRAPHY

ABA Antitrust Section, Merger Case Digest (1967).
Adams and Dirlan, *Brown Shoe: In Step With Antitrust,* 1963 Wash. U. L.Q. 158.
Adelman, *The Antimerger Act 1950–60,* 51 Am. Economic Rev. 236 (1961).
Adelman, *Economic Aspects of the Bethlehem Opinion,* 45 Va. L. Rev. 684 (1959).
Allen, *Only Yesterday* (1931).
Arnold, *Fair Fights and Foul* (1960).
Barnes, *The Primacy of Competition and the Brown Shoe Decision,* 51 Geo. L.J. 706 (1963).
The Backward Sweep Theory and the Oligopoly Problem, 32 ABA Antitrust L.J. 306 (1966).
Berle, *The Developing Law of Corporate Concentration,* 19 U. Chi. L. Rev. 639 (1952).
Bock, *Mergers and Markets* (1962).
Bok, *Section 7 of the Clayton Act and the Merging of Law and Economics,* 74 Harv. L. Rev. 226 (1960).
Bork, *Anticompetitive Enforcement Doctrine Under Section 7 of the Clayton Act,* 39 Texas L. Rev. 832 (1961).
Bowman, *Incipiency, Mergers and the Size Question: Section 7 of the Clayton Act,* 1 Antitrust Bull. 533 (1956).
Burns, *A Study of the Antitrust Laws* (1958).
Butters, Lintner, and Cary, *Effect of Taxation Upon Corporate Mergers* (1951).

Carter, *The Clayton Act, Original Section 7: Re-examination and Reappraisal,* 8 Antitrust Bull. 187 (1963).
Celler, *The Celler-Kefauver Act and the Quest for Market Certainty,* 50 A.B.A.J. 559 (1964).
Celler, *Facts About Antitrust Myths,* 9 Antitrust Bull. 607 (1964).
Celler, *An Antitrust Legislative Program,* in 1962 N.Y. State Bar Assoc. Antitrust Law Symposium, CCH Trade Regulation Rep., at 9.
Celler, *Corporation Mergers and Antitrust Laws,* 7 Mercer L. Rev. 267 (1956).
Celler, *The New Antimerger Statute: The Current Outlook,* 37 A.B.A.J. 897 (1951).
Comment, *ABC's of Clayton 7: Amendment of 1950; Brown Shoe; the court and current complexities,* 10 Vill. L. Rev. 734 (1965).
Cook, *Merger Law and Big Business: A Look Ahead,* 40 N.Y.U.L. Rev. 710 (1965).
Coyle, *Brown Shoe: Judicial Reaffirmance of Traditional Clayton Act Standards,* 1963 Wash. U. L.Q. 174.
Dean and Gustus, *Vertical Integration and Section 7,* 40 N.Y.U.L. Rev. 672 (1965).
Dirlam, *The Celler-Kefauver Act: A Review of Enforcement Policy, in Administered Prices: A Compendium on Public Policy* 125 (1963).
FTC, Report on Corporate Mergers and Acquisitions (1955).
FTC, Report on the Merger Movement: A Summary Report (1948).
Fusfeld, *The Economic Thought of F.D.R. and the Origins of the New Deal* (1958).
Garraty, *The American Nation Since 1865* (1966).
Goldman, *Rendezvous with Destiny* (1952).
Gwynne, *The Federal Trade Commission and Section 7,* 1 Antitrust Bull. 523 (1956).
Handler and Robinson, *A Decade of Administration of the Celler-Kefauver Antimerger Act,* 61 Colum. L. Rev. 629 (1961).
Handler, *Industrial Mergers and the Antitrust Laws,* 32 Colum. L. Rev. 179 (1932).
Hernacki, *Mergerism and Section 7 of the Clayton Act,* 20 Geo. Wash. L. Rev. 659 (1952).
H.R. Rep. No. 1191, 81st Cong., 1st Sess. (1949).
Kintner, *Section 7 Circa 1960—Recent Developments and Future Problems as Seen by a Federal Trade Commission Lawyer,* 39 Texas L. Rev. 823 (1961).
Kintner and Rockefeller, *What's Ahead in Section 7 Enforcement,* 39 U. Detroit L.J. 206 (1961)
Kintner, *Developments Under the Antimerger Act and Other Aspects of the Federal Trade Commission's Antitrust Programs,* 5 Antitrust Bull. 387 (1960).
Kintner, *The Revitalized Federal Trade Commission: A Two Year Evaluation,* 30 N.Y.U.L. Rev. 1143 (1955).
Lewyn and Mann, *Ten Years Under the New Section 7 of the Clayton Act: A Lawyer's Practical Approach to the Case Law,* 36 N.Y.U. L. Rev. 1067 (1961).
Lintner and Butters, *Effect of Mergers on Industrial Concentration 1940–1947,* 32 Rev. of Econ. & Statistics 30 (1950).
Lynch, *The Concentration of Economic Power* (1946).
Markham, *Merger Policy Under The New Section 7: A Six-Year Appraisal,* 43 Va. L. Rev. 489 (1957).
Markham, *Survey of the Evidence and Findings on Mergers, in Business Concentration and Price Policy* (1955).
Martin, *Mergers and the Clayton Act* (1959).
Mason, *Economic Concentration and the Monopoly Problem* (1957).
Mitchell, *Depression Decade* (1957).

Moley, *After Seven Years* (1939).
Montague, *The Celler Anti-Merger Act: An Administrative Problem in an Economic Crisis,* 37 A.B.A.J. 253 (1951).
Nelson, *Merger Movements in American Industry 1895–1956* (1959).
Note, *Section 7 of the Clayton Act: A Legislative History,* 52 Colum. L. Rev. 766 (1952).
Orrick, *The Clayton Act: Then and Now,* 24 ABA Antitrust Section 44 (1964).
Proceedings of the ABA Section of Antitrust Law Subcommittee on Section 7 of the Clayton Act, Implications of Brown Shoe for Merger Law and Enforcement, 8 Antitrust Bull. 225 (1963).
Reid, *Mergers, Managers and the Economy* (1968).
Roosevelt, *Public Papers and Addresses* (Rosenman, ed. 1938).
S. Rep. No. 1775, 81st Cong. 2d Sess. (1950).
Staff of the Bureau of Economics of the Federal Trade Commission, The Celler-Kefauver Act: Sixteen Years of Enforcement, in Economic Papers 1966–69 (1967).
Stigler, *Monopoly and Oligopoly by Merger,* 40 Am. Economic Rev. (1950).
Stocking and Watkins, *Monopoly and Free Enterprise* (1951).
Strichartz, *The Anti-Merger Act: A Legal-Economic Analysis,* 2 How. L.J. 57 (1956).
Symposium on the DuPont-General Motors Opinion, 3 Antitrust Bull. 3 (1958).
Symposium on the DuPont-General Motors Decision: The Merger Problem in a New Perspective, 46 Geo. L.J. 561 (1958).
Thorelli, *The Federal Antitrust Policy, Origination of an American Tradition* (1955).
Thorp, *The Persistence of the Merger Movement,* 21 Am. Economic Rev. 79 (1931).
TNEC, Final Report and Recommendations (1941).
Turner, *Conglomerate Mergers and Section 7 of the Clayton Act,* 78 Harv. L. Rev. 1313 (1965).
Van Cise, *The Modern Corporation and the Antitrust Laws: From Trust to Distrust,* 19 U. Chi. L. Rev. 639 (1952).
von Kalinowski, *Section 7 and Competitive Effects,* 48 Va. L. Rev. 827 (1962).
Vukasin, *The Anti-Merger Law of the United States: Yesterday, Today, Tomorrow,* Pt. 1, 3 Antitrust Bull. 309 (1958).
Weiner, *The New Deal and the Corporation,* 19 U. Chi. L. Rev. 724 (1952).
Weston, *The Role of Mergers in the Growth of Large Firms* (1953).
64 Stat. 1125 (1950), amending 15 U.S.C. §§18 and 22 (1964).

CASES

Arrow-Hart & Hegeman Electric Co. v. *FTC,* 291 U.S. 587 (1934).
Brown Shoe Co. v. *United States,* 370 U.S. 294 (1962).
Farm Journal, Inc., 53 F.T.C. 26 (1956).
Foremost Dairies, Inc., 60 F.T.C. 944 (1962).
Foremost Dairies, Inc., 52 F.T.C. 1480 (1946).
FTC v. *Consolidated Foods Corp.,* 380 U.S. 592 (1965).
FTC v. *Western Meat Co.,* 272 U.S. 554 (1926).
International Shoe Co. v. *FTC,* 280 U.S. 291 (1930).
United States v. *Brown Shoe Co.,* 179 F. Supp. 721 (E.D. Mo. 1959).
United States v. *Columbia Pictures Corp.,* 189 F. Supp. 153 (S.D.N.Y. 1960).
United States v. *Continental Oil Co.,* 1965 Trade Cases ¶ 71,557 (D.N.M.), *rev'd per curiam on other grounds,* 387 U.S. 424 (1967).
United States v. *E. I. du Pont de Nemours & Co.,* 353 U.S. 586 (1957).
United States v. *Lever Bros.,* 216 F. Supp. 887 (S.D.N.Y. 1963).

Chapter 15: Classification of Mergers

BIBLIOGRAPHY

"The Celler-Kefauver Act: Sixteen Years of Enforcement," *FTC Economic Papers 1966–69.*

Comment, *"Substantially to Lessen Competition . . ." Current Problems of Horizontal Mergers,* 68 Yale L.J. 1627 (1959).

Department of Justice Press Release, "Merger Guidelines" (May 30, 1968).

Mueller, *Mergers Among Large Firms,* Hearings on Economic Concentration, 89th Cong., 1st Sess., Pt. 2, 515 (1965).

Pitofsky, *Joint Ventures Under the Antitrust Laws: Some Reflections on the Significance of "Penn-Olin,"* 82 Harv. L. Rev. 1007 (1969).

Reed, *Mergers, Managers & the Economy* (1968).

Turner, *Conglomerate Mergers and Section 7 of the Clayton Act,* 78 Harv. L. Rev. 1313 (1965).

CASES

Brown Shoe Co. v. *United States,* 370 U.S. 294 (1962).

FTC v. *Consolidated Food Corp.,* 380 U.S. 592 (1965).

FTC v. *Procter & Gamble Co.,* 386 U.S. 568 (1967).

General Foods v. *FTC,* 386 F.2d 936 (3rd Cir. 1967), *cert. denied,* 391 U.S. 919 (1968).

Reynolds Metals Co. v. *FTC,* 309 F.2d 223 (D.C. Cir. 1962).

United States v. *E. I. du Pont de Nemours & Co.,* 353 U.S. 586 (1957).

United States v. *El Paso Natural Gas Co.,* 373 U.S. 930 (1964).

United States v. *Pabst Brewing Co.,* 384 U.S. 546 (1966).

United States v. *Penn-Olin Chemical Co.,* 378 U.S. 158 (1964).

United States v. *Philadelphia National Bank,* 374 U.S. 321 (1963).

United States v. *Von's Grocery Co.,* 384 U.S. 270 (1966).

Chapter 16: Relevant Market

BIBLIOGRAPHY

Report of the Attorney General's National Committee to Study the Antitrust Laws (Washington, D.C.: Government Printing Office, 1955).

CASES

Brown Shoe Co. v. *United States,* 370 U.S. 294 (1962).

FTC v. *Procter & Gamble Co.,* 386 U.S. 568 (1967).

General Foods Corp. v. *FTC,* 386 F.2d 936 (3rd Cir. 1967).

Reynolds Metals v. *FTC,* 309 F.2d 223 (D.C. Cir. 1962).

Tampa Electric Co. v. *Nashville Coal Co.,* 365 U.S. 320 (1960).

United States v. *Aluminum Co. of America,* 377 U.S. 271 (1964), *rehearing denied,* 377 U.S. 1010 (1964).

United States v. *Bethlehem Steel Corp.,* 168 F. Supp. 576 (S.D.N.Y. 1958).

United States v. *Columbia Pictures Corp.,* 189 F. Supp. 153 (S.D.N.Y. 1960).

United States v. *Continental Can Co.,* 378 U.S. 441 (1964).

United States v. *E. I. du Pont de Nemours & Co.,* 353 U.S. 586 (1957).

United States v. *E. I. du Pont de Nemours & Co.,* 351 U.S. 377 (1956).

United States v. *El Paso Natural Gas Co.,* 376 U.S. 651 (1964).

United States v. *Kennecott Copper Corp.,* 231 F. Supp. 95 (S.D.N.Y. 1964).

United States v. *Kimberley-Clark Corp.,* 264 F. Supp. 39 (N.D. Cal. 1967).

United States v. *Penn-Olin Chemical Co.,* 378 U.S. 158 (1964).

United States v. *Pennzoil Co.,* 252 F. Supp. 962 (W.D. Pa. 1965).
United States v. *Philadelphia National Bank,* 374 U.S. 321 (1963).
United States v. *Von's Grocery Co.,* 384 U.S. 270 (1966).

Chapter 17: Tests of Unlawfulness

BIBLIOGRAPHY

Comment, *Market Extension Mergers Found Invalid Without Examination of Relevant Markets,* 41 N.Y.U.L. Rev. 975 (1966).

Comment, *Proof of "Section of the Country" Not Necessary Under Section 7 of the Clayton Act,* 51 Minn. L. Rev. 582 (1966).

Comment, *Structural Reciprocity: New Attack on Conglomerates,* 58 Geo. L.J. 609 (1970).

Hall and Phillips, *Antimerger Criteria: Power, Concentration, Foreclosure and Size,* 9 Vill. L. Rev. 211 (1964).

Harvith, *Reciprocity and the Federal Antitrust Laws,* 40 Wash. L. Rev. 133 (1965).

Kaysen and Turner, *Antitrust Policy: An Economic and Legal Analysis* (1959).

Low, *Ease of Entry: A Fundamental Economic Defense in Merger Cases,* 36 Geo. Wash. L. Rev. 515 (1968).

Note, *Competition and the Geographic Market Under Section 7 of the Clayton Act,* 62 Nw.U.L. Rev. 58 (1967).

Note, *Determining the "Line of Commerce" Under Section Seven of the Clayton Act,* 18 Vand. L. Rev. 1506 (1965).

Note, *The ABC's of Clayton 7: Amendment of 1950,* 10 Vill. L. Rev. 734 (1965).

Report of the Attorney General's National Committee to Study the Antitrust Laws (Washington, D.C.: Government Printing Office, 1955).

Rill, *Conglomerate Mergers: The Problem of Superconcentration,* 14 U.C.L.A.L. Rev. 1028 (1967).

Shapiro and Karekcn, *Lines of Commerce, Standards of Illegality and Section 7 Predictability,* 40 N.Y.U.L. Rev. 628 (1965).

Solomon, *Why Uncle Sam Can't Lose a Case under Section 7 of the Clayton Act,* 53 A.B.A.J. 137 (1967).

Turner, *Conglomerate Mergers and Section 7 of the Clayton Act,* 78 Harv. L. Rev. 1313 (1965).

CASES

A. G. Spalding & Co., v. *FTC,* 301 F.2d 585 (3rd Cir. 1962).

Allis-Chalmers Mfg. Co. v. *White Consol. Indus., Inc.,* 414 F.2d 506 (3rd Cir. 1969), *cert. denied,* 396 U.S. 1009 (1970).

American Crystal Sugar Co. v. *Cuban-American Sugar Co.,* 152 F. Supp. 387 (S.D.N.Y. 1957), *aff'd,* 259 F.2d 528 (2d Cir. 1958).

Brown Shoe Co. v. *United States,* 370 U.S. 294 (1962).

Crown-Zellerbach Corp. v. *FTC,* 296 F.2d 800 (9th Cir. 1961).

Ekco Products Co., [1963–65 Transfer Binder] Trade Reg. Rep. ¶ 16,879 (FTC 1964), *aff'd,* 347 F.2d 745 (7th Cir. 1965).

FTC v. *Consolidated Foods Corp.,* 380 U.S. 592 (1965).

FTC v. *Procter & Gamble Co.,* 386 U.S. 568 (1967).

Ford Motor Co. v. *United States,* 92 S. Ct. 1142 (1972).

International Shoe Co. v. *FTC,* 380 U.S. 291 (1930).

National Tea Co., [1965–67 Transfer Binder] Trade Reg. Rep. ¶ 17,463 (FTC 1966).

Reynolds Metals Co. v. *FTC,* 309 F.2d 223 (D.C. Cir. 1962).

Scott Paper Co. v. *FTC,* 301 F.2d 579 (3rd Cir. 1962).
Transamerica Corp. v. *Board of Governors,* 206 F.2d 163 (3rd Cir. 1953), *cert. denied,* 346 U.S. 901 (1953).
United States v. *Bethlehem Steel Corp.,* 108 F. Supp. 576 (S.D.N.Y. 1958).
United States v. *Columbia Steel Co.,* 334 U.S. 495 (1948).
United States v. *Continental Can Co.,* 378 U.S. 441 (1964).
United States v. *E. I. du Pont de Nemours & Co.,* 353 U.S. 586 (1957).
United States v. *E. I. du Pont de Nemours & Co.* (The Cellophane Case), 351 U.S. 377 (1956).
United States v. *El Paso Natural Gas Co.,* 376 U.S. 651 (1964).
United States v. *First National Bank and Trust Co.,* 376 U.S. 665 (1964).
United States v. *Ingersoll-Rand Co.,* 320 F.2d 509 (3rd Cir. 1963).
United States v. *Pabst Brewing Co.,* 384 U.S. 546 (1966).
United States v. *Philadelphia National Bank,* 374 U.S. 321 (1963).
United States v. *Topco Associates, Inc.,* 31 L. Ed. 2d 515 (1972).
United States v. *Von's Grocery Co.,* 384 U.S. 270 (1966).

Chapter 18: Defenses

BIBLIOGRAPHY

Comment, *The Impact of the "Failing Company" Doctrine in the Federal Trade Commission's Pre-Merger Clearance Program,* 19 Syracuse L. Rev. 911 (1968).

CASES

Beatrice Foods Co., [1967–70 Transfer Binder] Trade Reg. Rep. ¶ 19,135 (1970).
Bendix Corp., 1971 Trade Reg. Rep. ¶ 19,288 (FTC 1970).
Brown Shoe Co. v. *United States,* 270 U.S. 294 (1962).
Citizen Publishing Co. v. *United States,* 394 U.S. 131 (1968).
Ford Motor Co. v. *United States,* 92 S. Ct. 1142 (1972).
General Portland Cement Co., [1967–70 Transfer Binder] Trade Reg. Rep. ¶ 19,129 (FTC 1970).
Grandaer v. *Public Bank,* 281 F. Supp. 120 (E.D. Mich. 1967), *aff'd,* 417 F.2d. 75 (6th Cir. 1969).
International Shoe Co. v. *FTC,* 280 U.S. 291 (1930).
Kirihara v. *The Bendix Corp.,* 306 F. Supp. 72 (D. Hawaii 1969).
National Tea Co., 1971 Trade Reg. Rep. ¶ 19,304 (FTC 1970).
National Tea Co., [1967–70 Transfer Binder] Trade Reg. Rep. ¶ 19,266 (FTC 1970).
United States v. *Diebold,* 369 U.S. 654 (1962).
United States v. *E. I. du Pont de Nemours & Co.,* 353 U.S. 586 (1957).
United States v. *First City National Bank of Houston,* 386 U.S. 361 (1967).
United States v. *Greater Buffalo Press, Inc.,* 327 F. Supp. 305 (W.D.N.Y. 1970), *rev'd,* 402 U.S. 549 (1971).
United States v. *Maryland and Virginia Milk Producers Association, Inc.* 167 F. Supp. 799 (D.D.C. 1958), *aff'd on other grounds,* 362 U.S. 458 (1960).
United States v. *Pabst Brewing Co.,* 296 F. Supp. 994 (E.D. Wisc. 1969).
United States v. *Tidewater Marine Services, Inc.,* 284 F. Supp. 324 (E.D. La. 1968).
United States v. *Wilson Sporting Goods Co.,* 288 F. Supp. 543 (N.D. Ill. 1968).
United States Steel Corp., [1967–70 Transfer Binder] Trade Reg. Rep. ¶ 18,626 (FTC 1968).
United States Steel Corp. v. *FTC,* 426 F.2d 592 (6th Cir. 1970).

Chapter 19: Miscellaneous Corporate Amalgamations

BIBLIOGRAPHY

Chevigny, *The Validity of Grant-Back Agreements Under the Antitrust Laws,* 34 Fordham L. Rev. 569 (1966).
Hale, *Joint Ventures: Collaborative Subsidiaries and the Antitrust Laws,* 42 Va. L. Rev. 927 (1956).
Heyman, *Patent Licensing and the Antitrust Laws—A Reappraisal at the Close of the Decade,* 14 Antitrust Bull. 537 (1969).
Mead, *The Competitive Significance of Joint Ventures,* 12 Antitrust Bull. 819 (1967).
Pitofsky, *Joint Ventures Under the Antitrust Laws: Some Reflections on the Significance of Penn-Olin,* 82 Harv. L. Rev. 1007 (1964).
Roberts, *Antitrust Problems in the Newspaper Industry,* 82 Harv. L. Rev. 319 (1968).
Stedman, *Acquisition of Patents and Know-How by Grant, Fraud, Purchase and Grantback,* 28 U. Pitt. L. Rev. 161 (1966).
Turner, *Patents, Antitrust & Innovation,* 28 U. Pitt. L. Rev. 151 (1966).

CASES

Bander v. *Hearst Corp.,* 152 F. Supp. 569 (D. Conn. 1957).
Citizen Publishing Co. v. *United States,* 394 U.S. 131 (1969).
Farm Journal, Inc., 53 F.T.C. 26 (1956) (Initial Order), adopted without appeal by the Commission, 53 F.T.C. 26, 32 (1956).
Northern Natural Gas Co. v. *Federal Power Commission,* 399 F.2d 953 (D.C. Cir. 1968).
United States v. *Columbia Pictures Corp.,* 189 F. Supp. 153 (S.D.N.Y. 1960).
United States v. *Lever Brothers Company,* 216 F. Supp. 887 (S.D.N.Y. 1963).
United States v. *Penn-Olin Chemical Co.,* 378 U.S. 158 (1964).
Western Geophysical Co. v. *Bolt Associates, Inc.,* 305 F. Supp. 1251 (D. Conn. 1969).

Chapter 20: Mergers Involving Foreign Commerce

BIBLIOGRAPHY

Brewster, *Antitrust & American Business Abroad* (1958).
Donovan, *Antitrust Considerations in the Organization and Operation of American Business Abroad,* 9 B. C. Ind. & Com. L. Rev. 239 (1968).
Donovan, *The Legality of Acquisitions and Mergers Involving American and Foreign Corporations Under the United States Antitrust Laws—Part I,* 39 So. Cal. L. Rev. 526 (1966); Part II, 40 So. Cal. L. Rev. 38 (1967).
Fulgate, *Foreign Commerce & the Antitrust Laws* (1958).
Graham, Hermann, and Marcus, *Section 7 of the Clayton Act & Mergers Involving Foreign Interests,* 23 Stan. L. Rev. 205 (1971).
Scott and Yablonski, *Transnational Mergers and Joint Ventures Affecting American Exports,* 14 Antitrust Bull. 1 (1969).

CASES

United States v. *Jos. Schlitz Brewing Co.,* 253 F. Supp. 129 (N.D. Cal.), *aff'd per curiam,* 385 U.S. 37 (1966).
United States v. *Minnesota Mining & Manufacturing Co.,* 92 F. Supp. 947 (D. Mass. 1950).

United States v. *Pan American World Airways, Inc.,* 193 F. Supp. 18 (S.D.N.Y. 1961), *rev'd on other grounds,* 371 U.S. 196 (1963).

Chapter 21: Recent Developments in the Antimerger Laws

BIBLIOGRAPHY

Comment, *The FTC's Power to Seek Preliminary Injunctions in Anti-Merger Cases,* 66 Mich. L. Rev. 142 (1967).

Decker, *The Department of Justice Merger Guidelines,* ABA Law Notes (July 1969).

Department of Justice, Press Release, "Merger Guidelines," (May 30, 1968).

Elman, *Rulemaking Procedures in the FTC's Enforcement of the Merger Law,* 78 Harv. L. Rev. 385 (1964).

FTC Announces Merger Notification Program as Mergers Hit Record Peak (FTC Press Release, April 13, 1969).

FTC Enforcement Policy with Respect to Mergers in the Food Distribution Industries (FTC Press Release, January 3, 1967).

FTC Enforcement Policy with Respect to Mergers in the Textile Mill Products Industry (FTC Press Release, November 27, 1968).

FTC Enforcement Policy with Respect to Product Extension Mergers in Grocery Products Manufacturing (FTC Press Release, May 15, 1968).

FTC Enforcement Policy with Respect to Vertical Mergers in the Cement Industry (FTC Press Release, January 3, 1967).

FTC Establishes New Procedure for Handling of Pre-Merger Clearance Requests, and Applications for Approval of Divestitures, Acquisitions, or Similar Transactions Subject to Commission Review Under Outstanding Orders (FTC Press Release, May 23, 1969).

Mueller, *The New Antitrust: A "Structural Approach,"* 12 Vill. L. Rev. 764 (1967).

Note, *FTC Merger Guidelines: Stemming the Tide,* 5 Colum. J.L. & Soc. Prob. 137 (1969).

Note, *Noncase Guidelines for Conglomerate Mergers Under Section 7 of the Clayton Act,* 45 N.Y.U.L. Rev. 90 (1970).

Note, *Present Guidelines for Conglomerate Mergers,* 44 N.D.L. Rev. 226 (1968).

O'Brien, *The Federal Trade Commission's Pre-Merger Notification Requirements,* 14 Antitrust Bull. 557 (1969).

CASES

Brown Shoe Co. v. *United States,* 370 U.S. 294 (1962).

Ford Motor Co. v. *United States,* 92 S. Ct. 1142 (1972).

FTC v. *Consolidated Foods Corp.,* 380 U.S. 592 (1965).

FTC v. *Procter & Gamble Co.,* 386 U.S. 568 (1967).

United States v. *Continental Can Co.,* 378 U.S. 441 (1964).

United States v. *Pabst Brewing Co.,* 384 U.S. 546 (1966).

United States v. *Philadelphia National Bank,* 374 U.S. 321 (1963).

United States v. *Von's Grocery Co.,* 384 U.S. 270 (1966).

Chapter 22: Justice Department Procedure and Enforcement

BIBLIOGRAPHY

Archer, *Techniques of Litigating Government Merger Cases,* 25 Bus. Law. 723 (1970).

Report of the Attorney General's National Committee to Study the Antitrust Laws (Washington, D.C.: Government Printing Office, 1955).
Comment, *Direct Appeals in Antitrust Cases,* 81 Harv. L. Rev. 1558 (1968).
Dabney, *Consent Decrees Without Consent,* 63 Colum. L. Rev. 1052 (1963).
Flynn, *Consent Decrees in Antitrust Enforcement: Some Thoughts and Proposals,* 53 Iowa L.J. 983 (1968).
Handler, *The Shift from Substantive to Procedural Innovations in Antitrust Suits,* 71 Colum. L. Rev. 1 (1971).
Hart and Wechsler, *The Federal Courts and the Federal System* (1953).
Hearings of the Subcomm. of the House Appropriations Comm., Part 1—The Judiciary, Dept. of Justice, 91st Cong., 2d Sess. 529 (1970).
The Nader Study Group Report on Antitrust Enforcement, The Closed Enterprise System 2 & 3 (1971).
Rashid, *New Trends in Antitrust Investigations,* 37 ABA Antitrust L.J. 188 (1968).
Reycraft, *Dealing with Enforcement Agencies Prior to Filing of Suit,* 25 Bus. Law. 715 (1970).
Thorelli, *The Federal Antitrust Policy* (1955).
Zimmerman, *Procedures for Settling with the Antitrust Division,* 37 ABA Antitrust L.J. 212 (1968).

CASES

Allis-Chalmers Mfg. Co. v. *White Consolidated Industries, Inc.,* 414 F.2d 506 (3rd Cir. 1969).
Brown Shoe Co. v. *United States,* 370 U.S. 294 (1962).
California v. *Federal Power Commission,* 369 U.S. 482 (1962).
Cascade Natural Gas Corp. v. *El Paso Natural Gas Corp.,* 386 U.S. 129 (1967).
Chattanooga Pharmaceutical Ass'n v. *United States,* 358 F.2d 864 (6th Cir. 1966).
Ford Motor Co. v. *United States,* 92 S. Ct. 1142 (1972).
Hyster Co. v. *United States,* 338 F.2d 183 (9th Cir. 1964).
Kennecott Copper Corp. v. *United States,* 381 U.S. 414 (1965).
Lightning Rod Manufacturers Ass'n v. *Staal,* 339 F.2d 346 (7th Cir. 1964).
Northern Securities Co. v. *United States,* 193 U.S. 197 (1904).
Petition of Gold Bond Stamp Co., 221 F. Supp. 391 (1963), *aff'd, Gold Bond Stamp Co.* v. *United States,* 325 F.2d 1018 (1964).
Standard Oil Co. of New Jersey v. *United States,* 221 U.S. 1 (1911).
Swift & Co. v. *United States,* 276 U.S. 311 (1928).
United States v. *Addyston Pipe & Steel Co.,* 85 F. 271 (6th Cir. 1898).
United States v. *Atlantic Richfield Co.,* 297 F. Supp. 1060 (S.D.N.Y. 1969).
United States v. *Ciba Corp.,* 1970 Trade Cas. ¶ 73,319 (S.D.N.Y. 1970).
United States v. *FMC Corp.,* 84 S. Ct. 4 (1963).
United States v. *Kaiser Aluminum & Chemical Corp.,* 1965 Trade Cas. ¶ 71,354 (D.R.I. 1962).
United States v. *Lucky Lager Brewing Co.,* 209 F. Supp. 665 (D. Utah 1962).
United States v. *Phillipsburg National Bank,* 399 U.S. 350 (1970).
United States v. *Procter & Gamble Co.,* 356 U.S. 677 (1958).
United States v. *Singer Mfg. Co.,* 374 U.S. 174 (1963).
United States v. *Swift & Co.,* 286 U.S. 106 (1932).
United States v. *Union Oil Co. of California,* 343 F.2d 29 (9th Cir. 1965).
United States v. *Von's Grocery Co.,* 384 U.S. 270 (1966).
Upjohn Co. v. *Bernstein,* 1966 Trade Cas. ¶ 71,830 (D.D.C. 1966).

Chapter 23: Federal Trade Commission Practice and Procedure

BIBLIOGRAPHY

Burrus and Savarese, *Institutional Decision-making and the Problem of Fairness in FTC Antitrust Enforcement,* 53 Geo. L.J. 656 (1965).
Burrus and Teter, *Antitrust: Rulemaking* v. *Adjudication in the FTC,* 54 Geo. L.J. 1106 (1966).
Comment, *Preliminary Relief for the Government under Section 7 of the Clayton Act,* 79 Harv. L. Rev. 391 (1965).

CASES

Atlantic Richfield Co. v. *Federal Trade Commission,* 381 U.S. 357 (1965).
Farmington Dowel Products Co. v. *Forster Mfg., Inc.,* 1967 Trade Cas. ¶ 72,262 (1st Cir. 1967).
FTC v. *American Tobacco Co.,* 264 U.S. 298 (1924).
FTC v. *Dean Foods, Inc.,* 384 U.S. 597 (1966).
FTC v. *OKC Corp.,* 1970 Trade Cas. ¶ 73,288 (5th Cir. 1970).
FTC v. *Rubberoid,* 343 U.S. 470 (1952).
Jacob Siegal Co. v. *FTC,* 327 U.S. 608 (1946).
Lippa & Co. v. *Lenox, Inc.,* 305 F. Supp. 175 (D. Vt. 1969).
Luria Bros. Co., 62 F.T.C. 243 (1963).
Minnesota Mining and Mfg. Co. v. *New Jersey Wood Finishing Co.,* 381 U.S. 311 (1965).
Nashville Milk Co. v. *Carnation Co.,* 335 U.S. 373 (1958).
United States v. *Morton Salt,* 338 U.S. 632 (1949).
United States v. *St. Regis Paper Co.,* 181 F. Supp. 862 (S.D.N.Y. 1960).

Chapter 24: Private Enforcement

BIBLIOGRAPHY

Greenwald, *The Measurement of Damages in Private Antitrust Suits,* 5 Antitrust Bull. 293 (1960).
Loevinger, *Private Action—The Strongest Pillar of Antitrust,* 3 Antitrust Bull. 167 (1958).
MacIntyre, *The Role of the Private Litigant in Antitrust Enforcement,* 7 Antitrust Bull. 113 (1962).
Note, *Availability of Divestiture in Private Litigation as a Remedy for Violation of Section 7 of the Clayton Act,* 49 Minn. L. Rev. 267 (1964).
Note, *Private Actions Under Section 4 and 7 of the Clayton Act: A Fresh Look at an Old Problem,* 29 Ohio St. L.J. 957 (1964).
Note, *Treble Damages for Violations of Section 7 of the Clayton Act,* 38 U. Chi. L. Rev. 404 (1971).
Stein, *Section 7 of the Clayton Act as a Basis for the Treble-Damage Action: When May the Private Litigant Bring His Suit?* 56 Calif. L. Rev. 968 (1968).
Timberlake, *Federal Treble Damage Antitrust Actions* (1965).

CASES

Bailey's Bakery, Ltd. v. *Continental Baking Co.,* 235 F. Supp. 205 (D. Hawaii 1964), *aff'd,* 401 F.2d 182 (9th Cir.), *cert. denied,* 393 U.S. 1086 (1968).
Dailey v. *Quality School Plan, Inc.,* 380 F.2d 484 (5th Cir. 1967).
Gottesman v. *General Motors Corp.,* 221 F. Supp. 488 (S.D.N.Y. 1963), *rev'd,* 414 F.2d 956 (2d Cir. 1969), *on remand,* 310 F. Supp. 1857 (S.D.N.Y. 1970), *aff'd,* 436 F.2d 1205 (2d Cir.), *cert. denied,* 403 U.S. 911 (1971).

Highland Supply Corp. v. *Reynolds Metals Co.,* 327 F.2d 725 (8th Cir. 1964).
Isidor Weinstein Investment Co. v. *Hearst Corp.,* 303 F. Supp. 646 (N.D. Calif. 1969).
Julius M. Ames Co. v. *Bostich, Inc.,* 240 F. Supp. 521 (S.D.N.Y. 1965).
Kirihara v. *Bendix Corporation,* 306 F. Supp. 72 (D. Hawaii 1964).
Metropolitan Liquor Co., Inc. v. *Heublein, Inc.,* 305 F. Supp. 946 (E.D. Wisc. 1969).
Sam S. Goldstein Industries, Inc. v. *Botany Industries, Inc.,* 301 F. Supp. 728 (S.D.N.Y. 1969).
Western Geophysical Co. v. *Bolt Assoc., Inc.,* 305 F. Supp. 1251 (D. Conn. 1969).

Chapter 25: Mergers in the Regulated Industries

BIBLIOGRAPHY

Adams, *Business Exemptions from the Antitrust Laws: Their Extent and Rationale, Perspectives on Antitrust Policy* (Phillips ed. 1965).
Baker, *The Antitrust Division, Department of Justice: The Role of Competition in Regulated Industries,* 11 B.C. Ind. & Com. L. Rev. 571 (1970).
Bennett, *Media Concentration and the FCC: Focusing with a Section Seven Lens,* 66 Nw.U.L. Rev. 159 (1971).
Bleakney, *The Interstate Commerce Commission,* 11 B.C. Ind. & Com. L. Rev. 785 (1970).
Comment, *Ocean Shipping Conferences and the Federal Maritime Commission,* 53 Cornell L. Rev. 1070 (1968).
Hale and Hale, *Mergers in Regulated Industries,* 59 Nw.U.L. Rev. 49 (1964).
Latta, *Primary Jurisdiction in the Regulated Industries and the Antitrust Laws,* 30 U. Cin. L. Rev. 261 (1961).
Levi, *Section 7 of the Clayton Act and the Regulated Industries,* 1959 Antitrust L. Symposium 136.
Posner, *Natural Monopoly and Its Regulations,* 21 Stan. L. Rev. 548 (1969).
Turner, *The Scope of Antitrust and Other Economic Regulatory Policies,* 82 Harv. L. Rev. 1207 (1969).

CASES

Algonquin Gas Transmission Co., 37 F.P.C. 1128 (1967).
Butler Aviation Co. v. *CAB,* 389 F.2d 517 (2d Cir. 1968).
California v. *FPC,* 369 U.S. 482 (1962).
Carnation Co. v. *Pacific Westbound Conf.,* 383 U.S. 213, *modified,* 383 U.S. 932 (1966).
Commonwealth Edison Co. & Central Illinois Electricity & Gas Co., 36 F.P.C. 927 (1966).
Denver & Rio Grande W.R.R. Co. v. *United States,* 387 U.S. 485 (1967).
FCC v. *Sanders Brothers Radio Station,* 309 U.S. 470 (1940).
FTC v. *Procter & Gamble,* 386 U.S. 568 (1967).
Great Northern Pacific Ry. Co. Acquisition, 162 I.C.C. 37 (ICC 1930).
Interstate Investors, Inc. v. *Transcontinental Bus Systems, Inc.,* 310 F. Supp. 1053 (S.D.N.Y. 1970).
Isbrandtsen Co. v. *United States,* 211 F.2d 51 (D.C. Cir. 1954), *cert. denied,* 347 U.S. 990 (1954).
Matson Navigation Co. v. *FMC,* 405 F.2d 796 (9th Cir. 1968).
McLean Trucking Co. v. *United States,* 321 U.S. 67 (1944).
Minneapolis & St. Louis Ry. v. *United States,* 361 U.S. 173 (1959).

National Aviation Trades Ass'n v. *CAB,* 420 F.2d 209 (D.C. Cir. 1969).
New York Cent. Sec. Co. v. *United States,* 287 U.S. 12 (1932).
Norfolk & Western Ry. Merger, 307 I.C.C. 407 (ICC 1959).
Northern Natural Gas Co. v. *FPC,* 399 F.2d 953 (1968).
Northern Sec. Co. v. *United States,* 193 U.S. 197 (1904).
Pacific Power & Light Co. v. *FPC,* 111 F.2d 1014 (9th Cir. 1940).
Pan American Airways v. *United States,* 371 U.S. 296 (1963).
Penn Central Merger Cases, 389 U.S. 486 (1968).
Seaboard Air Line R.R., 320 I.C.C. 122 (ICC 1963), *rev'd sub nom. Florida East Coast Ry.* v. *United States,* 242 F. Supp. 14 (M.D. Fla. 1965), *rev'd sub nom. Seaboard Air Line R.R.* v. *United States,* 382 U.S. 154 (1965).
United States v. *El Paso Natural Gas Co.,* 376 U.S. 651 (1969).
United States v. *ICC,* 396 U.S. 491 (1970).
United States v. *Penn-Olin Co.,* 378 U.S. 158 (1964).
United States v. *Philadelphia National Bank,* 374 U.S. 321 (1963).
United States v. *Radio Corporation of America,* 358 U.S. 334 (1959).
United States v. *R. J. Reynolds Tobacco Co.,* 1971 Trade Cas. ¶ 73,545 (D.N.J. 1971).
United States v. *Western Pacific Ry.,* 352 U.S. 59 (1956).
Volkswagenwerk v. *FMC,* 390 U.S. 261 (1968).

Chapter 26: Bank Mergers

BIBLIOGRAPHY

Address, Donald Baker, Director of Policy Planning, Antitrust Division, "The Brand New Ball Game—Bank Holding Company Competition in the 1970's," November 16, 1971.
Baker, *Competition's Role in the Regulation of Banking,* 154 The Bankers Magazine No. 3, 75 (1971).
Blaine, *Registered Bank Holding Companies and the One-Bank Holding Company,* 26 Bus. Law. 9 (1970).
Casson and Burrus, *Federal Regulation of Bank Mergers,* 18 American U. L. Rev. 677 (1969).
Cohen, *The Antitrust Laws Applied to Bank Mergers, Reciprocity and Tie-In Arrangements,* 26 Bus. Law. 1 (1970).
Darnell, *Phillipsburg National Bank,* 16 Antitrust Bull. 33 (1971).
Hale, *Mergers of Financial Institutions,* 21 Bus. Law. 211 (1965).
Lifland, *The Supreme Court, Congress and Bank Mergers,* 32 Law & Contemp. Prob. 15 (1969).
McLaren, "Statement Before the Senate Banking and Currency Committee on Legislation to Amend the Bank Holding Company Act," May 18, 1970.
Mogel, *Bank Mergers and the Antitrust Laws,* 17 American U.L. Rev. 57 (1967).
Reycraft, *Antitrust Problems in Banking,* 16 Antitrust Bull. 817 (1971).
Reycraft, *Bank Merger Compliance with the Antitrust Laws,* 12 Antitrust Bull. 445 (1967).
Searls and Reasoner, *The Bank Merger Act of 1966—Its Strange and Fruitless Odyssey,* 25 Bus. Law. 133 (1969).
Seeley, *Banks and Antitrust,* 21 Bus. Law. 917 (1966).
Shull and Horvitz, *The Bank Merger Act of 1960: A Decade After,* 16 Antitrust Bull. 859 (1971).
Waxberg and Robinson, *Chaos in Federal Regulation of Bank Mergers: A Need for Legislative Revision,* 82 Banking L. Rev. 377 (May 1965).
Whitesell, *Potential Competition and Bank Mergers,* 88 Banking L.J. 387 (May 1971).

CASES

Transamerica Corp. v. *Federal Reserve Board,* 206 F.2d 163 (3rd Cir.), *cert. denied,* 346 U.S. 901 (1953).
United States v. *Columbia Steel Corp.,* 334 U.S. 495 (1950).
United States v. *County National Bank of Bennington,* File No. 6088, January 27, 1972.
United States v. *Crocker-Anglo National Bank,* 277 F. Supp. 133 (N.D. Cal. 1967).
United States v. *Firstamerica Corp.,* Civil No. 38139 (N.D. Cal.), *cert. denied,* 361 U.S. 928 (1960).
United States v. *First National Bancorporation,* 1971 Trade Cas. ¶ 73,651 (C.D. Colo. 1971).
United States v. *First National Bank & Trust Co. of Lexington,* 376 U.S. 665 (1964).
United States v. *First National Bank of Houston,* 386 U.S. 361 (1967).
United States v. *First National Bank of Jackson,* 301 F. Supp. 1161 (S.D. Miss. 1969).
United States v. *First National Bank of Maryland,* 310 F. Supp. 157 (D. Md. 1970).
United States v. *Idaho First National Bank,* 315 F. Supp. 261 (D. Idaho 1970).
United States v. *Manufacturers Hanover Trust & Co.,* 240 F. Supp. 133 (S.D.N.Y. 1965).
United States v. *Philadelphia National Bank,* 374 U.S. 321 (1963).
United States v. *Phillipsburg National Bank,* 399 U.S. 350 (1970).
United States v. *Provident National Bank,* 386 U.S. 361 (1967).
United States v. *United Banks of Colorado,* 1971 Trade Cas. ¶ 73,421 (D. Colo. 1970).

Chapter 27: Conclusion—A Final Word on the Conglomerate

BIBLIOGRAPHY

Address, Herbert Brownell, Jr., Attorney General of the United States, "The Antitrust Aspects of Mergers," September 30, 1954.
Address, Willard F. Mueller, Address before the National Industrial Conference Board, March 6, 1969.
Adelman, *Economic Analysis and Critique of the Factors Considered in Judging the Legality of Mergers,* 21 Current Business Studies 21 (December 1954).
Bock and Forkas, *Concentration and Productivity: Some Preliminary Findings,* Studies in Business Economics No. 103, National Industrial Conference Board (1968).
Davidow, *Conglomerate Concentration and Section Seven: The Limitations of the Anti-Merger Act,* 68 Colum. L. Rev. 1231 (1968).
Galbraith, *The New Industrial State* (1967).
Weston, *The Nature and Significance of Conglomerate Firms,* 44 St. John's L. Rev. 66 (1970 Special Edition).

Appendix II

Sherman Act

[As amended by Public No. 314—75th Congress, August 17, 1937]
An Act to protect trade and commerce against unlawful restraints and monopolies.
Be it enacted by the Senate and House of Representatives of the United States of America in Congress assembled, that

Section 1. Every contract, combination in the form of trust or otherwise, or conspiracy, in restraint of trade or commerce among the several States, or with foreign nations, is declared to be illegal: *Provided,* That nothing contained in sections 1 to 7 of this title shall render illegal, contracts or agreements prescribing minimum prices for the resale of a commodity which bears, or the label or container of which bears, the trademark, brand, or name of the producer or distributor of such commodity and which is in free and open competition with commodities of the same general class produced or distributed by others, when contracts or agreements of that description are lawful as applied to intrastate transactions, under any statute, law, or public policy now or hereafter in effect in any State, Territory, or the District of Columbia in which such resale is to be made, or to which the commodity is to be transported for such resale, and the making of such contracts or agreements shall not be an unfair method of competition under section 45 of this title: *Provided further,* That the preceding proviso shall not make lawful any contract or agreement, providing for the establishment or maintenance of minimum resale prices on any commodity herein involved, between manufacturers, or between producers, or between wholesalers, or between brokers, or between factors, or between retailers, or between persons, firms, or corporations in competition with each other. Every person who shall make any contract or engage in any combination or conspiracy declared by sections 1 to 7 of this title to be illegal shall be deemed guilty of a misdemeanor, and, on conviction thereof, shall be punished by fine not exceeding fifty thousand dollars, or by imprisonment not exceeding one year, or by both said punishments, in the discretion of the court.

Section 2. Every person who shall monopolize, or attempt to monopolize, or combine or conspire with any other person or persons, to monopolize any part of the trade or commerce among the several States, or with foreign nations, shall be deemed guilty of a misdeameanor, and, on conviction thereof, shall be punished by fine not exceeding fifty thousand dollars, or by imprisonment not exceeding one year, or by both said punishments, in the discretion of the court.

Section 3. Every contract, combination in form of trust or otherwise, or conspiracy, in restraint of trade or commerce in any Territory of the United States or of the District of Columbia, or in restraint of trade or commerce between any such Territory and another, or between any such Territory or Territories and any State or States or the District of Columbia, or with foreign nations, or between the District of Columbia and any State or States or foreign nations, is declared illegal. Every person who shall make any such contract or engage in any such combination or conspiracy, shall be deemed guilty of a misdemeanor, and, on conviction thereof, shall be punished by fine not exceeding fifty thousand dollars, or by imprisonment not exceeding one year, or by both said punishments, in the discretion of the court.

Section 4. The several district courts of the United States are invested with jurisdiction to prevent and restrain violations of sections 1 to 7 of this title; and it shall be the duty of the several United States attorneys, in their respective districts, under the direction of the Attorney General, to institute proceedings in equity to prevent and restrain such violations. Such proceedings may be by way of petition setting forth the case and praying that such violation shall be enjoined or otherwise prohibited. When the parties complained of shall have been duly notified of such petition the court shall proceed, as soon as may be, to the hearing and determination of the case; and pending such petition and before final decree, the court may at any time make such temporary restraining order or prohibition as shall be deemed just in the premises.

Section 5. Whenever it shall appear to the court before which any proceeding under section 4 of this title may be pending, that the ends of justice require that other parties should be brought before the court, the court may cause them to be summoned, whether they reside in the district in which the court is held or not; and subpœnas to that end may be served in any district by the marshal thereof.

Section 6. Any property owned under any contract or by any combination, or pursuant to any conspiracy (and being the subject thereof) mentioned in section 1 of this title, and being in the course of transportation from one State to another, or to a foreign country, shall be forfeited to the United States, and may be seized and condemned by like proceedings as those provided by law for the forfeiture, seizure, and condemnation of property imported into the United States contrary to law.

Section 7. The word "person," or "persons," wherever used in sections 1 to 7 of this title shall be deemed to include corporations and associations existing under or authorized by the laws of either the United States, the laws of any of the Territories, the laws of any State, or the laws of any foreign country.

Approved July 2, 1890.
Amended August 17, 1937.

Appendix III

The Clayton Act

(Including the Robinson-Patman Amendment)

[Public—No. 212—63d Congress, As Amended by Public—No. 692—74th Congress, Public—No. 899—81st Congress and Public Law 86–107, 86th Congress]

H.R. 15657

An Act to supplement existing laws against unlawful restraints and monopolies, and for other purposes.

Be it enacted by the Senate and House of Representatives of the United States of America in Congress assembled, that

"Antitrust laws," as used herein, includes the Act entitled "An Act to protect trade and commerce against unlawful restraints and monopolies," approved July second, eighteen hundred and ninety; sections seventy-three to seventy-seven, inclusive, of an Act entitled "An Act to reduce taxation, to provide revenue for the Government, and for other purposes," of August twenty-seventh, eighteen hundred and ninety-four; an Act entitled "An Act to amend sections seventy-three and seventy-six of the Act of August twenty-seventh, eighteen hundred and ninety-four, entitled 'An Act to reduce taxation, to provide revenue for the Government, and for other purposes,'" approved February twelfth, nineteen hundred and thirteen; and also this Act.

"Commerce," as used herein, means trade or commerce among the several States and with foreign nations, or between the District of Columbia or any Territory of the United States and any State, Territory, or foreign nation, or between any insular possessions or other places under the jurisdiction of the United States, or between any such possession or place and any State or Territory of the United States or the District of Columbia or any foreign nation, or within the District of Columbia or any Territory or any insular possession or other place under the jurisdiction of the United States: *Provided,* That nothing in this Act contained shall apply to the Philippine Islands.

The word "person" or "persons" wherever used in this Act shall be deemed to include corporations and associations existing under or authorized by the laws of either the United States, the laws of any of the Territories, the laws of any State, or the laws of any foreign country.

Section 2. (a) It shall be unlawful for any person engaged in commerce, in the course of such commerce, either directly or indirectly, to discriminate in price between different purchasers of commodities of like grade and quality, where either or any of the purchases involved in such discrimination are in commerce, where such commodities are sold for use, consumption, or resale within the United States or any Territory thereof or the District of Columbia or any insular possession or other place under the jurisdiction of the United States, and where the effect of such discrimination may be substantially to lessen competition or tend to create a monopoly in any line of commerce, or to injure, destroy, or prevent competition with any person who either grants or knowingly receives the benefit of such discrimination, or with customers of either of them: *Provided,* That nothing herein contained shall prevent differentials which make only due allowance for differences in the cost of manufacture, sale, or delivery resulting from the differing methods or quantities in which such commodities are to such purchasers sold or delivered: *Provided, however,* That the Federal Trade Commission may, after due investigation and hearing to all interested parties, fix and establish quantity limits, and revise the same as it finds necessary, as to particular commodities or classes of commodities, where it finds that available purchasers in greater quantities are so few as to render differentials on account thereof unjustly discriminatory or promotive of monopoly in any line of commerce; and the foregoing shall then not be construed to permit differentials based on differences in quantities greater than those so fixed and established: *And provided further,* That nothing herein contained shall prevent persons engaged in selling goods, wares, or merchandise in commerce from selecting their own customers in bona fide transactions and not in restraint of trade: *And provided further,* That nothing herein contained shall prevent price changes from time to time where in response to changing conditions affecting the market for or the marketability of the goods concerned, such as but not limited to actual or imminent deterioration of perishable goods, obsolescence of seasonal goods, distress sales under court process, or sales in good faith in discontinuance of business in the goods concerned.

(b) Upon proof being made, at any hearing on a complaint under this section, that there has been discrimination in price or services or facilities furnished, the burden of rebutting the prima-facie case thus made by showing justification shall be upon the person charged with a violation of this section, and unless justification shall be affirmatively shown, the Commission is authorized to issue an order terminating the discrimination: *Provided, however,* That nothing herein contained shall prevent a seller rebutting the prima-facie case thus made by showing that his lower price or the furnishing of services or facilities to any purchaser or purchasers was made in good faith to meet an equally low price of a competitor, or the services or facilities furnished by a competitor.

(c) It shall be unlawful for any person engaged in commerce, in the course of such commerce, to pay or grant, or to receive or accept, anything of value as a commission, brokerage, or other compensation, or any allowance or discount in lieu thereof, except for services rendered in connection with the sale or purchase of goods, wares, or merchandise, either to the other party to such transaction or to an agent, representative, or other intermediary therein where such intermediary is acting in fact for or in behalf, or is subject to the direct or indirect control, of any party to such transaction other than the person by whom such compensation is so granted or paid.

(d) It shall be unlawful for any person engaged in commerce to pay or contract for the payment of anything of value to or for the benefit of a customer of such person in the course of such commerce as compensation or in consideration for any services or facilities furnished by or through such customer in connection with the processing, handling, sale, or offering for sale of any products or com-

modities manufactured, sold, or offered for sale by such person, unless such payment or consideration is available on proportionally equal terms to all other customers competing in the distribution of such products or commodities.
(e) It shall be unlawful for any person to discriminate in favor of one purchaser against another purchaser or purchasers of a commodity bought for resale, with or without processing, by contracting to furnish or furnishing, or by contributing to the furnishing of, any services or facilities connected with the processing, handling, sale, or offering for sale of such commodity so purchased upon terms not accorded to all purchasers on proportionally equal terms.
(f) It shall be unlawful for any person engaged in commerce, in the course of such commerce, knowingly to induce or receive a discrimination in price which is prohibited by this section.

Section 3. It shall be unlawful for any person engaged in commerce, in the course of such commerce, to lease or make a sale or contract for sale of goods, wares, merchandise, machinery, supplies, or other commodities, whether patented or unpatented, for use, consumption, or resale within the United States or any Territory thereof or the District of Columbia or any insular possession or other place under the jurisdiction of the United States, or fix a price charged therefor, or discount from, or rebate upon, such price, on the condition, agreement, or understanding that the lessee or purchaser thereof shall not use or deal in the goods, wares, merchandise, machinery, supplies, or other commodities of a competitor or competitors of the lessor or seller, where the effect of such lease, sale, or contract for sale or such condition, agreement, or understanding may be to substantially lessen competition or tend to create a monopoly in any line of commerce.

Section 4. Any person who shall be injured in his business or property by reason of anything forbidden in the antitrust laws may sue therefor in any district court of the United States in the district in which the defendant resides or is found or has an agent, without respect to the amount in controversy, and shall recover threefold the damages by him sustained, and the cost of suit, including a reasonable attorney's fee.

Section 4A. Whenever the United States is hereafter injured in its business or property by reason of anything forbidden in the antitrust laws it may sue therefor in the United States district court for the district in which the defendant resides or is found or has an agent, without respect to the amount in controversy, and shall recover actual damages by it sustained and the cost of suit.

Section 4B. Any action to enforce any cause of action under sections 15 or 15a of this Title shall be for ever barred unless commenced within 4 years after the cause of action accrued. No cause of action barred under existing law on the effective date of this section and sections 15a and 16 of this Title shall be revived by said sections.

Section 5. (a) A final judgment or decree heretofore or hereafter rendered in any civil or criminal proceeding brought by or on behalf of the United States under the antitrust laws to the effect that a defendant has violated said laws shall be prima facie evidence against such defendant in any action or proceeding brought by any other party against such defendant under said laws or by the United States under section 15a of this title, as to all matters respecting which said judgment or decree would be an estoppel as between the parties thereto: *Provided,* That this section shall not apply to consent judgments or decrees entered before any testimony has been taken or to judgments or decrees entered in actions under section 15a of this title.
(b) Whenever any civil or criminal proceeding is instituted by the United

States to prevent, restrain, or punish violations of any of the antitrust laws, but not including an action under section 15a of this title, the running of the statute of limitations in respect of every private right of action arising under said laws and based in whole or in part on any matter complained of in said proceeding shall be suspended during the pendency thereof and for one year thereafter: *Provided, however,* That whenever the running of the statute of limitations in respect of a cause of action arising under section 15 of this title is suspended hereunder, any action to enforce such cause of action shall be forever barred unless commenced either within the period of suspension or within four years after the cause of action accrued.

Section 6. The labor of a human being is not a commodity or article of commerce. Nothing contained in the antitrust laws shall be construed to forbid the existence and operation of labor, agricultural, or horticultural organizations, instituted for the purposes of mutual help, and not having capital stock or conducted for profit, or to forbid or restrain individual members of such organizations from lawfully carrying out the legitimate objects thereof; nor shall such organizations, or the members thereof, be held or construed to be illegal combinations or conspiracies in restraint of trade, under the antitrust laws.

Section 7. No corporation engaged in commerce shall acquire, directly or indirectly, the whole or any part of the stock or other share capital and no corporation subject to the jurisdiction of the Federal Trade Commission shall acquire the whole or any part of the assets of another corporation engaged also in commerce, where in any line of commerce in any section of the country, the effect of such acquisition may be substantially to lessen competition, or to tend to create a monopoly.

No corporation shall acquire, directly or indirectly, the whole or any part of the stock or other share capital and no corporation subject to the jurisdiction of the Federal Trade Commission shall acquire the whole or any part of the assets of one or more corporations engaged in commerce, where in any line of commerce in any section of the country, the effect of such acquisition, of such stocks or assets, or of the use of such stock by the voting or granting of proxies or otherwise, may be substantially to lessen competition, or to tend to create a monopoly.

This section shall not apply to corporations purchasing such stock solely for investment and not using the same by voting or otherwise to bring about, or in attempting to bring about, the substantial lessening of competition. Nor shall anything contained in this section prevent a corporation engaged in commerce from causing the formation of subsidiary corporations for the actual carrying on of their immediate lawful business, or the natural and legitimate branches or extensions thereof, or from owning and holding all or a part of the stock of such subsidiary corporations, when the effect of such formation is not to substantially lessen competition.

Nor shall anything herein contained be construed to prohibit any common carrier subject to the laws to regulate commerce from aiding in the construction of branches or short lines so located as to become feeders to the main line of the company so aiding in such construction or from acquiring or owning all or any part of the stock of such branch lines, nor to prevent any such common carrier from acquiring and owning all or any part of the stock of a branch or short line constructed by an independent company where there is no substantial competition between the company owning the branch line so constructed and the company owning the main line acquiring the property or an interest therein, nor to prevent such common carrier from extending any of its lines through the medium of the acquisition of stock or otherwise of any other common carrier where there is no substantial competition between the company extending its lines and the company whose stock, property, or an interest therein is so acquired.

Nothing contained in this section shall be held to affect or impair any right heretofore legally acquired: *Provided,* That nothing in this section shall be held or construed to authorize or make lawful anything heretofore prohibited or made illegal by the antitrust laws, nor to exempt any person from the penal provisions thereof or the civil remedies therein provided.

Nothing contained in this section shall apply to transactions duly consummated pursuant to authority given by the Civil Aeronautics Board, Federal Communications Commission, Federal Power Commission, Interstate Commerce Commission, the Securities and Exchange Commission in the exercise of its jurisdiction under section 79j of this title, the United States Maritime Commission, or the Secretary of Agriculture under any statutory provision vesting such power in such Commission, Secretary, or Board.

Section 8. No private banker or director, officer, or employee of any member bank of the Federal Reserve System or any branch thereof shall be at the same time a director, officer, or employee of any other bank, banking association, savings bank, or trust company organized under the National Bank Act or organized under the laws of any State or of the District of Columbia, or any branch thereof, except that the Board of Governors of the Federal Reserve System may by regulation permit such service as a director, officer, or employee of not more than one other such institution or branch thereof; but the foregoing prohibition shall not apply in the case of any one or more of the following or any branch thereof:

(1) A bank, banking association, savings bank, or trust company, more than 90 per centum of the stock of which is owned directly or indirectly by the United States or by any corporation of which the United States directly or indirectly owns more than 90 per centum of the stock.

(2) A bank, banking association, savings bank, or trust company which has been placed formally in liquidation or which is in the hands of a receiver, conservator, or other official exercising similar functions.

(3) A corporation, principally engaged in international or foreign banking or banking in a dependency or insular possession of the United States which has entered into an agreement with the Board of Governors of the Federal Reserve System pursuant to section 601 to 604a of Title 12.

(4) A bank, banking association, savings bank, or trust company, more than 50 per centum of the common stock of which is owned directly or indirectly by persons who own directly or indirectly more than 50 per centum of the common stock of such member bank.

(5) A bank, banking association, savings bank, or trust company not located and having no branch in the same city, town, or village as that in which such member bank or any branch thereof is located, or in any city, town, or village contiguous or adjacent thereto.

(6) A bank, banking association, savings bank, or trust company not engaged in a class or classes of business in which such member bank is engaged.

(7) A mutual savings bank having no capital stock.

Until February 1, 1939, nothing in this section shall prohibit any director, officer, or employee of any member bank of the Federal Reserve System, or any branch thereof, who is lawfully serving at the same time as a private banker or as a director, officer, or employee of any other bank, banking association, savings bank, or trust company, or any branch thereof, on August 23, 1935, from continuing such service.

The Board of Governors of the Federal Reserve System is authorized and directed to enforce compliance with this section, and to prescribe such rules and regulations as it deems necessary for that purpose.

No person at the same time shall be a director in any two or more corporations, any one of which has capital, surplus, and undivided profits aggregating more than $1,000,000, engaged in whole or in part in commerce, other than banks, banking associations, trust companies, and common carriers subject to the Act to regulate commerce, approved February fourth, eighteen hundred and eighty-seven, if such corporations are or shall have been theretofore, by virtue of their business and location of operation, competitors, so that the elimination of competition by agreement between them would constitute a violation of any of the provisions of any of the antitrust laws. The eligibility of a director under the foregoing provision shall be determined by the aggregate amount of the capital, surplus, and undivided profits, exclusive of dividends declared but not paid to stockholders, at the end of the fiscal year of said corporation next preceding the election of directors, and when a director has been elected in accordance with the provisions of this Act it shall be lawful for him to continue as such for one year thereafter.

When any person elected or chosen as a director or officer or selected as an employee of any bank or other corporation subject to the provisions of this Act is eligible at the time of his election or selection to act for such bank or other corporation in such capacity his eligibility to act in such capacity shall not be affected and he shall not become or be deemed amenable to any of the provisions hereof by reason of any change in the affairs of such bank or other corporation from whatsoever cause, whether specifically excepted by any of the provisions hereof or not, until the expiration of one year from the date of his election or employment.

Section 9. Recodified as 18 U.S.C. § 660 (1970).

Section 10. No common carrier engaged in commerce shall have any dealings in securities, supplies, or other articles of commerce, or shall make or have any contracts for construction or maintenance of any kind, to the amount of more than $50,000, in the aggregate, in any one year, with another corporation, firm, partnership, or association when the said common carrier shall have upon its board of directors or as its president, manager, or as its purchasing or selling officer, or agent in the particular transaction, any person who is at the same time a director, manager, or purchasing or selling officer of, or who has any substantial interest in, such other corporation, firm, partnership, or association, unless and except such purchases shall be made from, or such dealings shall be with, the bidder whose bid is the most favorable to such common carrier, to be ascertained by competitive bidding under regulations to be prescribed by rule or otherwise by the Interstate Commerce Commission. No bid shall be received unless the name and address of the bidder or the names and addresses of the officers, directors, and general managers thereof, if the bidder be a corporation, or of the members, if it be a partnership or firm, be given with the bid.

Any person who shall, directly or indirectly, do or attempt to do anything to prevent anyone from bidding, or shall do any act to prevent free and fair competition among the bidders or those desiring to bid, shall be punished as prescribed in this section in the case of an officer or director.

Every such common carrier having any such transactions or making any such purchases shall, within thirty days after making the same, file with the Interstate Commerce Commission a full and detailed statement of the transaction showing the manner of the competitive bidding, who were the bidders, and the names and addresses of the directors and officers of the corporations and the members of the firm or partnership bidding; and whenever the said commission shall, after investigation or hearing, have reason to believe that the law has been violated in and about the said purchases or transactions, it shall transmit all papers and documents and its own views or findings regarding the transaction to the Attorney General.

If any common carrier shall violate this section, it shall be fined not exceeding $25,000; and every such director, agent, manager, or officer thereof who shall have knowingly voted for or directed the act constituting such violation, or who shall have aided or abetted in such violation, shall be deemed guilty of a misdemeanor and shall be fined not exceeding $5,000 or confined in jail not exceeding one year, or both, in the discretion of the court.

Section 11. (a) Authority to enforce compliance with sections 13, 14, 18, and 19 of this title by the persons respectively subject thereto is vested in the Interstate Commerce Commission where applicable to common carriers subject to the Interstate Commerce Act, as amended; in the Federal Communications Commission where applicable to common carriers engaged in wire or radio communication or radio transmission of energy; in the Civil Aeronautics Board where applicable to air carriers and foreign air carriers subject to the Civil Aeronautics Act of 1938; in the Federal Reserve Board where applicable to banks, banking associations, and trust companies; and in the Federal Trade Commission where applicable to all other character of commerce to be exercised as follows:
(b) Whenever the Commission or Board vested with jurisdiction thereof shall have reason to believe that any person is violating or has violated any of the provisions of sections 13, 14, 18, and 19 of this title, it shall issue and serve upon such person and the Attorney General a complaint stating its charges in that respect, and containing a notice of a hearing upon a day and at a place therein fixed at least thirty days after the service of said complaint. The person so complained of shall have the right to appear at the place and time so fixed and show cause why an order should not be entered by the Commission or Board requiring such person to cease and desist from the violation of the law so charged in said complaint. The Attorney General shall have the right to intervene and appear in said proceeding and any person may make application, and upon good cause shown may be allowed by the Commission or Board, to intervene and appear in said proceeding by counsel or in person. The testimony in any such proceeding shall be reduced to writing and filed in the office of the Commission or Board. If upon such hearing the Commission or Board, as the case may be, shall be of the opinion that any of the provisions of said sections have been or are being violated, it shall make a report in writing, in which it shall state its findings as to the facts, and shall issue and cause to be served on such person an order requiring such person to cease and desist from such violations, and divest itself of the stock, or other share capital, or assets, held or rid itself of the directors chosen contrary to the provisions of sections 18 and 19 of this title, if any there be, in the manner and within the time fixed by said order. Until the expiration of the time allowed for filing a petition for review, if no such petition has been duly filed within such time, or, if a petition for review has been filed within such time then until the record in the proceeding has been filed in a court of appeals of the United States, as hereinafter provided, the Commission or Board may at any time, upon such notice and in such manner as it shall deem proper, modify or set aside, in whole or in part, any report or any order made or issued by it under this section. After the expiration of the time allowed for filing a petition for review, if no such petition has been duly filed within such time, the Commission or Board may at any time, after notice and opportunity for hearing, reopen and alter, modify, or set aside, in whole or in part, any report or order made or issued by it under this section, whenever in the opinion of the Commission or Board conditions of

fact or of law have so changed as to require such action or if the public interest shall so require: *Provided, however,* That the said person may, within sixty days after service upon him or it of said report or order entered after such a reopening, obtain a review thereof in the appropriate court of appeals of the United States, in the manner provided in subsection (c) of this section.

(c) Any person required by such order of the commission or board to cease and desist from any such violation may obtain a review of such order in the court of appeals of the United States for any circuit within which such violation occurred or within which such person resides or carries on business, by filing in the court, within sixty days after the date of the service of such order, a written petition praying that the order of the commission or board be set aside. A copy of such petition shall be forthwith transmitted by the clerk of the court to the commission or board, and thereupon the commission or board shall file in the court the record in the proceeding, as provided in section 2112 of Title 28. Upon such filing of the petition the court shall have jurisdiction of the proceeding and of the question determined therein concurrently with the commission or board until the filing of the record, and shall have power to make and enter a decree affirming, modifying, or setting aside the order of the commission or board, and enforcing the same to the extent that such order is affirmed, and to issue such writs as are ancillary to its jurisdiction or are necessary in its judgment to prevent injury to the public or to competitors pendente lite. The findings of the commission or board as to the facts, if supported by substantial evidence, shall be conclusive. To the extent that the order of the commission or board is affirmed, the court shall issue its own order commanding obedience to the terms of such order of the commission or board. If either party shall apply to the court for leave to adduce additional evidence, and shall show to the satisfaction of the court that such additional evidence is material and that there were reasonable grounds for the failure to adduce such evidence in the proceeding before the commission or board, the court may order such additional evidence to be taken before the commission or board, and to be adduced upon the hearing in such manner and upon such terms and conditions as to the court may see proper. The commission or board may modify its findings as to the facts, or make new findings, by reason of the additional evidence so taken, and shall file such modified or new findings, which if supported by substantial evidence, shall be conclusive, and its recommendation, if any, for the modification or setting aside of its original order, with the return of such additional evidence. The judgment and decree of the court shall be final, except that the same shall be subject to review by the Supreme Court upon certiorari, as provided in section 1254 of Title 28.

(d) Upon the filing of the record with its jurisdiction of the court of appeals to affirm, enforce, modify, or set aside orders of the commission or board shall be exclusive.

(e) Such proceedings in the court of appeals shall be given precedence over other cases pending therein, and shall be in every way expedited. No order of the commission or board or judgment of the court to enforce the same shall in anywise relieve or absolve any person from any liability under the antitrust laws.

(f) Complaints, orders, and other processes of the commission or board under this section may be served by anyone duly authorized by the commission or board, either (1) by delivering a copy thereof to the person to be served, or to a member of the partnership to be served, or to the president, secretary, or other executive officer or a director of the corporation to be served; or (2) by leaving a copy thereof at the residence or the principal office or place of business of such person; or (3) by mailing by registered or certified mail a copy thereof addressed to such person at his or its residence or principal office or place of business. The verified return by the person so serving said complaint, order, or

other process setting forth the manner of said service shall be proof of the same, and the return post office receipt for said complaint, order, or other process mailed by registered or certified mail as aforesaid shall be proof of the service of the same.
(g) Any order issued under subsection (b) of this section shall become final—

(1) upon the expiration of the time allowed for filing a petition for review, if no such petition has been duly filed within such time; but the commission or board may thereafter modify or set aside its order to the extent provided in the last sentence of subsection (b) of this section; or
(2) upon the expiration of the time allowed for filing a petition for certiorari, if the order of the commission or board has been affirmed, or the petition for review has been dismissed by the court of appeals, and no petition for certiorari has been duly filed; or
(3) upon the denial of a petition for certiorari, if the order of the commission or board has been affirmed or the petition for review has been dismissed by the court of appeals; or
(4) upon the expiration of thirty days from the date of issuance of the mandate of the Supreme Court, if such Court directs that the order of the commission or board be affirmed or the petition for review be dismissed.

(h) If the Supreme Court directs that the order of the commission or board be modified or set aside, the order of the commission or board rendered in accordance with the mandate of the Supreme Court shall become final upon the expiration of thirty days from the time it was rendered, unless within such thirty days either party has instituted proceedings to have such order corrected to accord with the mandate, in which event the order of the commission or board shall become final when so corrected.
(i) If the order of the commission or board is modified or set aside by the court of appeals, and if (1) the time allowed for filing a petition for certiorari has expired and no such petition has been duly filed, or (2) the petition for certiorari has been denied, or (3) the decision of the court has been affirmed by the Supreme Court then the order of the commission or board rendered in accordance with the mandate of the court of appeals shall become final on the expiration of thirty days from the time such order of the commission or board was rendered, unless within such thirty days either party has instituted proceedings to have such order corrected so that it will accord with the mandate, in which event the order of the commission or board shall become final when so corrected.
(j) If the Supreme Court orders a rehearing; or if the case is remanded by the court of appeals to the commission or board for a rehearing, and if (1) the time allowed for filing a petition for certiorari has expired, and no such petition has been duly filed, or (2) the petition for certiorari has been denied, or (3) the decision of the court has been affirmed by the Supreme Court, then the order of the commission or board rendered upon such rehearing shall become final in the same manner as though no prior order of the commission or board had been rendered.
(k) As used in this section the term "mandate," in case a mandate has been recalled prior to the expiration of thirty days from the date of issuance thereof, means the final mandate.
(l) Any person who violates any order issued by the commission or board under subsection (b) of this section after such order has become final, and while such order is in effect, shall forfeit and pay to the United States a civil penalty of not more than $5,000 for each violation, which shall accrue to the United States and may be recovered in a civil action brought by the United States. Each separate violation of any such order shall be a separate offense, except that in the case

of a violation through continuing failure or neglect to obey a final order of the commission or board each day of continuance of such failure or neglect shall be deemed a separate offense.

Section 12. Any suit, action, or proceeding under the antitrust laws against a corporation may be brought not only in the judicial district whereof it is an inhabitant, but also in any district wherein it may be found or transacts business; and all process in such cases may be served in the district of which it is an inhabitant, or wherever it may be found.

Section 13. In any suit, action, or proceeding brought by or on behalf of the United States subpœnas for witnesses who are required to attend a court of the United States in any judicial district in any case, civil or criminal, arising under the antitrust laws may run into any other district: *Provided,* That in civil cases no writ of subpœna shall issue for witnesses living out of the district in which the court is held at a greater distance than one hundred miles from the place of holding the same without the permission of the trial court being first had upon proper application and cause shown.

Section 14. Whenever a corporation shall violate any of the penal provisions of the antitrust laws, such violation shall be deemed to be also that of the individual directors, officers, or agents of such corporation who shall have authorized, ordered, or done any of the acts constituting in whole or in part such violation, and such violation shall be deemed a misdemeanor, and upon conviction therefor of any such director, officer, or agent he shall be punished by a fine of not exceeding $5,000 or by imprisonment for not exceeding one year, or by both, in the discretion of the court.

Section 15. The several district courts of the United States are invested with jurisdiction to prevent and restrain violations of this Act, and it shall be the duty of the several United States attorneys, in their respective districts, under the direction of the Attorney General, to institute proceedings in equity to prevent and restrain such violations. Such proceedings may be by way of petition setting forth the case and praying that such violation shall be enjoined or otherwise prohibited. When the parties complained of shall have been duly notified of such petition, the court shall proceed, as soon as may be, to the hearing and determination of the case; and pending such petition, and before final decree, the court may at any time make such temporary restraining order or prohibition as shall be deemed just in the premises. Whenever it shall appear to the court before which any such proceeding may be pending that the ends of justice require that other parties should be brought before the court, the court may cause them to be summoned whether they reside in the district in which the court is held or not, and subpœnas to that end may be served in any district by the marshal thereof.

Section 16. Any person, firm, corporation, or association shall be entitled to sue for and have injunctive relief, in any court of the United States having jurisdiction over the parties, against threatened loss or damage by a violation of the antitrust laws, including sections 13, 14, 18, and 19 of this title, when and under the same conditions and principles as injunctive relief against threatened conduct that will cause loss or damage is granted by courts of equity, under the rules governing such proceedings, and upon the execution of proper bond against damages for an injunction improvidently granted and a showing that the danger of irreparable loss or damage is immediate, a preliminary injunction may issue: *Provided,* That nothing herein contained shall be construed to entitle any person, firm, corporation, or association, except the United States, to bring suit in equity for injunctive relief against any common carrier subject to the provisions of the Act to regulate commerce, approved February fourth, eighteen hundred and eighty-seven, in respect of any matter subject to the regulation, supervision, or other jurisdiction of the Interstate Commerce Commission.

Sections 17–25. Recodified as 18 U.S.C. §§ 402, 3285, 3691 (1970).

Section 26. If any clause, sentence, paragraph, or part of this Act shall, for any reason, be adjudged by any court of competent jurisdiction to be invalid, such judgment shall not affect, impair, or invalidate the remainder thereof, but shall be confined in its operation to the clause, sentence, paragraph, or part thereof directly involved in the controversy in which such judgment shall have been rendered.

Approved, October 15, 1914.

Appendix IV

The Federal Trade Commission Act

[Public No. 203—63d Congress, as amended by Public No. 447—75th Congress, as amended by Public No. 459—81st Congress, as amended by Public No. 542—82d Congress, as amended by Public No. 85—791—85th Congress, as amended by Public No. 85—909—85th Congress, as amended by Public No. 91—452—91st Congress]

An Act to create a Federal Trade Commission, to define its powers and duties, and for other purposes.

Be it enacted by the Senate and House of Representatives of the United States of America in Congress assembled, that

Section 1. A commission is created and established, to be known as the Federal Trade Commission (hereinafter referred to as the Commission), which shall be composed of five Commissioners, who shall be appointed by the President, by and with the advice and consent of the Senate. Not more than three of the Commissioners shall be members of the same political party. The first Commissioners appointed shall continue in office for terms of three, four, five, six, and seven years, respectively, from September 26, 1914, the term of each to be designated by the President, but their successors shall be appointed for terms of seven years, except that any person chosen to fill a vacancy shall be appointed only for the unexpired term of the Commissioner whom he shall succeed: *Provided, however,* That upon the expiration of his term of office a Commissioner shall continue to serve until his successor shall have been appointed and shall have qualified. The President shall choose a chairman from the Commission's membership. No Commissioner shall engage in any other business, vocation, or employment. Any Commissioner may be removed by the President for inefficiency, neglect of duty, or malfeasance in office. A vacancy in the Commission shall not impair the right of the remaining Commissioners to exercise all the powers of the Commission.

The Commission shall have an official seal, which shall be judicially noticed.

Section 2. The Commission shall appoint a secretary, who shall receive a salary, payable in the same manner as the salaries of the judges of the courts of the United States, and it shall have authority to employ and fix the compensation of such attorneys, special experts, examiners, clerks, and other employees as it may from time to time find necessary for the proper performance of its duties and as may be from time to time appropriated for by Congress.

With the exception of the secretary, a clerk to each Commissioner, the attorneys, and such special experts and examiners as the Commission may from time to time find necessary for the conduct of its work, all employees of the Commission shall be a part of the classified civil service, and shall enter the service under such rules and regulations as may be prescribed by the Commission and by the Civil Service Commission.

All of the expenses of the Commission, including all necessary expenses for transportation incurred by the Commissioners or by their employees under their orders, in making any investigation, or upon official business in any other places than in the city of Washington, shall be allowed and paid on the presentation of itemized vouchers therefor approved by the Commission.

Until otherwise provided by law, the Commission may rent suitable offices for its use.

The General Accounting Office shall receive and examine all accounts of expenditures of the Commission.

Section 3. The principal office of the Commission shall be in the city of Washington, but it may meet and exercise all its powers at any other place. The Commission may, by one or more of its members, or by such examiners as it may designate, prosecute any inquiry necessary to its duties in any part of the United States.

Section 4. The words defined in this section shall have the following meaning when found in sections 41 to 46 and 47 to 58 of this title, to wit:

"Commerce" means commerce among the several States or with foreign nations, or in any Territory of the United States or in the District of Columbia, or between any such Territory and another, or between any such Territory and any State or foreign nation, or between the District of Columbia and any State or Territory or foreign nation.

"Corporation" shall be deemed to include any company, trust, so-called Massachusetts trust, or association, incorporated or unincorporated, which is organized to carry on business for its own profit or that of its members, and has shares of capital or capital stock or certificates of interest, and any company, trust, so-called Massachusetts trust, or association, incorporated or unincorporated, without shares of capital or capital stock or certificates of interest, except partnerships, which is organized to carry on business for its own profit or that of its members.

"Documentary evidence" includes all documents, papers, correspondence, books of account, and financial and corporate records.

"Acts to regulate commerce" means the Act entitled "An Act to regulate commerce," approved February 14, 1887 and all Acts amendatory thereof and supplementary thereto and the Communications Act of 1934 and all Acts amendatory thereof and supplementary thereto.

"Antitrust Acts" means the Act entitled "An Act to protect trade and commerce against unlawful restraints and monopolies," approved July 2, 1890; also sections 73 to 77, of an Act entitled "An Act to reduce taxation, to provide revenue for the Government, and for other purposes," approved August 27, 1894; also the Act entitled "An Act to amend sections 73 and 76 of the Act of August 27, 1894, entitled 'An Act to reduce taxation, to provide revenue for the Government, and for other purposes,' " approved February 12, 1913; and also the Act entitled "An Act to supplement existing laws against unlawful restraints and monopolies, and for other purposes," approved October 15, 1914.

Section 5. (a)

(1) Unfair methods of competition in commerce, and unfair or deceptive acts or practices in commerce, are declared unlawful.

(2) Nothing contained in this section or in any of the Antitrust Acts shall

render unlawful any contracts or agreements prescribing minimum or stipulated prices, or requiring a vendee to enter into contracts or agreements prescribing minimum or stipulated prices, for the resale of a commodity which bears, or the label or container of which bears, the trade-mark, brand, or name of the producer or distributor of such commodity and which is in free and open competition with commodities of the same general class produced or distributed by others, when contracts or agreements of that description are lawful as applied to intrastate transactions under any statute, law, or public policy now or hereafter in effect in any State, Territory, or the District of Columbia in which such resale is to be made, or to which the commodity is to be transported for such resale.

(3) Nothing contained in this section or in any of the Antitrust Acts shall render unlawful the exercise or the enforcement of any right or right of action created by any statute, law, or public policy now or hereafter in effect in any State, Territory, or the District of Columbia, which in substance provides that willfully and knowingly advertising, offering for sale, or selling any commodity at less than the price or prices prescribed in such contracts or agreements whether the person so advertising, offering for sale, or selling is or is not a party to such a contract or agreement, is unfair competition and is actionable at the suit of any person damaged thereby.

(4) Neither the making of contracts or agreements as described in paragraph (2) of this subsection, nor the exercise or enforcement of any right or right of action as described in paragraph (3) of this subsection shall constitute an unlawful burden or restraint upon, or interference with, commerce.

(5) Nothing contained in paragraph (2) of this subsection shall make lawful contracts or agreements providing for the establishment or maintenance of minimum or stipulated resale prices on any commodity referred to in paragraph (2) of this subsection, between manufacturers, or between producers, or between wholesalers, or between brokers, or between factors, or between retailers, or between persons, firms, or corporations in competition with each other.

(6) The Commission is empowered and directed to prevent persons, partnerships, or corporations, except banks, common carriers subject to the Acts to regulate commerce, air carriers and foreign air carriers subject to the Federal Aviation Act of 1958, and persons, partnerships, or corporations insofar as they are subject to the Packers and Stockyards Act, 1921, as amended, except as provided in section 406(b) of said Act, from using unfair methods of competition in commerce and unfair or deceptive acts or practices in commerce.

(b) Whenever the Commission shall have reason to believe that any such person, partnership, or corporation has been or is using any unfair method of competition or unfair or deceptive act or practice in commerce, and if it shall appear to the Commission that a proceeding by it in respect thereof would be to the interest of the public, it shall issue and serve upon such person, partnership, or corporation a complaint stating its charges in that respect and containing a notice of a hearing upon a day and at a place therein fixed at least thirty days after the service of said complaint. The person, partnership, or corporation so complained of shall have the right to appear at the place and time so fixed and show cause why an order should not be entered by the Commission requiring such person, partnership, or corporation to cease and desist from the violation of the law so charged in said complaint. Any person, partnership, or corporation may make application, and upon good cause shown may be allowed by the Commission to intervene and appear in said proceeding by counsel or in person. The testimony in any such proceeding shall be reduced to writing and filed in the office of the Commission. If upon such hearing the Commission shall be of the opinion that the method of competition or the act or practice in question is prohibited by sections 41 to 46 and 47 to 58 of this title, it shall make a report in writing in which it shall state its findings as to the facts and shall issue and cause to be served on such person, partnership, or corporation an order requiring such person, partnership, or corporation to cease and desist from using such method of competition or such act or practice. Until the expiration of the time allowed for filing a petition for review, if no such petition has been duly filed within such time, or, if a petition for review has been filed within such time then until the record in the proceeding has been filed in a court of appeals of the United States, as hereinafter provided, the Commission may at any time, upon such notice and in such manner as it shall deem proper, modify or set aside, in whole or in part, any report or any order made or issued by it under this section. After the expiration of the time allowed for filing a petition for review, if no such petition has been duly filed within such time, the Commission may at any time, after notice and opportunity for hearing, reopen and alter, modify, or set aside, in whole or in part, any report or order made or issued by it under this section, whenever in the opinion of the Commission conditions of fact or of law have so changed as to require such action or if the public interest shall so require: *Provided, however,* That the said person, partnership, or corporation may, within sixty days after service upon him or it of said report or order entered after such a reopening, obtain a review thereof in the appropriate court of appeals of the United States, in the manner provided in subsection (c) of this section.

(c) Any person, partnership, or corporation required by an order of the Commission to cease and desist from using any method of competition or act or practice may obtain a review of such order in the court of appeals of the United States, within any circuit where the method of competition or the act or practice in question was used or where such person, partnership, or corporation resides or carries on business, by filing in the court, within sixty days from the date of the service of such order, a written petition praying that the order of the Commission be set aside. A copy of such petition shall be forthwith transmitted by the clerk of the court to the Commission, and thereupon the Commission shall file in the court the record in the proceeding, as provided in section 2112 of Title 28. Upon such filing of the petition the court shall have jurisdiction of the proceeding and of the question determined therein concurrently with the Commission until the filing of the record and shall have power to make and enter a decree affirming, modifying, or setting aside the order of the Commission, and enforcing the same to the extent that such order is affirmed and to issue such writs as are ancillary to its jurisdiction or are necessary in its judgment to prevent injury to the public or to competitors pendente lite. The findings of the Commission as to the facts, if supported by evidence, shall be conclusive. To the extent that the order of the Commission is affirmed, the court shall thereupon issue its own order commanding obedience to the terms of such order of the Commission. If either party shall apply to the court for leave to adduce additional evidence, and shall show to the satisfaction of the court that such additional evidence is material and that there were reasonable grounds for the failure to adduce such evidence in the proceeding before the Commission, the court may order such additional evidence to be taken before the Commission and to be adduced upon the hearing in such manner and upon such terms and conditions as to the court may seem proper. The Commission may modify its findings as to the facts, or make new findings, by reason of the additional evidence so taken, and it shall file such modified or new findings, which, if supported by evidence, shall be conclusive, and its recommendation, if any, for the modification or setting aside of its original order, with the return of such additional evidence. The judgment and decree of the court shall be final, except that the same shall be subject to review by the Supreme Court upon certiorari, as provided in section 347 of Title 28.

(d) Upon the filing of the record with it the jurisdiction of the court of appeals of the United States to affirm, enforce, modify, or set aside orders of the Commission shall be exclusive.
(e) Such proceedings in the court of appeals shall be given precedence over other cases pending therein, and shall be in every way expedited. No order of the Commission or judgment of court to enforce the same shall in anywise relieve or absolve any person, partnership, or corporation from any liability under the Antitrust Acts.
(f) Complaints, orders, and other processes of the Commission under this section may be served by anyone duly authorized by the Commission, either (a) by delivering a copy thereof to the person to be served, or to a member of the partnership to be served, or the president, secretary, or other executive officer or a director of the corporation to be served; or (b) by leaving a copy thereof at the residence or the principal office or place of business of such person, partnership, or corporation; or (c) by mailing a copy thereof by registered mail or by certified mail addressed to such person, partnership, or corporation at his or its residence or principal office or place of business. The verified return by the person so serving said complaint, order, or other process setting forth the manner of said service shall be proof of the same, and the return post office receipt for said complaint, order, or other process mailed by registered mail or by certified mail as aforesaid shall be proof of the service of the same.
(g) An order of the Commission to cease and desist shall become final—

(1) Upon the expiration of the time allowed for filing a petition for review, if no such petition has been duly filed within such time; but the Commission may thereafter modify or set aside its order to the extent provided in the last sentence of subsection (b); or

(2) Upon the expiration of the time allowed for filing a petition for certiorari, if the order of the Commission has been affirmed, or the petition for review dismissed by the court of appeals, and no petition for certiorari has been duly filed; or

(3) Upon the denial of a petition for certiorari, if the order of the Commission has been affirmed or the petition for review dismissed by the court of appeals; or

(4) Upon the expiration of thirty days from the date of issuance of the mandate of the Supreme Court, if such Court directs that the order of the Commission be affirmed or the petition for review dismissed.

(h) If the Supreme Court directs that the order of the Commission be modified or set aside, the order of the Commission rendered in accordance with the mandate of the Supreme Court shall become final upon the expiration of thirty days from the time it was rendered, unless within such thirty days either party has instituted proceedings to have such order corrected to accord with the mandate, in which event the order of the Commission shall become final when so corrected.
(i) If the order of the Commission is modified or set aside by the court of appeals, and if (1) the time allowed for filing a petition for certiorari has expired and no such petition has been duly filed, or (2) the petition for certiorari has been denied, or (3) the decision of the court has been affirmed by the Supreme Court, then the order of the Commission rendered in accordance with the mandate of the court of appeals shall become final on the expiration of thirty days from the time such order of the Commission was rendered, unless within such thirty days either party has instituted proceedings to have such order corrected so that it will accord with the mandate, in which event the order of the Commission shall become final when so corrected.
(j) If the Supreme Court orders a rehearing; or if the case is remanded by the

court of appeals to the Commission for a rehearing, and if (1) the time allowed for filing a petition for certiorari has expired, and no such petition has been duly filed, or (2) the petition for certiorari has been denied, or (3) the decision of the court has been affirmed by the Supreme Court, then the order of the Commission rendered upon such rehearing shall become final in the same manner as though no prior order of the Commission had been rendered.
(k) As used in this section the term "mandate," in case a mandate has been recalled prior to the expiration of thirty days from the date of issuance thereof, means the final mandate.
(*l*) Any person, partnership, or corporation who violates an order of the Commission to cease and desist after it has become final, and while such order is in effect, shall forfeit and pay to the United States a civil penalty of not more than $5,000 for each violation, which shall accrue to the United States and may be recovered in a civil action brought by the United States. Each separate violation of such an order shall be a separate offense, except that in the case of a violation through continuing failure or neglect to obey a final order of the Commission each day of continuance of such failure or neglect shall be deemed a separate offense.

Section 6. The Commission shall also have power—
(a) To gather and compile information concerning, and to investigate from time to time the organization, business, conduct, practices, and management of any corporation engaged in commerce, excepting banks and common carriers subject to the Act to regulate commerce, and its relation to other corporations and to individuals, associations, and partnerships.
(b) To require, by general or special orders, corporations engaged in commerce, excepting banks and common carriers subject to the Act to regulate commerce, or any class of them, or any of them, respectively, to file with the Commission in such form as the Commission may prescribe annual or special, or both annual and special, reports or answers in writing to specific questions, furnishing to the Commission such information as it may require as to the organization, business, conduct, practices, management, and relation to other corporations, partnerships, and individuals of the respective corporations filing such reports or answers in writing. Such reports and answers shall be made under oath, or otherwise, as the Commission may prescribe, and shall be filed with the Commission within such reasonable period as the Commission may prescribe, unless additional time be granted in any case by the Commission.
(c) Whenever a final decree has been entered against any defendant corporation in any suit brought by the United States to prevent and restrain any violation of the antitrust Acts, to make investigation, upon its own initiative, of the manner in which the decree has been or is being carried out, and upon the application of the Attorney General it shall be its duty to make such investigation. It shall transmit to the Attorney General a report embodying its findings and recommendations as a result of any such investigation, and the report shall be made public in the discretion of the Commission.
(d) Upon the direction of the President or either House of Congress to investigate and report the facts relating to any alleged violations of the antitrust Acts by any corporation.
(e) Upon the application of the Attorney General to investigate and make recommendations for the readjustment of the business of any corporation alleged to be violating the antitrust Acts in order that the corporation may thereafter maintain its organization, management, and conduct of business in accordance with law.
(f) To make public from time to time such portions of the information obtained by it hereunder, except trade secrets and names of customers, as it shall deem

expedient in the public interest; and to make annual and special reports to the Congress and to submit therewith recommendations for additional legislation; and to provide for the publication of its reports and decisions in such form and manner as may be best adapted for public information and use.
(g) From time to time to classify corporations and to make rules and regulations for the purpose of carrying out the provisions of sections 41 to 46 and 47 to 58 of this title.
(h) To investigate, from time to time, trade conditions in and with foreign countries where associations, combinations, or practices of manufacturers, merchants, or traders, or other conditions, may affect the foreign trade of the United States, and to report to Congress thereon, with such recommendations as it deems advisable.

Section 7. In any suit in equity brought by or under the direction of the Attorney General as provided in the antitrust Acts, the court may, upon the conclusion of the testimony therein, if it shall be then of opinion that the complainant is entitled to relief, refer said suit to the Commission, as a master in chancery, to ascertain and report an appropriate form of decree therein. The Commission shall proceed upon such notice to the parties and under such rules of procedure as the court may prescribe, and upon the coming in of such report such exceptions may be filed and such proceedings had in relation thereto as upon the report of a master in other equity causes, but the court may adopt or reject such report, in whole or in part, and enter such decree as the nature of the case may in its judgment require.

Section 8. The several departments and bureaus of the Government when directed by the President shall furnish the Commission, upon its request, all records, papers, and information in their possession relating to any corporation subject to any of the provisions of sections 41 to 46 and 47 to 58 of this title, and shall detail from time to time such officials and employees to the Commission as he may direct.

Section 9. For the purposes of sections 41 to 46 and 47 to 58 of this title the Commission, or its duly authorized agent or agents, shall at all reasonable times have access to, for the purpose of examination, and the right to copy any documentary evidence of any corporation being investigated or proceeded against; and the Commission shall have power to require by subpœna the attendance and testimony of witnesses and the production of all such documentary evidence relating to any matter under investigation. Any member of the Commission may sign subpœnas, and members and examiners of the Commission may administer oaths and affirmations, examine witnesses, and receive evidence.

Such attendance of witnesses, and the production of such documentary evidence, may be required from any place in the United States, at any designated place of hearing. And in case of disobedience to a subpœna the Commission may invoke the aid of any court of the United States in requiring the attendance and testimony of witnesses and the production of documentary evidence.

Any of the district courts of the United States within the jurisdiction of which such inquiry is carried on may, in case of contumacy or refusal to obey a subpœna issued to any corporation or other person, issue an order requiring such corporation or other person to appear before the Commission, or to produce documentary evidence if so ordered, or to give evidence touching the matter in question; and any failure to obey such order of the court may be punished by such court as a contempt thereof.

Upon the application of the Attorney General of the United States, at the request of the Commission, the district courts of the United States shall have jurisdiction to issue writs of mandamus commanding any person or corporation to comply with the provisions of sections 41 to 46 and 47 to 58 of this title or any order of the Commission made in pursuance thereof.

The Commission may order testimony to be taken by deposition in any proceeding or investigation pending under said sections at any stage of such proceeding or investigation. Such depositions may be taken before any person designated by the Commission and having power to administer oaths. Such testimony shall be reduced to writing by the person taking the deposition, or under his direction, and shall then be subscribed by the deponent. Any person may be compelled to appear and depose and to produce documentary evidence in the same manner as witnesses may be compelled to appear and testify and produce documentary evidence before the Commission as hereinbefore provided.

Witnesses summoned before the Commission shall be paid the same fees and mileage that are paid witnesses in the courts of the United States, and witnesses whose depositions are taken and the persons taking the same shall severally be entitled to the same fees as are paid for like services in the courts of the United States.

No person shall be excused from attending and testifying or from producing documentary evidence before the Commission or in obedience to the subpoena of the Commission on the ground or for the reason that the testimony or evidence, documentary or otherwise, required of him may tend to criminate him or subject him to a penalty or forfeiture. But no natural person shall be prosecuted or subjected to any penalty or forfeiture for or on account of any transaction, matter, or thing concerning which he may testify, or produce evidence, documentary or otherwise, before the Commission in obedience to a subpoena issued by it: *Provided,* That no natural person so testifying shall be exempt from prosecution and punishment for perjury committed in so testifying.

Section 10. Any person who shall neglect or refuse to attend and testify, or to answer any lawful inquiry or to produce documentary evidence, if in his power to do so, in obedience to the subpœna or lawful requirement of the Commission, shall be guilty of an offense and upon conviction thereof by a court of competent jurisdiction shall be punished by a fine of not less than $1,000 nor more than $5,000, or by imprisonment for not more than one year, or by both such fine and imprisonment.

Any person who shall willfully make, or cause to be made, any false entry or statement of fact in any report required to be made under sections 41 to 46 and 47 to 58 of this title, or who shall willfully make, or cause to be made, any false entry in any account, record, or memorandum kept by any corporation subject to said sections, or who shall willfully neglect or fail to make, or to cause to be made, full, true, and correct entries in such accounts, records, or memoranda of all facts and transactions appertaining to the business of such corporation, or who shall willfully remove out of the jurisdiction of the United States, or willfully multilate, alter, or by any other means falsify any documentary evidence of such corporation, or who shall willfully refuse to submit to the Commission or to any of its authorized agents, for the purpose of inspection and taking copies, any documentary evidence of such corporation in his possession or within his control, shall be deemed guilty of an offense against the United States, and shall be subject, upon conviction in any court of the United States of competent jurisdiction, to a fine of not less than $1,000 nor more than $5,000, or to imprisonment for a term of not more than three years, or to both such fine and imprisonment.

If any corporation required by sections 41 to 46 and 47 to 58 of this title to file any annual or special report shall fail so to do within the time fixed by the Commission for filing the same, and such failure shall continue for thirty days after notice of such default, the corporation shall forfeit to the United States the sum of $100 for each and every day of the continuance of such failure, which forfeiture shall be payable into the Treasury of the United States, and shall be recoverable in a civil suit in the name of the United States brought in the district where the corporation has its principal office or in any district in which it shall do business. It shall be the duty of the various United States attorneys, under the direction of the Attorney General of the United States, to prosecute for the recovery of forfeitures. The costs and expenses of such prosecution shall be paid out of the appropriation for the expenses of the courts of the United States.

Any officer or employee of the Commission who shall make public any information obtained by the Commission without its authority, unless directed by a court, shall be deemed guilty of a misdemeanor, and, upon conviction thereof, shall be punished by a fine not exceeding $5,000, or by imprisonment not exceeding one year, or by fine and imprisonment, in the discretion of the court.

Section 11. Nothing contained in sections 41 to 46 and 47 to 58 of this title shall be construed to prevent or interfere with the enforcement of the provisions of the antitrust Acts or the Acts to regulate commerce, nor shall anything contained in said sections be construed to alter, modify, or repeal the said antitrust Acts or the Acts to regulate commerce or any part or parts thereof.

Section 12. (a) Unlawfulness.

It shall be unlawful for any person, partnership, or corporation to disseminate, or cause to be disseminated, any false advertisement—

(1) By United States mails, or in commerce by any means, for the purpose of inducing, or which is likely to induce, directly or indirectly the purchase of food, drugs, devices, or cosmetics; or

(2) By any means, for the purpose of inducing, or which is likely to induce, directly or indirectly, the purchase in commerce of food, drugs, devices, or cosmetics.

(b) Unfair or deceptive act or practice.

The dissemination or the causing to be disseminated of any false advertisement within the provisions of subsection (a) of this section shall be an unfair or deceptive act or practice in commerce within the meaning of section 45 of this title.

Section 13. (a) Power of Commission; jurisdiction of courts.

Whenever the Commission has reason to believe—

(1) that any person, partnership, or corporation is engaged in, or is about to engage in, the dissemination or the causing of the dissemination of any advertisement in violation of section 52 of this title, and

(2) that the enjoining thereof pending the issuance of a complaint by the Commission under section 45 of this title, and until such complaint is dismissed by the Commission or set aside by the court on review, or the order of the Commission to cease and desist made thereon has become final within the meaning of section 45 of this title, would be to the interest of the public,

the Commission by any of its attorneys designated by it for such purpose may bring suit in a district court of the United States or in the United States court of any Territory, to enjoin the dissemination or the causing of the dissemination of such advertisement. Upon proper showing a temporary injunction or restraining order shall be granted without bond. Any such suit shall be brought in the district in which such person, partnership, or corporation resides or transacts business.

(b) Whenever it appears to the satisfaction of the court in the case of a newspaper, magazine, periodical, or other publication, published at regular intervals—

(1) that restraining the dissemination of a false advertisement in any particular issue of such publication would delay the delivery of such issue after the regular time therefor, and

(2) that such delay would be due to the method by which the manufacture and distribution of such publication is customarily conducted by the publisher in accordance with sound business practice, and not to any method or device adopted for the evasion of this section or to prevent or delay the issuance of an injunction or restraining order with respect to such false advertisement or any other advertisement,

the court shall exclude such issue from the operation of the restraining order or injunction.

Section 14. (a) Any person, partnership, or corporation who violates any provision of section 52 (a) of this title shall, if the use of the commodity advertised may be injurious to health because of results from such use under the conditions prescribed in the advertisement thereof, or under such conditions as are customary or usual, or if such violation is with intent to defraud or mislead, be guilty of a misdemeanor, and upon conviction shall be punished by a fine of not more than $5,000 or by imprisonment for not more than six months, or by both such fine and imprisonment; except that if the conviction is for a violation committed after a first conviction of such person, partnership, or corporation, for any violation of such section, punishment shall be by a fine of not more than $10,000 or by imprisonment for not more than one year, or by both such fine and imprisonment: *Provided,* That for the purposes of this section meats and meat food products duly inspected, marked, and labeled in accordance with rules and regulations issued under the Meat Inspection Act, shall be conclusively presumed not injurious to health at the time the same leave official "establishments."
(b) No publisher, radio-broadcast licensee, or agency or medium for the dissemination of advertising, except the manufacturer, packer, distributor, or seller of the commodity to which the false advertisement relates, shall be liable under this section by reason of the dissemination by him of any false advertisement, unless he has refused, on the request of the Commission, to furnish the Commission the name and post-office address of the manufacturer, packer, distributor, seller, or advertising agency, residing in the United States, who caused him to disseminate such advertisement. No advertising agency shall be liable under this section by reason of the causing by it of the dissemination of any false advertisement, unless it has refused, on the request of the Commission, to furnish the Commission the name and post-office address of the manufacturer, packer, distributor, or seller, residing in the United States, who caused it to cause the dissemination of such advertisement.

Section 15. For the purposes of sections 52 to 54 of this title—
(a) (1) The term "false advertisement" means an advertisement, other than labeling, which is misleading in a material respect; and in determining whether any advertisement is misleading, there shall be taken into account (among other things) not only representations made or suggested by statement, word, design, device, sound, or any combination thereof, but also the extent to which the advertisement fails to reveal facts material in the light of such representations or material with respect to consequences which may result from the use of the commodity to which the advertisement relates under the conditions prescribed in said advertisement, or under such conditions as are customary or usual. No advertisement of a drug shall be deemed to be false if it is disseminated only to members of the medical profession, contains no false representation of a material

fact, and includes, or is accompanied in each instance by truthful disclosure of, the formula showing quantitatively each ingredient of such drug.

(2) In the case of oleomargarine or margarine an advertisement shall be deemed misleading in a material respect if in such advertisement representations are made or suggested by statement, word, grade designation, design, device, symbol, sound, or any combination thereof, that such oleomargarine or margarine is a dairy product, except that nothing contained herein shall prevent a truthful, accurate, and full statement in any such advertisement of all the ingredients contained in such oleomargarine or margarine.

(b) The term "food" means (1) articles used for food or drink for man or other animals, (2) chewing gum, and (3) articles used for components of any such article.

(c) The term "drug" means (1) articles recognized in the official United States Pharmacopœia, official Homœopathic Pharmacopœia of the United States, or official National Formulary, or any supplement to any of them; and (2) articles intended for use in the diagnosis, cure, mitigation, treatment, or prevention of disease in man or other animals; and (3) articles (other than food) intended to affect the structure or any function of the body of man or other animals; and (4) articles intended for use as a component of any article specified in clauses (1), (2), or (3); but does not include devices or their components, parts, or accessories.

(d) The term "device" (except when used in subsection (a) of this section) means instruments, apparatus, and contrivances, including their parts and accessories, intended (1) for use in the diagnosis, cure, mitigation, treatment, or prevention of disease in man or other animals; or (2) to affect the structure or any function of the body of man or other animals.

(e) The term "cosmetic" means (1) articles to be rubbed, poured, sprinkled, or sprayed on, introduced into, or otherwise applied to the human body or any part thereof intended for cleansing, beautifying, promoting attractiveness, or altering the appearance, and (2) articles intended for use as a component of any such article; except that such term shall not include soap.

(f) For the purposes of this section and section 347 of Title 21, the term "olemargarine" or "margarine" includes—

(1) all substances, mixtures, and compounds known as oleomargarine or margarine;

(2) all substances, mixtures, and compounds which have a consistence similar to that of butter and which contain any edible oils or fats other than milk fat if made in imitation or semblance of butter.

Section 16. Whenever the Federal Trade Commission has reason to believe that any person, partnership, or corporation is liable to a penalty under section 54 of this title or under subsection (*l*) of section 45 of this title, it shall certify the facts to the Attorney General, whose duty it shall be to cause appropriate proceedings to be brought for the enforcement of the provisions of such section or subsection.

Section 17. If any provision of sections 41 to 46 and 47 to 58 of this title, or the application thereof to any person, partnership, corporation, or circumstance, is held invalid, the remainder of said sections, and the application of such provision to any other person, partnership, corporation, or circumstance, shall not be affected thereby.

Section 18. Sections 41 to 46 and 47 to 58 of this title may be cited as the "Federal Trade Commission Act."

Approved September 26, 1914.
Amended March 21, 1938.

Appendix V

Justice Department Merger Guidelines

1. *Purpose*. The purpose of these guidelines is to acquaint the business community, the legal profession, and other interested groups and individuals with the standards currently being applied by the Department of Justice in determining whether to challenge corporate acquisitions and mergers under Section 7 of the Clayton Act. (Although mergers or acquisitions may also be challenged under the Sherman Act, commonly the challenge will be made under Section 7 of the Clayton Act and, accordingly, it is to this provision of law that the guidelines are directed.) The responsibilities of the Department of Justice under Section 7 are those of an enforcement agency, and these guidelines are announced solely as a statement of current Department policy, subject to change at any time without prior notice, for whatever assistance such statement may be in enabling interested persons to anticipate in a general way Department enforcement action under Section 7. Because the statements of enforcement policy contained in these guidelines must necessarily be framed in rather general terms, and because the critical factors in any particular guideline formulation may be evaluated differently by the Department than by the parties, the guidelines should not be treated as a substitute for the Department's business review procedures, which make available statements of the Department's present enforcement intentions with regard to particular proposed mergers or acquisitions.

2. *General Enforcement Policy*. Within the over-all scheme of the Department's antitrust enforcement activity, the primary role of Section 7 enforcement is to preserve and promote market structures conducive to competition. Market structure is the focus of the Department's merger policy chiefly because the conduct of the individual firms in a market tends to be controlled by the structure of that market, *i.e.,* by those market conditions which are fairly permanent or subject only to slow change (such as, principally, the number of substantial firms selling in the market, the relative sizes of their respective market shares, and the substantiality of barriers to the entry of new firms into the market). Thus, for example, a concentrated market structure, where a few firms account for a large share of the sales, tends to discourage vigorous price competition by the firms in the market and to encourage other kinds of conduct, such as use of inefficient methods of production or excessive promotional expenditures, of an economically undesirable nature. Moreover, not only does emphasis on market structure generally produce economic predictions that are fully adequate for the purposes

of a statute that requires only a showing that the effect of a merger "may be substantially to lessen competition, or to tend to create a monopoly," but an enforcement policy emphasizing a limited number of structural factors also facilitates both enforcement decision-making and business planning which involves anticipation of the Department's enforcement intent. Accordingly, the Department's enforcement activity under Section 7 is directed primarily toward the identification and prevention of those mergers which alter market structure in ways likely now or eventually to encourage or permit non-competitive conduct.

In certain exceptional circumstances, however, the structural factors used in these guidelines will not alone be conclusive, and the Department's enforcement activity will necessarily be based on a more complex and inclusive evaluation. This is sometimes the case, for example, where basic technological changes are creating new industries, or are significantly transforming older industries, in such fashion as to make current market boundaries and market structure of uncertain significance. In such unusual transitional situations application of the normal guideline standards may be inappropriate; and on assessing probable future developments, the Department may not sue despite nominal application of a particular guideline, or it may sue even though the guidelines, as normally applied, do not require the Department to challenge the merger. Similarly, in the area of conglomerate merger activity, the present incomplete state of knowledge concerning structure-conduct relationships may preclude sole reliance on the structural criteria used in these guidelines, as explained in paragraphs 17 and 20 below.

3. *Market Definition.* A rational appraisal of the probable competitive effects of a merger normally requires definition of one or more relevant markets. A market is any grouping of sales (or other commercial transactions) in which each of the firms whose sales are included enjoys some advantage in competing with those firms whose sales are not included. The advantage need not be great, for so long as it is significant it defines an area of effective competition among the included sellers in which the competition of the excluded sellers is, *ex hypothesi,* less effective. The process of market definition may result in identification of several appropriate markets in which to test the probable competitive effects of a particular merger.

A market is defined both in terms of its "product dimension" ("line of commerce") and its "geographic dimension" ("section of the country").

(i) *Line of commerce.* The sales of any product or service which is distinguishable as a matter of commercial practice from other products or services will ordinarily constitute a relevant product market, even though, from the standpoint of most purchasers, other products may be reasonably, but not perfectly, interchangeable with it in terms of price, quality, and use. On the other hand, the sales of two distinct products to a particular group of purchasers can also appropriately be grouped into a single market where the two products are reasonably interchangeable for that group in terms of price, quality, and use. In this latter case, however, it may be necessary also to include in that market the sales of one or more other products which are equally interchangeable with the two products in terms of price, quality, and use from the standpoint of that group of purchasers for whom the two products are interchangeable.

The reasons for employing the foregoing definitions may be stated as follows. In enforcing Section 7 the Department seeks primarily to prevent mergers which change market structure in a direction likely to create a power to behave noncompetitively in the production and sale of any particular product, even though that power will ultimately be limited, though not nullified, by the presence of other similar products that, while reasonably interchangeable, are less than perfect substitutes. It is in no way inconsistent with this effort also to pursue a policy designed to prohibit mergers between firms selling distinct products where the result of the merger may be to create or enhance the companies' market power due to the fact that the products, though not perfectly substitutable by purchasers, are significant enough alternatives to constitute substantial competitive influences on the production, development or sale of each.

(ii) *Section of the Country.* The total sales of a product or service in any commercially significant section of the country (even as small as a single community), or aggregate of such sections, will ordinarily constitute a geographic market if firms engaged in selling the product make significant sales of the product to purchasers in the section or sections. The market need not be enlarged beyond any section meeting the foregoing test unless it clearly appears that there is no economic barrier (*e.g.*, significant transportation costs, lack of distribution facilities, customer inconvenience, or established consumer preference for existing products) that hinders the sale from outside the section to purchasers within the section; nor need the market be contracted to exclude some portion of the product sales made inside any section meeting the foregoing test unless it clearly appears that the portion of sales in question is made to a group of purchasers separated by a substantial economic barrier from the purchasers to whom the rest of the sales are made.

Because data limitations or other intrinsic difficulties will often make precise delineation of geographic markets impossible, there may often be two or more groupings of sales which may reasonably be treated as constituting a relevant geographic market. In such circumstances, the Department believes it to be ordinarily most consistent with the purposes of Section 7 to challenge any merger which appears to be illegal in any reasonable geographic market, even though in another reasonable market it would not appear to be illegal.

The market is ordinarily measured primarily by the dollar value of the sales or other transactions (*e.g.*, shipments, leases) for the most recent twelve month period for which the necessary figures for the merging firms and their competitors are generally available. Where such figures are clearly unrepresentative, a different period will be used. In some markets, such as commercial banking, it is more appropriate to measure the market by other indicia, such as total deposits.

I. HORIZONTAL MERGERS

4. *Enforcement Policy.* With respect to mergers between direct competitors (*i.e.*, horizontal mergers), the Department's enforcement activity under Section 7 of the Clayton Act has the following interrelated purposes: (i) preventing elimination as an independent business entity of any company likely to have been a substantial competitive influence in a market; (ii) preventing any company or small group of companies from obtaining a position of dominance in a market; (iii) preventing significant increases in concentration in a market; and (iv) preserving significant possibilities for eventual deconcentration in a concentrated market.

In enforcing Section 7 against horizontal mergers, the Department accords primary significance to the size of the market share held by both the acquiring and the acquired firms. ("Acquiring firm" and "acquired firm" are used herein, in the case of horizontal mergers, simply as convenient designations of the firm with the larger market share and the firm with the smaller share, respectively, and do not refer to the legal form of the merger transaction.) The larger the market share held by the acquired firm, the more likely it is that the firm has been a substantial competitive influence in the market or that concentration in the market will be significantly increased. The larger the market share held by the acquiring firm, the more likely it is that an acquisition will move it toward, or further entrench it in, a position of dominance or of shared market power. Accordingly, the standards most often applied by the Department in determining whether to challenge horizontal mergers can be stated in terms of the sizes of the merging firms' market shares.

5. *Market Highly Concentrated.* In a market in which the shares of the four largest firms amount to approximately 75% or more, the Department will ordinarily challenge mergers between firms accounting for, approximately, the following percentages of the market:

Acquiring Firm	Acquired Firm
4%	4% or more
10%	2% or more
15% or more	1% or more

(Percentages not shown in the above table should be interpolated proportionately to the percentages that are shown.)

6. *Market Less Highly Concentrated.* In a market in which the shares of the four largest firms amount to less than approximately 75%, the Department will ordinarily challenge mergers between firms accounting for, approximately, the following percentages of the market:

Acquiring Firm	Acquired Firm
5%	5% or more
10%	4% or more
15%	3% or more
20%	2% or more
25% or more	1% or more

(Percentages not shown in the above table should be interpolated proportionately to the percentages that are shown.)

7. *Market With Trend Toward Concentration.* The Department applies an additional, stricter standard in determining whether to challenge mergers occurring in any market, not wholly unconcentrated, in which there is a significant trend toward increased concentration. Such a trend is considered to be present when the aggregate market share of any grouping of the largest firms in the market from the two largest to the eight largest has increased by approximately 7% or more of the market over a period of time extending from any base year 5–10 years prior to the merger (excluding any year in which some abnormal fluctuation in market shares occurred) up to the time of the merger. The Department will ordinarily challenge any acquisition, by any firm in a grouping of such largest firms showing the requisite increase in market share, of any firm whose market share amounts to approximately 2% or more.

8. *Non-Market Share Standards.* Although in enforcing Section 7 against horizontal mergers the Department attaches primary importance to the market shares of the merging firms, achievement of the purposes of Section 7 occasionally requires the Department to challenge mergers which would not be challenged under the market share standards of Paragraphs 5, 6, and 7. The following are the two most common instances of this kind in which a challenge by the Department can ordinarily be anticipated:

(a) acquisition of a competitor which is a particularly "disturbing," "disruptive," or otherwise unusually competitive factor in the market; and

(b) a merger involving a substantial firm and a firm which, despite an insubstantial market share, possesses an unusual competitive potential or has an asset that confers an unusual competitive advantage (for example, the acquisition by a leading firm of a newcomer having a patent on a significantly improved product or production process).

There may also be certain horizontal mergers between makers of distinct products regarded as in the same line of commerce for reasons expressed in Paragraph 3(i) where some modification in the minimum market shares subject to challenge may be appropriate to reflect the imperfect substitutability of the two products.

9. *Failing Company.* A merger which the Department would otherwise challenge will ordinarily not be challenged if (i) the resources of one of the merging firms are so depleted and its prospects for rehabilitation so remote that the firm faces the clear probability of a business failure, and (ii) good faith efforts by the failing firm have failed to elicit a reasonable offer of acquisition more consistent with the purposes of Section 7 by a firm which intends to keep the failing firm in the market. The Department regards as failing only those firms with no reasonable prospect of remaining viable; it does not regard a firm as failing merely because the firm has been unprofitable for a period of time, has lost market position or failed to maintain its competitive position in some other respect, has poor management, or has not fully explored the possibility of overcoming its difficulties through self-help.

In determining the applicability of the above standard to the acquisition of a failing division of a multi-market company, such factors as the difficulty in assessing the viability of a portion of a company, the possibility of arbitrary accounting practices, and the likelihood that an otherwise healthy company can rehabilitate one of its parts, will lead the Department to apply this standard only in the clearest of circumstances.

10. *Economies.* Unless there are exceptional circumstances, the Department will not accept as a justification for an acquisition normally subject to challenge under its horizontal merger standards the claim that the merger will produce economies (*i.e.,* improvements in efficiency) because, among other reasons, (i) the Department's adherence to the standards will usually result in no challenge being made to mergers of the kind most likely to involve companies operating significantly below the size necessary to achieve significant economies of scale; (ii) where substantial economies are potentially available to a firm, they can normally be realized through internal expansion; and (iii) there usually are severe difficulties in accurately establishing the existence and magnitude of economies claimed for a merger.

II. VERTICAL MERGERS

11. *Enforcement Policy.* With respect to vertical mergers (*i.e.,* acquisitions "backward" into a supplying market or "forward" into a purchasing market), the Department's enforcement activity under Section 7 of the Clayton Act, as in the merger field generally, is intended to prevent changes in market structure that are likely to lead over the course of time to significant anticompetitive consequences. In general, the Department believes that such consequences can be expected to occur whenever a particular vertical acquisition, or series of acquisitions, by one or more of the firms in a supplying or purchasing market, tends significantly to raise barriers to entry in either market or to disadvantage existing non-integrated or partly integrated firms in either market in ways unrelated to economic efficiency. (Barriers to entry are relatively stable market conditions which tend to increase the difficulty of potential competitor's entering the market as new sellers and which thus tend to limit the effectiveness of the potential competitors both as a restraint upon the behavior of firms in the market and as a source of additional actual competition.)

Barriers to entry resting on such factors as economies of scale in production and distribution are not questionable as such. But vertical mergers tend to raise barriers to entry in undesirable ways, particularly the following: (i) by foreclosing equal access to potential customers, thus reducing the ability of non-integrated firms to capture competitively the market share needed to achieve an efficient level of production, or imposing the burden of entry on an integrated basis (*i.e.,* at both the supplying and purchasing levels) even though entry at a single level would permit efficient operation; (ii) by foreclosing equal access to potential suppliers, thus either increasing the risk of a price or supply squeeze on the new entrant or imposing the additional burden of entry as an integrated firm; or (iii) by facilitating promotional product differentiation, when the merger involves a manufacturing firm's acquisition of firms at the retail level. Besides impeding the entry of new sellers, the foregoing consequences of vertical mergers, if present, also artificially inhibit the expansion of presently competing sellers by conferring on the merged firm competitive advantages, unrelated to real economies of production or distribution, over non-integrated or partly integrated firms. While it is true that in some instances vertical integration may raise barriers to entry or disadvantage existing competitors only as the result of the achievement of significant economies of production or distribution (as, for example, where the increase in barriers is due to achievement of economies of integrated production through an alteration of the structure of the plant as well as of the firm), integration accomplished by a large vertical merger will usually raise entry barriers or disadvantage competitors to an extent not accounted for by, and wholly disproportionate to, such economies as may result from the merger.

It is, of course, difficult to identify with precision all circumstances in which vertical mergers are likely to have adverse effects on market structure of the kinds indicated in the previous paragraph. The Department believes, however, that the most important aims of its enforcement policy on vertical mergers can be satisfactorily stated by guidelines framed primarily in terms of the market shares of the merging firms and the conditions of entry which already exist in the relevant markets. These factors will ordinarily serve to identify most of the situations in which any of the various possible adverse effects of vertical mergers may occur and be of substantial competitive significance. With all vertical mergers it is necessary to consider the probable competitive consequences of the merger in both the market in which the supplying firm sells and the market in which the purchasing firm sells, although a significant adverse effect in either market will ordinarily result in a challenge by the Department. ("Supplying firm" and "purchasing firm," as used herein, refer to the two parties to the vertical merger transaction, the former of which sells a product in a market in which the latter buys that product.)

12. *Supplying Firm's Market.* In determining whether to challenge a vertical merger on the ground that it may significantly lessen existing or potential competition in the supplying firm's market, the Department attaches primary significance to (i) the market share of the supplying firm, (ii) the market share of the purchasing firm or firms, and (iii) the conditions of entry in the purchasing firm's market. Accordingly, the Department will ordinarily challenge a merger or series of mergers between a supplying firm, accounting for approximately 10% or more of the sales in its market, and one or more purchasing firms, accounting *in toto* for approximately 6% or more of the total purchases in that market, unless it clearly appears that there are no significant barriers to entry into the business of the purchasing firm or firms.

13. *Purchasing Firm's Market.* Although the standard of paragraph 12 is designed to identify vertical mergers having likely anticompetitive effects in the supplying firm's market, adherence by the Department to that standard will also

normally result in challenges being made to most of the vertical mergers which may have adverse effects in the purchasing firm's market (*i.e.*, that market comprised of the purchasing firm and its competitors engaged in resale of the supplying firm's product or in the sale of a product whose manufacture requires the supplying firm's product) since adverse effects in the purchasing firm's market will normally occur only as the result of significant vertical mergers involving supplying firms with market shares in excess of 10%. There remain, however, some important situations in which vertical mergers which are not subject to challenge under paragraph 12 (ordinarily because the purchasing firm accounts for less than 6% of the purchases in the supplying firm's market) will nonetheless be challenged by the Department on the ground that they raise entry barriers in the purchasing firm's market, or disadvantage the purchasing firm's competitors, by conferring upon the purchasing firm a significant supply advantage over unintegrated or partly integrated existing competitors or over potential competitors. The following paragraph sets forth the enforcement standard governing the most common of these situations.

If the product sold by the supplying firm and its competitors is either a complex one in which innovating changes by the various suppliers have been taking place, or is a scarce raw material or other product whose supply cannot be readily expanded to meet increased demand, the merged firm may have the power to use any temporary superiority, or any shortage, in the product of the supplying firm to put competitors of the purchasing firm at a disadvantage by refusing to sell the product to them (supply squeeze) or by narrowing the margin between the price at which it sells the product to the purchasing firm's competitors and the price at which the end-product is sold by the purchasing firm (price squeeze). Even where the merged firm has sufficient market power to impose a squeeze, it may well not always be economically rational for it actually to do so; but the Department believes that the increase in barriers to entry in the purchasing firm's market arising simply from the increased risk of a possible squeeze is sufficient to warrant prohibition of any merger between a supplier possessing significant market power and a substantial purchaser of any product meeting the above description. Accordingly, where such a product is a significant feature or ingredient of the end-product manufactured by the purchasing firm and its competitors, the Department will ordinarily challenge a merger or series of mergers between a supplying firm, accounting for approximately 20% or more of the sales in its market, and a purchasing firm or firms, accounting *in toto* for approximately 10% or more of the sales in the market in which it sells the product whose manufacture requires the supplying firm's product.

14. *Non-Market Share Standards.*

(a) Although in enforcing Section 7 against vertical mergers the Department attaches primary importance to the market shares of the merging firms and the conditions of entry in the relevant markets, achievement of the purposes of Section 7 occasionally requires the Department to challenge mergers which would not be challenged under the market share standards of paragraphs 12 and 13. Clearly the most common instances in which challenge by the Department can ordinarily be anticipated are acquisitions of suppliers or customers by major firms in an industry in which (i) there has been, or is developing, a significant trend toward vertical integration by merger such that the trend, if unchallenged, would probably raise barriers to entry or impose a competitive disadvantage on unintegrated or partly integrated firms, and (ii) it does not clearly appear that the particular acquisition will result in significant economies of production or distribution unrelated to advertising or other promotional economies.

(b) A less common special situation in which a challenge by the Department can ordinarily be anticipated is the acquisition by a firm of a customer or supplier for the purpose of increasing the difficulty of potential competitors in entering the market of either the acquiring or acquired firm, or for the purpose of putting competitors of either the acquiring or acquired firm at an unwarranted disadvantage.

15. *Failing Company.* The standards set forth in paragraph 9 are applied by the Department in determining whether to challenge a vertical merger.

16. *Economies.* Unless there are exceptional circumstances, and except as noted in paragraph 14(a), the Department will not accept as a justification for an acquisition normally subject to challenge under its vertical merger standards the claim that the merger will produce economies, because, among other reasons, (i) where substantial economies of vertical integration are potentially available to a firm, they can normally be realized through internal expansion into the supplying or purchasing market, and (ii) where barriers prevent entry into the supplying or purchasing market by internal expansion, the Department's adherence to the vertical merger standards will in any event usually result in no challenge being made to the acquisition of a firm or firms of sufficient size to overcome or adequately minimize the barriers to entry.

III. CONGLOMERATE MERGERS

17. *Enforcement Policy.* Conglomerate mergers are mergers that are neither horizontal nor vertical as those terms are used in sections I and II, respectively, of these guidelines. (It should be noted that a market extension merger, *i.e.*, one involving two firms selling the same product, but in different geographic markets, is classified as a conglomerate merger.) As with other kinds of mergers, the purpose of the Department's enforcement activity regarding conglomerate mergers is to prevent changes in market structure that appear likely over the course of time to cause a substantial lessening of the competition that would otherwise exist or to create a tendency toward monopoly.

At the present time, the Department regards two categories of conglomerate mergers as having sufficiently identifiable anticompetitive effects as to be the subject of relatively specific structural guidelines: mergers involving potential entrants (Paragraph 18) and mergers creating a danger of reciprocal buying (Paragraph 19).

Another important category of conglomerate mergers that will frequently be the subject of enforcement action—mergers which for one or more of several reasons threaten to entrench or enhance the market power of the acquired firm—is described generally in Paragraph 20.

As Paragraph 20 makes clear, enforcement action will also be taken against still other types of conglomerate mergers that on specific analysis appear anticompetitive. The fact that, as yet, the Department does not believe it useful to describe such other types of mergers in terms of a few major elements of market structure should in no sense be regarded as indicating that enforcement action will not be taken. Nor is it to be assumed that mergers of the type described in Paragraphs 18 and 19, but not covered by the specific rules thereof, may not be the subject of enforcement action if specific analysis indicates that they appear anticompetitive.

18. *Mergers Involving Potential Entrants.*

(a) Since potential competition (*i.e.*, the threat of entry, either through internal expansion or through acquisition and expansion of a small firm, by firms not already or only marginally in the market) may often be the most significant competitive limitation on the exercise of market power by leading firms, as well as the most likely source of additional actual competition, the Department will ordinarily challenge any merger between one of the most likely entrants into the market and:

(i) any firm with approximately 25% or more of the market;

(ii) one of the two largest firms in a market in which the shares of the two largest firms amount to approximately 50% or more;

(iii) one of the four largest firms in a market in which the shares of the eight largest firms amount to approximately 75% or more, provided the merging firm's share of the market amounts to approximately 10% or more; or

(iv) one of the eight largest firms in a market in which the shares of these firms amount to approximately 75% or more, provided either (A) the merging firm's share of the market is not insubstantial and there are no more than one or two likely entrants into the market, or (B) the merging firm is a rapidly growing firm.

In determining whether a firm is one of the most likely potential entrants into a market, the Department accords primary significance to the firm's capability of entering on a competitively significant scale relative to the capability of other firms (*i.e.*, the technological and financial resources available to it) and to the firm's economic incentive to enter (evidenced by, for example, the general attractiveness of the market in terms of risk and profit; or any special relationship of the firm to the market; or the firm's manifested interest in entry; or the natural expansion pattern of the firm; or the like).

(b) The Department will also ordinarily challenge a merger between an existing competitor in a market and a likely entrant, undertaken for the purpose of preventing the competitive "disturbance" or "disruption" that such entry might create.

(c) Unless there are exceptional circumstances, the Department will not accept as a justification for a merger inconsistent with the standards of this paragraph 18 the claim that the merger will produce economies, because, among other reasons, the Department believes that equivalent economies can be normally achieved either through internal expansion or through a small firm acquisition or other acquisition not inconsistent with the standards herein.

19. *Mergers Creating Danger of Reciprocal Buying.*

(a) Since reciprocal buying (*i.e.*, favoring one's customer when making purchases of a product which is sold by the customer) is an economically unjustified business practice which confers a competitive advantage on the favored firm unrelated to the merits of its product, the Department will ordinarily challenge any merger which creates a significant danger of reciprocal buying. Unless it clearly appears that some special market factor makes remote the possibility that reciprocal buying behavior will actually occur, the Department considers that a significant danger of reciprocal buying is present whenever approximately 15% or more of the total purchases in a market in which one of the merging firms ("the selling firm") sells are accounted for by firms which also make substantial sales in markets where the other merging firm ("the buying firm") is both a substantial buyer and a more substantial buyer than all or most of the competitors of the selling firm.

(b) The Department will also ordinarily challenge (i) any merger undertaken for the purpose of facilitating the creation of reciprocal buying arrangements, and (ii) any merger creating the possibility of any substantial reciprocal buying where one (or both) of the merging firms has within the recent past, or the merged firm has after consummation of the merger, actually engaged in reciprocal buying, or attempted directly or indirectly to induce firms with which it deals to engage in reciprocal buying, in the product markets in which the possibility of reciprocal buying has been created.

(c) Unless there are exceptional circumstances, the Department will not accept as a justification for a merger creating a significant danger of reciprocal buying the claim that the merger will produce economies, because, among other reasons, the Department believes that in general equivalent economies can be achieved by the firms involved through other mergers not inconsistent with the standards of this paragraph 19.

20. *Mergers Which Entrench Market Power and Other Conglomerate Mergers.* The Department will ordinarily investigate the possibility of anticompetitive consequences, and may in particular circumstances bring suit, where an acquisition of a leading firm in a relatively concentrated or rapidly concentrating market may serve to entrench or increase the market power of that firm or raise barriers to entry in that market. Examples of this type of merger include: (i) a merger which produces a very large disparity in absolute size between the merged firm and the largest remaining firms in the relevant markets, (ii) a merger of firms producing related products which may induce purchasers, concerned about the merged firm's possible use of leverage, to buy products of the merged firm rather than those of competitors, and (iii) a merger which may enhance the ability of the merged firm to increase product differentiation in the relevant markets.

Generally speaking, the conglomerate merger area involves novel problems that have not yet been subjected to as extensive or sustained analysis as those presented by horizontal and vertical mergers. It is for this reason that the Department's enforcement policy regarding the foregoing category of conglomerate mergers cannot be set forth with greater specificity. Moreover, the conglomerate merger field as a whole is one in which the Department considers it necessary, to a greater extent than with horizontal and vertical mergers, to carry on a continuous analysis and study of the ways in which mergers may have significant anticompetitive consequences in circumstances beyond those covered by these guidelines. For example, the Department has used Section 7 to prevent mergers which may diminish long-run possibilities of enhanced competition resulting from technological developments that may increase interproduct competition between industries whose products are presently relatively imperfect substitutes. Other areas where enforcement action will be deemed appropriate may also be identified on a case-by-case basis; and as the result of continuous analysis and study the Department may identify other categories of mergers that can be the subject of specific guidelines.

21. *Failing Company.* The standards set forth in paragraph 9 are normally applied by the Department in determining whether to challenge a conglomerate merger, except that in marginal cases involving the application of Paragraph 18(a)(iii) and (iv) the Department may deem it inappropriate to sue under Section 7 even though the acquired firm is not "failing" in the strict sense.

Appendix VI

Federal Trade Commission Special Reports Relating to Large Corporate Mergers

REQUIREMENTS CONCERNING NOTIFICATION AND SUBMISSION

Notice is hereby given that the Federal Trade Commission will require firms undertaking large corporate mergers or acquisitions to notify the Commission and supply special reports pursuant to section 6 (a) and (b) of the Federal Trade Commission Act (15 U.S.C. 46 (a) and (b)).

The Commission's requirements apply to any merger or acquisition involving firms which (1) are subject to the Commission's jurisdiction, (2) have assets or sales of $10 million or more, and (3) have combined assets or sales of $250 million or more. For mergers and acquisitions meeting these criteria, the notification and reporting requirements are as follows:

(1) Within 10 days after any agreement or understanding in principle is reached to merge or to acquire assets of $10 million or more, and no less than 60 days prior to the consummation of the merger or acquisition, if the combined assets or sales of the acquiring and acquired corporations are $250 million or more, the parties to the agreement shall notify the Commission of the proposed merger or acquisition; and any such party with assets or sales of $250 million or more shall also be required to file a special report in response to an order of the Commission;

(2) Upon becoming a party to an agreement or understanding as defined in Item (1), above, any corporation with assets or sales of less than $250 million may also be required to file a Special Report in response to an order of the Commission;

(3) Within 10 days after amassing 10 percent or more of the voting stock of another corporation with assets or sales of $10 million or more, any acquiring corporation with assets or sales of $250 million or more shall notify the Commission of such stock holdings and shall also be required to file a special report in response to an order of the Commission; and any acquiring corporation with assets or sales of less than $250 million, if the combined assets or sales of the acquiring and acquired corporations are $250 million or more, shall notify the Commission and may also be required to file a special report;

(4) At least 60 days prior to effecting a stock acquisition which will result in the acquiring corporation holding 50 percent or more of the voting stock of another corporation with assets or sales of $10 million or more, any acquiring corporation with assets or sales of $250 million or more shall notify the Commis-

sion of the proposed acquisition and shall also be required to file a special report in response to an order of the Commission; and any acquiring corporation with assets or sales of less than $250 million, if the combined assets or sales of the acquiring and acquired corporations are $250 million or more, shall notify the Commission and may also be required to file a special report;

(5) Any corporation whose voting stock has been acquired in the amount set forth in Item (3), above, or whose voting stock is the subject of a proposed acquisition as set forth in Item (4), above, may be required to file a special report in response to an order of the Commission.

Notifications filed pursuant to these requirements will constitute a part of the public records of the Commission, but the special reports filed pursuant to order of the Commission will constitute a part of the Commission's confidential records. Special reports will be made available to the Commission's staff and, upon a request complying with § 4.11(c) of the Commission's rules of practice and procedure, may be made available to the Department of Justice and other governmental agencies.

The foregoing requirements pertaining to notification will become effective for all corporations within the coverage of such requirements on the date of publication of this notice in the FEDERAL REGISTER, and this publication constitutes notice to all such corporations that they are required to comply therewith. Proper notification will consist of a letter indicating the names and mailing addresses of the corporations involved, the type of (proposed) transaction, the date of the agreement (if any), and the consummation date of the (proposed) merger or acquisition.

The effective date of the requirements pertaining to filing of special reports will be, for each corporation, the date upon which that corporation receives an order requiring filing of special report from the Commission. The date upon which the special report must be filed will be the date designated as "Reporting Date" in the special report form.

The Commission's initiation of this procedure should not be interpreted to mean that corporations must request Commission approval prior to the consummation of any mergers or acquisitions, nor should the fact that the Commission has not challenged a merger or acquisition prior to its consummation be interpreted as Commission approval of the legality of the transaction. However, the Commission will continue to provide advisory opinions, as provided by its rules of practice and procedure, regarding the legality of particular mergers and acquisitions and invites those contemplating merger to avail themselves of this program in any situation in which they are uncertain as to the legality of the proposed transaction.

Issued: April 17, 1972.

By direction of the Commission.

[SEAL]

CHARLES A. TOBIN,
Secretary.

Index

Accounting aspects of mergers, 98–108
Acquisition agreement, 133–35
Acquisitions: ban on, 187–88
Air carriers: merger regulation of, 384, 394–97
Alcoa case, 290–92
Aldrich Commission Report, 7
American Institute of Certified Public Accountants, 99, 101–102, 104, 107
 guidelines of, for use of pooling method, 103
American Stock Exchange, 30
Antitrust Civil Process Act (1955), 330, 331
Antitrust considerations in selection of corporate structure, 39–42
Antitrust laws, 6, 145. *See also* Clayton Antitrust Act; Federal Trade Commission Act; Sherman Antitrust Act
 bank mergers and. *See* Bank mergers
 private enforcement of, 360–76
Antitrust theory: history of, 139–53
Appraisal rights, 29, 30, 31–32, 33–34, 35
Arnold, Thurmond, 10, 164, 194, 197
Assets, purchase of, 27, 31, 32–33
 assumption of liabilities in, 36–37
 difficulties in transaction of, 39
 shareholder approval for, 31

Bank-holding companies, 433, 439, 442, 443–48
 background of, 445
 growth of one-bank-holding companies, 445–46
 legislation concerning, 446
 reciprocity effect, 442
Bank Holding Company Act of 1956, 443, 445
 one-bank-holding company loophole in, 445, 446
Bank Holding Company Act of 1966, 433, 447
Bank Holding Company Act of 1970, 446–48
Bank Merger Act of 1960, 412, 416, 420, 421–22, 425
 provisions of, 417–19
 value of, 437–38
Bank Merger Act of 1966, 425–29
 legislative history of, 425–26
 main provisions of, 427
Bank mergers, 411–48
 antitrust laws and, 414–16, 420–25, 427, 437–38, 439
 approval rights of banking agencies over, 417–18, 427, 429
 cases after passage of Bank Merger Act of 1966, 429–36
 convenience-and-needs-of-the-community defense, 427, 429, 430, 432, 433, 434, 439
 effect of Celler-Kefauver amendment on, 415
 guidelines for, 434–36, 449–50
 horizontal, 438
 Houston-Provident decision, 429–31, 433, 439
  procedural issues, 429–31
  results of, 432–33
 Justice Department suits to enjoin, 418–19, 420–25, 437, 438, 443. *See also* Justice Department

Bank mergers (*Cont.*)
Lexington Bank case, 167–70, 423–25, 428
market-extension mergers, 438–42
Nashville Bank case, 432, 433
results of, 432–33
Philadelphia National Bank case. See *Philadelphia National Bank* case
Phillipsburg National Bank case, 433, 434–36, 437, 444
product-extension mergers, 442–43
reasons for, 413–14
trend of, prior to Bank Merger Act of 1960, 415–16
trend of, since passage of Bank Merger Act of 1960, 418
Banking Act of 1935, 412
Banking industry: competition and, 411–13
Bathtub conspiracy doctrine, 40, 41–42
Birnbaum doctrine, 80
"Boot," 111, 113, 115, 116
Broadcasting industry: regulation of, 397–400
Brown Shoe Company case, 204–210, 212, 215, 222, 225, 227, 228, 234, 235, 239, 240, 241, 242, 243, 246–47, 256–58, 259–60, 263, 310, 314, 343
Bulk-sales laws, 36–37
Bus companies, intercity, 393
Business review procedure of Justice Department, 323–24

Cease and desist orders of FTC, 351, 353
Celler, Emanuel, 196–97, 198–99, 200
Celler-Kefauver amendment (1950), 11, 12, 39, 152–53, 161, 172, 177, 191–210. *See also* Clayton Antitrust Act: Section 7 of
effect of, on bank mergers, 415
enactment of, 12, 197
historical background of, 191–97
revisions contained in, 198–99
Cement industry: FTC merger guidelines for, 309–310, 350, 359
Cheney, Richard, 22–23
Civil Aeronautics Board, 382, 383, 384, 386, 394–97
Civil investigative demand (CID) by Justice Department, 325, 326–31
Clayton Antitrust Act (1914), 7
deficiencies of, 158–60
provisions and amendments to, 484–94
Clayton Antitrust Act: Section 4 of, 360, 364, 486
Clayton Antitrust Act: Section 7 of, 167, 169–70, 172, 174, 175, 176, 181, 487–88
application of, to mergers in regulated industries, 383–84, 387, 388, 389, 414, 419, 420–23
FTC Act and, 173, 178–80, 181–83, 184–86, 188–89
1950 amendment to, 197–99. *See also* Celler-Kefauver amendment
applicability of, to foreign amalgamations, 287, 289, 294–98, 300, 302–303
application of, to joint venture, 274–80
checklist to determine whether acquisition is violation of, 201–203
defenses against complaints under, 256–72
determination of relevant market under, 221–31, 233–37
Justice Department merger guidelines under. *See* Merger guidelines of Justice Department
key concepts of. *See* Relevant geographic market; Relevant product market
litigation under, 178–80, 182–89, 203–210
tests of unlawfulness of mergers applicable to, 232–55
original of, 151, 152, 154–55
litigation under, 155–58
major loopholes in, 191–92, 414
Supreme Court and, 191
private actions for violations of, 361, 362, 363, 364–73, 375. *See also* Private enforcement of antitrust laws

Clayton Antitrust Act: Section 11 of, 490–91
application of, to mergers in regulated industries, 383–84, 387, 392–93, 397, 399, 400, 405, 414, 415, 419
Clayton Antitrust Act: Section 16 of, 361, 362–63, 493–94
Columbia Steel case, 165–66
Competition, potential, 251–52, 439–41
Comptroller of the Currency, 416, 417, 418–19, 420
Conglomerate mergers, 19, 449–53. *See also* Geographic market-extension merger; Joint ventures; Product-extension merger
cases under Section 5 of FTC Act, 183–86
defined, 217
involving foreign commerce, 301
Justice Department guidelines, 308–309, 440–41, 449–50, 513–15
legal standards applicable to, 217–20
rise of, 14
tests of unlawfulness of, applicable to Section 7, 248–55. *See also* Tests of unlawfulness
Consent decrees, Justice Department, 333–40
advantages of, 334–35
compliance and enforcement of, 340–41
entry of, 338–39
initiation of, 335–36
relief in, 336, 337–38
time limits of, 339–40
Consolidation, 110
Continuity-of-interest doctrine, 110–11
Convenience-and-needs-of-the-community defense, 427, 429, 430, 432, 433, 434, 439
Corporations: joining of. *See* Assets, purchase of; Merger(s); Stock, purchase of

De facto merger doctrine, 32–33, 35, 37
Debt-equity switching, 22, 70
Deep-pocket (or rich-parent), 252–53
Defenses against complaints
under Section 5 of FTC Act, 188–90
under Section 7 of Clayton Act, 256–72
failing-company doctrine, 261–70
overall procompetitive effects, 270–72
purpose of merger, 256–59
toehold acquisitions, 260–61
two-small-company situation, 259–60
Diversification as a reason for merging, 19–20
Divestiture, 187, 345–46, 352, 362–63
Du Pont-General Motors suit, 203–204, 216, 222–23, 243, 247, 258, 259, 364, 366, 425

Economic entity test, 40–41
Electric utilities: merger regulation of, 386, 407–408
Emergency Banking Act (1933), 412
Emergency Railroad Transportation Act (1933), 387
Entrenchment theory, 441–42, 515
Equity dilution, 103–105
Expediting Act (1903), 341–45

Failing-company defense, 261, 510
Fair Labor Standards Act (1938), 10
Federal Aviation Act, 384, 394
Federal Communications Commission, 383, 384–85, 386, 397–400
Federal Deposit Insurance Act, 414
Federal Deposit Insurance Corporation, 414, 416, 417, 420, 437
Federal Maritime Commission, 379, 383, 385, 400–404
Federal Power Act, 386, 404, 407
Federal Power Commission, 382, 383, 386, 404–408
Federal Reserve Act (1913), 7–8
Federal Reserve Board, 383, 414, 415, 416, 417, 418, 420, 437, 439, 446, 447–48
Federal Trade Commission, 382, 385, 415, 416, 420, 421, 449

Federal Trade Commission (*Cont.*)
cease and desist orders of, 351, 353
informal methods used by, to encourage compliance with laws, 355–58
merger guidelines of, 309–15. *See also* Merger guidelines of FTC
power of, to require special reports, 349–51, 500
premerger notification rules of, 315–16, 349–50, 516–17
procedures followed by, 174–76, 349–59
requirements of, concerning special reports relating to large corporate mergers, 516–17
structure of, 348–49
temporary injunction of, to block merger, 352
violation hearings of, 351
working relationship between Justice Department and, 358–59
Federal Trade Commission Act (1914), 7, 151, 171
applicability of, to foreign amalgamations, 288, 289
provisions of, 495–505
Federal Trade Commission Act: Section 5 of, 171–90, 348
Clayton Act and, 173, 178–80, 181–83, 184–86, 188–89, 348
defenses against complaints under, 188–90
FTC procedures in enforcement of, 174–76, 348–59. *See also* Federal Trade Commission
provisions of, 496–500
litigation under, 176–90
in conglomerate mergers, 183–86
in horizontal mergers, 177–80
in vertical mergers, 180–83
remedies for illegality under, 186–88
Sherman Act and, 174
Fibreboard Paper Products Corp. v. *NLRB*, 120–22
Food distribution industries: FTC merger guidelines for, 310–11, 350, 359
Ford Motor Co. v. *United States*, 244–45, 246, 270–72, 345–47
Foreclosure, 242–45
Foreign amalgamations, 285–304
conglomerate mergers, 301
horizontal mergers, 293–98
joint ventures, 301–304
jurisdiction over, 289–92
statutes aimed at, 286–89
vertical mergers, 298–301
"Funny money," 70

Gary, Elbert H., 149–50
Geographic market-extension merger, 178, 183, 184, 185, 217–18, 248, 295
in banking industry, 438–42
Glass-Steagall Act (1933), 443
Grocery products manufacturing industry: FTC merger guidelines for, 311–13, 359

Hand, Learned: opinion of, in *Alcoa* case, 290–92
Holding companies
bank. *See* Bank-holding companies
public utility, 8
SEC regulation of, 408–410
railroad, 162–64
Horizontal mergers, 6, 151, 165
in banking industry, 438
cases under Section 5 of FTC Act, 177–80
decline in, 14
defined, 6, 177, 211
during 1920s, 8–9
involving foreign commerce, 293–98
Justice Department guidelines, 306–307, 508–510
legal standards applicable to, 211–14
tests of unlawfulness of, applicable to Section 7, 237–42. *See also* Tests of unlawfulness
Houston-Provident decision, 429–31, 433, 439

Injunctions: action for, 361–62
"Instant earnings," 107–108

Interdepartmental Committee on Bank Mergers, 418
Interstate Commerce Act, 387
Interstate Commerce Commission, 7, 381, 382, 383, 384, 386, 387–94, 403

John Wiley & Sons v. *Livingston,* 119–20, 124, 125–27
Joint-operating agreement, 283
Joint ventures, 219–20, 273–80
  application of Section 7 to, 274–80
  involving foreign commerce, 301–304
  types of, violating Section 7, 278–80
Jurisdiction over foreign mergers, 289–92
  personal jurisdiction, 289–90, 294
  subject-matter jurisdiction, 290
Justice Department, Antitrust Division, 350, 382, 383, 385–86, 397, 398, 399–400, 449
  appeal of judgments, 332–33
  bank mergers and, 415, 416, 418–19, 420–25, 426, 432–33, 436, 437, 438, 440–41, 446
  business review procedure of, 323–24
  compliance and enforcement of judgments, 340–41
  consent decrees, 333–40. *See also* Consent decrees
  investigations of, 324–31
    civil investigative demand (CID), 325, 326–31
    preliminary investigation, 325
  merger guidelines of. *See* Merger guidelines of Justice Department
  structure of, 319–21
  working relationship between FTC and, 358–59

Labor aspects of mergers, 119–31
  balancing test, 119, 124, 125, 126
  buyer's obligations, 123–27
    duty of successor to bargain with predecessor union, 125
    John Wiley and the survival of contract obligations, 125–27
  seller's duties, 120–23
  "successor" doctrine, 125
Lexington Bank case, 167–70, 423–25, 428
Liabilities
  assumption of, in merger, 35–38
  warranties guaranteeing nature and amount of, 38
Licensing, 281–83
Line of commerce. *See* Relevant product market

Market: ease of entry into, 239–40, 245–46, 253–54, 307
Market-extension merger. *See* Geographic market-extension merger
Market share standards, 239, 306–307, 508–509, 511–12
Merger(s). *See also* Assets, purchase of; Stock, purchase of
  accounting aspects of, 98–108
    abuses in, 99
    equity dilution, 99, 103–105
    "instant earnings," 99, 107–108
    pooling concept, 99, 100–103
    resurrecting submerged data, 99, 105–107
  antitrust considerations in selection of corporate structure of, 39–42
  assumption of liabilities in, 35–38
  of banks, 411–48. *See also* Bank mergers
  buyer motivation for, 18–24
    diversification, 19–20
    to foreclose competition, 20
    merger vs. internal growth, 23–24
    operational reasons, 18–19
    stock market considerations, 20–21
    tax considerations, 21–23
  classification of, 211–20. *See also* Conglomerate mergers; Horizontal mergers; Vertical mergers
  de facto, 32–33, 35, 37

Mergers (*Cont.*)
dilution of shareholders' equity in, 38
involving foreign commerce, 285–304. *See also* Foreign amalgamations
joint ventures. *See* Joint ventures
labor aspects of, 119–31. *See also* Labor aspects of mergers
mcthods of, 27
in regulated industries, 379–448. *See also* Bank mergers; Regulated industries
retention of contractual and other rights in, 38
rights of shareholders in, 31–35
seller motivation for, 16–18
shareholder approval for, 29–31
short-form, 30, 31, 32
steps necessary for completion of, 132–36
tax-free reorganizations, 109–118. *See also* Tax-free reorganizations
tests of unlawfulness of, applicable to Section 7, 232–55. *See also* Tests of unlawfulness
time and effort in transaction of, 39
under original Clayton Antitrust Act, 154–61
under Section 5 of Federal Trade Commission Act, 171–90. *See also* Federal Trade Commission Act
under Sherman Antitrust Act, 162–70. *See also* Sherman Antitrust Act
Merger guidelines for banking industry, 434–36
Merger guidelines of FTC, 309–310, 321, 322, 350
for cement industry, 309–310, 359
for food distribution industries, 310–11, 359
for grocery products manufacturing industry, 311–13, 359
for textile mill products industry, 313–15, 359
Merger guidelines of Justice Department, 213–14, 216, 219, 259, 261, 268, 305–309, 322–23, 506–515
conglomerate mergers, 308–309, 440–41, 449–50, 513–15
horizontal mergers, 306–307, 508–510
vertical mergers, 307–308, 510–13
Merger movements
first (at end of 19th century), 5–8, 192, 193
prosperity and, 4
second (during the 1920s), 8–11, 192, 193
third (present period), 11–15
1943–1947, 12
1948 to date, 12–15
Minority shareholder interests: elimination of, by "squeeze-out," 30–31
Model Business Corporation Act, 28, 30, 35
Money damages, 364–67
Monopolies, 144

National Bank Consolidation Act, 414
National Committee to Study Antitrust Laws, 329–30
National Labor Relations Act, 121
National Labor Relations Board, 122, 128–29, 130
Natural Gas Act (1938), 386, 404, 405, 406
Natural gas industry: control of mergers in, 386, 404, 405–407
New York Stock Exchange, 30
disclosure rule of, 61

Pabst Brewing case, 213, 229–30, 235, 236, 245, 265
Patents, trademarks, and copyrights, 281–83
Patman, Wright, 426, 430, 445–46
Penn-Olin Chemical Co. case, 274–79, 302
Philadelphia National Bank case, 167–70, 212, 225, 228–29, 238, 239,

241, 242, 270–71, 273, 420–23, 425, 428, 430, 432, 439, 444
main points of decision, 421–23
Phillipsburg National Bank case, 433, 434–36, 437, 444
Pipeline industry: control of mergers in, 386, 404, 405–407
Pooling concept, 100–103
guidelines of AICPA for use of, 103
Potential competition theory, 251–52, 439–41
Private enforcement of antitrust laws, 360–76
equitable remedies of injunction and divestiture, 361–64
legal remedies of money damages, 364–67
litigant's burden of proof under Section 7, 367–73
proof of certain amount of damages, 370–73
proof of damage, 369–70
proof of violation, 367–69
proper plaintiffs in, 373–75
Procter & Gamble Co. case, 174, 176, 184–85, 190, 218–19, 252, 253–54, 255, 311
Product-extension merger, 183, 184, 217, 218–19, 248, 295–96, 311, 312
in banking industry, 442–43
Protective order, 330–31
Proxy fights, 67
Public utility holding companies, 8, 408–410
Public Utility Holding Company Act (1935), 194, 386, 408–410

Railroad industry
application of Sherman Act in cases, 162–65
holding companies, 162–64
mergers in, 387–90
Reciprocity, 219, 249–50, 308, 311, 442, 444
Reciprocity effect, 442, 444
Regulated industries, 379–448
anticompetitive effects of mergers in, 379–81, 383–84
banking industry. *See* Bank mergers
Civil Aeronautics Board, 382, 383, 384, 386
mergers and, 394–97
doctrine of primary jurisdiction, 381–83
Federal Communications Commission, 383, 384–85, 386
mergers and, 397–400
Federal Maritime Commission, 379, 383, 385
mergers and, 400–404
Federal Power Commission, 382, 383, 386
mergers and, 404–408
Interstate Commerce Commission, 381, 382, 383, 384, 386
mergers and, 387–94
Securities and Exchange Commission, 408
control of public utility holding companies by, 408–410
statutory provisions dealing with mergers in, 383–86
Relevant geographic market (or section of the country), 167–69, 199, 200–201, 202–203, 206, 209–210, 221, 299, 300, 305, 434, 440, 508
defined, 227–28, 508
determination of, 227–31, 235–37, 422
Relevant product market (or line of commerce), 167–68, 199, 200, 202–203, 205, 221, 299, 300, 305, 434, 440, 507–508
defined, 222, 507–508
determination of, 222–27, 233–34, 422
Remedies
equitable, of injunction and divestiture, 361–64
legal, of money damages, 364–67
Reverse merger, 112–14
"Robber barons," 144–45
Robertson, A. Willis, 425
Roosevelt, Franklin D., 10, 193–94

Roosevelt, Theodore, 7, 147
on monopolistic industries, 147–48

Section of the country. *See* Relevant geographic market
Securities
dealing in, 43–63. *See also* Securities registration
controlling shareholders, the, 55–57
determining investment intent of restricted securities, 47
disclosure rule of New York Stock Exchange, 61
misuse of inside information, 57–62
resale of restricted securities, 47–50
short-swing profits, 62–63
tender offer, 64–97. *See also* Tender offers
private offering of, 45–46
Securities Act of 1933, 43–44, 45, 46, 193
Rule 133, 50–53, 55, 112
leakage provisions of, 51–52
Rule 144, 46–50, 52
Rule 145, 51–53
Rule 237, 49–50
Securities Exchange Act of 1934, 44, 55, 62, 193
Rule 10b-5, 44, 58–59, 61, 62, 80–81
Williams amendments to. *See* Williams Act
Securities registration, 44–53
exemptions to, 44–45
no-sale exemption, 50–53
private-offering exemption, 45–50
Securities registration
shelf registration by acquiring corporation, 54–55
Shareholders
approval of, for merger, 29–31
controlling, 55–57
rights of, in merger, 31–35
Sherman, John, 145
Sherman Antitrust Act, 6–7, 145–47, 154, 157, 387, 398, 399, 414, 419, 420–21, 423–24, 427, 428
applicability of, to foreign amalgamations, 286–87, 289
Federal Trade Commission Act and, 174
litigation under, 162–70
Columbia Steel Company case, 165–66
Lexington Bank case, 167–70, 423–25, 428
Philadelphia National Bank case, 167–70. See also *Philadelphia National Bank* case
railroad cases, 162–65. *See also* Railroad industry
relevant market defined in, 167–69
provisions of, 482–83
Shipping Act (1916), 385, 400, 402, 403, 404
Shipping industry: regulation of, 385–86, 400–404
Short-form merger, 30, 31, 32
Short-tendering, 77
Small-company mergers, 259–60
Social Security Act (1935), 10
Spacek, Leonard, 102
Spin-off, 117
Split-off, 117
Split-up, 117
"Squeeze-out" methods to eliminate minority shareholder interests, 30–31
Statutory merger or consolidation, 27, 30, 32–33, 34. *See also* Merger(s)
"Step transaction," 111, 115, 116–17
Stock, purchase of, 27, 30–31
assumption of liabilities, 36
convenience of transaction of, 39
shareholder approval for, 30–31
Stock-for-stock exchange, 114–15

Taft, William H., 7
Take-over bid. *See* Tender offers
Tax considerations
as reason for merger, 21–23
as result of mergers and acquisitions, 109–118
Tax-free reorganizations, 109–118

"A" reorganization (or statutory merger or consolidation), 110–11, 112
"B" reorganization (or stock-for-stock exchange), 111, 114–15
"C" reorganization (or stock-for-assets acquisition), 111, 115–17
"D" reorganization (or divisive transaction), 117
"E" reorganization (or recapitalization), 117
"F" reorganization, 117–18
reverse merger, 112–14
triangular "A," 111–12, 114
Telephone and telegraph companies: merger regulation of, 384–85
Tender offer(s) (or take-over bids), 64–97
advantages of, 66–69
announcement of existence of, 81–82
defensive tactics, 90–97
after offer has been announced, 93–97
preplanning, 91–93
described, 65–66
information to be disclosed by offerer, 75
kinds of, 64–65
cash offers, 64, 65, 68, 70
exchange offers, 64–65, 68, 70
legal background of, 72–76
offensive tactics, 88–90
offerer's statement of its plans regarding target, 83–84
prohibition of short-tendering and open market purchases, 76–77
pros and cons of, 69–71
recommendations to shareholders by target company, 76
regulated by Williams Act, 65. *See also* Williams Act
regulation of, by state and federal laws other than Williams Act, 87–88
restrictions on terms of, 76
target's statement of reasons for recommendation for or against offer, 84–86
uncontested, 68
Tests of unlawfulness of mergers applicable to Section 7
conglomerate mergers, 248–55
deep-pocket or rich-parent, 252–53
ease of entry into market, 253–54
elimination of potential competition, 251–52, 439–41
miscellaneous tests, 254–55
reciprocity, 249–50, 442
size of company, 254
determination of relevant geographic market in, 227–31, 235–37
determination of relevant product market in, 222–27, 233–34
horizontal mergers, 237–42
concentration of firms, 238
ease of entry into market, 239–40
elimination of substantial competition, 237
history of acquisition in firm or industry, 242
market share of company, 239
possibility of future mergers, 240
reduction in number of independent businessmen, 241
size of company, 240–41
vertical mergers, 242–48
ease of entry into market, 245–46
expectations of acquiring company, 247
history of acquisition in industry, 247
miscellaneous tests, 247–48
nature and purpose of merger, 246–47
threat of foreclosure, 242–45
Texas Gulf Sulphur litigation, 59–60, 81–82, 85, 95
Textile mill products industry: FTC merger guidelines for, 313–15, 359
Toehold acquisitions, 260–61
Transportation Act (1920), 383–84, 387
Transportation Act (1940), 388, 389, 391, 392–93

Treble-damage actions, 360, 361, 364, 365, 367, 401–402
Triangular "A" reorganization, 111–12, 114
Trucking industry: mergers in, 391–92
Trust(s), 5–7, 144–45
  antitrust laws. *See* Antitrust laws
Trust-busting, 6, 10, 164–65
Turner, Donald, 40

Uniform Commercial Code, 36, 37

Vertical mergers, 6, 152, 165
  backward vertical integration merger, 215
  cases under Section 5 of FTC Act, 180–83
  decline in, 14
  defined, 6, 180, 214–15
  during 1920s, 8
  forward vertical integration merger, 215, 216
  involving foreign commerce, 298–301
  Justice Department guidelines, 307–308, 510–13
  legal standards applicable to, 215–16
  original Clayton Act and, 159
  tests of unlawfulness of, applicable to Section 7, 242–48. *See also* Tests of unlawfulness
Voting rights, 31–32, 33–34, 35

Warehousing, 74
Webb-Pomerene Act, 288–89
Williams, Harrison, 72, 73
Williams Act, 65, 95, 97. *See also* Tender offers
  antifraud provisions of, 80–83, 96
  critique of, 77–80
  development of, 72–73
  information required by, 83–86
  1970 amendments to, 74, 80, 88
  scope of, 74–77
Wilson, Woodrow, 7, 8
  on monopolistic industries, 148–49